Interpersonal Message Skills	Interpersonal Message Skills in Action	Interpersonal Message Skills' Benefits
Listening Skills Chapter 5 and Listen to This boxes	• Listening effectively by avoiding the barriers to listening in receiving, understanding, remembering, evaluating, and responding • Adjusting your listening on the basis of the type of interpersonal interaction	Learn, relate, influence, play, and help more effectively through listening
Verbal Message Skills Chapter 6	• Expressing confirmation while avoiding racist, heterosexist, sexist, and ageist language • Using verbal messages to symbolize reality, to distinguish between facts and inferences, and to identify and not obscure important distinctions	Communicate your meanings more accurately and effectively while avoiding the common distortions and obstacles that verbal messages can create
Nonverbal Message Skills Chapter 7	• Using nonverbal messages to manage impressions and relationships, structure social interaction, influence and deceive, express emotions, and reinforce verbal messages • Using all appropriate nonverbal cues to communicate your interpersonal messages	Communicate your meanings with (and decipher the meanings of others from) body, face, eye, space, touch, and a wide variety of other nonverbal cues
Conversation Skills Chapter 8	• Engaging in conversation that is dialogic, reciprocal, and responsive to the influences of power • Expressing your feelings appropriately, clearly, and without angry messages	Engage in conversation that is mutually satisfying and productive. Express emotions clearly and effectively
Relationship Skills Chapter 9	• Communicating to develop, maintain, and repair interpersonal relationships • Communicating in ways consistent with your relational stage	Strengthen healthy friendship, romantic, family, and work relationships
Conflict Management Skills Chapter 10	• Seeking win-win solutions, fighting actively and supportively, using face-enhancing strategies, and being argumentative rather than verbally aggressive • Managing interpersonal conflict in logical stages	Manage (perhaps resolve) interpersonal problems while maximizing the chances that everyone comes out a winner

Interpersonal Messages
Communication and Relationship Skills

Interpersonal
Messages
Communication and Relationship Skills

Joseph A. DeVito
Hunter College of the
City University of New York

PEARSON

Boston   New York   San Francisco
Mexico City   Montreal   Toronto   London   Madrid   Munich   Paris
Hong Kong   Singapore   Tokyo   Cape Town   Sydney

Editor-in-Chief: Karon Bowers
Associate Editor: Deb Hanlon
Series Editorial Assistant: Jenny Lupica
Marketing Manager: Suzan Czajkowski
Editorial Production Service: Nesbitt Graphics, Inc.
Composition Buyer: Linda Cox
Manufacturing Buyer: JoAnne Sweeney
Electronic Composition: Nesbitt Graphics, Inc.
Interior Design: Nesbitt Graphics, Inc.
Photo Researcher: Nesbitt Graphics, Inc.
Cover Designer: Joel Gendron

For related titles and support materials, visit our online catalog at www.ablongman.com.

Between the time website information is gathered and then published, it is not unusal for some sites to have closed. Also, the transcription of URLs can result in typographical errors. The publisher would appreciate notification where these errors occur so that they may be corrected in subsequent editions.

Library of Congress Cataloging-in-Publication Data

DeVito, Joseph A.
   Interpersonal messages: communication and relationship skills /
Joseph A. DeVito
     p. cm.
   Rev. ed. of: Messages. 2005.
   Includes bibliographical references and index.
   ISBN: 0-205-49111-1
  1. Interpersonal communication—Textbooks. I. DeVito, Joseph A.
Messages. II. Title.
   BF637.C45D5 2007
    158.2—dc22   2006050746

Printed in the United States of America

10 9 8 7 6 5 4 CKV 10 09

Brief Contents

Contents

Chapter 3 *The Self in Interpersonal Communication* 58

Chapter 4 *Perception and Interpersonal Communication*   84

Chapter 5 *Listening and Interpersonal Communication*   104

FEATURED BOXES

Chapter 8 *Conversation Messages*   180

FEATURED BOXES

Chapter 9 *Interpersonal Relationships* 206

FEATURED BOXES

Self-Tests: (1) Is Violence a Part of Your Relationship?   218, (2) What Kind of Lover Are You?   222

Listen to This: Listening to Stage Talk   216

Ethical Messages: Q and A   209

Skill Building Exercises: (1) Talking Cherishing   212, (2) Using Affinity-Seeking Strategies   222, (3) Interpersonal Relationships in Songs and Greeting Cards   229

Chapter 10 *Interpersonal Conflict Management* 240

Specialized Table of Contents

Self-Tests

These self-assessment tests will help you analyze your own communication patterns and strategies and make plans for achieving greater interpersonal effectiveness.

Listen to This

These discussions will help you improve your listening skills in a wide variety of specific interpersonal situations.

Ethical Messages

These discussions will encourage you to consider the ethical implications of your interpersonal messages and will help you formulate your own code of the ethics of interpersonal communication.

Dialogues for Analysis

These brief dialogues offer you the opportunity to analyze interactions focusing on the principles discussed in the text and will help you see these principles in operation.

Skill Building Exercises

These exercises will help you work actively with interpersonal communication concepts and principles and will help you practice the many and varied interpersonal skills discussed in the text.

WELCOME TO
Interpersonal Messages: Communication and Relationship Skills

It's a great pleasure to present this thoroughly new version of *Interpersonal Messages: Communication and Relationship Skills*. So new, in fact, that the title of the book (formerly *Messages: Building Interpersonal Communication Skills*) has been changed to signal the extensive revision and to reflect better the course for which this text is designed.

The changes in this new version are of two major types. First, the book has been reorganized to contain ten chapters, with some features deleted and new features added. And second, the material has been revised and updated throughout to incorporate more discussion of computer-mediated communication, new research, and new topics.

Amid these changes the book continues to have its original two interrelated purposes: (1) to present you with an overview of interpersonal communication—what it is and what we know about it—and (2) to provide you with numerous ideas for improving your interpersonal communication and relationship skills. These two purposes influence everything included in the text—the topics discussed, the way each topic is presented, the specific skills highlighted, and the pedagogy incorporated.

Major Themes

Several themes highlight the skills of interpersonal communication and—taken together—define the uniqueness of this text:

- an emphasis on *skill building* that offers guidelines and experiences to help you master the crucial skills of interpersonal communication and relationships, whether these are face-to-face or computer-mediated

- an integration of *listening skills* throughout the coverage of interpersonal communication

- an integration of *critical thinking principles and techniques* to help you think more logically about interpersonal communication (or about anything else)

- an emphasis on *culture and cultural sensitivity* as it influences all forms of interpersonal and intercultural interactions

- a full *integration of technology, especially computer-mediated communication.*

- a focus on *ethical issues* as they relate to a wide variety of interpersonal communication situations

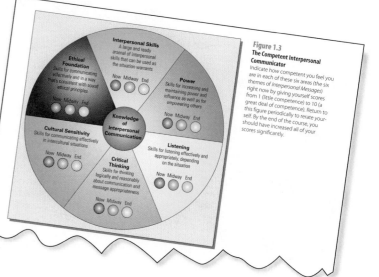

Figure 1.3
The Competent Interpersonal Communicator
Indicate how competent you feel you are in each of these six areas (the six themes of *Interpersonal Messages*) right now by giving yourself scores from 1 (little competence) to 10 (a great deal of competence). Return to this figure periodically to rerate yourself. By the end of the course, you should have increased all of your scores significantly.

- *power and empowerment skills* for increasing interpersonal effectiveness
- an *interactive presentation* to the greatest degree possible in a printed text

Skill Building

Interpersonal Messages continues the focused approach to skill development. **Interpersonal communication skills** are integral to the text discussions and appear in all chapters. But several features further highlight these skills and will facilitate your mastery of them.

First, thirty **Skill Building Exercises** appear throughout the text; these exercises will enable you to apply the material in the chapter to specific situations and thereby to increase and perfect your own interpersonal skills. These exercises are practice experiences aimed at increasing your ability to formulate more effective messages. All exercises, in fact, ask you to construct specific types of messages to demonstrate your mastery of skills. Examples include exercises focusing on reducing apprehension, formulating excuses, and confronting intercultural difficulties.

New to this edition are brief **Dialogues for Analysis** to illustrate concepts presented in each chapter. You'll be encouraged to apply as many of the chapter insights as you can to analyze the dialogue. Each chapter's dialogue exercise can be used to introduce the chapter, to summarize the chapter, or as a before-reading-the-chapter and an after-reading-the-chapter exercise.

The skills formerly presented in *Skills Toolboxes* have been now integrated into the basal text where appropriate. The *Message Skills* that appeared in the margins of the previous version have been moved to each chapter's summary, which includes both a summary of concepts and a summary of skills. The skills presented here have been reorganized around the topics of the ten chapters. A summary of these reorganized skills now appears on the inside covers, as a ready reference to these essential interpersonal skills.

Listening

Listening occupies an important place in *Interpersonal Messages*. First, Chapter 5 focuses exclusively on listening. It covers the importance of listening, the listening process from receiving to responding, guidelines for increasing listening effectiveness, and the role of culture and gender in listening.

To emphasize further that listening is a part of all types of interpersonal communication, each chapter contains a **Listen to This** box. These boxes discuss listening skills as they relate to the chapter content and cover such skills as listening to gender differences, listening to the emotions of others, and listening without bias. At the end of each box is a case for analysis that asks you to apply the relevant listening skills. A complete list of these boxes is given in the Specialized Contents.

Skill building exercise

Content and Relationship Messages

How would you communicate both the content and the relationship messages in the following situations?

1. After a date that you didn't enjoy and don't want to repeat ever again, you want to express your sincere thanks, but you don't want to be misinterpreted as communicating any indication that you would go on another date with this person.
2. You're tutoring a high school freshman in algebra, but your tutee is really terrible and isn't paying attention or doing the homework you assign. You need to change this behavior and motivate a great change, yet at the same time you don't want to discourage or demoralize the young student.
3. You're interested in dating a student in your sociology class, but you don't know if the feeling is mutual. So you decide to ask for the date but want to do it in such a way that if your invitation is refused, you will be able to save face.

Content and relationship messages serve different communication functions. Being able to distinguish between them is prerequisite to using and responding to them effectively.

Dialogue for Analysis

The Intercultural Relationship

Here's a dialogue centering on intercultural relationships. Analyze the dialogue and try to identify examples of effective and ineffective interpersonal communication. How might you have engaged in this dialogue to make it a more effective, satisfying, and culturally sensitive interaction?

The Cast

Spanish-American women.*

Sofia, Aida, Inez, and Serena, all in their early 30s

The Context

Four former college best friends now meet once a year for an elaborate reunion dinner.

Sofia: It's so great getting together every year.
Aida: I'm always anxious to hear what everyone's been up to.
Serena: Well, I got engaged.
Several at once: What? Engaged? When did this happen?
Sofia: You weren't even dating anyone the last time we met!

(continues)

Listen to this

Listening without Bias

Just as racist, sexist, heterosexist, and ageist attitudes influence your language, they also influence your listening. In biased listening you hear what the speaker says through your preconceptions. You assume that what the speaker is saying merely reflects, for example, the speaker's gender, race, affectional orientation, or age.

Such biased listening occurs in a wide variety of situations. For example, when you dismiss a valid argument or give credence to an invalid argument, when you refuse to give someone a fair hearing, or when you attribute less credibility (or more credibility) to a speaker *because* the speaker is of a particular gender, race, affectional orientation, or age—and when these characteristics have nothing to do with the position or argument advanced—you're listening with bias.

To be sure, there are many instances in which speakers' characteristics are relevant and pertinent to your evaluation of the message. For example, the gender of a speaker who is discussing pregnancy, fathering a child, birth control, or surrogate motherhood is, most probably relevant to the message. But it is not biased listening to hear the discussion in light of the gender of the speaker—or that what one sexist listening to assume that only one gender has anything to say that's worth hearing. The same is true in regard to a person's race, age, or affectional orientation.

Applying Listening Skills

Chloe, a good friend of yours, has been assigned to train under the supervision of someone of a different race. Chloe confides in you that she just can't get herself to work with this person; she admits she is just too prejudiced to appreciate anything her supervisor says or does. What listening advice would you give Chloe?

Critical and Creative Thinking

The critical thinking insights so popular in previous versions continue to be woven into the text. Equally important is creative thinking; to cover this, a separate booklet is available, entitled *Brainstorms: How to Think More Creatively about Communication or about Anything Else.* The *Brainstorms* booklet contains a variety of creative (and in many ways critical) thinking tools.

Culture and Intercultural Communication

The text presents interpersonal communication as taking place in an increasingly multicultural context. This version presents the chapter on culture, expanded from all previous versions, as Chapter 2 to emphasize the foundational role that culture plays in all interpersonal communication interactions. This chapter covers the relationship of culture to interpersonal communication, the major cultural differences, aspects of intercultural communication, and a series of important guidelines for improving intercultural communication.

In addition, **integrated discussions of culture** appear throughout the text. Some of the more important of these discussions include:

- Chapter 1: the role of culture in interpersonal communication
- Chapter 2: entire chapter devoted to culture and intercultural communication
- Chapter 3: the influence of culture on self-concept, self-disclosure, and communication apprehension
- Chapter 4: cultural sensitivity as a means to increasing your accuracy in interpersonal perception
- Chapter 5: listening differences among cultures and between men and women
- Chapter 6: culture and gender differences in directness; racism, heterosexism, ageism, and sexism
- Chapter 7: the influence of culture on gesture, facial expression, colors, touch, silence, and time
- Chapter 8: the role of culture in emotional conversation.
- Chapter 9: cultural differences in interpersonal relationships
- Chapter 10: gender and cultural influences on interpersonal conflict

In keeping with this cultural orientation, the names of many characters in the Dialogues for Analysis come from different cultures and languages: Chapter 1, Chinese (Mandarin); Chapter 2, Spanish; Chapter 3, Arabic; Chapter 4, French; Chapter 5, African; Chapter 7, English. The cultures and dialogues were matched randomly; no connection between the substance of any dialogue and any stereotypes about a specific culture should be drawn. Further, the names are not intended to signify that the interpersonal interactions are taking place in foreign countries; rather, visualize the characters as Chinese American, Spanish American, and so on.

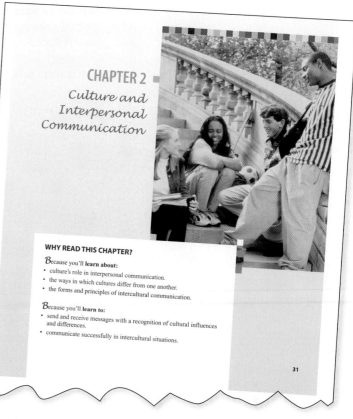

CHAPTER 2
Culture and Interpersonal Communication

WHY READ THIS CHAPTER?

Because you'll **learn about:**
- culture's role in interpersonal communication.
- the ways in which cultures differ from one another.
- the forms and principles of intercultural communication.

Because you'll **learn to:**
- send and receive messages with a recognition of cultural influences and differences.
- communicate successfully in intercultural situations.

31

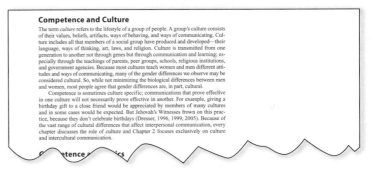

Competence and Culture

The term *culture* refers to the lifestyle of a group of people. A group's culture consists of their values, beliefs, artifacts, ways of behaving, and ways of communicating. Culture includes all that members of a social group have produced and developed—their language, ways of thinking, art, laws, and religion. Culture is transmitted from one generation to another not through genes but through communication and learning; especially through the teachings of parents, peer groups, schools, religious institutions, and government agencies. Because most cultures teach women and men different attitudes and ways of communicating, many of the gender differences we observe may be considered cultural. So, while not minimizing the biological differences between men and women, most people agree that gender differences are, in part, cultural.

Competence is sometimes culture specific; communications that prove effective in one culture will not necessarily prove effective in another. For example, giving a birthday gift to a close friend would be appreciated by members of many cultures and in some cases would be expected. But Jehovah's Witnesses frown on this practice, because they don't celebrate birthdays (Dresser, 1996, 1999, 2005). Because of the vast range of cultural differences that affect interpersonal communication, every chapter discusses the role of culture and Chapter 2 focuses exclusively on culture and intercultural communication.

Competence and Ethics

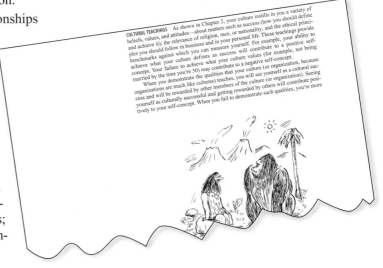

CULTURAL TEACHINGS As shown in Chapter 2, your culture instills in you a variety of beliefs, values, and attitudes—about matters such as success (how you should define and achieve it); the relevance of religion, race, or nationality; and the ethical principles you should follow in business and in your personal life. These teachings provide benchmarks against which you can measure yourself. For example, your ability to achieve what your culture defines as success will contribute to a positive self-concept. Your failure to achieve what your culture values (for example, not being married by the time you're 30) may contribute to a negative self-concept.

When you demonstrate the qualities that your culture (or organization, because organizations are much like cultures) teaches, you will see yourself as a cultural success and will be rewarded by other members of the culture (or organization). Seeing yourself as culturally successful and getting rewarded by others will contribute positively to your self-concept. When you fail to demonstrate such qualities, you're more tively to your self-concept.

These names were taken from a variety of websites (for example, www.babynology.com, http://www.namestatistics.com), www.babynames.org, www.20000-names.com, and Wikipedia, the online encyclopedia (http://wn.wikipedia.org/wiki/most_popular_names). In order to preserve the gender neutrality of the characters in the dialogues in Chapters 6, 8, 9, and 10 "Pat" and "Chris" are used.

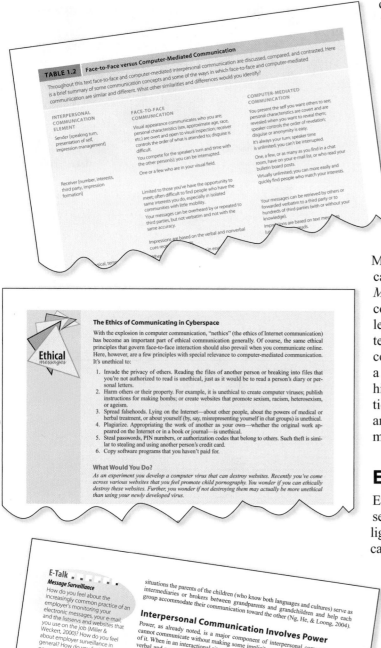

The impact of culture in interpersonal communication also relates to communication between people with and without various disabilities. Interpersonal communication between blind and sighted individuals, persons with and without physical disabilities, deaf and hearing people, and persons with and without speech and language disorders are covered in special tables in Chapters 1, 2, 5, and 8.

Computer-Mediated Communication and Technology

The new technologies of computer-mediated communication—communication between people that takes place through some computer connection (for example, e-mail, instant messaging, interactive websites and blogs, and social networks such as MySpace)—are a part of everyone's everyday communication and are now fully integrated into *Interpersonal Messages*. First, the varieties of computer-mediated communication are introduced and discussed at some length in Chapter 1 and compared with face-to-face interaction. Second, the role of technology in general is considered throughout the text where appropriate. Third, a new marginal feature, **E-Talk,** several per chapter, highlights the part that computer-mediated communication plays in today's interpersonal communication world and the ways in which it differs from face-to-face communication.

Ethics

Ethics receives focused attention throughout the text. A series of **Ethical Messages** boxes (one per chapter) highlight a variety of ethical issues in interpersonal communication; for example, the ethics of various cultural practices, outing, lying, and ethical fighting. These boxes will serve as frequent reminders that ethical considerations are an integral part of all interpersonal communication decisions you make. At the end of each box, you're given a specific real-life situation and asked, "What Would You Do?"

Power and Empowerment

Because power permeates all forms of interpersonal communication, **personal empowerment** and **empowering others** are integral parts of this text. *Interpersonal Messages* aims to give you the skills and experiences to become a more effective, more empowered, and more empowering individual. The material on power has been integrated throughout the text rather than being confined to the final chapter as in the previous version of *Messages*. This change enables the discussion of power issues to be positioned where they are most relevant. For example, the material on self-esteem is now integrated into the chapter on the self (Chapter 3), and the discussion of high-and low-power distances is now integrated into the chapter on culture (Chapter 2).

Interactive Presentation

Given the limitations of print, a printed text cannot literally be interactive. Yet the format of *Interpersonal Messages* is as interactive as possible, asking you to respond and get personally involved with the material throughout the entire text. This is a text that requires your active involvement. The book contains a variety of features to win your involvement:

- **Self-Tests** encourage you to assess yourself on a variety of interpersonal issues.
- **Skill Building Exercises** encourage you to interact with and personalize the concepts discussed in the text.
- **Vocabulary Quizzes** highlight key terms and make learning new terms easier and more enjoyable.
- Brief **What Do You Say?** scenarios placed in the margins invite you to apply what you're reading about to specific interpersonal situations.
- **E-Talk** items, also positioned in the margins, encourage you to compare face-to-face and computer-mediated communication.
- **Application exercises** (in the Ethical Messages and the Listen to This boxes) invite your active participation in the analysis and management of interpersonal situations.
- **Discussion questions** appear at the end of each chapter, inviting debate and challenge.
- **Integrated discussions** throughout the text encourage personalization of the material asking you to respond to bulleted lists of items.
- A **Dialogue for Analysis** appears in each chapter and invites you to analyze a brief interpersonal interaction.

Major Structural Changes

For those who used the previous version of *Messages*, let me identify some of the major structural changes in *Interpersonal Messages*:

- The number of chapters has been reduced from 12 to 10.

  The chapter on power has been deleted, with the material integrated throughout the text. For example, the types of power are introduced in Chapter 1 as one of the principles of interpersonal communication, power distances are discussed in Chapter 2 on culture, and the verbal and nonverbal cues to power are discussed in Chapter 8 on conversation.

  The chapters on conversation and emotion have been combined.

- New and more direct chapter openers have been introduced. The scenarios that opened the chapters from the last edition of *Messages* are available on the text's website at www.mycommunicationlab.com.

- Two new marginal features (one focusing on computer-mediated communication and one focused on making interpersonal communication decisions in a wide variety of situations) have been added. The Message Skills in the margins of the previous version are now included as the skills section of the chapter summary.

- Each chapter now contains a Dialogue for Analysis that can be used as an introductory and/or summary exercise.

- The Skills Toolbox material has been integrated into the basal text where appropriate.

Major Content Changes

In addition to the new features mentioned earlier, the updating of research and theory throughout the book, and new and varied examples integrated throughout the text, some of the major content changes are:

- A new feature appearing in the margins and called **E-Talk** discusses research findings and points out the similarities and differences between computer-mediated and face-to-face communication.

- Computer-mediated communication is discussed throughout the book, but especially in the discussions of the elements of interpersonal communication in Chapter 1 and in the discussion of relationships in Chapter 9.

- Also new to this version are marginal items called **What Do You Say?** These items present interpersonal choice points, points at which you have to make a decision as to what to say and how or to whom to say it. They are frequent reminders that the material you're reading about has very practical application in a variety of situations.

- A new feature, called **Dialogue for Analysis,** appears at the end of every chapter. These dialogues illustrate various concepts and principles discussed in the chapter; they represent a kind of interactive summary of the chapter and may be used as a springboard to preview and/or review the contents of the chapter.

- Chapter 2 is now dedicated to a more extended and focused discussion of culture in which all the dimensions of culture are considered together.

- One of the goals of this version was to incorporate more examples to illustrate the concepts and principles. These examples appear just about everywhere throughout the text.

- New self-tests include tests on self-esteem, apprehension in computer-mediated communication, conversation satisfaction, and relationship violence, as well as a revised shorter self-test for verbal aggressiveness.

- New and extensively revised listening boxes include Listening Nonverbally and Listening to Emotions (10 Easy Ways).

- All Skill Building Exercises were revised for added clarity, and new ones have been added to cover such topics as content and relationship messages, first impressions, reversing negative impressions, nonverbal impression formation, and interpersonal relationships in songs and greeting cards.

- New and extensively updated and revised sections include, for example:
  - reasons for studying interpersonal communication as well as the forms of computer-mediated communication and how they compare to face-to-face interaction in Chapter 1

- power distances, stereotyping, and a revised section on cultural principles (maxims) in Chapter 2
- expanded discussion of self-esteem in Chapter 3
- clarification of the self-serving bias and an explanation of the uses and abuses of perceptual shortcuts in Chapter 4
- clarification of the benefits of effective listening in Chapter 5
- discussions of racism, sexism, heterosexism, and ageism, including both individual and institutionalized bias, in Chapter 6
- expanded discussion of culture and nonverbal communication in Chapter 7
- dialogic communication in Chapter 8
- theories of interpersonal relationships, a revised section on family, and a new section on relationship violence in Chapter 9
- influences on conflict strategy selection, the principles of conflict, and verbal aggressiveness and argumentativeness in Chapter 10

The Internet

Interpersonal Messages provides both text and Internet resources for improving your interpersonal communication skills.

- MyCommunicationLab, a state-of-the-art, interactive and instructive online solution for interpersonal communication courses. Designed to be used as a supplement to a traditional lecture course, or completely administer an online course, MyCommunicationLab combines multimedia, video, activities, research support, tests, and quizzes to make teaching and learning fun! In addition, MyCommunicationLab for *Interpersonal Messages* includes wide variety of resources such as exercises and self-tests related to each chapter's concepts and skills. Writing resources and assignments are also available for your use. Each chapter of the book ends with an overview of some of the resources that can be found at www.mycommunicationlab.com (access code required). Available with this book for fall 2007 classes.

- Interpersonal Communication Companion Study Site at http://abinterpersonal .com contains a fully expanded set of practice tests for all major topics, flashcards, and links to other valuable web sources.

- The Communication Blog, maintained by the author and available at http:// tcbdevito.blogspot.com, provides a forum for users of *Interpersonal Messages* and offers periodic updates and suggestions for teaching interpersonal communication.

- Allyn & Bacon's Research Navigator website is a powerful and extensive online database of popular and academic articles in communication and other related areas of interest. Providing credible and reliable source material from, among others, the EBSCO Academic Journal and Abstract Database, *New York Times* Search by Subject Archive, "Best of the Web" Link Library, and *Financial Times* Article Archive and Company Financials, Research Navigator helps students quickly and efficiently make the most of their research time.

Supplements

Student Resources

PRINT SUPPLEMENTS *Study Guide,* by Kristal Lewis Menchaca of Texas Tech University. The Study Guide contains learning objectives, chapter summary grids, study methods, chapter outlines, vocabulary review, sample tests, suggested readings, and

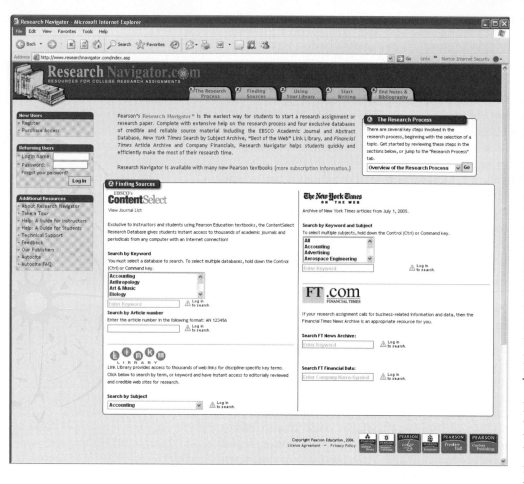

tips for learning. It also includes activities for reinforcing learning and demonstrating skills.

ResearchNavigator.com Guide: Speech Communication. This updated booklet by Steven L. Epstein of Suffolk County Community College, includes tips, resources, and URLs to aid students conducting research on Pearson Education's research website, **www.researchnavigator.com**. The guide contains a student access code for the Research Navigator database, offering students free, unlimited access to a collection of more than 25,000 discipline-specific articles from top-tier academic publications and peer-reviewed journals, as well as the *New York Times* and popular news publications. The guide introduces students to the basics of the Internet and the Wolrd Wide Web, and includes tips for searching for articles on the site, and a list of journals useful for research in their discipline. Also included are hundreds of web resources for the discipline, as well as information on how to correctly cite research. The guide is available packaged with new copies of the text.

Brainstorms, by Joseph A. DeVito. A guide to thinking more creatively about communication, or anything else; a perfect complement to the text's unique emphasis on critical thinking. Students find 19 practical, easy-to-use creative thinking techniques along with insights into the creative thinking process.

Study Card for Interpersonal Communication. Colorful, affordable, and packed with useful information, Allyn & Bacon's Study Cards make studying easier, more efficient, and more enjoyable. Course information is distilled down to the basics, helping you quickly master the fundamentals, review a subject for understanding, or prepare for an exam. Because they're laminated for durability, you can keep these Study Cards for years to come and pull them out whenever you need a quick review.

Pathways to Careers in Communication. The National Communication Association's booklet provides information about the discipline, its history and importance, information on career possibilities, and other available resources for investigating communication studies. Value-packed with any A&B Communication text.

ELECTRONIC SUPPLEMENTS *MyCommuncationLab* is an interactive and instructive online solution for introductory public speaking. Designed to be used as a supplement to a traditional lecture course, or completely administer an online course, *MyCommunicationLab* combines multimedia, video, research support, tests, and quizzes to make teaching and learning fun! Students benefit from a wealth of video clips, many of which are accompanied by activities, questions to consider, and helpful tips—all geared to help students learn to communicate more effectively. Go to www.mycommunicationlab.com for more information or contact your local Allyn & Bacon representative.

Interpersonal Communication Companion Website, accessed at www.abinterpersonal .com. The site contains a fully expanded set of practice tests for all major topics, flashcards, and links to other valuable web sources.

VideoWorkshop for Interpersonal Communication Student Learning Guide, by Christine North, Ohio Northern University. VideoWorkshop for Interpersonal Communication is a new way to bring video into your course for maximized learning! This total teaching and learning system includes quality video footage on an easy-to-use CD-ROM, plus a *Student Learning Guide* and an *Instructor's Teaching Guide*—both with textbook-specific correlation grids. The result? A program that brings textbook concepts to life with ease and helps your students understand, analyze, and apply the objectives of the course. VideoWorkshop is available for your students as a value-pack option with this textbook.

Allyn & Bacon Communication Studies Website, by Terrence Doyle, Northern Virginia Community College, and Tim Borchers, Minnesota State University at Moorhead. This site includes modules on interpersonal, small group communication, and public speaking, and includes web links, enrichment materials, and interactive activities to enhance students' understanding of key concepts. Access this site at www.ablongman.com/commstudies.

Instructor's Resources

PRINT SUPPLEMENTS *Instructor's Manual and Test Bank with Transparency Masters,* by Marylin S. Kelly of McLennan Community College. The Instructor's Manual provides chapter overviews, chapter outlines, skill objectives, and classroom strategies for each chapter. The manual provides ideas to activate class discussions and contains exercises to illustrate the concepts, principles, and skills of interpersonal communication. In addition, the Test Bank portion of the manual contains numerous multiple choice, true-false, fill in the blank, and essay test questions. The manual also includes more than 100 transparency masters that frame key concepts and skills.

The Blockbuster Approach: A Guide to Teaching Interpersonal Communication with Video, Third Edition, by Thomas E. Jewell, Bergen Community College. The guide provides lists and descriptions of commercial videos that can be used in the classroom to illustrate interpersonal concepts and complex interpersonal relationships. Sample activities are also available.

VideoWorkshop for Interpersonal Communication Instructor's Teaching Guide, by Christine North, Ohio Northern University. This guide provides teaching suggestions, quiz questions and answers, and discussion starters that will help you use the VideoWorkshop for Interpersonal Communication CD-ROM in class. A correlation guide helps you relate the materials to your text. The complete CD-ROM and Student Learning Guide are included in this guide. Go to www.ablongman.com/ html/videoworkshop for more details.

ELECTRONIC SUPPLEMENTS *MyCommuncationLab* is an interactive and instructive online solution for introductory public speaking. Designed to be used as a supplement to a traditional lecture course, or completely administer an online course, *MyCommunicationLab* combines multimedia, video, research support, tests, and quizzes to make teaching and learning fun! Students benefit from a wealth of video clips, many of which are accompanied by activities, questions to consider, and helpful tips—all geared to help students learn to communicate more effectively. Go to www.mycommunicationlab.com for more information or contact your local Allyn & Bacon representative.

TestGen EQ: Computerized Test Bank. The user-friendly interface enables instructors to view, edit, and add questions, transfer questions into tests, and print tests in a variety of fonts. Search and sort features allow instructors to locate questions quickly and arrange them in preferred order. Available on CD-ROM or downloadable through our Instructor's Resource Center at http://suppscentral.ablongman.com.

PowerPoint Presentation Package, by Keri Moe of El Paso Community College. This text-specific package consists of a collection of lecture outlines and graphic images keyed to every chapter in the text. Available at http://suppscentral.ablongman.com.

Allyn & Bacon Digital Media Archive CD-ROM for Communication, Version 3.0. This CD-ROM contains electronic images of charts, graphs, maps, tables, and figures, along with media elements such as video, audio clips, and related web links. These media assets are fully customizable to use with our preformatted PowerPoint outlines or to import into your own lectures. (Available in Windows and Mac formats.)

Allyn & Bacon Interpersonal Communication Video The interpersonal video contains three scenarios that illustrate key concepts in interpersonal communication. A faculty User's Guide featured transcripts and teaching activities. For adopters only. Restrictions apply. See your Allyn & Bacon/Longman representative for details.

InterWrite PRS (Personal Response System). Assess your students' progress with the Personal Response System—an easy-to-use wireless polling system that enables you to pose questions, record results, and display those results instantly in your classroom.

Designed by teachers, for teachers, PRS is easy to integrate into your lectures:

- Students use a cell-phone-sized transmitter which they bring to class.
- You ask multiple-choice, numerical-answer, or matching questions during class; students simply click their answer into their transmitter.
- A classroom receiver (portable or mounted) connected to your computer tabulates all answers and displays them graphically in class.
- Results can be recorded for grading, attendance, or simply used as a discussion point.

Our partnership with PRS allows us to offer student rebate cards bundled with any Allyn & Bacon/Longman text. The rebate card has a direct value of $20.00 and can be redeemed for the purchase a new PRS student transmitter.

Sandbox. With Sandbox Custom Publishing from Allyn & Bacon, you can build your own textbook—one designed specifically around the course you teach, with the material relevant to your specific course. Using texts from Allyn & Bacon, you can:

- Develop a book with a single look and feel throughout.
- Updated internal referencing! Table of contents, index, glossary, and figure numbering all match!
- Revise and print on demand.
- Previews available within two days.
- A one-time downloadable, printable evaluation copy is available on request.
- Minimum 25 units, minimum 150 pages.
- Black and white only for adoptions under 2,500 units.

Choose how your textbook looks both inside and out, with all the chapters you want, in the order you want them. With Sandbox, you can include your own class notes. You can remove chapters from one book and add chapters from another. And you can do it without having to sacrifice quality. Create a custom book as seamless as the original products used to construct it. Imagine the possibilities when you build your book in Sandbox! For more information, contact your local Allyn & Bacon representative or go to www.ablongmancustom.com.

The Communication Blog (http://tcbdevito.blogspot.com). Maintained by the author, this site offers a forum for people teaching basic courses in interpersonal communication as well as the hybrid and public speaking courses. Regular posts by the author update the text material and share ideas for teaching.

Acknowledgments

I want to thank those who reviewed the text at the various stages of revision; they gave generously of their time and expertise and I am, as always, in their debt. Thank you Lana Becker, Ivy Tech State College; Gary Kuhn, Chemeketa Community College; Amy London, Oxnard College; Kristal Lewis Menchaca, Texas Tech University.

I also want to thank the many people who worked so hard to turn a manuscript into this book. I'm especially grateful to Karon Bowers, editor-in-chief, who, as always, admirably guided the process of a revision that turned into a new book; Kristen Desmond Lefevre, developmental editor, who made numerous and valuable suggestions for improvement; Suzan Czajkowski, marketing manager, who likewise made valuable suggestions; Jenny Lupica, editorial assistant, who managed expertly the process and the relationships involved in doing this text; Jay Howland, copy editor, who did her customarily superb editing of this manuscript—the felicity of style is hers; and Tom Conville, project manager, who guided the manuscript-to-book process without the least snag or bump in the road.

Joseph A. DeVito
jadevito@earthlink.net
www.ablongman.com/devito
http://tcbdevito.blogspot.com

Interpersonal Messages
Communication and
Relationship Skills

CHAPTER 1 ■
Interpersonal Communication

WHY READ THIS CHAPTER?

Because you'll **learn about:**

- the nature of interpersonal communication.
- the essential elements of interpersonal communication.
- the principles that explain how interpersonal communication works.

Because you'll **learn to:**

- communicate with a clear understanding of the elements of interpersonal communication.
- communicate with an understanding of the principles of interpersonal communication.

$\mathcal{H}$ere we begin the study of interpersonal communication—a study you'll find both intellectually challenging and at the same time extremely practical. This chapter begins with offering a more complete answer to the question posed in the chapter opener, Why study interpersonal communication?

Why Study Interpersonal Communication?

Perhaps the most obvious reason to study interpersonal communication is that your interpersonal skills will influence how effective you are as a friend, relationship partner, coworker, or manager. For example, in a survey of 1,001 people over 18 years of age, 53 percent felt that a lack of effective communication was the major cause of marriage failure—a factor significantly greater than money (38 percent) or in-law interference (14 percent) (www.natcom.org/research/Roper/how_Americans_communicate.htm, accessed April 8, 2003). The relevance of interpersonal communication skills to relationships is a major theme of this text.

In a similar way, interpersonal skills are crucial to professional success, as has been widely documented (Morreale, Osborn, & Pearson, 2000). Interpersonal skills have become so important that the U.S. Department of Labor, in its report "What Work Requires of Schools"—a report based on interviews with managers, employers, and workers who described the skills they needed to function effectively at their jobs—identified interpersonal skills as one of five skills essential for a nation and an individual to be economically competitive in the world marketplace (*New York Times,* July 3, 1991, p. A17).

More recent evidence comes from a study by the *Wall Street Journal,* which reported that of the 23 attributes ranked as "very important" in recent business school graduates, "communication and interpersonal skills" was at the top of the list, being noted by 89 percent of the business recruiters surveyed (Alsop, 2004). This attribute was ranked far higher than the business schools' "faculty expertise" (noted by 25 percent of the recruiters) and "content of the core curriculum" (noted by 34 percent). And in a survey of employers it was the "soft skills" that distinguished the successful from the unsuccessful. Employers identified: "work ethic, communications, information gathering, and people skills at the top of the list, followed by analytical and problem-solving skills. These capabilities apply across all fields" (Coplin, 2004, p. 15A).

Interpersonal skills have long been recognized as critical to professional success in a wide variety of occupations (Morreale, Osborn, & Pearson, 2000). Here are just a few examples:

- Interpersonal skills are considered "key in [the] office of the future" (*TMA Journal,* 1999, p. 53).
- Interpersonal skills are a "key career advantage for finance professionals in the next century" (Messmer, 1999).
- Interpersonal skills are important for preventing workplace violence (Parker, 2004).
- Interpersonal skills figure prominently in the health care industry—for example, in enabling nurses to rise in the corporate hierarchy and in building patient trust (Nordhaus-Bike, 1999; Titlow, Rackoff, & Emanuel, 1999).
- Interpersonal skills are crucial in reducing medical mishaps and in improving doctor–patient communication (Sutcliffe, Lewton, & Rosenthal, 2004; Smith, 2004).
- Interpersonal skills are identified as one of six areas that define the professional competence of physicians and trainees (Epstein & Hundert, 2002).

■ **What Do You Say** ❓
Interpersonal Choice Points
Throughout the text you'll find marginal items that identify an interpersonal choice point, a point at which you need to make a decision and say something (or, of course, decide to remain silent). These *What Do You Say?* items are designed to encourage you to apply the skills discussed in the text to a wide variety of interpersonal situations.

- Interpersonal skills are one of the three "vitally important subjects" that need to be emphasized in the training of hotel and restaurant administrators (Dittman, 1997).
- Interpersonal skills are considered an essential part of business competence (Bassellier & Benbasat, 2004).

The importance of interpersonal communication skills, then, seems to extend over the entire spectrum of professions.

This book, in short, is about the nature and principles of interpersonal communication and about improving your own interpersonal skills so that you'll be more effective in a wide variety of interpersonal communication situations: with your family; with supervisors, coworkers, and subordinates; and with acquaintances, friends, and lovers.

Before beginning your study of this exciting and practical area, examine your own beliefs about interpersonal communication by taking the self-test below.

Test *Yourself* ■ ■ ■ ■ ■ ■ ■ ■ ■ ■ ■ ■ ■ ☑

What Do You Believe about Interpersonal Communication?

INSTRUCTIONS: Respond to each of the following statements with T (true) if you believe the statement is usually true or F (false) if you believe the statement is usually false.

_____ ❶ Good communicators are born, not made.

_____ ❷ The more you communicate, the better at communicating you will be.

_____ ❸ In your interpersonal communications, a good guide to follow is to be as open, empathic, and supportive as you can be.

_____ ❹ The best guide to follow when communicating with someone from another culture is to ignore the differences and treat the other person just as you'd treat members of your own culture.

_____ ❺ Fear of speaking is detrimental, and to be an effective speaker you must eliminate it.

_____ ❻ When there is conflict, your relationship is in trouble.

HOW DID YOU DO? As you probably figured out, all six statements are generally false. As you read this text, you'll discover not only why these beliefs are false but also the trouble you can get into when you assume they're true. For now, and in brief, here are some of the reasons why each statement is (generally) false: (1) Effective communication is learned; all of us can improve our abilities and become more effective communicators. (2) It isn't the amount of communication that matters, it's the quality. If you practice bad habits, you're more likely to grow less effective than more effective. (3) Because each interpersonal situation is unique, the type of communication appropriate in one situation may not be appropriate in another. (4) Ignoring differences will often merely create problems; people from different cultures may, for example, follow different rules for what is and what is not appropriate in interpersonal communication. (5) Most speakers are nervous; managing, not eliminating, the fear will enable you to become more effective regardless of your current level of apprehension. (6) All meaningful relationships experience conflict; the trick is to manage it effectively.

WHAT WILL YOU DO? This is a good place to start practicing the critical thinking skill of questioning commonly held assumptions—about communication and about yourself as a communicator. Do you hold beliefs that may limit your thinking about communication? For example, do you believe that certain kinds of communication are beyond your capabilities? Do you impose limits on how you see yourself as a communicator?

CMC/Computer-Mediated Communication

Throughout this text you'll find marginal items labeled "E-Talk," which draw your attention to the similarities and differences between computer-mediated and face-to-face communication. A definition from **TheFreeDictionary.com** will serve us well to begin: "Computer-mediated communication (CMC) is any form of communication between two or more individual people who interact and/or influence each other via separate computers" and generally refers to "e-mail, video, audio or text conferencing, bulletin boards, listservs, instant messaging, and multi-player video games."

*W*hat Is Interpersonal Communication?

Interpersonal communication is communication that occurs between persons who have a connection or relationship. **Communication** occurs when you send or receive messages and when you assign meaning to such messages. Interpersonal communication is always distorted by "noise," occurs within a context, and involves some opportunity for feedback.

Interpersonal communicators are conscious of each other and of their connection with each other. They're interdependent; what one person thinks and says impacts what the other thinks and says. Examples of interpersonal communication includes the conversations that take place between an interviewer and a potential employee, between a son and his father, between two sisters, between a teacher and a student, or between two lovers or two friends. Even the stranger asking for directions from a local resident has a relationship with that person and is communicating interpersonally.

Models of Interpersonal Communication

Some early theories viewed the communication process as linear. In this *linear* view of communication, the speaker spoke and the listener listened; after the speaker finished speaking, the listener would speak. Communication was seen as proceeding in a relatively straight line. Speaking and listening were seen as taking place at different times—when you spoke, you didn't listen; and when you listened, you didn't speak (Figure 1.1).

This linear **model,** or representation of the process, soon gave way to an *interactional* view in which the speaker and the listener were seen as exchanging turns at speaking and listening. For example, A spoke while B listened and then B (exchanging the listener's role for the speaker's role) spoke in response to what A said and A listened. Speaking and listening were still viewed as separate acts that did not overlap and that were not performed at the same time by the same person.

Figure 1.1
The Transactional View of Interpersonal Communication
The top figure represents a linear view of communication, in which the speaker speaks and the listener listens. The middle figure represents an interactional view, in which speaker and listener take turns speaking and listening; A speaks while B listens and then B speaks while A listens. The bottom figure represents a transactional view, in which each person serves simultaneously as speaker and listener; at the same time that you send messages, you also receive messages from your own communications as well as from the reactions of the other person(s).

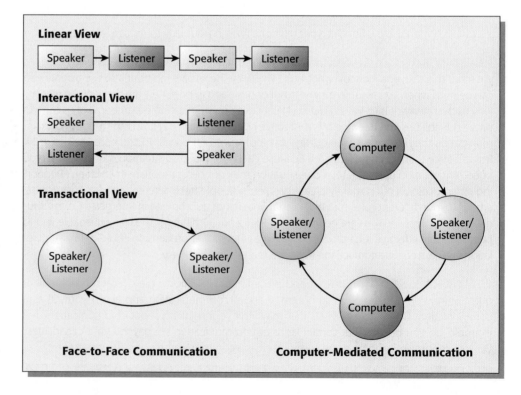

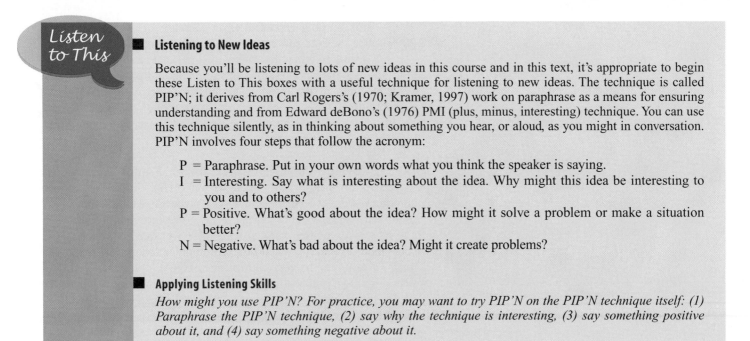

Listening to New Ideas

Because you'll be listening to lots of new ideas in this course and in this text, it's appropriate to begin these Listen to This boxes with a useful technique for listening to new ideas. The technique is called PIP'N; it derives from Carl Rogers's (1970; Kramer, 1997) work on paraphrase as a means for ensuring understanding and from Edward deBono's (1976) PMI (plus, minus, interesting) technique. You can use this technique silently, as in thinking about something you hear, or aloud, as you might in conversation. PIP'N involves four steps that follow the acronym:

P = Paraphrase. Put in your own words what you think the speaker is saying.
I = Interesting. Say what is interesting about the idea. Why might this idea be interesting to you and to others?
P = Positive. What's good about the idea? How might it solve a problem or make a situation better?
N = Negative. What's bad about the idea? Might it create problems?

Applying Listening Skills

How might you use PIP'N? For practice, you may want to try PIP'N on the PIP'N technique itself: (1) Paraphrase the PIP'N technique, (2) say why the technique is interesting, (3) say something positive about it, and (4) say something negative about it.

A more satisfying view, and the one currently held, sees communication as a *transactional* process in which each person serves simultaneously as speaker and listener. According to the **transactional view,** at the same time that you send messages, you're also receiving messages from your own communications and from the reactions of the other person. And at the same time that you're listening, you're also sending messages. In a transactional view, each person is seen as both speaker and listener, as simultaneously communicating and receiving messages (Watzlawick, Beavin, & Jackson, 1967; Watzlawick, 1977, 1978; Barnlund, 1970; Wilmot, 1987).

Also, in a transactional view the elements of communication are seen as *inter*dependent (never *in*dependent). Each exists in relation to the others. A change in any one element of this **process** produces changes in the other elements. For example, suppose you're talking with a group of your friends and your mother enters the group. This change in "audience" will lead to other changes; perhaps you'll change what you say or how you say it. Regardless of what change occurs, other changes will follow as a result.

Computer-Mediated Communication

Often interpersonal communication takes place face-to-face; examples are talking with other students before class, interacting with family or friends over dinner, trading secrets with intimates. These are the types of interactions that probably come to mind when you think of interpersonal communication. Because of technological advances, however, much communication today is computer-mediated. Online communication, or what is now called **computer-mediated communication** (and often abbreviated CMC), is now a major part of people's experience throughout the world. Such communication is important personally, socially, and professionally. For example, in 2004 (on an average day) approximately 70 million adult Americans logged on to the Internet to send and receive e-mail; catch up on the news; access information on genealogy, health, and government programs; make reservations; gamble; and look for friends and romantic partners, as well as for countless other purposes (Rainie & Horrigan,

❝The new source of power is not money in the hands of a few, but information in the hands of many.❞
—John Naisbitt

"I loved your E-mail, but I thought you'd be older."

2005). This number represented an increase of 37 percent since 2000, when the first survey of this type was completed.

According to a Pew Internet and American Life Project survey, "the internet fits seamlessly with in-person and phone encounters. With the help of the internet, people are able to maintain active contact with sizable social networks, even though many of the people in those networks do not live nearby" (Boase, Horrigan, Wellman, & Rainie, 2006).

TYPES OF COMPUTER-MEDIATED COMMUNICATION **E-mail** is today the most common use of the Internet (see Table 1.1). Unlike face-to-face communication, e-mail does not take place in real time. You may send your message today, but the receiver may not read it for a week and may take another week to respond. Consequently, much of the spontaneity created by real-time communication is lost here. You may, for example, be very enthusiastic about a topic when you send your e-mail but practically forget it by the time someone responds. E-mail is more like a postcard than a letter and so can be read by others along the route. It's also virtually unerasable, a feature that has important consequences and that is discussed later in this chapter.

The **listserv** or **mailing list group** consists of a group of people interested in a particular topic who communicate with one another through e-mail. Generally, you subscribe to a list and communicate with all other members by addressing your mail to the group e-mail address. Any message you send to this address will be sent to each member who subscribes to the list. Your message is sent to all members at the same time; there are no asides to the person sitting next to you (as in face-to-face groups).

Instant messaging (often abbreviated IM) is an Internet text-based system that allows you to communicate online by exchanging short messages in (essentially) real time. Through IM you can also play games, share files, listen to music, and send messages to cell phones. A 2004 study reported that approximately 42 percent of Internet users (more than 53 million Americans) use IM. Approximately 21 percent of IM users report that they use it at work; of these, 40 percent use it to communicate with coworkers, 33 percent to communicate with friends and family, and 21 percent to communicate with both groups (Shiu & Lenhart, 2004). Among college students, as you probably know, the major purpose of IM seems to be to maintain "social connectedness" (Kindred & Roper, 2004).

But it's in business that IM is growing most impressively. Some 80 percent of U.S. corporations use IM. Within IBM, for example, some 2.5 million IMs are exchanged daily (Strom, 2006). Because IM tells you who else is now online, it enables members of a geographically separated workforce to contact others immediately—a decided advantage over e-mail, in which you have no idea when the recipients are going to read your message and get back to you. A nurse can instantly contact a physician online to ask a question, and a salesperson can consult with a supervisor to answer a customer's question immediately. In addition, IM builds a sense of community among users, even though they may physically be in different parts of the world.

Chat groups enable you to converse in real time. Unlike mailing lists, chat communication lets you see a member's message as it's being sent; there's virtually no delay, and recent innovations now enable you to communicate with voice as well as text. At any one time there are thousands of groups, so your chances of finding a topic you're interested in are high. As with e-mail and face-to-face conversation, the purposes of chat groups vary from communication that simply maintains connection with others (what many would call "idle chatter" or "phatic communication") to extremely significant discussions in science, education, health, politics, and just about any field you can name. Like mailing lists, chat groups have the great advantage of enabling you to communicate with people you would never meet and interact with

E-Talk . ▪ ▪ ▪ ▪ ▪ .

Gendered E-Mail

Studies of gender differences find that women's e-mails are more relational and expressive and that they focus more on domestic and personal topics than do the e-mails of males (Colley, Todd, Bland, Holmes, Khanom, & Pike, 2004). Do you find this difference in your own e-mail experience? What other gender differences do you observe?

TABLE 1.1 The Uses of the Internet

Here are the 10 most frequent activities Americans engaged in online in the years 2000 and 2004. How many of these activities have you engaged in during, say, the last month?

ACTIVITY	NUMBER OF USERS 2000	NUMBER OF USERS 2004
Use e-mail	45,000,000	58,000,000
Get news	19,000,000	35,000,000
Check the weather	14,000,000	25,000,000
Conduct job-related research	14,000,000	24,000,000
Research a product before buying	12,000,000	19,000,000
Search for political news or information	9,000,000	24,000,000
Send instant message	10,000,000	15,000,000
Conduct research for school	9,000,000	14,000,000
Get travel information	6,000,000	10,000,000
Get health or medical information	6,000,000	7,000,000

Source: Rainie, Lee. Horrigan, John. A decade of adoption: how the internet has woven itself into American Life. Pew Internet & American Life Project, January 25, 2005, **www.pewinternet.org/PPF/r/148/report_display.asp.**

face-to-face. Because many chat groups are international, they provide excellent exposure to other cultures, other ideas, and other ways of communicating.

A particular subcategory of chat group includes the social networking services used by high school and college students—such as Facebook, MySpace, Friendster, LiveJournal, and Xanga, to name just a few. These services not only enable you to communicate with people you know but provide a useful and simple way to meet new people and thus to enlarge your network and perhaps meet a best friend or even a lifetime romantic partner. You can post your profile, in some cases in considerable detail and with music and video; have ready access to a wide social network; and voice your opinions about just anything. Depending on the source you read, these websites are among the most popular on the entire Internet and number their users in the millions.

Blogs and **interactive websites** now enable you to express your opinions for others to read and react to, and to communicate your reactions to what others say. Increasingly blogs are being used for more relational purposes, such as maintaining family or group ties and encouraging frequent communication among family or group members.

DIFFERENCES BETWEEN FACE-TO-FACE AND COMPUTER-MEDIATED COMMUNICATION One of the major differences between face-to-face and computer-mediated communication lies in the permanency of electronic communication as contrasted with the evanescence of face-to-face communication. Here are a few of the consequences of this difference—all of which suggest added caution when you communicate electronically, whether it's via e-mail, chat room conversations, or blog posts:

1. Electronic messages are difficult to destroy. Often e-mails that you think you deleted will remain on servers and workstations and may be retrieved by a clever hacker.

"Instant message, sire."

The Ethics of Communicating in Cyberspace

With the explosion in computer communication, "nethics" (the ethics of Internet communication) has become an important part of ethical communication generally. Of course, the same ethical principles that govern face-to-face interaction should also prevail when you communicate online. Here, however, are a few principles with special relevance to computer-mediated communication. It's unethical to:

1. Invade the privacy of others. Reading the files of another person or breaking into files that you're not authorized to read is unethical, just as it would be to read a person's diary or personal letters.
2. Harm others or their property. For example, it is unethical to create computer viruses; publish instructions for making bombs; or create websites that promote sexism, racism, heterosexism, or ageism.
3. Spread falsehoods. Lying on the Internet—about other people, about the powers of medical or herbal treatment, or about yourself (by, say, misrepresenting yourself in chat groups) is unethical.
4. Plagiarize. Appropriating the work of another as your own—whether the original work appeared on the Internet or in a book or journal—is unethical.
5. Steal passwords, PIN numbers, or authorization codes that belong to others. Such theft is similar to stealing and using another person's credit card.
6. Copy software programs that you haven't paid for.

What Would You Do?

As an experiment you develop a computer virus that can destroy websites. Recently you've come across various websites that you feel promote child pornography. You wonder if you can ethically destroy these websites. Further, you wonder if not destroying them may actually be more unethical than using your newly developed virus.

2. Electronic messages may easily be made public; the ease of forwarding e-mails or newsgroup postings makes it especially important that you consider that what you intend for one person may actually be received by many.
3. Electronic messages are not privileged communication and can easily be used against you, especially in the workplace. For example, criticism of others may one day give rise to accusations of discrimination.
4. Electronic messages provide permanent records, making it impossible for you to say, for example, "That's not exactly what I said" if it is indeed exactly what you said; it will be there in black and white.
5. Electronic message files may be accessed by others, whether by a nosy colleague at the next desk or by a visiting neighbor, and can then be forwarded to others.
6. Electronic messages and photos may be accessed by employers or by college administrators. Photos of you at a college party may not be the photos you'd want your prospective employer to see; nor would you want them to be used along with your graduate school application.

Table 1.2 presents some of the similarities and differences between face-to-face and computer-mediated communication. As you review the table, you may wish to add other similarities and differences or to take issue with the ones identified here.

The Elements of Interpersonal Communication

Given the basic definition of interpersonal communication, the transactional perspective, and an understanding that interpersonal communication occurs in many different forms, let's expand our model as in Figure 1.2 and look at each of the es-

Throughout this text face-to-face and computer-mediated interpersonal communication are discussed, compared, and contrasted. Here is a brief summary of some communication concepts and some of the ways in which face-to-face and computer-mediated communication are similar and different. What other similarities and differences would you identify?

INTERPERSONAL COMMUNICATION ELEMENT	FACE-TO-FACE COMMUNICATION	COMPUTER-MEDIATED COMMUNICATION
Sender [speaking turn, presentation of self, impression management]	Visual appearance communicates who you are; personal characteristics (sex, approximate age, race, etc.) are overt and open to visual inspection; receiver controls the order of what is attended to; disguise is difficult.	You present the self you want others to see; personal characteristics are covert and are revealed when you want to reveal them; speaker controls the order of revelation; disguise or anonymity is easy.
	You compete for the speaker's turn and time with the other person(s); you can be interrupted.	It's always your turn; speaker time is unlimited; you can't be interrupted.
Receiver [number, interests, third party, impression formation]	One or a few who are in your visual field.	One, a few, or as many as you find in a chat room, have on your e-mail list, or who read your bulletin board posts.
	Limited to those you've have the opportunity to meet; often difficult to find people who have the same interests you do, especially in isolated communities with little mobility.	Virtually unlimited; you can more easily and quickly find people who match your interests.
	Your messages can be overheard by or repeated to third parties, but not verbatim and not with the same accuracy.	Your messages can be retrieved by others or forwarded verbatim to a third party or to hundreds of third parties (with or without your knowledge).
	Impressions are based on the verbal and nonverbal cues receiver perceives.	Impressions are based on text messages (usually) receiver reads.
Context [physical, temporal social–psychological, cultural]	Where you both are; together in essentially the same physical space.	Where you and receiver each want to be, separated in space.
	As it happens; you have little control over the context once you're in a communication situation.	You can more easily choose the timing—when you want to respond.
	Communication is synchronous—messages are exchanged at the same time.	Communication may be synchronous, as in chat rooms and instant messaging, or asynchronous—messages are exchanged at different times—as in e-mail and bulletin board postings.
Channel	Auditory + visual + tactile + proxemic.	Visual for text (though the auditory and visual for graphics and video are available).
	Two-way channel enabling immediate interactivity.	Two-way channels, some enabling immediate and some delayed interactivity.
Messages [verbal, nonverbal, permanence, purposes]	Spoken words along with your gestures, eye contact, accent, paralinguistic cues, space, touch, clothing, hair and all the nonverbal cues.	Written words in purely text-based CMC, though that's changing.
	Temporary unless recorded; speech signals fade rapidly.	Permanent unless erased.
	Rarely are abbreviations verbally expressed.	Limited nonverbal cues; some can be created with emoticons or words and some (like smells and touch) cannot.
		Uses lots of abbreviations.
Feedforward	Conveyed nonverbally and verbally early in the interaction.	In e-mail it's given in the headings and subject line, as well as in the opening sentences.
Ethics and Deception	Presentation of false physical self is more difficult, though not impossible; false psychological and social selves are easier.	Presentation of false physical self as well as false psychological and social selves are relatively easy.
	Nonverbal leakage cues often give you away when you're lying.	Lying is probably relatively easy.

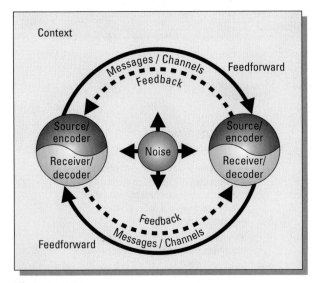

Figure 1.2

The Process of Interpersonal Communication

This model puts into visual form the various elements of the interpersonal communication process. How would you diagram the interpersonal communication process?

sential elements in interpersonal communication: source–receiver, messages, feedback, feedforward, channel, noise, context, and competence. Along with this discussion you may wish to visit the websites of some of the major communication organizations to see how they discuss communication. See, for example, www.natcom.org and www.icahdq.org for the two major academic associations in communication.

Source–Receiver

Interpersonal communication involves at least two persons. Each functions as a **source** (formulates and sends messages) and operates as a **receiver** (receives and understands messages). The linked term *source–receiver* emphasizes that each person is both source and receiver.

By putting your meanings into sound waves (or gestures, facial expressions, or body movements), you're putting your thoughts and feelings into a **code,** or a set of symbols—a process called *en*coding. By translating sound (and light) waves into ideas, you're taking them out of the code they're in, a process called *de*coding. So we can call speakers (or, more generally, senders) **encoders:** those who put their meanings *into* a code. And we can call listeners (or, more generally, receivers) **decoders:** those who take meanings *out of* a code. Since encoding and decoding activities are combined in each person, the term *encoding–decoding* is used to emphasize this inevitable dual function.

Usually you encode an idea into a code that the other person understands; for example, you use words and gestures for which both you and the other person have similar meanings. At times, however, you may want to exclude others; so, for example, you might speak in a language that only one of your listeners knows or use jargon to prevent others from understanding. At other times, you may assume incorrectly that the other person knows your code and, for example, unknowingly use words or gestures the other person simply doesn't understand.

For interpersonal communication to occur, then, meanings must be both encoded and decoded. If Jamie has his eyes closed and is wearing stereo headphones as his dad is speaking to him, interpersonal communication is not taking place—simply because the messages—both verbal and nonverbal—are not being received.

Messages

For interpersonal communication to exist, **messages** that express your thoughts and feelings must be sent and received. Interpersonal communication may be verbal or nonverbal, but it's usually a combination of both. You communicate interpersonally with words as well as with gestures and touch, for example. Even the clothes you wear communicate, as do the way you walk and the way you shake hands, comb your hair, sit, smile, or frown. Everything about you has the potential to send interpersonal messages, and every message has an **effect,** or outcome.

In face-to-face communication your messages are both verbal and nonverbal; you supplement your words with facial expressions, body movements, and variations in vocal volume and rate, for example. When you communicate through a keyboard, your message is communicated basically with words. This does not mean that you

  From listening comes wisdom, and from speaking repentance.

—Italian proverb

cannot communicate emotional meanings; in fact, some researchers have argued that diagrams, pictures, and varied typefaces enable you to communicate messages that are rich in emotional meaning (Lea & Spears, 1995). Similarly, you can use emoticons. But basically a keyboarded or written message is communicated with words. Because of this, sarcasm, for example, is difficult to convey unambiguously—whereas in face-to-face communication you might wink or smile to indicate that your message should not be taken seriously or literally.

METAMESSAGES One very special type of message is the **metamessage.** This type of message refers to other messages, it's a message about a message. Both verbal and nonverbal messages can be metacommunicational. Verbally, you can convey metamessages such as "Do you understand what I'm saying?" Nonverbally, you can wink to communicate that you're lying or being sarcastic. Your interpersonal effectiveness will often hinge on your competence in metacommunication. For example, in conflict situations it's often helpful to talk about the way you argue or what your raised voice means. In romantic relationships, it may be helpful to talk about what each of you means by "exclusive" or "love." On the job, it's often necessary to talk about the ways people delegate orders or express criticism.

MESSAGE OVERLOAD Message overload (often called information overload in business) is one of the greatest obstacles to communication efficiency and may even lead to health problems in corporate managers (Lee, 2000). The ease with which people can copy or forward e-mail and Internet messages has obviously contributed to message overload, as has the junk e-mail and spam that seems to grow every day. Invariably, you must select certain messages to attend to and other messages to ignore. Today, for example, the American worker is exposed to more messages in one year than a person living in 1900 was in his or her entire life. The average employee now receives more than 50 e-mails daily. And in one day the average manager sends and receives more than 100 documents.

One of the problems message overload creates is that it absorbs an enormous amount of time. The more messages you have to deal with, the less time you have for the most important messages or tasks. Similarly, errors are more likely under conditions of message overload, simply because you cannot devote the needed time to any one item. The more rushed you are, the more likely you are to make mistakes. Additionally, research shows that under conditions of message overload, you're more likely to respond to the simpler messages and to generate simpler responses (Jones, Ravid, & Rafaeli, 2004).

Another problem is that the overabundance of messages may make it difficult for you to determine efficiently which messages need immediate attention and which don't, which messages may be discarded and which must be retained.

FEEDBACK MESSAGES **Feedback** is a special type of message. When you send a spoken or written message to another person, you get feedback from your own message: You hear what you say, you feel the way you move, you see what you write. On the basis of this information, you may correct yourself, rephrase something, or perhaps smile at a clever turn of phrase. This is self-feedback.

You also get feedback from others. The person with whom you're communicating is constantly sending you messages that indicate how he or she is receiving and responding to your messages. Nods of agreement, smiles, puzzled looks, and questions asking for clarification are all examples of feedback.

Notice that in face-to-face communication you can monitor the feedback of the other person as you're speaking. In computer-mediated communication that feedback will come much later and thus is likely to be more clearly thought out and perhaps more closely monitored.

FEEDFORWARD MESSAGES Much as feedback contains information about messages already sent, **feedforward** conveys information about messages before you send them.

■ **What Do You Say**

Stopping Overload

Several relatives have developed chain e-mail lists and send you virtually everything they come across as they surf the Internet. You need to stop this e-mail overload. **What Do You Say?** To whom? Through what channel?

Giving Effective Feedback

Here are three situations in which you might want to give feedback. For each situation (a) indicate the kind of feedback that you would consider appropriate and (b) write one or two sentences in which you express this appropriate feedback.

1. A colleague persists in talking explicitly about sex despite your previous and frequent objections.
2. A telemarketer—the fifth this evening—asks you to change your long-distance carrier.
3. A homeless person smiles at you on the street and asks for some change.

Feedback comes in a variety of styles and serves a variety of purposes. Use it and read it; it's a significant part of the interpersonal interaction.

Opening comments such as "Wait until you hear this" or "I'm not sure of this, but . . ." or "Don't get me wrong, but . . ." are examples of feedforward. These messages tell the listener something about the messages to come or about the way you'd like the listener to respond. Nonverbally, you give feedforward by, for example, your facial expressions, eye contact, and physical posture; with these nonverbal messages you tell the other person something about the messages you'll be sending. A smile may signal a pleasant message; eye avoidance may signal that the message to come is difficult and perhaps uncomfortable to express. A book's table of contents, its preface, and (usually) its first chapter are also examples of feedforward. In computer-mediated communication the subject heading on your e-mail well illustrates this function of feedforward, as do the phone numbers and names that come up on your cell phone or call-waiting device.

Channel

The communication **channel** is the medium through which message signals pass. The channel works like a bridge connecting source and receiver. Normally two, three, or four channels are used simultaneously. For example, in face-to-face **speech** interactions, you speak and listen, using the vocal–auditory channel. You also, however, make gestures and receive these signals visually, using the visual channel. Similarly, you emit odors and smell those of others (using the chemical channel). Often you touch one another, and this too communicates (using the tactile channel).

Another way to classify channels is by the means of communication. Thus, face-to-face contact, telephones, e-mail, movies, television, smoke signals, and telegraph would be types of channels. Of most relevance today, of course, is the difference between face-to-face and computer-mediated interpersonal communication: interaction through e-mail, chat groups, instant messaging, news postings, film, television, radio, or fax.

At times one or more channels may be damaged. For example, in the case of people who are blind, the visual channel is impaired and so adjustments have to be made. Table 1.3 gives you an idea of how such adjustments between blind and sighted persons can make interpersonal communication more effective.

Noise

Noise is anything that interferes with your receiving a message. Just as messages may be auditory or visual, noise, too, comes in both auditory and visual forms. Four types of noise are especially relevant:

TABLE 1.3   *Interpersonal Communication Tips*

BETWEEN BLIND AND SIGHTED PEOPLE

People vary greatly in their visual abilities, some are totally blind, some are partially sighted, and some have unimpaired vision. Ninety percent of people who are "legally blind" have some vision. All, however, have the same need for communication and information. Here are some tips for making communication between blind and sighted people more effective.

If you're the sighted person and are talking with a blind person:

1. Identify yourself; don't assume the blind person will recognize your voice.
2. Face the blind person; you'll be easier to hear. At the same time, don't shout. People who are visually impaired are not hearing impaired. Speak at your normal volume.
3. Because your gestures, eye movements, and facial expressions cannot be seen, encode into speech all the meanings you wish to communicate.
4. Use audible turn-taking cues. When you pass the role of speaker to a person who's visually impaired, don't rely on nonverbal cues; instead, say something like "Do you agree with that, Joe?"
5. Use normal vocabulary and discuss topics that you'd discuss with sighted people. Don't avoid terms like *see* or *look* or even *blind*. Don't avoid discussing a television show or a painting or the way your new car looks; these are normal conversational topics for all people.
6. In guiding a person who is blind, follow these simple suggestions:
   a. If you want to offer assistance, ask first ("Would you like me to hold your arm as we go upstairs?") instead of just grabbing the person.
   b. Identify obstacles before reaching them: "There are three steps coming up."
   c. When you have to leave, make sure the blind person is comfortable where he or she is. For example, ask if the person would like to sit while you get the coffee.

If you're the blind person and are interacting with sighted person:

1. Help the sighted person meet your special communication needs. If you want your surroundings described, ask. If you want the person to read the road signs, ask.
2. Be patient with the sighted person. Many people are nervous talking with people who are blind for fear of offending. Put them at ease in a way that also makes you more comfortable.

Source: These suggestions were drawn from a variety of sources: **www.cincyblind.org/what _do_you_do_htm**, **www.abwa.asn.au/**, and **www.dol.gov** (all accessed March 26, 2005).

1. **Physical noise** is interference that is external to both speaker and listener; it hampers the physical transmission of the signal or message and includes impediments such as the screeching of passing cars, the hum of a computer, sunglasses, extraneous messages, illegible handwriting, blurred type or fonts that are too small or difficult to read, misspellings and poor grammar, and pop-up ads.

2. **Physiological noise** is created by barriers within the sender or receiver and includes impairments such as loss of vision, hearing loss, articulation problems, and memory loss.

3. **Psychological noise** is mental interference in speaker or listener and includes preconceived ideas, wandering thoughts, biases and prejudices, closed-mindedness, and extreme emotionalism.

4. **Semantic noise** is interference created when the speaker and listener have different meaning systems; types of semantic noise include linguistic or dialectical differences, the use of jargon or overly complex terms, and ambiguous or overly abstract terms whose meanings can be easily misinterpreted.

As you can see from these examples, noise is anything that distorts your reception of the messages of others or their reception of your messages.

A useful concept in understanding noise and its importance in communication is **signal-to-noise ratio.** In this phrase the term *signal* refers to information that you'd

E-Talk

Spamming and Spimming

Just as spam—unwanted e-mail—intrudes into your e-mail, spim—essentially spam except that it comes through in instant messaging, is likewise adding noise to your computer-mediated communications. How might you use spim (also written spIM) ethically to get people to visit your website? Would you support a "don't spam/spim" list on the analogy of the "don't call" list?

find useful; *noise* refers to information that is useless (to you). So, for example, mailing lists or newsgroups that contained lots of useful information would be high on signal and low on noise; those that contained lots of useless information would be high on noise and low on signal.

All communications contain noise. Noise cannot be totally eliminated, but its effects can be reduced. Making your language more precise, sharpening your skills for sending and receiving nonverbal messages, and improving your listening and feedback skills are some ways to combat the influence of noise.

Context

Communication always takes place within a context: an environment that influences the form and the content of communication. At times this context is so natural that you ignore it, like street noise. At other times the context stands out, and the ways in which it restricts or stimulates your communications are obvious. Think, for example, of the different ways you'd talk at a funeral, in a quiet restaurant, and at a rock concert. And consider how the same "How are you?" will have very different meanings depending on the context: Said to a passing acquaintance, it means "Hello," whereas said to a sick friend in the hospital, it means "How are you feeling?"

The **context of communication** has at least four dimensions: physical, social–psychological, temporal, and cultural. The room, workplace, or outdoor space in which communication takes place—the tangible or concrete environment—is the *physical dimension*. When you communicate with someone face-to-face, you're both in essentially the same physical environment. In computer-mediated communication you may be in drastically different environments; one of you may be on a beach in San Juan, and the other may be in a Wall Street office.

The *social–psychological* dimension includes, for example, the status relationships among the participants: distinctions such as who is the employer and who the employee, who is the salesperson and who the store owner. The formality or informality, the friendliness or hostility, the cooperativeness or competitiveness of the interaction are also part of the social–psychological dimension.

The *temporal* or *time dimension* has to do with where a particular message fits into a sequence of communication events. For example, if you tell a joke about sickness immediately after your friend tells you she is sick, the joke will be perceived differently from the same joke told as one of a series of similar jokes to your friends in the locker room of the gym.

The *cultural dimension* consists of the rules, norms, beliefs, and attitudes of the people communicating that are passed from one generation to another. For example, in some cultures it's considered polite to talk to strangers; in others that is something to be avoided.

*I*nterpersonal Competence

Your ability to communicate effectively is your **interpersonal competence** (Spitzberg & Cupach, 1989; Wilson & Sabee, 2003). A major goal of this text (and of your course) is to expand and enlarge your competence so you'll have a greater arsenal of communication options at your disposal. It's much like learning vocabulary: The more words you know, the more ways you'll have to express yourself. The greater your interpersonal competence, the more options you'll have for communicating with friends, lovers, and family; with colleagues on the job; and in just about any situation in which you'll talk with another person. The greater your competence, the greater your own power to accomplish successfully what you want to accomplish—to ask for a raise or a date; establish temporary work relationships, long-term friendships, or romantic relationships; communicate empathy and support; or gain

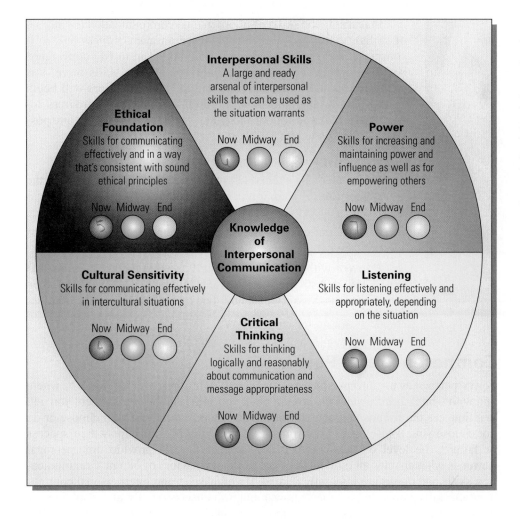

Figure 1.3
The Competent Interpersonal Communicator
Indicate how competent you feel you are in each of these six areas (the six themes of *Interpersonal Messages*) right now by giving yourself scores from 1 (little competence) to 10 (a great deal of competence). Return to this figure periodically to rerate yourself. By the end of the course, you should have increased all of your scores significantly.

compliance or resist the compliance tactics of others. Whatever your interpersonal goal, increased competence will help you accomplish it more effectively.

In short, interpersonal competence includes knowing how interpersonal communication works and how to best achieve your purposes by adjusting your messages according to the context of the interaction, the person with whom you're interacting, and a host of other factors discussed throughout this text. The process goes like this: Knowledge of interpersonal communication *leads to* greater interpersonal ability *leads to* a greater number of available choices or options for interacting *leads to* greater likelihood of interpersonal effectiveness.

As shown in Figure 1.3, interpersonal competence consists largely of understanding the way interpersonal communication works and mastering its **skills** (including **power** and the often neglected skills of **listening**). These skills depend on **critical thinking,** are specific to a given **culture,** and rest on an **ethical foundation.** Understanding the nature of these six themes of competence and how they are highlighted in this text will enable you to gain the most from studying and working with this material.

Competence and Interpersonal Skills

This text explains the theory and research in interpersonal communication in order to provide you with a solid understanding of how interpersonal communication works. With that understanding as a firm foundation, you'll be better able to develop and master the very practical skills of interpersonal communication.

In learning the skills of interpersonal communication (or any set of skills), you'll probably at first sense an awkwardness and self-consciousness; the new behaviors may not seem to fit comfortably. As you develop more understanding and use the skills more, this awkwardness will gradually fade and the new behaviors will begin to feel comfortable and natural. You'll facilitate your progress toward mastery if you follow a logical system of steps. Here's one possible system, called STEP (Skill, Theory, Example, Practice):

1. Get a clear understanding of what the *skill* is.

2. Understand the *theory;* if you understand the reasons for the suggestions offered, it will help make the skill more logical.

3. Develop *examples,* especially your own; this will help to make the material covered here a more integral part of communication behavior.

4. *Practice* with the Skill Building Exercises included in this text as well as with those on the website; practice alone at first, then with supportive friends, and then in general day-to-day interactions.

Competence and Power

Power permeates all interpersonal relationships. It influences what you do, when, and with whom. It influences the employment you seek and the employment you get. It influences the friends you choose and do not choose and those who choose or do not choose you. It influences your romantic and family relationships—their success or failure, the level of satisfaction or dissatisfaction they provide. Interpersonal **power** is what enables an individual to control the behaviors of others. Communication skills and power are integrally related. If you have strong interpersonal communication skills, you're likely to have power and influence—socially, at school, in your close relationships, at work, or just about any place where people interact. If you have poor interpersonal skills, you're likely to have much less power and influence. Because of the importance of power, discussions covering a wide range of issues relating to power are integrated throughout this text.

Competence and Listening

Often we tend to think of competence in interpersonal communication as "speaking effectiveness," paying little attention to listening. But listening is an integral part of interpersonal communication; you cannot be a competent communicator if you're a poor listener. Listening, therefore, is emphasized in this text in two major ways: (1) *Chapter 5 is devoted to listening* and covers the nature and importance of listening, the steps you go through in listening, the role of culture and gender in listening, and ways to increase your listening effectiveness. (2) *Ten "Listen to This" boxes are positioned throughout the text* to illustrate how listening relates to the topic of each chapter and to provide a variety of specific listening skills. Among the topics of these boxes are the importance of listening to yourself, the role of gender differences, and ways to listen during conflict.

Competence, Critical Thinking, and Mindfulness

Without critical thinking there can be no competent exchange of ideas. **Critical thinking** is logical thinking; it's thinking that is well reasoned, unbiased, and clear. It involves thinking intelligently, carefully, and with as much clarity as possible. It's the opposite of what you'd call sloppy, illogical, or careless thinking. And, not surprisingly, according to one study of corporate executives, critical thinking is one of the stepping stones to effective management (Miller, 1997, p. 71).

A special kind of critical thinking is mindfulness. **Mindfulness** is a state of awareness in which you're conscious of your reasons for thinking or behaving. In its opposite, mindlessness, you lack conscious awareness of what or how you're thinking (Langer, 1989). To apply interpersonal skills effectively in conversation, you need to be mindful of the unique communication situation you're in, of your available communication options, and of the reasons why one option is likely to be better than the others (Elmes & Gemmill, 1990; Burgoon, Berger, & Waldron, 2000).

To increase mindfulness, try the following suggestions (Langer, 1989).

- *Create and re-create categories.* Group things in different ways; remember that people are constantly changing, so the categories into which you may group them also should change. Learn to see objects, events, and people as belonging to a wide variety of categories. Try to see, for example, your prospective romantic partner in a variety of roles—child, parent, employee, neighbor, friend, financial contributor, and so on.

- *Be open to new information and points of view,* even when these contradict your most firmly held beliefs. New information forces you to reconsider what might be outmoded ways of thinking and can help you challenge long-held but now inappropriate beliefs and attitudes.

- *Beware of relying too heavily on first impressions* (Chanowitz & Langer, 1981; Langer, 1989). Treat first impressions as tentative, as hypotheses that need further investigation. Be prepared to revise, reject, or accept these initial impressions.

- *Think before you act.* Especially in delicate situations such as anger or commitment messages, it's wise to pause and think over the situation mindfully (DeVito, 2003b). In this way you'll stand a better chance of acting and reacting appropriately.

Competence and Culture

The term *culture* refers to the lifestyle of a group of people. A group's culture consists of their values, beliefs, artifacts, ways of behaving, and ways of communicating. Culture includes all that members of a social group have produced and developed—their language, ways of thinking, art, laws, and religion. Culture is transmitted from one generation to another not through genes but through communication and learning; especially through the teachings of parents, peer groups, schools, religious institutions, and government agencies. Because most cultures teach women and men different attitudes and ways of communicating, many of the gender differences we observe may be considered cultural. So, while not minimizing the biological differences between men and women, most people agree that gender differences are, in part, cultural.

Competence is sometimes culture specific; communications that prove effective in one culture will not necessarily prove effective in another. For example, giving a birthday gift to a close friend would be appreciated by members of many cultures and in some cases would be expected. But Jehovah's Witnesses frown on this practice, because they don't celebrate birthdays (Dresser, 1996, 1999, 2005). Because of the vast range of cultural differences that affect interpersonal communication, every chapter discusses the role of culture and Chapter 2 focuses exclusively on culture and intercultural communication.

Competence and Ethics

Interpersonal communication also involves questions of **ethics,** or right and wrong. There is a moral dimension to any interpersonal communication act (Jaksa & Pritchard, 1994; Bok, 1978). For example, although it might be effective to lie in selling a product, it would not be ethical. The decisions you make concerning com-

Flirting On and Off

One of the differences research finds between face-to-face and online flirting is that in the online situation reality and fantasy become somewhat blurred (Whitty, 2003). What other differences do you find between face-to-face and computer-mediated flirtations?

munication need to be guided by what you consider right as well as by what you consider effective.

Ethical dimensions of interpersonal communication are presented throughout the text in "Ethical Messages" features. Woven through these discussions of ethics are two overriding questions that will influence all your ethical decisions: (1) Are ethical principles objective or subjective? and (2) Does the end justify the means?

In an *objective* view, you'd argue that the rightness or wrongness of an act is absolute and exists apart from the values or beliefs of any individual or culture. With this view, you'd hold that there are standards that apply to all people in all situations at all times. If lying, false advertising, using illegally obtained evidence, or revealing secrets you've promised to keep were considered unethical, then they would be unethical regardless of circumstances or of cultural values and beliefs. In an objective view the end can never justify the means; an unethical act is never justified regardless of how good or beneficial its results (or ends) might be.

In a *subjective* view of ethics, you'd argue that absolute statements about right and wrong are too rigid and that the ethics of a message depends on the culture's values and beliefs as well as on the particular circumstances. Thus, a subjective position would claim that lying might be wrong to win votes or sell cigarettes, but that it might be quite ethical if good would result from it—as when we try to make friends feel better by telling them that they look great or that they'll get well soon. In a subjective view a good end would often justify the use of means that would in other situations be considered unethical.

As you read the Ethical Messages boxes and respond to the ethical issues raised, ask yourself to what extent your responses reflect an objective or a subjective view of ethics and to what extent you believe that the end may justify the means.

These six themes of competence are not separate and distinct from one another but rather interact and overlap. For example, as already noted, critical thinking pervades the entire interpersonal communication process, but it also serves as a foundation for your cultural awareness, listening effectiveness, and skill development. Similarly, an awareness of cultural differences will make you more effective as a listener, more discerning in using skills, and more conscious of the ethical dimension of interpersonal communication. So, as you read the text and work actively with the concepts, remember that everything in it—including the regular text, the boxed features, the material in the margins, and the summaries and vocabulary tests at the end of the chapters—is designed to contribute to one overarching aim: to increase your interpersonal communication competence.

*P*rinciples of Interpersonal Communication

Another way to define interpersonal communication is to consider its major principles. These principles are significant in terms of explaining theory and also, as you'll see, have very practical applications.

Interpersonal Communication Is a Package of Signals

Communication behaviors, whether they involve verbal messages, gestures, or some combination thereof, usually occur in "packages" (Pittenger, Hockett, & Danehy,

1960). Usually, verbal and nonverbal behaviors reinforce or support each other. All parts of a message system normally work together to communicate a particular meaning. You don't express fear with words while the rest of your body is relaxed. You don't express anger through your posture while your face smiles. Your entire body works together—verbally and nonverbally—to express your thoughts and feelings.

With any form of communication, whether interpersonal messages, small group communication, public speaking, or mass media, you probably pay little attention to its "packaged" nature. It goes unnoticed. But when there's an incongruity—when the chilly handshake belies the verbal greeting, when the nervous posture belies the focused stare, when the constant preening belies the expressions of being comfortable and at ease—you take notice. Invariably you begin to question the credibility, the sincerity, and the honesty of the individual.

Often contradictory messages are sent over a period of time. Note, for example, that in the following interaction the employee is being given two directives: (1) Use initiative, and (2) Don't use initiative. Regardless of what he or she does, rejection will follow.

> **Employer:** You've got to learn to take more initiative. You never seem to take charge, to take control.
> **Employee:** (Takes the initiative, makes decisions.)
> **Employer:** You've got to learn to follow the chain of command and not do things just because you want to.
> **Employee:** (Goes back to old ways, not taking any initiative.)
> **Employer:** Well, I told you. We expect more initiative from you.

Contradictory messages are particularly damaging when children are involved. Children can neither escape from such situations nor communicate about the communications. They can't talk about the lack of correspondence between one set of messages and another set. They can't ask their parents, for example, why they don't hold them or hug them when they say they love them.

Contradictory messages may be the result of the desire to communicate two different emotions or feelings. For example, you may like a person and want to communicate a positive feeling, but you may also feel resentment toward this person and want to communicate a negative feeling as well. The result is that you communicate both feelings; for example, you say that you're happy to see the person, but your facial expression and body posture communicate your negative feelings (Beier, 1974). In this example, and in many similar cases, the socially acceptable message is usually communicated verbally, whereas the less socially acceptable message is communicated nonverbally.

Interpersonal Communication Involves Content *and* Relationship Messages

Interpersonal messages combine **content and relationship dimensions.** That is, they refer to the real world, to something external to both speaker and listener; and at the same time they also refer to the relationship between the parties. For example, a supervisor may say to a trainee, "See me after the meeting." This simple message has a content message that tells the trainee to see the supervisor after the meeting. It also contains a **relationship message** that says something about the connection between the supervisor and the trainee. Even the use of the simple command shows there is a status difference that allows the supervisor to command the trainee. You can appreciate this most clearly if you visualize this command being made by the trainee to the supervisor. It appears awkward and out of place, because it violates the normal relationship between supervisor and trainee.

"It's not about the story. It's about Daddy taking time out of his busy day to read you the story."

Deborah Tannen, in her recent book *You're Wearing That?* (2006), gives lots of examples of content and relationship communication and the problems that can result from different interpretations. For example, the mother who says, "Are you going to quarter those tomatoes?" thinks she is communicating solely a content message. To the daughter, however, the message is largely relational and is in fact a criticism of the way she intends to cut the tomatoes. Questions, especially, may appear to be objective and focused on content but often are perceived as attacks, as in the title of Tannen's book. For example, here are some questions that you may have been asked—or that you yourself may have asked. Can you identify the potential relationship messages that the listener might receive in each case?

- *You're calling me?*
- *Did you say, you're applying to* medical *school?*
- *You're in love?*
- *You paid $100 for that?*
- *And that's* all *you did?*

Many conflicts arise because people misunderstand relationship messages and cannot clarify them. Other problems arise when people fail to see the difference between content messages and relationship messages. A good example occurred when my mother came to stay for a week at a summer place I had. On the first day she swept the kitchen floor six times. I had repeatedly told her that it did not need sweeping, that I would be tracking in dirt and mud from the outside. She persisted in sweeping, however, saying that the floor was dirty. On the content level, we were talking about the value of sweeping the kitchen floor. On the relationship level, however, we were talking about something quite different. We were each saying, "This is my house." When I realized this, I stopped complaining about the relative usefulness of sweeping a floor that did not need sweeping. Not surprisingly, she stopped sweeping.

Arguments over the content dimension of a message—such as what happened in a movie—are relatively easy to resolve. You may, for example, simply ask a third person what took place or see the movie again. Arguments on the relationship level, however, are much more difficult to resolve, in part because people seldom recognize that the argument is about relationship messages.

Skill building
exercise

Content and Relationship Messages

How would you communicate both the content and the relationship messages in the following situations?

1. After a date that you didn't enjoy and don't want to repeat ever again, you want to express your sincere thanks, but you don't want to be misinterpreted as communicating any indication that you would go on another date with this person.
2. You're tutoring a high school freshman in algebra, but your tutee is really terrible and isn't paying attention or doing the homework you assign. You need to change this behavior and motivate a great change, yet at the same time you don't want to discourage or demoralize the young student.
3. You're interested in dating a student in your sociology class, but you don't know if the feeling is mutual. So you decide to ask for the date but want to do it in such a way that if your invitation is refused, you will be able to save face.

Content and relationship messages serve different communication functions. Being able to distinguish between them is prerequisite to using and responding to them effectively.

Interpersonal Communication Is a Process of Adjustment

The principle of **adjustment** states that interpersonal communication can take place only to the extent that the people talking share the same communication system. We can easily understand this when dealing with speakers of two different languages; much miscommunication is likely to occur. The principle, however, takes on particular relevance when you realize that no two people share identical communication systems. Parents and children, for example, not only have very different vocabularies but also, more importantly, have different meanings for some of the terms they have in common. (Consider, for example, the differences between parents' and children's understanding of such terms as *music, success,* and *family*.) Different cultures and social groups, even when they share a common language, also have different nonverbal communication systems. To the extent that these systems differ, communication will be hindered.

Part of the art of interpersonal communication is learning the other person's signals, how they're used, and what they mean. People in close relationships—either as intimate friends or as romantic partners—realize that learning the other person's signals takes a long time and, often, great patience. If you want to understand what another person means—by smiling, by saying "I love you," by arguing about trivial matters, by making self-deprecating comments—you have to learn that person's system of signals. Furthermore, you have to share your own system of signals with others so that they can better understand you. Although some people may know what you mean by your silence or by your avoidance of eye contact, others may not. You cannot expect others to decode your behaviors accurately without help.

This principle is especially important in intercultural communication, largely because people from different cultures use different signals and sometimes the same signals to signify quite different things. In much of the United States, focused eye contact means honesty and openness. But in Japan and in many Hispanic cultures, that same behavior may signify arrogance or disrespect if engaged in by, say, a youngster with someone significantly older.

COMMUNICATION ACCOMMODATION An interesting theory largely revolving around adjustment is communication accommodation theory. This theory holds that speakers will adjust to or accommodate to the speaking style of their listeners so as to gain, for example, social approval and greater communication efficiency (Giles, Mulac, Bradac, & Johnson, 1987). For example, when two people have a similar speech rate, they seem to be attracted to each other more than to those with dissimilar rates (Buller, LePoire, Aune, & Eloy, 1992). Speech rate similarity has also been associated with greater sociability and intimacy (Buller & Aune, 1992). Also, the speaker who uses language intensity similar to that of listeners is judged to have greater credibility than the speaker who uses intensity different from that of listeners (Aune & Kikuchi, 1993). Other research found that roommates who had similar communication attitudes (both were high in communication competence and willingness to communicate, and low in verbal aggressiveness) were highest in roommate liking and satisfaction (Martin & Anderson, 1995). Still another study even showed that people accommodate in their e-mail. For example, responses to messages that contain politeness cues were significantly more polite than responses to e-mails that did not contain such cues (Bunz & Campbell, 2004). So, for example, if you say "thank you" and "please," others are more likely to use politeness cues as well.

In some instances intermediates may "broker" accommodation in an attempt to make communication easier between two different groups. For example, communication among Chinese immigrants in New Zealand is complicated by the fact that grandparents speak only Chinese and know only the Chinese culture, whereas their grandchildren speak only English and know only the New Zealand culture. In such

Message Surveillance

How do you feel about the increasingly common practice of an employer's monitoring your electronic messages, your e-mail, and the listservs and websites that you use on the job (Miller & Weckert, 2000)? How do you feel about employer surveillance in general? How do you feel about government surveillance?

situations the parents of the children (who know both languages and cultures) serve as intermediaries or brokers between grandparents and grandchildren and help each group accommodate their communication toward the other (Ng, He, & Loong, 2004).

Interpersonal Communication Involves Power

Power, as already noted, is a major component of interpersonal competence. You cannot communicate without making some implicit comment on your power or lack of it. When in an interactional situation, therefore, recognize that on the basis of your verbal and nonverbal messages, people will assess your power and will interact accordingly.

No interpersonal relationship exists without a power dimension. Look at your own relationships and those of your friends and relatives. In each relationship, who has the greater power? In interpersonal relationships among most Americans, the more powerful person is often the one who is more attractive or the one who has more money. In other cultures the factors that contribute to power may be different and may include a person's family background, age, knowledge, or wisdom.

Research has identified six types of power: legitimate, referent, reward, coercive, expert, and information or persuasion power (French & Raven, 1968; Raven, Centers, & Rodrigues, 1975). As you listen to the messages of others (and your own) and as you observe the relationships of others (and your own), consider the role of power, how it's expressed, and how it's responded to. The more sensitive you become to the expression of power—in messages and in relationships—the more effective your interpersonal messages are likely to be.

You hold **legitimate power** when others believe you have a right—by virtue of your position—to influence or control their behaviors. Your legitimate power comes from the roles that you occupy and from the belief that because you occupy these roles, you have a right to influence others. For example, as an employer, judge, manager, or police officer you'd have legitimate power by virtue of these roles. Relate your persuasive arguments and appeals to your own role and credibility.

You have **referent power** when others wish to be like you. Referent power holders are often attractive, have considerable prestige, and are well liked and well respected. For example, you might have referent power over a younger brother because he wants to be like you. Demonstrate those qualities admired by those you wish to influence.

You have **reward power** when you control the rewards that others want. Rewards may be material (for example, money, promotion, jewelry) or social (for example, love, friendship, respect). For example, teachers have reward power over students because they control grades, letters of recommendation, and social approval. Make rewards contingent on compliance, and follow through by rewarding those who comply with your requests.

You have **coercive power** when you have the ability to administer punishments to or remove rewards from others if they do not do as you wish. Usually, people who have reward power also have coercive power. For example, teachers may give poor grades or withhold recommendations. Make clear the negative consequences that are likely to follow noncompliance. But be careful, because this one can backfire; coercive power may reduce your other power bases and can have a negative impact when used, for example, by supervisors on subordinates in business (Richmond, Davis, Saylor, & McCroskey, 1984).

You have **expert power** when others see you as having expertise or knowledge. Your expert power increases when you're seen as unbiased with nothing personally to gain from exerting this power. For example, judges have expert power in legal matters and doctors have expert power in medical matters. Cultivate your own expertise and connect your persuasive appeals to this expertise.

You have **information or persuasion power** when others see you as having the ability to communicate logically and persuasively. For example, researchers and scientists may be given information power because of their being perceived as informed and critical thinkers. Increase your communication competence; this book's major function, of course, is to explain ways for you to accomplish this.

Interpersonal Communication Is Ambiguous

All messages are ambiguous to some degree. **Ambiguity** is a condition in which a message can be interpreted as having more than one meaning. Sometimes ambiguity results when we use words that can be interpreted differently. Informal time terms offer good examples; different people may interpret terms such as *soon, right away, in a minute, early,* and *late* very differently. The terms themselves are ambiguous. A more interesting type of ambiguity is grammatical ambiguity. You can get a feel for this type of ambiguity by trying to paraphrase—rephrase in your own words—the following sentences:

- *What has the cat in its paws?*
- *Visiting neighbors can be boring.*
- *They are frying chickens.*

Each of these ambiguous sentences can be interpreted and paraphrased in at least two different ways:

- *What monster has the cat in its paws? What does the cat have in its paws?*
- *To visit neighbors is boring. Neighbors who visit are boring.*
- *Those people are frying chickens. Those chickens are for frying.*

Although these examples are particularly striking, some degree of ambiguity exists in all interpersonal communication. When you express an idea, you never communicate your meaning exactly and totally; rather, you communicate your meaning with some reasonable accuracy—enough to give the other person a reasonably clear idea of what you mean. Sometimes, of course, you're less accurate than you anticipated and your listener "gets the wrong idea," or "gets offended" when you only meant to be humorous, or "misunderstands your emotional meaning." Because of this inevitable uncertainty, you may qualify what you're saying, give an example, or ask, "Do you know what I mean?" These clarifying tactics help the other person understand your meaning and reduce uncertainty (to some degree).

Similarly, all relationships contain uncertainty. Consider a close interpersonal relationship of your own, and ask yourself the following questions. Answer each question according to a six-point scale on which 1 means "completely or almost completely uncertain" and 6 means "completely or almost completely certain." How certain are you about these questions?

- *What can and can't you and your partner say to each other in this relationship?*
- *Do you and your partner feel the same way about each other?*
- *How would you and your partner describe this relationship?*
- *What is the future of the relationship?*

Very likely you were not able to respond with "6" for all four questions. And it's equally likely that your relationship partner would be unable to respond to every question with a 6. These questions from a relationship uncertainty scale (Knobloch & Solomon, 1999)—and similar others—illustrate that you probably experience some degree of uncertainty about the norms that govern your relationship communication (question 1), the degree to which the two of you see the relationship in similar ways (question 2), the definition of the relationship (question 3), and/or the relationship's future (question 4).

■ **What Do You Say** **?**
How to Disambiguate?
You've been dating someone for several months. You'd now like to invite your date to meet your parents, but you aren't sure how your date will perceive this invitation. Your purpose is to see if this relationship has a future. **What Do You Say?** In what context?

The skills of interpersonal communication presented throughout this text can give you tools for appropriately reducing ambiguity and making your meanings as unambiguous as possible.

Interpersonal Communication Is Inevitable, Irreversible, and Unrepeatable

Three characteristics often considered together are interpersonal communication's *inevitability, irreversibility,* and *unrepeatability.*

" Once a word is allowed to escape, it can never be recalled. **"**

—Horace

COMMUNICATION IS INEVITABLE Often communication is intentional, purposeful, and consciously motivated. Sometimes, however, you are communicating even though you may not think you are, or may not even want to. Take, for example, the student sitting in the back of the room with an "expressionless" face, perhaps staring out the window. The student may think that she or he is not communicating with the teacher or with the other students. On closer inspection, however, you can see that the student *is* communicating something— perhaps lack of interest or simply anxiety about a private problem. In any event, the student is communicating whether she or he wishes to or not—demonstrating the principle of **inevitability.** Similarly, the color and type of your cell phone, the wallpaper in your room, the screen saver on your computer, and even the type and power of your computer communicate messages about you. You cannot *not* communicate. In the same way, you cannot *not* influence the person you interact with (Watzlawick, 1978). Persuasion, like communication, is also inevitable. The issue, then, is not whether you will or will not persuade or influence another; rather, it's how you'll exert your influence.

COMMUNICATION IS IRREVERSIBLE Notice that only some processes can be reversed. For example, you can turn water into ice and then reverse the process by turning the ice back into water. Other processes, however, are irreversible. You can, for example, turn grapes into wine, but you cannot reverse the process and turn wine into grapes. Interpersonal communication is an irreversible process. Although you may try to qualify, deny, or somehow reduce the effects of your message, you cannot withdraw the message you have conveyed. Similarly, once you press the send key, your e-mail is in cyberspace and impossible to reverse. Because of **irreversibility,** be careful not to say things you may wish to withdraw later. Similarly, monitor carefully messages of commitment, messages sent in anger, or messages of insult or derision. Otherwise you run the risk of saying something you'll be uncomfortable with later.

COMMUNICATION IS UNREPEATABLE The reason for communication's unrepeatability is simple: Everyone and everything are constantly changing. As a result, you never can recapture the exact same situation, frame of mind, or relationship dynamics that defined a previous interpersonal act. For example, you never can repeat meeting someone for the first time, comforting a grieving friend, or resolving a specific conflict.

You can, of course, try again; you can say, "I'm sorry I came off so pushy, can we try again?" Notice, however, that even when you say this, you have not erased the initial (and perhaps negative) impression. Instead, you try to counteract this impression by going through the motions again. In doing so, you hope to create a more positive impact that will lessen the original negative effect.

Face-to-face communication is evanescent; it fades after you have spoken. There is no trace of your communications outside of the memories of the parties involved or of those who overheard your conversation. In computer-mediated communication, however, the messages are written and may be saved, stored, and printed. Both face-to-face and computer-mediated messages may be kept confidential or revealed pub-

Interpersonal Principles in Practice

Using the principles of interpersonal communication discussed in this chapter, describe what is going on in these several cases and offer any suggestions you think would help.

- Karla's fiancé, Tom, did not speak up in defense of her proposal at a company for which both work. Karla feels that Tom created a negative attitude and encouraged others to reject her ideas. Tom says that he felt he could not defend her proposal because others in the room would have seen his defense as motivated by their relationship.

- A couple have been together for 20 years but are arguing about seemingly insignificant things—who takes out the garbage, who does the dishes, who decides where to eat, and on and on. The arguments are so frequent and so unsettling that the pair are seriously considering separating.

- Pat and Chris have been online friends for the last two years, communicating with each other at least once a day. Recently Pat wrote several things that Chris interpreted as insulting and as ridiculing Chris's feelings and dreams. Pat has written every day for the last two weeks to try to patch things up, but Chris won't respond.

Theories are extremely practical; knowing *why* something happens often helps you figure out *how* to do something.

licly. But computer messages can be made public more easily and spread more quickly than face-to-face messages. And, of course, in the case of written messages there is clear evidence of what you said and when you said it.

Interpersonal Communication Is Purposeful

Interpersonal communication can be used to accomplish a variety of purposes. Understanding how interpersonal communication serves these varied purposes will help you more effectively achieve your own interpersonal goals.

Interpersonal communication enables you to *learn,* to better understand the external world—the world of objects, events, and other people. Although a great deal of information comes from the media and the Internet, you probably discuss and ultimately "learn" or internalize information through interpersonal interactions. In fact, your beliefs, attitudes, and values are probably influenced more by interpersonal encounters than by the media or even by formal education. Through interpersonal communication you also learn about yourself. By talking about yourself with others, you gain valuable feedback on your feelings, thoughts, and behaviors. Through these communications, you also learn how you appear to others—who likes you, who dislikes you, and why.

Interpersonal communication helps you *relate* to others, whether it's face-to-face or online. One of the greatest needs people have is to establish and maintain close relationships. You want to feel loved and liked, and in turn you want to love and like others. Such relationships help to alleviate loneliness and depression, enable you to share and heighten your pleasures, and generally make you feel more positive about yourself.

Very likely, you *influence* the attitudes and behaviors of others in your interpersonal encounters. You may wish another person to vote a particular way, try a new diet, buy a new book, listen to a record, see a movie, take a specific course, think in a particular way, believe that something is true or false, or value some idea—the list is endless. A good deal of your time is probably spent in interpersonal persuasion.

A new study called **captology**—"the study of computers as persuasive technologies"—has recently arisen. Captology focuses on the ways in which computers and computer mediated communication generally can influence beliefs, attitudes, and behaviors (http://captology.stanford.edu/notebook/archives/000087.html, accessed February 11, 2005). And, as you probably have noticed from your own e-mail, social movement organizations are increasingly using the Internet to further their aims (Fisher, 1998; Banerjee, 2005).

Talking with friends about your weekend activities, discussing sports or dates, interacting through MOOS and MUDS, telling stories and jokes, and, in general, just passing the time fulfill a *play* function. Far from frivolous, this play purpose is extremely important. It gives our activities a necessary balance and our mind a needed break from all the seriousness around us. Everyone has an inner child, and that child needs time to play.

Therapists of various kinds serve a helping function professionally by offering guidance through interpersonal interaction. But everyone interacts to *help* in everyday life: You console a friend who has broken off a love affair, counsel another student about courses to take, or offer advice to a colleague about work. Not surprisingly, much support and counseling take place through e-mail and chat groups (Wright & Chung, 2001).

Popular belief and recent research both agree that men and women use communication for different purposes. Generally, men seem to communicate more for information, whereas women seem to communicate more for relationship purposes (Shaw & Grant, 2002; Colley, Todd, Bland, Holmes, Khanom, & Pike, 2004). Gender differences also occur in computer communication. For example, women ICQ users chat more for relationship reasons, while men chat more to play and to relax (Leung, 2001).

Dialogue *for* Analysis

The Interpersonally Challenged Family

This dialogue is designed to illustrate several of the principles of interpersonal communication discussed in this chapter. As you read it, try to identify the concepts or principles discussed in the chapter. Look especially for problem communication, and consider how this might have been avoided and corrected.

As noted in the book's preface, the names used in these dialogues were chosen to represent names from different cultures (for this chapter it's Mandarin Chinese), but there is no connection between the content of the dialogue and the specific culture; dialogues and cultures were paired randomly. Here as in other dialogues, visualize the interpersonal interaction as taking place among Chinese Americans, Spanish Americans, and so on.

The Cast

A Chinese American family.*

Nessa:	mother, housewife, junior high school history teacher; 41 years old
Wei:	father, gas station attendant; 46 years old
Gillian:	daughter, receptionist in an art gallery; 22 years old
Wang:	son, college freshman; 18 years old

The Context

Nessa is in the kitchen finishing preparing dinner—lamb chops, Wei's favorite, though she doesn't much care for them herself. Gillian is going through some CDs. Wang is reading one of his textbooks. Wei comes in from work and throws his jacket over the couch; it falls to the floor.

Wei: [Bored but angry, looking at Wang] What did you do with the car last night? It stunk like hell. And you left all your damn school papers all over the back seat.

Wang: [As if expecting the angry remarks] What did I do now?

(continues)

(continued)

Wei: You stunk up the car with your damn pot or whatever you kids smoke, and you left the car looking like hell. Can't you hear?
[Wang says nothing; goes back to looking at his book but without really reading.]

Nessa: Dinner's almost ready. Come on. Wash up and sit down.
[At dinner]

Gillian: Mom, I'm going to go to the shore for the weekend with some friends from work.

Nessa: OK. When will you be leaving?

Gillian: Friday afternoon, right after work.

Wei: Like hell you're going. No more going to the shore with that group.

Nessa: Wei, they're nice people. Why shouldn't she go?

Wei: Because I said so, OK? Finished. Closed.

Gillian: [Mumbling] I'm 22 years old and he gives me problems. You make me feel like a kid, like some stupid little kid.

Wei: Get married and then you can tell your husband what to do.

Gillian: I wish I could.

Wang: But nobody'll ask her.

Nessa: Why should she get married? She's got a good life—good job, nice friends, good home. Listen, I was talking with Elizabeth and Cara this morning, and they both feel they've just wasted their lives. They raised a family and what have they got? They got nothing. [To Gillian] And don't think sex is so great either; it isn't, believe me.

Wei: Well, they're idiots.

Nessa: [Snidely] They're idiots? Yeah, I guess they are.
How's school, Wang?

Wang: I hate it. It's so big. Nobody knows anyone. You sit in these big lecture halls and listen to some creep talk. I really feel lonely and isolated, like nobody knows I'm alive.

Wei: Listen to that college-talk garbage. Get yourself a woman and you won't feel lonely, instead of hanging out with those friends of yours.
[Gillian looks to Nessa, giving a sigh as if to say, "Here we go again."]

Wang: [Pushing his plate away] I'm finished; I'm going out.

Wei: Sit down and finish your damn supper. You think I work all day for you to throw the food away? You wanna go smoke your dope?

Wang: No. I just want to get away from you—forever.

Nessa: You mean we both work all day.

Wei: No, I mean I work and you baby-sit.

Nessa: Teaching junior high school history isn't baby-sitting.

Wei: What the hell is it then? You don't teach them anything.

Nessa: [To Gillian] You see? You're better off single. I should've stayed single. Instead . . . Oh, well. I was young and stupid. It was my own fault for getting involved with a loser. Just don't you make the same mistake.

Wei: [To Wang] Go ahead. Leave the table. Leave the house. Who cares what you do?

*It's interesting to know that the people of China speak several different languages; Mandarin is spoken by the largest number, and Cantonese is second. With more than 800 million speakers, Mandarin is spoken by more people than any other language in the world. Mandarin is the official language of China, Taiwan, and Singapore. More than 64,000 college students currently come from China to study in the United States each year; only India sends more students (74,600). Asian students make up more than 50 percent of the total international student body.

Summary of Concepts and Skills

This chapter explored the nature of interpersonal communication, its essential elements, and several principles of interpersonal communication.

1. Interpersonal communication is a transactional process that takes place between two or more people who have a relationship.
2. Essential to an understanding of interpersonal communication are the following elements: source–receiver, encoding–decoding, messages (including metamessages, message overload, feedback, and feedforward), channel, noise (physical, physiological, psychological, and semantic), context (physical, cultural, social–psychological, and temporal), and competence.
3. Interpersonal communication is:
   - a package of signals that usually reinforce but also may contradict one another
   - both content and relationship messages; we communicate about objects and events in the world but simultaneously about relationships between sources and receivers
   - a process of adjustment in which each of us accommodates to the specialized communication system of the other
   - integrally connected with power
   - ambiguous to some extent
   - inevitable (communication will occur whether we want it to or not), irreversible (once something is received, it remains communicated and cannot be erased from a listener's memory), and unrepeatable (no communication act can ever be repeated exactly)
   - purposeful; through interpersonal communication we learn, relate, influence, play, and help

In addition to the above concepts, this chapter also covered several interpersonal skills. As you read over the list, place a check in front of those you feel you'd like to work on:

_____ 1. *Message Overload.* Combat message overload by organizing your messages and distinguishing between messages to save and throw away.

_____ 2. *Feedback.* Listen to both verbal and nonverbal feedback—from yourself and from others—and use these cues to help you adjust your messages.

_____ 3. *Feedforward.* Use feedforward when you feel your listener needs background or when you want to ease into a particular topic, such as bad news.

_____ 4. *Channel.* Assess your channel options (for example, face-to-face conversation versus e-mail or voicemail message) before communicating important messages.

_____ 5. *Noise Management.* Reduce physical, physiological, psychological, and semantic noise as best you can; use repetition and restatement and, when in doubt, ask if you're clear.

_____ 6. *Mindfulness.* Create and recreate categories, be open to new information and points of view, avoid relying too heavily on first impressions, and think before you act.

_____ 7. *Packaging.* Make your verbal and nonverbal messages consistent; inconsistencies often create uncertainty and misunderstanding.

_____ 8. *Content and Relationship.* Listen to both the content and the relationship aspects of messages, distinguish between them, and respond to both.

_____ 9. *Context Adjustment.* Adjust your messages to the physical, cultural, social–psychological, and temporal context.

_____ 10. *Accommodation.* Accommodate to the speaking style of your listeners in moderation. Too much mirroring of the other's style may appear manipulative.

_____ 11. *Communication Options.* Assess your communication options before communicating, in light of inevitability, irreversibility, and unrepeatability.

Match the terms of interpersonal communication with their definitions. Record the number of the definition next to the appropriate term.

_____ interpersonal communication

_____ captology

_____ feedback

_____ ambiguity

_____ cultural context

_____ feedforward

_____ relationship messages

_____ source–receiver

_____ encoding

_____ communication as a transactional process

1. Messages sent back to the source in response to the source's messages.
2. Each person in the interpersonal communication act.
3. Information about messages that are yet to be sent.
4. Presence of more than one potential meaning.
5. The rules and norms, beliefs and attitudes of the people communicating.
6. Communication as an ongoing process in which each part depends on each other part.
7. Communication that takes place between persons who have a relationship.
8. Messages referring to the connection between the two people communicating.
9. The study of the persuasive power of computer-mediated communication.
10. The process of sending messages; for example, in speaking or writing.

Four for Discussion

1. The popularity of American media and America's domination of the Internet, some researchers point out, foster an Americanization of different cultures worldwide. Some people find this an unpleasant prospect and see it as the loss of diversity; others may see it as inevitable and as the result of a democratic process whereby people select the values and customs they wish to adopt. How do you feel about global Americanization?

2. The "feedback theory of relationships" holds that in satisfying interpersonal relationships feedback is positive, person focused, immediate, low in monitoring, and supportive—and that in unsatisfying relationships feedback is negative, self-focused, nonimmediate, high in monitoring, and critical. How effective do you find this theory in explaining relationships with which you're familiar?

3. What characters in television sitcoms or dramas demonstrate superior interpersonal competence? What characters demonstrate obvious interpersonal incompetence?

4. Analyze the following two brief conversations in light of the principles of interpersonal communication covered in this chapter. What do you find is the major difference between the two interactions?

Conversation 1

Paul: I'm going bowling tonight. The guys are organizing a team.

Judy: [Looking annoyed] Why didn't you tell me? I could have arranged to do something myself.

Paul: What's the difference? I'm off. See you later.

Judy: Thanks for nothing.

Conversation 2

Paul: The guys are organizing a bowling team, and I'd sure like to go to the organizational meeting tonight. Is that okay?

Judy: Sounds great. It'll be good to see you bowl again; you haven't played in so long. But I'd love to go out to dinner tonight. Do you think there'd be time? What time will the meeting be over?

Paul: It shouldn't be too late; I'll call you on the cell when the meeting is about over and we can meet at The Watering Hole. How's that?

Explore www.mycommunicationlab.com to find a variety of exercises relevant to the content of this chapter; these include (1) Models of Interpersonal Communication, (2) Ethics in Interpersonal Communication, (3) How Can You Respond to Contradictory Messages? (4) I'd Prefer to Be, (5) Applying the Axioms, and (6) Analyzing an Interaction.

Also visit MyCommunicationLab for a wealth of study tools, activities, and video clips on the nature and varieties of interpersonal communication.

Explore our research resources at www.researchnavigator.com.

Research
Navigator.com

CHAPTER 2 ■
Culture and Interpersonal Communication

WHY READ THIS CHAPTER?

*B*ecause you'll **learn about:**
- culture's role in interpersonal communication.
- the ways in which cultures differ from one another.
- the forms and principles of intercultural communication.

*B*ecause you'll **learn to:**
- send and receive messages with a recognition of cultural influences and differences.
- communicate successfully in intercultural situations.

*C*entral to all forms of interpersonal communication is culture. The more you understand about culture, the more effective you'll be in a wide variety of interpersonal interactions. Here we explore the relationship between culture and interpersonal communication; the major differences among cultures; and intercultural communication, its forms and skills.

Culture and Interpersonal Communication

The word *culture,* you'll recall from Chapter 1, refers to the lifestyle of a group of people; their values, beliefs, artifacts, ways of behaving, and ways of communication. Culture includes everything that members of a social group have produced and developed—their language, ways of thinking, art, laws, and religion—and that is transmitted from one generation to another through communication rather than through genes.

Gender is considered a cultural variable, because cultures teach boys and girls different attitudes, beliefs, values, and ways of communicating and relating to other people. Gender is what culture makes out of biology. And all cultures distinguish between the two genders—but in very different ways, as you'll discover in this chapter.

The Importance of Culture

A walk through any large U.S. city or through many small towns, through schools and colleges, or into this country's business and manufacturing centers will convince you that the United States is largely a collection of lots of different cultures.

As a people, we've become increasingly sensitive to cultural differences. U.S. society has moved from a perspective that endorsed **cultural assimilation** (people should leave their native culture behind and adapt to their new culture) to a view that values cultural diversity (people should retain their native cultural ways). And with some notable exceptions—hate speech, racism, sexism, homophobia, and classism come quickly to mind—we're more concerned with saying the right thing and ultimately with developing a society in which all cultures can coexist and enrich one another. At the same time, the ability to interact effectively with members of other cultures often translates into financial gain, increased employment opportunities, and better advancement prospects.

Consider these facts (*The New York Times Almanac 2005*; *The World Almanac and Book of Facts 2005*): The foreign-born population of the United States is increasing dramatically. In 1980 the foreign-born population was 14 million (about 6.2 percent of the total population), in 1990 it was 19.8 million (7.9 percent), and in 2000 it was 28.4 million (10.4 percent). Increasingly frequent communication in a multicultural context is inevitable.

In your more immediate environment, consider the number of foreign students who come to the United States to continue their education. For the academic year 2002–2003, according to the Institute of International Education (www.parstimes.com/news/archive/2003/washfile028.html, accessed February 8, 2005), there were 586,323 international students studying in the United States. The number of students from the top 10 countries, along with the percentage of increase or decrease from the previous year are: India with 74,603 (up 12 percent), China with 64,757 (up 2 percent), South Korea with 51,519 (up 5 percent), Japan with 45,960 (down 2 percent), Taiwan with 28,017 (down 3 percent), Canada with 26,513 (unchanged), Mexico with 12,801 (up 2 percent), Turkey with 11,601 (down 4 percent), Indonesia with 10,432 (down 10 percent), and Thailand with 9,982 (down 14 percent). Students from the Middle East had declined the most—especially those from Saudi Arabia, Kuwait, and the United Arab Emirates—though the absolute numbers were still quite high: The total fell from 38,545 during the previous year to 34,803 for 2002–2003.

And if you're currently attending the University of Southern California, New York University, Columbia University, Purdue University, the University of Texas, or the University of Michigan, you're attending one of the six schools with the largest foreign student enrollment. In 2002–2003 there were 153 colleges and universities at which 1,000 or more international students were enrolled. And if you live in New York, Los Angeles, Boston, Washington, D.C., Chicago, Philadelphia, San Jose, Houston, Dallas, or San Francisco, you're living in one of the 10 cities hosting the most international students. As you can see from even these few figures, frequent intercultural communication is an inevitable part of college life today.

U.S. corporations, too, are becoming more and more intercultural. Increasingly you see large and small corporations announcing that future growth will depend on expansion into foreign countries. Manufacturing, media, information technology, and farming interests depend on foreign markets. Business opportunities, therefore, have an increasingly international dimension, making cultural awareness and intercultural communication competence essential skills for professional success.

Cultural awareness helps us understand that interpersonal competence is specific to a given culture; what proves effective in one culture may prove ineffective in another. For example, in the United States corporate executives get down to business during the first several minutes of a meeting. In Japan, however, business executives interact socially for an extended period and try to find out something about one another. Thus, the communication principle influenced by U.S. culture would advise participants to tackle the meeting's agenda during the first five minutes. The principle influenced by Japanese culture would advise participants to avoid dealing with business until everyone has socialized sufficiently and feels well enough acquainted to begin negotiations. Neither principle is right and neither is wrong. Each is effective within its own culture, and ineffective outside its own culture.

Today, most countries are economically dependent on one another. Our economic lives depend on our ability to communicate effectively across cultures. Similarly, our political well-being depends in great part on that of other cultures. Political

E-Talk

Internet: Rural and Urban

People living in rural and urban areas use the Internet for different reasons. For example, rural users are more likely to access religious content than are urban users, whereas urban users are more likely to buy and bank through the Internet than are rural users. The rural population lags the national average in Internet usage by approximately 10 percentage points (Rural Areas and the Internet, **www.pewinternet.org/PPF/r/ 112/report_display.asp**, dated February 17, 2004, accessed February 10, 2005). How would you account for these differences?

Listen to this

Listening without Bias

Just as racist, sexist, heterosexist, and ageist attitudes influence your language, they also influence your listening. In biased listening you hear what the speaker says through your preconceptions. You assume that what the speaker is saying merely reflects, for example, the speaker's gender, race, affectional orientation, or age.

Such biased listening occurs in a wide variety of situations. For example, when you dismiss a valid argument or give credence to an invalid argument, when you refuse to give someone a fair hearing, or when you attribute less credibility (or more credibility) to a speaker *because* the speaker is of a particular gender, race, affectional orientation, or age—and when these characteristics have nothing to do with the position or argument advanced—you're listening with bias.

To be sure, there are many instances in which speakers' characteristics are relevant and pertinent to your evaluation of the message. For example, the gender of a speaker who is discussing pregnancy, fathering a child, birth control, or surrogate motherhood is, most would agree, probably relevant to the message. On such topics it is not biased listening to hear the discussion in light of the gender of the speaker. But it is sexist listening to assume that only one gender has anything to say that's worth hearing—or that what one gender says can be discounted without a fair hearing. The same is true in regard to a person's race, age, or affectional orientation.

Applying Listening Skills

Chloe, a good friend of yours, has been assigned to train under the supervision of someone of a different race. Chloe confides in you that she just can't get herself to work with this person; she admits she is just too prejudiced to appreciate anything her supervisor says or does. What listening advice would you give Chloe?

E-Talk ▪ ▪ ▪ ▪ ▪

Cell Phone Etiquette
A survey of cell phone users found that people will more likely turn off their cell phones when entering a church or hospital than when entering a retail store, for example (**www.cellular-news.com/story/ 10000.shtml**, posted October 28, 2003, accessed September 10, 2004). Where are you most likely to turn off your cell phone? In what public situations are you likely to leave it on?

unrest in any part of the world affects our own security. Intercultural communication and understanding seem more crucial now than ever. Yet daily the media bombard us with reports of racial tensions, religious disagreements, sexual bias—in general, with evidence of the problems caused when intercultural communication fails.

On the positive side, technology has made intercultural communication easy, practical, and inevitable. Specifically, the Internet has made intercultural communication as easy as writing a note on your computer. You can now communicate by e-mail just as easily with someone in Europe or Asia, for example, as with someone in another city or state.

The Aim of a Cultural Perspective

As illustrated throughout this text, culture influences communications of all types (Moon, 1996). It influences what you say to yourself and how you talk with friends, lovers, and family in everyday conversation. It influences how you interact in groups and how much importance you place on the group versus the individual. It influences the topics you talk about and the strategies you use in communicating information or in persuading. And it influences how you use the media and the credibility you attribute to them. Adopting a cultural perspective will help you both to understand how interpersonal communication works and to develop successful interpersonal skills.

And, of course, you need cultural understanding in order to communicate effectively in a wide variety of intercultural situations. Success in interpersonal communication—on your job and in your social life—will depend on your ability to communicate effectively with persons who are culturally different from yourself.

This emphasis on culture does not imply that you should accept all cultural practices or that all cultural practices are equal (Hatfield & Rapson, 1996). For example, cockfighting, foxhunting, and bullfighting are parts of the culture of some Latin American countries, England, and Spain, respectively; but you need not find these activities acceptable or equal to a cultural practice in which animals are treated kindly. Further, a cultural emphasis does not imply that you have to accept or follow even the practices of your own culture. For example, even if the majority in your culture find cockfighting acceptable, you need not agree with or follow the practice. Similarly, you may reject your culture's values and beliefs; its religion or political system; or its attitudes toward the homeless, the handicapped, or the culturally different. Often, for example, personality factors (such as your degree of assertiveness, extroversion, or optimism) will prove more influential than culture (Hatfield & Rapson, 1996). Of course, going against your culture's traditions and values is often very difficult. But it's important to realize that culture only influences; it does not determine your values or behavior.

As demonstrated throughout this text, cultural differences exist across the interpersonal communication spectrum—from the way you use eye contact to the way you develop or dissolve a relationship (Chang & Holt, 1996). But these differences should not blind you to the great number of similarities existing among even the most widely separated cultures. Close interpersonal relationships, for example, are common in all cultures, even though people in different cultures enter into them for very different reasons. Further, remember that differences are usually matters of degree. For example, most cultures value honesty, although not all value it to the same degree. Also, the advances in media and technology and the widespread use of the Internet are influencing cultures and cultural change and are perhaps homogenizing different cultures to some degree, lessening differences and increasing similarities.

❝The highest result of education is tolerance.❞
—Helen Keller

The Ethics of Cultural Practices

Throughout history there have been numerous cultural practices that would be judged unethical and even illegal in much of today's world. Sacrificing virgins to the gods, burning people who held different religious beliefs, and sending children to fight religious wars are obvious examples. But even today there are practices woven deep into the fabric of different cultures that many people would find unethical. Consider just a few of these:

- Some cultures support bronco-riding events at which the bull's testicles are tied so that it will experience pain and will buck and try to throw off the rider.
- Some cultures support clitoridectomy, the practice of cutting a young girl's genitals so that she can never experience sexual intercourse without pain; the goal is to keep the girl a virgin until marriage.
- Some cultures support and enforce the belief that a woman must be subservient to her husband's will.
- Some cultures support the practice of wearing fur. In some cases this means catching wild animals in extremely painful traps; in others, raising captive animals so they can be killed when their pelts are worth the most money.

What Would You Do?

Imagine that you're on a television talk show dealing with the topic of cultural differences and diversity. During the discussion different members of the panel speak in support of each of the practices mentioned above, arguing that each culture is entitled to its own practices and beliefs and that no outsider has the right to object. Given your own beliefs about these issues and about cultural diversity in general, what ethical obligations do you have as a member of this panel?

Enculturation and Acculturation

You learn the values of your culture through the teachings of your parents, peer groups, schools, religious institutions, government agencies, and media; this process is known as **enculturation.** Such values might include "democracy is the best form of government," or "God is just" or "Charity is an obligation," or "Killing another human being is wrong." Through enculturation you develop an ethnic identity, a commitment to the beliefs and philosophy of your culture (Chung & Ting-Toomey, 1999). The degree to which you identify with your cultural group can be measured by your responses to such questions as the following (from Ting-Toomey, 1981). Using a five-point scale from 1 (strongly disagree) to 5 (strongly agree), indicate how true of you the following statements are:

❝From the moment of his birth, the customs into which [a person] is born shape his experience and behavior. By the time he can talk, he is the little creature of his culture.**❞**

—Ruth Benedict

- *I am increasing my involvement in activities with my ethnic group.*
- *I involve myself in causes that will help members of my ethnic group.*
- *It feels natural being part of my ethnic group.*
- *I have spent time trying to find out more about my own ethnic group.*
- *I am happy to be a member of my ethnic group.*
- *I have a strong sense of belonging to my ethnic group.*
- *I often talk to other members of my group to learn more about my ethnic culture.*

E-Talk . ▪ ▪ ▪ ▪ ▪

Helping Others?

You're more likely to help someone who is similar in race, attitude, and general appearance. Even the same first name is significant. For example, when an e-mail (asking receivers to fill out surveys of their food habits identified the sender as someone with the same first name as the receiver, there was a greater willingness to comply with the request (Gueguen, 2003). Why do you think people respond this way? Do you?

High scores (say, 5s and 4s) indicate a strong commitment to your culture's values and beliefs; low numbers (1s and 2s) indicate a relatively weak commitment.

Acculturation refers to the processes by which a person's culture is modified through direct contact with or exposure to (say, through the mass media) another culture (Kim, 1988). For example, when immigrants settle in the United States (the host culture), their own culture becomes influenced by the host culture. Gradually the values, ways of behaving, and beliefs of the host culture become more and more a part of the immigrants' culture. At the same time, of course, the host culture changes too. Generally, however, the culture of the immigrants changes more. As Young Yun Kim (1988) puts it, "a reason for the essentially unidirectional change in the immigrant is the difference between the number of individuals in the new environment sharing the immigrant's original culture and the size of the host society."

Immigrant groups' acceptance of the their adopted culture depends on several factors (Kim, 1988). Immigrants who come from cultures similar to the host culture will become acculturated more easily. Similarly, those who are younger and better educated become acculturated more quickly than do older and less educated persons. Personality factors also are relevant. Persons who are risk takers and open-minded, for example, have a greater acculturation potential. Also, persons who are familiar with the host culture before immigration—whether through interpersonal contact or through mass media—will be acculturated more readily.

Cultural Principles

As you learn about your culture's beliefs, values, and other aspects, you also learn the culture's principles (often referred to as "maxims") for communicating. Some of these cultural principles focus on enhancing communication efficiency (for example, how to make messages more easily understood) and some on maintaining interpersonal relationships (for example, how to get along with other people).

PRINCIPLES FOR COMMUNICATION EFFICIENCY   When you communicate interpersonally, you probably follow the general principle of cooperation; there's a mutually agreed-upon assumption that you'll both try to understand each other (Grice, 1975). You cooperate largely by adhering to four maxims—rules that speakers and listeners in the United States and in many other cultures follow in conversation. As you'll see, following these maxims ensures efficient interpersonal communication.

Skill Building
Exercise

Exploring Cultural Attitudes

One of the best ways to appreciate the influence of culture on communication is to consider the attitudes people have about central aspects of culture. In a group of five or six people—try for as culturally diverse a group as possible—discuss how you think most of the students at your school feel (not how you feel) about each of the following. Use a five-point scale on which 5 = most students strongly agree; 4 = most students agree; 3 = students are relatively neutral; 2 = most students disagree; 1 = most students strongly disagree.

_____ 1. Most feminists are just too sensitive about sexism.
_____ 2. Courses on sexism should be required in our schools.
_____ 3. Gay rights means gay men and lesbians demanding special privileges.
_____ 4. Homosexuals have made many contributions to their societies.
_____ 5. Racism isn't going to end overnight so minorities need to be patient.
_____ 6. White people benefit from racism whether they want to or not.

Attitudes strongly influence communication. Understanding your cultural attitudes is prerequisite to effective intercultural communication.

Source: These statements were taken from the Human Relations Attitude Inventory (Koppelman, with Goodhart, 2005). The authors note that this inventory is based on an inventory developed by Flavio Vega.

The **quantity principle** requires that you be only as informative as necessary to communicate your intended meaning. Thus, you include information that makes the meaning clear but omit what does not. The maxim of quantity requires that you give neither too little nor too much information. Spam is the perfect example of messages that violate this principle; spam messages are unwanted noise and intrude on your own communication.

The **quality principle** states that you should say what you know or believe to be true and not say what you know to be false. When you're communicating, you assume that the other person's information is true—at least as far as he or she knows. For example when a friend tells you what happened on a trip, you assume that it's true.

The **relation principle** asks that you talk about what is relevant to the conversation. Speakers who digress widely and frequently interject irrelevant comments violate the maxim of relation.

The **manner principle** requires that you be clear, avoid ambiguities, be relatively brief, and organize your thoughts into a meaningful sequence. Thus, you use terms that the listener will understand and omit or clarify terms that you suspect the listener will not understand. When you talk to a young child, for example, you normally use familiar words and short sentences. You can also see this principle operating in computer-mediated communication's reliance on acronyms—an extremely efficient method of communicating (when sender and receiver both know the meanings), much like macros and autocorrect features in word processors. Table 2.1 presents some popular CMC acronyms.

PRINCIPLES FOR MAINTAINING RELATIONSHIPS Some communication principles help to maintain peaceful relationships rather than foster efficiency.

The **peaceful relations principal,** observed among the Japanese, requires that you say only what preserves peaceful relationships with others. (Midooka, 1990). Under this principle you wouldn't contradict another person or point out errors in what the other person said. This maxim of peaceful relationships is much more important in public than in private conversations, in which the maxim may be and often is violated.

TABLE 2.1	Some Popular Acronyms

Here are some popular acronyms used widely in computer-mediated communication. For an ever-increasing list of acronyms see Net Lingua's website (**www.fun-with-words.com/ acronyms.html**).

ACRONYM	MEANING
BTW	By the way
IMHO	In my humble opinion
IMNSHO	In my not so humble opinion
NP	No problem
OTT	Over the top
OTOH	On the other hand
RUOK	Are you okay?
TIC	Tongue in cheek
TTYL	Talk to you later
TVM	Thanks very much

The **self-denigration principle,** observed in the conversations of Chinese speakers, may require that you avoid taking credit for some accomplishment—saying, for example, "My colleagues really did most of the work." Or you might be expected to make less of some ability or talent you have—to say, for example, "I still have much to learn" (Gu, 1990). Putting yourself down helps to elevate the person to whom you're speaking.

The **politeness principle** is probably universal across all cultures (Brown & Levinson, 1987). Cultures differ, however, in how they define politeness and in how important politeness is in comparison with, say, openness or honesty. In interpersonal communication politeness can refer to, for example, not interrupting, saying "please" and "thank you," maintaining a focused interaction with appropriate eye contact, and/or not criticizing someone in public. Cultures also differ in their rules for expressing politeness or impoliteness. Some cultures, for example, may require you to give a long speech of praise when meeting, say, an important scientist or educator; other cultures expect you to assume a more equal position regardless of the stature of the other person. And cultures differ in their punishments for violations of the accepted rules of politeness (Mao, 1994; Strecker, 1993).

There also are large gender differences (as well as some similarities) in the expression of politeness (Holmes, 1995). Generally, studies from several different cultures show that women use more polite forms than men (Brown, 1980; Wetzel, 1988; Holmes, 1995). For example, both in informal conversation and in conflict situations, women tend to seek areas of agreement more than do men. Young girls are more apt to try to modify expressions of disagreement, whereas young boys are more apt to express more "bald disagreements" (Holmes, 1995). There are also similarities. For example, both men and women in the United States and New Zealand seem to pay compliments in similar ways (Manes & Wolfson, 1981; Holmes, 1986, 1995), and both men and women use politeness strategies when communicating bad news in an organization (Lee, 1993).

Politeness also varies with the type of relationship. One researcher, for example, has proposed that politeness is considerably greater with friends than with either strangers or intimates (Wolfson, 1988; Holmes, 1995). Wolfson (1998) depicts this relationship as in Figure 2.1.

In Internet communication, politeness is covered very specifically by the rules of netiquette, which are very clearly stated in most computer books. For example: Find out what a group is talking about before breaking in with your own comment; be tolerant of newbies (those who are new to newsgroups or chat groups); don't send duplicate messages; don't flame.

*C*ultural Differences

For effective interpersonal communication in a global world, good will and good intentions are helpful but not enough. If you're

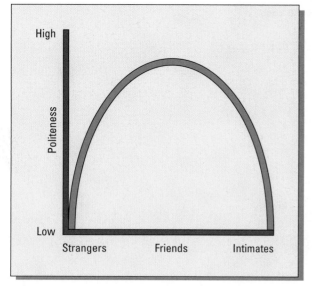

Figure 2.1
Wolfson's Bulge Model of Politeness
Do you find this model a generally accurate representation of your own level of politeness in different types of relationships? Can you build a case for an inverted U theory, in which politeness would be high with both strangers and intimates and low with friends?

going to be effective, you need to know how cultures differ and how these differences influence interpersonal communication. Research supports five major cultural distinctions that impact communication. Cultures differ in terms of their (1) orientation (whether individualist or collectivist), (2) context (whether high or low), (3) masculinity–femininity, (4) power structure, and (5) tolerance for ambiguity. Each of these dimensions of difference has a significant impact on interpersonal communication (Hofstede, 1997; Hall & Hall, 1987; Gudykunst, 1994).

Individualist and Collectivist Cultures

In an **individualist culture** you're responsible for yourself and perhaps your immediate family; in a **collectivist culture** you're responsible for the entire group. In an individualist culture success is measured by the extent to which you surpass other members of your group; you will take pride in standing out from the crowd, and your heroes—in the media, for example—are likely to be those who are unique and who stand apart. In a collectivist culture success is measured by your contribution to the achievements of the group as a whole; you will take pride in your similarity to other members of your group. Your heroes are more likely to be team players who do not stand out from the rest of the group's members.

In an individualist culture, you're responsible to your own conscience, and responsibility is largely an individual matter. In a collectivist culture you're responsible to the rules of the social group, and responsibility for an accomplishment or a failure is shared by all members. In individualist cultures competition is promoted; in collectivist cultures cooperation is promoted. Distinctions between in-group members and out-group members are extremely important in collectivist cultures. In individualistic cultures, which prize a person's individuality, these distinctions are likely to be less important.

Countries high on individualism include the United States, Australia, United Kingdom, Netherlands, Canada, New Zealand, Italy, Belgium, Denmark, and Sweden. Countries high on collectivism include Guatemala, Ecuador, Panama, Venezuela, Colombia, Indonesia, Pakistan, China, Costa Rica, and Peru.

The distinction between individualist and collectivist cultures revolves around the extent to which the individual's goals or the group's goals are given greater importance. Individualist and collectivist tendencies are not mutually exclusive; this is not an all-or-none orientation but rather one of emphasis. Thus, you may, for example, compete with other members of your basketball team for the most baskets or to get the most valuable player award. In a game, however, you will act in a way that will benefit the group. In actual practice, both individualist and collectivist tendencies will help you and your team each achieve your goals. Even so, at times these tendencies may conflict; for example, do you shoot for the basket and try to raise your own individual score, or do you pass the ball to another player who is better positioned to score the basket and thus benefit your team?

Today we have become familiar with suicide bombers, people who will give up their own life in support of a cause in which they believe. In individualistic cultures this is something difficult to understand; it's so foreign to everything such cultures teach and value. But for people from collectivist cultures, the larger social group is more important than the individual, so relinquishing life for the group is consistent with this cultural orientation.

High- and Low-Context Cultures

High-context cultures place a great deal of emphasis on the information that is in the context or in the person. For example, in high-context cultures, information that was communicated in previous interactions or through shared experiences is not explicitly stated in their verbal messages. **Low-context cultures** place more emphasis on the information that is explicitly stated in verbal messages or, in formal transactions, in written (contract) form.

■ **What Do You Say**

Culture versus Culture

Your friend is pressed for time and asks you to do the statistical analyses for a term project. Your first impulse is to say yes, because in your culture it would be extremely impolite to refuse someone you've known for so long a favor. Yet you're aware that providing this kind of help is considered unethical at colleges in the United States. You want to help your friend but avoid doing anything that would be considered deceitful and might be severely punished. **What Do You Say?**

To appreciate the distinction between high and low context, consider giving directions ("Where's the voter registration center?") to someone who knows the neighborhood and to a newcomer to your city. With someone who knows the neighborhood (a high-context situation), you can assume the person knows the local landmarks. So you can give directions such as "next to the laundromat on Main Street" or "the corner of Albany and Elm." With the newcomer (a low-context situation), you cannot assume the person shares any information with you. So you have to use directions that a stranger will understand; for example, "Turn left at the next stop sign" or "Go two blocks and then turn right."

High-context cultures are also collectivist cultures. These cultures (Japanese, Arabic, Latin American, Thai, Korean, Apache, and Mexican are examples) place great emphasis on personal relationships and oral agreements (Victor, 1992). Low-context cultures, on the other hand, are individualistic cultures. These cultures (German, Swedish, Norwegian, and American are examples) place less emphasis on personal relationships; they tend to emphasize explicit explanations and, for example, written contracts in business transactions.

Members of high-context cultures spend lots of time getting to know one another before engaging in any important transactions. Because of this prior personal knowledge, a great deal of information is already shared and therefore does not have to be explicitly stated. High-context cultures, for example, rely more on nonverbal cues in reducing uncertainty (Sanders, Wiseman, & Matz, 1991). Members of low-context cultures spend less time getting to know each other and therefore do not have that shared knowledge. As a result everything has to be stated explicitly. When this simple difference is not taken into account, misunderstandings can easily result. For example, the directness and explicitness characteristic of the low-context culture may be perceived as insulting, insensitive, or unnecessary by members of a high-context culture. Conversely, to members of a low-context culture, someone from a high-context culture may appear vague, underhanded, even dishonest in his or her reluctance to be explicit or to engage in communication that a low-context culture would consider open and direct.

Another frequent difference and source of misunderstanding between high- and low-context cultures is relative importance of maintaining a positive public self-image, or what is frequently called **face-saving** (Hall & Hall, 1987). People in high-context cultures place a great deal more emphasis on face-saving. For example, they are more likely to avoid argument for fear of causing others to lose face; people in low-context cultures (with their individualistic orientation) are more likely to use argument to win a point. Similarly, in high-context cultures negative comments should be made only in private so that the person can save face. For example, a manager in a high-context culture would criticize an employee only in private. Low-context cultures may not make this public-private distinction.

Members of high-context cultures are reluctant to say no for fear of offending and causing a person to lose face. So, for example, it's necessary to understand when a Japanese executive's yes means yes and when it means no. The difference is not in the words but in the way they are used. It's easy to see how a low-context individual may interpret this reluctance to be direct—to say no when you mean no—as a weakness or as an unwillingness to confront reality.

Members of high-context cultures also are reluctant to question the judgments of their superiors. So, for example, if a product were being manufactured with a defect, workers might be reluctant to communicate this back to management (Gross, Turner, & Cederholm, 1987). Similarly, workers might detect problems in procedures proposed by management but never communicate their concerns back to management. In an intercultural organization knowledge of this tendency would alert a low-context management to look more deeply into the absence of communication.

■ What Do You Say ?

Getting Your Foot Out of Your Mouth

At work you tell a homophobic joke, only to discover that it has been resented and clearly has violated the organizational norms for polite and unbiased talk. You need to make this situation less awkward and potentially damaging to your work experience. **What Do You Say?** In what context? Through what channel?

Masculine and Feminine Cultures

Cultures differ in the extent to which gender roles are distinct or overlap (Hofstede, 1997, 1998). When denoting cultural orientations, the terms *masculine* and *feminine*, and used by Gerte Hofstede to describe this cultural difference, should be taken not as perpetuating stereotypes but as reflecting some of the commonly held assumptions of a sizable number of people throughout the world.

In a highly **masculine culture,** men are valued for their aggressiveness, material success, and strength. Women, on the other hand, are valued for their modesty, focus on the quality of life, and tenderness. On the basis of Hofstede's (1997, 1998) research, the 10 countries with the highest masculinity scores are (beginning with the highest) Japan, Austria, Venezuela, Italy, Switzerland, Mexico, Ireland, Jamaica, Great Britain, and Germany. Of the 53 countries ranked, the United States ranks 15th most masculine. In masculine societies there is a very clear distinction between men's and women's gender roles and expectations. Further, masculine cultures emphasize success and so socialize their members to be assertive, ambitious, and competitive. For example, members of masculine cultures are more likely to confront conflicts directly and to fight out any differences competitively; they're more likely to emphasize win–lose conflict strategies.

A highly **feminine culture,** on the other hand, values modesty, concern for relationships and the quality of life, and tenderness in both men and women. Here gender distinctions are much more fluid than in masculine cultures. The 10 countries with the highest femininity score are (beginning with the highest) Sweden, Norway, Netherlands, Denmark, Costa Rica, Yugoslavia, Finland, Chile, Portugal, and Thailand. Feminine cultures emphasize the quality of life and so socialize their members to be modest and to highlight close interpersonal relationships. Feminine cultures, for example, are more likely to utilize compromise and negotiation in resolving conflicts; they're more likely to seek win–win solutions.

Like countries, organizations can be viewed as masculine or feminine. Masculine organizations emphasize competitiveness and aggressiveness. They stress the bottom line and reward their workers on the basis of their contribution to the organization. Feminine organizations are less competitive and less aggressive. They emphasize worker satisfaction and reward their workers on the basis of need; those who have large families, for example, may get better raises than single people, even if they haven't contributed as much to the organization.

High- and Low-Power-Distance Cultures

In some cultures power is concentrated in the hands of a few, and there's a great difference between the power held by these people and the power of the ordinary citizen. These are called **high-power-distance cultures;** examples are Mexico, Brazil, India, and the Philippines (Hofstede, 1997). In **low-power-distance cultures,** power is more evenly distributed throughout the citizenry; examples include Denmark, New Zealand, Sweden, and to a lesser extent the United States.

These differences influence communication in numerous ways. For example, in high-power-distance cultures there's a great power differential between students and teachers; students are expected to be modest, polite, and totally respectful. In contrast, in low-power-distance cultures (and you can see this clearly in U.S. college classrooms) students are expected to demonstrate their knowledge and command of the subject matter, participate in discussions with the teacher, and even challenge the teacher—something many members of high-power-distance cultures wouldn't even think of doing.

Friendship and dating relationships also are influenced by power distances between groups (Andersen, 1991). In India, for example, such relationships are expected to take place within your cultural class. In Sweden, a person is expected to

■ **What Do You Say**
Feminine and Masculine Cultures

You come from a highly feminine culture and are working with colleagues who epitomize the highly masculine culture. Assertiveness (even aggressiveness) is rewarded and paid attention to while your lack of assertiveness leads you to be ignored. You want to explain this cultural difference to your colleagues and at the same time ensure that your contributions will be listened to and evaluated fairly instead of being ignored. **What Do You Say?** To whom? In what channel?

select friends and romantic partners not on the basis of class or culture but on the basis of personality, appearance, and the like.

In low-power-distance cultures you're expected to confront a friend, partner, or supervisor assertively; there is in these cultures a general feeling of equality that is consistent with assertive behavior (Borden, 1991). An assistant who feels he or she is being treated unfairly is expected to bring the problem to the attention of the manager, for example. In high-power-distance cultures, however, direct confrontation and assertiveness may be viewed negatively, especially if directed at a superior.

Even in democracies in which everyone is equal under the law (or should be), there are still great power distances between those in authority—the employers, the police, the politicians—and ordinary citizens as there are between those who are rich and those who are poor.

High- and Low-Ambiguity-Tolerance Cultures

In some cultures people do little to avoid uncertainty and have little anxiety about not knowing what will happen next. In some other cultures, however, uncertainty is strongly avoided and there is much anxiety about uncertainty.

HIGH-AMBIGUITY-TOLERANCE CULTURES Members of high-ambiguity-tolerance cultures don't feel threatened by unknown situations; uncertainty is a normal part of life, and people accept it as it comes. Examples of such low-anxiety cultures include Singapore, Jamaica, Denmark, Sweden, Hong Kong, Ireland, Great Britain, Malaysia, India, Philippines, and the United States.

Because high-ambiguity-tolerance cultures are comfortable with ambiguity and uncertainty, they minimize the importance of rules governing communication and relationships (Hofstede, 1997; Lustig & Koester, 2006). People in these cultures readily tolerate individuals who don't follow the same rules as the cultural majority, and they may even encourage different approaches and perspectives.

Students in high-ambiguity-tolerance cultures appreciate freedom in education and prefer vague assignments without specific timetables. These students want to be rewarded for creativity and readily accept an instructor's lack of knowledge.

LOW-AMBIGUITY-TOLERANCE CULTURES Members of low-ambiguity-tolerance cultures do much to avoid uncertainty and have a great deal of anxiety about not knowing what

Skill Building
Exercise

Identifying Cultural Differences

Using any of the five dimensions of culture discussed here (individualism and collectivism, high and low context, masculinity and femininity, high and low power distance, and high and low tolerance for ambiguity), identify any potentially contradictory perceptions—and hence potential for miscommunication—that people may have in situations such as the following. What might you do to prevent such miscommunication from occurring in the first place?

- A young female supervisor criticizes the performance of an older male analyst at a department meeting.
- A teacher, noticing similarities between two students' term papers, accuses the students of plagiarizing and calls their parents in to meet with the principal.
- A CEO, leading a discussion among a group of new interns, asks for their opinions on how the company might improve communication among workers at all levels.

Cultural teachings and orientations exert powerful (but often unconscious) influences on the way people communicate. A knowledge of such influences will often help suggest remedies for misperceptions and misunderstandings.

will happen next; they see uncertainty as threatening and as something that must be counteracted. Examples of such low-ambiguity-tolerance cultures include Greece, Portugal, Guatemala, Uruguay, Belgium, El Salvador, Japan, Yugoslavia, Peru, France, Chile, Spain, and Costa Rica (Hofstede, 1997).

Low-ambiguity-tolerance cultures create very clear-cut rules for communication that must not be broken. For example, students in these uncertainty-avoidant cultures prefer highly structured learning experiences with little ambiguity; they prefer specific objectives, detailed instructions, and definite timetables. An assignment to write a term paper on "anything" would be cause for alarm; it wouldn't be clear or specific enough. These students expect to be judged on the basis of producing the right answers and expect the instructor to have all the answers all the time (Hofstede, 1997).

Keeping these five cultural distinctions in mind, let's now examine intercultural communication.

Intercultural Communication

Intercultural communication is communication between persons who have different cultural beliefs, values, or ways of behaving. The model in Figure 2.2 illustrates this concept. The larger circles represent the cultures of the individual communicators. The inner circles identify the communicators (the sources–receivers). In this model each communicator is a member of a different culture. In some instances the cultural differences are relatively slight—say, between persons from Toronto and New York. In other instances the cultural differences are great—say, between persons from Borneo and Germany, or between persons from rural Nigeria and industrialized England.

All messages originate from a specific and unique cultural context, and that context influences their content and form. You communicate as you do largely as a result of your culture. Culture (along with the processes of enculturation and acculturation) influences every aspect of your communication experience. And, of course, you receive messages through the filters imposed by a unique culture. Cultural filters, like filters on a camera, color the messages you receive. They influence what you receive and how you receive it. For example, some cultures rely heavily on television or newspapers for their news and trust them implicitly. Others rely on face-to-face interpersonal interactions, distrusting any of the mass communication systems. Some look to religious leaders as guides to behavior; others generally ignore them.

Forms of Intercultural Communication

The term *intercultural* is used broadly to refer to all forms of communication among persons from different groups as well as to the more narrowly defined area of communication between different cultures. The model of intercultural communication presented in Figure 2.2 applies equally to communication between a smaller culture and the dominant or majority culture, communication between different smaller cultures, and communication between groups of various other types. The following categories of communication all may be considered "intercultural"; more important, all are subject to the same barriers and gateways to effective communication identified in this chapter:

- Communication between cultures—for example, between Chinese and Portuguese, or between French and Norwegian individuals or groups.
- Communication between races (sometimes called *interracial communication*)—for example, between people of African American and Asian American heritages.
- Communication between ethnic groups (sometimes called *interethnic communication*)—for example, between Italian Americans and German Americans.

E-Talk ▪ ▪ ▪ ▪ ▪ ▪ ▪ ▪

Internet Religion

One study finds that nearly two-thirds of those using the Internet (or about 82 million people in the U.S.) have used it for religious or spiritual purposes such as e-mailing letters with spiritual content, sending an online greeting card celebrating a religious holiday, reading news of religious events, seeking information about celebrating religious holidays, and finding places of worship (Faith Online, **www.pewinterent.org/PPE/r/ 126/report_display.asp**, dated April 7, 2004, accessed February 10, 2005). How would you describe your own use of the Internet for such purposes?

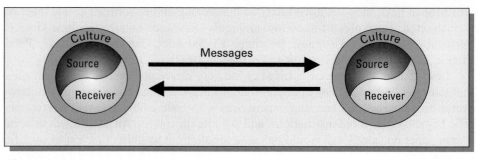

Figure 2.2
A Model of Intercultural Communication
This model of intercultural communication illustrates that culture is a part of every communication act. More specifically, it illustrates that the messages you send and the messages you receive will be influenced by your cultural beliefs, values, and attitudes.

- Communication between people of different religions—for example, between Roman Catholics and Episcopalians, or between Muslims and Jews.
- Communication between nations (sometimes called *international communication*)—for example, between the United States and Argentina, or between China and Italy.
- Communication between smaller cultures existing within the larger culture—for example, between doctors and patients, or between research scientists and the general public.
- Communication between a smaller culture and the dominant culture—for example, between homosexuals and heterosexuals, or between older people and the younger majority.
- Communication between genders—between men and women. Some researchers would consider intergender communication as a separate area—as a form of intercultural communication only when the two people are also from different races or nationalities. But gender roles are largely learned through culture, so it seems useful to consider male–female communication as intercultural (Tannen, 1994a, 1994b). That is, even though gender itself is transmitted genetically and not by communication, it is cultures that teach boys and girls different attitudes, beliefs, values, and ways of communicating and relating to one another (Payne, 2001). You act like a man or a woman partly because of

what your culture has taught you about how men and women should act. Further, you can view male–female communication as cross-cultural because of the numerous differences in the way men and women speak and listen (Eckstein & Goldman, 2001). This does not deny that biological differences also play a role. In fact, research continues to uncover biological roots of behaviors once thought to be entirely learned, such as happiness and shyness (McCroskey, 2001).

Regardless of your own cultural background, you will surely come into close contact with people from a variety of other cultures—people who speak different languages, eat different foods, practice different religions, and approach work and relationships in very different ways. It doesn't matter whether you're a longtime resident or a newly arrived immigrant: You are or soon will be living, going to school, working, and forming relationships with people who are from very different cultures. Your day-to-day experiences are sure to become increasingly intercultural.

Improving Intercultural Communication

Murphy's law ("If anything can go wrong, it will") is especially applicable to intercultural communication. Intercultural communications is, of course, subject to all the same barriers and problems as are the other forms of communication discussed throughout this text. In this section, however, we'll consider some suggestions designed to counteract the barriers that are unique to intercultural communications (Barna, 1997; Ruben, 1985; Spitzberg, 1991).

Above all, intercultural communication depends on the cultural sensitivity of both individuals. **Cultural sensitivity** is an attitude and way of behaving in which you're aware of and acknowledge cultural differences. Cultural sensitivity is crucial on a global scale, as in efforts toward world peace and economic growth; it's also essential for effective interpersonal communication and for general success in life (Franklin & Mizell, 1995). Without cultural sensitivity there can be no effective interpersonal communication between people who are different in gender or race or nationality or affectional orientation. So be mindful of the cultural differences between yourself and the other person. For example, the close physical distance that is normal in Arab cultures may prove too familiar or too intrusive in much of the United States and northern Europe. The empathy that most Americans welcome may be uncomfortable for most Koreans (Yun, 1976).

The following guidelines can help you achieve cultural sensitivity: (1) Prepare yourself, (2) reduce your ethnocentrism; (3) confront your stereotypes; (4) be mindful; (5) avoid overattribution; (6) reduce uncertainty; (7) recognize differences; (8) adjust your communication; and (9) recognize culture shock—its inevitability and its symptoms. We'll take a look at each guideline in turn.

PREPARE YOURSELF There's no better preparation for intercultural communication than learning about the other culture. Fortunately, there are numerous sources to draw on. View a video or film that presents a realistic view of the culture. Read what members of the culture as well as "outsiders" write about the culture. Scan magazines and websites from the culture. Talk with members of the culture. Chat on international IRC channels. Read materials addressed to people who need to communicate with those from other cultures. The easiest way to do this is to search the online bookstores (for example, Barnes and Noble at **www.bn.com**, Borders at **www.borders.com**, and Amazon at **www.Amazon.com**) for such keywords as *culture, international,* and *foreign travel.*

Another part of this preparation is to recognize and face fears that may stand in the way of effective intercultural communication (Gudykunst, 1994; Stephan & Stephan, 1985). For example, you may fear for your self-esteem. You may be anxious about your ability to control the intercultural situation, or you may worry about your own level of discomfort. You may fear saying something that will be considered politically incorrect or culturally insensitive and thereby losing face.

E-Talk ▪ ▪ ▪ ▪ ▪ ▪ ▪ ▪
Take a Cultural Tour
Virtual tours offer an interesting way of viewing a wide variety of areas. Currently, the most popular tours— which 54 million Americans have already taken—include visits to museums, vacation spots, schools, real estate, historical exhibits, parks, places such as the Taj Mahal and the White House, and hotels (Virtual Tours, Pew/Internet, Data Memo 202-419-4500, **www.pewinternet.org**, dated December 2004, accessed February 10, 2005). What are some of the virtual tours currently available that you might use to learn about different cultures?

You may fear that you'll be taken advantage of by a member of the other culture. Depending on your own stereotypes, you may fear being lied to, financially duped, or made fun of.

You may fear that members of this other group will react to you negatively. You may fear, for example, that they will not like you or will disapprove of your attitudes or beliefs or perhaps even reject you as a person. Conversely, you may fear negative reactions from members of your own group. They might, for example, disapprove of your socializing with culturally different people.

Some fears, of course, are reasonable. In many cases, however, fears are groundless. Either way, you need to assess your concerns logically and weigh their consequences carefully. Then you'll be able to make informed choices about your communications.

REDUCE YOUR ETHNOCENTRISM Before reading about reducing ethnocentrism, examine your own cultural thinking by taking the self-test below.

Test Yourself ✓

How Ethnocentric Are You?

INSTRUCTIONS: Here are 18 statements representing your beliefs about your culture. For each statement indicate how much you agree or disagree, using the following scale: strongly agree = 5, agree = 4, neither agree nor disagree = 3, disagree = 2, and strongly disagree 1.

_____ ① Most cultures are backward compared to my culture.

_____ ② My culture should be the role model for other cultures.

_____ ③ Lifestyles in other cultures are just as valid as those in my culture.

_____ ④ Other cultures should try to be like my culture.

_____ ⑤ I'm not interested in the values and customs of other cultures.

_____ ⑥ People in my culture could learn a lot from people in other cultures.

_____ ⑦ Most people from other cultures just don't know what's good for them.

_____ ⑧ I have little respect for values and customs of other cultures.

_____ ⑨ Most people would be happier if they lived like people in my culture.

_____ ⑩ People in my culture have just about the best lifestyles of anywhere.

_____ ⑪ Lifestyles in other cultures are not as valid as those in my culture.

_____ ⑫ I'm very interested in the values and customs of other cultures.

_____ ⑬ I respect the values and customs of other cultures.

_____ ⑭ I do not cooperate with people who are different.

_____ ⑮ I do not trust people who are different.

_____ ⑯ I dislike interacting with people from different cultures.

_____ ⑰ Other cultures are smart to look up to my culture.

_____ ⑱ People from other cultures act strange and unusual when they come into my culture.

HOW DID YOU DO? This test was presented to give you the opportunity to examine some of your own cultural beliefs, particularly those cultural beliefs that contribute to ethnocentrism. The person low in ethnocentrism would have high scores (4s and 5s) for items 3, 6, 12, and 13 and low scores (1s and 2s) for all the others. The person high in ethnocentrism would have low scores for items 3, 6, 12, and 13 and high scores for all the others.

WHAT WILL YOU DO? Use this test to bring your own cultural beliefs to consciousness so you can examine them logically and objectively. Ask yourself if your beliefs are productive and will help you achieve your professional and social goals, or if they're counterproductive and will actually hinder your achieving your goals.

Source: Adapted from James W. Neuliep & James C. McCroskey (1997). The development of a U.S. and generalized ethnocentrism scale, *Communication Research Reports, 14,* 393.

☑

■ **What Do You Say**
Dating an Ethnocentric
You've been dating this wonderful person for the last few months but increasingly are discovering that your "ideal" partner is extremely ethnocentric and sees little value in other religions, other races, other nationalities. You want to educate your possible life partner. **What Do You Say?** In what context?

As you've probably gathered from taking this test, **ethnocentrism** is the tendency to see others and their behaviors through your own cultural filters, often as distortions of your own behaviors. It's the tendency to evaluate the values, beliefs, and behaviors of your own culture as superior; as more positive, logical, and natural than those of other cultures. To achieve effective interpersonal communication, you need to see yourself and others as different but as neither inferior nor superior—not a very easily accomplished task.

Ethnocentrism exists on a continuum. People are not either ethnocentric or non-ethnocentric; rather, most people are somewhere along the continuum (Table 2.2) and we're all ethnocentric to at least some degree. Most important for out purposes is that your degree of ethnocentrism will influence your interpersonal (intercultural) communications.

CONFRONT YOUR STEREOTYPES Stereotypes, especially when they operate below the level of conscious awareness, can create serious communication problems (Lyons &

"Well, they look pretty undocumented to me."

TABLE 2.2 **The Ethnocentrism Continuum**

Drawing from several researchers (Lukens, 1978; Gudykunst & Kim, 1992; Gudykunst, 1994), this table summarizes some interconnections between ethnocentrism and communication. The table identifies five levels of ethnocentrism; the general terms under "Communication Distances" characterize the major communication attitudes that dominate the various levels. Under "Communications" are some ways people might behave given their particular degree of ethnocentrism. How would you rate yourself on this scale?

DEGREE OF ETHNOCENTRISM	COMMUNICATION DISTANCES	COMMUNICATIONS
Low	Equality	Treats others as equals; evaluates other ways of doing things as equal to own ways
	Sensitivity	Wants to decrease distance between self and others
	Indifference	Lacks concern for others but is not hostile
	Avoidance	Avoid and limits interpersonal interactions with others; prefers to be with own kind
High	Disparagement	Engages in hostile behavior; belittles others; views own culture as superior to other cultures

Kashima, 2003). Originally, the word *stereotype* was a printing term that referred to a plate that printed the same image over and over. A sociological or psychological **stereotype** is a fixed impression of a group of people. Everyone has attitudinal stereotypes—of national groups, religious groups, or racial groups, or perhaps of criminals, prostitutes, teachers, or plumbers. Consider, for example, if you have any stereotypes of, say, bodybuilders, the opposite sex, a racial group different from your own, members of a religion very different from your own, hard drug users, or college professors. It is very likely that you have stereotypes of several, or perhaps all, of these groups. Although we often think of stereotypes as negative ("They're lazy, dirty, and only interested in getting high"), they may also be positive ("They're smart, hardworking, and extremely loyal").

The New Yorker Collection 1996 Tom Cheney from cartoonbank.com. All rights reserved.

If you have these fixed impressions, you may, on meeting a member of a particular group, see that person primarily as a member of that group. Initially this may provide you with some helpful orientation. However, it creates problems when you apply to the person all the characteristics you assign to members of that group without examining the unique individual. If you meet a politician, for example, you may have a host of characteristics for politicians that you can readily apply to this person. To complicate matters further, you may see in this person's behavior the manifestation of various characteristics that you would not see if you did not know that this person was a politician. Because there are few visual and auditory cues in online communication, it's not surprising to find that people form impressions of their online communication partner with a heavy reliance on stereotypes (Jacobson, 1999).

" If you see in any given situation only what everybody else can see, you can be said to be so much a representative of your culture that you are a victim of it. "
—S. I. Hayakawa

Consider, however, another kind of stereotype: You're driving along a dark road and are stopped at a stop sign. A car pulls up beside you and three teenagers jump out and rap on your window. There may be a variety of reasons for this: Perhaps they need help or want to ask directions—or perhaps they are planning a carjacking. Your self-protective stereotype may help you decide on "carjacking" and may lead you to pull away and into the safety of a busy service station. In doing that, of course, you may have escaped being carjacked, or you may have failed to help people who needed your assistance.

Stereotyping can lead to two major barriers. First, the tendency to group a person into a class and to respond to that person primarily as a member of that class can lead you to perceive that a person possesses those qualities (usually negative) that you believe characterize the group to which he or she belongs. If that happens, you will fail to appreciate the multifaceted nature of all people and all groups. For example, consider your stereotype of a high-frequency computer user. Very likely your image of such a person is quite different from the research findings, which show that such users are as often female as male and are as sociable, popular, and self-assured as their peers who are not into heavy computer use (Schott & Selwyn 2000). And second, because stereotyping also can lead you to ignore the unique characteristics of an individual, you may fail to benefit from the special contributions each person can bring to an encounter.

BE MINDFUL Being mindful rather than mindless (a distinction considered in Chapter 1) is especially helpful in intercultural communication (Hajek & Giles, 2003). When you're in a mindless state, you behave in accordance with assumptions that would not normally pass intellectual scrutiny. For example, you know that cancer is not contagious, and yet many people will avoid touching cancer patients. You know that people who cannot see do not have hearing problems, and yet many people use a louder voice when talking to persons without sight. When the discrepancies between available evidence and behaviors are pointed out and your mindful state is awakened, you quickly realize that these behaviors are not logical or realistic.

When you deal with people from other cultures, you're often in a mindless state and therefore may function nonrationally in many ways. When your mindful state is awakened, you may then shift to a more critical thinking mode—and recognize, for example, that other people and other cultural systems are different but not inferior or superior. Thus, these suggestions for increasing intercultural communication effectiveness may appear logical (even obvious) to your mindful state, even though they are probably frequently ignored in your mindless state.

AVOID OVERATTRIBUTION **Overattribution** is the tendency to attribute too much of a person's behavior or attitudes to one of that person's characteristics ("She thinks that

"Because my genetic programming prevents me from stopping to ask directions—that's why!"

way because she's a woman," "He believes that because he was raised a Catholic"). In intercultural communication situations, overattribution takes two forms. First, it's the tendency to see too much of what a person believes or does as caused by the person's cultural identification. Second, it's the tendency to see a person as a spokesperson for his or her particular culture—for example, to assume because a man is African American (as in the cartoon on page 48) that he is therefore knowledgeable about the entire African American experience or that his thoughts are always focused on African American issues. People's ways of thinking and ways of behaving are influenced by a wide variety of factors; culture is only one factor of many.

REDUCE UNCERTAINTY All communication interactions involve uncertainty and ambiguity. Not surprisingly, this uncertainty and ambiguity is greater when there are wide cultural differences (Berger & Bradac, 1982; Gudyknust, 1989, 1993). Because of this, in intercultural communication it takes more time and effort to reduce uncertainty and thus to communicate meaningfully. Reducing your uncertainty about another person is worth the effort, however; it not only will make your communication more effective but also will increase your liking for the person (Douglas, 1994).

Techniques such as active listening (Chapter 5) and perception checking (Chapter 4) help you check on the accuracy of your perceptions and allow you to revise and amend any incorrect perceptions. Also, being specific reduces ambiguity and the chances of misunderstandings; misunderstanding is a lot more likely if you talk about "neglect" (a highly abstract concept) than if you refer to "forgetting my last birthday" (a specific event).

Finally, seeking feedback helps you correct any possible misconceptions almost immediately. Seek feedback on whether you're making yourself clear ("Does that make sense?" "Do you see where to put the widget?"). Similarly, seek feedback to make sure you understand what the other person is saying ("Do you mean that you'll never speak with them again? Do you mean that literally?").

RECOGNIZE DIFFERENCES To communicate interculturally you need to recognize the differences between yourself and people who are culturally different, the differences within the culturally different group, and the numerous differences in meaning that arise from cultural differences.

Differences between Yourself and Culturally Different People A common barrier to intercultural communication is the assumption that similarities exist but that differences do not. For example, although you may easily accept different hairstyles, clothing, and foods, you may assume that in basic values and beliefs, everyone is really alike. But that's not necessarily true. When you assume similarities and ignore differences, you'll fail to notice important distinctions. As a result, you'll risk communicating to others that your ways are the right ways and that their ways are not important to you. Consider: An American invites a Filipino coworker to dinner. The Filipino politely refuses. The American is hurt, feels that the Filipino does not want to be friendly, and does not repeat the invitation. The Filipino is hurt and concludes that the invitation was not extended sincerely. Here, it seems, both the American and the Filipino assume that their customs for inviting people to dinner are the same—when, in fact, they aren't. A Filipino expects to be invited several times before accepting a dinner invitation. In the Philippines, an invitation given only once is viewed as insincere.

Or consider age. If you were raised in the United States, you probably grew up with a youth bias (young is good, old is not so good—an attitude the U.S. media re-

E-Talk ▪ ▪ ▪ ▪ ▪ ▪

Similarities and Differences

People who interact in online political discussions see themselves to be interacting with people very different from themselves. Yet, and contrary to the research showing that we communicate most with people we perceive as similar to ourselves, they enjoy this diversity of people and differences of opinions (Stromer-Galley, 2003). Is this true of your own experiences in online discussions?

inforce daily) and may well have assumed that this reverence for youth was universal across all cultures. But it isn't; and if you assume it is, you may be in line for intercultural difficulties. A good example is the case of the American journalist in China who remarked to a government official that the official was probably too young to remember a particular event. The comment would have been taken as a compliment by most youth-oriented Americans. But the official perceived it as an insult—as a suggestion that he was too young to deserve respect (Smith, 2002).

Differences within the Culturally Different Group Within every cultural group there are wide and important differences. Just as all Americans are not alike, neither are all Indonesians, Greeks, Mexicans, and so on. When you ignore these differences—when you assume that all persons covered by the same label (in this case a national or racial label) are the same—you're guilty of stereotyping. A good example of this is the use of the term "African American." The term stresses the unity of Africa and those who are of African descent and is analogous to "Asian American" or "European American." At the same time, if the term is used in the same sense as "German American" or "Japanese American," it ignores the great diversity within the African continent. More analogous terms would be "Nigerian American" or "Ethiopian American." Within each culture there are smaller cultures that differ greatly from one another and from the larger culture as well as from other large cultures.

Differences in Meaning Meanings exist not in words but in people (Chapter 6). Consider, for example, the different meanings of the word *woman* to an American and a Muslim, of *religion* to a born-again Christian and an atheist, or of *lunch* to a Chinese rice farmer and a Madison Avenue advertising executive. Even though different groups may use the same word, its meanings will vary greatly depending on the listeners' cultural definitions.

Similarly, nonverbal messages have different meanings in different cultures. For example, a left-handed American who eats with the left hand may be seen by a Muslim as obscene. Muslims do not use the left hand for eating or for shaking hands but solely to clean themselves after excretory functions. So using the left hand to eat or to shake hands is considered insulting and obscene.

ADJUST YOUR COMMUNICATION Intercultural communication (in fact, all interpersonal communication) takes place only to the extent that you and the person you're trying to communicate with share the same system of symbols. Your interaction will be hindered to the extent that your language and nonverbal systems differ. Therefore, it's important to adjust your communication to compensate for cultural differences.

This principle takes on particular relevance when you realize that even within a given culture, no two persons share identical symbol systems. Parents and children, for example, not only have different vocabularies but also, even more important, associate different meanings with some of the terms they both use. People in close relationships—either as intimate friends or as romantic partners—realize that learning the other person's signals takes a long time and, often, great patience. If you want to understand what another person means—by smiling, by saying "I love you," by arguing about trivial matters, by self-deprecating comments—you have to learn the person's system of signals.

In the same way, part of the art of intercultural communication is learning the other culture's signals, how they're used, and what they mean. Furthermore, you have to share you own system of signals with others so that they can better understand you. Although some people may know what you mean by your silence or by your avoidance of eye contact, others may not. You cannot expect others to decode your behaviors accurately without help.

Adjusting your communication is especially important in intercultural situations, largely because people from different cultures use different signals—or sometimes use the same signals to signify quite different things. For example, focused eye

■ What Do You Say?
Privileged Language
You enter a group of racially similar people using terms normally considered negative to refer to themselves. Trying to be one of the group, you too use such terms only to be met with extremely negative nonverbal feedback. You need to lessen this negative reaction and let the group know that you don't normally use such racial terms. **What Do You Say?**

Skill Building Exercise

Confronting Cultural Differences

Here are a few cases of obvious intercultural differences. Select any one of them and indicate how you might communicate. For example: (1) What attitude would you approach the situation with? (2) What specific purposes would you hope to achieve? And (3) what would you say, and how would you say it?

1. You're in an interracial, interreligious relationship. Your partner's family ignores your "couplehood." For example, you and your partner are never invited to dinner as a couple or included in any family affairs. You decide to confront your partner's family.
1. Your parents persist in holding and verbalizing stereotypes about other religious, racial, and ethnic groups. You feel you must tell your parents how incorrect you think these stereotypes are.
3. Marsha, a colleague at work, recently underwent a religious conversion. She now persists in trying to get you and everyone else to undergo this same conversion. You decide to tell her that you find this behavior offensive.

Confronting intercultural insensitivity is extremely difficult, especially because most people will deny it. So approach these situations carefully, relying heavily on the skills of interpersonal communication identified throughout this text.

contact means honesty and openness in much of the United States. But in Japan and in many Hispanic cultures, that same behavior may signify arrogance or disrespect, particularly if engaged in a youngster with someone significantly older.

Communication accommodation theory, as explained in Chapter 1, holds that speakers will adjust or accommodate to the communication style of their listeners in order to interact more pleasantly and efficiently (Giles, Mulac, Bradac, & Johnson, 1987). As you adjust your messages, recognize that each culture has its own rules and customs for communication (Barna, 1997; Ruben, 1985; Spitzberg, 1991). These rules identify what is appropriate and what is inappropriate. Thus, for example, in U.S. culture you would call a person you wished to date three or four days in advance. In certain Asian cultures you might call the person's parents weeks or even months in advance. In U.S. culture you say, as a general friendly gesture and not as a specific invitation, "Come over and pay us a visit sometime." To members of other cultures, this comment is sufficient to prompt the listeners actually to visit at their convenience. Table 2.3 presents a good example of a set of cultural rules—guidelines for communicating with an extremely large and important culture that many people don't know.

RECOGNIZE CULTURE SHOCK Culture shock is the psychological reaction you experience when you encounter a culture very different from your own (Furnham & Bochner, 1986). Culture shock is normal; most people experience it when entering a new and different culture. Going away to college, moving in together, or joining the military, for example, can also result in culture shock. Nevertheless, it can be unpleasant and frustrating. Entering a new culture often engenders feelings of alienation, conspicuousness, and difference from everyone else. When you lack knowledge of the rules and customs of the new society, you cannot communicate effectively. You're apt to blunder frequently and seriously. In your culture shock you may not know basic things:

- how to ask someone for a favor or pay someone a compliment
- how to extend or accept an invitation
- how early or how late to arrive for an appointment, or how long to stay
- how to distinguish seriousness from playfulness and politeness from indifference

TABLE 2.3 *Interpersonal Communication Tips*

BETWEEN PEOPLE WITH AND WITHOUT DISABILITIES

Consider communication between people with general disabilities—such as people in wheelchairs or people with cerebral palsy—and those who have no such disability. Note that the suggestions offered here are considered appropriate in the United States but not necessarily in other cultures. For example, although most people in the United States accept the phrase "person with mental retardation," it's considered offensive to many in the United Kingdom (Fernald, 1995).

If you're the one without a general disability:

1. Avoid negative terms and terms that define the person in terms of the disability, such as "the disabled" or "the handicapped." Instead, say "person with a disability," putting the person, not the disability, first. Similarly, say "seizure" instead of "fit," "person with cerebral palsy" instead of "cerebral palsy victim" and "wheelchair user" instead of "wheelchair bound."

2. Treat assistive devices such as wheelchairs, canes, walkers, or crutches as the personal property of the user; be careful not to move these out of your way, as they're needed by the person with a disability.

3. If you shake hands with others in a group, also shake hands with the person with a disability. Don't avoid shaking hands, say, because the individual's hand is crippled.

4. Avoid talking about the person with a disability in the third person. For example, don't make remarks like "Doesn't he get around beautifully with the new crutches." Always direct your comments directly to the individual.

5. Don't assume that people who have a disability (such as slurred speech, as may occur with people who have cerebral palsy or cleft plate) are intellectually impaired. This definitely may not be the case, so be especially careful not to talk down to such people as research shows many people do (Unger, 2001).

6. If you're not sure how to act—for example, whether or not to offer walking assistance—ask: "Would you like me to help you into the dining room?"

7. If the person is in a wheelchair, it may be helpful for you to sit down or kneel down to get on the same eye level.

If you're the one with a disability:

1. Let the other person know if he or she can do anything to assist you in communicating. For example, if you want someone to speak louder, ask. If you want to relax and have someone push your wheelchair, say so.

2. Be patient and understanding with those who may not know how to act or what to say. Put them at ease as best you can.

3. If you detect discomfort in the other person, you might talk a bit about your disability to show that you're not uncomfortable and that you understand that others may not know how you feel. But, of course, you are under no obligation to educate the public—so don't feel this is something you ought to or have to do. If it makes you more comfortable, then do it, otherwise, don't.

These suggestions are based on a wide variety of sources, for example, **www.empowermentzone.com/etiquet.txt** (the website for the National Center for Access Unlimited), **www.dol.gov/dol/odep/, www.drc.uga.edu, www.ucpa.org/** (all accessed March 26, 2005).

- how to dress for an informal, formal, or business function
- how to order a meal in a restaurant or how to summon a waiter

The amount of culture shock you experience and the accompanying stress and difficulty you may experience seem proportional to the distance between your own culture and that of the new culture in which you find yourself. Visiting a culture similar to your own will lead to less stress and fewer problems than visiting a culture very different from your own (Furnham, 2004).

Culture shock occurs in four general stages, which apply to a wide variety of encounters with the new and the different (Oberg, 1960).

Stage One: The Honeymoon At first you experience fascination, even enchantment, with the new culture and its people. You finally have your own apartment. You're your own boss. Finally, on your own! Among people who are culturally different, the early (and superficial) relationships of this stage are characterized by cordiality and friendship. Many tourists remain at this stage, because their stays in foreign countries are so brief.

Stage Two: The Crisis In the crisis stage the differences between your own culture and the new one create problems. For example, students no longer find dinner ready or their clothes washed or ironed unless they do these chores themselves. Feelings of frustration and inadequacy come to the fore. This is the stage at which you experience the actual shock of the new culture. For example, in a study of students from more than 100 countries who were studying in 11 foreign countries, 25 percent of the students experienced depression (Klineberg & Hull, 1979).

Stage Three: The Recovery During the recovery period you gain the skills necessary to function effectively in the new culture. You learn how to shop, cook, and plan a meal. You find a local laundry and figure you'll learn how to iron later. You learn the language and ways of the society. Your feelings of inadequacy subside.

Stage Four: The Adjustment At the final stage you adjust to and come to enjoy the new culture and the new experiences. You may still experience periodic difficulties and strains, but on a whole, the experience is pleasant. Actually you're now a pretty decent cook. You're even coming to enjoy it. And you're making a good salary, so why learn to iron?

People also may experience a kind of reverse culture shock when they return to their original culture after living in a foreign culture (Jandt, 2000). Consider, for example, Peace Corps volunteers who work in economically deprived rural areas around the world. On returning to Las Vegas or Beverly Hills, they too may experience culture shock. Sailors who serve long periods aboard ship and then return to, for example, isolated farming communities may also experience culture shock. In these cases, however, the recovery period is shorter and the sense of inadequacy and frustration is less.

The suggestions outlined in the preceding subsections will go a long way in helping you communicate more effectively in all situations, and especially in intercultural interactions. These suggestions are, however, most effective when they are combined with the essential skills of all interpersonal communication (listed on the inside covers).

Dialogue *for* **Analysis**

The Intercultural Relationship

Here's a dialogue centering on intercultural relationships. Analyze the dialogue and try to identify examples of effective and ineffective interpersonal communication. How might you have engaged in this dialogue to make it a more effective, satisfying, and culturally sensitive interaction?

The Cast

Spanish-American women.*

Sofia, Aida, Inez, and Serena, all in their early 30s

The Context

Four former college best friends now meet once a year for an elaborate reunion dinner.

Sofia: It's so great getting together every year.
Aida: I'm always anxious to hear what everyone's been up to.
Serena: Well, I got engaged.
Several at once: What? Engaged? When did this happen?
Sofia: You weren't even dating anyone the last time we met!

(continues)

(continued)

Serena: I guess I just met the man I've been look for all my life. And he's not even from our country.

Aida: You couldn't find someone right here? In this entire country?

Sofia: What did your parents say?

Serena: They were furious.

Sofia: I bet they were.

Serena: They were furious; they told me all the reasons it wouldn't work and all the reasons I should get my head examined. And they want nothing to do with any children we might have. They don't even want to see their own future grandchildren.

Aida: You know interracial relationships don't work.

Inez: And it's just not accepted—despite what you see on TV.

Aida: And TV is NOT reality.

Inez: And don't be fooled into thinking everything will be OK—it won't.

Sofia: And what about the kids?

Aida: Is he—tell me, he is—at least a Christian?

Serena: No—surprise number three—he's an atheist and a communist.

Sofia: Your parents are right; you should have your head examined.

Inez: You need to reconsider this, honey. You're going to make the rest of your life very difficult. And what about the kids?

Aida: Your kids are the ones to suffer. They won't know who they are or where they belong. I know this for a fact. You know my cousin married that creep from Lebanon or some such third world country.

Sofia: And you're going to bring your kids up as little atheists? That'll make them real popular.

Serena: Well, we intend to expose the children to a variety of religious viewpoints and let them make up their own minds. I mean isn't that more logical than shoving one religion down their throats?

Inez: You're pregnant, aren't you?

Serena: No, I'm not pregnant, but we are trying.

Aida: And where will you live?

Serena: We'll live partly in North Korea—he has a big family there, and he's very close to them and we get along real well. And we'll live partly right here in Miami. By the way, his name is Kwon and we love each other.

*It's interesting to know that Spanish is the official language of 21 countries (representing more 300 million people); Mexico is the largest Spanish-speaking country, with more than 85 million people. Approximately 20 million Americans consider Spanish their first language. Of all the Spanish-speaking countries, Mexico sends the most international students to the United States; in 2002–03, Mexican students in this country numbered almost 13,000.

Summary of Concepts and Skills

This chapter explored culture and intercultural communication, the ways in which cultures differ, and ways to improve intercultural communication.

1. A culture is the specialized lifestyle of a group of people—their values, beliefs, artifacts, ways of behaving, and ways of communicating. Each generation transmits its culture to the next generation through the process of enculturation. In acculturation, one culture is modified through direct contact with or exposure to another culture.

2. Intercultural communication encompasses a broad range of interactions. Among them are communication between cultures, between races, between genders, between socioeconomic and ethnic groups, between age groups, between religions, and between nations.

3. Cultures differ in the degree to which they teach an individualist orientation (the individual is the most important consideration) or a collectivist orientation (the group is the most important consideration).

4. In high-context cultures much information is in the context or in the person's nonverbals; in low-context cultures most of the information is explicitly stated in the message.

5. Cultures differ in the degree to which gender roles are distinct or overlap. Highly "masculine" cultures view men as assertive, oriented to material success, and strong and view women as modest, focused on the quality of life, and tender. Highly feminine cultures encourage both men and women to be modest, oriented to maintaining the quality of life, and tender and socialize people to emphasize close relationships.

6. Cultures differ in their power structures; in high-power-distance cultures there is much difference in power between rulers and the ruled, whereas in low-power-distance cultures power is more evenly distributed.

7. Cultures differ in the degree to which they tolerate ambiguity and uncertainty. High-ambiguity-tolerance cultures are comfortable with uncertainty, whereas low-ambiguity-tolerance cultures are not.

8. Many tactics can help make intercultural communication more effective. For example, prepare yourself by learning about the culture, reduce ethnocentrism, confront your stereotypes, communicate mindfully, avoid overattribution, reduce uncertainty, recognize differences, adjust your communication on the basis of cultural differences, and recognize culture shock.

In addition, this chapter considered some important skills. Check those you wish to work on.

_____ 1. *Cultural influences.* Communicate with an understanding that culture influences communication in all its forms.

_____ 2. *Individualist and collectivist cultures.* Adjust your messages and your listening with an awareness of differences in individualist and collectivist cultures.

_____ 3. *High- and low-context cultures.* Adjust your messages and your listening in light of the differences between high- and low-context cultures.

_____ 4. *Masculine and feminine cultures.* Adjust your messages and your listening to differences in masculinity and femininity.

_____ 5. *High- and low-power-distance cultures.* Adjust your messages on the basis of the power structure that is written into the culture.

_____ 6. *High and low tolerance for ambiguity.* Adjust your messages on the basis of the degree of the ambiguity tolerance of the other people.

_____ 7. *Ethnocentric thinking.* Recognize your own ethnocentric thinking and how it influences your verbal and nonverbal messages.

_____ 8. *Intercultural communication.* Become mindful of (1) the differences between yourself and the culturally different, (2) the differences within the cultural group, (3) the differences in meanings, and (4) the differences in cultural customs.

_____ 9. *Appreciating cultural differences.* Look at cultural differences not as deviations or deficiencies but as the differences they are. Recognizing differences, however, does not necessarily mean accepting them.

Vocabulary Quiz: The Language of Intercultural Communication

Match the terms of intercultural communication with their definitions. Record the number of the definition next to the appropriate term.

_____ high-context culture

_____ acculturation

_____ intercultural communication

_____ low-context culture

_____ ethnocentrism

_____ culture

_____ low-power-distance cultures

_____ enculturation

_____ individualist cultures

_____ collectivist cultures

1. A culture in which most information is explicitly encoded in the verbal message.

2. The values, beliefs, artifacts, and ways of communicating of a group of people.
3. The process by which culture is transmitted from one generation to another.
4. Communication that takes place between persons of different cultures or persons who have different cultural beliefs, values, or ways of behaving.
5. The process through which a person's culture is modified through contact with another culture.
6. The tendency to evaluate other cultures negatively and our own culture positively.
7. Cultures in which power is relatively evenly distributed.
8. Cultures that emphasize competition and individual success, and in which your responsibility is largely to yourself.
9. A culture in which much information is in the context or the person and is not made explicit in the verbal message.
10. Cultures that emphasize the member's responsibility to the group.

Four for Discussion

1. In this age of multiculturalism, how do you feel about Article II, Section 1 of the U.S. Constitution? The relevant section reads: "No person except a natural born citizen, or citizen of the United States at the time of the adoption of this Constitution, shall be eligible to the office of President."

2. Social Darwinism holds that much as the human species evolved from lower life forms to homo sapiens, cultures also evolve. Consequently, some cultures may be considered "advanced" and others "primitive." Cultural relativism, on the other hand, holds that although all cultures are different, no culture is either superior or inferior to any other (Berry, Poortinga, Segall, & Dasen, 1992). What arguments can you advance in support of or against each position?

3. Men and women from different cultures were asked the following question: "If a man (woman) had all the other qualities you desired, would you marry this person if you were not in love with him (her)?" (LeVine, Sato, Hashimoto, & Verma, 1994). Fifty percent of the respondents from Pakistan, 49 percent from India, and 19 percent from Thailand said yes. At the other extreme were respondents from Japan (only 2 percent said yes), the United States (3.5 percent), and Brazil (4 percent). How would you answer this question? How is your answer influenced by your culture?

4. Some cultures frown on sexual relationships outside of marriage; others consider sex a normal part of intimacy. Intercultural researchers (Hatfield & Rapson, 1996) recall a discussion between colleagues from Sweden and the United States on ways of preventing AIDS. When researchers from the United States suggested promoting abstinence, their Swedish counterparts asked, "How will teenagers ever learn to become loving, considerate sexual partners if they don't practice?" "The silence that greeted the question," note Hatfield and Rapson (1996, p. 36), "was the sound of two cultures clashing." How have your cultural beliefs and values influenced what you consider appropriate relationship behavior?

MyCommunicationLab Explorations

Explore www.mycommunicationlab.com to find exercises on culture and intercultural communication; including (1) Random Pairs, (2) Cultural Beliefs, (3) From Culture to Gender, (4) Cultural Identities, and (5) The Sources of Your Cultural Beliefs. Three relevant self-tests are (6) How Open Are You Interculturally? (7) Can You Distinguish Universal from Culture-Specific Icons? and (8) What Are Your Cultural Beliefs and Values?

Also visit MyCommunicationLab for a variety of study aids, exercises, and video clips on the nature and importance of culture in all aspects of interpersonal communication.

Explore our research resources at
www.researchnavigator.com.

Research
Navigator.com

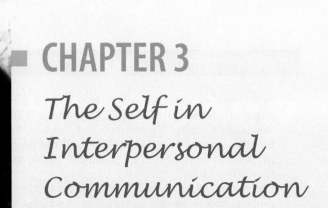

CHAPTER 3
The Self in Interpersonal Communication

WHY READ THIS CHAPTER?

*B*ecause you'll **learn about:**
- self-concept, self-awareness, and self-esteem.
- self-disclosure.
- fear in communication.

*B*ecause you'll **learn to:**
- clarify your self-concept and increase your self-awareness and self-esteem.
- appropriately regulate self-disclosures and your responses to the disclosures of others.
- manage your fear of communication in a variety of interpersonal situations.

*I*n this chapter we look at self-concept, self-awareness, and self-esteem and particularly at how you develop your image of yourself and how you can increase your own self-awareness and self-esteem. With this as a foundation, we then look at self-disclosure, the process of revealing yourself to another person; and we consider speaker apprehension and some ways to reduce your own fear of communication.

Self-Concept, Self-Awareness, and Self-Esteem

Central to all forms of interpersonal communication is your self-concept—the image you have of yourself—and how that image is formed. Equally significant is your self-awareness, the degree to which you know yourself. Let's look first at self-concept.

Self-Concept

Your **self-concept** is your image of who you are. It's how you perceive yourself: your feelings and thoughts about your strengths and weaknesses and your abilities and limitations. Self-concept develops from the image that others have of you; the comparisons you draw between yourself and others; your cultural experiences in the realms of race, ethnicity, gender, and gender roles; and your evaluation of your own thoughts and behaviors (Figure 3.1).

OTHERS' IMAGES OF YOU   If you wished to see the way your hair looked, you'd probably look in a mirror. But what would you do if you wanted to see how friendly or how assertive you are? According to the concept of the *looking-glass self* (Cooley, 1922), you would look at the image of yourself that others reveal to you through their behaviors, and especially through the way they treat you and react to you.

You don't want to seek such information from just anyone, however. People who are overly negative, who have personal agendas, or who know you only slightly are

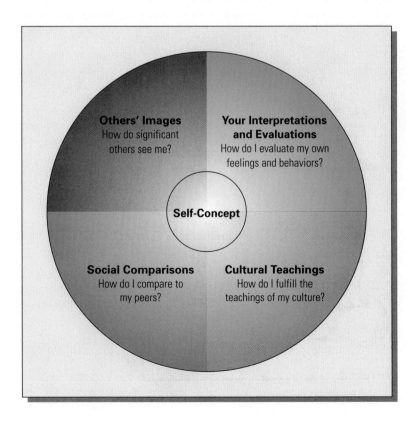

Figure 3.1
The Sources of Self-Concept
This diagram depicts the four sources of self-concept, the four contributors to how you see yourself. As you read about self-concept, consider the influence of each of these four factors throughout your life. For example, which factor influenced you most as a preteen? Which influences you the most now? Which will influence you the most 20 years from now?

generally poor sources for seeking self-insight. Rather, you would look to those who are most significant in your life—to your *significant others*. As a child, for example, you would look to your parents and then to your elementary school teachers. As an adult you might look to your friends and romantic partners. If these significant others think highly of you, you will see a positive self-image reflected in their behaviors; if they think little of you, you will see a more negative image.

SOCIAL COMPARISONS   Another way you develop self-concept is to compare yourself with others, to engage in what are called *social comparisons* (Festinger, 1954). Again, you don't choose just anyone. Rather, when you want to gain insight into who you are and how effective or competent you are, you look to your peers. For example, after an examination you probably want to know how you performed relative to the other students in your class. This gives you a clearer idea as to how effectively you performed. If you play on a baseball team, it's important to know your batting average in comparison with the batting averages of others on the team. Your absolute score on the exam or your batting average may be helpful in telling you something about your performance, but you gain a different perspective when you see your scores in comparison with those of your peers.

CULTURAL TEACHINGS   As shown in Chapter 2, your culture instills in you a variety of beliefs, values, and attitudes—about matters such as success (how you should define and achieve it); the relevance of religion, race, or nationality; and the ethical principles you should follow in business and in your personal life. These teachings provide benchmarks against which you can measure yourself. For example, your ability to achieve what your culture defines as success will contribute to a positive self-concept. Your failure to achieve what your culture values (for example, not being married by the time you're 30) may contribute to a negative self-concept.

When you demonstrate the qualities that your culture (or organization, because organizations are much like cultures) teaches, you will see yourself as a cultural success and will be rewarded by other members of the culture (or organization). Seeing yourself as culturally successful and getting rewarded by others will contribute positively to your self-concept. When you fail to demonstrate such qualities, you're more

"You remind me of myself—you know—a while ago."

likely to see yourself as a cultural failure and to be punished by other members of the culture, contributing to a more negative self-concept.

Because you belong to a variety of cultures and because each of these cultures exerts influence on your attitudes and beliefs, you may find that some of these influences contradict one another. For example, you may have been taught that it's important to be financially successful—but that the love of money is the root of all evil or, recalling religious scripture, that "it's easier for a camel to pass through the eye of a needle than for a rich man to get into heaven." Or you may have been taught to be the best in your field but also to be cooperative and helpful to others, perhaps even those you find yourself competing against. Such contradictory beliefs may easily cause intrapersonal conflicts. In extreme cases you may decide to reject the attitudes and beliefs of one culture—often the "old-world" culture—in favor of those of the culture with which you feel more comfortable.

YOUR OWN OBSERVATIONS, INTERPRETATIONS, AND EVALUATIONS   You also observe, interpret, and evaluate your own behavior. For example, let's say you believe that lying is wrong. If you lie, you will probably evaluate this behavior in terms of your internalized beliefs about lying and will react negatively to your own behavior. You may, for example, experience guilt as a result of your behavior's contradicting your beliefs. On the other hand, let's say that you pull someone out of a burning building at great personal risk. You will probably evaluate this behavior positively; you will feel good about this behavior and, as a result, about yourself.

The more you understand why you view yourself as you do, the better you'll understand who you are. You can gain additional insight into yourself by looking more closely at self-awareness—and especially at the Johari model of the self.

Self-Awareness

The term **self-awareness** refers to your awareness of or your insight into or consciousness of yourself—of your physical self and personality traits, your thoughts and feelings, and your behaviors. A high level of self-awareness will enable you to control your thoughts and behaviors and will help you to identify your strengths and weaknesses so that you can capitalize on your strengths and direct your energies to correcting weaknesses. The **Johari window,** a model of four selves, is particularly helpful in explaining the self and in offering suggestions on how to increase self-awareness (Figure 3.2).

	Known to self	**Not known to self**
Known to others	**Open Self** Information about yourself that you and others know	**Blind self** Information about yourself that you don't know but that others do know
Not known to others	**Hidden self** Information about yourself that you know but others don't know	**Unknown self** Information about yourself that neither you nor others know

Figure 3.2

The Johari Window

This diagram is a tool commonly used for examining what you know and don't know about yourself. It will also prove an effective way of explaining the nature of self-disclosure, covered later in this chapter. The window gets its name from its inventors, *Joseph Luft* and *Harry* Ingham. When interacting with your peers, which self is your largest? Your smallest?

Source: From *Group Processes: An Introduction to Group Dynamics,* 3rd ed., by Joseph Luft. Copyright © 1984 by Mayfield Publishing. Reprinted with permission of The McGraw-Hill Companies.

YOUR FOUR SELVES   Assume that the model in Figure 3.2 represents you. The model is divided into quadrants, each of which contains a different self. Visualize the entire Johari window as of constant size but each section as variable: sometimes small, sometimes large. That is, changes in one quadrant will cause changes in the other quadrants. For example, if you enlarge the open self, then another self must get smaller (see Figure 3.3).

The Johari model emphasizes that the several aspects of the self are not separate and distinct pieces. Rather, they're parts of a whole that interact with one another. Like the model of interpersonal communication, this model of the self is transactional: Each part is dependent on each other part.

Your *open self* represents all the information, behaviors, attitudes, feelings, desires, motivations, and ideas that characterize you. The types of information included here might vary from your name and sex to your age, religious affiliation, and batting average. The size of your open self changes depending on the situation and the individuals you're interacting with. Some people probably make you feel comfortable and support you. To them, you may open yourself wide. To others you might prefer to leave most of yourself closed or unknown.

Your *blind self* represents all the things about yourself that others know but that you do not. These include, for example, your habit of rubbing your nose when you get angry, your defense mechanisms, and your repressed experiences. Interpersonal communication depends on both parties' sharing the same basic information about each other. Where blind areas exist, communication will be more difficult. Yet blind areas always exist. You can shrink your blind area, but you can never totally eliminate it.

Your *hidden self* contains all that you know of yourself but that you keep to yourself. This area includes all your successfully kept secrets. In any interaction, this area includes everything you have not revealed and perhaps seek actively to conceal. When you move information from this area to the open area—as in, say, telling someone a secret—you're self-disclosing, a process examined later in this chapter.

Your *unknown self* represents truths that exist but that neither you nor others know. We infer the existence of this unknown self from dreams, psychological tests, or therapy. For example, through therapy you might become aware of your high need for acceptance and of how this influences the way you allow people to take advantage of you. With this insight, this information moves from the unknown self to the hidden self and perhaps to the open self.

INCREASING SELF-AWARENESS   Embedded in the discussion of the Johari window were suggestions on how to increase your own self-awareness. Let's make them a bit more specific.

Figure 3.3
The Johari Window of Varied Structures
Notice that as one self grows, one or more of the other selves shrink. Assume that each of these models depicts the self-awareness and self-disclosure of different people. How would you describe the type of interpersonal communication (especially self-disclosure) that characterizes each of these four people?

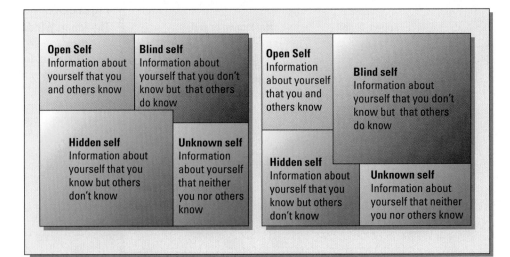

Reveal Yourself.   You can increase your self-awareness—oddly enough—by revealing yourself to others and thereby enlarging your open self. At the very least, this will help you bring into focus what you may have buried within. As you discuss yourself, you may see connections that you had previously missed. For example, as you discuss your previous failed relationships, you may recall common mistakes you made or things you might have done differently. With feedback from others, you may gain still more insight. Also, by increasing your open self, you increase the chances that others will reveal what they know about you, further increasing self-awareness.

Listen to Others.   You can learn a great deal about yourself from *listening to others* and seeing yourself as others do. Conveniently, others are constantly giving you the very feedback you need to increase self-awareness. In every interpersonal interaction, people comment on you in some way—on what you do, what you say, how you look. Sometimes these comments are explicit: "Loosen up," "Don't take things so hard," "You seem angry." Often, however, they're hidden in the way others look at you or in what they talk about. Pay close attention to this kind of information (both explicit and hidden) and use it to increase your own self-awareness.

Seek Out Information to Reduce Your Blind Self.   Encouraging people to reveal what they know about you will further help increase your awareness. You need not be so blatant as to say, "Tell me about myself" or "What do you think of me?" You can, however, use some situations that arise every day to gain self-information. "Do you think I came down too hard on the kids today?" "Do you think I was assertive enough when asking for a raise?" But use this route to self-awareness in moderation. If you do it too often, your friends will soon look for someone else to talk with.

Another way to seek out information about yourself is to visualize how you're seen by your parents, teachers, friends, the stranger on the bus, your neighbor's child. Recognize that each of these people sees you differently; to each you're a different person. Yet you're really *all* those persons. The experience will surely give you new and valuable perspectives on yourself. It will convince you that you're actually a different person, depending on the person you're interacting with. For example, my colleagues see me as serious and always doing a hundred things at the same time. My students, however, see me as humorous and laid back.

"I've tried a lot of life strategies, and being completely self-serving works best for me."

Self-Esteem

Self-esteem is a measure of how valuable you think you are; people with high self-esteem think very highly of themselves, whereas people with low self-esteem view themselves negatively. Before reading further about this topic, consider your own self-esteem by taking the following self-test.

Test *Yourself*

How's Your Self-Esteem?

INSTRUCTIONS: Respond to each of the following statements with T (true) if the statement describes you at least some significant part of the time, or with F (false) if the statement describes you rarely or never.

_____ ❶ Generally, I feel I have to be successful in all things.

_____ ❷ Many of my acquaintances are often critical of what I do and how I think.

_____ ❸ I often tackle projects that I know are impossible to complete to my satisfaction.

_____ ❹ When I focus on the past, I tend to focus on my failures more often than on my successes and on my negative rather than my positive qualities.

_____ ❺ I make little effort to improve my personal and interpersonal skills.

HOW DID YOU DO?   "True" responses to these questions would generally be seen as reflecting attitudes or choices that would get in the way of building positive self-esteem. "False" responses would indicate that you are thinking much the way a self-esteem coach would want you to think.

WHAT WILL YOU DO?   The following discussion elaborates on the patterns suggested by these five questions and illustrates why each of them creates problems for the development of healthy self-esteem. So this discussion is a good starting place for working on your self-esteem. You might also want to log into the National Association for Self-Esteem's website (**www.self-esteem-nase.org**). There you'll find a variety of materials for examining and bolstering self-esteem.

The basic idea behind self-esteem is that when you feel good about yourself—about who you are and what you're capable of doing—you will perform better. When you think like a success, you're more likely to act like a success. When you think you're a failure, you're more likely to act like a failure. Increasing self-esteem will, therefore, help you to function more effectively in school, in interpersonal relationships, and in your career. Here are five suggestions for increasing self-esteem that parallel the questions in the self-test.

ATTACK SELF-DESTRUCTIVE BELIEFS   Challenge those beliefs you have about yourself that are unproductive or that make it more difficult for you to achieve your goals—for example, the belief that you have to succeed in everything you do, the belief that you have to be loved by everyone, the belief that you must be strong at all times, or the belief that you must please others (Butler, 1981). Replace these self-destructive beliefs with more productive ones, such as "I succeed in many things, but I don't have to succeed in everything" and "It would be nice to be loved by everyone, but it isn't necessary to my happiness."

SEEK OUT NOURISHING PEOPLE   Psychologist Carl Rogers (1970) drew a distinction between *noxious* and *nourishing* people. Noxious people criticize and find fault with

It's All About You © Tony Murphy.

just about everything. Nourishing people, on the other hand, are positive and optimistic. Most important, they reward us, they stroke us, they make us feel good about ourselves. To enhance your self-esteem, seek out these people; also, avoid noxious others, those who make you feel negatively about yourself. At the same time, seek to become more nourishing yourself so that you and others will build up one another's self-esteem.

WORK ON PROJECTS THAT WILL RESULT IN SUCCESS   Some people want to fail, or so it seems. Often, they select projects that will result in failure simply because they are impossible to complete. Avoid this trap and select projects that will result in success. Each success will help build self-esteem, and each success will make the next success a little easier. When a project does fail, recognize that this does not mean that you're a failure. Everyone fails somewhere along the line. Failure is something that happens; it's not something you've created, and it's not something inside you. Further, your failing once does not mean that you will fail the next time. So put failure in perspective.

REMIND YOURSELF OF YOUR SUCCESSES   Some people have a tendency to focus, sometimes too much, on their failures, their missed opportunities, their social mistakes. If your objective is to correct what you did wrong or to identify the skills that you need to correct these failures, then focusing on failures can have some positive value. But if you focus mainly on failure without any plans for correction, then you're probably making life more difficult for yourself and limiting your self-esteem. To counteract the tendency to recall failures, remind yourself of your successes. Recall these successes both intellectually and emotionally. Realize why you succeeded, and relive the emotional experience when you sank that winning basket or aced that test or helped that friend overcome personal problems. And while you're at it, recall too your positive qualities. For a start read down the list of the essential interpersonal skills on the inside covers of this book and check off those you'd consider among your assets. To this list add any other qualities you number among your positive qualities.

SECURE AFFIRMATION   It's frequently recommended that you remind yourself of your successes—that you focus on your good deeds; on your positive qualities, strengths, and

" Even when we are quite alone, how often do we think with pleasure or pain of what others think of us—of their imagined approbation or disapprobation. "

—Charles Darwin

virtues; and on your productive and meaningful relationships with friends, loved ones, and relatives (Aronson, Cohen, & Nail, 1998; Aronson, Wilson, & Akert, 1999). The idea behind this advice is that the way you talk to yourself will influence what you think of yourself. If you *affirm* yourself—if you tell yourself that you're a success, that others like you, that you will succeed on the next test, that you will be welcomed when asking for a date—you will soon come to feel more positive about yourself. Self-affirmations include statements like "I'm a worthy person," "I'm responsible and can be depended upon," "I'm capable of loving and being loved," "I'm a good team player," and "I can accept my past but also let it go."

However, not all researchers agree with this advice. Some argue that such affirmations—although extremely popular in self-help books—may not be very helpful. These critics contend that if you have low self-esteem, you're not going to believe your self-affirmations, because you don't have a high opinion of yourself to begin with (Paul, 2001). Such critics propose that the alternative to self-affirmation is to secure affirmation from others. You'd do this by, for example, becoming more interpersonally competent and interacting with more positive people. In this way you'd get more positive feedback from others—which, these researchers argue, is more helpful than self-talk in raising self-esteem.

Identification with people similar to yourself also seems to increase self-esteem. For example, one study found that deaf people who identified with the larger deaf community had greater self-esteem than those who didn't so identify (Jambor & Elliott, 2005). Similarly, identification with your cultural group also seems helpful in developing positive self-esteem (McDonald, McCabe, Yeh, Lau, Garland, & Hough, 2005).

Self-Disclosure

When you move information from the hidden self into the open self, you're self-disclosing; you're revealing information about yourself to others. You can self-disclose through overt statements as well as through slips of the tongue and unconscious nonverbal movements. **Self-disclosure** may involve information that you tell others freely or information that you normally keep hidden. It may supply information ("I earn $45,000") or reveal feelings ("I'm feeling really depressed"). Self-disclosure can vary from the insignificant ("I'm a Sagittarius") to the highly revealing ("I'm currently in an abusive relationship," "I'm always depressed").

Skill building
exercise

Empowering Others

Here are three situations in which you might wish to empower the individuals involved. For each situation, describe the kinds of messages (verbal and nonverbal) that would empower the other person, using such strategies as (a) raising the other person's self-esteem; (b) listening actively and supportively; (c) being open, positive, and empathic; and (d) avoiding verbal aggressiveness or any unfair conflict strategies.

1. Your partner is having lots of difficulties—lost two jobs in the last six months, received poor grades in a night class, and has been gaining a lot of weight. At the same time, you're doing extremely well—you just got promoted, got admitted to a great MBA program, and are looking your best. You want to give your partner confidence. How might you raise your partner's self-esteem?
2. You're supervising four college interns, three men and one woman, who are redesigning your company's website. The men are extremely supportive of one another and regularly contribute ideas. Although equally competent, the woman doesn't contribute; she seems to lack confidence. But the objective of this redesign is to increase the number of female visitors, so you really need her input and want to empower her. What can you do to empower the lone woman on your team?
3. You're a third-grade teacher. Most of your students are from the same ethnic–religious group; three, however, are from a very different group. The problem is that these students don't participate successfully; for example, they stumble when they have to read in front of the class (although they read well in private), and they make lots of arithmetic mistakes at the chalkboard. You want to empower these students to help them realize their potential. What can you say or do to help empower these students?

Empowering others enables you to help others but also to benefit yourself. Empowered partners and colleagues, for example, are likely to be happier, a lot less prone to violence or verbal abuse, and more satisfied with the relationship than those lacking in power.

Only new knowledge represents "disclosure." To tell someone something about yourself that he or she already knows is not self-disclosure. And self-disclosure involves at least one other individual. It cannot be *intra*personal communication (communication with yourself). Nor may you "disclose" in a way that makes the message impossible for another person to understand. For a communication to be self-disclosure, someone must receive and understand the information.

Factors Influencing Self-Disclosure

Many factors influence whether or not you disclose, what you disclose, and to whom you disclose. Among the most important factors are who you are, your culture, your gender, who your listeners are, and what your topic is.

WHO YOU ARE Highly sociable and extroverted people self-disclose more than those who are less sociable and more introverted. People who are apprehensive about talking in general also self-disclose less than those who are more comfortable in communicating.

Competent people engage in self-disclosure more than less competent people. Perhaps competent people have greater self-confidence and more positive things to reveal. Similarly, their self-confidence may make them more willing to risk possible negative reactions (McCroskey & Wheeless, 1976).

YOUR CULTURE People from different cultures self-disclose differently. People in the United States, for example, disclose more than those in Great Britain, Germany, Japan, or Puerto Rico (Gudykunst, 1983). American students also disclose more than students from most Middle East countries (Jourard, 1971). Americans also reported greater self-disclosure when communicating with other Americans than when communicating interculturally (Allen, Long, O'Mara, & Judd, 2003). Similarly, American

What Do You Say

Corrective Self-Disclosing

When you met your current partner—with whom you want to spend the rest of your life—you minimized the extent of your romantic past. You now want to come clean and disclose your "sordid" history. **What Do You Say?** Through what channel?

students self-disclose more about controversial issues and to different types of people than do Chinese students (Chen, 1992). Chinese Singaporean students consider more topics to be taboo and inappropriate for self-disclosure than their British peers (Goodwin & Lee, 1994). Among the Kabre of Togo, secrecy is a major part of everyday interaction (Piot, 1993).

In some cultures—for example, Mexican—there's a strong emphasis on discussing all matters in a positive mode, and this undoubtedly influences the way Mexicans approach self-disclosure as well. Negative self-disclosures, for example, are usually made only to close intimates and then only after considerable time has elapsed in a relationship. This reluctance to disclose negative information extends to people's HIV-positive status and thus is creating serious problems in Mexico's efforts to prevent and treat HIV infection (Szapocznik, 1995). In contrast to this generalization about Mexicans and self-disclosure, however, one study has found that Argentineans disclose more than Americans (Horenstein & Downey, 2003).

Other research indicates that Indians are reluctant to self-disclose, for fear that what they say will reflect negatively on their reputation and family (Hastings, 2000). Religious traditions may also affect self-disclosure; in a study of Muslim, Druze, and Jewish adolescents in Israel, Muslim students disclosed most, Jewish students next, and Druze students least (Shechtman, Hiradin, & Zina, 2003).

There is some indication that the political climate today will influence the cross-cultural self-disclosure patterns of all people. Significant self-disclosure between Muslim and non-Muslim Americans, for example, are likely to be more guarded than before September 11, 2001, and the Iraqi war, as are self-disclosures between recent immigrants and other Americans (Barry, 2003).

These differences aside, there are also important similarities across cultures. For example, people from Great Britain, Germany, the United States, and Puerto Rico are all more apt to disclose certain kinds of personal information—such as details about hobbies, interests, attitudes, and opinions on politics and religion—than to discuss finances, sex, personality, and interpersonal relationships (Jourard, 1971). Similarly, one study showed self-disclosure patterns between American males to be virtually identical to those between Korean males (Won-Doornink, 1991).

YOUR GENDER   The popular stereotype of gender differences in self-disclosure emphasizes the male's reluctance to speak about himself. For the most part, research supports this view and shows that women disclose more than men. This is especially true in same-sex dyads (two-person groups); women disclose more intimately (and with more emotion) when talking with other women than with men (Shaffer, Pegalis, & Bazzini, 1996). Men and women, however, make negative disclosures nearly equally (Naifeh & Smith, 1984).

More specifically, women disclose more than men about their previous romantic relationships, their feelings about their closest same-sex friends, their greatest fears, and what they don't like about their partners (Sprecher, 1987). Women also seem to increase the depth of their self-disclosures as the relationship becomes more intimate, whereas men seem not to change their self-disclosure levels. Finally, women even self-disclose more to members of the extended family than men do (Komarovsky, 1964; Argyle & Henderson, 1985; Moghaddam, Taylor, & Wright, 1993). One notable exception occurs in initial encounters. Here men will disclose more intimately than women, perhaps "in order to control the relationship's development" (Derlega, Winstead, Wong, & Hunter, 1985). In another exception to the general gender trend, a study of Americans and Ar-

In order to have a conversation with someone, you must reveal yourself.

—James Baldwin

gentineans found that in Argentina males indicated a significantly greater willingness to self-disclose than females (Horenstein & Downey, 2003).

Although to some extent men and women give different reasons for avoiding self-disclosure (Rosenfeld, 1979), both genders share this reason: "If I disclose, I might project an image I do not want to project." In a society in which image is so important—in which a person's image is often the basis for success or failure—this explanation is not surprising.

YOUR LISTENERS Self-disclosure occurs more readily in small groups than in large groups. Dyads, or groups of two people, are the most hospitable setting for self-disclosure. With one listener, you can attend to the responses carefully. You can monitor the disclosures, continuing if there is support from your listener and stopping if there is not. With more than one listener, such monitoring becomes difficult, because the listeners' responses are sure to vary.

Because you disclose, generally at least, on the basis of support you receive, you probably disclose to people you like (Derlega, Winstead, Wong, & Greenspan, 1987; Collins & Miller, 1994), to people you trust (Wheeless & Grotz, 1977), to people who show you concern and affection (Roberts & Aruguete, 2000), and to people you feel understand you (Martin, Anderson, & Mottet, 1999). You probably also come to like those to whom you disclose (Berg & Archer, 1983; Collins & Miller, 1994).

At times self-disclosure occurs more in temporary than in permanent relationships—for example, between strangers on a train or plane, a kind of "in-flight intimacy" (McGill, 1985). In this kind of situation, two people set up an intimate self-disclosing relationship during a brief travel period, but they don't pursue it beyond that point. You're also more likely to disclose information you received from a low-level intimate (say a casual acquaintance) to a higher-level intimate (say a best friend) than you are to disclose information you received from a high-level intimate to a low-level intimate. This is a specific instance of the more general principle that you're more likely to communicate important information upward (to those of greater intimacy) than downward (to those of less intimacy) (Yovetich & Drigotas, 1999).

You're more likely to disclose when the person you're with discloses. This **dyadic effect** (what one person does, the other person does likewise) probably leads you to feel more secure and reinforces your own self-disclosing behavior. Disclosures also are more intimate when they're made in response to the disclosures of others (Berg & Archer, 1983). Research finds, too, that reciprocal self-disclosure occurs more quickly and at higher levels online than it does in face-to-face interactions (Levine, 2000; Joinson, 2001). This dyadic effect is not universal across all cultures, however. For example, Americans in dyads are likely to follow the dyadic effect and to reciprocate with explicit, verbal self-disclosure, but Koreans are not (Won-Doornink, 1985). As you can appreciate, this can easily cause intercultural differences; for example, an American may feel hurt or insulted if his or her Korean counterpart doesn't reciprocate with self-disclosures that are similar in depth.

YOUR TOPIC AND CHANNEL You're also more likely to disclose about some topics than others. For example, as mentioned earlier, you're probably more likely to self-disclose information about your job or hobbies than about your sex life or financial situation (Jourard, 1968, 1971). You're also more likely to disclose favorable information than unfavorable information. And dating couples are more likely to disclose information about nonsexual topics than about sexual ones (Byers & Demmons, 1999). Generally, the more personal and negative the topic, the less likely people are to self-disclose.

Consider your own willingness to self-disclose. How willing would you be to disclose such topics as the following to, say, members of this class?

E-Talk
Self-Esteem and CMC
An investigation of self-esteem found that when people engaged in a communication situation involving interpersonal risk, low-self-esteem persons preferred e-mail, whereas high-self-esteem persons preferred face-to-face interaction (Joinson, 2004). How would you explain this finding?

- *your attitudes toward different nationalities and races*
- *your feelings about your parents*
- *your sexual fantasies*
- *your past sexual experiences*
- *your ideal mate*
- *your drinking and/or drug-taking behavior*
- *your personal goals*
- *your unfulfilled desires*
- *your major weaknesses*
- *your feelings about the people in the class*

Recently, research has addressed differences in self-disclosure in relation to communication channels, whether face-to-face or computer mediated. Some research finds that people experience greater closeness and self-disclosure in face-to-face groups than in Internet chat groups (Mallen, Day, & Green, 2003). Other research, however, seems to indicate that self-disclosure occurs more quickly and at higher levels of intimacy online than in face-to-face situations (Joinson, 2001; Levine, 2000). Some researchers have pointed to a "disinhibition effect" that occurs in online communication. People often seem less inhibited in communicating in e-mail or in chat groups, for example, than they do face-to-face. Among the reasons for this seem to be that in online communication there is a certain degree of anonymity and invisibility (Suler, 2004).

The Rewards and Dangers of Self-Disclosure

Like other forms of interpersonal communication, self-disclosure entails both potential rewards and potential dangers. Let's look first at the rewards.

REWARDS OF SELF-DISCLOSURE   Research shows that self-disclosure helps to increase self-knowledge, communication and relationship effectiveness, and physiological well-being. Let's look at each of these.

Self-Knowledge.   One reward of self-disclosure is that you gain a new perspective on yourself, a deeper understanding of your own behavior. Through self-disclosure you may bring to consciousness a great deal that you might otherwise keep from conscious analysis. For example, as Tony talks about the difficulties he had living with an alcoholic father, he may remember details of his early life or entertain new feelings.

Even **self-acceptance** is difficult without self-disclosure. You accept yourself largely through the eyes of others. Through self-disclosure and subsequent support, you may be in a better position to see the positive responses to you. And you're more likely to respond by developing a more positive self-concept.

Communication Effectiveness.   You understand the messages of another person largely to the extent that you understand the person. For example, you can tell when a friend is serious or joking, when someone you know well is being sarcastic out of fear and when out of resentment. Self-disclosure is an essential condition for getting to know another individual.

Couples who engage in significant self-disclosure are found to remain together longer than couples who do not (Sprecher, 1987). Self-disclosure helps us achieve a closer relationship with the person to whom we self-disclose (Schmidt & Cornelius, 1987). Within a sexual relationship self-disclosure increases sexual rewards and general relationship satisfaction. These two benefits in turn increase sexual satisfaction (Byers & Demmons, 1999). Without self-disclosure, meaningful relationships seem impossible to develop. Interestingly enough, we also come to increase our affection for our partner when we self-disclose.

E-Talk ▪ ▪ ▪ ▪ ▪ ▪

Self-Disclosure On and Off

What has been your experience with online self-disclosure? Do you disclose more or less online than you do in face-to-face encounters? Do you hear more disclosures online or in face-to-face situations?

Physiological Health. People who self-disclose are less vulnerable to illnesses and less likely to feel depressed (Pennebacker, 1991). These health effects, not surprisingly, also result from disclosing in e-mails (Sheese, Brown, & Graziano, 2004). For example, bereavement over the death of someone very close is linked to physical illness for those who bear this alone and in silence, but bereavement is unrelated to any physical problems for those who share their grief with others. Similarly, women who suffer sexual trauma normally experience a variety of illnesses (among them headaches and stomach problems). Women who keep these experiences to themselves, however, suffer these illnesses to a much greater extent than those who talk with others about these traumas. The physiological effort required to keep your burdens to yourself seems to interact with the effects of the trauma to create a combined stress that can lead to physical illness.

" Failure is the opportunity to begin again, more intelligently. "
—Henry Ford

DANGERS OF SELF-DISCLOSURE There are risks to self-disclosure, however. The more you reveal about yourself to others, the more areas of your life you expose to possible attack. Especially in the competitive contexts of work or romance, the more others know about you, the more they'll be able to use against you. This simple fact has prompted power watcher Michael Korda (1975, p. 302) to advise that you "never reveal all of yourself to other people, hold something back in reserve so that people are never quite sure if they really know you." This advice is not necessarily to suggest that you be secretive; rather, Korda is advocating "remaining slightly mysterious, as if [you] were always capable of doing something surprising and unexpected."

As you weigh decisions whether to self-disclose or not, keep Korda's advice in mind. Let's consider some of the potential personal, relational, and professional risks to self-disclosure.

Personal Risks. If you self-disclose certain aspects of your life, you may face rejection from even the closest friends and family members. Those who disclose that they have thoughts of suicide, bouts of depression, or dishonest activities, for example, may find that their friends and family no longer want to be quite as close as before.

Relationship Risks. Even in close and long-lasting relationships, self-disclosure can cause problems. Total self-disclosure may prove threatening to a relationship by decreasing trust. Self-disclosures concerning infidelity, romantic fantasies, past indiscretions or crimes, lies, or hidden weaknesses and fears could easily have such negative effects.

Professional Risks. Revealing political views or attitudes toward different religious or racial groups may create problems on the job—as may disclosing health problems, such as HIV-positive status (Fesko, 2001). Teachers who disclose former or current drug use or cohabitation with students may find themselves being denied tenure, teaching at undesirable hours, and eventually falling victim to "budget cuts." Teachers or students who, in the supportive atmosphere of their interpersonal communication course, disclose details about their sex life or financial condition or reveal self-doubts, anxieties, or fantasies may find some less-than-sympathetic listeners later using that information against them. Openly gay and lesbian personnel in the military—as well as in education, fire departments, law enforcement, or health care agencies, to cite just a few examples—may find themselves confined to desk jobs, barred from further advancement, or even charged with criminal behavior and fired.

■ **What Do You Say**
Discouraging Self-Disclosure
Your colleague at work reveals too much private information for your liking. You're really not interested in this person's sex life, financial woes, and medical problems. **What Do You Say?** What can you do to eliminate this too-personal self-disclosure, at least to you?

Guidelines for Self-Disclosure

Because self-disclosure is an important type of interpersonal communication with the potential for great rewards and great dangers, here are some guidelines—first, for making self-disclosures; second, for facilitating and responding to the disclosures of others; and third, for resisting pressures to self-disclose.

GUIDELINES FOR MAKING SELF-DISCLOSURES   Should you disclose? Consider the following guidelines.

Assess Your Motivation.   Self-disclose out of a concern for the relationship, for the others involved, and for yourself. Some people self-disclose out of a desire to hurt the listener rather than from a desire to improve the relationship—as when children tell their parents that they never loved them or when a person informs a relationship partner that he or she stifled emotional development. However, let's say that you feel ignored and unimportant because your partner devotes all available time to professional advancement. Instead of letting these feelings smolder and turn into resentment, it might be helpful to the relationship to disclose them.

Consider Appropriateness.   Appropriate self-disclosures include honest expressions of feelings ("I feel uncomfortable when you criticize me in front of my friends"), past behaviors that another has a right to know ("I was married when I was 17; we divorced two years later"), or personal abilities (or lack of them) that affect others ("I've never hung wallpaper before but I'll do my best"). Self-disclose in an appropriate atmosphere in which your listener can give open and honest responses. Don't wait until you're boarding the bus to say to your friend, "I got some really bad news today. I'll tell you about it later."

Take Cues from the Other Person.   During your disclosures, give the other person a chance to reciprocate with his or her own disclosures. If the other person does not do so, then reassess your own self-disclosures. The lack of reciprocity may signal that this person, at this time and in this context, does not welcome your disclosures. Therefore, disclose gradually and in small increments so that you can retreat if the responses are not positive enough. Lack of reciprocity may also be due to cultural differences; in some cultures, significant self-disclosure takes place only after an extremely long acquaintanceship or may be considered inappropriate among, say, opposite-sex friends.

Consider Any Possible Negatives.   Carefully weigh the potential problems that the self-disclosure may cause. Could you, if you were to disclose your previous prison record, afford to lose your job? If you were to disclose your previous failed romantic relationships, would you be willing to risk discouraging your present relational partner?

Ask yourself whether you're making unreasonable demands on the listener. For example, consider the person who discloses in confidence to his or her mother-in-law an affair with a neighbor. This type of situation places an unfair burden on the mother-in-law. She is now in a bind: Should she break her promise of secrecy or allow her own child to believe a lie? Often such disclosures do not improve a relationship. Instead, they may simply add tension and friction.

In making your choice between disclosing and not disclosing, keep in mind—besides the advantages and dangers already noted—the irreversible nature of communication discussed in Chapter 1. No matter how many times you may try to qualify something or take it back, once you have said something, you cannot withdraw it. You cannot erase the conclusions and inferences listeners have made on the basis of your disclosures.

GUIDELINES FOR FACILITATING AND RESPONDING TO SELF-DISCLOSURES   When someone discloses to you, it's usually a sign of trust and affection. In serving this most important receiver function, keep the following guidelines in mind. These guidelines will also help you facilitate the disclosures of another person.

■ What Do You Say?

Disclosure Encouragement

Your teenaged nephew seems on edge, and you think he needs to talk about what's on his mind. You want to encourage greater disclosure but don't want to seem pushy or nosy. **What Do You Say?**

Practice the Skills of Effective and Active Listening.   The skills of effective listening (Chapter 5) are especially important when you are listening to self-disclosures: Listen actively, listen for different levels of meaning, listen with empathy, and listen with an open mind. Paraphrase the speaker so that you can be sure you understand both the thoughts and the feelings communicated. Express an understanding of the speaker's feelings to allow the speaker the opportunity to see his or her emotions more objectively and through the eyes of another. Ask questions to ensure your own understanding and to signal your interest and attention.

Support and Reinforce the Discloser.   Express support for the person during and after the disclosures. Try to refrain from evaluation. Concentrate on understanding and empathizing with the discloser. Allow the discloser to choose the pace; don't rush the discloser with a too-frequent "So how did it all end?" response. Make your supportiveness clear to the discloser through your verbal and nonverbal responses: Maintain eye contact, lean toward the speaker, ask relevant questions, and echo the speaker's thoughts and feelings. Generally, women are more supportive in these situations than men—and recent experiments suggest that the reason men are reluctant to provide sensitive emotional support (to the degree that women do, for example) is that men don't want their behavior to be seen as feminine (Burleson, Holmstrom, & Gilstrap, 2005).

❝ Confiding a secret to an unworthy person is like carrying grain in a bag with a hole. **❞**
—Ethiopian proverb

Be Willing to Reciprocate.   When you make relevant and appropriate disclosures of your own in response to the other person's disclosures, you're demonstrating your understanding of the other's meanings and at the same time a willingness to communicate on this meaningful level.

Keep the Disclosures Confidential.   When a person discloses to you, it's because she or he wants you to know the feelings and thoughts that are communicated. If you reveal these disclosures to others, negative effects are inevitable. Revealing what was said will probably inhibit future disclosures by this individual in general and to you in particular, and it's likely that your relationship will suffer considerably. But most importantly, betraying a confidence is unfair; it debases what could be and should be a meaningful interpersonal experience.

It's interesting to note that one of the netiquette rules of e-mail is that you shouldn't forward mail to third parties without the writer's permission. This rule is useful for self-disclosure generally: Maintain confidentiality; don't pass on disclosures made to you to others without the person's permission.

Don't Use the Disclosures against the Person.   Many self-disclosures expose some kind of vulnerability or weakness. If you later turn around and use disclosures against the person, you betray the confidence and trust invested in you. Regardless of how angry you may get, resist the temptation to use the disclosures of others as weapons—the relationship is sure to suffer and may never fully recover.

GUIDELINES FOR RESISTING PRESSURES TO SELF-DISCLOSE   You may, on occasion, find yourself in a position in which a friend, colleague, or romantic partner pressures you to self-disclose. In such situations you may wish to weigh the pros and cons of self-disclosure and then make your decision as to whether and what you'll disclose. If your decision is not to disclose and you're still being pressured, then you need to say something. Here are a few suggestions.

Don't Be Pushed.   Although there may be certain legal or ethical reasons for disclosing, generally, if you don't want to disclose, you don't have to. Don't be pushed into disclosing because others are doing it or because you're asked to. Realize that you're in control of what you reveal and of when and to whom you reveal it. Remember that self-

Outing

An interesting variation on self-disclosure occurs when someone else takes information from your hidden self and makes it public. Although this third-party disclosure can concern any aspect of a person's hidden self—for example, an athlete's prison record or drug habit, a movie star's ill health or alcoholism, or a politician's friends or financial dealings—the media have made a special case out of revealing a person's affectional orientation, or **outing** (Gross, 1991; Signorile, 1993; Johansson & Percy, 1994).

Those against outing argue that people have a right to privacy and say no one else should take that right from them. Because outing can lead to severe consequences—for example, loss of a job, expulsion from the military, or social and physical harassment—no one but the individual himself or herself has the right to reveal such information. Those in favor of outing argue that it's an expedient political and social weapon to silence gay men and lesbians who support homophobic policies.

What Would You Do?

An excellent staff reporter and regular contributor to the college newspaper brings the editor a story revealing that a particular professor is a lesbian. This professor has repeatedly voted against adding any gay or lesbian courses to the curriculum and is an advisor to an exclusive sorority that has repeatedly refused admission to lesbians. What would be the ethically responsible thing for this editor to do? What would you do in this situation, if you were the editor and final judge as to whether to publish the article?

disclosure has significant consequences; so if you're not sure you want to reveal something, at least not until you've had additional time to think about it, then don't.

Be Assertive in Your Refusal to Disclose. You may wish to say, very directly, "I'd rather not talk about that now" or "Now is not the time for this type of discussion." More specific guidelines for communicating assertiveness are offered in Chapter 6.

Be Indirect and Move to Another Topic. Alternatively, you can avoid the question that asks you to disclose and change the subject. This tactic often is a polite way of saying, "I'm not talking about it," and may be the preferred choice in certain situa-

Skill building
exercise

Self-Disclosing Appropriately

Whether you should self-disclose is one of the most difficult decisions you have to make in interpersonal communication. Here are several instances of impending self-disclosure. For each situation, indicate: (a) the channel of communication you'd recommend (for example, face-to-face, e-mail); (b) the context you'd suggest the person arrange to self-disclose in; and (c) a few sentences that you'd recommend the speaker might say in effectively self-disclosing

1. Tom is engaged to Cathy, but over the past few months he has fallen in love with another woman. He now wants to end his relationship with Cathy. Tom wants to break his engagement and disclose his new relationship. How should Tom break this news?
2. Sam has been living in a romantic relationship with another man for the past several years. Sam wants to tell his parents, with whom he has been very close throughout his life. How should Sam reveal this part of his life to his family?
3. Kathy and Kelley have been friends since grade school and are currently seniors in college. The problem is that Kathy has been secretly dating Kelley's boyfriend, Hogan. Kathy plans to disclose this affair and to tell Kelley that she and Hogan are getting engaged. What should Kathy say?

Self-disclosure is a complex communication process with significant advantages and disadvantages. Disclose only after mindfully considering the potential effects.

tions and with certain people. Most often people will get the hint and understand your refusal to disclose. If they don't, then the more direct and assertive approach might have to be used.

Interpersonal Apprehension

You'll profit most from this discussion if you first take the following self-test. This test measures your communication **apprehension,** or fear or anxiety in interpersonal communication situations.

Test *Yourself* ◼◼◼◼◼◼◼◼◼◼◼◼◼◼◼◼◼◼ ☑

How Apprehensive Are You?

INSTRUCTIONS: This questionnaire consists of six statements concerning your feelings about communication with other people. Please indicate in the space provided the degree to which each statement applies to you by marking whether you (1) strongly agree, (2) agree, (3) are undecided, (4) disagree, or (5) strongly disagree with each statement. There are no right or wrong answers. Work quickly; record your first impression.

_____ ❶ While participating in a conversation with a new acquaintance, I feel very nervous.

_____ ❷ I have no fear of speaking up in conversations.

_____ ❸ Ordinarily I am very tense and nervous in conversations.

_____ ❹ Ordinarily I am very calm and relaxed in conversations.

_____ ❺ While conversing with a new acquaintance, I feel very relaxed.

_____ ❻ I'm afraid to speak up in conversations.

HOW DID YOU DO?   Compute your score as follows:

_____ ❶ Begin with the number 18; it's used as a base so that you won't wind up with negative numbers.

_____ ❷ To 18, add your scores for items 2, 4, and 5.

_____ ❸ Subtract your scores for items 1, 3, and 6 from your step 2 total.

_____ ❹ The result (which should be somewhere between 6 and 30) is your apprehension score for interpersonal conversations. The higher the score, the greater your apprehension. A score above 18 indicates some degree of apprehension.

WHAT WILL YOU DO?   Try first to identify those interpersonal situations that create the greatest communication apprehension for you. What factors can you identify that contribute to apprehension? What can you do to reduce the impact of those factors?

Source: From James C. McCroskey, *Introduction to Rhetorical Communication,* 8/e. Published by Allyn & Bacon, Boston, MA. Copyright © 2001 by Pearson Education. Adapted by permission of the publisher.

── ☑

Fear and anxiety cause some people to develop negative feelings about communication and therefore to expect the worst of themselves when they're called on to speak. To those who feel high anxiety in such circumstances, it just doesn't seem worthwhile to try. This is not to say that apprehensives are ineffective or unhappy people. Most of them have learned or can learn to deal with their communication anxiety or fear.

■ **What Do You Say** ?
Refusing to Self-Disclose
You've dated someone three or four times, but each time you're pressured to self-disclose your past experiences and personal information you're just not ready to talk about—at least, not at this early stage of the relationship. **What Do You Say?** What are some of the things you can say or do to resist this pressure to self-disclose? What might you say to discourage further requests that you reveal yourself?

E-Talk . . . . . .

Shy Communication

Some research claims that shy people communicate with less anxiety on the Internet than in face-to-face situations (cf. Scealy, Phillips, & Stevenson, 2002; Stritzke, Nguyen, & Durkin, 2004). Do you think that shy people experience different reactions and communicate differently in face-to-face and in computer-mediated situations? If so, in what way? Why?

"Communication apprehension," researchers note, "is probably the most common handicap . . . suffered by people in contemporary American society" (McCroskey & Wheeless, 1976). According to surveys of college students, between 10 and 20 percent suffer "severe, debilitating communication apprehension"; another 20 percent suffer from "communication apprehension to a degree substantial enough to interfere to some extent with their normal functioning."

Of course, these comments and the preceding apprehension self-test focus on face-to-face interpersonal communication. You also may experience apprehension in computer-mediated communication, however. You might want to take the following self-test and compare your relative apprehension.

Test *Yourself* ☑

How Apprehensive Are You in Computer-Mediated Communication?

INSTRUCTIONS: Respond to each of the following using a scale on which

5 = strongly disagree, **4** = disagree, **3** = neither agree nor disagree, **2** = agree, and **1** = strongly agree.

_____ ❶ I look forward to the opportunity to interact with others on the computer.

_____ ❷ I feel that I am more skilled than most others when interacting with people online.

_____ ❸ I would enjoy giving a presentation to others online.

_____ ❹ I look forward to expressing myself during online meetings.

_____ ❺ I like to get involved in computer-based group discussion.

HOW DID YOU DO? Add up your responses; your score should range from 5 to 25. Low scores, say between 5 and 10, indicate little apprehension; high scores, say between 20 and 25 indicate significant apprehension. Are you more apprehensive in face-to-face communication? Most people are (Rockwell & Singleton, 2002, Campbell & Neer, 2001).

WHAT WILL YOU DO? If computer-mediated communication causes you significant apprehension, can you pinpoint the reasons for this? If so, what possible remedies can you suggest? For example, if you're apprehensive because you fear making spelling or grammatical mistakes, then consider writing your messages using software with spelling and grammar aids and then copying the messages to e-mail.

Source: From Scott and Timmerman (2005). The authors note that these test items are modified from McCroskey (1970).

☑

Apprehensive Behaviors

We can also look at apprehension in more behavioral terms (Richmond & McCroskey, 1998). Generally, apprehension causes a decrease in the frequency, strength, and likelihood of engaging in communication transactions. High apprehensives avoid communication situations; when forced to participate, they do so as little as possible.

This reluctance to communicate shows itself in a variety of forms. For example, in small group situations, apprehensives not only will talk less but also will avoid the "seats of influence" in the group leader's direct line of sight. Even in classrooms high-apprehension individuals avoid seats where they can easily be called on, and they maintain little direct eye contact with the instructor, especially when a question is likely to be asked. Closely related to this behavior is the finding that apprehensives have more negative attitudes toward school, earn poorer grades, and are more likely to drop out of college (McCroskey, Booth-Butterfield, & Payne, 1989).

Apprehensives disclose little and avoid occupations with heavy communication demands (for example, teaching or public relations). Within their occupations, they're less desirous of advancement than others, largely because with advancement comes an increase in the need to communicate. High apprehensives are even less likely to get job interviews.

Apprehensives also engage more in steady dating, a finding that is not unexpected. One of the most difficult communication situations is asking for a date—especially a first date—and developing a new relationship. Consequently, once a dating relationship has been established, the apprehensive is reluctant to give this up and go through the anxiety of another first date and another get-acquainted period.

Your level of communication apprehension will even influence your satisfaction with dating (Powers & Love, 2000). Ask yourself if the following statements are basically true (yes) or basically false (no) about your own feelings about communicating with your dating partner:

- *I am comfortable in developing intimate conversations with my partner.*
- *I feel I am an open communicator with my partner.*
- *I am hesitant to develop a "deep" conversation with my partner.*
- *Even in casual conversations with my partner, I feel I must guard what I say.*

If you said yes to the first two statements and no to the last two, then, research shows, you're more likely to experience interpersonal communication satisfaction. If, on the other hand, you said no to the first two and yes to the last two, then you're likely to experience a lack of satisfaction.

Culture and Apprehension

Interacting with members of cultures different from your own can create uncertainty, fear, and anxiety, all of which contribute to apprehension (Stephan & Stephan, 1992).

When you're speaking with people from cultures very different from your own, you're likely to be more uncertain about the situation and about your hearers' possible responses (Gudykunst & Nishida, 1984; Gudykunst, Yang, & Nishida, 1985). When you're sure of a situation and can predict what will happen, you're more likely to feel comfortable and at ease. But when you cannot predict what will happen, you're likely to become more apprehensive (Gudykunst & Kim, 1992).

Such situations can also engender fear. You might, for example, have a greater fear of saying something that might prove offensive or of revealing your own prejudices. The fear is easily transformed into apprehension. These situations can also create anxiety. For example, if your prior relationships with members of a culturally different group were few, or if they were unpleasant, then you're likely to experience greater anxiety when dealing with other members of that group than if your prior experiences were numerous and positive (Stephan & Stephan, 1985, 1992).

Your thoughts and feelings about the other people also will influence your apprehension. For example, if you hold stereotypes and prejudices, or if you feel that you're very different from these other people, you're likely to experience more apprehension than you would if you saw them as similar to you.

There are also gender differences in intercultural apprehension. For example, men report greater apprehension about intercultural communication than do women. Men also report greater ethnocentrism and less willingness to communicate interculturally than do women (Lin & Rancer, 2003a, 2003b).

Managing Apprehension

Although most of us suffer from some communication apprehension, we can successfully manage it and control it—at least to some degree. Here are some suggestions (Beatty, 1988; McCroskey, 2001; Richmond & McCroskey, 1998).

ACQUIRE COMMUNICATION SKILLS AND EXPERIENCE If you lack skills in typing, you can hardly expect to type very well. Yet we rarely assume that a lack of interpersonal skills

Skill building
exercise

Reducing Apprehension

This approach to reducing apprehension, called *performance visualization,* is designed to reduce your outward signs of nervousness and also to reduce negative thinking (Ayres & Hopf, 1993, 1995). Try reducing your own communication apprehension by following these simple suggestions.

1. The first part of performance visualization is to develop a positive attitude and a positive self-perception. So visualize yourself as an effective speaker. Imagine yourself communicating as a fully and totally confident individual. Look at your listeners and speak. Throughout your conversation, see yourself as fully in control of the situation. See your listeners in rapt attention from the time you begin to the time you stop. Throughout this visualization, avoid all negative thoughts. As you visualize yourself as an effective speaker, take special note of how you walk, look at your listeners, and respond to questions, and especially of how you feel about the whole experience.
2. The second part of performance visualization can help you model your performance on that of an especially effective speaker. View a particularly competent speaker and make a mental "movie" of what happens. Try also selecting a video you can replay several times. As you review the actual video and the mental movie, begin to shift yourself into the role of speaker. Become this effective speaker.

You may not be able to eliminate your apprehension, but you can manage and in many cases reduce its effects.

and experience can cause difficulty with communication and create apprehension. It can. After all, if you had never asked for a date and had no idea how to do it, it would be natural to feel apprehension in doing so. In this course you're gaining the skills of effective interpersonal interaction. Engage in experiences—even if they prove difficult at first—that will help you acquire the skills you need most. The more preparation and practice you put into something, the more comfortable you will feel with it.

FOCUS ON SUCCESS   The more you perceive a situation as one in which others will evaluate you, the greater your apprehension will be (Beatty, 1988). Employment interviews and asking for a date, for example, are anxiety-provoking largely because they're highly evaluative. Your prior history in similar situations also influences the way you respond to new ones. Prior success generally (though not always) reduces apprehension. Prior failure generally (though not always) increases apprehension. If you see yourself succeeding, you'll stand a good chance of doing just that. So think positively. Concentrate your energies on doing the best job you can in any situation you find yourself in. You now have new skills and new experiences, and these will increase your chances for success. Do be careful, however, that your focus on success does not translate into the need to appear perfect, an attitude that is likely to increase your interpersonal apprehension (Saboonchi, Lundh, & Oest, 1999).

REDUCE UNPREDICTABILITY   The more unpredictable the situation, the greater your apprehension is likely to be. Ambiguous situations and new situations are unpredictable. Therefore, you naturally become anxious. In managing apprehension, therefore, try to reduce any unpredictability. When you're familiar with the situation and with what is expected of you, you're better able to predict what will happen. This will reduce the ambiguity and perceived newness of the situation. So, for example, if you're going to ask the boss for a raise, become familiar with as much of the situation as you can. If possible, sit in the chair you will sit in; then rehearse your statement of the reasons you deserve the raise and the way in which you'll present them.

Put Apprehension in Perspective.   Whenever you engage in a communication experience, remember that the world won't end if you don't succeed. Also remember that other people are not able to perceive your apprehension as sharply as you do. You may feel a dryness in your throat and a rapid heartbeat; however, no one knows this but you.

Empowering Apprehensives

At the same time that you want to manage and perhaps lessen your own apprehension, consider the values and means of empowering others to manage and better control their own apprehension. Here are some suggestions, based largely on the insights of shyness and apprehension researchers (Carducci & Zimbardo, 1996; Richmond & McCroskey, 1998).

- Don't overprotect the shy person, especially the shy child. If you constantly rush to a child's aid every time he or she experiences social anxiety, the child will never learn how to cope with it. Instead, be supportive (indirectly). Nudge, instead of push, a child or an adult to try out new communication situations. In this way you can help the shy person to interact in small doses and eventually to develop the self-confidence needed for more extended interaction.

- Demonstrate your understanding and empathy for apprehensives' shyness. Don't minimize their fear of communication situations—something those with little apprehension often do. Practice active listening, should you sense that an apprehensive person wishes to discuss his or her anxiety and shyness.

- Avoid making shy people the center of attention. That is exactly what they don't want. And never make their shyness the topic of a group conversation. Saying, "Oh, James; he's so bright, but he's so shy" only makes it more difficult for James to open his mouth. At the same time, make sure that you give shy people opportunities to speak and that you don't monopolize the conversation. For example, ask their opinions; when appropriate, try to steer the conversation in the direction of a shy person's expertise and area of competence.

■ What Do You Say ?
Lessening Apprehension

You've heard people say that you're not sociable; in truth, you'd love to be more sociable, but you're extremely apprehensive, especially when meeting new people or people you think you might become romantically interested in. **What Do You Say?** What are some of the things you can do to lessen your apprehension in social situations?

The Facilitation of Self-Disclosure

Dialogue *for* Analysis

Here are two dialogues, one illustrating the failure and one illustrating the success of facilitating self-disclosure. After reading both dialogues, identify the principles that make one interaction ineffective and the other effective, focusing especially on self-disclosure and how disclosure may be hindered or facilitated.

The Cast

An Arab-American family.

Abdul:	12-year-old son
Habib:	Abdul's father
Gemma:	Abdul's mother
Alexandra:	Abdul's 16-year-old sister

The Context

Abdul enters the living room of the family's apartment, throws his books down on the coffee table, and goes to the kitchen, where he opens the refrigerator.

Act I. The Failure

Habib (to Gemma): What's wrong with him?
Gemma: I don't know. He's been acting strange the last few days.
Alexandra: *Acting* strange? He *is* strange. Weird.
[Abdul comes back into the living room, sits down, and stares into space.]

(continues)

(continued)

Habib: Well, when you're twelve years old, that's the way it is. I remember when I was twelve. When I was your age, the big thing was girls. You got a girl, Abdul?

Alexandra: Hey Mom, how about driving me to the mall? I gotta get a new dress for next week.

Gemma: Okay. I need a few things at Target. You need anything Abdul? You don't want to come with us, do you?

Alexandra: Please say no. If people see us together, they'll think we're related. God! My life would be ruined. People would ignore me. No one would talk to me.

Habib: Okay. Okay. That's enough. You two go to the mall. I'm going bowling with Pete and Joe. Abdul will be okay home alone.

Abdul: Yeah.

Alexandra: Mom, let's go.

Gemma: All right. I just have to call Grandma and see if she's okay.

Alexandra: Oh, that reminds me. I have to call Jack. Lori left him for a college guy and he's really down in the dumps. I thought I'd call to cheer him up.

Gemma: Can't you do that when we get back?

Alexandra: Yeah, I guess.

Habib: Well, you guys have fun. I'm off to bowl another two-hundred game. Joe is still bowling under one-forty, so Pete and I are going to try to give him a few tips.

Gemma: Hello, Mom? How are you doing? Is the arthritis acting up? I figure that with this weather it must be really bad.

Alexandra: Come on, Mom.

[Habib exits; Abdul turns on TV.]

Act II. The Success

Habib (calling into the kitchen): Hey, Abdul, what's up? You look pretty angry.

Abdul: It's nothing. Just school.

Alexandra: He's just weird, Dad.

Habib: You mean "weird" like the mad scientist in the old movies?

Alexandra: No. You know what I mean—he's different.

Habib: Oh, well, that's something else. That's great. I'm glad Abdul is different. The world doesn't need another clone, and Abdul is certainly no clone. At twelve years old, it's not easy being unique. Right, Abdul?

Abdul (to Alexandra): Yeah, unique.

Habib (to Gemma and Alexandra): Are you still planning to go to the mall?

Alexandra: Yeah, I have to get a new dress.

Gemma: And I need some things at Target. Are you going bowling?

Habib: Well, I was planning on it, but I thought I might cancel and stay home. Abdul, you got any plans? If not, how about doing something together?

Abdul: No. You want to go bowling.

Habib: I can bowl anytime. After all, what's another two-hundred game? It's hardly a challenge. Come on. How about we take a drive to the lake and take a swim—just the two of us. And I'd like to hear about what's going on in school.

Abdul: Okay, let's go. I need to put on my trunks. You know I can swim four lengths without stopping.

Habib: Four lengths? Well, I got to see that. Get those trunks on and we're out of here.

Alexandra: Mom, let's go-o-o-o.

Gemma: Okay. Okay. Okay. But, I have to call Grandma first to see if she's all right.

Habib: Let me say hello too.

Gemma (to Abdul and Alexandra): You two want to talk to Grandma too?

Alexandra: Of course. I got to tell her about this great new guy at school.

Gemma: Oh, I want to hear about this too. Well, we'll have plenty of time to talk in the car.

Abdul: Hey Mom, I gotta tell Grandma about my new bike. So let me talk first so Dad and I can get to the lake.

[later, Abdul and Habib in car]

Habib (puts arm on Abdul's shoulder): School got you down?

Abdul: It's this new teacher. What a pain. I can't understand what he's talking about. Maybe I'm just stupid.

Habib: What don't you understand?

Abdul: I don't know. He calls it pre-geometry. What's pre-geometry?

*It's interesting to know that Arabic is the official language of 25 countries (representing some 200 million people); only French and English are spoken in a greater number of countries. Because the Quran is written in Arabic, it is the second language for many other countries that have dominant or largely Muslim populations, such as Indonesia, India, and Iran. In 2002–03 almost 35,000 international strudents came to the United States from the largely Arab Middle East, a number that has recently decreased.

Summary of Concepts and Skills

This chapter explored the self in interpersonal communication, looking first at self-concept and self-awareness along with ways to increase self-esteem; second at the process of self-disclosure along with some of its advantages and disadvantages; and third at apprehension, including what causes it and how you can manage it.

1. The self-concept is the image that you have of yourself. It develops from the images of you that others have and that they reveal to you, the comparisons you make between yourself and others, and the ways you interpret and evaluate your own thoughts and behaviors.

2. The four selves are the open self (what we and others know about us), the blind self (what others know but we do not know), the hidden self (what we know but keep hidden from others), and the unknown self (what neither we nor others know).

3. We may increase self-awareness by asking ourselves about ourselves, listening to others, actively seeking information about ourselves, seeing ourselves from different perspectives, and increasing our open selves.

4. Self-esteem has to do with the value you place on yourself. Research differs on the value of self-esteem.

5. Self-disclosure is a type of communication in which we reveal information about ourselves to others.

6. Self-disclosure is generally reciprocal; the self-disclosures of one person stimulate the self-disclosures of the other person.

7. Both men and women avoid self-disclosure for fear of projecting a negative image.

8. Through self-disclosure you may gain self-knowledge, increase communication effectiveness, enhance the meaningfulness of your interpersonal relationships, and promote physical health.

9. There are also serious dangers in self-disclosing. Your interpersonal, social, and business relationships may suffer if your self-disclosures are not positively received.

10. Communication apprehension is a feeling of fear or anxiety about interpersonal communication situations.

11. Persons with high apprehension behave differently from persons with low apprehension. High apprehensives communicate less and avoid situations and occupations that

demand lots of communication. High apprehensives have more negative attitudes toward school, are more likely to drop out of college, are less likely to advance in their jobs, and tend to engage more in steady dating.

12. Techniques for managing communication apprehension include acquiring communication skills and experience, focusing on success, reducing unpredictability, and becoming familiar with the situation.

In addition, this chapter covered several significant skills. Check those you wish to work on:

_____ 1. *Self-concept.* See yourself, as objectively as you can, through the eyes of others; compare yourself to similar (and admired) others; examine the influences of culture; and observe and evaluate your own message behaviors.

_____ 2. *Self-awareness.* Increase self-awareness by listening to others, increasing your open self, and seeking out information to reduce blind spots.

_____ 3. *Self-esteem.* Increase your self-esteem by attacking self-destructive beliefs, seeking out nourishing others, working on projects that will result in success, and securing affirmation.

_____ 4. *Deciding to self-disclose.* Consider the potential benefits (for example, self-knowledge, increased communication effectiveness, and physiological health) as well as the potential personal, relationship, and professional risks.

_____ 5. *Appropriateness of self-disclosure.* When thinking of disclosing, consider the legitimacy of your motives, the appropriateness of the disclosure, the listener's responses (is the dyadic effect operating?), and the potential burdens such disclosures might impose.

_____ 6. *Responding to others' disclosures.* Listen actively, support the discloser, and keep the disclosures confidential.

_____ 7. *Communication apprehension management.* To reduce anxiety, acquire necessary communication skills and experiences, focus on prior successes, reduce unpredictability, and put apprehension in perspective.

Vocabulary Quiz: The Language of the Self

Match the terms listed here with their definitions. Record the number of the definition next to the appropriate term.

_____ Johari window

_____ the open self

_____ self-esteem

_____ the hidden self

_____ the unknown self

_____ self-awareness

_____ self-disclosure

_____ the dyadic effect

_____ communication apprehension

_____ gender and culture

1. Fear or anxiety in interpersonal communication situations.
2. The part of the self that contains information known to others but unknown to yourself.
3. The tendency for the behaviors of one person to stimulate similar behaviors in the other person.
4. The part of the self that contains information known to yourself and to others.
5. The part of the self that contains information known to yourself but unknown to others.
6. A model of the four selves.
7. Self-knowledge.
8. The process of revealing something significant about yourself to another individual or to a group.
9. The value you place on yourself.
10. Two of the factors influencing self-disclosure.

Four for Discussion

1. Some people engage primarily in downward social comparison; they compare themselves to those they know are worse off than they are on a particular quality. Others engage primarily in upward social comparison; they compare themselves to those who are better looking, more successful, smarter, and so on (Aspinwall & Taylor, 1993). What do you see as the advantages and disadvantages of each type of comparison?

2. Popular psychology and many television talk shows (especially Oprah) emphasize the importance of self-esteem. The self-esteem camp has come under attack from critics, however (for example, Bushman & Baumeister, 1998; Baumeister, Bushman, & Campbell, 2000; Bower, 2001; Coover & Murphy, 2000; Hewitt, 1998). Much current thinking holds that high self-esteem is not desirable: It does nothing to improve academic performance, it does not predict success, and it even may lead to antisocial (especially aggressive) behavior. On the other hand, it's difficult to imagine how a person would function successfully without positive self-feelings. How do you feel about the benefits or liabilities of self-esteem? Would you have included this topic in this text?

3. Shyness researchers have argued that the people we single out as heroes are those who call attention to themselves, such as rock stars and media personalities; "people who are most likely to be successful are those who are able to

obtain attention and feel comfortable with it" (Carducci & Zimbardo, 1996, p. 66). Who are your heroes? Are they the people who call attention to themselves? Are any of your heroes high communication apprehensives or shy individuals?

4. Much has been written about the unwillingness of men to reveal their feelings and to self-disclose on intimate levels. Do you find that men and women disclose differently? Do men and women expect the same level of self-disclosure from their partners?

MyCommunicationLab Explorations

Explore www.mycommunicationlab.com to find exercises and self-tests relevant to the self in interpersonal communication. These include (1) Disclosing Your Hidden Self, (2) Weighing the Rewards and Dangers of Self-Disclosure [additional cases], (3) Time for Self-Disclosure, (4) Reducing Apprehension with Systematic Desensitization, (5) How Willing to Disclose Are You? (6) What Do You Have a Right to Know? (7) How Shy Are You? (8) How Apprehensive Are You in Employment Interviews? (9) How Apprehensive Are You in Group Discussions? and (10) How Apprehensive Are You of Public Speaking?

Also visit MyCommunicationLab for additional study aids, activities, and video clips on the role of the self in interpersonal communication.

Research Navigator.com

Explore our research resources at www.researchnavigator.com.

CHAPTER 4
Perception and Interpersonal Communication

WHY READ THIS CHAPTER?

*B*ecause you'll **learn about:**
- interpersonal perception.
- the influences on your perceptions of others and on their perceptions of you.

*B*ecause you **learn to:**
- avoid common errors that people make when they perceive people and messages.
- use a variety of strategies to increase your own accuracy in perceiving other people and their messages.

$\mathcal{P}$erception is the process by which you become aware of things in the world through your senses: sight, smell, taste, touch, and hearing. **Interpersonal perception** is the process by which you become aware of people and by extension of interpersonal messages. Your perceptions (whether of objects or of people) result from a combination of what exists in the outside world and your own experiences, desires, needs and wants, loves and hatreds.

One of the reasons why perception is so important in interpersonal communication is that it influences your communication choices. The messages you send and listen to will depend on how you see the world, on how you size up specific situations, on what you think of the people with whom you interact.

$\mathcal{T}$he Stages of Perception

Interpersonal perception is a continuous series of processes that blend into one another. For convenience, we can separate these processes into five stages: (1) You sense, you pick up some kind of stimulation; (2) you organize the stimuli in some way; (3) you interpret and evaluate what you perceive; (4) you store your perception in memory; and (5) you retrieve it when needed (see Figure 4.1). Notice that perception in an active process; in each stage you do something—you actively pick up stimulation, actively organize stimuli in some way, actively interpret and evaluate what you perceive, and so on.

Stage One: Stimulation

At this first stage, your sense organs encounter a **stimulus**—you hear a new CD, you see a friend, you smell someone's perfume, you taste an orange, you feel another's sweaty palm. Naturally, you don't perceive everything; rather, you engage in **selective perception.** This general term includes selective attention and selective exposure. In **selective attention,** you attend to those things that you anticipate will fulfill your needs or will prove enjoyable. For example, when daydreaming in class, you don't hear what the instructor is saying until your name is called. Your selective attention mechanism focuses your senses on your name.

Through **selective exposure** you expose yourself to people or messages that will confirm your existing beliefs, that will contribute to your objectives, or that will prove satisfying in some way. For example, after you buy a car, you're more apt to read and listen to advertisements for the car you just bought, because these messages tell you that you made the right decision. At the same time, you will tend to avoid advertisements for the cars that you considered but eventually rejected, because these messages would tell you that you made the wrong decision.

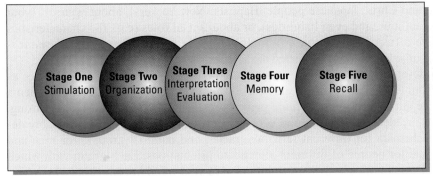

Figure 4.1
The Five Stages of Perception
This model depicts the stages involved in perception.

> " Manage every second of a first meeting. Do not delude yourself that a bad impression can be easily corrected. Putting things right is a lot harder than getting them right the first time. "
>
> —David Lewis

You're also more likely to perceive stimuli that are greater in intensity than surrounding stimuli and those that have novelty value. For example, television commercials normally play at a greater volume than regular programming to ensure that you take special notice. You're also more likely to notice the coworker who dresses in a novel way than you are to notice the one who dresses like everyone else. You will quickly perceive someone who shows up in class wearing a tuxedo or who appears at a formal party in shorts.

Stage Two: Organization

At the second stage, you organize the information your senses pick up. Three interesting ways in which people organize their perceptions are by rules, by schemata, and by scripts. Let's look at each briefly.

ORGANIZATION BY RULES One frequently used rule is that of *proximity* or physical closeness. The rule, simply stated, would say: Things that are physically close together constitute a unit. Thus, using this rule, you would perceive people who are often together, or messages spoken one immediately after the other, as units—as belonging together. For example, if you frequently see Pat and Chris together—taking walks through your neighborhood, eating lunch together, or shopping at the mall together, you'd probably view Pat and Chris as a unit. You also assume that verbal and nonverbal signals sent at about the same time are related and constitute a unified whole; you assume they follow a *temporal rule,* which says that things occurring together in time belong together.

Another rule is *similarity:* Things that are physically similar, things that look alike, belong together and form a unit. This principle of similarity would lead you to see people who dress alike as belonging together. Similarly, you might assume that people who work at the same jobs, who are of the same religion, who live in the same building, or who talk with the same accent belong together.

You use the principle of *contrast* when you note that some items (people or messages, for example) don't belong together—that they are too different from each other to be part of the same perceptual organization. So, for example, if the sports reporter covering your favorite basketball team delivered the commentary in a slow, subdued manner, you'd probably begin to focus on the contrast between the rate and style of speaking and the fast-paced nature of the game.

ORGANIZATION BY SCHEMATA Another way you organize material is by creating **schemata,** mental templates or structures that help you organize the millions of items of information you come into contact with every day as well as those you already have in memory. Schemata may thus be viewed as general ideas about people (e.g., Pat and Chris, Japanese people, Baptists, New Yorkers), about yourself (your qualities, abilities, and even liabilities), or about social roles (e.g., the characteristics of a police officer, a professor, or a multibillionaire CEO). (The word *schemata* is the plural of *schema* and is preferred to the alternative plural *schemas.*)

You develop schemata from your own experience—from actual experiences as well as from television, reading, and hearsay. For example, you might have a schema for college athletes; it might include perceptions that athletes are physically strong, ambitious, academically weak, and egocentric. And, of course, you've probably developed schemata for different religious, racial, and national groups; for men and women; and for people of different affectional orientations. Each group with which you have some familiarity will be represented in your mind in some kind of schema.

Schemata help you organize your perceptions by allowing you to classify millions of people into a manageable number of categories or classes. As we'll see below, however, schemata can also create problems—they can lead you to see what is not there or to miss seeing what is there.

ORGANIZATION BY SCRIPTS   A script is a type of schema; but because it's a special type, it's given a different name. Like a schema, a **script** is also an organized body of information—but instead of being about people, it's about some action, event, or procedure. It's a general idea of how some event should play out or unfold; it's the rules governing events and their sequence. For example, you probably have a script for eating in a restaurant with the actions organized into a pattern something like this: Enter, take a seat, review the menu, order from the menu, eat your food, ask for the bill, leave a tip, pay the bill, exit the restaurant. Similarly, you probably have scripts for how you do laundry, conduct an interview, introduce someone to someone else, or ask for a date.

In the organization of perceptions, everyone relies heavily on shortcuts. Rules, schemata, and scripts, for example, are all useful shortcuts that simplify your understanding, remembering, and recalling information about people and events. If you didn't have these shortcuts, then you'd have to treat every person, role, or action differently from each other person, role, or action. This would make every experience new and totally unrelated to anything you already know. If you didn't use these shortcuts, you'd be unable to generalize, draw connections, or otherwise profit from previously acquired knowledge. Shortcuts, however, may mislead you; they may contribute to your remembering things that are consistent with your schemata even if they didn't occur, and to your distorting or forgetting information that is inconsistent.

Further, because your schemata and scripts are created on the basis of your own cultural beliefs and experiences, you can easily (but inappropriately) apply these to members of other cultures. So it's easy to infer that when members of other cultures do things that conform to your scripts, they're right, and when they do things that contradict your scripts, they're wrong—a classic example of ethnocentric thinking. As you can appreciate, this tendency can easily contribute to intercultural misunderstandings.

A similar problem arises when you base your scripts for different cultural groups on stereotypes you may have derived from television or movies. For example, you may have scripts for religious Muslims based on stereotypes presented in the media. If you then apply these scripts to all Muslims, you may tend to see what conforms to your scripts and may distort or fail to see what does not conform.

Stage Three: Interpretation–Evaluation

The interpretation–evaluation stage of perception (the two processes cannot be separated) is inevitably subjective and is greatly influenced by your experiences, needs, wants, values, beliefs about the way things are or should be, expectations, physical and emotional state, and so on. Your interpretation–evaluation will be influenced by your rules, schemata, and scripts as well as by your gender; for example, women have been found to view others more positively than men (Winquist, Mohr, & Kenny, 1998).

For example, upon meeting a new person who is introduced to you as a college football player,

❝ I make up my mind about people in the first ten seconds, and I very rarely change it. **❞**

—Margaret Thatcher

E-Talk . ▪ . ▪ . ▪ .

Dating Online

According to a *New York Times* survey a few years ago, online dating was losing its stigma as a place for losers (June 29, 2003, p. A1). Why do you think perceptions have changed in the direction of greater acceptance of online relationships?

you will tend to apply your schema to this person and view him as physically strong, ambitious, academically weak, and egocentric. You will, in other words, see this person through the filter of your schema and evaluate him according to your schema for college athletes. Similarly, when viewing someone performing some series of actions (say, eating in a restaurant), you apply your script to this event and view the event through the script. You interpret the actions of the diner as appropriate or inappropriate depending on your script for this behavior and the ways in which the diner performs the sequence of actions.

Stage Four: Memory

Your perceptions and their interpretations–evaluations are put into memory; they're stored so that you may ultimately retrieve them at some later time. But what you remember about a person or an event generally isn't an objective recollection but is more likely heavily influenced by your preconceptions or your schemata about what belongs and what doesn't belong, what fits neatly into the templates in your brain and what doesn't fit. Your reconstruction of an event or person contains a lot of information that was not in the original sensory experience, and it may omit a lot that was in the experience. So, for example, you have in memory your schema for college athletes and the fact that Ben Williams is a football player. Ben Williams is then stored in memory with "cognitive tags" that tell you that he's strong, ambitious, academically weak, and egocentric. Now, despite the fact that you've not witnessed Ben's strength or ambitions and have no idea of his academic record or his psychological profile, you still may store your memory of Ben along with the qualities that make up your schema for "college athletes."

Now let's say that at different times you hear that Ben failed Spanish I (normally an A or B course at your school), that Ben got an A in chemistry (normally a tough course), and that Ben is transferring to Harvard as a theoretical physics major. Schemas act as filters or gatekeepers; they allow certain information to get stored in relatively objective form, much as you heard or read it, but may distort or prevent other information from getting stored. As a result, these three items of information

---

Listen to this

■ **Listening to Other Perspectives**

"Galileo and the Ghosts" is a technique for altering your perception of a problem, person, or situation by seeing it through the eyes of different people (DeVito, 1996). It involves setting up a mental "ghost thinking" team, much the way executives and politicians hire ghostwriters to write their speeches or corporations and research institutes maintain think tanks. In this ghost thinking technique, you select a team of about four to eight "people" you admire; for example, historical figures like Aristotle or Picasso, fictional figures like Wonder Woman or Batman, contemporary figures like Oprah Winfrey or Jerry Springer, or persons from other cultures or of a different gender or affectional orientation.

You pose a problem or question and then ask yourself how each of your team of ghosts would perceive the problem or answer the question, allowing yourself to listen to their perceptions. Of course, you're really listening to yourself—but to yourself taking the role of another person. The technique forces you to step outside your normal role and to consider the perspective of someone totally different from you. As a result, your own perception of the problem will change. You can also use this technique to appreciate—and ultimately empathize with—the perspective of your romantic partner, friend, parent, or child.

■ **Applying Listening Skills**

Pat and Chris, a couple in their 40s who have been together for the last 15 years, have been having tremendous difficulty communicating; each claims the other doesn't understand and doesn't empathize. What suggestions would you offer to help them listen more effectively to other perspectives?

about Ben may get stored very differently in your memory along with your schema for college athletes.

For example, you may readily store the information that Ben failed Spanish, because it's consistent with your schema; it fits neatly into the template you have for college athletes. Information that's consistent with your schema—such as in this example—will strengthen your schema and make it more resistant to change (Aronson, Wilson, & Akert, 1999). Depending on the strength of your schema, you may also store in memory, even though you didn't hear it, a perception that Ben did poorly in other courses as well. The information that Ben got an A in chemistry, because it contradicts your schema (it just doesn't seem right), may easily be distorted or lost. The information that Ben is transferring to Harvard, however, is a bit different. This information is also inconsistent with your schema; but it is so drastically inconsistent that you may begin to look at this mindfully and may even begin to question your schema, or perhaps to view Ben as an exception to the general rule. In either case, you're going to etch Ben's transferring to Harvard very clearly in your mind.

Memory is especially unreliable when the information is ambiguous—when it can be interpreted in different ways. Thus, for example, consider the statement, "Ben didn't do as well in his other courses as he would have liked." If your schema of Ben is "brilliant" then you may "remember" that Ben got B's. But if, as in our example, your schema is of the academically weak athlete, you may "remember" that Ben got D's. Conveniently, but unreliably, schemata reduce ambiguity.

Stage Five: Recall

At some later date, you may want to recall or access the information you have stored in memory. Let's say you want to retrieve your information about Ben because he's a topic of conversation among you and a few friends. As we'll see in our discussion of listening in Chapter 5, memory isn't reproductive; you don't simply reproduce what you've heard or seen. Rather, you reconstruct what you've heard or seen into a whole that is meaningful to you—depending in great part on your schemata and scripts—and it's this reconstruction that you store in memory. Now, when you want to retrieve this information from memory, you may recall it with a variety of inaccuracies. Specifically, you're likely to

- recall information that is consistent with your schema. In fact, you may not even be recalling the specific information (say about Ben) but may actually be recalling your schema (which contains the information about college athletes and, because of this, also about Ben).
- fail to recall information that is inconsistent with your schema. You have no place to put that information, so you easily lose it or forget it.
- recall information that drastically contradicts your schema, because it forces you to think (and perhaps rethink) about your schema and its accuracy. It may even force you to revise your schema for college athletes in general.

*T*he Processes of Perception

Before reading about the specific processes that you use in perceiving other people, examine your own perception strategies by taking the self-test on the next page.

■ What Do You Say❓
Reversing First Impressions
You made a bad impression at work—you drank too much at an office party and played the clown. This is not the impression you want to give, and you need to change it fast. **What Do You Say?** To whom? Through what channel?

STIVERS   ©1991 *Stivers*

© 1991 Mark Stivers. Reprinted by permission.

How Accurate Are You at People Perception?

INSTRUCTIONS: Respond to each of the following statements with T (true) if the statement is usually or generally accurate in describing your behavior, or with F (false) if the statement is usually or generally inaccurate in describing your behavior.

_____ ❶ When I know some things about another person, I can pretty easily fill in what I don't know.

_____ ❷ I make predictions about people's behaviors that generally prove to be true.

_____ ❸ I base most of my impressions of people on the first few minutes of our meeting.

_____ ❹ I generally find that people I like possess positive characteristics and people I don't like possess negative characteristics.

_____ ❺ I generally attribute people's attitudes and behaviors to their most obvious physical or psychological characteristic.

_____ ❻ I believe that the world is basically just, that good things happen to good people and bad things happen to bad people.

HOW DID YOU DO? This test was designed to preview issues to be considered in this chapter. All statements refer to perceptual processes that you may use but that can lead you to form inaccurate impressions. The first four statements refer to implicit personality theory (question 1), self-fulfilling prophecy (2), primary—recency (3), and consistency (4). Statements 5 and 6 refer to two mistakes we may make in attributing motives to other people's—and even our own—behaviors: overattribution (5) and the self-serving bias (6), which often involves a belief that the world is fundamentally just. Ideally, you would have responded with "false" to all six statements, indicating that you regularly avoid falling into these potential traps.

WHAT WILL YOU DO? As you read this chapter, think about perceptual processes and consider how you might use your awareness of these processes to make your perceptions of people more accurate. At the same time, recognize that situations vary widely and that the suggestions offered will prove useful most but not all of the time.

☑

Implicit Personality Theories

Each person has a subconscious or implicit system of rules—an **implicit personality theory**—that says which characteristics of an individual go with other characteristics. Consider, for example, the following brief statements. What word in parentheses do you think best completes each sentence?

- *Carlo is energetic, eager, and (intelligent, stupid).*
- *Kim is bold, defiant, and (extroverted, introverted).*
- *Joe is bright, lively, and (thin, heavy).*
- *Ava is attractive, intelligent, and (likable, unlikable).*
- *Susan is cheerful, positive, and (outgoing, shy).*
- *Angel is handsome, tall, and (friendly, unfriendly).*

What makes some of these choices seem right and others wrong is your implicit personality theory. Your theory may, for example, have told you that a person who is energetic and eager is also intelligent, not stupid—even though there is no logical reason why a stupid person could not be energetic and eager.

"Be careful. Any man who wears earplugs at the gym is liable to wear a pocket protector at work."

The well-documented **halo effect** is a function of the implicit personality theory (Dion, Berscheid, & Walster, 1972; Riggio, 1987). If you believe a person has some positive qualities, you're likely to infer that she or he also possesses other positive qualities. For example, you're likely to perceive attractive people as more generous, sensitive, trustworthy, and interesting than those who are less attractive. And the "horns effect" or "reverse halo effect" will lead you to perceive those who are unattractive as mean, dishonest, antisocial, and sneaky (Katz, 2003).

In using implicit personality theories, apply them carefully and critically so as to avoid perceiving qualities in an individual that your theory tells you should be present when they really aren't. Similarly, be careful of ignoring or distorting qualities that don't conform to your theory but that are actually present in the individual, as research shows many people do (Plaks, Grant, & Dweck, 2005).

As might be expected, the implicit personality theories that people hold differ from culture to culture, from group to group, and even from person to person. For example, the Chinese have a concept called *shi gu* that refers to "someone who is worldly, devoted to his or her family, socially skillful, and somewhat reserved" (Aronson, Wilson, & Akert, 1999, p. 117). This concept isn't easily encoded in English. English, on the other hand, has a concept of the "artistic type," a generalization that seems absent in Chinese. Thus, although it is easy for speakers of English or Chinese to refer to specific concepts—as in describing someone as socially skilled or creative—each language creates its own generalized categories. In Chinese the qualities that make up *shi gu* are seen as going together more easily than they might be for an English speaker; they're part of the implicit personality theory of more Chinese speakers than English speakers.

"That dawg won't hunt."

The Self-Fulfilling Prophecy

A **self-fulfilling prophecy** occurs when you make a prediction that comes true because you act on it as if it were true; you act on your schema as if it were true and in doing so make it true (Merton, 1957). There are four basic steps in the self-fulfilling prophecy:

1. You make a prediction or formulate a belief about a person or a situation. For example, you predict that Pat is friendly in interpersonal encounters.
2. You act toward that person or situation as if that prediction or belief were true. For example, you act as if Pat were a friendly person.
3. Because you act as if the belief were true, it becomes true. For example, because of the way you act toward Pat, Pat becomes comfortable and friendly.
4. You observe what is in fact *your* effect on the person or the resulting situation, and what you see strengthens your beliefs. For example, you observe Pat's friendliness, and this reinforces your belief that Pat is in fact friendly.

The self-fulfilling prophecy can also be seen when you make predictions about yourself and fulfill them. Perhaps you enter a group situation convinced that the other members will dislike you. Almost invariably you'll be proved right; the other members will appear to you to dislike you. What you may be doing is acting in a way that encourages the group to respond to you negatively. In this way you fulfill your prophecies about yourself.

A widely known example of the self-fulfilling prophecy is the **Pygmalion effect.** In a well-known study, teachers were told that certain pupils were expected to do exceptionally well, although they were late bloomers. The names of these students were actually selected at random by the experimenters. The results, however, were not random. The students whose names were given to the teachers actually performed at a higher level than others. In fact, these students' IQ scores even improved more than did the other students'. The teachers' expectations probably prompted them to give extra attention to the selected students, thereby positively affecting their performance (Rosenthal & Jacobson, 1968; Insel & Jacobson, 1975). Studies have found the same general effect in military training and in business settings; trainees and workers performed better when their supervisors were given positive information about them (McNatt, 2001). In fact, researchers have identified the Pygmalion effect in contexts as varied as leadership, athletic coaching, and effective stepfamilies (Eden, 1992; Solomon et al., 1996; Einstein, 1995; McNatt, 2001).

Self-fulfilling prophecies can short-circuit critical thinking and influence another person's behavior (or your own) so that it conforms to your prophecy. As a result, they can lead you to see what you predicted rather than what is really there—for example, to perceive yourself as a failure because you have predicted it rather than because of any actual failures.

To understand one's self is the classic form of consolation; to delude one's self is the romantic.
—George Santayana

Primacy–Recency

Assume for a moment that you're enrolled in a course in which half the classes are extremely dull and half extremely exciting. At the end of the semester, you evaluate the course and the instructor. Will your evaluation be more favorable if the dull classes occur in the first half of the semester and the exciting classes in the second? Or will it be more favorable if the order is reversed? If what comes first exerts the most influence, you have a *primacy effect*. If what comes last (or most recently) exerts the most influence, you have a *recency effect*.

In the classic study on the effects of **primacy and recency** in interpersonal perception, college students perceived a person who was described as "intelligent, industrious, impulsive, critical, stubborn, and envious" more positively than a person described as "envious, stubborn, critical, impulsive, industrious, and intelligent" (Asch, 1946). Clearly, there's a tendency to use early information to get a general idea about a person and to use later information to make this impression more specific. The initial information helps you form a schema for the person. Once that schema is formed, you're likely to resist information that contradicts it.

One interesting practical implication of primacy–recency is that the first impression you make on others is likely to be the most important. The reason for this is that the schema that others form of you functions as a filter to admit or block additional information about you. If the initial impression or schema is positive, others are likely to readily remember additional positive information, because it confirms this original positive image or schema. Similarly, they are likely to forget or distort negative information, because it contradicts this original positive schema. They are also more likely to place a positive interpretation on information that is really ambiguous. If the initial impression is positive, then, you win all three ways.

The tendency to give greater weight to early information and to interpret later information in light of early impressions can lead you to formulate a total picture of an individual on the basis of initial impressions that may not be typical or accurate. For example, if you judge a job applicant as generally nervous when he or she may simply be showing normal nervousness at being interviewed for a much needed job, you will have misperceived this individual.

■ What Do You Say ?
Presenting Yourself
At an interview you're asked about your competence with Microsoft Excel. In truth you have no competence; however, you are extremely fast in learning computer programs, and Excel should be no exception. **What Do You Say?** What might you say to convince the interviewer that you're the person to hire?

Skill building *exercise*

First Impressions

Although people know (mindfully) that first impressions are often wrong, this doesn't deter anyone from forming opinions from early impressions. For each of the following people, (1) describe the physical person with at least three adjectives, (2) describe the person's personality with at least three qualities, (3) identify the person's gender, and (4) identify the person's cultural affiliations. Share and compare your responses with those of others. What can you learn about the origin of these first impressions? How might these first impressions facilitate communication? How might they hinder meaningful communication?

- a 19-year-old high-fashion model who has been modeling over the last four years
- a 25-year-old gay activist who was recently jailed for leading a protest march
- a 40-year-old migrant farm worker
- a 50-year-old college classics professor, a specialist in Ancient Greek literature
- a 75-year-old housekeeper who supports four grandchildren

First impressions are extremely inevitable, extremely difficult to change, and often wrong; it's a lot easier to collect more evidence and information and then make the judgment.

Similarly, this tendency can lead you to discount or distort subsequent perceptions so as not to disrupt your initial impression or upset your original schema. For example, you may fail to see signs of deceitfulness in someone you like because of your early impression that this person is good and honest.

Consistency

The tendency to maintain balance among perceptions or attitudes is called **consistency** (McBroom & Reed, 1992). You expect certain things to go together and other things not to go together. On a purely intuitive basis, for example, respond to the following sentences by noting your *expected* response:

- *I expect a person I like to (like, dislike) me.*
- *I expect a person I dislike to (like, dislike) me.*
- *I expect my friend to (like, dislike) my friend.*
- *I expect my friend to (like, dislike) my enemy.*
- *I expect my enemy to (like, dislike) my friend.*
- *I expect my enemy to (like, dislike) my enemy.*

According to most consistency theories, your expectations would be as follows: You would expect a person you liked to like you (1) and a person you disliked to dislike you (2). You would expect a friend to like a friend (3) and to dislike an enemy (4). You would expect your enemy to dislike your friend (5) and to like your other enemy (6). All these expectations are intuitively satisfying.

Further, you would expect someone you liked to possess characteristics you like or admire. And you would expect your enemies not to possess characteristics you like or admire. Conversely, you would expect people you liked to lack unpleasant characteristics and those you disliked to possess unpleasant characteristics.

Uncritically assuming that an individual is consistent can lead you to ignore or distort your perceptions of behaviors that are inconsistent with your picture of the whole person. For example, you may misinterpret Kim's basic shyness because your image of Kim is "bold, defiant, and extroverted." Consistency can also lead you to see certain behaviors as positive if you interpreted other behaviors positively (the halo effect) or as negative if you interpreted other behaviors negatively (the reverse halo effect).

E-Talk . . . .

First and Last Impressions

How would you describe the operation of primacy and recency in online communication? Which has more influence on your perceptions of another person—their earliest messages or their more recent messages?

Attribution

Attribution is the process by which we try to explain the motivation for a person's behavior. Perhaps the major way we do this is to ask ourselves if the person was in control of the behavior. If people are in control of their own behavior, then we feel justified in praising them for positive behaviors and blaming them for negative behaviors. You probably make similar judgments based on controllability in many situations. Consider, for example, how you would respond to situations such as Doris's failing her history exam or Sidney's having his car repossessed because he failed to keep up the payments.

Very likely you would be sympathetic to Doris and Sidney if you feel that they were *not* in control of what happened; for example, if the examination was unfair or if Sidney couldn't make his car payments because he lost his job as a result of discrimination. On the other hand, you probably would not be sympathetic or might blame these people for their problems if you felt that they were in control of what happened; for example, if Doris partied instead of studying or if Sidney gambled his payments away.

Generally, research shows that if we feel people are in control of negative behaviors, we will come to dislike them. If we feel people are not in control of negative behaviors, we will not blame them for their negative circumstances.

Three major attribution problems can interfere with the accuracy of your interpersonal perceptions: the self-serving bias, overattribution, and the fundamental attribution error.

After getting a poor performance evaluation, you may well attribute it to the difficulty of the job or to unfairness on the part of the supervisor (that is, to uncontrollable factors). After getting an extremely positive evaluation, however, you're more likely to attribute it to your ability or hard work (that is, to controllable factors). This tendency is the **self-serving bias,** our tendency to take credit for the positive and deny responsibility for the negative (Bernstein, Stephan, & Davis, 1979). A great deal of research supports the prevalence of this bias. For example, you're likely to take credit for your computer's effective performance but to blame the device for negative outcomes (Moon, 2003). Similarly, you're likely to favor your own group by attributing successful outcomes to internal factors and negative outcomes to external factors (Sherman & Kim, 2005). You also are apt to assume that your own behavior will be more positive than the behaviors of others. For example, when people were asked to indicate the changes that would take place in their lives if they won the lottery, they indicated that their own changes would be significantly more positive than other people's changes (Nelson & Beggan, 2004). Even young children, when reporting conflicts, will attribute positive actions to themselves and less positive actions to their siblings (Ross, Smith, Spielmacher, & Recchia, 2004).

To prevent the self-serving bias from distorting your attributions, consider the potential influences of both internal and external factors on both your positive and negative behaviors. Ask yourself to what extent your negative behaviors may be due to internal (controllable) factors and your positive behaviors to external (uncontrollable) factors. Just asking the question will prevent you from mindlessly falling into the self-serving bias trap.

If someone you work with had alcoholic parents or is blind or was born into great wealth, there's often a tendency to attribute everything that person does to such factors. And so you might say, "Sally has difficulty working on a team because she grew up in a home of alcoholics," "Alex overeats because he's blind," or "Lillian lacks ambition because she always got whatever she wanted without working for it." As discussed in Chapter 2, this is called *overattribution*—the tendency to single out one or two obvious characteristics and attribute everything a person does to these one or two characteristics. To prevent overattribution, recognize that most behaviors result from a lot of factors and that you almost always make a mistake when you select one factor and attribute everything to it. When you make a judgment, ask yourself if other factors might underlie the behaviors that seem at first glance to stem solely from one factor.

■ What Do You Say ?

Overattribution

Your friends attribute your behavior, attitudes, values, and just about everything you do to your racial origins—a clear case of overattribution. You want to explain the illogic of this thinking. **What Do You Say?** Through what channel?

Perceiving Differences

Examine each of the following situations and indicate how each of the persons identified might conceivably view the situation.

1. Pat, a single parent, has two small children (ages 7 and 12) who often lack some of the important things children their age should have—such as school supplies, sneakers, and toys—because Pat can't afford them. Yet Pat smokes two packs of cigarettes a day.

   Pat sees . . .

   The 12-year-old daughter sees . . .

   The children's teacher sees . . .

2. Chris has extremely high standards and feels that getting all A's in college is an absolute necessity. In fear of earning that first B (after three and a half years of nothing but A's), Chris cheats on an examination in a course on communication ethics and gets caught by the instructor.

   Chris sees . . .

   The instructor sees . . .

   The average B student sees . . .

3. Pat, a supervisor in an automobile factory, has been ordered to increase production or be fired. In desperation Pat gives a really tough message to the workers—many of whom are greatly insulted and, as a result, slow down rather than increase their efforts.

   Pat sees . . .

   The average worker sees . . . .

   Pat's supervisor sees . . .

Each person perceives the world differently. For effective communication to take place, each person needs to understand the perceptions of the other.

When Pat is late for a meeting, you're more likely to conclude that Pat is inconsiderate or irresponsible or "scatterbrained" than to attribute the lateness to a bus breakdown or a traffic accident. This tendency to conclude that people do what they do because that's the kind of people they are, not because of the situation they're in, is known as the **fundamental attribution error.** When you commit this error, you overvalue the contribution of internal factors and undervalue the influence of external factors. To avoid making this error, ask yourself if you're giving undue emphasis to internal factors, and consider what external factors might have accounted for another's behavior. Interestingly enough, this tendency may be culture specific, not universal as previously thought (Goode, 2000). For example, research finds that Asians are less likely to commit this fundamental attribution error than Americans. In one study researchers presented American and Korean students with a speech endorsing a particular position and told them that the writer had been instructed to write this and really had no choice. Americans were more likely to decide that the speaker believed in the position endorsed; they concluded that the speech expressed what the speaker really believed (and not the external circumstances of being forced to write the speech). Korean students, on the other hand, were less likely to believe in the sincerity of the speaker and gave greater weight to the external factor that the speaker was forced to write the speech.

*I*ncreasing Your Accuracy in Interpersonal Perception

Your effectiveness in interpersonal communication depends largely on the accuracy of your perceptions. Here are four suggestions to help you perceive other people more accurately.

Analyze Your Perceptions

When you become aware of your perceptions, you'll be able to subject them to logical and critical analysis. Here are some suggestions.

- Recognize your own role in perception. Your emotional and physiological state will influence the meaning you give to your perceptions. A movie may seem hysterically funny when you're in a good mood but just plain stupid if you're in a bad mood or preoccupied with family problems. Know when your perceptual evaluations are unduly influenced by your own biases; for example, by a tendency to perceive only the positive in people you like and only the negative in people you don't like. Even your gender will influence your perceptions. Women consistently evaluate other people more positively than do men on such factors as agreeableness, conscientiousness, and emotional stability (Winquist, Mohr, & Kenny, 1998).

- Avoid early conclusions. On the basis of your observations, formulate hypotheses to test against additional information and evidence rather than drawing conclusions you then look to confirm.

- Look for a variety of cues before making a judgment. For example, in making a judgment about a place to work, you'd logically use a variety of cues—salary, opportunity for advancement, benefits package, the working environment, and probably lots of other factors as well. After examining these cues, you'd make a judgment about the suitability of this job. In a similar way, it's useful to use a variety of cues when making judgments of people.

- Be alert to any *confirmation bias*—a tendency to seek out and believe information that supports your position or bias. Conversely, a *disconfirmation bias* may lead you to avoid any information that would contradict your position or bias. When

CURTIS © 1993 Ray Billingsley. Reprinted with special permission of King Features Syndicate.

❝ We must always tell what we see. Above all, and this is more difficult, we must always see what we see. ❞
—Charles Peguy

evaluating information, ask yourself if you're being influenced by either of these biases. Bringing this possibility to consciousness will help you think more critically about the information (Edwards & Smith, 1996; Kuhn, Weinstock, & Flaton, 1994).

Check Your Perceptions

Perception checking is another way to reduce uncertainty and to make your perceptions more accurate. The goal of perception checking is to explore further the thoughts and feelings of the other person, not to prove that your initial perception is correct. With this simple technique, you lessen your chances of misinterpreting another's feelings. At the same time, you give the other person an opportunity to elaborate on his or her thoughts and feelings. In its most basic form, perception checking consists of two steps:

● Describe what you see or hear, recognizing that even descriptions are not really objective but are heavily influenced by who you are, your emotional state, and so on. At the same time, you may wish to describe what you think is happening. Again, try to do this as descriptively (not evaluatively) as you can. Sometimes you may wish to offer several possibilities: "You've called me from work a lot this week. You seem concerned that everything is all right at home." Or, "You've not wanted to talk

Censoring Messages and Interactions

A *gatekeeper* is a person or institution that regulates what information gets through from a source to a receiver. Television programmers, for example, are gatekeepers in determining which programs people will see. Teachers, authors, newsgroup moderators, and parents also are gatekeepers—passing on certain information and preventing other information from getting through.

Similarly, relational gatekeepers encourage certain relationships and discourage or even prevent other relationships. Parents, for example, often encourage their children to play with and become friends with children from the same ethnic background, national group, and religion and at the same time discourage friendships with children from different cultures. Your friends may exert pressure on you to date one person and not another, to associate with some types of people but not others.

What Would You Do?

Tom has become interested in Ann and so approaches Sara, Ann's best friend, to ask how she feels about him. Tom has been charged with physical abuse and an indictment for additional charges is pending. Ann, on the other hand, is extremely vulnerable and would surely be tempted by Tom's fast talk. Sara is convinced that Tom would be bad for Ann and so tells him that Ann is not interested and is seeing someone else, both untrue statements. Sara also decides not to tell Ann anything about Tom's interest. Is Sara ethical in lying to Tom? Is Sara ethical in concealing Tom's expression of interest from Ann? If you were Ann's best friend, what would you do in this situation?

with me all week. You say that my work is fine but you don't seem to want to give me the same responsibilities that other editorial assistants have."

- Seek confirmation. Ask the other person if your description is accurate. Be careful that your request for confirmation does not sound as though you already know the answer; ask for confirmation in as supportive a way as possible, for example, "Are you worried about me or the kids?" or "Are you displeased with my work? Is there anything I can do to improve my job performance?"

Reduce Your Uncertainty

Reducing uncertainty enables you to achieve greater accuracy in perception. A variety of strategies can help reduce uncertainty (Berger & Bradac, 1982; Gudykunst, 1994):

- Observing another person while he or she is engaged in an active task, preferably interacting with others in relatively informal social situations, will often reveal a great deal about the person. The reason is that in informal situations people are less apt to monitor their behaviors and more likely to reveal their true selves.

- You can manipulate situations to observe people in more revealing contexts. Employment interviews, theatrical auditions, and student teaching are typical situations designed to reveal how people act and react—and thus to help reduce uncertainty.

- When you log on to a chat group for the first time and you lurk, reading the exchanges among other group members before saying anything yourself, you're learning about the people in the group and about the group itself and thus reducing uncertainty. When uncertainty is reduced, you're more likely to make contributions that will be appropriate to the group and less likely to violate any of the group's norms; in short, you're more likely to communicate effectively.

- Another way to reduce uncertainty is to collect information by asking others about a person. For example, you might ask a colleague if a third person finds you interesting and might like to have dinner with you.

> ■ **What Do You Say**?
> **Relationship Uncertainty**
> You've been dating someone casually over the past six months and want to take the relationship to the next level. But first you want to find out if your partner feels the same way. **What Do You Say?** To whom? Through what channel?

Skill building
exercise

Reversing Negative Perceptions

What might you do in each of the following situations to maintain a positive public image? You may want to return to these scenarios after reading about verbal and nonverbal communication (Chapters 6 and 7).

- At a club, you had a few drinks and exchanged a few kisses with someone who now turns up as a freshman student in a class you're teaching. You fear it will be common knowledge when your class meets the next time.

- When coming out of a sex therapist's office, you bump into a work colleague who, you discover, lives in the same building in which your therapist has an office. You're embarrassed and don't want to appear to be someone in need of sexual therapy.

- A fellow student, with whom you have broken off a romantic relationship, is now spreading false rumors about you. Although totally untrue, the rumors are causing damage to your formerly popular image.

Reversing negative impressions is an extremely difficult task. In fact, attempting to improve your image doesn't always work; yet in some instances your only choice is to make the effort.

And of course you can interact with the individual. For example, you can ask questions: "Do you enjoy sports?" "What did you think of that computer science course?" "What would you do if you got fired?" You also gain knowledge of another by disclosing information about yourself. Your disclosures will help create an environment that encourages disclosures from the person about whom you wish to learn more.

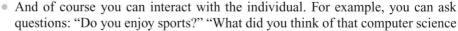
❝ The choice of a point of view is the initial act of culture. ❞
—Ortega y Gasset

Increase Your Cultural Sensitivity

Recognizing and being sensitive to cultural differences will help increase your accuracy in perception. For example, Russian or Chinese artists such as ballet dancers will often applaud their audience by clapping. Americans seeing this may easily interpret the behavior as egotistical. Similarly, a German man will enter a restaurant before the woman in order to see if the place is respectable enough for the woman to enter. This simple custom can easily seem rude to members of cultures in which courtesy means allowing the woman to enter first (Axtell, 1993).

Within every cultural group there are wide and important differences. As not all Americans are alike, neither are all Indonesians, Greeks, Mexicans, and so on. When you make assumptions that all people of a certain culture are alike, you're thinking in stereotypes. Recognizing not only the differences between another culture and your own but also the differences among members of any given culture will help you perceive situations more accurately.

Cultural sensitivity will help counteract the considerable difficulty most people have in understanding the nonverbal messages of people from other cultures. For example, it's easier to decode the emotions communicated facially by members of your own culture than to read facial expressions in members of other cultures (Weathers, Frank, & Spell, 2002). This "in-group advantage" can assist your perceptional accuracy with members of your own culture but will often hinder your accuracy with members of other cultures (Elfenbein & Ambady, 2002).

E-Talk ▪ ▪ ▪ ▪ ▪

Perceptual Accuracy

How would you describe your own perceptual accuracy in face-to-face versus online relationships? What perceptual cues do you use in each situation? For example, what cues do you use to judge the honesty of an online acquaintance? The degree of attraction the person feels for you? The person's financial assets?

The Parental Difference

Here is a dialogue written to illustrate how different people see the same incident very differently. As you read the dialogue, identify the principles of perception that might help this couple communicate more effectively.

The Cast

A French-American family.*
Mom (Nicole) and Dad (Gaetan), who are in their 40s

The Context

Nicole and Gaetan are in the kitchen getting ready for dinner; their conversation centers on Alain, their eighth-grade son, the youngest of their five children,

Nicole (hanging up the phone): That was Alain's teacher. She caught him in the locker room drinking beer.

Gaetan: Alain? Wow! I could have expected it from Phillipe or Alexandre or even Vanessa but not Alain. Wow!

Nicole: Is that all you want to say? Wow! The kid is thirteen; he shouldn't be drinking.

Gaetan: What's the big deal? Didn't I do it? And I didn't wait until I was thirteen. And you weren't so innocent either. Don't worry; it's not a problem.

Nicole: That's always your response. It's not a problem; just like when Gerard was caught buying pot.

Gaetan: And it wasn't a problem, was it?

Nicole: Yes, it was and it is a problem. Do you know I found pot in his room last week?

Gaetan: What did you do with it?

Nicole: I flushed it down the toilet—what do you think I did with it?

Gaetan: Well, we could have shared it like we did when we were in college.

Nicole: Will you stop? This is serious.

Gaetan: Look, all kids smoke a little pot. It's no big deal.

Nicole: And what happens when he wants something stronger and becomes a coke addict?

Gaetan: He's not going to become a coke addict. And if he's going to use coke, it's not because he smokes a little grass.

Nicole: Well, I hope you don't take that attitude when we meet the assistant principal—Thursday at four.

Gaetan: Maybe I'd better not go. I'd tell that overpaid teacher to go to hell. So what if the kid had a beer. Let's not make a federal case out of it.

*It's interesting to know that French is the first language for approximately 100 million people. French is the native tongue of far fewer people than Mandarin, Spanish, or Arabic, but its importance rests on its being an official language of 32 countries. France, with 55 million people, is the largest French-speaking country, followed by Canada, the Democratic Republic of the Congo, Belgium, Cameroon, and Switzerland. In comparison with Asian countries, for example, France sends relatively few students to study in the United States. However, English is required of all French high school students, and French remains a popular foreign language in high schools and colleges throughout the United States.

Summary of Concepts and Skills

This chapter discussed how perception works, the processes that influence perception, and how you can make your perceptions more accurate.

1. Perception is the process by which you become aware of the many stimuli impinging on your senses. It occurs in five stages: sensory stimulation occurs, sensory stimulation is organized, sensory stimulation is interpreted and evaluated, sensory stimulation is held in memory, and sensory stimulation is recalled.

2. Processes that influence perception include: (1) implicit personality theories, (2) self-fulfilling prophecy, (3) primacy–recency, (4) consistency, and (5) attribution.

3. Implicit personality theories are the private personality theories people hold, which influence how they perceive other people.

4. The self-fulfilling prophecy occurs when you make a prediction or formulate a belief that comes true because you have made the prediction and acted as if it were true.

5. Primacy–recency has to do with the relative influence of stimuli as a result of their order. If what occurs first exerts greater influence, you have a primacy effect. If what occurs last exerts greater influence, you have a recency effect.

6. Consistency influences you to see what is consistent with your expectations and not to see what is inconsistent.

7. Attribution is the process through which you try to understand the behaviors of others (and your own, in self-attribution)—particularly the reasons or motivations for these behaviors. Perceptions of controllability often influence attributions. Errors of attribution include the self-serving bias, overattribution, and the fundamental attribution error.

8. To increase the accuracy of your interpersonal perceptions: (1) Critically analyze your perceptions; formulate hypotheses rather than conclusions, look for a variety of cues (especially contradictory ones), and be aware of your own biases. (2) Check your perceptions, describing what you see or hear and asking for confirmation. (3) Reduce uncertainty by, for example, interacting with a person or lurking before joining a group. (4) Be culturally sensitive, recognizing the differences between your own and other cultures and also differences among members of any specific culture.

This chapter considered a variety of skills to help make your perceptions more accurate:

_____ 1. *Perceptual shortcuts.* Be mindful of your perceptual shortcuts so that they don't mislead you and result in inaccurate perceptions.

_____ 2. *Implicit personality theory.* Bring your implicit personality theory to your mindful state to subject your perceptions and conclusions to logical analysis.

_____ 3. *Self-fulfilling prophecy.* Take a second look at your perceptions when they correspond very closely to your initial expectations; the self-fulfilling prophecy may be at work.

_____ 4. *Initial impressions.* Guard against drawing impressions too quickly or from too little information; remember that initial impressions can function as filters that prevent you from forming more accurate perceptions on the basis of more information.

_____ 5. *Self-serving bias.* Become mindful of giving too much weight to internal factors (when explaining your positives) and too little weight to external factors (when explaining your negatives).

_____ 6. *Overattribution.* Avoid overattribution; rarely is any one factor an accurate explanation of complex human behavior.

_____ 7. *Fundamental attribution error.* Avoid the fundamental attribution error, whereby you attribute someone's behavior solely to internal factors while minimizing or ignoring situational forces.

_____ 8. *Analyzing your perceptions.* Increase accuracy in interpersonal perception by identifying the influence of your physical and emotional state and making sure that you're not drawing conclusions from too little information.

_____ 9. *Checking perceptions.* Increase accuracy in perception by: (1) describing what you see or hear and the meaning you assign to it and (2) asking the other person if your perceptions are accurate.

_____ 10. *Reducing uncertainty.* Use passive, active, and interactive strategies to reduce uncertainty.

_____ 11. *Culture and perception.* Increase accuracy in perception by learning as much as you can about the cultures of those with whom you interact.

Match the terms dealing with interpersonal perception with their definitions. Record the number of the definition next to the appropriate term.

_____ script

_____ implicit personality theory

_____ selective attention

_____ proximity

_____ the fundamental attribution error

_____ self-fulfilling prophecy

_____ halo effect

_____ perception checking

_____ self-serving bias

_____ schemata

1. Overvaluing internal factors and undervaluing external factors in explaining behavior.
2. Increasing accuracy in perception by describing what you think is going on and asking for confirmation.
3. A theory about people that you have and through which you perceive others.
4. Physical closeness, which encourages perception of things as belonging together, as forming a unit.
5. An organized mental template for the way an action or procedure should take place.
6. Perception of stimuli that you anticipate will fulfill your needs.
7. The mental templates or structures that help you organize information in memory.
8. The situation in which we make a prediction and then act in a way that makes the prediction come true.
9. A tendency to take credit for positive outcomes and to deny responsibility for negative events.
10. The tendency to generalize a person's virtue or expertise from one area to another.

Four for Discussion

1. In making evaluations of other people, we tend to assume that we first think about the situation and then make the evaluation. Some research claims, however, that we really don't think before assigning any perception a positive or negative value. This research argues that all perceptions have a positive or negative value attached to them and that these evaluations are most often automatic, involving no conscious thought. Immediately upon perceiving a person, idea, or thing, we attach a positive or negative value (*New York Times*, August 8, 1995, pp. C1, C10). What do you think of this claim? Can you think of examples from your own experience that would support or contradict this view?

2. Although most of the research on the self-fulfilling prophecy illustrates its distorting effect on behavior, it's been argued that organizations could use the self-fulfilling prophecy to stimulate higher performance (Eden, 1992; Field, 1989). For example, managers could be told that employees had extremely high capabilities; managers would then act as if this were true and thus promote high-level performance in the workers. Consider how you might go about using the self-fulfilling prophecy to encourage behaviors you wanted to increase in strength and frequency. For example, what might you do to encourage persons who are high in communication apprehension to speak up with greater confidence, or to encourage people who are reluctant to self-disclose to reveal more of their inner selves? How might this strategy be used in the college classroom or in parenting?

3. Writers to advice columnists generally attribute their problems to external sources (argumentative in-laws, a negative climate at work). The columnists' responses, however, more often focus on internal sources (the writer's temper, an unwillingness to compromise). The columnists' advice, therefore, is usually directed at the writer (you shouldn't have done that; apologize; get out of the relationship) (Schoeneman & Rubanowitz, 1985). Do you find that this happens when people discuss their problems with you, whether face-to-face, in letters, or in e-mails? Do you generally respond as the columnists do?

4. What stereotypes do you think men entertain about women? What stereotypes do you think women entertain about men? How might these stereotypes influence their interpersonal interactions?

MyCommunicationLab Explorations

Explore www.mycommunicationlab.com where you'll find exercises relevant to perception in interpersonal communication: (1) Perceiving My Selves, (2) How Do You Make Attributions? (3) Taking Another's Perspective, (4) Checking Perceptions, and (5) What Are Your Cultural Perceptions?

Also visit MyCommunicationLab for study guides, activities, and video clips on the nature of interpersonal perception and how it influences the messages you send and receive.

Research Navigator.com

Explore our research resources at
www.researchnavigator.com.

CHAPTER 5

Listening and Interpersonal Communication

WHY READ THIS CHAPTER?

*B*ecause you'll **learn about:**
- the process of listening.
- the styles of listening you can use.
- the role of culture and gender differences in listening.

*B*ecause you'll **learn to:**
- listen more effectively during each of stage of the process.
- regulate your listening style on the basis of the unique situation.
- listen with sensitivity to cultural and gender differences.

This chapter examines **listening,** which, according to the International Listening Association, is "the process of receiving, constructing meaning from, and responding to spoken and/or nonverbal messages" (Emmert, 1994, cited in Brownell, 2006). Although an essential part of every interpersonal communication event, listening is often neglected. Perhaps people assume that all they have to do is open their ears (and that even that is automatic) and they'll listen. As we'll see, this assumption is far from accurate. Listening is a lot more than hearing. It consists of a series of skills that are covered in this chapter; other chapter topics include the importance of listening, the nature of the listening process, the varied styles of listening you might use in different situations, and some cultural and gender differences in listening. Throughout this chapter I'll emphasize ways to avoid the major barriers to listening as well as guidelines for more effective listening.

The Importance of Listening: Task and Relationship Benefits

Regardless of what you do, listening will prove a crucial communication component and will serve both task and relationship functions. In terms of task functions, for example, one study concluded that in this era of technological transformation, employees' interpersonal skills are especially significant; workers' advancement will depend on their ability to speak and write effectively, to display proper etiquette, and *to listen attentively.* And in a survey of 40 CEOs of Asian and Western multinational companies, respondents cited a lack of listening skills as *the major shortcoming* of top executives (Witcher, 1999).

Listening also is crucial to developing and maintaining relationships of all kinds. You expect a friend or a romantic partner to listen to you, and you are expected to listen to them in turn. Listening also plays a significant role in the management of interpersonal conflict; listening effectively to the other person, even during a heated argument, will go a long way toward helping you manage the conflict and preventing it from escalating into a major blowup.

Another way to look at the importance of listening is to realize that effective listening brings the same array of benefits or payoffs as those identified for interpersonal communication in Chapter 1: It enables you to learn, relate, influence, play, and help (Johnson & Bechler, 1998; Kramer, 1997; Castleberry & Shepherd, 1993; Levine, 2004; Brownell, 2006). Listening helps you *learn;* it lets you acquire knowledge of others, the world, and yourself so as to avoid problems and make more reasonable decisions. Listening enables you to *relate,* to form and maintain relationships with others, to gain social acceptance and popularity, simply because people come to like those who are attentive and listen supportively. You also exert *influence* through listening; people are more likely to respect and follow those who they feel have listened to and understood them. Knowing when to suspend critical and evaluative listening and simply to enjoy absurdities or incongruities enables you to fulfill the *play* function. And, of course, listening enables you to *help* others, to assist other people by hearing more, empathizing more, and coming to understand others more deeply.

The Stages of Listening

Listening is a five-stage process of (1) receiving, (2) understanding, (3) remembering, (4) evaluating, and (5) responding to oral messages, as visualized in Figure 5.1. As you'll see from the following discussion, listening involves a collection of skills that work together at each of these five stages. Listening can go wrong at any stage; by the same token, you can enhance your listening ability by strengthening the skills needed for each step of the process.

All five stages overlap. When you listen, you're performing all five processes at essentially the same time. For example, when listening in conversation, you're not only processing what you hear for understanding, but you're also putting it into memory storage, critically evaluating what was said, and responding (nonverbally and perhaps with verbal messages as well).

Receiving

Unlike listening, hearing begins and ends with this first stage—receiving. Hearing is something that just happens when you get within earshot of auditory stimuli. Listening is quite different. Listening begins, but does not end, with receiving messages the speaker sends. In listening, you receive both the verbal and the nonverbal messages—not only the words but also the gestures, facial expressions, variations in volume and rate, and lots more.

The following suggestions should help you receive messages more effectively. Analyze your own receiving; do you:

- *focus attention on the speaker's verbal and nonverbal messages, on both what is said and what is not said, rather than on what you'll say next?*
- *maintain your role as listener and avoid interrupting the speaker until he or she is finished?*

❝The opposite of talking isn't listening. The opposite of talking is waiting. **❞**

—Fran Lebowitz

Figure 5.1
The Five Stages of Listening
Both this model and the suggestions for listening improvement throughout this chapter draw on theories and models that listening researchers have developed (for example, Nichols & Stevens, 1957; Nichols, 1995; Barker & Gaut, 2002; Steil, Barker, & Watson, 1983; Brownell, 2006).

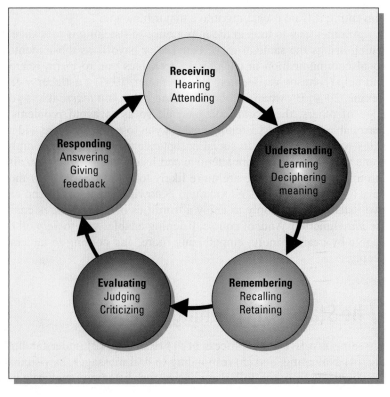

TABLE 5.1 *Interpersonal Communication Tips*

BETWEEN DEAF AND HEARING PEOPLE

People differ greatly in their hearing ability; some are totally deaf and can hear nothing, others have some hearing loss and can hear some sounds, and still others have impaired hearing but can hear most speech. Although many people with profound hearing loss can speak, their speech may seem labored and less clear than the speech of those with unimpaired hearing. Here are some suggestions to help deaf and hearing people communicate more effectively.

If you have unimpaired hearing:

1. Set up a comfortable context. Reduce the distance between yourself and the person with a hearing impairment. Reduce the background noise. Turn off the television and even the air conditioner.

2. Face the person and avoid any interference with the visual cues from your speech; for example, avoid smoking, chewing gum, or holding your hand over your mouth. Make sure the lighting is adequate.

3. Speak with an adequate volume, but don't shout. Shouting can distort your speech and may insult the person. Be especially careful to avoid reducing volume at the ends of your sentences.

4. Because some words are easier to lip-read than others, it often helps if you can rephrase your ideas in different ways.

5. In group situations only one person should speak at a time. Similarly, avoid the tendency to talk to a person with hearing loss through a third party. Elementary school teachers, for example, have been found to direct fewer comments to deaf children than to hearing students (Cawthon, 2001). So direct your comments to the person himself or herself.

6. Ask the person if there is anything you can do to make it easier for him or her to understand you.

7. Don't avoid terms like *hear, listen, music,* or *deaf* when they're relevant to the conversation. Trying to avoid these common terms will make your speech sound artificial.

8. Use nonverbal cues that help communicate your meaning; gestures indicating size or location and facial expressions indicating emotions and feelings are often helpful.

If you have impaired hearing:

1. Do your best to eliminate background noise.

2. Move closer to the speaker if this helps. Alert the other person that this closer distance will help you hear better.

3. If you feel the speaker can make adjustments that will make it easier for you to understand, ask. For example, ask the speaker to repeat a message, to speak more slowly or more distinctly, or to increase his or her volume.

4. If you hear better in one ear than another, position yourself accordingly; if necessary, clue the other person in to this fact.

5. If necessary, ask the person to write down certain information, such as phone numbers or website addresses. Carrying a pad and pencil will prove helpful, both for this purpose and in the event that you wish to write something down for others.

Sources: These suggestions were drawn from a variety of sources: *Tips for Communicating with Deaf People* (Rochester Institute of Technology, National Technical Institute for the Deaf, Division of Public Affairs); **www.his.com/~lola/deaf.html** and **www.zak.co.il/deaf-info/old/comm_strategies.html.** All websites accessed July 18, 2006.

● *avoid assuming you understand what the speaker is going to say before he or she actually says it?*

In this brief discussion of receiving (and in this entire chapter on listening), the unstated assumption is that both individuals can receive auditory signals without difficulty. For the many people who have hearing impairments, however, listening presents a variety of problems. Table 5.1 provides tips for communication between deaf and hearing people.

Understanding

Understanding occurs when you learn what the speaker means, when the meaning you get is essentially the same as what the speaker sent. Understanding includes both the thoughts that are expressed and the emotional tone that accompanies them, for example, the urgency or the joy or sorrow expressed in the message.

E-Talk . ▪ . ▪ . ▪ .

Cell Phone Annoyances

One researcher has argued that listening to the cell phone conversations of others is particularly annoying because you can hear only one side of the conversation; survey respondents rated cell phone conversations as more intrusive than two people talking face-to-face (Monk, Fellas, & Ley, 2004). Do you find the cell phone conversations of people near you on a bus or in a store annoying, perhaps for the reason given here?

In understanding, do you:

- *see the speaker's messages from the speaker's point of view? Avoid judging the message until you've fully understood it—as the speaker intended it?*
- *ask questions to clarify or to secure additional details or examples if necessary?*
- *rephrase (paraphrase) the speaker's ideas in your own words?*

Remembering

Messages that you receive and understand need to be remembered for at least some period of time. What you remember is not what was actually said but what you think (or recall) was said. Memory for speech is *reconstructive,* not *reproductive.* In other words, you don't simply reproduce in your memory what the speaker said; rather, as noted in the discussion of perception in Chapter 4, you reconstruct the messages you hear into a system that makes sense to you. Your goal should be to reproduce the message you hear in your memory as accurately as you can with as little personal re-contructing as possible.

In remembering, do you:

- *identify the central ideas in a message?*
- *summarize the message in a more easily retained form?*
- *repeat names and key concepts to yourself or, if appropriate, aloud?*

Evaluating

Evaluating consists of judging messages in some way. At times you may try to evaluate the speaker's underlying intent, often without conscious awareness. For example, Elaine tells you that she is up for a promotion and is really excited about it. You may then try to judge her intention. Does she want you to use your influence with the company president? Is she preoccupied with her accomplishment and thus telling everyone about it? Is she looking for a pat on the back? Generally, if you know the person well, you'll be able to identify the intention and therefore be able to respond appropriately.

In evaluating, do you:

- *resist evaluation until you fully understand the speaker's point of view?*
- *assume that the speaker is a person of goodwill? Give the speaker the benefit of any doubt by asking for clarification on issues that you feel you must object to?*
- *distinguish facts from opinions and personal interpretations as well as identify any biases, self-interests, or prejudices that may lead the speaker to slant unfairly what is presented?*

Responding

Responding takes place in two phases: (1) responding that occurs while the speaker is talking and (2) responding that occurs after the speaker has stopped talking. Responses are feedback—information that you send back to the speaker and that tells the speaker how you feel and think about his or her messages. Responses made while the speaker is talking should be supportive and should acknowledge that you're listening. Such responses include what researchers on nonverbal communication call **backchanneling cues** and may serve the following functions (Burgoon & Bacue, 2003; Burgoon & Hoobler, 2002):

1. You can use backchanneling cues to indicate agreement or disagreement by smiling, nodding approval, making brief comments such as "right" and "of course," frowning, shaking your head, or making brief comments such as "no" or "never."

TABLE 5.2	Problem-Causing Listening Responses
LISTENER TYPE	LISTENING RESPONDING BEHAVIOR
The static or overly expressive listener	Gives no feedback and remains relatively motionless, revealing no expressions—or responds with excessive feedback to just about everything said.
The monotonous feedback giver	Seems responsive, but the responses never vary; regardless of what you say, the response is the same.
The eye avoider	Looks all around the room and at others but never at you.
The preoccupied listener	Listens to other things at the same time, often with headphones or with the television on
The waiting listener	Listens for a cue that will let him or her take over the speaking turn.
The thought-completing listener	Listens a little and then finishes your thought.

2. You can indicate your degree of involvement by an attentive or inattentive posture, by leaning forward or slouching while looking around the room, and by focused or wandering eye movements.

3. You can regulate the speaker by asking him or her to slow down or get to the point or by raising your hand near your ear to indicate that he or she should speak louder.

4. You can ask for clarification by a puzzled facial expression, perhaps coupled with a forward lean, or by directly interjecting "Who?" or "What was that?"

In responding, do you:

- *express support and understanding for the speaker throughout the conversation?*
- *use varied backchanneling cues (for example, nodding, using appropriate facial expressions, or saying "I see") that tell the speaker that you're listening?*
- *own your own responses; that is, state your thoughts and feelings as your own, using "I-messages"—for example, saying, "I don't agree" rather than "No one will agree with that"?*

Table 5.2 presents another way of looking at appropriate and inappropriate listening responses.

Before reading about the styles and principles of effective listening, examine your own listening habits and tendencies by taking the accompanying self-test. Even

Skill building *exercise*

Obstacles to Listening

Taking into consideration your own attitudes, beliefs, values, and opinions, what obstacles to listening would you identify for each of the following interpersonal situations?

1. Colleagues at work are discussing how they can persuade management to restrict the company gym to men only.
2. Students in your computer science class are talking about planting a virus in the college computer as a way of protesting recent decisions by the administration.
3. A campus religious group is conferring about its plan to prevent same-sex couples from attending the college prom.
4. A group of faculty and students are discussing a campaign to prevent the military from recruiting on campus.

No one can listen apart from his or her own attitudes, beliefs, values, and opinions; these always get in the way of accurate listening. Your objective should be to minimize these effects.

Listening Ethically

As a listener you have ethical obligations. First, you owe it to the speaker to give the speaker's message an honest hearing and to avoid prejudgment. Try to put aside prejudices and preconceptions so you can evaluate the message fairly. At the same time, try to empathize with the speaker. You don't have to agree with the speaker, but try to understand emotionally as well as intellectually what the speaker means. Then accept or reject the speaker's ideas on the basis of the information offered, not on the basis of misunderstanding.

Second, you owe the speaker honest responses. Just as you should be honest with the listener when speaking, you should be honest with the speaker when listening. This means giving open and honest feedback. It also means reflecting honestly on what the speaker says. Much as the listener has a right to expect an active speaker, the speaker has the right to expect an active listener.

Applying Listening Skills

You're in conversation with a friend and your friend's friend (whom you're meeting for the first time). During the conversation this individual expresses political and social beliefs that you personally find reprehensible. How do you adjust your listening to give this person both an honest hearing and honest responses?

though the "desirable" answers will be obvious, try to give responses that are true for you in most of your listening experiences.

Styles of Listening Effectively

Listening is situational (Brownell, 2006). As we've seen, the way you listen should depend on the situation you are in. You don't listen to a State of the Union address in the same way that you listen to Jay Leno's monologue or to a proposal for a date. At the least you need to adjust your listening on the basis of (1) your purposes (are you listening to learn? To give comfort?) and (2) your knowledge of and relationship to

"Of course I'm paying attention—I've pressed the mute button."

the other person (does this person exaggerate or lie? or need support or perhaps a reality check?). The following discussion will provide specific suggestions for how to adjust your listening style and how you can avoid the pitfalls and barriers to ineffective listening. We'll look at four dimensions of listening: the empathic–objective, nonjudgmental–critical, surface–deep, and active–inactive dimensions.

Test *Yourself*  ✓

How Do You Listen?

INSTRUCTIONS: Respond to each statement using the following scale:

1 = always, **2** = frequently, **3** = sometimes, **4** = seldom, and **5** = never.

_____ ❶ I listen actively, communicate acceptance of the speaker, and prompt the speaker to further explore his or her thoughts.

_____ ❷ I listen to what the speaker is saying and feeling; I try to feel what the speaker feels.

_____ ❸ I listen without judging the speaker.

_____ ❹ I listen to the literal meanings that a speaker communicates; I don't look too deeply into hidden meanings.

_____ ❺ I listen without active involvement; I generally remain silent and take in what the other person is saying.

_____ ❻ I listen objectively; I focus on the logic of the ideas rather than on the emotional meaning of the message.

_____ ❼ I listen critically, evaluating the speaker and what the speaker is saying.

_____ ❽ I look for the hidden meanings, the meanings that are revealed by subtle verbal or nonverbal cues.

HOW DID YOU DO? These statements focus on the ways of listening discussed in this chapter. All of these ways are appropriate at some times but not at other times. It depends. So the only responses that are really inappropriate are "always" and "never." Effective listening is listening that is tailored to the specific communication situation.

WHAT WILL YOU DO? Consider how you might use these statements to begin to improve your listening effectiveness. A good way to begin doing this is to review these statements, trying to identify situations in which each statement would be appropriate and situations in which each statement would be inappropriate.

✓

Empathic and Objective Listening

If you're going to understand what a person means and what a person is feeling, you need to listen with some degree of **empathy** (Rogers, 1970; Rogers & Farson, 1981). To **empathize** with others is to feel with them, to see the world as they see it, to feel what they feel. When you listen empathically as a neighbor tells of having her apartment burgled and all her prized possessions taken, you can share on some level the loss and emptiness she feels. Only when you achieve empathy can you fully understand another person's meaning. Empathic listening will also help you enhance your relationships (Barrett & Godfrey, 1988; Snyder, 1992).

Although for most communication situations empathic listening is the preferred mode of responding, there are times when you need to go beyond it and to measure the speaker's meanings and feelings against some objective reality. It's important to

E-Talk ▪ ▪ ▪ ▪ ▪ ▪ ▪ ▪ ▪

Limited Storage

There's no limit to your brain's long-term memory, but there is limited storage space on your computer—and the less free space there is, the longer it takes to load web pages. So, if you want to increase the speed of loading web pages, close programs you don't need, whether they're visible or operating in the background. In what other ways might you increase storage capacity?

Ethical messages

A Question of Choice

One way of looking at interpersonal communication ethics is in light of the theory of "information ethics," a theory based on the notion of choice. The assumption in information ethics is that people have a right to make their own choices and that interpersonal communications (and, in fact, all forms of communication) are ethical to the extent that they facilitate a person's freedom of choice by presenting the person with accurate information. Communications are unethical to the extent that they interfere with people's freedom of choice by preventing them from securing information relevant to the choices they will make. The ethical communicator, then, provides others with the kinds of information they will need in making their own choices.

This position argues that you have the right to information about yourself that others possess and that influences the choices you'll make. Thus, for example, you have the right to face your accusers, to know what witnesses will be called to testify against you, to see your credit ratings, and to know what Social Security benefits you'll receive. On the other hand, you don't have the right to information about others; for example, information about whether your neighbors are happy or what they argue about or how much money they have.

Information ethics also obligates you to reveal information that you possess that bears on the choices of your society. Thus, for example, you have an obligation to identify wrongdoing that you witness, to identify someone in a police lineup, to report suspicions of child abuse, and to testify at a trial when you possess pertinent information. This information is essential for society to accomplish its purposes and to make its legitimate choices.

What Would You Do?

Pat and Chris are weekend pot smokers and smoke only when the children are out of the house. Their teenager, however, has heard rumors about the smoking and asks them if they smoke pot. Will it be ethical for Pat and Chris to lie and say they don't smoke? Will it be ethical for them to tell the truth and say they do smoke? If you were one of the parents, what would you do in this situation?

listen to Peter tell you how the entire world hates him and to understand how Peter feels and why he feels this way. But then you need to look a bit more objectively at the situation and perhaps see Peter's paranoia or self-hatred. Sometimes you have to put your empathic responses aside and listen with objectivity and detachment.

In adjusting your empathic and objective listening focus, keep the following recommendations in mind.

- Punctuate from the speaker's point of view (Chapter 1). That is, see the sequence of events as the speaker does and try to figure out how this perspective can influence what the speaker says and does.

- Engage in equal, two-way conversation. To encourage openness and empathy, try to eliminate any physical or psychological barriers to equality. For example, step from behind the large desk separating you from your employees. Avoid interrupting the speaker—a sign that what you have to say is more important.

- Seek to understand both thoughts and feelings. Don't consider your listening task finished until you've understood what the speaker is feeling as well as what he or she is thinking.

- Avoid "offensive listening"—the tendency to listen to bits and pieces of information that will enable you to attack the speaker or find fault with something the speaker has said (Floyd, 1985).

- Strive especially to be objective when listening to friends or foes alike. Your attitudes may lead you to distort messages—to block out positive messages about a foe or negative messages about a friend. Guard against "expectancy hearing," in which you fail to hear what the speaker is really saying and instead hear what you expect.

■ What Do You Say?
Listening Empathically
Your neighbors, who've avoided work all their lives and lived off unfairly obtained government disability payments, have just won the lottery for $16 million. They want you to share their joy, and they invite you over for a champagne toast. **What Do You Say?**

Nonjudgmental and Critical Listening

Effective listening includes both nonjudgmental and critical responses. You need to listen *nonjudgmentally*—with an open mind and with a view toward understanding. But you also need to listen *critically*—with a view toward making some kind of evaluation or judgment. Clearly, it's important to listen first for understanding while suspending judgment. Only after you've fully understood the relevant messages should you evaluate or judge.

Supplement nonjudgmental listening with critical listening. When you listen critically, you think logically and dispassionately about, for example, the stories your friends tell you or the sales pitch of the car dealer. Listening with an open mind will help you understand the messages better; listening with a critical mind will help you analyze and evaluate the messages. In adjusting your nonjudgmental and critical listening, focus on the following guidelines:

- Keep an open mind. Avoid prejudging. Delay your judgments until you fully understand both the content and the intention the speaker is communicating. Avoid either positive or negative evaluation until you have a reasonably complete understanding. Even when a friend tells you he or she did something you disapprove of, nonjudgmental listening requires you to withhold making value judgments (in your mind as well as in your responses) that can get in the way of your understanding your friend.

- Avoid filtering out or oversimplifying complex messages. Similarly, avoid filtering out undesirable messages. Clearly, you don't want to hear that something you believe is untrue, that people you care for are unkind, or that ideals you hold are self-destructive. Yet it's important that you reexamine your beliefs by listening to these messages.

- Recognize your own biases. These may interfere with accurate listening and cause you to distort message reception through a process of assimilation—the tendency to integrate and interpret what you hear or think you hear in keeping with your own biases, prejudices, and expectations. For example, are your ethnic, national, gender, or religious biases preventing you from appreciating a speaker's point of view?

- Avoid uncritical listening when you need to make evaluations and judgments.

- Recognize and combat the natural tendency to *sharpen*—to highlight, emphasize, and perhaps embellish one or two aspects of a message. Often the concepts that we tend to sharpen are incidental remarks that somehow stand out from the rest of the message. Be careful, therefore, about sharpening your blind date's "Thank you, I had a nice time" and assuming that the date was a big success—while ignoring the signs that it was just so-so, such as the lack of eye contact, the awkward silences, and the cell phone interruptions.

Surface and Depth Listening

In most messages there's an obvious meaning that you can derive from a literal reading of the words and sentences. But in reality, most messages have more than one level of meaning. Sometimes the other level is the opposite of the literal meaning; at other times it seems totally unrelated. Consider some frequently heard types of messages. Carol asks you how you like her new haircut. On one level, the meaning is clear: Do you like the haircut? But there's also another and perhaps more important level: Carol is asking you to say something positive about her appearance. In the same way, the parent who complains about working hard at the office or in the

" The first duty of love is to listen. "

—Paul Tillich

home may, on a deeper level, be asking for an expression of appreciation. The child who talks about the unfairness of the other children on the playground may be asking for comfort and love, for some expression of caring.

To appreciate these other meanings, you need to engage in *depth* listening. If you respond only to the *surface-level* communication (the literal meaning), you miss the opportunity to make meaningful contact with the other person's feelings and needs. If you say to the parent, "You're always complaining. I bet you really love working so hard," you fail to respond to the person's call for understanding and appreciation. In regulating your surface and depth listening, consider the following guidelines:

- Focus on both verbal and nonverbal messages. Recognize both consistent and inconsistent "packages" of messages and use these as guides for drawing inferences about the speaker's meaning. Ask questions when in doubt. Listen also to what is omitted. Remember that speakers communicate by what they leave out as well as by what they include. When Harry says things will be okay now that his relationship is finally over, but says it with downcast eyes, deep breathing, and clenched hands, consider the possibility that Harry is really hurting and that things are not okay.

- Listen for both content and relational messages. The student who constantly challenges the teacher is on one level communicating disagreement over content. However, on another level—the relationship level—the student may be voicing objections to the instructor's authority or authoritarianism. The instructor needs to listen and respond to both types of messages.

- Make special note of statements that refer back to the speaker. Remember that people inevitably talk about themselves. Whatever a person says is, in part, a function of who that person is. Attend carefully to those personal, self-referential messages. Realize that when Sara tells you that she fears that the economy is not going well, she may be voicing her own financial worries but phrasing them in the abstract.

- Don't, however, disregard the literal meaning of interpersonal messages in trying to uncover the more hidden meanings. Balance your listening between surface and underlying meanings. Respond to the different levels of meaning in the messages of others as you would like others to respond to yours—sensitively but not obsessively, readily but not overambitiously. When Tommy tells you he's not feeling well, don't ignore this literal meaning and assume that Tommy is just looking for attention.

Active and Inactive Listening

One of the most important communication skills you can learn is that of active listening (Gordon, 1975). Consider the following interaction. You're disappointed that you have to redo your entire budget report, and you say, "I can't believe I have to redo this entire report. I really worked hard on this project, and now I have to do it all over again." To this you get three different responses:

Apollo: That's not so bad; most people find they have to redo their first reports. That's the norm here.

Athena: You should be pleased that all you have to do is a simple rewrite. Peggy and Michael both had to completely redo their entire projects.

Diana: You have to rewrite that report you've worked on for the last three weeks? You sound really angry and frustrated.

All three listeners are probably trying to make you feel better. But they go about it in very different ways and, we can be sure, with very different results. Apollo tries to lessen the significance of the rewrite. This type of well-intended response is extremely common but does little to promote meaningful communication and understanding. Athena tries to give the situation a positive spin. With these responses, however, both these listeners are also suggesting that you should not be feeling the way you do. They're also implying that your feelings are not legitimate and should be replaced with more logical feelings.

Diana's response, however, is different from the others. Diana uses active listening. **Active listening** owes its development to Thomas Gordon (1975), who made it a cornerstone of his P-E-T (Parent Effectiveness Training) technique; it is a process of sending back to the speaker what you as a listener think the speaker meant—both in content and in feelings. Active listening, then is not merely repeating the speaker's exact words, but rather putting together into some meaningful whole your understanding of the speaker's total message.

" Listening is not merely talking, though even that is beyond most of our powers; it means taking a vigorous, human interest in what is being told to us. "
—Alice Duer Miller

FUNCTIONS OF ACTIVE LISTENING   Active listening serves several important functions.

To Check Understanding.   First, it helps you as a listener check your understanding of what the speaker said and, more important, what he or she meant. Reflecting back perceived meanings to the speaker gives the speaker an opportunity to offer clarification and correct any misunderstandings.

To Acknowledge the Speaker's Feelings.   Second, through active listening you let the speaker know that you acknowledge and accept his or her feelings. In the sample responses given, the first two listeners challenged your feelings. Diana, the active listener, who reflected back to you what she thought you meant, accepted what you were feeling. In addition, she also explicitly identified your emotions; she commented that you sounded "angry and frustrated," allowing you an opportunity to correct her interpretation if necessary. A word of caution, however: In understanding the other person and in communicating this understanding back to the person, be especially careful to avoid sending what Gordon (1975) calls "solution messages." Solution messages tell the person how he or she *should* feel or what he or she *should* do. The four types of messages that send solutions and that you'll want to avoid in your active listening are:

- ordering messages—*Do this . . . , Don't touch that . . .*
- warning and threatening messages—*If you don't do this, you'll . . . , If you do this, you'll . . .*
- preaching and moralizing messages—*People should all . . . , We all have responsibilities . . .*
- advising messages—*Why don't you . . . , What I think you should do is . . .*

To Stimulate the Speaker to Explore Feelings.   Third, active listening stimulates the speaker to explore his or her feelings and thoughts. For example, Diana's response encourages you to elaborate on your feelings. This opportunity to elaborate also helps you deal with your feelings by talking them through.

TECHNIQUES OF ACTIVE LISTENING   Three simple techniques may help you succeed in active listening: Paraphrase the speaker's meaning, express understanding, and ask questions.

- *Paraphrase the speaker's meaning.* Stating in your own words what you think the speaker means and feels can help ensure understanding and also shows interest in the speaker. Paraphrasing gives the speaker a chance to extend what was originally said. Thus, when Diana echoes your thoughts, you're given the opportunity to elaborate on why rewriting the budget report is so daunting to you.

Paraphrasing to Ensure Understanding

Here are a few messages for which you might want to use paraphrasing to ensure that you understand the speaker's thoughts and feelings. For each message, (a) identify the thoughts and feelings you think the speaker is expressing, and (b) put these thoughts and feelings into a paraphrase.

1. "Did you hear I got engaged to Jerry? Our racial and religious differences are really going to cause difficulties for both of us. But we'll work it through."
2. "I got a C on that paper. That's the worst grade I've ever received. I just can't believe that I got a C. This is my major. What am I going to do?"
3. "That rotten, inconsiderate pig just up and left. He never even said goodbye. We were together for six months and after one small argument he leaves without a word."
4. "I'm just not sure what to do. I really love Sofia. But she really wants to get married. I do too, and yet I don't want to make such a commitment. I really don't need that kind of pressure."

Paraphrasing helps you check your understanding of the speaker and better remember what the speaker said. It also helps reinforce and support the speaker.

But in paraphrasing, be objective; be especially careful not to lead the speaker in the direction you think he or she should go. Also, be careful that you don't overdo paraphrase; only a very small percentage of statements need paraphrasing. Paraphrase when you feel there's a chance for misunderstanding or when you want to express support for the other person and keep the conversation going.

- *Express understanding of the speaker's feelings.* In addition to paraphrasing the content, echo the feelings the speaker expressed or implied ("You must have felt horrible"). This expression of feelings will help you further check your perception of the speaker's feelings. This also will allow the speaker to see his or her feelings more objectively—especially helpful when they're feelings of anger, hurt, or depression—and to elaborate on these feelings.

- *Ask questions.* Asking questions strengthens your own understanding of the speaker's thoughts and feelings and elicits additional information ("How did you feel when you read your job appraisal report?"). Ask questions to provide just enough stimulation and support so the speaker will feel he or she can elaborate on these thoughts and feelings. These questions should further confirm your interest and concern for the speaker but not pry into unrelated areas or challenge the speaker in any way.

Consider this dialogue and note the active listening techniques used throughout:

Pat: That jerk demoted me. He told me I wasn't an effective manager. I can't believe he did that, after all I've done for this place.

Chris: I'm with you. You've been manager for three or four months now, haven't you?

Pat: A little over three months. I know it was probationary, but I thought I was doing a good job.

Chris: Can you get another chance?

Pat: Yes, he said I could try again in a few months. But I feel like a failure.

Chris: I know what you mean. It sucks. What else did he say?

Pat: He said I had trouble getting the paperwork done on time.

Chris: You've been late filing the reports?

Pat: A few times.

Chris: Is there a way to delegate the paperwork?

Pat: No, but I think I know now what needs to be done.

■ **What Do You Say** ?

Listening Actively

Your life partner comes home from work and is visibly upset. Your partner clearly has a need to talk about what happened but simply says, "Work sucks!" You're determined to use active listening techniques. **What Do You Say?** Through what channel?

Chris: You sound as though you're ready to give that manager's position another try.

Pat: Yes, I think I am, and I'm going to let him know that I intend to apply in the next few months.

Even in this brief interaction, Pat has moved from unproductive anger and feelings of failure to a determination to correct an unpleasant situation. Note, too, that Chris didn't offer solutions but "simply" listened actively.

As stressed throughout this discussion, listening is situational; the type of listening that is appropriate varies with the situation. You can visualize a listening situation as one in which you have to make choices among at least the four styles of effective listening just discussed. Each listening situation should call for a somewhat different configuration of listening responses; the art of effective listening is largely one of making appropriate choices along these four dimensions.

Listening, Culture, and Gender

Listening is difficult in part because of the inevitable differences in communication systems between speakers and listeners. Because each person has had a unique set of experiences, each person's communication and meaning system is going to be different from each other person's. When speaker and listener come from different cultures or are of different genders, the differences and their effects are naturally so much greater. Let's look first at culture.

Culture and Listening

The culture in which you were raised will influence your listening in a variety of ways. Here we look at some of these: language and speech, direct and indirect styles, nonverbal differences, and feedback.

Even when speaker and listener speak the same language, they speak it with different meanings and different accents. No two speakers speak exactly the same language. Every speaker speaks an *idiolect:* a unique variation of the language (King &

"I can't get off the phone, he won't stop listening!"

Reprinted by permission of Jerry Marcus.

DiMichael, 1992). Speakers of the same language will, at the very least, have different meanings for the same terms because they have had different experiences.

Speakers and listeners who have different native languages and who may have learned English as a second language will have even greater differences in meaning. Translations are never precise and never fully capture the meaning in the other language. If you learned your meaning for *house* in a culture in which everyone lived in their own house with lots of land around it, then communicating with someone whose meaning was learned in a neighborhood of high-rise tenements is going to be difficult. Although each of you will hear the word *house,* the meanings you'll develop will be drastically different. In adjusting your listening—especially when in an intercultural setting—understand that the speaker's meanings may be very different from yours even though you're speaking the same language.

Some cultures—those of western Europe and the United States, for example—favor **direct speech** in communication; they advise people to "say what you mean and mean what you say." Many Asian cultures, on the other hand, favor **indirect speech;** they emphasize politeness and maintaining a positive public image rather than literal truth. Listen carefully to persons with different styles of directness. Consider the possibility that the meanings the speaker wishes to communicate with, say, indirectness, may be very different from the meanings you would communicate with indirectness.

Another area of difference is that of accents. In many classrooms throughout the United States, there will be a wide range of accents. Those whose native language is a tonal one such as Chinese (in which differences in pitch signal important meaning differences) may speak English with variations in pitch that may be puzzling to others. Those whose native language is Japanese may have trouble distinguishing *l* from *r,* because Japanese does not include this distinction. The native language acts as a filter and influences the accent given to the second language.

Speakers from different cultures also have different *display rules:* cultural rules that govern which nonverbal behaviors are appropriate and which are inappropriate in a public setting. As you listen to other people, you also "listen" to their nonverbals. If these are drastically different from what you expect on the basis of the verbal message, you may perceive a kind of noise or interference or even contradictory messages. Also, of course, different cultures may give very different meanings to the same nonverbal gesture, a topic considered in detail in Chapter 7.

Variations in directness are often especially clear when people give feedback. Members of some cultures tend to give direct and honest feedback. Speakers from these cultures—the United States is a good example—expect feedback to be an honest reflection of what their listeners are feeling. In other cultures—Japan and Korea are good examples—it's more important to be positive than to be truthful; listeners may respond with positive feedback (say, in commenting on a business colleague's proposal) even though they don't feel positive. Listen to feedback, as you would all messages, with a full recognition that various cultures view feedback very differently.

Gender and Listening

Deborah Tannen opened her chapter on listening in her best-selling *You Just Don't Understand: Women and Men in Conversation* (1990) with several anecdotes illustrating that when men and women talk, men lecture and women listen. The lecturer is positioned as the superior—as the teacher, the expert. The listener is positioned as the inferior—as the student, the nonexpert.

Women, according to Tannen, seek to build rapport and establish a closer relationship and so use listening to achieve these ends. For example, women use more listening cues, which let the other person know they are paying attention and are interested. Men not only use fewer listening cues but interrupt more; and they will often change the topic to one they know more about or one that is less relational or people oriented or more factual, such as sports statistics, economic developments, or political problems. Men, research shows, play up their expertise, emphasize it, and use it in dominating the conversation. Women play down their expertise.

Now, you might be tempted to conclude from this that women play fair in conversation and that men don't; for example, that men consistently seek to put themselves in a position superior to women. But that may be too simple an explanation. Research shows that men communicate this way not only with women but also with other men. Men are not showing disrespect for their female conversational partners but are simply communicating as they normally do. Women, too, communicate as they do not only with men but also with other women.

Tannen argues that the goal of a man in conversation is to be accorded respect; so a man seeks to display his knowledge and expertise even if he has to change the topic to one he knows a great deal about. Women, on the other hand, seek to be liked; so a woman expresses interest, rarely interrupts a man to take her turn as speaker, and gives lots of cues (verbally and nonverbally) to indicate that she is listening.

Men and women also show that they are listening in different ways. A woman is more apt to give lots of listening cues, such as interjecting "yeah" or "uh-huh," nodding in agreement, and smiling. Women also make more eye contact when listening than do men, who are more apt to look around and often away from the speaker (Brownell, 2006). A man is more likely to listen quietly without giving lots of listening cues as feedback. Tannen also argues, however, that men do listen less to women than women listen to men. The reason, says Tannen, is that listening places the person in an inferior position, whereas speaking places the person in a superior position.

There is no evidence to show that these differences represent any negative motives—desires on the part of men to prove themselves superior or on the part of women to ingratiate themselves. Rather, these differences in listening are largely the result of the way in which men and women have been socialized.

Further, not all researchers agree that there is sufficient evidence to make the claims that Tannen and others make about gender differences (Goldsmith & Fulfs, 1999). Gender differences are changing drastically and quickly, so it's best to take generalizations about gender as starting points for investigation and not as airtight conclusions.

■ What Do You Say
Giving Listening Cues
People very frequently ask you if they are getting their message across clearly or making sense to you. It seems that they doubt that you're listening. But, usually at least, you are. You need to show people that you are listening to them and are interested in what they're saying. **What Do You Say?** Through what channels?

The Reluctant Listeners

Here is a simple dialogue that illustrates the difficulty people have listening to things they don't want to hear. As you read the dialogue, try to identify the principles of listening that these individuals violate and indicate what they might have done to make listening more effective.

Dialogue *for* Analysis

The Cast

An African-American family.*
Gathee (the father)
Akello (the mother)
Jomo (son, age 16)
Felistas (daughter, age 19)
Pili (son, age 13)

(continues)

(continued)

The Context

The family is watching television.

Gathee: Akello, pass the popcorn; this is great stuff.

Jomo: Hey, Mom, Dad? I need to say something.

Felistas: What's up? Let's hear.

Pili: I need to get new sneakers.

Akello: Oh, I forgot all about them. Let's go on Saturday, and I need to get a new toaster, coffee filters, and a hundred other things.

Gathee: And pick me up some duct tape—a six-roll pack.

Felistas: So, Jomo, you wanted to say something.

Akello: Yes, dear, what is it?

Gathee: You're not getting a car—not until you're eighteen. And not unless you start college.

Jomo: It's not a car. It's me. I don't know how to say this exactly, but I think I'm gay. I mean I am gay. I know I'm gay.

Gathee: Holy shit! You mean you're a faggot? My son is a faggot?

Akello: Hold on, Gathee. He's only sixteen; he doesn't really know what he is. Lots of boys go through this phase.

Jomo: It's not a phase, Mom.

Gathee: Well, it better be a phase—if you want to live in this house, that is.

Pili: Tricia's brother is gay; she told me.

Akello: Pili, don't say things like that.

Felistas: I think it's great that Jomo's come out.

Gathee: Come out! Out where? The neighbors don't know, do they?

Akello: I'm not sure what to say. Do you want to go to therapy? Do you want to get cured?

Jomo: Mom, being gay isn't a disease that you get cured of. I'm gay and I will always be gay.

Akello: But I can't bear to see you unhappy.

Jomo: Mom, I'm not unhappy; I'm gay.

Akello: Well, I don't care; you're not gay; you're going to see Reverend Wilson. You'll see, it'll all work out. You're not gay. He's not gay, Gathee.

Jomo: Mom, I am gay. Aren't you listening?

Gathee: You better not be; no faggot is going to live in this house, under my roof, and eat my food. I'm going to the bar. [exits]

Felistas: So, what's the big deal—he'll listen to Barbra Streisand and sing Broadway show tunes—[sings] "I am what I am and what I am needs no excuses."

Jomo: Felistas! She's kidding, Mom.

Felistas: Yes, Mom, I'm kidding.

Akello: Let's not talk anymore about this. Pili, what kind of sneakers do we have to get?

*It's interesting to know that Africa is a continent of some 870 million people who speak a variety of languages. Some languages are native to Africa, such as Hausa (the most widely spoken, with some 24 million speakers), Swahili, Yoruba, and Ibo. Other languages widely spoken in Africa were brought in largely from Europe, such as English, French, and Spanish. The names of the characters in this dialogue come from Kenya and are largely Swahili in origin. African students make up only about 7 percent of the international student body studying in the United States, a total of about 41,000. Of all the African countries, Kenya sends the most students to study in the United States (about 7,900).

This chapter first defined listening and discussed some of the benefits to be derived from listening; then explored the five stages of listening; next, explained the styles of listening and how best to adjust your listening to achieve maximum effectiveness; and, last, looked at the wide cultural and gender differences in listening.

1. Listening has both task and relationship benefits and serves the same purposes as communication: to learn, to relate, to influence, to play, and to help.
2. Listening may be viewed as a five-step process: receiving, understanding, remembering, evaluating, and responding. Listening difficulties and obstacles exist at each of these stages.
3. Effective listening depends on finding appropriate balances among empathic and objective, nonjudgmental and critical, surface and depth, and active and inactive listening.
4. Cultural differences in accents, in nonverbal behaviors, in directness, and in the feedback people give and expect may create listening difficulties.
5. Men and women seem to listen with different purposes in mind and with different behaviors.

This chapter also covered a wide variety of listening skills. Check those that you wish to work on.

_____ 1. *Receiving*. Focus attention on both the verbal and the nonverbal messages; both communicate essential parts of the total meaning.
_____ 2. *Understanding*. Relate new information to what you already know, ask questions, and paraphrase what you think the speaker said to make sure you understand.
_____ 3. *Remembering*. Identify the central ideas of a message, summarize the message in an easier-to-retain form, and repeat ideas (aloud or to yourself) to help you remember.
_____ 4. *Evaluating*. Try first to understand fully what the speaker means; then look to identify any biases or self-interests that might lead the speaker to give an unfair presentation.
_____ 5. *Responding*. Express support for the speaker by using I-messages instead of you-messages.
_____ 6. *Empathic and objective listening*. Punctuate the interaction from the speaker's point of view, engage in dialogue, and seek to understand the speaker's thoughts and feelings.
_____ 7. *Nonjudgmental and critical listening*. Keep an open mind, avoid filtering out difficult messages, and recognize your own biases. When listening to make judgments, listen extra carefully, ask questions when in doubt, and check your perceptions before criticizing.
_____ 8. *Surface and depth listening*. Focus on both verbal and nonverbal messages, on both content and relationship messages, and on statements that refer back to the speaker. At the same time, do not avoid the surface or literal meaning.
_____ 9. *Active and inactive listening*. Be an active listener: Paraphrase the speaker's meaning, express understanding of the speaker's feelings, and ask questions when necessary.
_____ 10. *Cultural differences in listening*. Be especially flexible when listening in a multicultural setting, realizing that people from other cultures give different listening cues and may operate with different rules for listening.
_____ 11. *Gender differences in listening*. Understand that women give more cues that they're listening and appear more supportive in their listening than men.

Match these terms about listening with their definitions. Record the number of the definition next to the appropriate term.

_____ listening
_____ offensive listening
_____ receiving
_____ empathic listening
_____ supportive listening
_____ backchanneling cues
_____ active listening
_____ memory
_____ paraphrase
_____ evaluating

1. A reconstructive (not a reproductive) process.
2. A process of sending back to the speaker what the listener thinks the speaker means.
3. Hearing.
4. A stage in the listening process in which you make judgments about a message.
5. A restatement of something said in your own words.
6. Listening for ideas to attack.
7. A process of receiving, understanding, remembering, evaluating, and responding to messages.
8. Listening in which you place yourself in the position of the speaker so that you feel as the speaker feels.
9. Responses listeners send back to the speaker as a kind of feedback.
10. Listening without judgment or evaluation; listening for understanding.

1. The term *false memory syndrome* refers to the tendency to "remember" past experiences that never actually occurred. Most of the studies on false memory syndrome have centered on beliefs of abuse and other traumatic experiences. Often these false memories are implanted by therapists and interviewers whose persistent questioning over a period of time creates such a realistic scenario that the individual comes to believe these things actually occurred (Porter, Brit, Yuille, & Lehman, 2000). In what other, less dramatic ways can false memory syndrome occur?

2. Although empathy has an almost universally positive image, some evidence suggests that it also has a negative side. For example, people are most empathic with those who are similar—racially and ethnically as well as in appearance and social status. The more empathy you feel toward members of your own group, the less empathy—and possibly even the more hostility—you probably feel toward members of other groups. The same empathy that increases your understanding of your own group decreases your understanding of other groups. So although empathy may encourage group cohesiveness and identification, it can also create dividing lines between your group and "them" (Angier, 1995). Have you ever experienced or witnessed these negative effects of empathy?

3. The popular belief is that men listen the way they do to prove themselves superior and that women listen as they do to ingratiate themselves. Although there is no evidence to support this belief, it persists in the assumptions people make about the opposite sex. What do you believe accounts for the differences in the way men and women listen?

4. What types of listening would you use (and what types would you not use) in each of the following situations? (A) Your steady dating partner for the last five years tells you that spells of depression are becoming more frequent. (B) An instructor lectures on the contributions of ancient China to modern civilization. (C) A physician discusses your recent physical tests and makes recommendations. (D) A salesperson tells you the benefits of the new computer. (E) A gossip columnist details the life of your favorite celebrity.

MyCommunicationLab Explorations

Explore www.researchnavigator.com to find exercises on listening, including (1) Experiencing Active Listening, (2) Regulating Your Listening Perspective (3) Sequential Communication, (4) Reducing Barriers to Listening, (5) Typical Man, Typical Woman, (6) Paraphrasing to Ensure Understanding, and (7) How Can You Express Empathy? While you're online, you may also want to check out the International Listening Association to get an overview of a professional academic organization devoted to listening; visit www.listen.org.

Also visit MyCommunicationLab for additional study aids, exercises, activities, and video clips on the nature and importance of listening.

Explore our research resources at www.researchnavigator.com.

Research Navigator.com

CHAPTER 6 ■
Verbal Messages

WHY READ THIS CHAPTER?

*B*ecause you'll **learn about:**

- the principles of verbal messages.
- how verbal messages communicate sexism, heterosexism, racism, and ageism.

*B*ecause you'll **learn to:**

- communicate your meanings the way you want them to be communicated.
- regulate your verbal messages to avoid sexism, heterosexism, racism, and ageism.
- avoid the major verbal barriers to critical thinking and mutual understanding.

In interpersonal communication you use two major signal systems—the verbal and the nonverbal. This chapter focuses on the verbal system and covers the principles of verbal messages, the ways in which you use language to confirm or to disconfirm another person, and ways to make your verbal messages more effective. The next chapter focuses on the nonverbal system.

Principles of Verbal Messages

Perhaps the best way to study verbal messages is to examine the principles that govern the way verbal messages work. Here we look at five such principles: (1) Message meanings are in *people;* (2) verbal messages are both denotative and connotative and communicate objective meanings as well as attitudes and values; (3) messages vary in directness; (4) messages vary in abstraction; and (5) messages vary in assertiveness.

Message Meanings Are in People

If you wanted to know the meaning of the word *love,* you'd probably turn to a dictionary. There you'd find, according to Webster's: "the attraction, desire, or affection felt for a person who arouses delight or admiration or elicits tenderness, sympathetic interest, or benevolence." This is the denotative meaning.

But where would you turn if you wanted to know what Pedro means when he says, "I'm in love"? Of course, you'd turn to Pedro to discover his meaning. It's in this sense that meanings are not in words but in people. Consequently, to uncover meaning, you need to look into people and not merely into words.

Also, recognize that as you change, you also change the meanings you created out of past messages. Thus, although the message sent may not change, the meanings you created from it yesterday and the meanings you create today may be quite different. Yesterday, when a special someone said, "I love you," you created certain meanings. But today, when you learn that the same "I love you" was said to three other people, or when you fall in love with someone else, you drastically change the meanings you draw from those three words.

Messages Are Denotative and Connotative

Two general types of meaning are essential to identify: denotation and connotation. The term **denotation** refers to the meaning you'd find in a dictionary; it's the meaning that members of the culture assign to a word. **Connotation** is the emotional meaning that specific speakers/listeners give to a word. Take as an example the word *death.* To a doctor this word might mean (denote) the time when the heart stops. This is an objective description of a particular event. On the other hand, to a mother who is informed of her son's death, the word means (connotes) much more. It recalls her son's youth, ambitions, family, illness, and so on. To her *death* is a highly emotional, subjective, and personal word. These emotional, subjective, or personal associations make up the word's connotative meaning. The denotation of a word is its objective definition. The connotation of a word is its subjective or emotional meaning.

Semanticist S. I. Hayakawa (Hayakawa & Hayakawa, 1989) coined the terms "snarl words" and "purr words" to further clarify

““ It is not only true that the language we use puts words in our mouths; it also puts notions in our heads. ””
—Wendell Johnson

the distinction between denotative and connotative meaning. Snarl words are highly negative ("She's an idiot," "He's a pig," "They're a bunch of losers"). Sexist, racist, heterosexist, and ageist language, and hate speech generally, provide lots of other examples. Purr words are highly positive ("She's a real sweetheart," "He's a dream," "They're the greatest").

Snarl and purr words, although they may sometimes seem to have denotative meaning and to refer to the "real world," are actually connotative in meaning. These terms do not describe people or events in the real world but rather reflect the speaker's feelings about these people or events. Compare the term *migrants* (used to designate Mexicans coming into the United States to better their economic condition) with the term *settlers* (used to designate Europeans who came to the United States for the same reason) (Koppelman with Goodhart, 2005). Though both terms describe people engaged in essentially the same activity (and are essentially the same denotatively), one label is often negatively evaluated and the other is more often positively valued (so that the terms differ widely in their connotations).

Messages Vary in Directness

Consider your own tendency to be direct or indirect. Imagine you're talking with a friend. Of the seven paired sentences below, how many would you use from the Indirect column? How many from the Direct column?

Indirect Messages	Direct Messages
Would you like to watch a movie?	I'd like to watch a movie.
I'd really like some ice cream.	Would you get me a plate of ice cream?
Isn't it chilly in here?	Jenny, please close the window.
It must have been expensive.	How much did you pay?

E-Talk
Irony
One of the differences often predicted between computer-mediated and face-to-face interaction has been that irony (subtle sarcasm, such as calling a poorly reasoned argument "a brilliant deduction" or a dead-end job "the fast track") would be used less in CMC largely because of the absence of nonverbal cues and the greater likelihood of miscommunication. In at least one study, however, the exact opposite was found (Hancock, 2004). What reasons might you offer to account for this counterintuitive result?

Ethical *messages*

Lying

Lying occurs when "one person intends to mislead another, doing so deliberately, without prior notification of this purpose, and without having been explicitly asked to do so by the target [the person the liar intends to mislead]" (Ekman, 1985b, p. 28). As this definition makes clear, a person can lie by omission (leaving out crucial information) as well as by commission (saying something you know to be false) (Bok, 1978).

Similarly, although most lies are verbal, some are nonverbal—and most seem to involve at least some nonverbal elements. Common examples of nonverbal lying include the innocent facial expression and focused eye contact despite the consciousness of unethical behavior and the knowing nod despite the inner awareness of ignorance. And, of course, some lies occur face-to-face and others online—self-misrepresentation in chat rooms and on dating services is perhaps the most obvious example.

What Would You Do?

On the basis of your own ethical beliefs about lying, which probably are greatly influenced by your culture, what would you do in the following situations? Would you

- lie to make another person feel good? For example, would you tell someone that he or she looked great or had a great sense of humor even if these statements were factually untrue?
- lie to enable another person to save face? For example, would you voice agreement with an idea you found foolish, say you enjoyed meeting a person when you didn't, or praise someone's work when the praise was totally undeserved?
- lie to get what you deserved but couldn't get any other way? For example, would you lie to get a well-earned promotion, a raise, or another chance with your relationship partner?
- lie to get yourself out of an unpleasant situation? For example, would you lie to get out of an unwanted date, an extra office chore, or a boring conversation?

Indirect Messages	Direct Messages
I really need to find someone to mind the dog for the weekend.	Would you mind watching my dog next weekend?
Doing anything this weekend?	I'd like to go to the movies; want to come?
Phone's ringing.	Would you please answer the phone?

The messages in the *Indirect* column, in large part, attempt to get the listener to say or do something without committing the speaker. The messages in the *Direct* column, on the other hand, express the speaker's preferences clearly and/or ask the listener to do or say something. (Note that direct and indirect messages also can be nonverbal. For example, to communicate that it's late, you might use an indirect message such as glancing at your watch; or you might use a more direct message such as getting up and putting on your jacket.)

ADVANTAGES AND DISADVANTAGES OF INDIRECT MESSAGES   Indirect messages have both advantages and disadvantages. On the positive side, indirect messages can allow you to express a thought without insulting or offending anyone; they allow you to observe the rules of polite interaction. So instead of saying, "I'm bored with this group," you say, "It's getting late, and I have to get up early tomorrow." Instead of saying, "This food tastes like cardboard," you say, "I just started my diet" or "I just ate." In each instance, you're stating a preference indirectly so as to avoid offending someone. Not all direct messages, however, are impolite. The examples in the Direct column above, for example, would not be considered impolite. One study of Spanish and English speakers, for example, found no evidence to support the assumption that politeness and directness were incompatible (Mir, 1993).

Sometimes indirect messages allow you to ask for compliments in a socially acceptable manner. A person who says, "I was thinking of getting a nose job" may hope to get the response, "A nose job? You? Your nose is perfect." Indirect messages, however, also have disadvantages and can create problems. Consider the following dialogue:

> **Pat:** You wouldn't like to have my parents over for dinner this weekend, would you?
> **Chris:** I really wanted to go to the shore and just relax.
> **Pat:** Well, if you feel you have to go to the shore, I'll make the dinner myself. You go to the shore. I really hate having them over and doing all the work myself. It's such a drag shopping, cooking, and cleaning all by myself.

Given this situation, Chris has two basic alternatives. One is to stick with the plan to go to the shore and relax. If this happens, Pat is going to be upset and Chris is going to feel guilty for not helping with the dinner. A second alternative is to give in to Pat, help with the dinner, and not go to the shore. In this outcome, Chris is going to have to give up a much-desired plan and is likely to resent Pat's "manipulative" tactics. Regardless of which decision is made, this "win–lose" strategy creates resentment, competition, and often an "I'll get even" attitude. With direct requests, this type of situation is much less likely to develop. Consider:

> **Pat:** I'd like to have my parents over for dinner this weekend. What do you think?
> **Chris:** Well, I really wanted to go to the shore and just relax.

Regardless of what develops next, both individuals are starting out on relatively equal footing. Each has clearly and directly stated a wish. Although at first these wishes seem mutually exclusive, it may be possible to fulfill both persons' desires. For example, Chris might say, "How about going to the shore this weekend and having your parents over next weekend? I'm really exhausted; I could use the rest." Here is a direct response to a direct request. Unless there is some pressing need to have

■ **What Do You Say**❓
Confronting a Lie
You ask about the previous night's whereabouts of your romantic partner of two years and are told something you know beyond any doubt to be false. You don't want to break up the relationship over this, but you do want the truth and an opportunity to resolve the problems that contributed to this situation. **What Do You Say?** Through what channel?

Pat's parents over for dinner this weekend, this response may enable each partner to meet the other's needs.

GENDER AND CULTURAL DIFFERENCES IN DIRECTNESS A popular stereotype in much of the United States holds that women are indirect in making requests and in giving orders—and that this indirectness communicates powerlessness, a discomfort with authority. Men, the stereotype continues, are direct, sometimes to the point of being blunt or rude. This directness communicates men's power and comfort with their own authority.

Deborah Tannen (1994b) provides an interesting perspective on these stereotypes. Women are, it seems, more indirect in giving orders; they are more likely to say, for example, "It would be great if these letters could go out today" rather than "Have these letters out by three." But Tannen (1994b, p. 84) argues that "issuing orders indirectly can be the prerogative of those in power" and in no way shows powerlessness. Power, to Tannen, is the ability to choose your own style of communication.

"" The finest language is mostly made up of simple, unimposing words. ""
—George Eliot

Listen to This

Listening to Gender Differences

Think about your own beliefs about gender differences in language. Your beliefs are important, because these beliefs influence what you hear (or think you hear) and the interpretations you give to what you hear.

Here are 10 phrases that have been used to describe "women's speech." Which do you think are accurate?

1. emotional rather than logical
2. vague and ambiguous
3. sprawling, tending to jump from one idea to another
4. highly personal and unbusinesslike
5. more polite than men's speech
6. weak (for example, uses weak intensifiers like *so* and *such* and few exclamations)
7. oriented toward seeking permission by, for example, using tag questions (as in "Let's meet at ten o'clock, *OK*?")
8. more euphemistic than men's speech (containing more polite words as substitutes for taboo or potentially offensive terms) and using less slang and swear terms
9. less effective than men's speech generally
10. less forceful and less in control than men's speech

These 10 characteristics were drawn from the research of Cheris Kramarae (1974a, 1974b, 1977, 1981; also see Coates & Cameron, 1989; Gamble & Gamble, 2003; and Stewart, Cooper, Stewart, with Friedley, 2003). There is some evidence to support "true" for numbers 5, 7, and 8; women's speech often is more polite and does contain more "tag" questions. The other phrases are likely more stereotypes than actual descriptions.

Applying Listening Skills

James is convinced that women's speech is exactly as described in these 10 statements and admits that because of this he has difficulty listening fairly and openly to women, both on the job and in his personal interactions. What listening skills would you suggest James learn?

■ **What Do You Say**

Rejecting Directly

A colleague at work repeatedly asks you out, but you're just not interested in dating this person. You've used every polite excuse in the book and now feel you have to be more direct and more honest; at the same time, you don't want to alienate or insult your colleague. **What Do You Say?** To whom? Through what channel?

Men, moreover, also are indirect—but in different situations (Rundquist, 1992). According to Tannen, men are more likely to use indirectness when they express weakness, reveal a problem, or admit an error. Men also are more likely to speak indirectly in expressing emotions (other than anger). In addition, men are more indirect when they shrink from expressions of increased romantic intimacy. Men are thus indirect, the theory goes, when they're saying something that goes against the masculine stereotype.

Many Asian and Latin American cultures stress the values of indirectness, largely because indirectness enables a person to avoid being overtly critical or contradicting others and thereby causing others to lose face. An example of a somewhat different kind of indirectness is the greater use of intermediaries to resolve conflict among the Chinese than among North Americans (Ma, 1992). In most of the United States, however, you're taught that directness is the preferred style. "Be up-front" and "Tell it like it is" are commonly heard communication guidelines. Contrast these with the following two Japanese principles of indirectness (Tannen, 1994b):

- *Omoiyari,* a concept close to empathy, says that a listener needs to understand the speaker without the speaker's being specific or direct.

- *Sassuru* advises listeners to anticipate a speaker's meanings and to use subtle cues from the speaker to infer his or her total meaning.

In thinking about direct and indirect messages, it's important to be aware of the ease with which misunderstandings can occur. For example, a person who uses an indirect style of speech may be doing so to be polite and may have been taught this style by his or her culture. If you assume, because of your own culture, that the person is using indirectness to be manipulative, then miscommunication is inevitable.

Messages Vary in Abstraction

Abstract terms refer to concepts and ideas that have no physical dimensions (freedom, love, happiness, equality, democracy). **Concrete terms,** on the other hand, refer to objects, people, and happenings that you perceive with your senses of sight, smell, touch, hearing, or taste. But between these extremes are degrees of abstraction. Consider the following list of terms:

- entertainment
- film
- American film
- classic American suspense film
- *Psycho*

At the top is the general or abstract word *entertainment.* Note that the category "entertainment" includes all the other items on the list plus various other items—television, novels, drama, comics, and so on. The next term, *film,* is more specific and concrete. It includes all of the items below it as well as various other items such as Indian film or Russian film. It excludes, however, all entertainment that is not film. *American film* is again more specific than *film* and excludes all films that are not American. *Classic American suspense film* further limits American film to a genre and time period. *Psycho* specifies concretely the one item to which reference is made.

A verbal message that uses the most general term—in this case, *entertainment*—will conjure up many different images in listeners' minds. One person may focus on television, another on music, another on comic books, and still another on radio. To some listeners the word *film* may bring to mind the early silent films; to others it may connote high-tech special effects; to still others it will recall Disney's animated cartoons. *Psycho* guides listeners still further—in this case, to one film. But note that

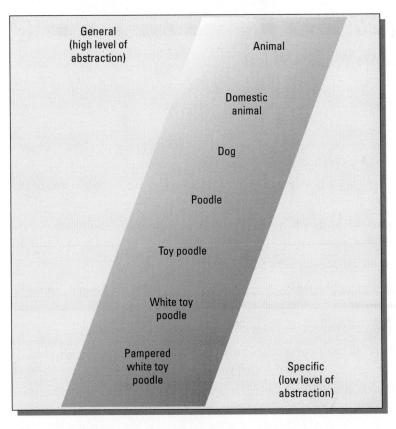

Figure 6.1
The Abstraction Ladder
As you go up in abstraction, you get more general; as you go down in abstraction, you get more specific. How would you arrange the following terms in order of abstraction, from most specific to most general: vegetation, tree, elm tree, thing, organic thing, blooming elm tree?

even though *Psycho* identifies a specific film, different listeners are likely to focus on different aspects of the film: perhaps its theme, perhaps the acting, perhaps its financial success. So, as you get more specific—less abstract—you more effectively guide the images that come to your listeners' minds.

Effective verbal messages include words that range widely in abstractness (Figure 6.1). At times a general term may suit your needs best; at other times a more specific term may serve better. The widely accepted recommendation for effective communication is to use abstractions sparingly and to express your meanings explicitly with words that are low in abstraction. However, are there situations in which terms high in abstraction would be more effective than concrete terms? How would you describe advertisements for cosmetics in terms of high and low abstraction? Advertisements for cereals? Advertisements for cat and dog food? How would you describe a political campaign speech in terms of abstraction?

Messages Vary in Assertiveness

Assertive messages express your real thoughts—even if they involve disagreeing or arguing with others—but are nevertheless respectful of the other person. Consider your own message behavior. If you disagree with other people in a group, do you speak your mind? Do you allow others to take advantage of you because you're reluctant to say what you want? Do you feel uncomfortable when you have to state your opinion in a group? Questions such as these revolve around your degree of **assertiveness**. Increasing your level of assertiveness will enable you to deal with these experiences positively and productively. Before reading further about this type of communication, take the self-test on the following page.

Test *Yourself* ■ ■■ ■ ■ ■■ ■ ■ ■ ■ ■ ■ ☑

How Assertive Are Your Messages?

INSTRUCTIONS: Indicate how true each of the following statements is about your own communication. Respond instinctively rather than in the way you feel you should respond. Use a scale on which

5 = always or almost always true; **4** = usually true; **3** = sometimes true, sometimes false; **2** = usually false; and **1** = always or almost always false.

_____ ❶ I would express my opinion in a group even if it contradicted the opinions of others.

_____ ❷ When asked to do something that I really don't want to do, I can say no without feeling guilty.

_____ ❸ I can express my opinion to my superiors on the job.

_____ ❹ I can start up a conversation with a stranger on a bus or at a business gathering without fear.

_____ ❺ I voice objection to people's behavior if I feel it infringes on my rights.

HOW DID YOU DO? All five items in this test identify characteristics of assertive communication. So high scores (say about 20 and above) would indicate a high level of assertiveness. Low scores (say about 10 and below) would indicate a low level of assertiveness.

WHAT WILL YOU DO? The remaining discussion in this section clarifies the nature of assertive communication and offers guidelines for increasing your own assertiveness. These suggestions can help you not only to increase your assertiveness but also, when appropriate, to reduce your aggressive tendencies.

☑

NONASSERTIVE, AGGRESSIVE, AND ASSERTIVE MESSAGES   In addition to identifying some specific assertive behaviors (as in the self-test above), we can further understand the nature of assertive communication by distinguishing it from nonassertiveness and aggressiveness (Alberti, 1977).

Nonassertive Messages.   The term *nonassertiveness* refers to a lack of assertiveness in certain types of (or even in all) communication situations. People who are nonassertive fail to stand up for their rights. In many instances these people do what others tell them to do—parents, employers, and the like—without questioning and without concern for what is best for them. They operate with a "you win, I lose" philosophy; they give others what they want without concern for themselves (Lloyd, 2001). Nonassertive people often ask permission from others to do what is their perfect right. Social situations create anxiety for these individuals, and their self-esteem is generally low.

Aggressive Messages.   *Aggressiveness* is the other extreme. Aggressive people operate with an "I win, you lose" philosophy; they care little for what the other person wants and focus only on their own needs. Some people communicate aggressively only under certain conditions or in certain situations (for example, after being taken advantage of over a long period of time); others communicate aggressively in all or at least most situations. Aggressive communicators think little of the opinions, values, or beliefs of others and yet are extremely sensitive to others' criticisms of their own behavior. Consequently, they frequently get into arguments with others.

Assertive Messages.   Assertive behavior—behavior that enables you to act in your own best interests without denying or infringing on the rights of others—is the gen-

E-Talk ∙ ▪ ∙ ▪ ∙ ▪ ∙

Assertiveness

How would you describe the level of assertiveness you use when talking face-to-face versus the level you use in e-mail and chat rooms? If you notice differences, to what do you attribute them?

erally desired alternative to nonassertiveness (which wil prevent you from expressing yourself) or aggressiveness (which will create resentment and conflict). Assertive people operate with an "I win, you win" philosophy; they assume that both people can gain something from an interpersonal interaction, even from a confrontation. Assertive people are willing to assert their own rights without hurting others in the process. Assertive people speak their minds and welcome others' doing likewise.

People who are assertive in interpersonal communication display four major behavior patterns (Norton & Warnick, 1976). To what extent do these patterns apply to you? Do you:

- *express your feelings frankly and openly to people in general as well as to those in whom you may have a romantic interest?*
- *volunteer opinions and beliefs and deal directly with interpersonal communication situations that may be stressful, and question others without fear?*
- *stand up and argue for your rights, even if this may entail a certain degree of disagreement or conflict with relatives or close friends?*
- *make up your own mind on the basis of evidence and argument instead of just accepting what others say?*

" Language exerts hidden power, like a moon on the tides. "

—Rita Mae Brown

Research shows that people who are assertive generally answer yes to these questions. Assertive people are more open, less anxious, more contentious, and less likely to be intimidated or easily persuaded than nonassertive people. Assertive people also are more positive and more hopeful than nonassertive people (Velting, 1999). People who are low in assertiveness generally answer no to the questions above. Such unassertive people are less open, more anxious, less contentious, and more likely to be intimidated and easily persuaded.

Table 6.1 contrasts assertive and aggressive styles in several aspects of interpersonal communication.

PRINCIPLES FOR INCREASING ASSERTIVENESS   Most people are nonassertive in certain situations. If you're one of these people and if you wish to modify your behavior in some situations, there are steps you can take to increase your assertiveness. (If you're

TABLE 6.1	Assertive and Aggressive Messages

As you read this table, consider your customary ways of interacting, especially when you feel angry or threatened. How often do you use assertive messages? How often do you use aggressive messages?

ASSERTIVE MESSAGES	AGGRESSIVE MESSAGES
I-messages that accept responsibility for your own feelings (*I feel angry when you . . .*)	You-messages that attribute your feelings to others (*You make me angry when you. . .*)
Descriptive and realistic expressions (*Last Saturday, you . . .*)	Allness and extreme expressions (*You never . . . ; you always . . .*)
Equality messages that recognize the essential equality of oneself and others (*We need to . . .*)	Inequality messages that may be insulting or condescending (*You don't know . . .*)
Relaxed and erect body posture	Tense or overly rigid posture
Expressive and genuine facial expressions; focused but not threatening eye contact	Unexpressive or overly hostile facial expressions; intense eye contact or excessive eye-contact avoidance
Normal vocal volume and rhythm pattern	Overly soft or overly loud and accusatory tone

nonassertive always and everywhere and are unhappy about this, then you may need to work with a therapist to change your behavior.)

Analyze Assertive Messages.   The first step in increasing your assertiveness skills is to understand the nature of these communications. Observe and analyze the messages of others. Learn to distinguish the differences among assertive, aggressive, and nonassertive messages. Focus on what makes one behavior assertive and another behavior nonassertive or aggressive.

After you've gained some skills in observing the behaviors of others, turn your analysis to yourself. Analyze situations in which you're normally assertive and situations in which you're more likely to act nonassertively or aggressively. What circumstances characterize these situations? What do the situations in which you're normally assertive have in common? How do you speak? How do you communicate nonverbally?

Rehearse Assertive Messages.   To rehearse assertiveness, select a situation in which you're normally nonassertive. Build a ladder (or hierarchy) whose first step is a relatively nonthreatening message, and whose second step would be a bit more risky but still safe, and so on until the final step, the desired communication. For example, let us say that you have difficulty voicing your opinion to your supervisor at work. The desired behavior, then, is to tell your supervisor your opinions. Construct a ladder or hierarchy of situations leading up to this desired behavior. Such a hierarchy might begin with visualizing yourself talking with your boss. Visualize this scenario until you can do it without any anxiety or discomfort. Once you have mastered this visualization, visualize a step closer to your goal; say, walking into your boss's office. Again, do this until your visualization creates no discomfort. Continue with these successive visualizations until you can visualize yourself telling your boss your opinion. As with the other visualizations, practice this until you can do it while totally relaxed. This is the mental rehearsal.

You might add a vocal dimension to this by actually acting out (with voice and gesture) your telling your boss your opinion. Again, do this until you experience no difficulty or discomfort. Next, try doing this in front of a trusted and supportive friend or group of friends. Ideally this interaction will provide you with useful feedback. After this rehearsal, you're probably ready for the next step: putting assertiveness into action.

Communicate Assertively.   Communicating assertively is naturally the most difficult step, but obviously the most important. Here's a generally effective pattern to follow:

1. Describe the problem; don't evaluate or judge it. "We're all working on this advertising project together. You're missing half our meetings, and you still haven't produced your first report."

2. State how this problem affects you. Be sure to use I-messages and to avoid messages that accuse or blame the other person. "My job depends on the success of this project, and I don't think it's fair that I have to do extra work to make up for what you're not doing."

3. Propose solutions that are workable and that allow the person to save face. "If you can get your report to the group by Tuesday, we'll still be able to meet our deadline. And I could give you a call an hour before the meetings to remind you."

4. Confirm understanding. "Is it clear that we just can't produce this project if you're not going to pull your own weight? Will you have the report to us by Tuesday?"

5. Reflect on your own assertiveness. Think about what you did. How did you express yourself verbally and nonverbally? What would you do differently next time?

■ **What Do You Say** ?
Acting Assertively
The person you've been dating for the last few months is wonderful and you're looking forward to continuing this relationship. The only problem is that your partner uses language more vulgar than you can stand. You've expressed your displeasure about this, but nothing has changed. You need to be more assertive. **What Do You Say?** Through what channel?

Practicing Assertiveness

For any one of the following situations, write (a) an aggressive, (b) a nonassertive, and (c) an assertive response. Then, in one sentence of 15 words or less, explain why your assertiveness message will prove more effective than the aggressive or nonassertive message.

1. You've just redecorated your apartment, expending considerable time and money in making it exactly as you want it. A good friend of yours brings you a house gift—the ugliest poster you've ever seen—and insists that you hang it over your fireplace, the focal point of your living room.
2. A friend borrows $30 and promises to pay you back tomorrow. But tomorrow passes, as do 20 subsequent tomorrows, and there is still no sign of the money. You know that your friend has not forgotten about the debt, and you also know that the person has more than enough money to pay you back.
3. A next-door neighbor repeatedly asks you to take care of her four-year-old while she runs some errand or another. You don't mind helping out in an emergency, but this occurs almost every day. You feel you're being taken advantage of and simply do not want to do this anymore.

Assertiveness is the most direct and honest response in situations such as these. Usually it's also the most effective.

Be cautious, however. It's easy to visualize a situation in which, for example, people are talking behind you in a movie and, with your newfound enthusiasm for assertiveness, you tell them to be quiet. It's also easy to see yourself getting smashed in the teeth as a result. In applying the principles of assertive communication, be careful that you do not go beyond what you can handle effectively.

Confirmation and Disconfirmation

The terms *confirmation* and *disconfirmation* refer to the extent to which you acknowledge another person. **Disconfirmation** is a communication pattern in which you ignore someone's presence as well as that person's communications. You say, in effect, that this person and what this person has to say are not worth serious attention or effort; that this person and this person's contributions are so unimportant or insignificant that there is no reason to concern yourself with them.

Note that disconfirmation is not the same as **rejection.** In rejection you acknowledge but disagree with the person; you indicate your unwillingness to accept something the other person says or does. In disconfirming someone, however, you deny that person's significance; you claim that what this person says or does simply does not count.

Confirmation is the opposite communication pattern. In **confirmation** you not only acknowledge the presence of the other person but also indicate your acceptance of this person, of this person's self-definition, and of your relationship as defined or viewed by this other person.

Consider this situation. You've been living with someone for the last six months and you arrive home late one night. Your partner, let's say Pat, is angry and complains about your being so late. Which of the following is most likely to be your response?

- Stop screaming. I'm not interested in what you're babbling about. I'll do what I want, when I want. I'm going to bed.
- What are you so angry about? Didn't you get in three hours late last Thursday when you went to that office party? So knock it off.

■ **What Do You Say** ❓
Discouraging Disconfirmation
For the last several months you've noticed how disconfirming your neighbors are toward their preteen children; it seems the children can never do anything to the parents' satisfaction. You'd like to make your neighbors more aware of their communication patterns and the possible negative effect these might have, but at the same time you don't want to appear the nosy, intrusive neighbor. **What Do You Say?** To Whom? Through what channel?

- You have a right to be angry. I should have called to tell you I was going to be late, but I got involved in an argument at work, and I couldn't leave until it was resolved.

In the first response, you dismiss Pat's anger and even indicate dismissal of Pat as a person. In the second response, you reject the validity of Pat's reasons for being angry but do not dismiss either Pat's feelings of anger or Pat as a person. In the third response, you acknowledge Pat's anger and the reasons for it. In addition, you provide some kind of explanation and, in doing so, show that both Pat's feelings and Pat as a person are important and that Pat has the right to know what happened. The first response is an example of disconfirmation, the second of rejection, and the third of confirmation.

You can gain insight into a wide variety of offensive language practices by viewing them as types of disconfirmation—as language that alienates and separates. One such practice is "ableism," or discrimination against people with disabilities. This particular practice is handled throughout this text in a series of tables offering tips for communication between people with and without a variety of disabilities. These tables address communication

- between blind and sighted people (Chapter 1);
- between people with and without disabilities (Chapter 2);
- between deaf and hearing people (Chapter 5); and
- between people with and without speech and language disorders (Chapter 8).

Skill Building *exercise*

Confirming, Rejecting, and Disconfirming

For each of the following scenarios, (1) write a confirming, a rejecting, and a disonfirming response, and (2) indicate what effects each type of response is likely to generate.

1. Enrique receives this semester's grades in the mail; they're a lot better than previous semesters' grades but are still not great. After opening the letter, Enrique says: "I really tried hard to get my grades up this semester." Enrique's parents respond:

   With disconfirmation

   With rejection

   With confirmation

2. Pat, who has been out of work for the past several weeks, says: "I feel like such a failure; I just can't seem to find a job. I've been pounding the pavement for the last five weeks and still nothing." Pat's friend responds:

   With disconfirmation

   With rejection

   With confirmation

3. Judy's colleague at work comes to her, overjoyed, and tells her that she has just been promoted to vice president of marketing, skipping three steps in the hierarchy and tripling her salary. Judy responds:

   With disconfirmation

   With rejection

   With confirmation

Although each type of response serves a different purpose, confirming responses seem most likely to promote communication satisfaction.

Here we'll consider four additional disconfirming practices—racism, heterosexism, ageism, and sexism. We'll then look at preferred "cultural identifiers," or confirming language practices, that are recommended for use with many groups.

Racism

Racism—like all the "isms" discussed in this section—exists on both an individual and an institutional level, as pointed out by educational researchers Kent Koppelman and R. Lee Goodhart (2005) and others. *Individual* racism consists of negative attitudes and beliefs that people hold about specific races or ethnic groups. The assumption that certain groups are intellectually inferior to others or are incapable of certain achievements are clear examples of individual racism. Prejudices against American Indians, African Americans, Hispanics, Arabs, and others have existed throughout history and are still a part of many people's lives today.

Institutionalized racism is seen in organizational behaviors such as de facto school segregation, corporations' reluctance to hire members of minority groups, and banks' unwillingness to extend mortgages and business loans to members of some groups or residents of some neighborhoods. Racial profiling, in which people become crime suspects solely because of their apparent race, is another form of institutionalized racism.

Racist language is used by members of one culture to disparage members of other cultures, their customs, or their accomplishments. Racist language emphasizes differences rather than similarities and separates rather than unites members of different cultures. Generally, the dominant group uses racist language to establish and maintain power over other groups.

According to Andrea Rich (1974), "any language that, through a conscious or unconscious attempt by the user, places a particular racial or ethnic group in an inferior position is racist." Racist language expresses racist attitudes. It also, however, contributes to the development of racist attitudes in those who use or hear the language. Even when racism is subtle, unintentional, or even unconscious, its effects are systematically damaging (Dovidio, Gaertner, Kawakami, & Hodson, 2002).

Examine your own language racism. Do you:

- *use derogatory terms for members of a particular race or group of people?*
- *interact with members of other races through stereotypes perpetuated by the media?*
- *include reference to race when it's irrelevant, as in referring to "an African American surgeon" or "an Asian athlete"?*
- *attribute economic or social problems to the race of individuals rather than to institutionalized racism or to general economic problems that affect everyone?*

Heterosexism

Heterosexism also exists on both an individual and an institutional level. On an individual level, the term **heterosexism** refers to attitudes, behaviors, and language that disparage gay men and lesbians and in the belief that all sexual behavior that is not heterosexual is unnatural and deserving of criticism and condemnation. Beliefs such as these are at the heart of antigay violence and "gay bashing." Individual heterosexism also includes such beliefs as the ideas that homosexuals are more likely to commit crimes (there's actually no difference) and to molest children than are heterosexuals (actually, heterosexual married men are overwhelmingly the child molesters) (Abel & Harlow, 2001; Koppelman with Goodhart, 2005). It also includes the belief that homosexuals cannot maintain stable relationships or effectively raise children, beliefs that contradict research evidence (Fitzpatrick, Jandt, Myrick, & Edgar, 1994; Johnson & O'Connor, 2002).

■ What Do You Say

Hate Speech

Your work colleagues frequently use derogatory racial terms. You want to protest this kind of talk, but at the same time you don't want to alienate people you're going to have to work closely with for some time to come. **What Do You Say?** To whom? Through what channel?

What Do You Say
Homophobia

You're bringing your college roommate home for the holidays; he's an outspoken gay activist whereas your family is extremely homophobic, though you suspect it's largely because of a lack of knowledge. You want to prepare your family and your roommate for their holiday get-together. **What Do You Say?** To whom? Through what channel?

Institutional heterosexism is easy to identify. For example, the ban on gay marriage in many states and the fact that at this time only one state (Massachusetts) allows gay marriage is a good example of institutional heterosexism. Other examples include the Catholic Church's ban on homosexual priests, the U.S. military's "don't ask, don't tell" policy, and the many laws prohibiting adoption of children by gay people. In some countries homosexual relations are illegal (for example, in India, Liberia, Malaysia, Pakistan, and Singapore) and carry penalties ranging from a misdemeanor-level punishment in Liberia to life in jail in Singapore and death in Pakistan.

Heterosexist language includes derogatory terms used for lesbians and gay men. For example, surveys in the military showed that 80 percent of those surveyed had heard "offensive speech, derogatory names, jokes or remarks about gays" and that 85 percent believed that such derogatory speech was "tolerated" (*New York Times*, March 25, 2000, p. A12). You also see heterosexism in more subtle forms of language usage; for example, when you qualify a professional—as in "gay athlete" or "lesbian doctor"—and, in effect, say that athletes and doctors are not normally gay or lesbian.

Still another instance of heterosexism is the presumption of heterosexuality. Usually, people assume the person they're talking to or about is heterosexual. And usually they're correct, because most people are heterosexual. At the same time, however, this presumption denies the lesbian or gay identity a certain legitimacy. The practice is very similar to the presumptions of whiteness and maleness that we have made significant inroads in eliminating.

Here are a few additional suggestions for avoiding heterosexist (or what some call homophobic) language. Do you:

- *avoid offensive nonverbal mannerisms that parody stereotypes when talking about gay men and lesbians? Do you use the "startled eye blink" with which some people react to gay couples (Mahaffey, Bryan, & Hutchison, 2005)?*

- *avoid "complimenting" gay men and lesbians by saying that they "don't look it"? To gay men and lesbians, this is not a compliment. Similarly, expressing disappointment that a person is gay—often intended to be complimentary, as in comments such as "What a waste!"—is not really flattering.*

- *avoid making the assumption that every gay or lesbian knows what every other gay or lesbian is thinking? It's very similar to asking a Japanese person why Sony is investing heavily in the United States or, as one comic put it, asking an African American, "What do you think Jesse Jackson meant by that last speech?"*

- *avoid denying individual differences? Comments like "Lesbians are so loyal" or "Gay men are so open with their feelings," which ignore the reality of wide differences within every group, are potentially insulting to members of any group.*

- *avoid overattribution, the tendency to attribute just about everything a person does, says, and believes to the fact that the person is gay or lesbian? This tendency helps to activate and perpetuate stereotypes.*

- *remember that relationship milestones are important to all people? Ignoring anniversaries or birthdays of, say, a relative's partner is likely to cause hurt and resentment.*

As you think about heterosexism, recognize that using heterosexist language will create barriers to communication. In contrast, refraining from heterosexist language will foster more meaningful communication: Your listeners will respond with greater comfort, an increased willingness to disclose personal information, and a greater willingness to engage in future interactions (Dorland & Fisher, 2001).

Ageism

Ageism is discrimination based on age and also comes in individual and institutionalized forms. On an individual level ageism is seen in the general disrespect many have for older people. More specifically, it's seen in negative stereotypes that many people have about those who are older.

Although used mainly to refer to prejudice against older people, the word *ageism* can also refer to prejudice against other age groups. For example, if you describe all teenagers as selfish and undependable, you're discriminating against a group purely because of their age and thus are ageist in your statements. In some cultures—some Asian and some African cultures, for example—the old are revered and respected. Younger people seek them out for advice on economic, ethical, and relationship issues.

Institutional ageism is seen in mandatory retirement laws and in age restrictions in certain occupations, such as those of pilot or air traffic controller (which impose age cutoffs rather than basing requirements on demonstrated competence). In some countries people in their 70s are not able to rent cars. In less obvious forms, institutional ageism is seen in the media's portrayal of old people as incompetent, complaining, and—perhaps most clearly evidenced in television and films—without romantic feelings. Rarely, for example, do TV shows or films show older people working productively, being cooperative and pleasant, and engaging in romantic and sexual relationships.

Popular language is replete with ageist phrases; as with racist and heterosexist language, we can all provide plenty of examples. Similarly, qualifying a description of someone in terms of his or her age demonstrates ageism. For example, if you refer to "a quick-witted 75-year-old" or "an agile 65-year-old" or "a responsible teenager," you are implying that these qualities are unusual in people of these ages and thus need special mention. You're saying that "quick-wittedness" and "being 75" do not normally go together; you imply the same abnormality for "agility" and "being 65" and for "responsibility" and "being a teenager." The problem with this kind of stereotyping is that it's simply wrong. There are many 75-year-olds who are extremely quick-witted (and many 30-year-olds who aren't).

You also communicate ageism when you speak to older people in overly simple words or explain things that don't need explaining. Nonverbally, you demonstrate ageist communication when, for example, you avoid touching an older person but touch others, or when you avoid making direct eye contact with an older person but readily do so with others. Also, it's a mistake to speak to an older person at an overly high volume; this suggests that all older people have hearing difficulties, and it tends to draw attention to the fact that you are talking down to the older person.

One useful way to avoid ageism is to recognize and avoid the illogical stereotypes that ageist language is based on. Do you:

- *avoid talking down to a person because he or she is older? Older people are not mentally slow; most people remain mentally alert well into old age.*
- *refrain from refreshing an older person's memory each time you see the person? Older people can and do remember things.*
- *avoid implying that relationships are no longer important? Older people continue to be interested in relationships.*
- *speak at a normal volume and maintain a normal physical distance? Being older does not necessarily mean being hard of hearing or being unable to see; most older people hear and see quite well, sometimes with hearing aids or glasses.*
- *engage older people in conversation as you would wish to be engaged? Older people are interested in the world around them.*

Even though you want to avoid ageist communication, there are times when you may wish to make adjustments when talking with someone who does have language or communication difficulties. The American Speech and Hearing Association offers several useful suggestions (www.asha.org, accessed July 17, 2006):

■ **What Do You Say** ?
Ageism
One of your instructors is extremely sensitive in talking about women, different races, and different affectional orientations but consistently speaks of old people using stereotypical and insulting language. You want to say something but feel awkward, after all you're in your early 20s and your instructor is at least 65. Yet, you want to object to this type of talk. **What Do You Say?** To whom? Through what channel?

- Reduce as much background noise as you can.
- Ease into the conversation by beginning with casual topics and then moving into more familiar topics. Stay with each topic for a while; avoid jumping too quickly from one topic to another.
- Speak in relatively short sentences and questions.
- Give the person added time to respond. Some older people react more slowly and need extra time.
- Listen actively. Practice the skills of active listening discussed in Chapter 5.

Sexism

The term **sexism** refers to the prejudicial attitudes and beliefs about men or women based on rigid beliefs about gender roles. Individual sexism may take the form of beliefs such as the ideas that women should be caretakers, should be sensitive at all times, and should acquiesce to men's decisions concerning political or financial matters. It also includes beliefs such as the notions that men are insensitive, are interested only in sex, and are incapable of communicating feelings, as the accompanying cartoon clearly illustrates.

Institutional sexism, on the other hand, consists of customs and practices that discriminate against people because of their gender. Two very clear examples are the widespread practice of paying women less than men for the same job and the discrimination against women in the upper levels of management. Another clear example of institutionalized sexism is the practice of automatically or near-automatically granting child custody to the mother rather than the father in divorce cases.

Of particular interest here is **sexist language:** language that puts down someone because of his or her gender (usually, language derogatory toward women). The National Council of Teachers of English has proposed guidelines for nonsexist (gender-free, gender-neutral, or sex-fair) language. These guidelines concern the use of the generic word *man,* the use of generic *he* and *his,* and sex role stereotyping (Penfield, 1987).

"Did you ever have that baby you wanted so much?"

Consider your own communication behavior. Do you

- *use the word* man *generically? The word* man *refers most clearly to an adult male. To use the term to refer to both men and women emphasizes maleness at the expense of femaleness. Gender-neutral terms can easily be substituted. Instead of* mankind, *you can say* humanity, people, *or* human beings. *Instead of the* common man, *you can say* the average person *or* ordinary people. *Similarly, the use of terms such as* policeman *or* fireman *and other terms that presume maleness as the norm—and femaleness as a deviation from this norm—are clear and common examples of sexist language.*

- *use the words* he *and* his *as generic? There seems no legitimate reason why the feminine pronoun cannot alternate with the masculine pronoun to refer to hypothetical individuals, or why terms such as* he and she *or* her and him *cannot be used instead of just* he *or* him. *Alternatively, you can restructure your sentences to eliminate any reference to gender. For example, the NCTE Guidelines (Penfield, 1987) suggest that instead of saying, "The average student is worried about his grades," you say, "The average student is worried about grades." Instead of saying, "Ask that each student hand in his work as soon as he is finished," say, "Ask students to hand in their work as soon as they're finished."*

- *use sex role stereotyping? The words you use often reflect a sex role bias—the assumption that certain roles or professions belong to men and others belong to women. When you make the hypothetical elementary school teacher female and the college professor male, or when you refer to doctors as male and nurses as female, you're sex role stereotyping. This is also true when you include the sex of a professional, as in referring to a "female doctor" or a "male nurse."*

HARASSMENT   This discussion of sexism leads naturally into a consideration of **sexual harassment,** a form of behavior that violates Title VII of the Civil Rights Act of 1964 as amended by the Civil Rights Act of 1991 (**www.eeoc.gov/policy/cra91. html**, last modified January 15, 1997; accessed May 4, 2002). There are two general categories of sexual harassment: quid pro quo (a term borrowed from the Latin that literally means "something for something") harassment and the creation of a hostile environment.

In **quid pro quo harassment,** employment opportunities (as in hiring and promotion) are made dependent on the granting of sexual favors. Conversely, quid pro quo harassment also includes situations in which reprisals and various negative consequences would result from the failure to grant such sexual favors. Put more generally, quid pro quo harassment occurs when employment consequences (positive or negative) hinge on a person's response to sexual advances.

Hostile environment harassment is broader and includes all sexual behaviors (verbal and nonverbal) that make a worker uncomfortable. Putting sexually explicit pictures on the bulletin board, using sexually explicit screen savers, telling sexual jokes and stories, and using sexual and demeaning language or gestures all constitute hostile environment harassment.

The Equal Employment Opportunity Commission (EEOC) definition of sexual harassment sums up these two basic types. In the definition below items 1 and 2 refer to quid pro quo harassment and item 3 to hostile environment harassment:

Unwelcome sexual advances, requests for sexual favors and other verbal or physical conduct of a sexual nature constitute sexual harassment when (1) submission to such conduct is made either explicitly or implicitly a term or condition of an individual's employment, (2) submission to or rejection of such conduct by an individual is used as the basis for employment decisions affecting such individual, or (3) such conduct has the purpose or effect of unreasonably interfering with an individual's work

E-Talk . ▪ . ▪ . ▪ . ▪

Harassment

In one study, 10 to 15 percent of the students surveyed reported being harassed via e-mail or instant messaging (Finn, 2004). What is the state of online harassment on your campus? What can you do about it?

performance or creating an intimidating, hostile, or offensive working environment. (Friedman, Boumil, & Taylor, 1992)

If you are trying to determine whether behavior constitutes sexual harassment, the following questions will help you assess your own situation objectively rather than emotionally (VanHyning, 1993):

1. Is it real? Does this behavior have the meaning it seems to have?
2. Is it job related? Does this behavior have something to do with or will it influence the way you do your job?
3. Did you reject this behavior? Did you make your rejection of unwanted messages clear to the other person?
4. Have these unwanted messages persisted? Is there a pattern, a consistency to these messages?

If you answer yes to all four questions, then the behavior is likely to constitute sexual harassment (VanHyning, 1993).

Keep in mind three additional facts that are often misunderstood. First, people of either gender may sexually harass either gender. Although most cases brought to public attention are committed by men against women, women may also harass men. Further, harassment may be committed by men against men and by women against women. Second, anyone in an organization can be guilty of sexual harassment. Although most cases of harassment involve persons in authority who harass subordinates, this is not a necessary condition. Coworkers, vendors, and even customers may be charged with sexual harassment. Third, sexual harassment is not limited to business organizations but can and does occur in schools, in hospitals, and in social, religious, and political organizations.

What can you do about sexual harassment? If you encounter sexual harassment and wish to do something, consider these suggestions recommended by workers in the field (Petrocelli & Repa, 1992; Bravo & Cassedy, 1992; Rubenstein, 1993):

1. Talk to the harasser. Tell this person, assertively, that you do not welcome the behavior and that you find it offensive. Simply informing Fred that his sexual jokes aren't appreciated and are seen as offensive may be sufficient to make him stop.
2. Collect evidence—perhaps corroboration from others who have experienced similar harassment at the hands of the same individual, and/or perhaps a log of the offensive behaviors.
3. Utilize appropriate channels within the organization. Most organizations have established channels to deal with such grievances. In most cases this step will eliminate any further harassment.
4. If necessary, file a complaint with an organization or governmental agency or perhaps take legal action.

Cultural Identifiers

Perhaps the best way to avoid sexism, heterosexism, racism, and ageism in language is to examine the preferred cultural identifiers to use (and not to use) in talking about members of different groups. As always, when in doubt, find out. The preferences and many of the specific examples identified here are drawn largely from the findings of the Task Force on Bias-Free Language of the Association of American University Presses (Schwartz, 1995). Do realize that not everyone would agree with these recommendations; they're presented here—in the words of the Task Force—"to encourage sensitivity to usages that may be imprecise, misleading, and needlessly offensive" (Schwartz, 1995, p. ix). They're not presented so that you can "catch" someone being "politically incorrect" or label someone "culturally insensitive."

Generally: The term *girl* should be used only to refer to a very young female and is equivalent to *boy*. Neither term should be used for people older than 13 or 14. *Girl* is never used to refer to a grown woman; nor is *boy* used to refer to persons in blue-collar positions, as it once was. *Lady* is negatively evaluated by many, because it connotes the stereotype of the prim and proper woman. *Woman* or *young woman* is preferred. *Older person* is preferred to *elder, elderly, senior,* or *senior citizen* (technically, someone older than 65).

Generally: *Gay* is the preferred term to refer to a man who has an affectional preference for other men, and *lesbian* is the preferred term for a woman who has an affectional preference for other women. (*Lesbian* means "homosexual woman," so the phrase *lesbian woman* is redundant.) This preference for the term *lesbian* is not universal among homosexual women, however; in one survey, for example, 58 percent preferred *lesbian*, but 34 percent preferred *gay* (Lever, 1995). *Homosexual* refers to both gay men and lesbians but more often merely denotes a sexual orientation to members of a person's own sex. *Gay* and *lesbian* refer to a lifestyle and not simply to sexual orientation. *Gay* as a noun, although widely used, may prove offensive in some contexts; for example, "We have two gays on the team." Although used within the gay community in an effort to remove the negative stigma through frequent usage, the term *queer*—as in "queer power"—is often resented when used by outsiders. Because most scientific thinking holds that one's sexuality is genetically determined rather than being a matter of choice, the term *sexual orientation* rather than *sexual preference* or *sexual status* (which is also vague) is preferred.

Generally: Most African Americans prefer *African American* to *black* (Hecht, Jackson, & Ribeau, 2003), though *black* is often used with *white* and is used in a variety of other contexts (for example, Department of Black and Puerto Rican Studies, *Journal of Black History,* and Black History Month). The American Psychological Association recommends that both terms be capitalized, but *The Chicago Manual of Style* (a manual used by most newspapers and publishing houses) recommends using lowercase. The terms *Negro* and *colored*, although used in the names of some organizations (for example, the United Negro College Fund and the National Association for the Advancement of Colored People), are not used outside of these contexts.

Generally: *White* is used to refer to those whose roots are in European cultures, but not to Hispanics. A parallel to *African American* is the phrase *European American*. Few European Americans, however, would want to be called that; most would prefer to specify their national origins; for example, to use *German American* or *Greek American*. This preference may well change as Europe becomes a more cohesive and united entity. *People of color*—a somewhat literary-sounding term appropriate perhaps to public speaking but awkward to use in most conversations—is preferred to *nonwhites,* which implies that whiteness is the norm and *nonwhiteness* is a deviation from that norm. The same is true of the term *non-Christian*.

Generally: The term *Hispanic* refers to anyone who identifies himself or herself as belonging to a Spanish-speaking culture. People born in Spain prefer to be called *Spanish* rather than *Hispanic*. *Latina* (female) and *Latino* (male) refer to persons whose roots are in one of the Latin American countries, such as the Dominican Republic, Nicaragua, or Guatemala. *Hispanic American* refers to United States residents from Spanish-speaking cultures and includes people from Mexico, the Caribbean,

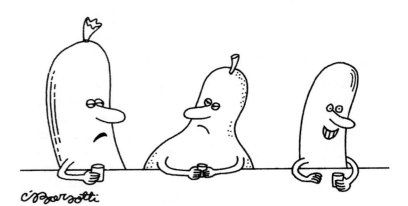

"It doesn't have a damn thing to do with political correctness, pal. I'm a sausage, and that guy's a wienie."

"When you say 'my people,' do you mean your tribe or your reps?"

■ **What Do You Say**
Cultural Identifiers
You're at an international students open house and all students are asked to talk about the cultural identifiers they prefer to have used in reference to themselves and well as the cultural identifiers they do not like. **What Do You Say?**

and Central and South America. In emphasizing a Spanish heritage, however, the term is really inaccurate, because of the large numbers in the Caribbean and in South America whose origins and languages are French or Portuguese. *Chicana* (female) and *Chicano* (male) refer to persons with roots in Mexico, though these terms often connote a nationalist attitude (Jandt, 2000) and are considered offensive by many Mexican Americans. *Mexican American* is preferred.

Inuk (plural, *Inuit*) was officially adopted at the Inuit Circumpolar Conference to refer to the indigenous peoples of Alaska, Northern Canada, Greenland, and Eastern Siberia. *Inuk* is preferred to *Eskimo* (a term the U.S. Census Bureau uses), which was applied to the indigenous peoples of Alaska by Europeans and derives from a word that means "raw meat eaters" (Maggio, 1997).

The word *Indian* technically refers only to someone from India, not to members of other Asian countries or to the indigenous peoples of North America. *American Indian* or *Native American* is preferred, even though many Native Americans do refer to themselves as *Indians* and *Indian people*. The term *native American* (with a lowercase *n*) is most often used to refer to persons born in the United States. Although the term technically could refer to anyone born in North or South America, people outside the United States generally prefer more specific designations such as *Argentinean, Cuban*, or *Canadian*. The term *native* means an indigenous inhabitant; it's not used to mean "member of a less developed culture." The word *squaw*, used to refer to a Native American woman and still used in the names of some places in the United States and in some textbooks, is clearly a term to be avoided; its usage is almost always negative and insulting (Koppelman with Goodhart, 2005).

Muslim is the preferred form (rather than the older *Moslem*) to refer to a person who adheres to the religious teachings of Islam. *Quran* (rather than *Koran*) is the preferred term for the scriptures of Islam. The terms "Mohammedan" or "Mohammedanism" are not considered appropriate; they imply worship of Muhammad, the prophet, which is "considered by Muslims to be a blasphemy against the absolute oneness of God" (Maggio, 1997, p. 277).

Although there is no universal agreement, *Jewish people* is often preferred to *Jews;* and *Jewess* (a Jewish female) is considered derogatory. *Jew* should be used only as a noun and is never correctly used as a verb or an adjective (Maggio, 1997).

When history was being written with a European perspective, Europe was taken as the focal point and the rest of the world was defined in terms of its location relative to that continent. Thus, Asia became the East or the Orient, and Asians became *Orientals*—a term that is today considered inappropriate or "Eurocentric." People from Asia are *Asians,* just as people from Africa are *Africans* and people from Europe are *Europeans*.

$\mathcal{U}$sing Verbal Messages Effectively and Critically

A chief concern in using verbal messages is to recognize what critical thinking theorists call "conceptual distortions": mental mistakes, misinterpretations, or reasoning fallacies. Avoiding these distortions and substituting a more critical, more realistic analysis is probably the best way to improve your own use of verbal messages. Let's explore conceptual distortions by examining three general princples of verbal messages: (1) Messages symbolize reality but are not the reality itself; (2) messages can express facts and/or inferences but may not always make the necessary distinctions between these two types of statements; and (3) messages can obscure important distinctions.

Messages Symbolize Reality

Language merely symbolizes reality; it's not the reality itself. The word *rose* is not the flower; the word doesn't make you sneeze or attract bees. The word is not the thing. Of course, this is obvious. But consider: Have you ever reacted to the way something was labeled or described rather than to the actual item? Have you ever bought something because of its name rather than because of the actual object? If so,

Skill Building *exercise*

Thinking and Talking in E-Prime

The term **E-prime** (E´) refers to normal English without the verb *to be* (Bourland, 1965–66, 2004; Wilson, 1989; Klein, 1992; Maas, 2002). Statements in E-prime can be more accurate and descriptive than conventional sentences. For example, the statement "The movie was great" implies that "greatness" is in the movie rather than in your perception of the movie. E-prime versions (for example, "I loved the movie" or "The movie kept my interest throughout the two hours") make it clear that you're talking about how you perceived the movie and not about something that is in the movie. When you say "The movie was great" you also imply that everyone will see it in the same way. On the other hand, when you say "I loved the movie" you leave open the possibility for differences of opinion. To appreciate the difference between statements that use the verb to be and those that do not, (1) in the second column below rewrite the sentences without using the verb to be in any of its forms—*is, are, am, was,* and so on. Then (2), in the third column, indicate the differences in meaning between the statements using to be and the E-prime rewrites.

Regular "to be" form	E-prime rewrite	Differences in meaning
1. I'm a poor student.		
2. They're inconsiderate.		
3. Is this valuable?		

The verb *to be* suggests that qualities are *in the person* or thing rather than *in the observer*. The verb *to be* also implies a permanence that is not true of the world in which you live.

you were probably responding as if language were reality, a distortion called intensional orientation.

INTENSIONAL ORIENTATION The term **intensional orientation** (the *s* in *intensional* is intentional) refers to our tendency to view people, objects, and events in the way they're talked about—the way they're labeled. For example, if Sally were labeled "uninteresting," you would, responding intensionally, evaluate her as uninteresting even before listening to what she had to say. You'd see Sally through a filter imposed by the label "uninteresting." **Extensional orientation,** on the other hand, is the tendency to look first at the actual people, objects, and events and only afterwards at their labels. In this case, it would mean looking at Sally without any preconceived labels, guided by what she says and does, not by the words used to label her.

The way to avoid intensional orientation is to extensionalize. Recognize that language provides labels for things and should never be given greater attention than the actual thing. Give your main attention to the people, things, and events in the world as you see them and not as they're presented in words. For example, when you meet Jack and Jill, observe and interact with them. Then form your impressions. Don't respond to them as "greedy, money-grubbing landlords" simply because Harry labeled them this way. Don't respond to Carmen as "lazy and inconsiderate" because Elaine told you she was.

ALLNESS A related distortion is to forget that language symbolizes only a portion of reality, never the whole. When you assume that you can know all or say all about anything, you're into a pattern of behavior called **allness.** You never see all of anything. You never experience anything fully. You see a part, then conclude what the whole is like. You have to draw conclusions on the basis of insufficient evidence (because you always have insufficient evidence). A useful **extensional device** to help combat the tendency to think that all can or has been said about anything is to end each statement mentally with **et cetera**—a reminder that there is more to learn, more to know, and more to say; that every statement is inevitably incomplete (Korzybski, 1933). To be sure, some people overuse "et cetera." They use it not as a mental reminder but as a substitute for being specific. This obviously is to be avoided and merely adds to the distortions in communication.

To achieve **nonallness,** recognize that language symbolizes only a part of reality, never the whole. Whatever someone says—regardless of what it is or how extensive it is—is only part of the story.

Messages Express Facts and Inferences

Technically, a **factual statement** is a statement that you make only after you observe the person or event and is limited to what you have observed (for example, "She's standing at the lectern") (Weinberg, 1959). An **inferential statement,** on the other hand, can be made without observation or can go beyond what you've observed. It's a guess ("She's feeling uncomfortable at that lectern"). Barriers to clear thinking can be created when you treat an inferential statement as if it were factual.

We sometimes construct statements of both facts and inferences without making any linguistic distinction between the two. Similarly, when we articulate or listen to such statements, we often don't make a clear distinction between statements of facts and statements of inference. Yet there are great differences between the two. Barriers to clear thinking can be created when inferences are treated as facts, a tendency called **fact–inference confusion.**

For example, you can say, "She's wearing a blue jacket," and you can say, "He's harboring an illogical hatred." Although the sentences have similar structures, they're different. You can observe the jacket and the blue color, but how do you observe "illogical hatred"? Obviously, this is not a factual statement but an inferential statement. It's one you make on the basis not only of what you observe, but of what you infer.

There is nothing wrong with making inferential statements. You must make them to talk about much that is meaningful to you. The problem arises when you act as if those inferential statements are factual. To test your ability to distinguish facts from inferences, try taking the self-test below (based on tests constructed by Haney, 1973).

Test *Yourself*

Can You Distinguish Facts from Inferences?

INSTRUCTIONS: Carefully read the following report and the observations based on it. Indicate whether you think, on the basis of the information presented in the report, that the observations are true, false, or doubtful. Write T if the observation is definitely true, F if the observation is definitely false, and ? if the observation may be either true or false. Judge the observations in order. Do not reread the observations after you have indicated your judgment, and do not change any of your answers.

> A well-liked college teacher had just completed making up the final examinations and had turned off the lights in the office. Just then a tall, broad figure with dark glasses appeared and demanded the examination. The professor opened the drawer. Everything in the drawer was picked up and the individual ran down the corridor. The dean was notified immediately.

_____ ❶ The thief was tall and broad and wore dark glasses.

_____ ❷ The professor turned off the lights.

_____ ❸ A tall figure demanded the examination.

_____ ❹ The examination was picked up by someone.

_____ ❺ The examination was picked up by the professor.

_____ ❻ A tall, broad figure appeared after the professor turned off the lights in the office.

_____ ❼ The man who opened the drawer was the professor.

_____ ❽ The professor ran down the corridor.

_____ ❾ The drawer was never actually opened.

_____ ❿ Three persons are referred to in this report.

HOW DID YOU DO? After you answer all 10 questions, form small groups of five or six and discuss the answers. Look at each statement from each member's point of view. For each statement, ask yourself, "How can you be absolutely certain that the statement is true or false?" You should find that only one statement can be clearly identified as true and only one as false; eight should be marked "?".

WHAT WILL YOU DO? Try to formulate specific guidelines that will help you distinguish facts from inferences.

To avoid fact–inference confusion, phrase your own inferential statements as tentative and leave open the possibility of being proved wrong. For example, treat the statement "Our biology teacher was fired for poor teaching" as the inferential statement it is; this allows you to consider other explanations and psychologically prepares you to be proved wrong.

This distinction is equally important when you are listening. Most talk is inferential, so beware of the speaker who presents everything as fact. Analyze closely and you'll uncover a world of inferences.

"Since the food you serve is not organically grown, is it safe to assume that the meat is laced with antibiotics and the salad is chockful of pesticides?"

Messages Can Obscure Distinctions

Messages can obscure distinctions, both by generalizing about people or events that are covered by the same label but are really quite different (indiscrimination) and by making it easy to focus on extremes rather than on the vast middle ground (polarization).

INDISCRIMINATION   Each word in a language can refer to lots of things; most general terms refer to a wide variety of individuals. Words such as *teacher* or *textbook* or *computer program* refer to lots of specific people and things. When you allow the general term to obscure the specific differences (say, among teachers or textbooks), you're into a pattern called indiscrimination.

Indiscrimination is the failure to distinguish between similar but different persons, objects, or events. It occurs when you focus on classes and fail to see that each phenomenon is unique and needs to be looked at individually.

Everything is unlike everything else. Our language, however, provides you with common nouns such as *teacher, student, friend, enemy, war, politician,* and *liberal.* Such terms lead you to focus on similarities—to group together all teachers, all students, all politicians. At the same time, the terms divert attention away from the uniqueness of each person, each object, and each event.

This kind of misevaluation is at the heart of stereotyping on the basis of nationality, race, religion, gender, age, or affectional orientation. A stereotype, you'll remember from previous discussions, is a fixed mental picture of a group that is applied to each individual in the group without regard to his or her unique qualities. Most stereotypes are negative and denigrate the group to which they refer. Some, however, are positive. A particularly glaring example is the popular stereotype of Asian American students as successful, intelligent, and hardworking.

Whether stereotypes are positive or negative, they create the same problem: They provide you with shortcuts that are often inappropriate. For instance, when you meet a particular person, your first reaction may be to pigeonhole him or her into some category—perhaps religious, national, or academic. Then you assign to this person all the qualities that are part of your stereotype ("She's a typical academic: never thinks of the real world"). Regardless of the category you use or the specific qualities you're ready to assign, you fail to give sufficient attention to the individual's unique characteristics. Two people may both be Christian, Asian, and lesbian, for example, but each will be different from the other. Indiscrimination is a denial of another's uniqueness.

A useful extensional device that can serve as an antidote to indiscrimination (and stereotyping) is the **index**. This mental subscript identifies each individual as an individual even though both may be covered by the same label. Thus, politician$_1$ is not politician$_2$; teacher$_1$ is not teacher$_2$. The index helps you to discriminate among without discriminating against. Although a label ("politician," for example) covers all politicians, the index makes sure that each politician is thought about as an individual.

POLARIZATION   Language also obscures differences because it has lots of terms to denote extremes and few terms to denote middle ground, a situation that often leads to **polarization.** You can appreciate the role language plays in fostering polarization by trying to identify the opposites of the following terms: *happy, long, wealth, life, healthy, up, left, legal, heavy, strong.* This should be relatively easy; you probably can identify the opposites very quickly. Now, however, identify the middle terms, the terms referring to the middle ground between the italicized terms and the opposites. These terms should be more difficult to come up with and should take you more time and effort. Further, if you compare your responses with those of others, you'll find that most people agree on the opposites; most people would have said *unhappy, short, poverty,* and so on. But when it comes to the middle terms, the degree of agreement will be much less. Thus, language makes it easy to focus on opposites and relatively difficult to talk about the middle areas.

Polarization, then, is the tendency to look at the world in terms of opposites and to describe it in extremes—good or bad, positive or negative, healthy or sick, intelligent or stupid. Polarization is often referred to as the fallacy of "either/or" or "black and white." Most of life exists somewhere between the extremes. Yet there's a strong tendency to view only the extremes and to categorize people, objects, and events in terms of these polar opposites.

Problems are created when opposites are used in inappropriate situations. For example, "The politician is either for us or against us." These two options do not include all possibilities. The politician may be for us in some things and against us in other things, or may be neutral.

To correct this polarizing tendency, beware of implying (and believing) that two extreme classes include all possible classes—that an individual must be one or the other, with no alternatives ("Are you pro-abortion or pro-life?"). Most people, most events, most qualities exist between polar extremes. When others imply that there are only two sides or two alternatives, look for the middle ground.

STATIC EVALUATION   Another distinction language often obscures is that of change. Language changes only very slowly, especially when compared to the rapid pace at which people and things change. The statements you make about an event or person need to change as quickly and as dramatically as people and events change. When you retain an evaluation (most often in the form of an internalized message), despite the changes in the person or thing, you're engaging in **static evaluation.**

It's important to act in accordance with the notion of change, not merely to accept it intellectually. If you failed at something once, that does not necessarily mean that you'll fail again. If you were rejected once, that does not mean you'll be rejected again. You've changed since the first failure and the first rejection. You're a different person now, and you need to make new evaluations and initiate new efforts.

The mental **date** is a useful extensional device for keeping language (and thinking) up to date and for guarding against static evaluation. Date your statements and especially your evaluations; remember that Pat Smith$_{2000}$ is not Pat Smith$_{2007}$, that academic abilities$_{2003}$ are not academic abilities$_{2007}$. In talking and in listening, look carefully at messages that claim that what was true still is. It may or may not be. Look for change; be suspicious of the implication of nonchange.

The Uncritical Observers

Here is a brief dialogue written to illustrate the various barriers to communication discussed in this chapter as they might apply to interpersonal relationships. Try identifying the barriers illustrated. Also think about why these statements establish barriers and how the people in the dialogue might have avoided the barriers.

Dialogue for Analysis

The Cast*

Pat and Chris, in their late 20s, have been in a committed relationship for the last several years, ever since graduating from college.

The Context

Pat and Chris are sitting in the living room watching television.

(continues)

Dialogue *for* **Analysis**

Pat: Look, do you care about me or don't you? If you do, then you'll go away for the weekend with me as we planned.

Chris: I know we planned to go, but I got this opportunity to put in some overtime, and I really need the extra money.

Pat: Look, a deal is a deal. You said you'd go, and that's all that really matters.

Chris: Pat! You never give me a break, do you? I just can't go; I have to work.

Pat: All right, all right. I'll go alone.

Chris: Oh, no you don't. I know what will happen.

Pat: What will happen?

Chris: You'll go back to drinking again. I know you will.

Pat: I will not. I don't drink anymore.

Chris: Pat, you're an alcoholic and you know it.

Pat: I am not an alcoholic.

Chris: You drink, don't you?

Pat: Yes, occasionally.

Chris: Occasionally? Yeah, you mean two or three times a week, don't you?

Pat: That's occasionally. That's not being an alcoholic.

Chris: Well, I don't care how much you drink or how often you drink. You're still an alcoholic.

Pat: Anyway, what makes you think I'll drink if I go away for the weekend?

Chris: All those weekend ski trips are just excuses to drink. I've been on one of them—remember?

Pat: Well, see it your way, my dear. See it your way. I'll be gone right after I shower. [thinks: "I can't wait to get away for the weekend."]

Chris: [thinks: "Now what have I done? Our relationship is finished."]

*This dialogue—as well as the dialogues in Chapters 8, 9, and 10—uses the names *Pat* and *Chris* in order to preserve the gender neutrality of the characters.

Summary of Concepts and Skills

This chapter looked at verbal messages: the nature of language and the ways in which language works; the concept of disconfirmation and how it relates to racism, heterosexism, ageism, and sexist language; and the ways in which you can use language more effectively.

1. Verbal messages are both denotative (objective and generally easily agreed upon) and connotative (subjective and generally highly individual in meaning).
2. Verbal messages vary in directness; they can state exactly what you mean, or they can hedge and state your meaning very indirectly.
3. Verbal messages vary in abstraction; they can vary from extremely general to extremely specific.
4. Message meanings are in people, not in things.
5. Messages vary in assertiveness.
6. Disconfirmation is the process of ignoring the presence and the communications of others. Confirmation means

accepting, supporting, and acknowledging the importance of the other person.

7. Racist, heterosexist, ageist, and sexist messages unfairly put down and negatively evaluate groups and are seen in both individual and institutionalized forms.
8. Using verbal messages effectively involves eliminating conceptual distortions and substituting more accurate assumptions about language, the most important of which are:

   • Language symbolizes reality; it's not the reality itself.
   • Language can express both facts and inferences, and distinctions need to be made between them.
   • Language can obscure distinctions in its use of general terms that lead us to ignore differences (indiscrimination), in its emphasis on extreme rather than middle terms (polarization), and in its emphasis on nonchange (static evaluation).

In addition, this chapter discussed a variety of verbal message skills. Check those you want to work on.

_____ 1. *Connotative meanings.* Clarify your connotative meanings if you have any concern that your listeners might misunderstand you; as a listener, ask questions if you have doubts about the speaker's connotations.

_____ 2. *Indirect messages.* Use indirect messages when a more direct style might prove insulting or offensive, but be aware that indirect messages also may create misunderstanding.

_____ 3. *Abstractions.* Use both abstract and concrete language when describing or explaining.

_____ 4. *Meanings in people.* When you are deciphering meaning, the best source is the person; meanings are in people. When in doubt, find out—from the source.

_____ 5. *Meanings depend on context.* Look at the context for cues as to how you should interpret the meanings of messages.

_____ 6. *Confirmation.* When you wish to be confirming, acknowledge (verbally and/or nonverbally) others in your group and their contributions.

_____ 7. *Disconfirming language.* Avoid racist, heterosexist, ageist, and racist language, which is disconfirming and insulting and invariably creates communication barriers.

_____ 8. *Cultural identifiers.* Use cultural identifiers that are sensitive to the desires of others; when appropriate, make clear the cultural identifiers you prefer.

_____ 9. *Intensional orientation.* Avoid intensional orientation. Look to people and things first and to labels second.

_____ 10. *Allness.* Avoid allness statements; they invariably misstate the reality and will often offend the other person.

_____ 11. *Facts and inferences.* Distinguish facts (verifiably true past events) from inferences (guesses or hypotheses), and act on inferences with tentativeness.

_____ 12. *Indiscrimination.* Treat each situation and each person as unique (when possible) even when they're covered by the same label. Index key concepts.

_____ 13. *Polarization.* Avoid thinking and talking in extremes by using middle terms and qualifiers. But remember that too many qualifiers may make you appear unsure of yourself.

_____ 14. *Dating statements.* Date your statements to avoid thinking of the world as static and unchanging. Reflect the inevitability of change in your messages.

Vocabulary Quiz: The Language of Language

Match these terms about language with their definitions. Record the number of the definition next to the appropriate term.

_____ polarization

_____ intensional orientation

_____ connotative meaning

_____ fact–inference confusion

_____ confirmation

_____ static evaluation

_____ indiscrimination

_____ ageism

_____ level of abstraction

_____ ableism

1. Treating inferences as if they were facts.
2. The denial of change in language and in thinking.
3. The emotional, subjective aspect of meaning.
4. A communication pattern of acknowledgement and acceptance.
5. Discrimination against people with disabilities.
6. The degree of generality or specificity of a term.
7. Discrimination based on age.
8. The failure to see the differences among people or things covered by the same label.
9. A focus on the way things are talked about rather than on the way they exist.
10. A focus on extremes to the neglect of the middle.

Four for Discussion

1. Visualize yourself seated with a packet of photographs before you. You're asked to scratch out the eyes in each photograph. You're further told that this is simply an experiment and that the individuals (all strangers) whose pictures you have will not be aware of anything that has happened here. As you progress through the pictures, scratching out the eyes, you come upon a photograph of your mother. What do you do? Are you able to scratch

out the eyes as you have done with the pictures of the strangers? Are you responding intensionally or extensionally? Can you identify other examples of how you or those you know act intensionally instead of extensionally?

2. One of your instructors persists in calling the female students girls, refers to gay men and lesbians as queers, and refers to various racial groups in ways that most people would consider inappropriate. When told that these terms are offensive, the instructor claims the right to free speech and argues that a restriction on free speech would be a far greater wrong than being culturally insensitive or politically incorrect. How would you comment on this argument?

3. Using a good search engine such as Google (www.google.com), Vivisimo (www.vivisimo.com), or AskJeeves (www.ask.com), look up "hate speech" and campus codes on hate speech. After reading about hate speech and the codes that have been developed, formulate your own position on campus codes for hate speech. Are you in favor of or opposed to such codes? What reasons can you offer in support of your position? If you're in favor of codes, how would you write such a code of conduct?

4. Still another "ism" is classism, "attitudes and discriminatory actions stemming from prejudice against poor people" (Koppelman with Goodhart, 2005, p. 247). What examples can you give to illustrate the existence of classism on an individual and on an institutional level?

My CommunicationLab Explorations

Explore www.mycommunicationlab.com to find exercises to help you work actively with the concepts discussed in this chapter: (1) Integrating Verbal and Nonverbal Messages, (2) Using the Abstraction Ladder as a Creative Thinking Tool, (3) How Can You Vary Directness for Greatest Effectiveness? (4) How Can You Rephrase Clichés? (5) Identifying the Barriers to Communication, (6) How Do You Talk? As a Woman? As a Man? (7) How Do You Talk about the Middle? and (8) "Must Lie" Situations. Two self-tests will help you examine some of your own language skills: (9) How Direct Are You? and (10) Can You Distinguish between Commonly Confused Words?

Also visit MyCommunicationLab for video clips, study aids, and activities that will further your understanding and mastery of the verbal message system.

Explore our research resources at
www.researchnavigator.com.

Research
Navigator.com

CHAPTER 7
Nonverbal Messages

WHY READ THIS CHAPTER?

*B*ecause you'll **learn about:**

- the world of nonverbal communication.
- the ways nonverbal messages can be sent and received.
- the cultural differences in nonverbal communication.

*B*ecause you'll **learn to:**

- send and receive nonverbal messages more effectively.
- use nonverbal signals more effectively in intercultural situations.

Nonverbal communication is communication without words. You communicate nonverbally when you gesture, smile or frown, widen your eyes, move your chair closer to someone, wear jewelry, touch someone, raise your vocal volume, or even say nothing. The crucial aspect is that the message you send is in some way received by one or more other people. If you gesture while you are alone in your room and no one is there to see you, then, most theorists would argue, communication has not taken place. The same is true of verbal messages, of course; if you recite a speech and no one hears it, then communication has not taken place.

The Benefits of Effective Nonverbal Communication

Competence in nonverbal communication can yield two principal benefits (Burgoon & Hoobler, 2002). First, the greater your ability to encode and decode nonverbal signals, the higher your popularity and psychosocial well-being are likely to be. (Not surprisingly, encoding and decoding abilities are highly correlated; if you're good at expressing yourself nonverbally, then you're likely to also be good at reading the nonverbal cues of others.) This relationship is likely part of a more general relationship: Research indicates that people who are high in interpersonal skills generally are perceived to be high on such positive qualities as expressiveness, self-esteem, outgoingness, social comfort, sociability, and gregariousness. Interpersonal skills really do matter. Second, the greater your nonverbal skills, the more successful you're likely to be at influencing and deceiving others. Skilled nonverbal communicators are highly persuasive. This persuasive power can be used to help or support another, or it can be used to deceive and fool.

As you begin your study of nonverbal communication, keep the following suggestions in mind.

- Analyze your own nonverbal communication patterns. If you're to use this material in any meaningful way to change some of your behaviors, for example, then self-analysis is essential.
- Observe. Observe. Observe. Observe the behaviors of those around you and your own. See in everyday behavior what you read about here and discuss in class.
- Resist the temptation to draw conclusions from nonverbal behaviors. Instead, develop hypotheses (educated guesses) about what is going on, and test the validity of your hypotheses on the basis of other evidence.
- Connect and relate. Although textbooks (like this one) must present the areas of nonverbal communication separately, the various elements all work together in actual communication situations.
- Nonverbal messages may be used alone; may function as the primary channel of communication, with the verbal message in a secondary role; or may serve in a secondary role (Burgoon & Hoobler, 2002).

E-Talk ▪ ▪ ▪ ▪ ▪ ▪

A Nonverbal Blog

An interesting blog dealing with nonverbal communication is available at **www.geocities.com/ marvin_hecht/nonverbal.html** (accessed May 5, 2005). Visit this site and examine the wide variety of information available. What do you find on this site that you would add to a chapter on nonverbal messages in interpersonal communication?

The Functions of Nonverbal Messages

To appreciate the many functions of nonverbal communication, let's look at (1) the ways in which nonverbal communication messages are integrated with verbal messages and (2) the functions that researchers have focused on most extensively (Burgoon & Hoobler, 2002; Burgoon & Bacue, 2003).

Integrating Nonverbal and Verbal Messages

In face-to-face communication, you blend verbal and nonverbal messages to best convey your meanings; you say "I'm happy to meet you" with a welcoming smile, focused eye contact, and a warm handshake. Here are six ways in which nonverbal messages are used with verbal messages; these will help to highlight the important interaction and integration of nonverbal and verbal messages (Knapp & Hall, 1996).

- Nonverbal communication often serves to *accent* or emphasize some part of the verbal message. You might, for example, raise your voice to underscore a particular word or phrase, bang your fist on the desk to stress your commitment, or look longingly into someone's eyes when saying "I love you."

- Nonverbal communication may *complement* or add nuances of meaning not communicated by your verbal message. Thus, you might smile when telling a story (to suggest that you find it humorous) or frown and shake your head when recounting someone's deceit (to suggest your disapproval). In computer-mediated communication, you may compensate for not being able to register volume changes or facial expressions with a variety of emoticons. Table 7.1 provides just a few examples of the growing number of emoticons used in computer-mediated communication of all types.

- You may deliberately *contradict* your verbal messages with nonverbal movements— for example, by crossing your fingers or winking to indicate that you're lying.

- Movements may serve to *regulate*—to control, or indicate your desire to control, the flow of verbal messages, as when you purse your lips, lean forward, or make hand gestures to indicate that you want to speak. You might also put up your hand or vocalize your pauses (for example, with "um" or "ah") to indicate that you have not finished and are not ready to relinquish the floor to the next speaker.

- You can *repeat* or restate the verbal message nonverbally. You can, for example, follow your verbal "Is that all right?" with raised eyebrows and a questioning look, or motion with your head or hand to repeat your verbal "Let's go."

- You may also use nonverbal communication to *substitute* or take the place of verbal messages. For instance, you can signal "OK" with a hand gesture. You can nod your head to indicate yes or shake your head to indicate no.

TABLE 7.1	Some Popular Emoticons

Here are just a few of the hundreds of popular emoticons used in computer-mediated communication. If you want more, take a look at Netlingo's website (**www.netlingo.com/smiley.cfm**).

EMOTICON	MEANING
:-[	Anger
>:-(	Annoyance
(((H)))	Big hug
:-!	Boredom
:")	Embarrassment
:-x	My lips are sealed; I'll keep this a secret
:-(	Feeling sad
:-d	Said with a smile
:->	Sarcasm
:0	Surprise

E-Talk

Establishing Closeness with Immediacy

How would you establish a psychological closeness in face-to-face and in computer-mediated communication? After you've developed your responses, take a look at O'Sullivan, Hunt, and Lippert (2004).

Researching Nonverbal Communication Functions

Although nonverbal communication serves the same functions as verbal communication, nonverbal researchers have singled out several functions in which nonverbal messages play particularly important roles (Burgoon, Buller, & Woodall, 1996; Burgoon & Hoobler, 2002).

FORMING AND MANAGING IMPRESSIONS   It is largely through the nonverbal communications of others that you form impressions of them. Based on a person's body size, skin color, and dress, as well as on the way the person smiles, maintains eye contact, and expresses himself or herself facially, you form impressions—you judge who the person is. One nonverbal researcher groups these impressions into four categories (Leathers, 1997): credibility (how competent and believable you find the person), likability (how much you like or dislike the person), attractiveness (how attractive you find the person), and dominance (how dominant the individual is).

Of course, you reveal yourself to others largely through the same nonverbal signals you use to size up others. But not only do you communicate your true self nonverbally; you also manage the impression that you give to others. Impression management may, for example, mean appearing brave when you're really scared or happy when you're really sad.

FORMING AND DEFINING RELATIONSHIPS   Much of your relationship life is lived nonverbally. Largely through nonverbal signals, you communicate the nature of your relationship to another person; and you and that person communicate nonverbally with each other. Holding hands, looking longingly into each other's eyes, and even dressing alike are ways in which you communicate closeness in your interpersonal relationships.

You also use nonverbal signals to communicate your relationship dominance and status (Knapp & Hall, 1996). The large corner office with the huge desk communicates high status just as the basement cubicle communicates low status.

STRUCTURING CONVERSATION AND SOCIAL INTERACTION   When you're in conversation, you give and receive cues—signals that you're ready to speak, to listen, to comment on what the speaker just said—that regulate and structure the interaction. These turn-taking cues may be verbal (as when you say, "What do you think?"), but most often they're nonverbal: A nod of the head in the direction of someone else signals that you're ready to give up your speaking turn and want this other person to say something. You also show that you're listening and that you want the conversation to continue (or that you're not listening and want the conversation to end) largely through nonverbal signals.

INFLUENCE AND DECEPTION   You can influence others not only through what you say but also through your nonverbal signals. A focused glance that says you're committed; gestures that further explain what you're saying; appropriate dress that says, "I'll easily fit in with this organization"—these are a few examples of ways in which you can exert nonverbal influence.

And with the ability to influence, of course, comes the ability to deceive—to lie, to mislead another person into thinking something is true when it's false or that something is false when it's true. One common example of nonverbal deception is using your eyes and facial expressions to communicate a liking for other people, when you're really interested only in gaining their support in some endeavor. Not surprisingly, you also use nonverbal signals

❝ Without wearing any mask we are conscious of, we have a special face for each friend. ❞
—Oliver Wendell Holmes

Integrating Verbal and Nonverbal Messages

To demonstrate that the way you say something influences the meanings you communicate, try reading each of the following aloud—first to communicate the statement's literal meaning and then to convey a meaning opposite to the literal one. As you communicate these meanings, try to identify the nonverbal differences between the ways in which you express the literal meanings and their opposites. Look specifically at (a) how you read the statements in terms of rate, pauses, and volume and (b) how your facial and eye expressions differ.

1. Yes, I have the relationship of a lifetime.
2. I can't wait to receive my test results.
3. Wow! I had some fantastic date last night.
4. Did you see him pitch that great game last night?
5. Did you see the way she decorated her apartment—real style, don't you think?

You cannot speak a sentence without using nonverbal signals, and these signals influence the meaning you send to the receiver.

to detect deception in others. For example, you may well suspect a person of lying if he or she avoids eye contact, fidgets, and conveys verbal and nonverbal messages that are inconsistent.

EMOTIONAL EXPRESSION   Although people often explain and reveal emotions verbally, nonverbal expressions probably communicate more about emotional experience. For example, you reveal your level of happiness or sadness or confusion largely through facial expressions. Of course, you also reveal your feelings by posture (for example, whether tense or relaxed), gestures, eye movements, and even the dilation of your pupils.

Nonverbal messages often help people communicate unpleasant messages, messages they might feel uncomfortable putting into words (Infante, Rancer, & Womack, 2002). For example, you might avoid eye contact and maintain large distances between yourself and someone with whom you didn't want to interact or with whom you wanted to decrease the intensity of your relationship.

The Channels of Nonverbal Messages

Nonverbal communication is probably most easily explained in terms of the various channels through which messages pass. Here we'll survey 10 channels: body, face, eye, space, artifactual, touch, paralanguage, silence, time, and smell.

Body Messages

Two aspects of the body are especially important in communicating messages: first, the movements you make with your body, and second, the general appearance of your body.

BODY MOVEMENTS   Nonverbal researchers identify five major types of body movements: emblems, illustrators, affect displays, regulators, and adaptors (Ekman & Friesen, 1969; Knapp & Hall, 1996).

Emblems are body gestures that directly translate into words or phrases; for example, the OK sign, the thumbs-up for "good job," and the V for victory. You use these consciously and purposely to communicate the same meaning as the words. But emblems are culture specific, so be careful when using your culture's emblems in other cultures. For example, when President Nixon visited Latin America and gestured with the OK sign, intending to communicate something positive, he was quickly informed that this gesture was not universal. In Latin America the gesture has a far more negative meaning. Here are a few cultural differences in the emblems you may commonly use (Axtell, 1993):

- In the United States, to say "hello" you wave with your whole hand moving from side to side but in a large part of Europe that same signal means "no." In Greece such a gesture would be considered insulting to the person to whom you're waving.

- The V for victory is common throughout much of the world; but if you make this gesture in England with the palm facing your face, it's as insulting as the raised middle finger is in the United States.

- In Texas the raised fist with little finger and index finger raised is a positive expression of support, because it represents the Texas longhorn steer. But in Italy it's an insult that means "Your spouse is having an affair with someone else." In parts of South America it's a gesture to ward off evil, and in parts of Africa it's a curse: "May you experience bad times."

- In the United States and in much of Asia, hugs are rarely exchanged among acquaintances; but among Latins and Southern Europeans hugging is a common greeting gesture, and failing to hug someone may communicate unfriendliness.

Illustrators enhance (literally "illustrate") the verbal messages they accompany. For example, when referring to something to the left, you might gesture toward the left. Most often you illustrate with your hands, but you can also illustrate with head and general body movements. You might, for example, turn your head or your entire body toward the left. You might also use illustrators to communicate the shape or size of objects you're talking about.

Research points to still another advantage of illustrators—namely, that they increase your ability to remember. In one study people who illustrated their verbal messages with gestures remembered some 20 percent more than those who didn't gesture (Goldin-Meadow, Nusbaum, Kelly, & Wagner, 2001).

Affect displays include movements of the face (smiling or frowning, for example), as well as of the hands and general body (body tension or relaxation, for example), that communicate emotional meaning. You use affect displays to accompany and reinforce your verbal messages, but also as substitutes for words; for example, you might smile while saying how happy you are to see your friend, or you might simply smile. Or you might rush to greet someone with open arms. Because affect displays are centered primarily in the facial area, we'll consider these in more detail in the "Facial Messages" section beginning on page 157. Affect displays are often unconscious; frequently, for example, you smile or frown without awareness. At other times, however, you may smile with awareness, consciously trying to convey pleasure or friendliness.

Regulators are behaviors that monitor, control, coordinate, or maintain the speaking of another individual. When you nod your head, for example, you tell the speaker to keep on speaking; when you lean forward and open your mouth, you tell the speaker that you would like to say something.

Adaptors are gestures that satisfy some personal need. **Self-adaptors** are self-touching movements; for example, rubbing your nose, scratching to relieve an itch, or moving your hair out of your eyes. **Alter-adaptors** are movements directed at the

❝ The body says what words cannot. ❞

—Martha Graham

person with whom you're speaking, such as removing lint from a person's jacket, straightening a person's tie, or folding your arms in front of you to keep others a comfortable distance from you. **Object-adaptors** are gestures focused on objects; for example, doodling on or shredding a Styrofoam coffee cup.

Table 7.2 summarizes these five types of body movements.

BODY APPEARANCE   Your general body appearance also communicates. Height, for example, has been shown to be significant in a wide variety of situations. Tall presidential candidates have a much better record of winning elections than do their shorter opponents. Tall people seem to be paid more and are favored by personnel interviewers over shorter job applicants (Keyes, 1980; Guerrero, DeVito & Hecht, 1999; Knapp & Hall, 1996; Jackson & Ervin, 1992). Taller people also have higher self-esteem and greater career success than do shorter people (Judge & Cable, 2004).

Your body also reveals your race (through skin color and tone) and may even give clues as to your specific nationality. Your weight in proportion to your height will also communicate messages to others, as will the length, color, and style of your hair.

Your general **attractiveness,** which includes both visual appeal and pleasantness of personality, is also a part of body communication. Attractive people have the advantage in just about every activity you can name. They get better grades in school, are more valued as friends and lovers, and are preferred as coworkers (Burgoon, Buller, & Woodall, 1996). Although we normally think of attractiveness as culturally determined—and to some degree it is—research seems to suggest that definitions of attractiveness are becoming universal (Brody, 1994). A person rated as attractive in one culture is likely to be rated as attractive in other cultures, even in cultures whose people are widely different in appearance.

Facial Messages

Throughout your interpersonal interactions, your face communicates many things, especially your emotions. Facial movements alone seem to communicate messages about pleasantness, agreement, and sympathy; the rest of the body doesn't provide any additional information in those realms. But for other emotional messages—for example, the intensity with which an emotion is felt—both facial and bodily cues enter in (Graham, Bitti, & Argyle, 1975; Graham & Argyle, 1975).

TABLE 7.2	Five Body Movements
Can you give at least one additional example of each of these five body movements?	

NAME AND FUNCTION	EXAMPLES
EMBLEMS directly translate words or phrases	"OK" sign, "come here" wave, hitchhiker's sign
ILLUSTRATORS accompany and literally "illustrate" verbal messages	Circular hand movements when talking of a circle; hands far apart when talking of something large
AFFECT DISPLAYS communicate emotional meaning	Expressions of happiness, surprise, fear, anger, sadness, disgust/contempt
REGULATORS monitor, maintain, or control the speaking of another	Facial expressions and hand gestures indicating "keep going," "slow down," or "what else happened?"
ADAPTORS satisfy some need	Scratching head

■ **Listening Nonverbally**

Much as you can communicate power and authority with words and nonverbal expressions, you can also communicate power through listening. Here are some suggestions:

- Respond visibly but in moderation; an occasional nod or a facial expression that says "that's interesting" is usually sufficient. Too little response says you aren't listening, and too much says you aren't listening critically.

- Avoid adaptors such as playing with your hair or a pencil or doodling. These signal discomfort and hence a lack of power.

- Maintain an open posture. Resist covering your face, chest, or stomach with your hands. These gestures may communicate defensiveness and vulnerability and hence powerlessness.

- You can also signal power through "visual dominance behavior" (Exline, Ellyson, & Long, 1975). For example, the average speaker maintains lots of eye contact while listening and less while speaking. To signal dominance, you can reverse this pattern and maintain lots of eye contact while talking but much less while listening.

■ **Applying Listening Skills**

Sumitra, a new project director at a conservative advertising company, comes from a culture very different from the one she'll be working in. What additional suggestions for nonverbal communication would you offer Sumitra?

Some researchers in nonverbal communication claim that facial movements may express at least the following eight emotions: happiness, surprise, fear, anger, sadness, disgust, contempt, and interest (Ekman, Friesen, & Ellsworth, 1972). Others propose that in addition, facial movements may also communicate bewilderment and determination (Leathers, 1997).

Try to express surprise using only facial movements. Do this in front of a mirror and try to describe in as much detail as possible the specific movements of the face that make up a look of surprise. If you signal surprise like most people, you probably use raised and curved eyebrows, long horizontal forehead wrinkles, wide-open eyes, a dropped-open mouth, and lips parted with no tension. Even if there were differences from one person to another—and clearly there would be—you probably could recognize the movements listed here as indicative of surprise.

Of course, some emotions are easier to communicate and to decode than others. For example, in one study, participants judged happiness with 55 to 100 percent accuracy, surprise with 38 to 86 percent accuracy, and sadness with 19 to 88 percent accuracy (Ekman, Friesen, & Ellsworth, 1972). Research finds that women and girls are more accurate judges of facial emotional expression than men and boys (Hall, 1984; Argyle, 1988).

As you've probably experienced, you may interpret the same facial expression differently depending on the context in which it occurs. For example, in a classic study, when researchers showed participants a smiling face looking at a glum face, the participants judged the smiling face to be vicious and taunting. But when presented with the same smiling face looking at a frowning face, they saw it as peaceful and friendly (Cline, 1956).

Not surprisingly, people who smile are judged to be more likable and more approachable than people who don't smile or people who pretend to smile (Gladstone & Parker, 2002; Kluger, 2005).

FACIAL MANAGEMENT As each of us learns our culture's nonverbal system of communication, we also learn certain **facial management techniques** that enable us to communicate our feelings to achieve the effect we want—for example, to hide certain emotions and to emphasize others. Consider your own use of such facial management techniques. As you do so, think about the types of interpersonal situations

■ **What Do You Say**

Smiling to Bad Effect

Sally smiles almost all the time. Even when she criticizes or reprimands a subordinate, she ends with a smile, and this dilutes the strength of her message. As Sally's supervisor, you need her to realize what she's doing and to change her nonverbals. **What Do You Say?** Through what channel?

in which you would use each of these facial management techniques (Malandro, Barker, & Barker, 1989; Metts & Planalp, 2002). Would you:

- *Intensify? Would you exaggerate surprise when friends throw you a party to make your friends feel better?*
- *Deintensify? Would you cover up your own joy in the presence of a friend who didn't receive such good news?*
- *Neutralize? Would you cover up your sadness to keep from depressing others?*
- *Mask? Would you express happiness in order to cover up your disappointment at not receiving the gift you expected?*
- *Simulate? Would you express an emotion you don't feel?*

These facial management techniques help you display emotions in socially acceptable ways. For example, when someone gets bad news in which you may secretly take pleasure, the display rule dictates that you frown and otherwise nonverbally signal your displeasure. If you place first in a race and your best friend barely finishes, the display rule requires that you minimize your expression of pleasure in winning and avoid any signs of gloating. If you violate these display rules, you'll be judged as insensitive. So, although these techniques may be deceptive, they're also expected—and, in fact, required—by the rules of polite interaction.

FACIAL FEEDBACK The **facial feedback hypothesis** holds that your facial expressions influence physiological arousal (Lanzetta, Cartwright-Smith, & Kleck, 1976; Zuckerman, Klorman, Larrance, & Spiegel, 1981). In one study, for example, participants held a pen in their teeth to simulate a sad expression and then rated a series of photographs. Results showed that mimicking sad expressions actually increased the degree of sadness the participants reported feeling when viewing the photographs (Larsen, Kasimatis, & Frey, 1992).

Further support for this hypothesis comes from a study that compared (1) participants who felt emotions such as happiness and anger with (2) those who both felt and expressed these emotions. In support of the facial feedback hypothesis, participants who felt and expressed the emotions became emotionally aroused faster than did those who only felt the emotion (Hess, Kappas, McHugo, Lanzetta, et al., 1992).

Generally, research finds that facial expressions can produce or heighten feelings of sadness, fear, disgust, and anger. But this effect does not occur with all emotions; smiling, for example, doesn't seem to make us feel happier (Burgoon, Buller, & Woodall, 1996). Further, it has not been demonstrated that facial expressions can eliminate one feeling and replace it with another. So if you're feeling sad, smiling will not eliminate the sadness and replace it with gladness. A reasonable conclusion seems to be that your facial expressions can influence some feelings but not all (Burgoon, Buller, & Woodall, 1996; Cappella, 1993).

Eye Messages

Research on communication via the eyes (a study known technically as *oculesis*) shows that these messages vary depending on the duration, direction, and quality of the eye behavior. For example, in every culture there are strict, though unstated, rules for the proper duration for eye contact. In our culture, the average length of gaze is 2.95 seconds. The average length of mutual gaze (two persons gazing at each other) is 1.18 seconds (Argyle & Ingham, 1972; Argyle, 1988). When eye contact falls short of this amount, you may think the person is uninterested, shy, or preoccupied. When the appropriate amount of time is exceeded, you may perceive the person as showing unusually high interest. Some researchers also note that eye contact serves to enable gay men and lesbians to signal their homosexuality and perhaps their interest in the other person—an ability referred to as "gaydar" (Nicholas, 2004; Lawson, 2005).

■ **What Do You Say**
Confronting a Misconception
You've been doing exceptionally well in English—after two previous semesters of earning a C and a C−. During a conference on your "A" paper, the instructor implies (very indirectly) that your paper looks plagiarized. You did not plagiarize the paper and you want that made very clear verbally and nonverbally. At the same time, you don't want to appear guilty by protesting too much. **What Do You Say?**

An eye can threaten like a loaded and leveled gun, or it can insult like hissing or kicking; or, in its altered mood, by beams of kindness, it can make the heart dance for joy. **"**
—Ralph Waldo Emerson

The direction of the eye glance also communicates. In much of the United States, you're expected to glance alternately at the other person's face, then away, then again at the face, and so on. The rule for the public speaker is to scan the entire audience, not focusing for too long on or ignoring any one area of the audience. When you break these directional rules, you communicate different meanings—abnormally high or low interest, self-consciousness, nervousness over the interaction, and so on. The quality of eye behavior—how wide or how narrow your eyes get during interaction—also communicates meaning, especially interest level and such emotions as surprise, fear, and disgust.

EYE CONTACT   With eye contact you send a variety of messages. One such message is a request for feedback. In talking with someone, we look at her or him intently, as if to say, "Well, what do you think?" As you might predict, listeners gaze at speakers more than speakers gaze at listeners. In public speaking, you may scan hundreds of people to secure this feedback.

Another type of message informs the other person that the channel of communication is open and that he or she should now speak. You see this regularly in conversation, when one person asks a question or finishes a thought and then looks to you for a response.

Eye contact may also send messages about the nature of the relationship. For example, if you engage in prolonged eye contact coupled with a smile, you'll signal a positive relationship. If you stare or glare at the person while frowning, you'll signal a negative relationship.

Eye contact messages enable you to psychologically lessen the physical distance between yourself and another person. When you catch someone's eye at a party, for example, you become psychologically close though physically far apart.

EYE AVOIDANCE   The eyes are "great intruders," observed sociologist Erving Goffman (1967). When you avoid eye contact or avert your glance, you help others to maintain their privacy. You may do this when you see a couple arguing in public: You turn your eyes away (though your eyes may be wide open) as if to say, "I don't mean to intrude; I respect your privacy." Goffman refers to this behavior as **civil inattention.**

Eye avoidance can also signal lack of interest—in a person, a conversation, or some visual stimulus. At times you may hide your eyes to block off unpleasant stimuli (a particularly gory or violent scene in a movie, for example) or close your eyes to block out visual stimuli and thus heighten other senses. For example, you may listen to music with your eyes closed. Lovers often close their eyes while kissing, and many prefer to make love in a dark or dimly lit room.

Spatial Messages

Space is an especially important factor in nonverbal interpersonal communication, although we seldom think about it. Edward T. Hall (1959, 1963, 1966), who has pioneered the study of spatial communication, called this study **proxemics.** We can examine this broad area by looking at the messages communicated by distance and territory.

PROXEMIC DISTANCES   Four proxemic distances correspond closely to the major types of relationships: intimate, personal, social, and public (see Table 7.3).

TABLE 7.3   Relationships and Proxemic Distances

These four distances can be further divided into close and far phases; the far phase of one level (say, personal) blends into the close phase of the next level (social). Do your relationships also blend into one another? Or are, say, your personal relationships totally separated from your social relationships?

RELATIONSHIP		DISTANCE
	Intimate Relationship	**Intimate Distance** 0 _____ 18 inches close phase far phase
	Personal Relationship	**Personal Distance** $1\frac{1}{2}$ _____ 4 feet close phase far phase
	Social Relationship	**Social Distance** 4 _____ 12 feet close phase far phase
	Public Relationship	**Public Distance** 12 _____ 25+ feet close phase far phase

In **intimate distance,** ranging from actual touching to 18 inches, the presence of the other individual is unmistakable. Each person experiences the sound, smell, and feel of the other's breath. You use intimate distance for lovemaking, comforting, and protecting. This distance is so short that most people do not consider it proper in public.

Personal distance refers to the protective "bubble" that defines your personal space, ranging from 18 inches to 4 feet. This imaginary bubble keeps you protected and untouched by others. You can still hold or grasp another person at this distance, but only by extending your arms; this allows you to take certain individuals such as loved ones into your protective bubble. At the outer limit of personal distance, you can touch another person only if both of you extend your arms. At this distance you conduct much of your interpersonal interactions; for example, talking with friends and family.

At **social distance,** ranging from 4 to 12 feet, you lose the visual detail you have at personal distance. You conduct impersonal business and interact at a social gathering at this social distance. The more distance you maintain in your interactions, the more formal they appear. In offices of high officials, the desks are positioned so the official is assured of at least this distance from clients.

Public distance, from 12 to 25 feet or more, protects you. At this distance you could take defensive action if threatened. On a public bus or train, for example, you might try to keep at least this distance from a drunken passenger. Although at this distance you lose fine details of the face and eyes, you're still close enough to see what is happening.

The specific distances that you maintain between yourself and other individuals depend on a wide variety of factors (Burgoon, Buller, & Woodall, 1996). Among the most significant factors are *gender* (women in same-sex dyads sit and stand closer to each other than do men, and people approach women more closely than they approach men); *age* (people maintain closer distances with similarly aged others than they do with those much older or much younger); and *personality* (introverts and highly anxious people maintain greater distances than do extroverts). Not surpris-

■ **What Do You Say**?

Close Talking

Like the close-talker in an episode of *Seinfeld,* one of your team members at work maintains an extremely close distance when talking. Also, this person is a heavy smoker and reeks of tobacco. So you need to say something. **What Do You Say?** Through what channel?

"Never let her catch you in her garden . . . Humans are *very* territorial."

© 2001. Reprinted courtesy of Bunny Hoest and *Parade* magazine.

ingly, you'll tend to maintain shorter distances with people you're familiar with than with strangers, and with people you like than with those you don't like.

TERRITORIALITY   Another type of communication having to do with space is **territoriality,** a possessive reaction to an area or to particular objects. You interact basically in three types of territories (Altman, 1975):

- **Primary territories** are areas that you might call your own; these areas are your exclusive preserve. Primary territories might include your room, your desk, or your office.

- **Secondary territories** are areas that don't belong to you but which you have occupied and with which you're associated. They might include your usual table in the cafeteria, your regular seat in the classroom, or your neighborhood turf.

- **Public territories** are areas that are open to all people; they may be owned by some person or organization, but they are used by everyone. They are places such as movie houses, restaurants, and shopping malls.

When you operate in your own primary territory, you have an interpersonal advantage, often called the **home field advantage.** In their own home or office, people take on a kind of leadership role: They initiate conversations, fill in silences, assume relaxed and comfortable postures, and maintain their positions with greater conviction. Because the territorial owner is dominant, you stand a better chance of getting your raise approved, your point accepted, or a contract resolved in your favor if you're in your own territory (your office, your home) rather than in someone else's (your supervisor's office, for example) (Marsh, 1988).

Like animals, humans mark both their primary and secondary territories to signal ownership. Humans use three types of **markers:** central markers, boundary markers, and earmarkers (Goffman, 1971). **Central markers** are items you place in a territory to reserve it for you—for example, a drink at the bar, books on your desk, or a sweater over a library chair.

Boundary markers serve to divide your territory from that of others. In the supermarket checkout line, the bar placed between your groceries and those of the person behind you is a boundary marker, as are fences, armrests that separate your chair from those on either side, and the contours of the molded plastic seats on a bus.

Earmarkers—a term taken from the practice of branding animals on their ears—are identifying marks that indicate your possession of a territory or object. Trademarks, nameplates, and initials on a shirt or attaché case are all examples of earmarkers.

Markers are also important in giving you a feeling of belonging. For example, one study found that students who marked their college dorm rooms by displaying personal items stayed in school longer than did those who didn't personalize their spaces (Marsh, 1988).

Again, like animals, humans use territory to signal their status. For example, the size and location of your territory (your home or office, say) indicates something about your status. Status is also signaled by the unwritten law governing the right of invasion. Higher-status individuals have a "right" to invade the territory of lower-status persons, but the reverse is not true. The boss of a large company, for example, can barge into the office of a junior executive, but the reverse would be unthinkable. Similarly, a teacher may invade a student's personal space by looking over her or his shoulder as the student writes, but the student cannot do the same to the teacher.

Some teenagers, perhaps because they can't yet own territories, often use markers to indicate their pseudo-ownership or their appropriation of someone else's space or a public territory for their own use (Childress, 2004). Examples of graffiti and the markings of gang boundaries come quickly to mind.

Sitting at the Company Meeting

The graphic here represents a meeting table with 12 chairs, one of which is already occupied by the boss. Below are listed five messages you might want to communicate. For each of these messages, indicate (a) where you would sit to communicate the desired message, (b) any other possible messages that your choice of seat would likely communicate, and (c) the messages that your choice of seat would make it easier for you to communicate.

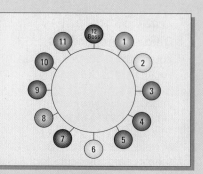

1. You want to polish the apple and ingratiate yourself with your boss.
2. You aren't prepared and want to be ignored.
3. You want to challenge your boss on a certain policy that will come up for a vote.
4. You want to help your boss on a certain policy that will come up for a vote.
5. You want to be accepted as a new (but important) member of the company.

Nonverbal choices (such as the seat you select or the clothes you wear) have an impact on communication and on your image as a communicator.

Artifactual Messages

Artifactual messages are messages conveyed through objects or arrangements made by human hands—such as color, clothing, jewelry, and the decoration of space. Let's look at each of these briefly.

COLOR   There is some evidence that colors affect us physiologically. For example, respiratory movements increase with red light and decrease with blue light. Similarly, eye blinks increase in frequency when eyes are exposed to red light and decrease when exposed to blue. This seems consistent with our intuitive feelings that blue is more soothing and red more arousing. When a school changed the color of its walls from orange and white to blue, the blood pressure of the students decreased and their academic performance increased (Malandro, Barker, & Barker, 1989).

   Color communication also influences perceptions and behaviors (Kanner, 1989). People's acceptance of a product, for example, can be largely determined by its packaging, especially its color. In one study, participants described the very same coffee taken from a yellow can as weak, from a dark brown can as too strong, from a red can as rich, and from a blue can as mild. Even your acceptance of a person may depend on the colors the person wears. Consider, for example, the comments of one color expert (Kanner, 1989): "If you have to pick the wardrobe for your defense lawyer heading into court and choose anything but blue, you deserve to lose the case. . . ." Black is so powerful it could work against the lawyer with the jury. Brown lacks sufficient authority. Green would probably elicit a negative response.

CLOTHING AND BODY ADORNMENT   People make inferences about who you are, at least in part, from the way you dress. Whether accurate or not, these inferences will affect what people think of you and how they react to you. Your socioeconomic class, your seriousness, your attitudes (for example, whether you're conservative or liberal), your concern for convention, your sense of style, and perhaps even your creativity will all be judged in part by the way you dress (Molloy, 1977; Burgoon, Buller, & Woodall, 1995; Knapp & Hall, 1996). In the business world your clothing may communicate your position within the hierarchy and your willingness and desire to conform to the clothing norms of the organization. It may also communicate your professionalism, which seems to be the reason why some organizations favor dress codes (Smith, 2003). In the college classroom, research indicates, college students tend to perceive an instructor dressed informally as friendly, fair, enthusiastic, and flexible and the same instructor dressed formally as prepared, knowledgeable, and organized (Malandro, Barker, & Barker, 1989).

Body adornment also communicates about aspects of who you are—from a concern about being up to date, to a desire to shock, to perhaps a lack of interest in appearances. Your jewelry, too, sends messages about you. Some jewelry is a form of **cultural display,** indicating a particular cultural or religious affiliation. Wedding and engagement rings are obvious examples that communicate specific messages. College rings and political buttons likewise convey messages. If you wear a Rolex watch or large precious stones, others are likely to infer that you're rich. Men who wear earrings will be judged differently from men who don't. What judgments people make will depend, of course, on who the receiver is, on the communication context, and on all the other factors identified throughout this text.

Body piercings have become increasingly popular, especially among the young. Nose and nipple rings and tongue and belly-button jewelry send a variety of messages. Although people wearing such jewelry may wish to communicate different meanings, those interpreting the messages of body piercings seem to infer that the wearers are communicating an unwillingness to conform to social norms and a willingness to take greater risks than those without such piercings (Forbes, 2001). It's worth noting that in a study of employers' perceptions, employers rated and ranked applicants with eyebrow piercings significantly lower than those without such piercings (Acor, 2001). Nose-pierced job candidates received lower scores on measures of credibility such as character and trust as well as on sociability and hirability (Seiter & Sandry, 2003). Further, health care providers sometimes see tattoos and piercings as signs of such undesirable traits as impulsiveness, unpredictability, and a tendency toward being reckless or violent (Rapsa & Cusack, 1990; Smith, 2003).

Tattoos—whether temporary or permanent—likewise communicate a variety of messages, often the name of a loved one or some symbol of allegiance or affiliation. Tattoos also communicate to the wearers themselves. For example, tattooed students see themselves (and perhaps others do as well) as more adventurous, creative, individualistic, and risk prone than those without tattoos (Drews, Allison, & Probst, 2000).

"I try not to judge my doctors by the art work in their waiting rooms."

SPACE DECORATION   The way you decorate your private spaces speaks about you. The office with a mahogany desk and bookcases and oriental rugs communicates your importance and status within the organization, just as a metal desk and bare floor indicate a worker much farther down in the hierarchy.

Similarly, people will make inferences about you based on the way you decorate your home. The expensiveness of the furnishings may communicate your status and wealth; their coordination, your sense of style. The magazines you choose may reflect your interests, and the arrangement of chairs around a television set may reveal how important watching television is to you. The contents of bookcases lining the walls reveal the importance of reading in your life. In fact, there is probably little in your home that would not send messages from which others would draw inferences about you. Computers, wide-screen televisions, well-equipped kitchens, and oil paintings of great grandparents, for example, all say something about the people who live in the home.

People also will make judgments as to your personality on the basis of room decorations. Research finds, for example, that people will make judgments as to your openness to new experiences (distinctive decorating usually communicates this, as do different types of books and magazines and travel souvenirs), conscientiousness, emotional stability, degree of extroversion, and agreeableness. Not surprisingly, bedrooms prove more revealing than offices (Gosling, Ko, Mannarelli, & Morris, 2002).

Similarly, the absence of certain items will communicate something about you. Consider what messages you would get from a home where no television, phone, or books could be seen.

Touch Messages

Touch communication, or **tactile communication,** is perhaps the most primitive form of communication (Montagu, 1971). Touch develops before the other senses; even in the womb the child is stimulated by touch. Soon after birth the child is fondled, caressed, patted, and stroked. In turn, the child explores its world through touch and quickly learns to communicate a variety of meanings through touch. The nature of touch communication also varies with relationship stages. In the early stages of a relationship you touch little, in intermediate stages (involvement and intimacy) you touch a great deal, and at stable or deteriorating stages you again touch little (Guerrero & Andersen, 1991).

THE MEANINGS OF TOUCH   Researchers in the field of **haptics**—the study of touch—have identified the major meanings of touch (Jones & Yarbrough, 1985):

- *Positive emotion.* Touch may communicate such positive feelings as support, appreciation, inclusion, sexual interest or intent, or affection.
- *Playfulness.* Touch often communicates our intention to play, either affectionately or aggressively.
- *Control.* Touch may direct the behaviors, attitudes, or feelings of the other person. To get attention, for example, you may touch a person as if to say, "Look at me" or "Look over here."
- *Ritual.* Ritualistic touching centers on greetings and departures; for example, shaking hands to say hello or goodbye or hugging, kissing, or putting your arm around another's shoulder when greeting or saying farewell.
- *Task-relatedness.* Task-related touching occurs while you're performing some function, such as removing a speck of dust from another person's face or helping someone out of a car.

Do recognize that different cultures will view these types of touching differently. For example, some task-related touching, viewed as acceptable in much of the United States, would be viewed negatively in some cultures. Among Koreans, for

What Do You Say

Violating Touch Boundaries

A colleague at work continually touches you in passing—your arm, your shoulder, your waist. These touches are becoming more frequent and more intimate. You want this touching to stop. **What Do You Say?** To whom? Through what channel?

example, it's considered disrespectful for a storekeeper to touch a customer in, say, handing back change; it's considered too intimate a gesture. But members of other cultures, expecting some touching, may consider the Koreans' behavior cold and insulting.

TOUCH AVOIDANCE Much as we touch and are touched, we also avoid touch from certain people and in certain circumstances. Researchers in nonverbal communication have found some interesting relationships between **touch avoidance** and other significant communication variables (Andersen & Leibowitz, 1978; Hall, 1996). Among research findings, for example, is the fact that touch avoidance is positively related to communication apprehension; those who fear oral communication also score high on touch avoidance. Touch avoidance is also high with those who self-disclose little. Both touch and self-disclosure are intimate forms of communication; thus, people who are reluctant to get close to another person by self-disclosing also seem reluctant to get close by touching.

Older people have higher touch-avoidance scores for opposite-sex persons than do younger people. As we get older we're touched less by members of the opposite sex, and this decreased frequency may lead us to avoid touching.

Males score higher on same-sex touch avoidance than do females, a finding that confirms popular stereotypes. Men avoid touching other men, but women may and do touch other women. On the other hand, women have higher touch-avoidance scores for opposite-sex touching than do men.

Paralanguage Messages

The term **paralanguage** refers to the vocal but nonverbal dimensions of speech. It refers to how you say something, not what you say. A traditional exercise students use to increase their ability to express different emotions, feelings, and attitudes is to repeat a sentence while accenting or stressing different words. One popular sentence is "Is this the face that launched a thousand ships?" Examine your own sensitivity to paralanguage variations by seeing if you get different meanings for each of the following questions based on where the emphasis is.

- Is *this the face that launched a thousand ships?*
- *Is* this *the face that launched a thousand ships?*
- *Is this the* face *that launched a thousand ships?*
- *Is this the face that* launched *a thousand ships?*
- *Is this the face that launched* a thousand ships*?*

In addition to stress and **pitch** (highness or lowness), paralanguage includes such **voice qualities** or vocal characteristics as **rate** (speed), **volume** (loudness), and rhythm as well as the vocalizations you make in crying, whispering, moaning, belching, yawning, and yelling (Trager, 1958, 1961; Argyle, 1988). A variation in any of these features communicates. When you speak quickly, for example, you communicate something different from when you speak slowly. Even though the words may be the same, if the speed (or volume, rhythm, or pitch) differs, the meanings people receive also will differ.

JUDGMENTS ABOUT PEOPLE We often use paralanguage cues as a basis for judgments about people; for example, evaluations of their emotional state or even their personality. A listener can accurately judge the emotional state of a speaker from vocal expression alone, if both speaker and listener speak the same language. Paralanguage cues are not so accurate when used to communicate emotions to those who speak a different language (Albas, McCluskey, & Albas, 1976). In studies in this field, speakers recite the alphabet or numbers while expressing emotions. Some emotions are easier to

Nonverbal Impression Formation

Earlier in this chapter we saw that impression formation is one of the major functions of non-verbal communication. Now that you've covered the types of nonverbal messages, consider how you would manage yourself nonverbally in the following situations. For each of these situations, indicate (1) the impressions you'd want to create (for example, an image as a hardworking self-starter); (2) the nonverbal cues you'd use to create these impressions; and (3) the nonverbal cues you'd be especially careful to avoid.

- You want a job at a conservative, prestigious law firm.
- You want a part in a movie in which you'd play a homeless drug addict.
- You're single and you're applying to adopt a child.

Interpersonal messages are a combination of verbal and nonverbal signals; even subtle variations in, say, eye movements or intonation can drastically change the impression communicated.

identify than others; it's easy to distinguish between hate and sympathy but more difficult to distinguish between fear and anxiety. And, of course, listeners vary in their ability to decode, and speakers in their ability to encode emotions (Scherer, 1986).

Less reliable are judgments made about personality. Some people, for example, may conclude that those who speak softly feel inferior, believing that no one wants to listen and nothing they say is significant, or that people who speak loudly have overinflated egos and think everyone in the world wants to hear them. Such conclusions may be mistaken, however. There are lots of reasons why people might speak softly (to communicate sorrow and understanding in consoling someone) or loudly (to override the noise or to emphasize a point).

JUDGMENTS ABOUT COMMUNICATION EFFECTIVENESS   The rate or speed at which people speak is the aspect of paralanguage that has received the most attention (MacLachlan, 1979). Rates of speech are of interest to the advertiser, the politician, and, in fact, anyone who tries to convey information or influence others. They are especially important when time is limited or expensive.

In one-way communication (when one person is doing all or most of the speaking and the other person is doing all or most of the listening), those who talk fast (about 50 percent faster than normal) are more persuasive. People agree more with a fast speaker than with a slow speaker and find the fast speaker more intelligent and objective.

When we look at comprehension, rapid speech shows an interesting effect. When the speaking rate is increased by 50 percent, the comprehension level drops only by 5 percent. When the rate is doubled, the comprehension level drops only 10 percent. These 5 and 10 percent losses are more than offset by the increased speed; thus, the faster rates are much more efficient in communicating information. If speeds are more than twice the rate of normal speech, however, comprehension begins to fall dramatically.

Do exercise caution in applying this research to all forms of communication (MacLachlan, 1979). For example, if you increase your rate to increase efficiency, you may create an impression so unnatural that others will focus on your speed instead of your meaning.

Silence Messages

Like words and gestures, **silence,** too, communicates important meanings and serves important functions (Johannesen, 1974; Jaworski, 1993). Silence allows the speaker *time to think,* time to formulate and organize his or her verbal communications. Before messages of intense conflict, as well as before those confessing undying love,

■ **What Do You Say**

Silence as Consent
Your college roommate has developed a small business selling term papers and uses your jointly owned computer to store them. Though you've remained silent about this activity for some time, you've become increasingly uncomfortable about it and want to distance yourself from an enterprise that you feel is unethical. **What Do You Say?** To whom? Through what channel?

there is often silence. Again, silence seems to prepare the receiver for the importance of these messages.

Some people use silence as a *weapon* to hurt others. We often speak of giving someone "the silent treatment." After a conflict, for example, one or both individuals may remain silent as a kind of punishment. Silence used to hurt others may also take the form of refusal to acknowledge the presence of another person, as in disconfirmation (see Chapter 6); here silence is a dramatic demonstration of the total indifference one person feels toward the other.

Sometimes silence is used as a *response to personal anxiety,* shyness, or threats. You may feel anxious or shy among new people and prefer to remain silent. By remaining silent you preclude the chance of rejection. Only when you break your silence and make an attempt to communicate with another person do you risk rejection.

Silence may be used *to prevent communication* of certain messages. In conflict situations, silence is sometimes used to prevent certain topics from surfacing and to prevent one or both parties from saying

> **&&** Well-timed silence hath more eloquence than speech. **""**
> —Martin Farquahr Tupper

things they may later regret. In such situations silence often allows us time to cool off before expressing hatred, severe criticism, or personal attacks—which, as we know, are irreversible.

Like the eyes, face, or hands, silence can also be used *to communicate emotional responses* (Ehrenhaus, 1988). Sometimes silence communicates a determination to be uncooperative or defiant; by refusing to engage in verbal communication, you defy the authority or the legitimacy of the other person's position. Silence is often used to communicate annoyance, particularly when accompanied by a pouting expression, arms crossed in front of the chest, and nostrils flared. Silence may express

Ethical *messages*

Interpersonal Silence

In the U.S. legal system, you have the right to remain silent and to refuse to reveal information about yourself that could be used against you or to incriminate you. But you don't have the right to refuse to reveal information about, for example, the criminal activities of others that you may have witnessed. Rightly or wrongly (and this in itself is an ethical issue), psychiatrists, clergy, and lawyers are often exempt from this general rule. Similarly, a wife can't be forced to testify against her husband or a husband against his wife.

In interpersonal situations, however, there are no such written rules; so it is not always clear if or when silence is ethical or unethical. For example, most people (but not all) would agree that you have the right to withhold information that has no bearing on the matter at hand. Thus, your previous relationship history, affectional orientation, or religion is usually irrelevant to your ability to function as a doctor or police officer and may thus be kept private in most job-related situations. If these issues become relevant—say, if you're about to enter a new relationship—then there may be an obligation to reveal certain information.

What Would You Do?

At the supermarket you witness a father verbally abusing his three-year-old child. You worry that the father might psychologically harm the child, and your first impulse is to speak up and tell this man that verbal abuse can have lasting effects on a child—and that it often leads to physical abuse. At the same time, you don't want to interfere with a father's right to say what he wants to his child. What is your ethical obligation in this case? What would you do in this situation?

affection or love, especially when coupled with long and longing gazes into each other's eyes.

Silence also may be used strategically, *to achieve specific effects*. You may, for example, strategically position a pause before what you feel is an important comment to make your idea stand out. A prolonged silence after someone voices disagreement may give the appearance of control and superiority. It's a way of saying, "I can respond in my own time." Generally research finds that people use silence strategically more with strangers than they do with close friends (Hesegawa & Gudykunst, 1998).

Of course, you may use silence when you simply have *nothing* to say—when nothing occurs to you, or when you do not want to say anything. Or you may use silence to avoid responsibility for wrongdoing (Beach, 1990–1991).

Time Messages

The study of **temporal communication,** known technically as **chronemics,** concerns the use of time—how you organize it, react to it, and communicate messages through it (Bruneau, 1985, 1990). Consider, for example, **psychological time:** the emphasis you place on the past, present, or future. In a *past orientation,* you have special reverence for the past. You relive old times and regard the old methods as the best. You see events as circular and recurring, so the wisdom of yesterday is applicable also to today and tomorrow. In a *present orientation,* however, you live in the present: for now, not tomorrow. In a *future orientation,* you look toward and live for the future. You save today, work hard in college, and deny yourself luxuries because you're preparing for the future. Before reading more about time, take the following self-test.

E-Talk

Speech Speed

When you have lots to communicate in a short time, the best you can do when speaking is to increase your rate. When you have a lot to communicate electronically, you can significantly compress your files to reduce the time they take to send and receive and to reduce the amount of storage space they take up. For instructions on how to do this, see **www.winzip.com**. In what other ways might you speed up your e-messages?

Test *Yourself* ☑

What Time Do You Have?

INSTRUCTIONS: For each statement, indicate whether the statement is true (T) or untrue (F) of your general attitude and behavior.

_____ ① Meeting tomorrow's deadlines and doing other necessary work comes before tonight's partying.

_____ ② I meet my obligations to friends and authorities on time.

_____ ③ I complete projects on time by making steady progress.

_____ ④ I am able to resist temptations when I know there is work to be done.

_____ ⑤ I keep working at a difficult, uninteresting task if it will help me get ahead.

_____ ⑥ If things don't get done on time, I don't worry about it.

_____ ⑦ I think that it's useless to plan too far ahead, because things hardly ever come out the way you planned anyway.

_____ ⑧ I try to live one day at a time.

_____ ⑨ I live to make better what is rather than to be concerned about what will be.

_____ ⑩ It seems to me that it doesn't make sense to worry about the future, since fate determines that whatever will be, will be.

_____ ⑪ I believe that getting together with friends to party is one of life's important pleasures.

_____ ⑫ I do things impulsively, making decisions on the spur of the moment.

_____ ⑬ I take risks to put excitement in my life.

_____ ⑭ I get drunk at parties.

_____ ⑮ It's fun to gamble.

_____ ⑯ Thinking about the future is pleasant to me.

_____ ⑰ When I want to achieve something, I set subgoals and consider specific means for reaching those goals.

_____ ⑱ It seems to me that my career path is pretty well laid out.

_____ ⑲ It upsets me to be late for appointments.

_____ ⑳ I meet my obligations to friends and authorities on time.

_____ ㉑ I get irritated at people who keep me waiting when we've agreed to meet at a given time.

_____ ㉒ It makes sense to invest a substantial part of my income in insurance premiums.

_____ ㉓ I believe that "A stitch in time saves nine."

_____ ㉔ I believe that "A bird in the hand is worth two in the bush."

_____ ㉕ I believe it is important to save for a rainy day.

_____ ㉖ I believe a person's day should be planned each morning.

_____ ㉗ I make lists of things I must do.

_____ ㉘ When I want to achieve something, I set subgoals and consider specific means for reaching those goals.

_____ ㉙ I believe that "A stitch in time saves nine."

HOW DID YOU DO? This time test measures seven different factors. If you selected true (T) for all or most of the questions within any given factor, you're high on that factor. If you selected untrue (F) for all or most of the questions within any given factor, you're low on that factor.

The first factor, measured by questions 1–5, is a future, work motivation, perseverance orientation. These people have a strong work ethic and are committed to completing a task despite difficulties. The second factor (questions 6–10) is a present, fatalistic, worry-free orientation. High scorers on this factor live one day at a time, not necessarily to enjoy the day but to avoid planning for the next day.

The third factor (questions 11–15) is a present, pleasure-seeking, partying orientation. These people enjoy the present, take risks, and engage in a variety of impulsive actions. The fourth factor (questions 16–18) is a future, goal-seeking, and planning orientation. These people derive pleasure from planning and achieving a variety of goals.

The fifth factor (questions 19–21) is a time-sensitivity orientation. People who score high are especially sensitive to time and its role in social obligations. The sixth factor (questions 22–25) is a future, practical action orientation. These people do what they have to do—take practical actions—to achieve the future they want.

The seventh factor (questions 26–29) is a future, somewhat obsessive daily planning orientation. High scorers make daily "to do" lists and devote great attention to detail.

WHAT WILL YOU DO? Now that you have some idea of how you treat time, consider how these attitudes and behaviors work for you. For example, will your time orientations help you achieve your social and professional goals? If not, what might you do about changing these attitudes and behaviors?

Source: From "Time in Perspective" by Alexander Gonzalez and Philip G. Zimbardo. Reprinted with permission from _Psychology Today_ magazine. Copyright © 1985 Sussex Publishers, Inc.

The time orientation you develop depends to a great extent on your socioeconomic class and your personal experiences (Gonzalez & Zimbardo, 1985). For example, parents with unskilled and semiskilled occupations are likely to teach their children a present-orientated fatalism and a belief that enjoying yourself is more important than planning for the future. Parents who are teachers, managers, or other professionals teach their children the importance of planning and preparing for the future, along with other strategies for success. In the United States, not surprisingly, future income is positively related to future orientation; the more future oriented you are, the greater your income is likely to be.

Different time perspectives also account for much intercultural misunderstanding, as different cultures often teach their members drastically different time orientations. For example, people from some Latin cultures would rather be late for an appointment than end a conversation abruptly or before it has come to a natural end. So the Latin may see an individual's lateness as a result of politeness. But others may see the lateness as impolite to the person with whom the individual had the appointment (Hall & Hall, 1987).

Similarly, the future-oriented person who works for tomorrow's goals will frequently see the present-oriented person as lazy and poorly motivated for enjoying today and not planning for tomorrow. In turn, the present-oriented person may see those with strong future orientations as obsessed with amassing wealth or rising in status.

Smell Messages

Smell communication, or **olfactory communication,** is extremely important in a wide variety of situations and is now big business (Kleinfeld, 1992). There is some evidence (though clearly not very conclusive evidence) that the smell of lemon contributes to a perception of health; the smells of lavender and eucalyptus seem to increase alertness; and the smell of rose oil seems to reduce blood pressure. The smell of chocolate seems to reduce theta brain waves and thus produces a sense of relaxation and a reduced level of attention (Martin, 1998). Findings such as these have contributed to the growth of aromatherapy and to a new profession of aromatherapists (Furlow, 1996). Because humans possess "denser skin concentrations of scent glands than almost any other mammal," it has been argued that it only remains for us to discover how we use scent to communicate a wide variety of messages (Furlow, 1996, p. 41). Here are some of the most important messages scent seems to communicate.

- *Attraction messages.* Humans use perfumes, colognes, after-shave lotions, powders, and the like to enhance their attractiveness to others and to themselves. After all, you also smell yourself. When the smells are pleasant, you feel better about yourself. Although we often think of women as the primary users of perfumes and scents, increasingly men are using them as well—not only the colognes and aftershave lotions they have long used but, more recently, body sprays; these sprays have become big business, with a market estimated at $180 million (Dell, 2005). Interestingly enough, women prefer the scent of men who bear a close genetic similarity to themselves—a finding that may account, in part, for humans' attraction to people much like themselves (Ober, Weitkamp, Cox, Dytch, Kostyu, & Elias, 1997; Wade, 2002).
- *Taste messages.* Without smell, taste would be severely impaired. For example, without smell it would be extremely difficult to taste the difference between a raw potato and an apple.

❝ For the sense of smell, almost more than any other, has the power to recall memories and it is a pity that you use it so little. ❞

—Rachel Carson

"It may be expensive for fragrance, but it's cheap for aromatherapy."

Street vendors selling hot dogs, sausages, and similar foods are aided greatly by the smells, which stimulate the appetites of passersby.

- *Memory messages.* Smell is a powerful memory aid; you often recall situations from months and even years ago when you happen upon a similar smell.
- *Identification messages.* Smell is often used to create an image or an identity for a product. Advertisers and manufacturers spend millions of dollars each year creating scents for cleaning products and tooth pastes, for example. These scents have nothing to do with the products' cleaning power; instead, they function solely to help create an image. There is also evidence that we can identify specific significant others by smell. In one study, for example, young children were able to identify the T-shirts of their brothers and sisters solely on the basis of smell (Porter & Moore, 1981). And one researcher goes so far as to advise: "If your man's odor reminds you of Dad or your brother, you may want genetic tests before trying to conceive a child" (Furlow, 1996, p. 41).

Culture and Nonverbal Communication

We have already seen several cultural and gender differences in nonverbal communication. The impact of culture on certain areas of nonverbal communication, however, has become the focus of sustained research. Here we consider just a sampling of research on these areas—on gestures, facial expressions, colors, silence, touch, and time.

Culture and Gesture

There is much variation in gestures and their meanings among different cultures. Consider a few common gestures that you might use even without thinking but that could easily get you into trouble if you used them in another culture (Axtell, 1993):

■ **What Do You Say**
Smelling
A co-worker in the next cubicle wears extremely strong cologne that you find horrendous. You can't continue smelling this horrible scent any longer; it's making it impossible for you to work efficiently.
What Do You Say?

- Folding your arms over your chest would be considered disrespectful in Fiji.
- Waving your hand would be insulting in Nigeria and Greece.
- Gesturing with the thumb up would be rude in Australia.
- Tapping your two index fingers together would be considered an invitation to sleep together in Egypt.
- Pointing with your index finger would be impolite in many Middle Eastern countries.
- Bowing to a lesser degree than your host would be considered a statement of your superiority in Japan.
- Inserting your thumb between your index and middle finger in a clenched fist would be viewed as a wish that evil fall on the person in some African countries.
- Resting your feet on a table or chair would be insulting in some Middle Eastern cultures.

Culture and Facial Expression

The wide variations in facial communication that we observe in different cultures seem to reflect which reactions are publicly permissible, rather than a difference in the way emotions are facially expressed. For example, Japanese and American students watched a film of a surgical operation (Ekman, 1985a). The students were videotaped both while being interviewed about the film, and alone while watching the film. When alone the students showed very similar reactions. In the interview, however, the American students displayed facial expressions indicating displeasure, whereas the Japanese students did not show any great emotion. Similarly, it's considered "forward" or inappropriate for Japanese women to reveal broad smiles, and so many Japanese women will hide their smile, sometimes with their hands (Ma, 1996). Women in the United States, on the other hand, have no such restrictions, and so are more likely to smile openly. Thus, the difference may not be in the way different cultures express emotions but rather in the **cultural display rules** for showing emotions in public (Matsumoto, 1991).

Similarly, cultural differences exist in decoding the meaning of a facial expression. In one study, for example, American and Japanese students judged the meaning of a smiling and a neutral facial expression. The Americans rated the smiling face as more attractive, more intelligent, and more sociable than the neutral face. The Japanese, however, rated the smiling face as more sociable but not as more attractive—and they rated the neutral face as more intelligent (Matsumoto & Kudoh, 1993).

Culture and Colors

Colors vary greatly in their meanings from one culture to another. Some of these cultural differences are illustrated in Table 7.4. Before looking at the table, however, think about the meanings given in your own culture(s) to such colors as red, green, black, white, blue, yellow, and purple.

Culture and Touch

The several functions and examples of touching discussed in the previous section have been based on studies in North America; in other cultures these functions are not served in the same way. For example, Muslim children are socialized

" 'There is a very simple rule about touching,' the manager continued, 'When you touch, don't take. Touch the people you manage only when you are giving them something— reassurance, support, encouragement, whatever.' "
—Kenneth Blanchard and Spencer Johnson

TABLE 7.4   Some Cultural Meanings of Color

This table, constructed from research reported by various culture watchers, illustrates only some of the different meanings that colors may communicate and especially how they are viewed in different cultures (Dreyfuss, 1971; Hoft, 1995; Dresser, 2005; Singh & Pereira, 2005). As you read this table, consider the meanings you give to these colors and where your meanings came from.

COLOR	CULTURAL MEANINGS AND COMMENTS
Red	In China red signifies prosperity and rebirth and is used for festive and joyous occasions; in France and the United Kingdom, it indicates masculinity; in many African countries, blasphemy or death; and in Japan, anger and danger. Red ink, especially among Korean Buddhists, is used only to write a person's name at the time of death or on the anniversary of the person's death; this can create problems when American teachers use red ink to mark homework.
Green	In the United States green signifies capitalism, go-ahead, and envy; in Ireland, patriotism; among some Native Americans, femininity; to the Egyptians, fertility and strength; and to the Japanese, youth and energy.
Black	In Thailand black signifies old age; in parts of Malaysia, courage; and in much of Europe, death.
White	In Thailand white signifies purity; in many Muslim and Hindu cultures, purity and peace; and in Japan and other Asian countries, death and mourning.
Blue	In Iran blue signifies something negative; in Ghana, joy; among the Cherokee, defeat; for Egyptians, virtue and truth; and for Greeks, national pride.
Yellow	In China yellow signifies wealth and authority; in the United States, caution and cowardice; in Egypt, happiness and prosperity; and in many countries throughout the world, femininity.
Purple	In Latin America purple signifies death; in Europe, royalty; in Egypt, virtue and faith; in Japan, grace and nobility; in China, barbarism; and in the United States, nobility and bravery.

not to touch members of the opposite sex, a practice which can easily be interpreted as unfriendly by American children who are used to touching each other (Dresser, 2005).

Similarly, when one study on touch surveyed college students in Japan and in the United States (Barnlund, 1975); students from the United States reported being touched twice as much as did the Japanese students. In Japan there is a strong taboo against strangers touching, and the Japanese are therefore especially careful to maintain sufficient distance.

Some cultures—including many in southern Europe and the Middle East—are *contact cultures,* and others—such as those of northern Europe and Japan—are *noncontact cultures*. Members of contact cultures maintain close distances, touch one another in conversation, face each other more directly, and maintain longer and more focused eye contact. Members of noncontact cultures maintain greater distance in their interactions, touch each other rarely (if at all), avoid facing each other directly, and maintain much less direct eye contact. As a result, northern Europeans and Japanese may be perceived as cold, distant, and uninvolved by southern Europeans—who may in turn be perceived as pushy, aggressive, and inappropriately intimate.

Culture, Paralanguage, and Silence

Cultural differences also need to be taken into consideration in evaluating the results of the studies on speech rate, since different cultures view speech rate differently. In one study, for example, Korean male speakers who spoke rapidly were given unfavorable credibility ratings, as opposed to the results obtained by Americans who spoke rapidly (Lee & Boster, 1992). Researchers have suggested that in individualistic societies a rapid-rate speaker is seen as more competent than a slow-rate speaker, whereas in collectivist cultures a speaker who uses a slower rate is judged more competent.

Similarly, not all cultures view silence as functioning in the same way (Vainiomaki, 2004). In the United States, for example, silence is often interpreted negatively. At a business meeting or even in informal social groups, a silent person may be seen as not listening or as having nothing interesting to add, not understanding the issues, being insensitive, or being too self-absorbed to focus on the messages of others. Other cultures, however, view silence more positively. In many situations in Japan, for example, silence is a response that is considered more appropriate than speech (Haga, 1988).

In Iranian culture there's an expression, *qahr*, which means not being on speaking terms with someone, giving someone the silent treatment. For example, when children disobey their parents, or are disrespectful, or fail to do their chores as they should, they are given this silent treatment. With adults *qahr* may be instituted when one person insults or injures another. After a cooling-off period, *ashti* (making up after *qahr*) may be initiated. *Qahr* lasts for a relatively short time when between parents and children but longer when between adults. *Qahr* is more frequently initiated between two women than between two men, but when men experience *qahr* it lasts much longer and often requires the intercession of a mediator to establish *ashti* (Behzadi, 1994).

The traditional Apache, to consider another example, see silence very differently than European Americans (Basso, 1972). Among the Apache mutual friends do not feel the need to introduce strangers who may be working in the same area or on the same project. The strangers may remain silent for several days. This period enables them to observe each other and to come to a judgment about each other. Once this assessment is made, the individuals talk. When courting, especially during the initial stages, the Apache remain silent for hours; if they do talk, they generally talk very little. Only after a couple has been dating for several months will they have lengthy conversations. These periods of silence are generally attributed to shyness or self-consciousness. But in reality the use of silence is explicitly taught to Apache women, who are especially discouraged from engaging in long discussions with their dates. Silence during courtship is a sign of modesty to many Apache.

Culture and Time

Culture influences our approaches to time in a variety of ways. Here we look at three types of **cultural time:** formal and informal time, monochronism and polychronism, and the social clock.

FORMAL AND INFORMAL TIME   In the United States and in most of the world, **formal time** is divided into seconds, minutes, hours, days, weeks, months, and years. Some cultures, however, may use seasons or phases of the moon to delineate their most important time periods. In the United States, if your college is on the semester system, your courses are divided into 50- or 75-minute periods that meet two or three times a week for 14-week periods. Eight semesters of 15 or 16 periods per week equal a college education. As these examples illustrate, formal time units are arbitrary. The culture establishes them for convenience.

In contrast, the term **informal time** refers to people's understanding of general time terms—for example, expressions such as "forever," "immediately," "soon," "right away," and "as soon as possible." Communication about informal time creates the most problems, because the terms have different meanings for different people. And this is especially true when these terms are used interculturally. For example, what does "late" mean when applied to a commuter train? Apparently, it depends on your culture. In the New York area, "late" means six minutes, and in Britain it means five minutes. But in Japan it means one minute. And recently, the most deadly train crash in Japan in the last 40 years—which killed 90 people—was attributed to speeding resulting from the Japanese concern (or obsession) with being on time (Onishi, 2005).

Other attitudes toward time also vary from one culture to another. In one study, for example, the accuracy of clocks was measured in six countries—Japan, Indonesia, Italy, England, Taiwan, and the United States. Japan had the most accurate and Indonesia had the least accurate clocks. The researchers also measured the speed at

"Hello, I'm Nesbit. I'm three, and I'm right on track."

which people in these six cultures walked, and results showed that the Japanese walked the fastest, the Indonesians the slowest (LeVine & Bartlett, 1984).

MONOCHRONISM AND POLYCHRONISM   Another important distinction is that between **monochronic** and **polychronic time orientations** (Hall, 1959, 1976; Hall & Hall, 1987). Monochronic people or cultures—such as those of the United States, Germany, Scandinavia, and Switzerland—schedule one thing at a time. In these cultures, time is compartmentalized and there is a time for everything. Polychronic people or cultures—such as those of Latin America, Mediterranean peoples, and Arab peoples—on the other hand, schedule multiple things at the same time. Members of these cultures feel comfortable eating, conducting business with several different people, and taking care of family matters all at the same time.

No culture is entirely monochronic or polychronic; rather, these are general tendencies that are found across a large part of the culture. Some cultures combine both time orientations; Japanese and parts of American culture are examples where both orientations are found. Table 7.5 identifies some of the distinctions between these two time orientations.

THE SOCIAL CLOCK   Another interesting aspect of cultural time is your "social clock" (Neugarten, 1979). Your culture, as well as your more specific society, maintains a schedule for the right time to do a variety of important things; for example, the right time to start dating, to finish college, to buy your own home, to have a child. And you no doubt learned about this "clock" as you were growing up, as has Nesbit in the cartoon. You may tend to evaluate your own social and professional development on the basis of this social clock. If you're on time relative to the rest of your peers—for example, if you all started dating at around the same age or you're all finishing college at around the same age—then you will feel well adjusted, competent, and a part of the group. If you're late, you will probably experience feelings of dissatisfaction. Research in recent decades, however, shows that this social clock is becoming more flexible; people are becoming more willing to tolerate deviations from the established, socially acceptable timetable for accomplishing many of life's transitional events (Peterson, 1996).

TABLE 7.5	Monochronic and Polychronic Time
Can you identify specific potentials for miscommunication that these differences might create when M-time and P-time people interact?	

THE MONOCHRONIC PERSON	THE POLYCHRONIC PERSON
Does one thing at a time	Does several things at one time
Treats time schedules and plans very seriously; they may be broken only for the most serious of reasons	Treats time schedules and plans as useful, but not sacred; they may be broken for a variety of causes
Considers the job the most important part of life, ahead of even family	Considers the family and interpersonal relationships more important than the job
Considers privacy extremely important; seldom borrows or lends to others; works independently	Is actively involved with others; works in the presence of and with lots of people at the same time

The Nonverbal Interview

This dialogue was written to raise questions about the importance of nonverbal messages when you wish to make an impression and to accomplish goals you have set for yourself. As you read the dialogue, consider how you would have handled the interview if you had been the interviewer and if you had been the job applicant.

Dialogue *for* Analysis

The Cast*

Ms. Johnson: the interviewer for a prestigious financial institution
Ms. Smith: a 20-something applicant for the position

The Context

Interviewer's office.

Johnson:	Sit right here, Ms. Smith
Smith:	[Sits] Wow! Sure is soft. Do you have an ashtray?
Johnson:	I'm sorry; this is a no-smoking building.
Smith:	OK, no problem. [Unwraps some gum and begins to chew]
Johnson:	So, I see you like body jewelry. Is that what it's called?
Smith:	Yeah, body jewelry. I just got this tongue jewel last week. It's still healing. I have eight pieces now; you can't see them all, but I have eight.
Johnson:	Interesting. Tell me about your education and a little about your last job.
Smith:	Well, you know. I went to college—Princeton—for computers and economics—and then to work at JJ&J. I've been there for three years.
Johnson:	And what did you do at JJ&J?
Smith:	I reorganized their billing procedures—they were a real mess—and I trained new people in data processing. And I edited their computer newsletter.
Johnson:	What did they think about your body piercings? I mean they're a pretty conservative firm.
Smith:	They were a little tight-assed about it—and about the way I dress.
Johnson:	The way you dress?
Smith:	I only wear black.
Johnson:	Always?
Smith:	It's the only clothes I have—the only clothes I buy. Why do you ask? You look surprised.
Johnson:	Well, I guess it's that it's not very executive looking. Not the kind of thing I'd expect from a Princeton graduate who—I see on your résumé—was on academic scholarship for four years and graduated in the top one percent of your class.
Smith:	Well, do you want the truth?
Johnson:	Yes, of course; tell me the truth.
Smith:	Well, I'm so good at what I do that anyone would be a fool not to hire me because of my body piercings or the way I dress.

***It's interesting to know** that English is spoken by approximately one-third of the world's population and is the official language of 58 countries.

(continues)

Dialogue *for* **Analysis**

(continued)

The United States is the largest English-speaking country, followed by the United Kingdom, the Philippines, India, Canada, Australia, and Nigeria. The names used here are the two most common surnames in the United States. Canada is one of the largest English-speaking countries sending students to study in the United States (about 26,500); approximately 8,000 students come from the United Kingdom.

Summary of Concepts and Skills

This chapter explored nonverbal communication—communication without words—and considered such areas as body language, facial and eye messages, spatial and territorial communication, artifactual communication, touch communication, paralanguage, silence, and time communication.

1. Nonverbal messages often interact with verbal messages to accent, complement, contradict, regulate, repeat, or substitute.

2. Nonverbal researchers have focused their efforts on understanding how nonverbal messages function to form and manage impressions, form and define relationships, structure conversation and social interaction, influence or deceive, and allow for the expression of emotion.

3. The five categories of body movements are emblems (which rather directly translate words or phrases); illustrators (which accompany and literally "illustrate" verbal messages); affect displays (which communicate emotional meaning); regulators (which coordinate, monitor, maintain, or control the speaking of another individual); and adaptors (which usually are unconscious and serve some kind of need, as in scratching an itch).

4. Facial movements may communicate a variety of emotions. The most frequently studied are happiness, surprise, fear, anger, sadness, and disgust/contempt. Facial management techniques enable you to control your facial expression of emotions. The facial feedback hypothesis claims that facial display of an emotion can lead to physiological and psychological changes.

5. Eye movements may seek feedback, invite others to speak, signal the nature of a relationship, or compensate for physical distance.

6. The study of proxemics investigates the communicative functions of space and spatial relationships. Four major proxemic distances are: (1) intimate distance, ranging from actual touching to 18 inches; (2) personal distance, ranging from 18 inches to 4 feet; (3) social distance, ranging from 4 to 12 feet; and (4) public distance, ranging from 12 to 25 or more feet.

7. Your treatment of space is influenced by such factors as status, culture, context, subject matter, sex, age, and positive or negative evaluation of the other person.

8. Territoriality involves people's possessive reactions to particular spaces or objects.

9. Artifactual communication consists of messages conveyed by objects or arrangements created by humans; for example, by the use of color, clothing, body adornment, or space decoration.

10. Touch communication, or haptics, may communicate a variety of meanings, the most important being positive affect, playfulness, control, ritual, and task-relatedness. Touch avoidance is the desire to avoid touching and being touched by others.

11. Paralanguage has to do with the vocal but nonverbal dimension of speech. It includes rate, pitch, volume, resonance, and vocal quality as well as pauses and hesitations. Based on paralanguage we make judgments about people, sense conversational turns, and assess believability.

12. Silence communicates a variety of meanings, from anger (as in the "silent treatment") to deep emotional responses.

13. Time communication, or chronemics, consists of messages communicated by our treatment of time.

14. Smell can communicate messages of attraction, taste, memory, and identification.

15. Cultural variations in nonverbal communication are great. Different cultures, for example, assign different meanings to gestures, facial expressions, and colors; have different spatial rules; and treat time very differently.

This chapter also covered some significant nonverbal communication skills. Check those you wish to work on.

_____ 1. *Body movements.* Use body and hand gestures to reinforce your communication purposes.

_____ 2. *Facial messages.* Use facial expressions to communicate involvement. In listening, look to the emotional expressions of others as cues to their meaning.

_____ 3. *Eye movements.* Use eye movements to seek feedback, exchange conversational turns, signal the nature of your relationship, or compensate for increased physical distance.

_____ 4. *Spatial and proxemic conversational distances.* Maintain distances that are comfortable and that are appropriate to the situation and to your relationship with the other person.

_____ 5. *Giving space.* Give others the space they need. Look to the other person for any signs of spatial discomfort.

_____ 6. *Artifactual communication.* Use artifacts (for example, color, clothing, body adornment, space decoration) to communicate desired messages.

_____ 7. *Touch and touch avoidance.* Respect the touch-avoidance tendencies of others; pay special attention to cultural and gender differences in touch preferences.

_____ 8. *Paralanguage.* Vary paralinguistic features to communicate nuances of meaning and to add interest and color to your messages.

_____ 9. *Silence.* Examine silence for meanings just as you would eye movements or body gestures.

_____ 10. *Time cues.* Interpret time cues from the perspective of the person with whom you're interacting. Be especially sensitive to the person's leave-taking cues—remarks such as "It's getting late" or glances at his or her watch.

_____ 11. *Nonverbal communication and culture.* Interpret the nonverbal cues of others from the perspective of the other person's cultural meanings (insofar as you can).

Vocabulary Quiz: The Language of Nonverbal Communication

Match the terms of nonverbal communication with their definitions. Record the number of the definition next to the appropriate term.

_____ emblems

_____ affect displays

_____ proxemics

_____ territoriality

_____ haptics

_____ paralanguage

_____ chronemics

_____ artifactual communication

_____ social clock

_____ psychological time

1. Movements of the facial area that convey emotional meaning.
2. The study of how time communicates.
3. The time that a culture establishes for achieving certain milestones.
4. Nonverbal behaviors that directly translate words or phrases.
5. Communication by touch.
6. Your orientation to the past, present, or future.
7. The meanings communicated by clothing, jewelry, buttons, or the furniture in your house, for example.
8. The study of how space communicates.
9. A possessive or ownership reaction to an area of space or to particular objects.
10. The vocal but nonverbal aspects of speech; for example, rate and volume.

Four for Discussion

1. A popular defense tactic in trials of individuals charged with sex crimes against women, gay men, or lesbians is to blame the victim by referring to the way the victim was dressed—to imply that the victim, by wearing certain clothing, provoked the attack. Although some states prohibit such tactics, this approach is still common in much of the United States and in other countries as well. What do you think of this tactic?

2. A "Pygmalion gift" is a gift designed to change the person into what the donor wants that person to become. The parent who gives a child books or science equipment may be asking the child to be a scholar. What messages have you recently communicated in your gift-giving behavior? What messages do you think others have communicated to you by gifts they've given you?

3. On a 10-point scale, with 1 indicating "not at all important" and 10 indicating "extremely important," how important is body appearance to your own romantic interest in another person? Do the men and women you know conform to the stereotypes that say males are more concerned with physical appearance and females with personality?

4. As discussed in the text, research clearly shows that women are better encoders and decoders of nonverbal signals than are men. Among the reasons advanced for this are: (1) Women through the ages were subordinate and powerless and so needed to become more competent in nonverbal communication; (2) women are socialized to be more accommodating and need nonverbal information to accomplish this; and (3) biological differences cause women to be more expressive and men to hold back emotional expression (Burgoon & Hoobler, 2002). Why do you think research finds that women are better than men at nonverbal communication?

MyCommunicationLab Explorations

Explore www.mycommunicationlab.com to find exercises to help explain further the dynamics of nonverbal communication including (1) Facial Expressions, (2) Eye Contact, (3) Interpersonal Interactions and Space, (4) The Meanings of Color, (5) Artifacts and Culture: The Case of Gifts, (6) Who? and (7) Praising and Criticizing. A self-test on touch avoidance will help you analyze your own touch tendencies: (8) Do You Avoid Touch?

Also visit MyCommunicationLab for additional study tools, activities, and video clips on nonverbal communication. Explore our research resources at www.researchnavigator.com.

Research
Navigator.com

CHAPTER 8
Conversation Messages

WHY READ THIS CHAPTER?

*B*ecause you'll **learn about:**
- the process of conversation.
- the principles for satisfying conversation.
- the special principles that apply to emotional conversations.

*B*ecause you'll **learn to:**
- open, maintain, and close conversations more effectively.
- communicate your feelings and respond to the feelings of others more effectively.

Most often, conversation takes place face-to-face; this is the type of interaction that probably comes to mind when you think of conversation. But today much conversation also takes place online. Online communication is becoming a part of people's experience worldwide. Such communications are important personally, socially, and professionally. Recall from earlier discussions of online conversation (e-mail or listservs and chat groups, for example) the ways in which they differ from face-to-face interaction. Keep online communication in mind as we explore conversation messages in this chapter.

The Process of Conversation

With the understanding that conversation can take place in a wide variety of channels, let's look at the way conversation works. **Conversation** is a process that involves five steps: opening, feedforward, business, feedback, and closing (Figure 8.1).

When reading about the process of conversation, of course, keep in mind that not everyone speaks with the fluency and ease that many textbooks often assume. Speech and language disorders, for example, can seriously disrupt the conversation process when some elementary guidelines aren't followed. Table 8.1 offers suggestions for making such conversations run more smoothly.

Opening

The first step in the conversational process is to open the interaction, usually with some verbal or nonverbal greeting: "Hi," "How are you?" "Hello, this is Joe," a smile, or a wave.

TABLE 8.1	*Interpersonal Communication Tips*

BETWEEN PEOPLE WITH AND WITHOUT SPEECH AND LANGUAGE DISORDERS

Speech and language disorders vary widely—from fluency problems in stuttering, to indistinct articulation, to difficulty in finding the right word in aphasia. Here are some guidelines that will help facilitate communication between people with and without speech and language disorders.

If you're the person without a speech or language disorder:

1. Avoid finishing sentences for someone who stutters or has difficulty in finding words (aphasia). Finishing sentences may communicate the idea that you're impatient and don't want to spend the extra time necessary to interact effectively.

2. Avoid giving directions to the person with a speech disorder. Saying things like "slow down" or "relax" will often prove insulting and will make further communication more difficult.

3. Maintain eye contact and avoid showing any signs of impatience or embarrassment.

4. If you don't understand what the person said, ask him or her to repeat it. Don't pretend that you understand when you don't.

5. Don't treat people who have language problems like children. A person with aphasia, say, may have difficulty with names or with nouns generally but is in no way childlike.

If you're the person with a speech or language disorder:

1. Let the other person know what your special needs are. For example, if you stutter, you might tell others that you have difficulty with certain sounds and that they need to be patient.

2. Demonstrate your comfort with and positive attitude toward the interpersonal situation. If you appear comfortable and positive, others will also.

Sources: These suggestions were drawn from the websites of the National Stuttering Association, **www.nsastutter.org**, the National Aphasia Association, **www.aphasia.org**, and Constance Dugan, M.A./CCC-SLP, **www.conniedugan.com**, all accessed April 5, 2002.

Figure 8.1

The Conversation Process

The process is viewed as occurring in five basic steps: opening, feedforward, business, feedback, and closing. Can you break down the conversation process into steps or stages that are significantly different from those identified here?

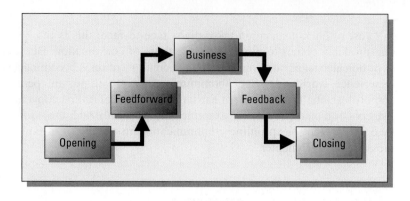

You can accomplish a great deal in your opening (Krivonos & Knapp, 1975). First, your greeting can tell others that you're accessible, that you're available to them for conversation. For example, greeting a work colleague with "How was your weekend?" clearly indicates a readiness for conversation, whereas a simple "Hi," especially if coupled with a refocusing of eye contact toward someone else, might not. You can also reveal important information about the relationship between yourself and the other person. For example, a big smile and a warm "Hi, it's been a long time" may signal that your relationship is still friendly, that you aren't angry any longer, or any of numerous other messages. Your greeting also helps maintain the relationship. You see this function served between workers who pass each other frequently. This greeting-in-passing assures both people that even though they do not stop and talk for an extended period, they still have access to each other.

Depending on the situation, you might open a conversation by shaking hands or exchanging a social or cheek kiss. Interestingly enough, this kind of kissing seems to be growing in popularity in the United States, even in some business settings. Among the possible reasons one etiquette watcher notes are the increased Latin influence, the growing informality of the workplace, the increased number of women in the workplace, and perhaps a trend toward imitating European interaction styles (Olson, 2006). But because the social kiss is still relatively new—as, say, a greeting among work colleagues—it's not always easy to know whether to extend your hand or pucker your lips.

In any case, in normal conversation your greeting is returned by the other person with a greeting that is similar in its formality and intensity. When it isn't—when the other person turns away or responds coldly to your friendly "Good morning"—you know that something is wrong. Similarly, openings are generally consistent in tone with the main part of the conversation; you would not normally follow a cheery "How ya doing today, big guy?" with news of a family death.

Feedforward

The second step usually involves some kind of feedforward (see Chapter 1). Here you give the other person a general idea of what the conversation will focus on: "I got to tell you about Jack," "Did you hear what happened in class yesterday?" or "We need to talk about our vacation plans." When feedforwards are misused—for example, when they are overly long or insensitive—they can create conversational problems.

As with the greeting, you can accomplish a great deal with feedforward. For example, you can (1) open the channels of communication, (2) preview the message, (3) altercast, and (4) disclaim. Let's look at each in more detail.

Open the Channels of Communication. Phatic communication is a perfect example of feedforward. Phatic communication con-

"Would you mind talking to me for a while? I forgot my cell phone."

sists of the "How are you" and "Nice weather" category of greetings—messages that are designed to maintain rapport and friendly relationships (Placencia, 2004; Burnard, 2003). Similarly, listeners' short comments that are unrelated to the content of the conversation but that indicate interest and attention also may be considered phatic communication (McCarthy, 2003). Phatic communication tells us that the normal, expected, and accepted rules of interaction will be in effect. It's information that tells us another person is willing to communicate.

Preview Future Messages. Feedforward messages frequently preview other messages. Feedforward may, for example, preview the content ("I'm afraid I have bad news for you"), the importance ("Listen to this before you make a move"), the form or style ("I'll tell you all the gory details"), and the positive or negative quality ("You're not going to like this, but here's what I heard") of subsequent messages.

" There is only one thing in the world worse than being talked about, and that is not being talked about. "
—Oscar Wilde

Altercast. Feedforward is often used to place someone in a specific role and to request that he or she respond to you in terms of this assumed role. This process, known as **altercasting**, asks the person to approach your message from a particular perspective or even as someone else (Weinstein & Deutschberger, 1963; McLaughlin, 1984). For example, you might ask a friend, "As an advertising executive, what would you think of corrective advertising?" This question casts your friend in the role of advertising executive (rather than that of, for example, parent, Democrat, or Baptist). It asks your friend to respond from a particular point of view.

Disclaim. A **disclaimer** is a statement that aims to ensure that your message will be understood and will not reflect negatively on you (Hewitt & Stokes, 1975; McLaughlin, 1984). Suppose, for example, that you fear that your listeners will think your comment is inappropriate, or that they may rush to judge you without hearing your full account, or that they may think you're not in full possession of your faculties. In such cases you may use some form of disclaimer and say, for example, "This may not be the place to say this, but . . ." or "Just hear me out before you hang up."

Business

The third step in the conversational process is the "business," the substance or focus of the conversation. The business is conducted through exchanges of speaker and listener roles. Usually, brief (rather than long) speaking turns characterize most satisfying conversations.

Business is a good word to use for this stage, because the term emphasizes that most conversations are goal-directed. You converse to fulfill one or several of the purposes of interpersonal communication: to learn, relate, influence, play, or help (Chapter 1). The term is also general enough to include all kinds of interactions. During the business stage you talk about Jack, what happened in class, or your vacation plans. This is obviously the longest part of the conversation and the reason for both the opening and the feedforward. Not surprisingly, each culture has its own conversational **taboos**—topics or language that should be avoided, especially by visitors from other cultures (see Table 8.2 on page 184).

Sometimes the business of conversation is gossip. **Gossip** is social talk that involves making evaluations about a person who is not present during the conversation and generally occurs when two people talk about a third party (Eder & Enke, 1991).

■ **What Do You Say**
Chatting for Free
A casual friend, who now has a cell phone with free unlimited long-distance calling, calls you several times a week just to chat about nothing you're really interested in. You don't want to offend this person or kill the friendship, but you don't want to spend a few hours a week on the phone. **What Do You Say?** Through what channel?

TABLE 8.2   **Conversational Taboos around the World**

This table lists several examples of topics that Roger Axtell (in *Do's and Taboos Around the World,* 1993) recommends that visitors from the United States avoid when in other countries. These examples are not intended to be exhaustive, but rather should serve as a reminder that each culture defines what is and what is not an appropriate topic of conversation. Note that this list was published in 1993. How would you revise this list to better represent today's conversational taboos?

COUNTRY	CONVERSATIONAL TABOOS
Belgium	Politics, language differences between French and Flemish, religion
Norway	Salaries, social status
Spain	Family, religion, jobs, negative comments on bullfighting
Egypt	Middle Eastern politics
Nigeria	Religion
Libya	Politics, religion
Iraq	Religion, Middle Eastern politics
Japan	World War II
Pakistan	Politics
Philippines	Politics, religion, corruption, foreign aid
South Korea	Internal politics, socialism or communism, criticism of the government
Bolivia	Politics, religion
Colombia	Politics, criticism of bullfighting
Mexico	Mexican-American war, illegal aliens
Caribbean nations	Race, local politics, religion

As you doubtless know, a large part of your conversation at work and in social situations is spent gossiping (Lachnit, 2001; Waddington, 2004). In fact, one study has estimated that approximately two-thirds of conversation time is devoted to social topics and that most of these can be considered gossip (Dunbar, 2004). Gossiping seems universal among all cultures (Laing, 1993), and among some groups it's a commonly accepted ritual (Hall, 1993).

Feedback

The feedback step is the reverse of the feedforward step. Here you reflect back on the conversation to signal that the business is completed: "So, you may want to send Jack a get-well card," "Wasn't that the craziest class you ever heard of?" or "I'll call for reservations while you shop for what we need."

In another sense, as described in Chapter 1, feedback takes place throughout the interpersonal communication process. Speakers and listeners constantly exchange feedback—messages sent back to the speaker concerning reactions to what is said (Clement & Frandsen, 1976). Feedback tells the speaker what effect he or she is having on listeners. On the basis of this feedback, the speaker may adjust, modify, strengthen, deemphasize, or change the content or form of the messages.

Feedback can take many forms. A frown or a smile, a yea or a nay, a pat on the back or a punch in the mouth—all are types of feedback. We can think about feedback in terms of five important dimensions: positive–negative, person-focused–message-focused, immediate–delayed, low-monitored–high-monitored, and supportive–critical. To use feedback effectively, you need to make educated choices along these dimensions.

Opening and Closing a Conversation

Effectively opening and closing conversations often can be challenging. Consider, first, a few situations in which you might want to open a conversation. For each situation develop a possible opening message in which you seek to accomplish one or more of the following: (a) telling others that you're accessible and open to communication, (b) showing that you're friendly, and/or (c) showing that you like the other person.

1. You're one of the first guests to arrive at a friend's party and are now there with several other people to whom you've only just been introduced. Your friend, the host, is busy with other matters.
2. You're in the college cafeteria eating alone. You see another student who is also eating alone and whom you recognize from your English literature class. But you're not sure if this person has noticed you in class.

Here are two situations in which you might want to bring a conversation to a close. For each situation develop a possible closing message in which you seek to accomplish one or more of the following: (a) end the conversation without much more talk, (b) leave the other person with a favorable impression of you, and/or (c) keep the channels of communication open for future interaction.

1. You and a friend have been talking on the phone for the last hour, but not much new is being said. You have a great deal of work to do and want to wrap it up. Your friend just doesn't seem to hear your subtle cues.
2. You're at a party and are anxious to meet a person with whom you've exchanged eye contact for the last 10 minutes. The problem is that a friendly and talkative older relative of yours is demanding all your attention. You don't want to insult your relative, but at the same time you want to make contact with this other person.

Opening and closing conversations are often difficult; your handling of these steps is going to help create an impression that's likely to be long-lasting and highly resistant to change.

Positive feedback (applause, smiles, head nods signifying approval) tells the speaker that his or her message is being well received and that essentially the speaker should continue speaking in the same general mode. **Negative feedback** (boos, frowns and puzzled looks, gestures signifying disapproval) tells the speaker that something is wrong and that some adjustment needs to be made. The art of feedback involves giving positive feedback without strings and giving negative feedback positively.

Feedback may be *person focused* ("You're sweet," "You have a great smile") or *message focused* ("Can you repeat that phone number?" "Your argument is a good one"). Especially when you are giving criticism, it's important to make clear that your feedback relates to, say, the organization of the budget report and not to the person himself or herself.

Feedback can be *immediate* or *delayed*. Generally, the most effective feedback is that which is most immediate. In interpersonal situations feedback is most often sent immediately after the message is received. Interpersonal feedback, like reinforcement, loses its effectiveness with time. The longer you wait to praise or punish, for example, the less effect it will have. In other communication situations, however, the feedback may be delayed. Instructor evaluation questionnaires completed at the end of the course provide feedback long after the class is over. In job interview situations the feedback may come weeks afterwards.

Feedback varies from the spontaneous and totally honest reaction (*low-monitored* feedback) to the carefully constructed response designed to serve a specific purpose (*high-monitored* feedback). In most interpersonal situations you probably give feedback spontaneously; you allow your responses to show without any monitoring. At other times, however, you may be more guarded, as when your boss asks you how you like your job or when your grandfather asks what you think of his new motorcycle outfit.

Feedback is *supportive* when you console another or when you simply encourage another to talk or affirm another's self-definition. *Critical* feedback, on the other hand, is evaluative. When you give critical feedback, you judge another's performance—as in, for example, evaluating a speech or coaching someone who is learning a new skill.

Closing

The fifth and last step in conversation, the opposite of the first step, is the closing, the good-bye (Knapp, Hart, Friedrich, & Shulman, 1973; Knapp & Vangelisti, 2000). Most obviously, this step signals the end of accessibility. Just as the opening signaled access, the closing signals the end of access. The closing may also signal some degree of supportiveness; for example, you might express your pleasure in interacting through a comment such as "Well, it was good talking with you."

In some conversations the closing summarizes the interaction. Like the opening, the closing may be verbal or nonverbal but is usually a combination of both. Examples of verbal closings include expressions of appreciation ("Well, I appreciate the time you've given me"), concern for the other's welfare ("Do take care of yourself"), or reinforcement ("It was great seeing you again") as well as leave-taking phrases ("Good-bye," "So long"). Nonverbal closings include breaking eye contact, positioning your legs or feet toward the door and away from the person you're talking with, leaning forward, and placing your hands on your knees or legs (often accompanied by forward leaning) to signal the intention to stand up. As with openings, usually the verbal and the nonverbal are combined; for example, you might say "It was good seeing you again" while leaning forward with hands on your knees.

Repairing

At times it's necessary to repair a conversation that has hit a snag. Unfortunately, even if you realize you've said the wrong thing, you can't erase the message—communication really is irreversible. So you may try to account for it. Perhaps the most common way of doing this is with an excuse (Snyder, 1984; Snyder, Higgins, & Stucky, 1983).

You learn early in life that when you do something that others will view negatively, an **excuse** is in order to justify your performance. In conversation, you're especially likely to offer an excuse when you say or are accused of saying something that runs counter to what is expected, sanctioned, or considered "right" by your listeners. Ideally, the excuse lessens the negative impact of the message.

Motives for Excuse Making.   The major motive for excuse making seems to be to maintain self-esteem, to project a positive image to yourself and to others. You also may offer an excuse to reduce the stress that may result from a bad performance. In other words, you may feel that if you can offer an excuse—especially a good one that is accepted by those around you—it will reduce the negative reaction to your performance and the subsequent stress.

Excuses also enable you to maintain effective interpersonal relationships, even after some negative behavior. For example, after criticizing a friend's behavior and observing the friend's negative reaction to your criticism, you might offer an excuse such as "Please forgive me; I'm really exhausted. I'm just not thinking straight." Excuses place your messages—even your failures—in a more favorable light.

Types of Excuses.   One categorization describes three basic classes of excuses (Snyder, 1984). Think of recent excuses you have used or heard. Did they fall into any of these classes?

- *I didn't do it.* You deny that you did what you're accused of: "I never said that." "I wasn't even near the place when it happened." "She did it, not me."

- *It wasn't so bad.* You admit to doing it, but you claim that the offense was not really so bad or perhaps that there was justification for it: "I only padded the expense account by a few dollars." "Sure, I hit him, but he was asking for it."

- *Yes, but.* You claim that extenuating circumstances account for the behavior: "It was the liquor talking." "I was too upset to think clearly."

■ What Do You Say ?

Apologizing

You borrowed a friend's car and got into an accident. To make matters worse, the collision was totally your fault. You need to explain the situation, alleviate any anxiety your friend will have over the accident, and pave the way for a request to borrow the car again next week—for the most important date of your life!

What Do You Say?

Through what channel?

Good Excuses.   The most important question to most people is what makes a good excuse (Snyder, 1984; Slade, 1995). Bad excuses only make matters worse—so how can you make good excuses and thus get out of problems?

What makes one excuse effective and another ineffective will vary from one culture to another and will depend on cultural characteristics already discussed, such as the culture's level of individualism versus collectivism, its degree of power distance, the values it places on assertiveness, and various other factors (Tata, 2000). But, in the United States at least, researchers seem to agree that the best excuses contain five elements (Slade, 1995; Coleman, 2002):

1. You demonstrate that you really see the problem and that your partner's feelings are legitimate and justified. Avoid minimizing the issue or your partner's feelings ("You're overreacting," "I was only two hours late").

2. You acknowledge your responsibility for doing what you did. Avoid qualifying responsibility ("I'm sorry *if* I did anything wrong") or expressing a lack of sincerity ("OK, I'm sorry; it's obviously my fault—*again*"). Excuse makers who accept responsibility will be perceived as more credible, competent, and likeable than those who deny responsibility (Dunn & Cody, 2000). Alternatively, if you can demonstrate that you had no control over what happened and therefore cannot be responsible, your excuse is likely to be highly persuasive (Heath, Stone, Darley, & Grannemann, 2003).

3. You say that you regret what you did; you make it clear that you're not happy with yourself for doing what you did.

4. You request forgiveness for what you did. It's important to be specific.

5. You make it clear that this will never happen again.

Table 8.3 provides examples of how you might deploy these five messages in excuses in romantic and business situations.

TABLE 8.3   **Excuses in Romantic and Workplace Relationships**

Here are the five key excuse messages along with some specific examples. As you read this table, visualize a specific situation in which you recently made an excuse. Can you reorganize what you said (or should have said) into this five-step sequence?

MESSAGE	IN ROMANTIC RELATIONSHIPS	AT WORK
1. I see	I should have asked you first; you have a right to be angry.	I understand that we lost the client because of this.
2. I did it	I was totally responsible.	I should have acted differently.
3. I'm sorry	I'm sorry that I didn't ask you first.	I'm sorry I didn't familiarize myself with the client's objections to our last offer.
4. Forgive me	Forgive me?	I'd really like another chance.
5. I'll do better	I'll never loan anyone money without first discussing it with you.	This will never happen again.

Skill building *exercise*

Formulating Excuses

Although excuses are not always appropriate, they're often helpful in lessening the possible negative effects of a mishap. Here are several situations in which you might want to offer an excuse. For any one situation, write an excuse that includes all five parts of the effective excuse as discussed in the text.

1. Your boss confronts you with your office telephone log. The log shows that you've been making lots of long-distance personal phone calls, a practice that is explicitly forbidden.
2. In talking with your supervisor, you tell a joke that puts down lesbians and gay men. Your supervisor tells you she finds the joke homophobic and offensive; she adds that she has a gay son and is proud of it. Because you just started the job, this supervisor's approval is important to you.
3. You're caught in a lie. You told your romantic partner that you were going to visit your parents, but you actually went to visit a former lover. Your partner has found out and confronts you.

Excuses will not reverse your errors or eliminate their negative impacts, but they may help repair—at least to some extent—conversational or relationship damage.

Effective Conversation

Effective conversation is characterized by three main principles: Effective conversation (1) is dialogic, (2) is reciprocal, and (3) involves power. Before reading about these principles, consider your own conversations and how satisfying they usually are by taking the following self-test.

Test *Yourself* ☑

How Satisfying Is Your Conversation?

INSTRUCTIONS: Respond to each of the following statements by recording the number best representing your feelings, using this scale:

1 = strongly agree, **2** = moderately agree, **3** = slightly agree, **4** = neutral, **5** = slightly disagree, **6** = moderately disagree, **7** = strongly disagree.

_____ ❶ The other person let me know that I was communicating effectively.

_____ ❷ Nothing was accomplished.

_____ ❸ I would like to have another conversation like this one.

_____ ❹ The other person genuinely wanted to get to know me.

_____ ❺ I was very dissatisfied with the conversation.

_____ ❻ I felt that during the conversation I was able to present myself as I wanted the other person to view me.

_____ ❼ I was very satisfied with the conversation.

_____ ❽ The other person expressed a lot of interest in what I had to say.

_____ ❾ I did *not* enjoy the conversation.

_____ ❿ The other person did *not* provide support for what he or she was saying.

_____ ⓫ I felt I could talk about anything with the other person.

_____ ⓬ We each got to say what we wanted.

_____ ⑬ I felt that we could laugh easily together.

_____ ⑭ The conversation flowed smoothly.

_____ ⑮ The other person frequently said things which added little to the conversation.

_____ ⑯ We talked about something I was *not* interested in.

HOW DID YOU DO? To compute your score, follow these steps:

1. Add the scores for items 1, 3, 4, 6, 7, 8, 11, 12, 13, and 14.

2. Reverse the scores for items 2, 5, 9, 10, 15, and 16 such that 7 becomes, 1, 6 becomes 2, 5 becomes 3, 4 remains 4, 3 becomes 5, 2 becomes 6, and 1 becomes 7.

3. Add the reversed scores for items 2, 5, 9, 10, 15, and 16.

4. Add the totals from steps 1 and 3 to yield your communication satisfaction score.

You may interpret your score along the following scale:

16	32	48	64	80	96	112
Extremely satisfying	Quite satisfying	Fairly satisfying	Average	Fairly unsatisfying	Quite unsatisfying	Extremely unsatisfying

WHAT WILL YOU DO? Before reading the remainder of this chapter, try to identify those qualities that make a conversation satisfying for you. What interpersonal qualities contribute most to making a person a satisfying conversational partner? How might you cultivate these qualities?

Source: This test was developed by Michael Hecht and appeared in "The Conceptualization and Measurement of Interpersonal Communication Satisfaction," *Human Communication Research* 4(1978): 253–264. It is reprinted by permission of the author.

Effective Conversation Is Dialogic

Often the term *dialogue* is used as a synonym for *conversation*. But **dialogue** is more than simple conversation; it's conversation in which there is genuine two-way interaction (Buber, 1958; Yaufair Ho, Chan, Peng, & Ng, 2001; McNamee & Gergen, 1999). It's useful to distinguish the ideal dialogic communicator from his or her opposite, the totally monologic communicator. Of course, no one totally and always engages in dialogue, and no one is totally monologic. These types are extremes and are intended to clarify the differences between these two types of communicators—and, at the same time, to illustrate interpersonal communication patterns to be emulated and patterns to avoid.

In dialogue each person is both speaker and listener, sender and receiver. Dialogue is conversation in which there is deep concern for the other person and for the relationship between the two. The objective of dialogue is mutual understanding, supportiveness, and empathy. There is respect for the other person, not because of what this person can do or give but simply because this person is a human being and therefore deserves to be treated honestly and sincerely.

In a dialogic interaction you respect the other person enough to allow that person the right to make his or

❝ Their remarks and responses were like a Ping-Pong game, with each volley clearing the net and flying back to the opposition. ❞
—Maya Angelou

"Of course we've already had this conversation. There isn't a conversation we haven't already had."

her own choices without coercion, without the threat of punishment, without fear or social pressure. A dialogic communicator believes that other people can make decisions that are right for them and implicitly or explicitly lets others know that whatever choices they make, they will still be respected as people.

The dialogic communicator avoids negative criticism and negative personal judgments and instead practices using positive criticism ("I liked those first explanations best; they were really well reasoned").

The dialogic communicator avoids dysfunctional communication patterns and keeps the channels of communication open by displaying a willingness to listen. This person lets you know that he or she is paying attention by giving listening cues such as nonverbal nods, brief verbal expressions of agreement, or paraphrasing. When in doubt about something that was said, the dialogic communicator asks for clarification or asks for your point of view or your perspective and thus signals a real interest in you and in what you say.

The dialogic communicator doesn't manipulate the conversation to try to get you to say something positive about him or her or to force you to think, believe, or behave in any particular way.

Monologue, or monologic communication, is the opposite: It's communication in which one person speaks and the other listens, and there's no real interaction between participants. The monologic communicator is focused only on his or her own goals and has no real concern for the listener's feelings or attitudes; this speaker is interested in the other person only insofar as that person can serve his or her purposes.

The monologic communicator frequently uses negative criticism ("I didn't like that explanation") and negative judgments ("You're not a very good listener, are you?"). This communicator also often uses dysfunctional communication patterns; for example, he or she may express an unwillingness to talk or to listen to what the other person has to say. Monologic communicators rarely demonstrate that they understand you; they give no cues that they are listening (for example, by paraphrasing or expressing agreement with what you say). Nor would monologic communicators request clarification of your ideas, because these individuals are less interested

■ What Do You Say ?

Expressing Thanks

Because of family problems you fell behind in your rent and were threatened with eviction. Your next-door neighbor and friend bailed you out by paying the overdue rent. You want to express your deep appreciation. **What Do You Say?** Through what channel?

Keeping Secrets Secret

You likely confide certain of your secrets to others; when you do, you assume that these messages will be kept secret and not revealed to third parties. Similarly, you probably hear secrets from friends, lovers, and family members; and people who are close to you likely assume that you will not reveal their secrets to others. So when is it and when is it not ethical to reveal someone's secrets? In *Secrets* (1983) ethicist Sissela Bok identifies three types of situations in which she argues it is unethical to reveal the secrets of another person:

1. It's unethical to reveal what you have promised to keep secret.
2. It's unethical to talk about another person when you know the information is false.
3. It's unethical to invade the privacy to which everyone has a right, to reveal information that no one else has a right to know. This is especially unethical when such disclosures can hurt the individual involved.

What Would You Do?

As Bok suggests, consider an 18-year-old friend who confides that he intends to commit suicide. Using Bok's guidelines, how would you evaluate the ethics involved in revealing this secret? What ethical justification might be offered for revealing such a secret? What would you do in this situation?

in you than in themselves. Still another characteristic of these people is to manipulate the conversation so as to lead you to say positive things about them ("How did you like the way I handled that?") or to secure agreement with their beliefs or values.

Effective Conversation Is Reciprocal

The defining feature of conversation is that the roles of speaker and listener are exchanged throughout the interaction. We use a wide variety of verbal and nonverbal cues to signal **conversational turns**—the changing (or maintaining) of the speaker or listener roles during the conversation. Figure 8.2 summarizes the various turn-taking cues and how they correspond to the conversational wants or desires of speaker and listener. Combining the insights of a variety of communication researchers (Duncan, 1972; Burgoon, Buller, & Woodall, 1996; Pearson & Spitzberg, 1990), let's examine conversational turns in terms of speaker cues and listener cues.

	To speak	To listen
Speaker	1 Turn-maintaining cues	2 Turn-yielding cues
Listener	3 Turn-requesting cues	4 Turn-denying cues

Figure 8.2
Turn-Taking and Conversational Wants
Quadrant 1 represents the speaker who wishes to continue to speak and uses turn-maintaining cues; quadrant 2, the speaker who wishes to listen and uses turn-yielding cues. Quadrant 3 represents the listener who wishes to speak and uses turn-requesting cues; quadrant 4, the listener who wishes to continue listening and uses turn-denying cues. Backchanneling cues would appear in quadrant 4, as they are cues that listeners use while they continue to listen. Interruptions would appear in quadrant 3, though they are not so much cues that request a turn as actual takeovers of the speaker's position.

> It is alright to hold a conversation, but you should let go of it now and then.
>
> —Richard Armour

Speaker Cues. As a speaker you regulate the conversation through two major types of cues. *Turn-maintaining cues* enable you to maintain the role of speaker. You communicate these cues by, for example, audibly inhaling breath to show that you have more to say; continuing a gesture to show that your thought is not yet complete; avoiding eye contact with the listener so as not to indicate that you're passing the speaking turn on to the listener; or vocalizing **pauses** ("er," "umm") rather than pausing silently, so as to prevent the listener from speaking and to show that you're still talking.

Turn-yielding cues tell the listener that you're finished and wish to exchange the role of speaker for the role of listener. You may communicate these cues by dropping your intonation, by a prolonged silence, by making direct eye contact with a listener, by asking a question, or by nodding in the direction of a particular listener.

Listener Cues. As a listener you can regulate the conversation by using three types of cues. First, *turn-requesting cues* tell the speaker that you would like to take a turn as speaker; you might transmit these cues by using some vocalized "er" or "um" that tells the speaker that you would now like to speak, by opening your eyes and mouth as if to say something, by beginning to gesture with a hand, or by leaning forward.

Second, through *turn-denying cues* you indicate your reluctance to assume the role of speaker by, for example, intoning a slurred "I don't know"; giving the speaker some brief grunt that signals you have nothing to say; avoiding eye contact with the speaker who wishes you now to take on the speaker role; or engaging in some behavior that is incompatible with speaking—for example, coughing or blowing your nose.

Third, through *backchanneling cues* (see Chapter 5) you communicate various meanings back to the speaker—but without assuming the role of the speaker. For example, you can indicate your *agreement* or *disagreement* with the speaker through smiles or frowns, nods of approval or disapproval; brief comments such as "right," "exactly," or "never"; or vocalizations such as "uh-huh" or "uh-uh." You convey your *involvement* or *boredom* with the speaker through attentive posture, forward leaning, and focused eye contact, which tell the speaker that you're involved in the conversation—or through an inattentive posture, backward leaning, and avoidance of eye contact, which communicate your lack of involvement. You can also request that the speaker *pace* the conversation differently, perhaps asking the speaker to slow down by raising your hand near your ear and leaning forward, or to speed up by continually nodding your head. Or you can signal the speaker to give you *clarification;* a puzzled facial expression, perhaps coupled with a forward lean, will probably tell most speakers that you need something clarified.

Some backchanneling cues are actually *interruptions.* Backchanneling interruptions, however, are generally confirming rather than disconfirming. They tell the speaker that you're listening and are involved (Kennedy & Camden, 1988). Other interruptions are not as confirming and simply take the speaking turn away from the speaker, either temporarily or permanently. Sometimes the interrupter may apologize for breaking in; at other times the interrupter may not even seem aware of interrupting.

Interruptions can, of course, serve a variety of specific functions. For example, interruptions may be used to change the topic ("I gotta tell you this story before I bust"); to correct the speaker ("You mean four months, not years, don't you?"); to seek information or clarification ("Are you talking about Jeff's cousin?"); or to introduce essential information ("Your car's on fire"). And, of course, you can interrupt to end the conversation ("I hate to interrupt, but I really have to get back to the office").

Not surprisingly, research finds that superiors (bosses, supervisors) and those in positions of authority (police officers, interviewers) interrupt those in inferior positions more than the other way around (Carroll, 1994; Ashcraft, 1998). In fact, it would probably strike you as strange to see a worker repeatedly interrupting a supervisor or a student repeatedly interrupting a professor.

Another and even more often studied aspect of interruption is that of gender difference. Do men or women interrupt more? Research here is conflicting. These few research findings will give you an idea of the differing results (Pearson, West, & Turner, 1995):

- The more malelike the person's gender identity—regardless of the person's biological sex—the more likely it is that the person will interrupt (Drass, 1986).
- There are no significant differences between boys and girls (aged two to five) in interrupting behavior (Greif, 1980).
- Fathers interrupt their children more than mothers do (Greif, 1980).
- Women judge "simultaneous talk" as being interruptions more than men do (Bresnahan & Cai, 1996).
- Men interrupt more than women do (Zimmerman & West, 1975; West & Zimmerman, 1977).
- Men and women do not differ in their interrupting behavior (Roger & Nesshoever, 1987).
- No single linguistic feature has been found that definitely identifies a message as an interruption (Coon & Schwanenflugel, 1996).

Effective Conversation Involves Power

Regardless of what you communicate, there is an element of power in your verbal and nonverbal message. Perhaps most times you'll want to express yourself with powerful messages. There are times, however, when you might want to use less powerful forms—for example, if you wanted to make the other person feel superior, as you might in interacting with an older person in certain cultures, or if you wanted to make up for previous verbal aggressiveness.

The ways in which people communicate powerfulness and powerlessness through speech have received lots of research attention (Molloy, 1981; Kleinke, 1986; Johnson, 1987; Dillard & Marshall, 2003). Generally, research finds that men use more powerful language forms than do women (Lakoff, 1975; Timmerman, 2002). Listed below are the major characteristics of powerless speech. As you consider this list, think of your own speech. Do you avoid the following speech behaviors?

- *Hesitations* make the speaker sound unprepared and uncertain. Example: "I, er, want to say that, ah, this one is, er, the best, you know?"
- *Too many intensifiers* make your speech monotonous and don't allow you to stress what you do want to emphasize. Example: "Really, this was the greatest; it was truly phenomenal."
- *Disqualifiers* signal a lack of competence and a feeling of uncertainty. Examples: "I didn't read the entire article, but. . . ." "I didn't actually see the accident, but. . . ."
- *Tag questions* ask for another's agreement and therefore may signal your need for agreement—and your own uncertainty. Examples: "That was a great movie, wasn't it?" "She's brilliant, don't you think?"

Turn-Taking and Empowerment

A study of Thai women shows that females participate in chat discussions more than males. Thai women also are responded to by both males and females more than males are. Despite the fact that these women live in a male-dominated society, they are quite dominant and empowered on the Internet (Panyametheekul & Herring, 2003). Can you think of other instances in which access to the Internet has empowered people?

- *Self-critical statements* signal a lack of confidence and may make public your own inadequacies. Examples: "I'm not very good at this." "This is my first public speech."
- *Slang and vulgar language* signal low social class and hence little power. Examples: "No problem!" "@*+#?$!!"

Just as you communicate your power (or lack of power) verbally, you also communicate it nonverbally. Here, for example, are some things you might do that are likely to enhance your power (Lewis, 1989; Burgoon & Bacue, 2003; Burgoon & Hoobler, 2002; Guerrero, DeVito, & Hecht, 1999):

- Avoid self-manipulations (playing with your hair or touching your face, for example) and backward leaning; these signals communicate a lack of comfort and an ill-at-ease feeling and are likely to damage your persuasiveness.
- Walk slowly and deliberately. To appear hurried is to appear powerless, as if you were rushing to meet the expectations of those who have power over you.
- Use facial expressions and gestures as appropriate; these help you express your concern for the other person and for the interaction and help you communicate your comfort and control of the situation.
- Select chairs you can get in and out of easily; avoid deep plush chairs that you sink into and have trouble getting out of.
- To communicate dominance with your handshake, exert more pressure than usual and hold the grip a bit longer than normal.
- Use consistent packaging; in other words, be careful that your verbal and non-verbal messages do not contradict each other, a signal of uncertainty and a lack of conviction.

   Most conversations are monologues delivered in the presence of witnesses. "

—Margaret Millar

Principles of Emotional Conversation

Communicating emotions is both difficult and important. It's difficult because your thinking often gets confused when you're intensely emotional. It's also difficult because you probably weren't taught how to communicate emotions—and you probably have few effective models to imitate. Communicating emotions is also most important. Feelings constitute a great part of your meanings. If you leave your feelings out, or if you communicate them inadequately, you will fail to communicate a great part of your meaning. Consider what your communications would be like if you left out your feelings when talking about failing a recent test, winning the lottery, becoming a parent, getting engaged, driving a car for the first time, becoming a citizen, or being promoted to supervisor. Emotional expression is so much a part of communication that even in the cryptic e-mail message style, emoticons are becoming more popular. (Two excellent websites contain extensive examples of smileys, emoticons, acronyms, and shorthand abbreviations: www.netlingo.com/smiley.cfm and www.netlingo.com/emailsh .cfm.) Let's look at several general principles of emotions and emotional expression.

Emotions Are Influenced by Body, Mind, and Culture

Emotion involves at least three parts: bodily reactions (such as blushing when you're embarrassed); mental evaluations and interpretations (as in calculating the odds of drawing an inside straight at poker); and cultural rules and beliefs (such as the pride parents feel when their child graduates from college).

Bodily reactions are the most obvious aspect of our emotional experience, because we can observe them easily. Such reactions span a wide range. They include, for example, the blush of embarrassment, the sweating palms that accompany nervousness, and the self-touching that goes with discomfort. When you judge people's emotions, you probably look to these nonverbal behaviors. You conclude that Ramon is happy to see you because of his smile and his open body posture. You conclude that Lisa is nervous from her damp hands, vocal hesitations, and awkward movements.

The mental or cognitive part of emotional experience involves the evaluations and interpretations you make on the basis of your behaviors. For example, leading psychotherapist Albert Ellis (1988; Ellis & Harper, 1975), whose insights are used throughout this chapter, claims that your evaluations of what happens have a greater influence on your feelings than what actually happens. Let us say, for example, that your best friend, Sally, ignores you in the college cafeteria. The emotions you feel will depend on what you think this behavior means. You may feel pity if you figure that Sally is depressed because her father died. You may feel anger if you believe that Sally is simply rude and insensitive and snubbed you on purpose. Or you may feel sadness if you believe that Sally is no longer interested in being friends with you.

The culture you were raised in and live in gives you a framework for both expressing feelings and interpreting the emotions of others. A colleague of mine gave a lecture in Beijing, China, to a group of Chinese college students. The students listened politely but made no comments and asked no questions after her lecture. At first my colleague concluded that the students were bored and uninterested. Later, she learned that Chinese students show respect by being quiet and seemingly passive. They think that asking questions would imply that she was not clear in her lecture. In other words, the culture—whether American or Chinese—influenced the interpretation of the students' feelings.

Emotions May Be Primary or Blends

How would you feel in each of the following situations?

- *You won the lottery!*
- *You got the job you applied for.*
- *Your best friend just died.*
- *Your parents tell you they're getting divorced.*

You would obviously feel very differently in each of these situations. In fact, each feeling is unique and unrepeatable. Yet amid all these differences, there are some similarities. For example, most people would claim that the feelings in the first two examples are more similar to each other than they are to the last two. Similarly, the last two are more similar to each other than they are to the first two.

To capture the similarities among emotions, many researchers have tried to identify basic or primary emotions. Robert Plutchik (1980; Havlena, Holbrook, & Lehmann, 1989) developed a most helpful model. In this model there are eight basic emotions (Figure 8.3): joy, acceptance, fear, surprise, sadness, disgust, anger, and anticipation. Emotions that are close to each other on this wheel are also close to each other in meaning. For example, joy and anticipation are more closely related than are joy and sadness or acceptance and disgust. Emotions that are opposite each other on the wheel are also opposite each other in their meaning. For example, joy is the opposite of sadness; anger is the opposite of fear.

In this model there are also blends. These are emotions that are combinations of the primary emotions. These are noted outside the emotion wheel. For example,

E-Talk . . . .
Gender Differences
Back in the mid-1990s, men used the Internet much more than women. Although the difference is lessening, women still remain less frequent and less intense users than men (Ono & Zavodny, 2003). How would you describe the way men and women use the Internet?

What Do You Say
Expressing Sympathy
A colleague's father just died. You don't know this person well, nor do you know what kind of relationship he had with his father. Yet you feel you want to express some sympathy. **What Do You Say?** Through what channel?

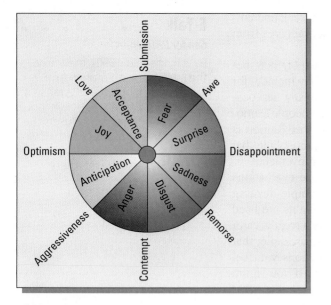

Figure 8.3

A Model of the Emotions

Do you agree with the basic assumptions of this model? For example, do you see love as a combination of joy and acceptance, and optimism as a combination of joy and anticipation.

From Robert Plutchik, *Emotion: A Psychoevolutionary Synthesis,* © 1980. Published by HarperCollins. Copyright © 2000 by Pearson Education. Reprinted by permission of the publisher.

according to this model, love is a blend of joy and acceptance. Remorse is a blend of disgust and sadness.

Emotional Expression Is Governed by Display Rules

As explained in Chapter 7, different cultures' display rules govern what is and what is not permissible emotional communication. Even within U.S. culture itself, there are differences. For example, in one study Americans classified themselves into four categories: Caucasian, African American, Asian, and Hispanic/Latino. Just to make the point that different cultures teach different rules for the display of emotions, here are a few of the study's findings (Matsumoto, 1994): (1) Caucasians found the expression of contempt more appropriate than did Asians; (2) African Americans and Hispanics felt disgust was less appropriate than did Caucasians; (3) Hispanics rated public displays of emotion as less appropriate than did Caucasians; and (4) Caucasians rated the expression of fear as more appropriate than Hispanics.

Researchers agree that men and women experience emotions similarly (Oatley & Duncan, 1994; Cherulnik, 1979; Wade & Tavris, 1998). The differences that are observed are differences in emotional expression. Men and women seem to have different **gender display rules,** much as different cultures have different cultural display rules.

Women talk more about feelings and emotions and use communication for emotional expression more than men (Barbato & Perse, 1992). Perhaps because of this, they also express themselves facially more than men. Even junior and senior high schoolers show this gender difference. Research findings suggest that this difference may be due to differences in the brains of men and women; women's brains have a significantly larger inferior parietal lobule, which seems to account for women's greater awareness of feelings (Barta, 1999).

Women are also more likely to express socially acceptable emotions than are men (Brody, 1985). For example, women smile significantly more than men. In fact, women smile even when smiling is not appropriate—for example, when reprimanding a subordinate. Men, on the other hand, are more likely than women to express anger and aggression (Fischer, 1993; DePaulo, 1992; Wade & Tavris, 1998). Similarly, women are more effective at communicating happiness and men are more effective at communicating anger (Coats & Feldman, 1996). Women also cry more than men (Metts & Planalp, 2002).

Women also seem to respond well to men who express emotions (Werrbach, Grotevant, & Cooper, 1990). In one study, while watching a movie, a confederate of the experimenter displayed a variety of emotions; the experimenter then asked participants what they thought of this person. Results showed that people liked men best when they cried and women best when they did not cry (Labott, Martin, Eason, & Berkey, 1991).

Effective Emotional Conversation

When strong emotions are involved, conversation becomes more difficult. Here are a few suggestions for making emotional communication—talking about feelings—more effective and more satisfying.

"I've been thinking—it might be good for Andrew if he could see you cry once in a while."

Confront the Obstacles to Communicating Emotions

Three major obstacles stand in the way of effective emotional communication: (1) societal rules and customs, (2) fear, and (3) inadequate interpersonal skills.

SOCIETAL RULES AND CUSTOMS   If you grew up in the United States, you probably learned that many people frown on emotional expression. This is especially true for men and has been aptly called "the cowboy syndrome," after a pattern of behavior seen in the old Westerns (Balswick & Peck, 1971). The cowboy syndrome describes the closed and unexpressive male. This man is strong but silent. He never feels any of the softer emotions (such as compassion, love, or contentment). He would never ever cry, experience fear, or feel sorry for himself. And he would never ask for "a bigger emotional share." Unfortunately, many men grow up trying to live up to this unrealistic image. It's a syndrome that prevents open and honest expression. Researcher Ronald Levant (*Time,* January 20, 1992, p. 44) has argued that men's inability to deal with emotions as effectively as women is a "trained incompetence." Such training begins early in life when boys are taught not to cry and to ignore pain. This is not necessarily to suggest, however, that men should communicate their emotions more openly. Unfortunately, there are many who will negatively evaluate men who express emotions openly and often; such men may be judged ineffective, insecure, or unmanly.

Nor are women exempt from the difficulties of emotional expression. At one time our society permitted and encouraged women to express emotions openly. The tide now is turning, especially for women in executive and managerial positions. Today the executive woman is being forced into the same cowboy syndrome. She is not allowed to cry or to show any of the once acceptable "soft" emotions. She is especially denied these feelings while she is on the job.

For both men and women, the best advice (as with self-disclosure or any of the characteristics of communication effectiveness discussed in this book) is to express your emotions selectively. Carefully weigh the arguments for and against expressing your emotions. Consider the situation, the people you're with, the emotions themselves, and all the elements that make up the communication act. And, most important, consider your options for communicating—not only what you'll say but also how you'll say it.

FEAR   A variety of types of fear stand in the way of emotional expression. Emotional expression exposes a part of you that makes you vulnerable to attack. For example, if you express your love for another person, you risk being rejected. That is, by exposing a "weakness," you can now easily be hurt by the uncaring and the insensitive. Of course, you may also fear hurting someone else by, say, voicing your feelings about past loves. Or you may be angry and want to say something but fear that you might hurt the person and then feel guilty yourself.

In addition, you may not reveal your emotions for fear of causing a conflict. Expressing your dislike for Pat's friends, for example, may create difficulties for the two of you, and you may not be willing to risk the argument and its aftermath.

Because of fears such as these, you may deny to others and perhaps even to yourself that you have certain feelings. In fact, this kind of **denial** is the way many people were taught to deal with emotions.

INADEQUATE INTERPERSONAL SKILLS   Perhaps the most important obstacle to effective emotional communication is lack of interpersonal skills. Many people simply don't know how to express their feelings. Some people, for example, can express anger only through violence or avoidance. Others can deal with anger only by blaming and accusing others. And many people cannot express love. They literally cannot say, "I love you."

E-Talk ▪ ▪ ▪ ▪ ▪ ▪ ▪

An Expression of Sympathy

In what ways do you express grief differently in online and in face-to-face situations? In what ways do you express sympathy?

Listening to Emotions (Ten Easy Ways)

Expressing your feelings is only half of the process of emotional communication; the other half is listening to the feelings of others. Here are a few guidelines for making an often difficult process a little easier.

1. Confirm the other person and his or her emotions. A simple "You must be worried about finding another position" confirms the person's feelings.

2. Show interest by encouraging the person to explore his or her feelings. Use simple encouragers like "I see" or "I understand." Or ask questions to let the speaker know that you're listening and that you're interested.

3. Give the person permission to express feelings. Let the person know that it's acceptable and okay with you if he or she expresses feelings in the ways that feel most comfortable—for example, by crying or talking about old times.

4. Don't try to force the person to talk about experiences or feelings she or he may not be willing to share.

5. Be especially sensitive to leave-taking cues. Don't overstay your welcome.

6. Empathize. See the situation from the point of view of the speaker. Avoid comments such as "Don't cry; it wasn't worth it," which can easily be interpreted to as a rejection of the person's feelings.

7. Focus on the other person; don't refocus the conversation on yourself.

8. Don't feel that responding to the emotions of others means that you have to solve their problems. Instead, provide a supportive atmosphere that encourages the person to express his or her feelings.

9. Avoid trying to focus on the bright side. Avoid expressions such as "You're lucky you have some vision left" or "It was better this way; Pat was suffering so much."

10. Avoid interrupting, even when the other person's pauses are overly long. Emotional expression frequently involves extra-long pauses.

Applying Listening Skills

Your best friend comes to you extremely upset and tells you that he suspects his lover of four years of seeing someone else. He tells you that he wants to confront the lover with his suspicions but is afraid of what he'll hear. What listening skills would you suggest he use if he goes through with this confrontation?

Expressing negative feelings is doubly difficult. Many of us suppress or fail to communicate negative feelings for fear of offending the other person or making matters worse. But failing to express negative feelings will probably not help the relationship, especially if these feelings are concealed frequently and over a long time.

Describe Your Feelings

Verbally articulate your feelings, being as specific as possible. Consider, for example, the frequently heard "I feel bad." Does it mean "I feel guilty" (because I lied to my best friend)? "I feel lonely" (because I haven't had a date in the last two months)? "I feel depressed" (because I failed that last exam)? Specificity helps. Describe also the intensity with which you feel the emotion: "I feel so angry I'm thinking of quitting the job." "I feel so hurt I want to cry." Learn the vocabulary to describe your emotions and feelings in specific and concrete terms.

Here is a list of terms for describing your emotions verbally. It's based on the eight primary emotions identified by Plutchik. Notice that the terms included for each basic emotion provide you with lots of choices for expressing the intensity level you're feeling. For example, if you're extremely happy, then *bliss, ecstasy,* or *enchantment* might be an appropriate description. If you're mildly happy, then perhaps *contentment, satisfaction,* or *well-being* would be more descriptive. Look over the list and try grouping the terms into three levels of intensity: high, middle, and low. Before doing that, however, look up the meanings of any words that are unfamiliar to you.

Happiness: bliss, cheer, contentment, delight, ecstasy, enchantment, enjoyment, felicity, joy, rapture, gratification, pleasure, satisfaction, well-being

Surprise: amazement, astonishment, awe, eye-opener, incredulity, jolt, revelation, shock, unexpectedness, wonder, startle, catch off-guard, unforeseen

Fear: anxiety, apprehension, awe, concern, consternation, dread, fright, misgiving, phobia, terror, trepidation, worry, qualm, terror

Anger: acrimony, annoyance, bitterness, displeasure, exasperation, fury, ire, irritation, outrage, rage, resentment, tantrum, umbrage, wrath, hostility

Sadness: dejected, depressed, dismal, distressed, grief, loneliness, melancholy, misery, sorrowful, unhappiness

Disgust: abhorrence, aversion, loathing, repugnance, repulsion, revulsion, sickness, nausea, offensiveness

Contempt: abhorrence, aversion, derision, disdain, disgust, distaste, indignity, insolence, ridicule, scorn, snobbery, revulsion, disrespect

Interest: attention, appeal, concern, curiosity, fascination, notice, spice, zest, absorb, engage, engross

Describe the reasons you're feeling as you are. "I'm feeling guilty because I lied to my best friend." "I feel lonely; I haven't had a date for the last two months." "I'm really depressed from failing that last exam." If your feelings were influenced by something the person you're talking to did or said, describe this also. For example, "I felt so angry when you said you wouldn't help me." "I felt hurt when you didn't invite me to the party."

Anchor Your Emotional Expression to the Present

In expressing feelings—inwardly or outwardly—try to link your emotions to the present. Coupled with specific description and the identification of the reasons for your feelings, such statements might look like this: "I feel like a failure right now; I've erased this computer file three times today." "I felt foolish when I couldn't think of that formula." "I feel stupid when you point out my grammatical errors."

Own Your Own Feelings

Perhaps the most important guideline for effective emotional communication is: Own your feelings, take personal responsibility for your feelings. Consider the following statements: "You make me angry." "You make me feel like a loser." "You make me feel stupid." "You make me feel like I don't belong here." In each of these statements, the speaker blames the other person for the way he or she is feeling. Of course, you know, on more sober reflection, that no one can make you feel anything. Others may do things or say things to you, but it is you who interpret them. That is, you develop feelings as a result of the interaction between what these people say, for example, and your own interpretations. **Owning feelings** means taking responsibility for them—acknowledging that your feelings are *your* feelings. The best way to own your statements is to use **I-messages** rather than the kinds of **you-messages** given above. With this acknowledgment of responsibility, the above statements would look like these: "I get angry when you come home late without calling." "I begin to think of myself as a loser when you criticize me in front of my friends." "I feel so stupid when you use medical terms that I don't understand." "When you ignore me in public, I feel like I don't belong here."

These rephrased statements identify and describe your feelings about those behaviors; they don't attack the other person or demand that he or she change certain

E-Talk ▪ ▪ ▪ ▪ ▪ ▪ ▪ ▪ ▪

Driving and the Cell Phone

One of the great advantages of cell phone communication is that you can talk wherever you are. When you are driving, however, using the cell phone creates problems—as both common sense and research agree (Charlton, 2004; Gugerty, Rakauskas, & Brooks, 2004). What can you do to guard against the dangers of talking on the phone while driving? Do you support the laws banning cell phone use by drivers that some municipalities have enacted?

Responding to Emotions

Perhaps even more difficult than communicating emotions is responding appropriately to the emotions of others. Here are some situations to practice on. Visualize yourself in each of the following situations. For each scenario indicate an appropriate response in which you (a) reflect the feelings of the other person to show you understand, (b) confirm the person's feelings, and (c) ask if there's anything you can do.

1. A neighbor who has lived in the apartment next door to you for the last 10 years and who has had many difficult financial times has just won a lottery worth several million dollars. Your ecstatic neighbor meets you in the hallway.
2. Your grandmother is dying and calls you to spend some time with her. She says that she knows she is dying, that she wants you to know how much she has always loved you, and that her only regret in dying is not being able to see you anymore.
3. A young child about six or seven years old is crying because the other children won't play with her.

Responding appropriately to the emotions of others requires you to know the other person and to have a firm grasp on the skills of effective interpersonal communication.

behaviors, and consequently they don't encourage defensiveness. With I-message statements, it's easier for the other person to acknowledge behaviors and to offer to change them.

Also use I-messages to describe what, if anything, you want the listener to do: "I'm feeling sorry for myself right now; just give me some space. I'll give you a call in a few days." Or, more directly: "I'd prefer to be alone right now."

Handle Your Anger: A Special Case

As a kind of summary of emotional communication, this section looks at anger. Anger is one of the eight basic emotions identified in Plutchik's model (Figure 8.3, page 196). It's also an emotion that can create considerable problems if not managed properly. Anger varies from mild annoyance to intense rage; increases in pulse rate and blood pressure usually accompany these feelings.

Anger is not always necessarily bad. In fact, anger may help you protect yourself, energizing you to fight or flee. Often, however, anger does prove destructive—as when, for example, you allow it to obscure reality or to become an obsession.

Anger doesn't just happen; you make it happen by your interpretation of events. Yet life events can contribute mightily. There are the road repairs that force you to detour so you wind up late for an important appointment. There are the moths that attack your favorite sweater. There's the water leak that ruins your carpet. People, too, can contribute to your anger: the driver who tailgates, the clerk who overcharges you, the supervisor who ignores your contributions to the company. But it is you who interpret these events and people in ways that stimulate you to generate anger.

Writing more than a hundred years ago, Charles Darwin observed in his *The Expression of the Emotions in Man and Animals* (1872): "The free expression by outside signs of an emotion intensifies it . . . the repression, as far as this is possible, of all outside signs softens our emotions. He who gives way to violent gestures will increase his rage." Popular psychology ignored Darwin's implied admonition in the 1960s and '70s, when the suggested prescription for dealing with anger was to "let it all hang out" and "tell it like it is." Express your anger, many people advised, or risk its being bottled up and eventually exploding. Later thinking has returned to Darwin, however, and suggests that venting anger may not be the best strategy (Tavris, 1989). Expressing anger doesn't get rid of it but makes it grow: Angry expression increases anger, which promotes more angry expression, which increases anger, and on and on.

■ **What Do You Say**

Saying the Right Thing

Your roommate just made the dean's list and as a reward received a new Lexus from a rich uncle. Your roommate is ecstatic and runs to you to share the news. You want to demonstrate empathy, but you're really annoyed that some people just seem to get everything. **What Do You Say?**

A better strategy seems to be to reduce the anger. With this principle in mind, here are some suggestions for analyzing and communicating anger.

E-Talk ....

Anger Online

How do you express anger online and in face-to-face communication? How do the consequences of your expression of anger differ in the different media?

ANGER MANAGEMENT: SCREAM BEFORE YOU SCREAM   Perhaps the most popular recommendation for dealing with anger is to count to 10. The purpose is to give you a cooling-off period, and the advice is not bad. A somewhat more difficult but probably far more effective strategy would be to use that cooling-off period not merely for counting but for mindfully analyzing and ultimately managing your anger. The procedure offered here is similar to those available in popular books on anger management but is couched in a communication framework. It's called SCREAM, an acronym for the major issues (that is, the major components of the communication process) that you need to consider:

- *Self.* How important is this to you? Is it worth the high blood pressure and the general aggravation? For example, are you interpreting the "insult" as the other person intended, or could you be misperceiving the situation or the intent? Is "insult" _to you_ the same as "insult" _to your mother-in-law_? Are you confusing factual with inferential knowledge? Are you sure that what you think happened really happened? Or might you be filling in the gaps with what could have or might have happened or with what you expected to happen?

- *Context.* Is this the appropriate time and place to express your anger? Do you have to express your anger right now? Do you have to express it right here? Might a better time and place be arranged?

- *Receiver.* Is this person the one to whom you wish to express your anger? For example, do you want to express your anger to your life partner if you're really angry with your supervisor for not recommending your promotion?

- *Effect* (immediate). What effect do you want to achieve? Do you want to express your anger to help you get the promotion? To hurt the other person? To release pent-up emotions? To stand up for your rights? Each purpose would obviously require a different communication strategy. Consider, too, what may be the likely immediate effect of your anger display. For example, will the other person

❝ Nothing lowers the level of conversation more than raising the voice. ❞
—Stanley Horowitz

also become angry? And if so, is it possible that the entire situation will snowball and get out of hand?

- *Aftermath* (long-range). What are the likely long-term repercussions of this expression of anger? What will be the effects on your relationship? Your continued employment?

- *Messages.* Suppose that after this rather thorough analysis, you do decide to express your anger. What messages would be appropriate? How can you best communicate your feelings to achieve your desired results? This question brings us to the subject of anger communication.

ANGER COMMUNICATION   Anger communication is not angry communication. In fact, it might be argued that the communication of anger ought to be especially calm and dispassionate. Here, then, are a few suggestions for communicating your anger in a nonangry way.

1. Get ready to communicate calmly and logically. First, relax. Try to breathe deeply; think pleasant thoughts; perhaps tell yourself to "take it easy," "think rationally," and "calm down." Try to get rid of any unrealistic ideas you may have that might contribute to anger; for example, is what this person did so reprehensible, or was it perhaps just a selfish act of a frightened individual?

2. Examine your communication options. In most situations there are lots of different ways to express yourself, so don't jump to the first possibility that comes to mind. Assess your options for the form of the communication—should you communicate face-to-face? By e-mail? By telephone? Similarly, assess your options for the timing of your communication, for the specific words and gestures you might use, for the physical setting, and so on.

3. Consider the advantages of delaying the expression of anger. For example, consider writing the e-mail but sending it to yourself, at least until the next morning. Then the options of revising it or not sending it at all will still be open to you.

4. Remember that different cultures have different display rules—norms for what is and what is not appropriate to display. Assess the culture you're in as well as the cultures of the other people involved, especially these cultures' display rules for communicating anger.

5. Apply the relevant skills of interpersonal communication. For example, be specific, use I-messages, avoid allness, avoid polarized terms, and in general communicate with all the competence you can muster.

6. Recall the irreversibility of communication. Once you say something, you'll not be able to erase or delete it from the mind of the other person.

These suggestions are not going to solve the problems of road rage, gang warfare, or domestic violence. Yet they may help—a bit—in reducing some of the negative consequences of anger and perhaps even some of the anger itself.

Dialogue *for* **Analysis**

The Conversation among Old "Friends"

This dialogue illustrates some common conversational problems. As you read it, try to identify alternative ways of communicating and the problems these new patterns might avoid.

The Cast

Pat, 30-something
Chris, a friend, also 30-something

(continues)

Dialogue *for* Analysis

The Context

Pat and Chris meet on the street; they haven't seen or talked with each other for a few weeks.

Pat: Hey, Chris.

Chris: Hey stranger. What's been going on; you haven't called in weeks.

Pat: Yeah. I've been kind of out of it.

Chris: What's the matter? You look terrible.

Pat: Lee left me. I found a Post-it note last week with "It's over" written on it.

Chris: What? Well, geez, I mean . . . you're better off, you know? I never understood what you saw in such a negative, arrogant know-it-all anyway. You can do a lot better.

Pat: Maybe. I don't know. Lately I just want to go to sleep and never wake up.

Chris: Totally. That's totally the way I felt when I broke up with Smitty.

Pat: Who?

Chris: You remember; we went out for like four or five weeks. It was really intense right up until it ended.

Pat: Yeah, I guess, but this was the last six years of my life, and I just thought we were. . . .

Chris: [Interrupting] Six weeks, six years; it's all the same. I mean, you know, my relationships are all very intense.

Pat: Sure. I know.

Chris: Remember that affair I had with B.B.? What a train wreck waiting to happen. And the one with that one from Oklahoma?

Pat: Yeah, I kind of remember the one from Oklahoma, I think.

Chris: Man, it's crazy to think back to those crazy flings, isn't it? I'm telling you!

Pat: Whatever; I mean, not right now.

Chris: Oh, come on, you'll be back out there again soon, I know it. By the way, how about grabbing a late dinner tonight at that new Moroccan restaurant?

Pat: Thanks, but I'm going to pass.

Chris: Suit yourself. Great seeing you. Don't be a stranger. Give me a call and we'll go out.

Summary of Concepts and Skills

This chapter examined conversation and also highlighted emotional conversation, explaining the basic principles and identifying important skills.

1. Conversation consists of five general stages: opening, feedforward, business, feedback, and closing.

2. Initiating conversations can be accomplished in various ways; for example, with self, other, relational, and context references.

3. People maintain conversations by taking turns at speaking and listening. Turn-maintaining and turn-yielding cues are used by the speaker; turn-requesting, turn-denying, and backchanneling cues are used by the listener.

4. You can close a conversation through a variety of methods. For example: Reflect back on the conversation, as in summarizing; directly state your desire to end the conversation; refer to future interaction; ask for closure; and/or state your pleasure with the interaction.

5. Conversational repair is frequently undertaken through excuses (statements of explanation designed to lessen the negative impact of a speaker's messages). "I didn't do it," "It wasn't so bad," and "Yes, but" are the major general categories of excuses.

6. Effective conversation is dialogic, reciprocal, and involves power.

7. Emotions consist of a physical part (our physiological reactions), a cognitive part (our interpretations of our

feelings), and a cultural part (our cultural traditions' influence on our emotional evaluations and expressions).

8. Emotions may be primary or blends. The primary emotions, according to Robert Plutchik, are joy, acceptance, fear, surprise, sadness, disgust, anger, and anticipation. Other emotions, such as love, awe, contempt, and aggressiveness, are blends of primary emotions.

9. Cultural and gender display rules identify what emotions may be expressed, where, how, and by whom.

10. The following guidelines should help make your emotional expression more meaningful: First, confront the obstacles to effective communication of feelings—societal rules and customs, fear of making yourself vulnerable, and inadequate communication skills. Further, describe your feelings as accurately as possible, identifying the reasons behind them. Anchor your feelings and their expression to the present time. Own your own feelings. Finally, handle your anger as appropriate.

11. In responding to the emotions of others, try to see the situation from the perspective of the other person. Avoid refocusing the conversation on yourself. Show interest and provide the speaker with the opportunity to talk and explore his or her feelings. Avoid evaluating the feelings of the other person.

This chapter also identified some significant conversational and emotional communication skills. Check those on which you'd like to focus for added skill development.

_____ 1. *Disclaimers.* Use disclaimers if you feel you might be misunderstood. But avoid them when they're not necessary; too many disclaimers can make you appear unprepared or unwilling to state an opinion.

_____ 2. *Conversational rules.* Observe the general rules for conversation (for example, using relatively short speaking turns and avoiding interruptions) but break them when there seems logical reason to do so.

_____ 3. *Conversational turns.* Maintain relatively short conversational turns; after taking your turn, pass the speaker's turn to another person nonverbally or verbally.

_____ 4. *Turn-taking cues.* Respond to both the verbal and the nonverbal conversational turn-taking cues given you by others, and make your own cues clear to others.

_____ 5. *Making excuses.* Repair conversational problems by offering excuses that demonstrate understanding, acknowledge your responsibility, acknowledge your regret, request forgiveness, and make clear that this will never happen again.

_____ 6. *Emotionality in interpersonal communication.* Recognize the inevitable emotionality in your thoughts and feelings, and include emotions as appropriate in your verbal and nonverbal messages.

_____ 7. *Emotional understanding.* Identify and describe emotions (both positive and negative) clearly and specifically. Learn the vocabulary of emotional expression.

_____ 8. *Emotional display.* Express emotions and interpret the emotions of others in light of the cultural rules dictating what is and what isn't "appropriate."

_____ 9. *Listening to the feelings of others.* Empathize, focus on the other person, and encourage the person to explore his or her feelings.

_____ 10. *I-messages.* Use I-messages when communicating your feelings; take responsibility for your own feelings rather than attributing them to others.

_____ 11. *Emotional communication.* Communicate emotions effectively: (1) Confront the obstacles to emotional expression; (2) describe your feelings, identifying the reasons behind them; (3) anchor feelings to the present; and (4) own your feelings and messages.

_____ 12. *Anger management.* Calm down as best you can and then consider your communication options and the relevant communication skills for expressing your feelings.

Vocabulary Quiz: The Language of Conversation

Match the following conversation-related terms with their definitions. Record the number of the definition next to the appropriate term.

_____ excuse

_____ I-messages

_____ disclaimer

_____ turn-yielding cues

_____ gender display rules

_____ backchanneling cues

_____ altercasting

_____ phatic communication

_____ owning feelings

_____ display rules

1. A form of conversation repair.
2. Messages about messages to follow.
3. Cues that announce that the speaker is finished and wishes to assume the listener's role.
4. A process by which the speaker or listener assumes a specific role.
5. Conversational messages through which the listener communicates information back to the speaker but does not ask to assume the speaker's role.
6. Messages that open the channels of communication.
7. The opposite of attributing feelings to others.
8. Messages that explicitly acknowledge responsibility for your own feelings.
9. Rules for the appropriate expression of emotions.
10. Rules for the appropriate expression of emotions for men and women.

Four for Discussion

1. In dialogic interaction between, say, a fluent speaker and a speaker who has a severe physical or psychological communication problem, the more fluent speaker tries to help the speaker with the problem communicate more effectively. In fact, some researchers have argued that the more competent communicator has an ethical responsibility to equalize the interaction by helping the other person to better convey his or her meaning (von Tetzchner & Jensen, 1999). Do you consider this an ethical responsibility?

2. Not surprisingly, each culture has its own conversational taboos—topics that should be avoided, especially by visitors from other cultures. Table 8.2 (p. 184) listed a few examples. Are there certain taboo topics that you do not want members of other cultures to talk about? Why?

3. If you were compiling a book on The World's Worst Excuses, which ones would you include? Which would you include in The World's Best Excuses? What standards would you use to classify excuses as bad or good?

4. Some societies permit and even expect men to show strong emotions. They expect men to cry, to show fear, to express anger openly. Other societies—including many groups within general U.S. culture—criticize men for experiencing and expressing such emotions. What did your culture teach you about gender and the expression of emotions—in particular, the expression of strongly felt emotions and emotions that show weakness (such as fear, discomfort, or uncertainty)?

MyCommunicationLab Explorations

Explore www.mycommunicationlab.com to find exercises on the varied aspects of conversation. These include (1) Conversational Analysis: A Chance Meeting, (2) Giving and Taking Directions, (3) Gender and the Topics of Conversation, (4) Responding Effectively in Conversation, (5) The Qualities of Effectiveness, (6) Communicating Emotions Nonverbally, (7) Communicating Your Emotions, (8) Expressing Negative Feelings, and (9) Emotional Advice.

Several self-tests on qualities of conversation also are available: (10) How Flexible Are You in Conversation? (11) How Polite Is Your Conversation? and (12) How Much Do You Self-Monitor?

And visit MyCommunicationLab for study guides, exercises, and video clips on varied aspects of conversation.

Explore our research resources at www.researchnavigator.com.

Research Navigator.com

CHAPTER 9
Interpersonal Relationships

WHY READ THIS CHAPTER?

*B*ecause you'll **learn about:**

- interpersonal relationships.
- why you form relationships.
- the ways in which culture and technology influence your relationships.

*B*ecause you'll **learn to:**

- communicate to develop and maintain meaningful interpersonal relationships.
- use messages appropriate to your relationship stage and the direction in which you want to move the relationship.
- communicate more effectively in friendship, love, family, and work relationships.
- communicate more effectively in different cultures and in different media.

*I*nterpersonal relationships are among the most important assets you have, and your ability to form meaningful and satisfying relationships rests largely on your interpersonal communication competencies.

As illustrated throughout this chapter, interpersonal relationships come in a variety of forms. Although the romantic relationship perhaps comes to mind most quickly, interpersonal relationships exist between—for example—friends, mentors and protégés, family members, and work team colleagues.

Relationship Stages

It's useful to look at interpersonal relationships as created and constructed by the individuals. Looked at in this way, there are many relationships in any interpersonal relationship. For example, in the interpersonal relationship between Pat and Chris, there are (1) the relationship that Pat sees, (2) the relationship as Chris sees it, (3) the relationship that Pat wants and is striving for, (4) the relationship that Chris wants. And of course there are the many relationships that friends and relatives see and that they reflect back in their communications. That is, the relationship that Pat's mother (who dislikes Chris) sees and reflects in her communication with Pat and Chris is very likely to influence Pat and Chris in some ways. And then there's the relationship that a dispassionate researcher/observer would see.

This is not to say that there is no real relationship, but it is to say that there are many real relationships. And because there are these differently constructed relationships, partners often disagree about a wide variety of issues and of course evaluate their relationship very differently. If you watch Jerry Springer or similar shows, you'll notice that many of the guest couples see their relationship very differently. The first guest thinks all is going well until the second guest comes on and explodes—often identifying long-held dissatisfactions and behaviors that shock the partner.

The quality that makes a relationship interpersonal is *interdependency:* The actions of one person impact on the other; one person's actions have consequences for the other person. The actions of a stranger—such as working overtime or flirting with a coworker—will have no impact on you; you and the proverbial stranger are independent, and your actions have no effect on each other. If, however, you were in an interpersonal relationship and your partner worked overtime or flirted with a coworker, these actions would affect you and the relationship in some way.

The six-stage model shown in Figure 9.1 on page 208 describes the significant stages you may go through as you try to achieve your relationship goals. As a general description of relationship development (and sometimes dissolution), the stages seem standard: They apply to all relationships, whether friendship or love, whether face-to-face or computer mediated. The six stages are contact, involvement, intimacy, deterioration, repair, and dissolution. Each stage can be divided into an initial and a final phase.

Contact

At the **contact** stage there is first perceptual contact—you see what the person looks like, you hear what the person

❝ **Laughter is not at all a bad beginning for a friendship.** ❞
—Oscar Wilde

Figure 9.1
The Six Stages of Relationships

Can you provide a specific example or examples, from literature or from your own experience, that would illustrate some or all of these six stages?

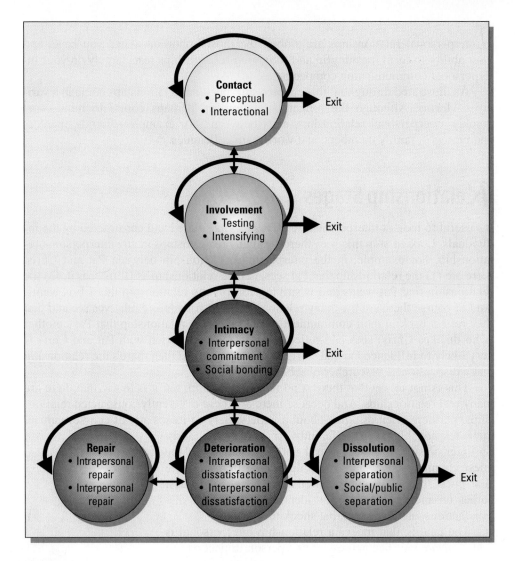

sounds like, you may even smell the person. From this contact you get a physical picture: gender, approximate age, height, and so on. If this is an online relationship, this initial perception relies on a different set of cues. Depending on your expectations for this relationship, you might develop a visual image based on the written messages exchanged or, if you have audio and video capabilities, on the sound of the person's voice, facial features, the way the person moves, and so on. From these cues you develop a physical picture.

After this perception, there is usually interactional contact. Here the interaction is superficial and impersonal. This is the stage of "Hello, my name is Joe"—the stage at which you exchange basic information that needs to come before any more intense involvement. This interactional contact also may be nonverbal, as in, for example, exchanging smiles, concentrating your focus on one person, or decreasing the physical distance between the two of you.

This is the stage at which you initiate interaction ("May I join you?") and engage in invitational communication ("May I buy you a drink?"). The invitational messages in computer-mediated communication may involve moving to a face-to-face meeting. According to some researchers, it's at this contact stage—within the first four minutes of initial interaction—that you decide if you want to pursue the relationship or not (Zunin & Zunin, 1972).

Physical appearance is especially important in the initial development of attraction, because it's the characteristic most readily available to sensory inspection. Yet

TABLE 9.1   **Where People Meet**

Here are the major places at which couples say they met.

Where?	How Many?
At work or school	38 %
Through friends and family	34%
At a night club, bar, or social gathering	13%
Through the Internet	3%
At a religious institution	2%
Through living in the same neighborhood	1%
At a recreational facility	1%
On a blind date or through a dating service	1%

Source: Madden, Mary. Lenhart, Amanda. Online dating. Pew Internet & American Life Project, March 5, 2006 , http://www.pewinternet.org/PPF/r/177/report_display.asp

E-Talk

Gender Flirting Online

Some research finds that men make themselves seem attractive online by describing themselves as financially secure, and women by describing themselves as physically attractive (Whitty, 2003). At the same time, one study found that personal ads describing women as ambitious, financially independent, and successful got more responses than those describing them as attractive, lovely, and slim (Strassberg & Holty, 2003). What types of qualities would you look for in a potential romantic partner?

through both verbal and nonverbal behaviors, qualities such as friendliness, warmth, openness, and dynamism also are revealed at the contact stage.

Not surprisingly, people make contact through various means. Table 9.1 provides the results of one survey on the places at which couples (all of whom were Internet users) met.

Involvement

At the **involvement** stage, a sense of mutuality, of being connected, develops. During this stage you experiment and try to learn more about the other person. At the early

Ethical *messages*

Q & A

One of the most difficult issues in interpersonal relationships occurs when you're asked a question and there is a tension between your desire to be truthful and your wish to be effective in achieving your relationship goals.

What Would You Do?

Here are a few questions that others might ask you. For each question, however, certain circumstances may make it difficult for you to respond fully or even truthfully; these are noted as the "Thoughts" you have as you consider your possible answers. What would you do in each of these three situations?

Question: *[A supervisor asks]: I need you to tell Pat I stayed late at the office with you last night. OK?*

Thought: *I don't want to get into their relationship problems, and I don't want to lie. But neither do I want to create problems with my boss.*

Question: *[A 15-year-old asks]: Was I adopted? Who are my real parents?*

Thought: *Yes, you were adopted, but I fear that if you find your biological parents I'll lose your love.*

Question: *[A romantic partner asks]: I love you. [Although not grammatically a question, this "declarative sentence" is a message asking for an answer.]*

Thought: *I don't want to commit myself, but I don't want to end the relationship, either. I want to allow the relationship to progress further before making any commitment.*

■ **What Do You Say**

"Clarifying" Your Relationship Résumé

Although you've been mostly honest in your two-month Internet relationship, you have padded your relationship résumé—lopped off a few years and pounds and made your temporary job seem like the executive fast-track. You now want to come clean. **What Do You Say?** Through what channel?

phase of involvement, a kind of preliminary testing goes on. You want to see if your initial judgment—made perhaps at the contact stage—proves reasonable. So you may ask questions— "Where do you work?" "What are you majoring in?"

If you're committed to getting to know the person even better, you continue your involvement by intensifying your interaction. Here, you not only try to get to know the other person better, but also begin to reveal yourself. It's at this stage that you begin to share your feelings and your emotions. If this is to be a romantic relationship, you might date. If it's to be a friendship, you might share in activities related to mutual interests—go to the movies or to some sports event together.

And throughout the relationship process—but especially during involvement and the early stages of intimacy—partners continue testing each other. Each person tests the other; each tries to find out how the other feels about the relationship. For example, you might ask your partner directly how he or she feels; or you might disclose your own feelings, on the assumption that your partner will also self-disclose; or you might joke about a shared future together, touch more intimately, or hint that you're serious about the relationship; or you might question mutual friends as to your partner's feelings (Bell & Buerkel-Rothfuss, 1990; Baxter & Wilmot, 1984).

Intimacy

One way to define **intimacy** is that in this stage you feel you can be honest and open when talking about yourself; you can express thoughts and feelings that you don't reveal in other relationships (Mackey, Diemer, & O'Brien, 2000). At the intimacy stage you commit yourself still further to the other person, establishing a kind of relationship in which this individual becomes your best or closest friend, lover, or companion. Your communication becomes more personalized, more synchronized, and easier (Gudykunst, Nishida, & Chua, 1987). Usually the intimacy stage divides itself quite neatly into two phases: an interpersonal commitment phase in which you commit yourselves to each other in a kind of private way, and a social bonding phase in which the commitment is made public—perhaps to family and friends, perhaps to the public at large through formal marriage. Here the two of you become a unit, a pair.

In addition, in intimacy you display affiliative cues (signs that show you love the other person), including head nods, gestures, and forward leaning. You also give *Duchenne smiles,* smiles that are beyond voluntary control and that signal genuine joy (Gonzaga, Keltner, Londahl, & Smith, 2001). Duchenne smiles give you crow's-feet around the eyes, raise up your cheeks, and puff up the lower eyelids (Lemonick, 2005a).

Commitment may take many forms; it may involve engagement or marriage, a commitment to help the person or to be with the person, or a commitment to reveal your deepest secrets. It may consist of living together or agreeing to become lovers. Or it may consist of becoming a romantic pair either in face-to-face or in online relationships. In a computer-mediated relationship, meeting face-to-face may be a possibility but not necessarily a requirement. The type of commitment varies with the relationship and with the individuals. The important characteristic is that the commitment made is special; it's a commitment that you do not make lightly or to everyone. Each of us reserves this level of intimacy for very few people at any given time—sometimes just one person; sometimes two, three, or perhaps four. In computer-mediated communication, of course, there is the potential for a much greater number of intimates.

INTIMACY AND RISK To some people, relational intimacy seems extremely risky. To others, it involves only low risk. Consider your own view of relationship risk by responding to the following questions.

- *Is it dangerous to get really close to people?*
- *Are you afraid to get really close to someone because you might get hurt?*
- *Do you find it difficult to trust other people?*

"I'm sure 'till death do you part' was only an estimate."

● *Do you believe that the most important thing to consider in a relationship is whether you might get hurt?*

People who answer yes to these and similar questions see intimacy as involving considerable risk (Pilkington & Richardson, 1988). Such people have fewer close friends, are less likely to have romantic relationships, have less trust in others, have lower levels of dating assertiveness, have lower self-esteem, are more possessive and jealous, and are generally less sociable and extroverted than those who see intimacy as involving little risk (Pilkington & Woods, 1999).

The nature of risk in online relationships is similar to that in face-to-face relationships; for example, in both kinds of relationships you risk losing face and damaging your self-esteem. So there's likely to be considerable similarity in any given individual's attitudes toward risk in both types of relationships.

INTIMACY AND IMMEDIACY   You can view **immediacy** as the interpersonal communication equivalent of relationship intimacy—it's the joining of speaker and listener; it's the creation of a sense of togetherness, of oneness. When you communicate immediacy you convey a sense of interest and attention, a liking for the other person. People respond to communication that is immediate more favorably than they respond to communication that is not. In various studies, for example, students of instructors who communicated immediacy felt that the instruction was better and the course more valuable than students of instructors who did not communicate immediacy (Moore, Masterson, Christophel, & Shea, 1996; Witt & Wheeless, 2001). Students and teachers liked each other largely on the basis of immediacy (Wilson & Taylor, 2001; Baringer & McCroskey, 2000).

Here are a few suggestions for communicating immediacy, whether to achieve intimacy or to simply further interpersonal interaction.

E-Talk ▪ ▪ ▪ ▪ ▪ ▪ ▪ ▪

Privacy and Emotional Closeness

In face-to-face relationships, emotional closeness compromises privacy; the closer you become, the less privacy you have. In online relationships, however, because you're more in control of what you reveal, you can develop close emotional relationships but also maintain your privacy (Ben-Ze'ev, 2003). Do you find this to be true? If not, how would you express the relationship between emotional closeness and privacy?

Talking Cherishing

Cherishing behaviors are those small gestures you enjoy receiving from your partner (a smile, a wink, a phone call, an e-mail saying "I'm thinking of you," a kiss). They are specific and positive—nothing overly general or negative; focused on the present and future rather than related to issues about which the partners have argued in the past; capable of being performed daily; and easily executed—nothing you really have to go out of your way to accomplish. Cherishing behaviors are an especially effective way to affirm another person and to increase "favor exchange," a concept that comes from the work of William Lederer (1984).

Prepare a list of 10 cherishing behaviors that you would like to receive from your real or imagined relationship partner. After each partner prepares a list, they exchange lists and, ideally, perform the desired cherishing behaviors. At first these behaviors may seem self-conscious and awkward. In time, however, they'll become a normal part of your interaction, which is exactly what you want.

Lists of cherishing behaviors—yours or your partner's—will also give you insight into your relationship needs and the kind of communicating partner you want.

- Express psychological closeness and openness by, for example, maintaining physical closeness and arranging your body to exclude third parties. Maintain appropriate eye contact and limit looking around at others.
- Smile and express your interest in the other person.
- Use the other person's name; for example, say, "Joe, what do you think?" instead of "What do you think?"
- Focus on the other person's remarks. Make the speaker know that you heard and understood what he or she said, and give the speaker appropriate verbal and nonverbal feedback.
- Express immediacy with cultural sensitivity. In the United States immediacy is generally seen as friendly and appropriate. In other cultures, however, the same behaviors may be viewed as overly familiar, as presuming that relationship is close when it's only one of acquaintanceship (Axtell, 1993).

Deterioration

Although many relationships remain at the intimacy stage, some enter the stage of **deterioration**—the stage that sees the weakening of bonds between the parties and that represents the downside of the relationship progression. Relationships deteriorate for many reasons. When the reasons for coming together are no longer present or change drastically, relationships may deteriorate. Thus, for example, when your relationship no longer lessens your loneliness or provides stimulation or self-knowledge, or when it fails to increase your self-esteem or to maximize pleasures and minimize pains, it may be in the process of deteriorating. Among the other reasons for deterioration are third-party relationships, sexual dissatisfaction, dissatisfaction with work, or financial difficulties (Blumstein & Schwartz, 1983).

The first phase of deterioration is usually *intrapersonal dissatisfaction*. You begin to feel that this relationship may not be as important as you had previously thought. You may experience personal dissatisfaction with everyday interactions and begin to view the future together negatively. If this dissatisfaction continues or grows, you may pass to the second phase, *interpersonal deterioration,* in which you discuss these dissatisfactions with your partner.

During the process of deterioration, communication patterns change drastically. These patterns are in part a response to the deterioration; you communicate as you do because of the way you feel your relationship is deteriorating. However, the way you communicate (or fail to communicate) also influences the fate of your relationship. During the deterioration stage you may, for example, increase withdrawal, communicate less, respond to computer messages more briefly and with greater delays, and self-disclose less.

Repair

The first phase of **repair** is *intrapersonal repair,* in which you analyze what went wrong and consider ways of solving your relational difficulties. At this stage you may consider changing your behaviors or perhaps changing your expectations of your partner. You may also weigh the rewards of your relationship as it is now against the rewards you could anticipate if your relationship ended.

If you decide that you want to repair your relationship, you may discuss this with your partner at the *interpersonal repair* level. Here you may talk about the problems in the relationship, the corrections you would want to see, and perhaps what you would be willing to do and what you would want the other person to do. This is the stage of negotiating new agreements, new behaviors. You and your partner may try to solve your problems yourselves, or you may seek the advice of friends or family or perhaps enter professional counseling.

You can look at the strategies for repairing a relationship in terms of the following six suggestions—which conveniently spell out the word REPAIR, a useful reminder that repair is not a one-step but a multistep process: Recognize the problem, Engage in productive conflict resolution, Pose possible solutions, Affirm each other, Integrate solutions into normal behavior, and Risk.

- *Recognize* the problem. What, in concrete terms, is wrong with your present relationship? What changes would be needed to make it better—again, in specific terms? Create a picture of your relationship as you would want it to be and compare that picture to the way the relationship looks now.
- *Engage* in productive conflict resolution. Interpersonal conflict is an inevitable part of relationship life. It's not so much the conflict that causes relationship difficulties as the way in which the conflict is approached (Chapter 10). If it's confronted through productive strategies, the conflict may be resolved, and the relationship may actually emerge stronger and healthier. If, however, unproductive and destructive strategies are used, the relationship may well deteriorate further.
- *Pose* possible solutions. Ideally, each person will ask, "What can we do to resolve the difficulty that will allow both of us to get what we want?"
- *Affirm* each other. For example, happily married couples engage in greater positive behavior exchange—that is, they communicate more agreement, approval, and positive affect—than do unhappily married couples (Dindia & Fitzpatrick, 1985).
- *Integrate* solutions into your life—make the solutions a part of your normal behavior.
- *Risk.* Risk giving favors without any certainty of reciprocity. Risk rejection by making the first move to make up or say you're sorry. Be willing to change, to adapt, to take on new tasks and responsibilities.

Dissolution

The **dissolution** stage, in both friendship and romance, is the cutting of the bonds that tie you together. The first phase of dissolution usually takes the form of interpersonal separation, in which you may not see each other anymore or may not return messages. If you live together, you move into separate apartments and begin to lead lives apart from each other. If this relationship is a marriage, you may seek a legal separation. If this separation period proves workable and if the original relationship is not repaired, you may enter the second phase: social or public separation. In marriage, this phase corresponds to divorce. Avoidance of each other and a return to

■ What Do You Say
Ending the Relationship
You want to break up your 8-month romantic relationship and still remain friends. Your desire to break up is likely to come as a major surprise to your dating partner. **What Do You Say?** Through what channel?

" Falling out of love is very enlightening; for a short while, you see the world with new eyes. "

—Iris Murdoch

being "single" are among the primary identifiable features of dissolution. In some cases, however, the former partners change the definition of their relationship; for example, ex-lovers become friends, or ex-friends become "just" business partners.

This final, "good-bye," phase of dissolution is the point at which you become an ex-lover or ex-friend. In some cases this is a stage of relief and relaxation; finally it's over. In other cases this is a stage of anxiety and frustration, of guilt and regret, of resentment over time ill spent and now lost. In more materialistic terms, the good-bye phase is the stage when property is divided and when legal battles may ensue over who should get what.

No matter how friendly the breakup, there is likely to be some emotional difficulty. Here are some suggestions for dealing with this:

- *Break the loneliness–depression cycle.* Avoid sad passivity, a state in which you feel sorry for yourself, sit alone, and perhaps cry. Instead, try to engage in active solitude (exercise, write, study, play computer games) and seek distraction (do things to put loneliness out of your mind; for example, take a long drive or shop). The most effective way to deal with loneliness is through social action, especially through helping people in need.

- *Take time out.* Take some time for yourself. Renew your relationship with yourself. Get to know yourself as a unique individual, standing alone now but fully capable of entering a meaningful relationship in the future.

- *Bolster self-esteem.* Positive and successful experiences are most helpful in building self-esteem. As in dealing with loneliness, helping others is one of the best ways to raise your own self-esteem.

- *Seek the support of others.* Avail yourself of your friends and family for support; it's an effective antidote to the discomfort and unhappiness that occur when a relationship ends.

- *Avoid repeating negative patterns.* Ask yourself, at the start of a new relationship, if you're entering a relationship modeled on the previous one. If the answer is yes, be especially careful that you do not repeat the problems. At the same time, avoid becoming a prophet of doom. Do not see in every new relationship vestiges of the old. Use past relationships and experiences as guides, not filters.

Reflections on the Model of Relationships

Before moving on to examine relationship types, let's consider some of the implications of the six-stage model of relationships.

1. Because relationships differ so widely, it's best to think of any relationship model as a tool for talking about relationships, rather than as a specific map that indicates how you move from one relationship stage to another. The six-stage model is certainly not the only way you can look at relationships. Table 9.2, for example, presents a somewhat different model of relationship stages.

2. Within each relationship and within each relationship stage, there are dynamic tensions. According to **relational dialectics theory,** all relationships can be defined by a series of pairs of competing opposite desires or motivations. For example: (1) The tension between *autonomy* and *connection* reflects your desire to remain an individual but also to be intimately connected to another person and

TABLE 9.2   Knapp's Model of Relationship Stages

The first five stages of Knapp's model describe the processes of coming together and moving toward greater connection and intimacy.

- *Initiation* is the stage at which you first perceive and interact with the other person. Here you try to present yourself in a positive light and to open the channels of communication.
- *Experimenting* involves trying to learn about the other person.
- *Intensifying* involves interacting on a more personal and intimate level; your speech becomes more informal, and you use lots of terms that have meaning only for the two of you.
- *Integrating* consists of a fusion of the two individuals, a stage when mutual opinions and attitudes are cultivated.
- *Bonding* has to do with the social naming of the relationship; for example, as marriage or domestic partnership or exclusive partnership.

The next five stages describe the stages of coming apart and moving away from intimacy.

- *Differentiating* is the process by which the individuals begin to think of themselves as different and distinct from each other.
- *Circumscribing* involves restricting communication, perhaps to topics that are safe and will not cause conflict.
- *Stagnating* is the stage of inactive communication; when you do communicate it's with difficulty and awkwardness.
- *Avoiding* involves active physical separation and the absence of face-to-face interaction.
- *Terminating* involves the breaking of the bonds that once held the relationship together.

Source: Adapted from Mark L. Knapp & Anita L. Vangelisti, *Interpersonal Communication and Human Relationships,* 4/e. Published by Allyn & Bacon, Boston, MA. Copyright © 2000 by Pearson Education. Reprinted by permission of the publisher.

to a relationship. (2) The tension between *novelty* and *predictability* focuses on your desires for newness and adventure on the one hand and for sameness and comfortableness on the other. (3) The tension between *closedness* and *openness* relates to your desires to be in an exclusive relationship yet at the same time to be in a relationship that is open to different people (Baxter, 1988, 1990; Baxter & Simon, 1993).

"Your wife's also asking that you rot in hell for eternity, but I think that's negotiable."

Listening to Stage Talk

Listening for **stage-talk messages**—messages expressing a desire to move the relationship in a particular way or to maintain it at a particular stage—will help you understand and manage your interpersonal relationships, whether business or personal. It will help you see when, for example, your partner's messages are inconsistent with the stage you think the relationship is at, or when your partner wants to intensify or deintensify the relationship. Stage-talk messages can be classified in the following categories.

1. *Contact messages* express a desire for contact: "Hi, my name is Joe."
2. *Closeness messages* express a desire for increased closeness, involvement, or intimacy: "I'd like to see you more often."
3. *Maintenance messages* express a desire to stabilize the relationship at one stage: "Let's stay friends for now; I'm afraid to get more involved at this point."
4. *Distancing messages* express a desire for more "space": "I think we need a few weeks apart."
5. *Repair messages* express a desire to repair the relationship: "Let's discuss this issue again. I didn't mean to hurt your feelings."
6. *Dissolution messages* express a desire to break up or dissolve the existing relationship: "It's just not working out; let's go on Jerry Springer."

Applying Listening Skills

Your dating partner of about five or six weeks gives you a gift that clashes with the way you see the relationship. The gift is much too intimate and too expensive for the casual relationship you perceive. You feel that if you accept it, you'll be making a major commitment that you're not ready to make just yet. Still, you want to maintain the relationship and see where it goes. How do you explain how you feel?

3. More accurate than a linear progression from stage to stage is the movement depicted in Figure 9.1 (p. 208) by the different types of arrows. The exit arrows show that each stage offers the opportunity to exit the relationship; for example, after saying hello you can say good-bye and exit. The vertical or movement arrows going to the next stage and back again represent the fact that you can move either to a more intense stage (say, from involvement to intimacy) or to a less intense stage (say, from intimacy to deterioration). The self-reflexive arrows—the arrows that return to the beginning of the same level or stage—signify that any relationship may become stabilized at any point. You may, for example, remain at the contact stage without getting any further involved, a situation that exists among residents in many large apartment complexes.

4. Movement from one stage to another depends largely on your **relationship communication** skills—the skills you deploy to initiate and open a relationship, to present yourself as likable, to express affection, and to self-disclose appropriately—and, in fact, on all the interpersonal skills you've been acquiring throughout this course (cf. Dindia & Timmerman, 2003). Recognize that these skills will prove relevant both in face-to-face and in computer-mediated relationships, though the specific ways in which you express empathy (for example) will vary depending on whether you're expressing it with only written cues or with facial and vocal and verbal cues.

■ **What Do You Say** ?

Relationship Stage

Your partner gives you a gift that contradicts your perceived relationship stage. The gift is much too intimate and too expensive for the casual relationship you believe you have. **What Do You Say?** Through what channel?

*A*dvantages and Disadvantages of Interpersonal Relationships

All relationships have advantages and disadvantages, and it is helpful to consider what these may be.

Advantages of Interpersonal Relationships

Among the most important advantages of interpersonal relationships is that they help to lessen loneliness (Rokach, 1998; Rokach & Brock, 1995). They make you feel that someone cares, that someone likes you, that someone will protect you, that someone ultimately will love you.

Relationships also provide stimulation (M. Davis, 1973). Human contact is one of the best ways to secure intellectual, physical, and emotional stimulation. And through this stimulation and contact with others you learn about yourself and see yourself from different perspectives and in different roles: as a child or parent, as a coworker, as a friend.

Healthy interpersonal relationships help enhance self-esteem and self-worth. Research consistently shows that interpersonal relationships contribute significantly to physical and emotional health (Rosen, 1998; Goleman, 1995a; Rosengren et al., 1993; Pennebacker, 1991) and to personal happiness (Berscheid & Reis, 1998). Without close interpersonal relationships you're more likely to experience depression, which contributes significantly to physical illness. Isolation, in fact, correlates as closely with mortality as does high blood pressure, high cholesterol, obesity, smoking, or lack of physical exercise (Goleman, 1995a).

Perhaps above all, interpersonal relationships maximize pleasure and minimize pain. Good friends, family, or romantic partners will make you feel even better at times of good fortune and less hurt in the face of hardships. Repeatedly research has shown that people in relationships are happier than people not in relationships (http://pewresearch.org/social/pack.php?PackID=1, accessed 2/20/06).

Disadvantages of Interpersonal Relationships

But there are also disadvantages to interpersonal relationships. Close relationships put pressure on you to reveal yourself and to expose your vulnerabilities. This is generally worthwhile in the context of a supporting and caring relationship—but if the relationship deteriorates, these weaknesses can be used against you. Do you really want to reveal all of your past relationships or your secret fantasies to anyone? You may simply want to keep some things to yourself.

Close relationships increase your obligations, sometimes to a great extent. Although you enter relationships in order to spend more time with special people, you also incur time commitments (and perhaps financial obligations) with which you may not be happy. A close relationship may prevent you from doing much of what you enjoyed as a single (going to the gym, talking on the phone for hours, or just lounging around).

Close interpersonal relationships can limit other relationships. Sometimes this issue involves contact with someone you like but your partner can't stand. More often, however, it's simply a matter of time and energy: You have less to give to other and less intimate relationships. And so you may turn down invitations to play on a company team, attend conferences, or join colleagues for a drink after work.

The closer your relationship, the more emotionally difficult it is to dissolve. A deteriorating relationship can cause distress or depression. In some cultures religious pressures may prevent unhappily married couples from separating. And if lots of money is at stake, the end of a relationship can involve a huge financial blow.

And, of course, your partner may break your heart. If you care a great deal, you're likely to experience great hurt. Ironically, if you care less, the hurt will be less.

The Dark Side of Interpersonal Relationships

In any interpersonal interaction there is the potential for productive and meaningful communication, as there is the potential for unproductive and destructive communication. But it's in the area of interpersonal relationships that the dark side, including various forms of psychological and physical violence, is most obvious and perhaps most significant. Before reading about this important but often neglected topic, take the following self-test.

Test *Yourself*

Is Violence a Part of Your Relationship?

INSTRUCTIONS: Based on your own current relationship or on a relationship you are familiar with, respond to the following questions. Write Yes if you do see yourself in the question or No if you do not see yourself here.

_____ ❶ Do you fear your partner's anger?

_____ ❷ Does your partner ever threaten you?

_____ ❸ Has your partner ever verbally abused you?

_____ ❹ Has your partner ever forced you to do something you didn't want to do?

_____ ❺ Has your partner ever hit (slapped, kicked, pushed) you?

_____ ❻ Has your partner isolated you from your friends or relatives?

HOW DID YOU DO? These six items all reflect signs of a violent partner and a violent relationship. You might also want to change the questions around a bit and ask yourself if your partner would answer Yes to any of these questions about you.

WHAT WILL YOU DO? If any of these questions describes your relationship, you may wish to seek professional help. Discussing these questions with your partner, which may seem the logical first step, may well create additional problems and perhaps incite violence. So you're better off discussing this with a school counselor or some other professional. At the same time, if any of these apply to you—if you yourself are prone to relationship violence—do likewise: Seek professional help. Additional suggestions are offered in the text of this section.

Source: These questions were drawn from a variety of sources, including SUNY at Buffalo Counseling Services (http://ub-counseling.buffalo.edu/warnings.shtml, accessed February 1, 2006); The American College of Obstetricians and Gynecologists, Women's Health Care Physicians (www.acog.org/departments/dept_notice.cfm?recno=17&bulletin=198, accessed February 1, 2006); and The University of Texas at Austin, The Counseling and Mental Health Center (www.utexas.edu/student/cmhc/booklets/relavio/relaviol.html, accessed February 1, 2006).

What Is Relationship Violence?

Three types of relationship violence may be distinguished: physical abuse, verbal or emotional abuse, sexual abuse (Rice, 2006—the U.S. Department of Veterans' Affairs, www.ncptsd.va.gov/facts/specific/fs_domestic_violence.html?printable=no, accessed February 1, 2006).

- *Physical abuse* involves threats of violence as well as acts such as pushing, hitting, slapping, kicking, choking, throwing things, and breaking things.
- *Verbal or emotional abuse* involves humiliating a partner; economic abuse such as controlling the finances or preventing the partner from working; and isolating, criticizing, or stalking the partner.
- *Sexual abuse* involves touching that is unwanted, accusations of sexual infidelity without reason, forced sex, and referring to a partner with abusive sexual terms.

A great deal of research has centered on identifying the warning signs of relationship violence. Here, for example, are a few signs compiled by the State University of New York at Buffalo (http://ub-counseling.buffalo.edu/warnings/shtml, accessed February 1, 2006). Your partner:

- belittles, insults, or ignores you.
- controls pieces of your life; for example, the way you dress or who you can be friends with.
- gets jealous without reason.
- can't handle sexual frustration without anger.
- is so angry or threatening that you've changed your life so as not to provoke additional anger.

The Effects of Violence

As you might expect, relationship violence has a variety of serious consequences: Physical, psychological, and economic injuries all are likely to result (www.cdc.gov/ncic/factsheets/ipvfacts.htm).

PHYSICAL INJURIES   Most obviously, relationship violence often causes physical injuries. These range from scratches and bruises to broken bones, knife wounds, and damage to the central nervous system.

PSYCHOLOGICAL INJURIES   Even when physical injuries are relatively minor the psychological injuries caused by relationship violence may be major. They may include, for example, depression, anxiety, fear of intimacy, and of course low self-esteem.

ECONOMIC INJURIES   Consider the cost to society. It's been estimated that each year in the United States, relationship violence costs approximately $6.2 billion for physical assaults and almost $500 million for rape. Interpersonal violence also results in lost days of work. The Center for Disease Control estimated that interpersonal violence costs the equivalent of 32,000 full-time jobs in lost work each year. Additional economic costs are incurred when interpersonal violence prevents a woman from maintaining a job or continuing her education.

The Alternatives to Violence

Here are some ways in which a nonviolent relationship differs from a violent relationship (www.utexas.edu/student/cmhc/booklets/relavio/relaviol.html), accessed February 1, 2006).

- Instead of emotional abuse, there is fairness; you look for resolutions to conflict that will be fair to both of you.
- Instead of control and isolation, there is communication that makes the partner feel safe and comfortable expressing himself or herself.
- Instead of intimidation, there is mutual respect, mutual affirmation, and valuing of each other's opinions.
- Instead of economic abuse, the partners make financial decisions together.
- Instead of threats, there is accountability—each person accepts responsibility for his or her own behavior.
- Instead of a power relationship in which one person is the boss and the other the servant, there is a fair distribution of responsibilities.
- Instead of sexual abuse, there is trust and respect for what each person wants and doesn't want.

Dealing with Violence

Whether you're a victim or a perpetrator of relationship violence, in addition to seeking professional help (and of course the help of friends and family where appropri-

■ **What Do You Say**
Impending Violence
You now see the signs of impending violence in someone you've been dating off and on for the last several months. You're not sure what to do but feel this may be a serious problem. **What Do You Say?** To whom? Through what channel?

ate), please consider the following suggestions (**www.utexas.edu/student/cmhc/ booklets/relavio/relaviol.html**, accessed February 1, 2006).

If your partner has been violent:

- Realize that you're not alone.
- Realize that you are not at fault. You did not deserve to be the victim of violence.
- Plan for your safety. Violence, if it occurred once, is likely to occur again.
- Know your resources—the phone numbers you need to contact help, the location of money and a spare set of keys.

If you are the violent partner:

- Realize that you too are not alone. Review the statistics.
- Know that you can change. It won't necessarily be easy or quick, but you can change.
- Own your own behaviors; take responsibility. This is an essential step if any change is to occur.

Relationship violence is not an inevitable part of interpersonal relationships; in fact, it occurs in a minority of relationships. Yet it's important to know that there is the potential for violence in all relationships, as there is the potential for friendship, love, support, and all the positive things we look for in relationships. Knowing the difference between productive and destructive relationships seems the best way to make sure that your own relationships are as you want them to be.

Relationship Types

In this section we look at some of the major types of relationships: friendship, love, family, and work relationships.

Friendship

Friendship is an interpersonal relationship between two people that is mutually productive and characterized by mutual positive regard.

Friendship is an interpersonal relationship; communication interactions must have taken place between the people. Further, the interpersonal relationship involves a "personalistic focus" (Wright, 1978, 1984). That is, friends react to each other as complete persons; as unique, genuine, and irreplaceable individuals.

Friendships must be mutually productive; by definition, they cannot be destructive to either person. Once destructiveness enters into a relationship, it no longer qualifies as friendship. For example, a relationship in which one person intimidates, controls, or ridicules the other can hardly be called a friendship. Love relationships, marriage relationships, parent–child relationships, and just about any other possible relationship can be either destructive or productive. But friendship must enhance the potential of each person and can only be productive.

Friendships are characterized by mutual positive regard. Liking people is essential if we are to call them friends. Three major characteristics of friendship—trust, emotional support, and sharing of interests (Blieszner & Adams, 1992)—testify to this positive regard.

The closer friends are, the more *interdependent* they become; that is, when friends are especially close, the actions of one will impact more significantly on the other than they would if the friends were just casual acquaintances. At the same time, however, the closer friends are, the more *independent* they are of, for example, the attitudes and behaviors of others. Also, they're less influenced by the societal rules that govern more casual relationships. In other words, close friends are likely to

Why Internet Friendships?

Research on young people (ages 10–17) finds that for both girls and boys, those who form close online relationships are more likely to have low levels of communication with their parents and to be more "highly troubled" than those who don't form such close online relationships (Wolak, Mitchell, & Finkelhor, 2003). Based on your knowledge and memory of yourself and your friends at this age group, did you see similar patterns? What other characteristics do you think might differentiate young people who form close relationships online from those who don't?

make up their own rules for interacting with each other; they decide what they will talk about and when, what they can say to each other without offending and what they can't, when and for what reasons one friend can call the other, and so on.

Because you and your friend know each other well (for example, you know each other's values, opinions, and attitudes), your uncertainty about each other has been significantly reduced—you're able to predict each other's behaviors with considerable accuracy. This knowledge makes significant interaction management possible, as well as greater positivity, supportiveness, and openness (Oswald, Clark, & Kelly, 2004). It also would seem logical to predict that you could read close friends' nonverbal signals accurately and could use these signals as guides to your interactions—avoiding certain topics at certain times or offering consolation on the basis of facial expressions. However, there is some evidence to suggest that less close friends are better at judging when a friend is concealing sadness and anger than are more intimate friends (Sternglanz & DePaulo, 2004). At this stage, you exchange significant messages of affection, messages that express fondness, liking, loving, and caring for the other person. Openness, self-disclosure, and emotional support become more important than shared activities (Fehr, 2004).

Friends serve a variety of needs; as your needs change, the qualities you look for in friendships also change. In many instances, old friends are dropped from your close circle to be replaced by new friends who better meet new needs. For example, as your own experience is likely to confirm, friendships serve such needs as *utility* (friends may have special talents, skills, or resources that prove useful to you), *affirmation* (friends may affirm your personal value), *ego support* (friends help you to view yourself as a worthy and competent individual), *stimulation* (friends introduce you to new ideas and new ways of seeing the world), and *security* (friends do nothing to hurt you or to emphasize your inadequacies or weaknesses) (Wright, 1978, 1984). And you'll be better able to serve such friendship needs when you apply the interpersonal communication skills discussed throughout this text (cf. Samter, 2003).

TYPES OF FRIENDSHIPS   Not all friendships are the same. But how do they differ? One way of answering this question is by distinguishing among the three major types of friendship: reciprocity, receptivity, and association (Reisman, 1979, 1981).

The friendship of *reciprocity* is the ideal type, characterized by loyalty, self-sacrifice, mutual affection, and generosity. A friendship of reciprocity is based on equality: Each individual shares equally in giving and receiving the benefits and rewards of the relationship. In the friendship of *receptivity*, in contrast, there is an imbalance in giving and receiving; one person is the primary giver and one the primary receiver. This imbalance, however, is a positive one, because each person gains something from the relationship. The different needs of both the person who receives and the person who gives are satisfied. This is the friendship that may develop between a teacher and a student or between a doctor and a patient. In fact, a difference in status is essential for the friendship of receptivity to develop.

The friendship of *association* is a transitory one. It might be described as a friendly relationship rather than a true friendship. Associative friendships are the kind we often have with classmates, neighbors, or coworkers. There is no great loyalty, no great trust, no great giving or receiving. The association is cordial but not intense.

■ **What Do You Say**

Projecting an Image

You're entering a new job and want to be perceived as likable and friendly but also serious and conscientious. **What Do You Say?** To whom? Through what channel?

❝ It is wise to apply the oil of refined politeness to the mechanisms of friendship. ❞

—Colette

Skill building *exercise*

Using Affinity-Seeking Strategies

Here are a few **affinity-seeking strategies**—behaviors that people use to make others like them, to draw people closer to them (Bell & Daly, 1984). As you read and think about such strategies, try composing at least one message that would help you communicate the desired qualities. Be sure to coordinate both verbal and nonverbal messages.

Affinity-Seeking Strategies

Altruism: Be of help to the other person.

Assumption of equality: Present yourself as socially equal to the other.

Comfortable self: Present yourself as comfortable and relaxed with the other.

Conversational rule-keeping: Follow the cultural rules for polite, cooperative conversation.

Dynamism: Appear active, enthusiastic, and dynamic.

Self-concept confirmation: Show respect for the other person and help the person feel positive about himself or herself.

All communication abounds with such strategies; practicing with these strategies will help increase your arsenal of ways to best achieve one of your most important interpersonal purposes.

Love

Although there are many theories about **love,** a model that has long interested interpersonal researchers is Lee's (1976) proposal that not one but six types of love exist. View the following descriptions of the six types as broad characterizations that are generally but not always true. As a preface to this discussion of the types of love, you may wish to respond to the self-test below.

Test *Yourself* ☑

What Kind of Lover Are You?

INSTRUCTIONS: Respond to each of the following statements with T if you believe the statement to be a generally accurate representation of your attitudes about love, or with F if you believe the statement does not adequately represent your attitudes about love.

_____ ❶ My lover and I have the right physical "chemistry" between us.

_____ ❷ I feel that my lover and I were meant for each other.

_____ ❸ My lover and I really understand each other.

_____ ❹ I believe that what my lover doesn't know about me won't hurt him/her.

_____ ❺ My lover would get upset if he/she knew of some of the things I've done with other people.

_____ ❻ When my lover gets too dependent on me, I want to back off a little.

_____ ❼ I expect to always be friends with my lover.

_____ ❽ Our love is really a deep friendship, not a mysterious, mystical emotion.

_____ ❾ Our love relationship is the most satisfying because it developed from a good friendship.

_____ ❿ In choosing my lover, I believed it was best to love someone with a similar background.

_____ ⓫ An important factor in choosing a partner is whether or not he/she would be a good parent.

_____ ⑫ One consideration in choosing my lover was how he/she would reflect on my career.

_____ ⑬ Sometimes I get so excited about being in love with my lover that I can't sleep.

_____ ⑭ When my lover doesn't pay attention to me, I feel sick all over.

_____ ⑮ I cannot relax if I suspect that my lover is with someone else.

_____ ⑯ I would rather suffer myself than let my lover suffer.

_____ ⑰ When my lover gets angry with me, I still love him/her fully and unconditionally.

_____ ⑱ I would endure all things for the sake of my lover.

HOW DID YOU DO? This scale is from Hendrick and Hendrick (1990) and is based on the work of Lee (1976), as is the text's discussion of the six types of love. The statements refer to the six types of love described in the text: eros, ludus, storge, pragma, mania, and agape. Statements 1–3 are characteristic of the eros lover. If you answered "true" to these statements, you have a strong eros component to your love style; if you answered "false," you have a weak eros component. Statements 4–6 refer to ludus love, 7–9 to storge love, 10–12 to pragma love, 13–15 to manic love, and 16–18 to agapic love.

WHAT WILL YOU DO? Are there things you can do to become more aware of the different love styles and to become a more well-rounded lover? Incorporating the qualities of effective interpersonal communication—for example, being more flexible, more polite, and more other-oriented—will go a long way toward making you a more responsive love partner.

Source: Scale from "A Relationship-Specific Version of the Love Attitudes Scale" by Clyde Hendrick and Susan Hendrick, *Journal of Social Behavior and Personality, 5,* 1990. Reprinted by permission of Select Press.

☑

TYPES OF LOVE The self-test above identified six types of love: *eros, ludus, storge, pragma, mania,* and *agape.*

Eros: Beauty and Sexuality. Like Narcissus, who fell in love with the beauty of his own image, the *erotic* lover focuses on beauty and physical attractiveness, sometimes to the exclusion of qualities you might consider more important and more lasting. Also like Narcissus, the erotic lover has an idealized image of beauty that is unattainable in reality. Consequently, the erotic lover often feels unfulfilled. Not surprisingly, erotic lovers are particularly sensitive to physical imperfections in the ones they love.

Ludus: Entertainment and Excitement. *Ludus* love is experienced as a game, as fun. The better the lover can play the game, the greater the enjoyment. Love is not to be taken too seriously; emotions are to be held in check lest they get out of hand and make trouble; passions never rise to the point where they get out of control. A ludic lover is self-controlled, always aware of the need to manage love rather than allowing it to be in control. Perhaps because of this need to control love, some researchers have proposed that ludic love tendencies may reveal tendencies to sexual aggression (Sarwer, Kalichman, Johnson, Early, et al., 1993). Not surprisingly, the ludic lover retains a partner only as long as he or she is interesting and amusing. When interest fades, it's time to change partners. Perhaps because love is a game, sexual fidelity is of little importance to ludic lovers. In fact, research shows that people who score high on ludic love are more likely to engage in extradyadic (outside-the-couple) dating and sex than those who score low on ludus (Wiederman & Hurd, 1999).

❝ True love comes quietly, without banners or flashing lights. If you hear bells, get your ears checked. ❞

—Erich Segal

Storge: Peace and Slowness. *Storge* love lacks passion and intensity. Storgic lovers set out not to find a lover but to establish a companionable relationship with someone they know and with whom they can share interests and activities. Storgic love is a gradual process of unfolding thoughts and feelings; the changes seem to come so slowly and so gradually that it's often difficult to define exactly where the relationship is at any point in time. Sex in storgic relationships comes late, and when it comes it assumes no great importance.

Pragma: Practicality and Tradition. The *pragma* lover is practical and seeks a relationship that will work. Pragma lovers want compatibility and a relationship in which their important needs and desires will be satisfied. They're concerned with the social qualifications of a potential mate even more than with personal qualities; family and background are extremely important to the pragma lover, who relies not so much on feelings as on logic. The pragma lover views love as a useful relationship, a relationship that makes the rest of life easier. So the pragma lover asks such questions of a potential mate as "Will this person earn a good living?" "Can this person cook?" "Will my family get along with this person?" Pragma lovers' relationships rarely deteriorate. This is partly because pragma lovers choose their mates carefully and emphasize similarities. Another reason is that they have realistic romantic expectations.

Mania: Elation and Depression. *Mania* is characterized by extreme highs and extreme lows. The manic lover loves intensely and at the same time worries intensely about the loss of the love. This fear often prevents the manic lover from deriving as much pleasure as possible from the relationship. With little provocation, the manic lover may experience extreme jealousy. Manic love is obsessive; the manic lover has to possess the beloved completely. In return, the manic lover wishes to be possessed, to be loved intensely. The manic lover's poor self-image seems capable of being improved only by being loved; self-worth comes from being loved rather than from any sense of inner satisfaction. Because love is so important, danger signs in a relationship are often ignored; the manic lover believes that if there is love, then nothing else matters.

Agape: Compassion and Selflessness. *Agape* (ah-guh-pay) is a compassionate, egoless, self-giving love. The agapic lover loves even people with whom he or she has no close ties. This lover loves the stranger on the road even though they will probably never meet again. Agape is a spiritual love, offered without concern for personal reward or gain. This lover loves without expecting that the love will be reciprocated. Jesus, Buddha, and Gandhi practiced and preached this unqualified love (Lee, 1976). In one sense, agape is more a philosophical kind of love than a love that most people have the strength to achieve.

Family

Today, you hear a great deal about "family," as if there were one kind of family. Actually, there are many types of families.

TYPES OF FAMILIES The "traditional" family of a husband, a wife, and one or more children is now just one of many family types. And in fact, as you can see from Table 9.3, which provides some statistics on the American family, families headed by married couples decreased from about 87 percent in 1970 to about 76 percent in 2002.

Another type of family consists of people living together in an exclusive relationship who are not married. For the most part these cohabitants live much like married couples: There is an exclusive sexual commitment; there may be children; there are shared financial responsibilities, shared time, and shared space. As Table 9.3 shows, while the number of families headed by married couples is decreasing, cohabitating (nonmarried couples) are increasing.

Also increasing are single-parent families. Some such families result from the death of a spouse or from a divorce. Increasingly, however, single people are opting

TABLE 9.3   The Changing Face of Family

There are a few statistics on the nature of the American family for 1970 and 2002, as reported by the *New York Times Almanac 2005* and *The World Almanac and Book of Facts 2005*, along with some trends these figures may indicate. What other trends do you see occurring in the family?

FAMILY CHARACTERISTIC	1970	2002	TRENDS
Number of members in average family	3.58	3.21	Reflects the tendency toward smaller families
Families without children	44.1%	52%	Reflects the growing number of families that are opting not to have children
Families headed by married couples	86.8%	76.3%	Reflects the growing trend for heterosexual couples to live as a family without marriage, for singles to have children, and for gay men and lesbians to form families
Females as heads of households	10.7%	17.7%	Reflects the growing number of women who have children without marriage and the increase in divorce and separation
Married-couple families	86.8%	76.3%	Reflects the growing trend for couples to form families without being married
Single-parent families	13%	27.8%	Reflects the growing trend for women (especially) to maintain families without a partner
Households headed by never-married women with children	248,000	4.3 million	Reflects the growing trend for women to have children and maintain a family without marriage
Children living with only one parent	12%	23%	Reflects the growing divorce rate and the increased number of children born to unwed mothers
Children between 25 and 34 living at home with parents	8% (11.9 million)	9.3% (19.2 million)	Reflects the increased economic difficulty of establishing a household and perhaps the increased divorce rate and later dates for marriage (especially true for men)

to have children and to form families. As you can see from the table, the number of single-parent families doubled in the 32 years covered by the research.

The gay male or lesbian couple who live together as "domestic partners" or are married are yet another kind of family. Many of these couples have children, whether from previous heterosexual unions, through artificial insemination, or by adoption. Although accurate statistics are difficult to secure, gay and lesbian couples seem also to be increasing. Some 30 years ago, a major study of couples concluded: " 'Couplehood', either as a reality or as an aspiration, is as strong among gay people as it is among heterosexuals" (Blumstein & Schwartz, 1983). More recent studies continue to support this conclusion (Fitzpatrick, Jandt, Myrick, & Edgar, 1994; Kurdek, 2003, 2004; Gottman, 2004).

Another way of looking at family types is to consider whether the partners are traditionals, independents, or separates (Fitzpatrick, 1983, 1988, 1991; Noller & Fitzpatrick, 1993).

Traditional Couples.   *Traditional couples* share a basic belief system and philosophy of life. They see themselves as a blending of two persons into a single couple rather than as two separate individuals. They're interdependent and believe that each partner's independence must be sacrificed for the good of the relationship.

" Although all those who fall in love do so in the same way, not all fall in love for the same reason. There is no single quality which is universally loved. "
—Jose Ortega y Gasset

"We're a traditional gay couple—we don't have kids."

Traditionals believe in mutual sharing and do little separately. This couple holds to the traditional sex roles, and there are seldom any role conflicts. There are few power struggles and few conflicts, because each person knows and adheres to a specified role within the relationship. In their communications traditionals are highly responsive to each other. Traditionals lean toward each other, smile, talk a lot, interrupt each other, and finish each other's sentences.

Independent Couples. *Independent couples* stress their individuality. The relationship is important, but never more important than each person's individual identity. Although independents spend a great deal of time together, they don't ritualize it, for example, with schedules. Each individual spends time with outside friends. Independents see themselves as relatively androgynous, as individuals who combine the traditionally feminine and the traditionally masculine roles and qualities. The communication between independents is responsive. They engage in conflict openly and without fear. Their disclosures are quite extensive and include high-risk and negative disclosures that are typically absent among traditionals.

Separate Couples. *Separate couples* live together but view their relationship more as a matter of convenience than as a result of their mutual love or closeness. They seem to have little desire to be together; in fact, they usually are together only at ritual functions, such as mealtime or holiday get-togethers. It's important to these separates that each has his or her own physical as well as psychological space. Separates share little; each seems to prefer to go his or her own way. Separates hold relatively traditional values and beliefs about sex roles, and each person tries to follow the behaviors normally assigned to each role. What best characterizes this type, however, is that each person sees himself or herself as a separate individual and not as a part of a "we."

In addition to these three pure types, there are also combinations. For example, in the separate–traditional couple one individual is a separate and one a traditional. Another common pattern is the traditional–independent, in which one individual believes in the traditional view of relationships and one in autonomy and independence.

CHARACTERISTICS OF FAMILIES Despite this diversity, all families have some characteristics in common. We can define **family** as a relationship characterized by defined roles, recognition of mutual responsibilities, a shared history and future, shared living space, and rules for communicating.

Defined Roles. Family members have relatively defined roles that each person is expected to play in relation to the others and to the relationship as a whole. Each member has acquired the rules of the culture and social group; each knows approximately what his or her obligations, duties, privileges, and responsibilities are. The partners' roles might include those of wage earner, cook, housecleaner, child caregiver, social secretary, home decorator, plumber, carpenter, food shopper, money manager, nurturer, philosopher, comedian, organizer, and so on. At times the roles may be shared, but even then it's often assumed that one person has *primary* responsibility for certain tasks and the other person for others.

Recognition of Responsibilities. Family members recognize their responsibilities to one another—for example, the responsibilities to help others financially; to offer comfort when family members are distressed; to take pleasure in family members' pleasures, to feel their pain, to raise their spirits. Each person in a couple also has a temporal obligation to reserve some large block of time for the other. Time sharing seems important to all relationships, although each couple may define it a bit differently.

Shared History and Future. Family members have a history that is at least partly shared by other members and the prospect is that they will share the future together as well. This history has enabled the members to get to know each other, to understand each other a little better, and ideally to like and even love each other. And, in most cases, family members view the relationship as persisting into the future.

Shared Living Space. Most American families share their living space. There is, however, a growing minority of couples who retain their original apartments or houses and may spend substantial time apart. These relationships, it should be stressed, are not necessarily less satisfying. After a thorough review of the research, one researcher concluded that "there is little, if any, decrease in relationship satisfaction, intimacy, and commitment as long as lovers are able to reunite with some frequency (approximately once a month)" (Rohlfing, 1995, pp. 182–183). In some traditional cultures, in fact, men and women don't share the same living space; the women may live with the children while the men live together in a communal arrangement (Harris, 1993).

Communication Rules. All families teach rules for communication. Some of these are explicit, such as "Never contradict the family in front of outsiders" or "Never talk finances with outsiders." Other rules are unspoken; you deduce them as you learn the communication style of your family. For example, if financial issues are always discussed in secret and in hushed tones, then you can infer that you shouldn't tell others about family finances. Family communication research points to the importance of rules in defining the family (Galvin, Bylund, & Brommel, 2004). You can view rules as concerning three main interpersonal communication issues (Satir, 1983):

1. What can you talk about? Can you talk about Grandpa's drinking? Your sister's lifestyle?

2. In what way can you talk about a given topic? Can you joke about your brother's disability? Can you directly address questions of family history or family skeletons?

3. To whom can you talk? Can you talk openly to extended family members such as cousins and aunts and uncles? Can you talk to close neighbors about family health issues?

Not surprisingly, the rules a family develops are greatly influenced by the wider culture. Although there are many similarities among families throughout the world,

E-Talk ▪ ▪ ▪ ▪ ▪ ▪ ▪
The Internet and Generational Conflict
Internet use seems to be contributing further to the already significant generational conflict between children and parents in South Korea (Rhee & Kim, 2004). Has computer-mediated communication contributed to generational gaps within your own family network?

What Do You Say ?

Establishing Family Communication Rules

You hope to begin your family in the very near future (hopefully with the person you've been dating for the last two years) and this notion of family communication rules seems intriguing; you begin to wonder what types of rules you'd like to see in your own soon-to-be family. **What Do You Say?**

there are also differences (Georgas et al., 2001). For example, members of collectivist cultures (Chapter 2) are more likely to restrict family information from outsiders as a way of protecting the family than are members of individualist cultures. As already noted, this tendency to protect the family can create serious problems in cases of wife abuse. Many women will not report spousal abuse becuase of this desire to protect the family image—this need not to let others know that things aren't perfect at home (Dresser, 2005).

Workplace

Workplace relationships are becoming more and more important as we spend growing amounts of time in work relationship situations, whether face-to-face in the traditional office or online. Online work groups are also on the increase—and have been found to be more task oriented and more efficient than face-to-face groups (Lantz, 2001). Online groups can provide a sense of belonging that may once have been thought possible only in face-to-face interactions (Silverman, 2001). Here we look at one particular kind of workplace relationship: workplace romance.

ROMANTIC RELATIONSHIPS IN THE WORKPLACE In television depictions coworkers always seem to be best friends who would do anything for one another, and characters move in and out of interoffice romances with no difficulties—at least with no difficulties that can't be resolved in 24 minutes. Real life is quite different.

Opinions concerning workplace romances vary widely. Some organizations, on the assumption that romantic relationships are basically detrimental to the success of the workplace, have explicit rules prohibiting such relationships. In some organizations workers can even be fired for getting involved in workplace romances.

On the positive side, the work environment seems a perfect place to meet a potential romantic partner. After all, by virtue of the fact that you're working in the same office, you both are probably interested in the same field, have similar training and ambitions, and will spend considerable time together—all factors that foster the development of a successful interpersonal relationship.

Similarly, office romances can lead to greater work satisfaction. If you're romantically attracted to another worker, it can make going to work, working together, and even working added hours more enjoyable and more satisfying. If the relationship is good and mutually satisfying, the individuals are likely to develop empathy for each other and to act in ways that are supportive, cooperative, and friendly; in short, the workers are more likely to act with all the characteristics of effective communication noted throughout this book.

However, even when the relationship is good for the two individuals, it may not necessarily be positive for other workers. Seeing the loving couple every day in every way may generate destructive office gossip. Or fellow workers may see the lovers as a team that has to be confronted as a pair, feeling that they can't criticize one lover without incurring the wrath of the other.

Similarly, such relationships may cause problems for management when, for example, promotion or relocation decisions are necessary. Can you legitimately ask one lover to move to Boston and the other to move to San Francisco? Will it prove difficult for management to put one lover in the position of supervising the other?

The workplace also puts pressure on the individuals. Most organizations in the United States are highly competitive, and one person's success often means another's failure. In this environment a romantic couple may find, for example, that the self-disclosures that normally accompany increased intimacy (and which often reveal weaknesses, self-doubts, and misgivings), may actually prove a competitive liability.

There's a popular belief that women see office romances as a route to some kind of personal gain. For example, researchers who surveyed 218 male and female business school graduates found that despite a lack of any evidence, people perceived women as entering office romances in order to achieve advancement (Anderson &

Interpersonal Relationships in Songs and Greeting Cards

The objectives of this exercise are (1) to become familiar with some of the popular sentiments concerning interpersonal relationships as they're expressed in songs and greeting cards and (2) to provide a stimulus for considering significant concepts and theories in interpersonal relationships. Bring to class a recording of one song or a greeting card that expresses a sentiment that is significant to the study of interpersonal relationships for any one of the following reasons:

- It expresses a sentiment that can assist us in understanding interpersonal relationships.
- It illustrates a concept or theory that is important in the study of interpersonal relationships.
- It suggests a useful question concerning interpersonal relationships.
- It illustrates a popular relational problem or difficulty.
- It illustrates a method for dealing with some kind of relationship problem or difficulty.

Songs and greeting cards are just two ways in which you're "taught" about relationships. But television sitcoms, news stories, movies, and most other media also send relationship messages.

Fisher, 1991). So the woman who does participate in an office romance may have to deal with both male and female colleagues' assumptions that she is in this relationship to advance her career.

When an office romance goes bad or when it's one-sided, there are even more disadvantages. One obvious problem is that it can be stressful for the former partners to see each other regularly and perhaps to work together. And other workers may feel they have to take sides, being supportive of one partner and critical of the other. This can easily cause friction throughout the organization. Another and perhaps more serious issue is the potential for charges of workplace sexual harassment, especially if the romance is between a supervisor and a worker. Whether the charges are legitimate or merely the result of an unhappy love affair that has nothing to do with the organization, management will find itself in the middle, facing the expenditure of time and money to investigate and ultimately act on the charges—or, still worse, to defend against lawsuits.

On balance, the generally negative attitude of management toward office love affairs and the problems of dealing with the normal stress of both work and romance seem to outweigh the positive benefits that could be derived from such relationships, so workers are generally advised not to romance their colleagues. Friendships seem the much safer course.

Relationship Theories

Numerous theories attempt to explain the hows and whys of interpersonal relationships. Let's take a look at four of the most interesting approaches. As you'll see when you read the following discussions, each theory offers considerable insight into relationships, but none provides a complete explanation.

Attraction Theory

Attraction theory holds that people develop relationships on the basis of three major factors: attractiveness (physical appearance and personality), proximity, and similarity.

PHYSICAL APPEARANCE AND PERSONALITY Not surprisingly, you probably prefer physically attractive to physically unattractive people, and you probably like people who

E-Talk ▪ ▪ ▪ ▪ ▪ ▪ ▪

Organizational Hierarchies

Some theorists believe that computer-mediated communication will eventually eliminate the hierarchical structure of organizations, largely because CMC "encourages wider participation, greater candor, and an emphasis on merit over status" (Kollock & Smith, 1996, p. 109). If prediction came true, it would mean that high-power-distance cultures would move in the direction of lower power distances and would gradually become more democratic. What evidence can you find bearing on this issue?

"If I had known I was going to meet somebody like you, I would have lost some weight, got some hair plugs, and made more money."

possess a pleasant rather than an unpleasant personality. Generally, you also will tend to attribute positive characteristics to people you find attractive and negative characteristics to people you find unattractive (Buss & Schmitt, 1993; Sergios & Cody, 1985; Rowatt, Cunningham, & Druen, 1999). Those you perceive as attractive, you'll also see as competent; conversely, those who are perceived as competent—say, as a team member working on a project or in social situations—are also seen as more attractive (Duran & Kelly, 1988).

Similarly, you'll find those with whom you have positive interactions more attractive than those with whom you have negative interactions (Albada, 2002).

Although culture influences what people think is physical attractiveness and what isn't, some research indicates that certain facial characteristics seem to be thought attractive in all cultures—that there is a kind of universal attractiveness (Brody, 1994). For example, a study comparing the very different cultures of England and Japan found that both men and women preferred (for long-term relationships) opposite-sex faces that were on the feminized side; these faces were seen as more sensitive and honest (Penton-Voak, Jacobson, & Trivers, 2004). This finding fits neatly with other research that finds that, contrary to popular opinion, nice guys don't finish last but instead are seen as more attractive than those described as "less nice" (Urbaniak & Kilmann, 2003).

You're more likely to find those who are culturally similar as more attractive than those who are culturally different (Pornpitakpan, 2003). You're also more likely to help someone who is similar in race, attitude, and general appearance. Even the same first name is significant. For example, when an e-mail asking recipients to fill out surveys of their food habits identified the sender as someone with the same name as the recipient, there was a greater willingness to comply with the request (Gueguen, 2003).

PROXIMITY   Generally, we find people who live or work close to us as more attractive than those who are less physically close. Repeated interaction—if the initial interaction is positive—will generally lead to increased attraction. You can easily test this out for yourself. Just take a look around your class and make a mental assessment of the attractiveness of the other students. Then take a look at a class of students you've not seen before and make a mental assessment of their attractiveness. According to the principle of **proximity,** you're likely to find the students in your own class more attractive than students with whom you've not spent time.

SIMILARITY   Although there are exceptions, the principle of **similarity** states that you're probably attracted to your own mirror image—to people who are similar to you in nationality, race, ability, physical characteristics, intelligence, and so on. What's more, all cultures seem to be similar in being attracted to people of similar attitudes (Hatfield & Rapson, 1992). People who are similar in attitude become more attracted to each other over time, whereas people who are dissimilar in attitude become less attracted to each other over time (Neimeyer & Mitchell, 1988; Honeycutt, 1986). The alternative explanation—that "opposites attract"—has received much less research support; similarity clearly wins out over differences.

Social Exchange Theory

Social exchange theory, based on an economic model of profits and losses, claims that you seek to develop the relationships (friendship and romantic) that will give you the greatest profit—relationships in which the rewards are greater than the costs. The preferred relationships, according to this theory, are those that are most profitable and thus give you the greatest rewards with the least costs (Chadwick-Jones, 1976; Gergen, Greenberg, & Willis, 1980; Thibaut & Kelley, 1959). The theory begins with the following equation:

Profits = Rewards − Costs

Rewards are anything that you want, that you enjoy, and that you'd be willing to incur costs to obtain. For example, to acquire the reward of financial gain, you might have to work rather than play. Love, affection, status, money, gifts, security, social acceptance, companionship, friendship, and intimacy are just a few examples of rewards for which you would be willing to work (that is, incur costs). **Costs** are those things that you normally try to avoid—things you consider unpleasant or difficult. Working overtime, washing dishes and ironing clothes, or watching a television show that your partner enjoys but you find boring might all be considered costs.

❝ If you have ever loved, been loved, or wanted to be in love, you have had to face a frustrating fact: different people can mean different things by that simple phrase 'I love you.' ❞

—John Alan Lee

Equity Theory

Equity theory uses the concepts of social exchange, but it goes a step farther. This theory claims that you develop and maintain relationships in which your ratio of rewards to costs is approximately equal to your partner's (Walster, Walster, & Berscheid, 1978; Messick & Cook, 1983). In equitable relationship both partners should derive rewards that are proportional to their costs. For example, you work harder for the relationship than your partner does, then equity demands that you should get greater rewards than your partner. If you both work equally hard for the relationship, then equity demands that each of you should get approximately equal rewards.

Much research finds that people in Western societies want equity and feel that relationships should be characterized by equity (Ueleke et al., 1983). As you can appreciate, however, this theory is decidedly a product of Western culture. For example, in Europe and the United States, each person is paid according to his or her contributions; the more you contribute to an organization—or to a relationship—the more rewards you should get out of it. In other cultures, especially collectivist cultures, a principle of equality or need might operate. According to the *principle of equality,* each person would get equal rewards, regardless of his or her individual contribution. According to the *principle of need,* each person would get rewards according to his or her need (Moghaddam, Taylor, & Wright, 1993).

Rules Theory

Rules theory is a theory of a different type; it doesn't so much explain why you *enter* a relationship as account for why you *stay* in the relationship. Rules theory describes relationships as interactions governed by a series of rules that a couple agrees to follow. When the rules are followed, the relationship is maintained; when they're broken, the relationship experiences difficulty and perhaps deteriorates or even dissolves.

For example, friendships are maintained by such rules as the following (Argyle & Henderson, 1984; Blieszner & Adams, 1992):

- Stand up for the friend in his or her absence.
- Share information and feelings about successes.
- Demonstrate emotional support.

■ **What Do You Say** ❓
Achieving Equity
After thinking about equity, you realize that you put a lot more effort into the relationship (you pay much more than half the relationship "costs") than your partner. You want this imbalance corrected, but at the same time don't want to create problems or destroy the relationship. **What Do You Say?** Through what channel?

- Trust each other.
- Offer to help when help is needed.

Romantic relationships also may be viewed as being maintained by rules. Here, for example, drawn from two research studies (Baxter, 1986; Kline & Stafford, 2004), are rules that enhance romantic relationship quality. As you read the list, consider your own relationship behaviors. Do you:

- *acknowledge each other's individual identities and lives beyond the relationship?*
- *express similar attitudes, beliefs, values, and interests?*
- *enhance each other's self-worth and self-esteem?*
- *remain loyal and faithful to each other?*
- *have substantial shared time together?*
- *attempt to make the interactions enjoyable?*
- *listen and try not to judge?*
- *act cheerful and positive?*
- *compliment each other's achievements?*
- *try to avoid embarrassing each other?*

As you can see, looking at relationships in terms of rules can help you distinguish successful from destructive relationship behavior and can help pinpoint why relationships break up and how they may be repaired.

Relationships, Culture, and Technology

Although this chapter has mentioned cultural and technological factors in relationships from time to time, it's helpful to bring these topics together now that we've covered a major part of our exploration of relationships. The material discussed here derives in great part from research conducted in the United States and on heterosexual couples. Accordingly, this research and the corresponding theory reflect the way most heterosexual relationships are viewed in the United States.

Relationships and Culture

In U.S. society it is assumed in discussions of relationship development—such as the model presented in this text—that you voluntarily choose your relationship partners. You consciously choose to pursue certain relationships and not others. In some cultures, however, your romantic partner is chosen for you by your parents. In some cases your husband or wife is chosen to unite two families or to bring some financial advantage to your family or village. An arrangement such as this may have been entered into by your parents when you were an infant or even before you were born. And even in cultures where arranged marriages are not the norm, of course, there's pressure to marry the "right" person and to be friends with certain people and not others.

Similarly, U.S. researchers study and textbook authors write about dissolving relationships and how to survive relationship breakups. It's assumed that you have the right to exit an undesirable relationship. But in some cultures you cannot simply dissolve a relationship once it's formed or once there are children. In the Roman Catholic church, once people are validly married, they're always married and cannot dissolve that relationship. More important in such cultures may be such issues as "How do you maintain a relationship that has problems?" "What can you do to survive in this unpleasant relationship?" or "How can you repair a troubled relationship?" (Moghaddam, Taylor, & Wright, 1993).

Further, your culture will influence the difficulty that you go through when relationships do break up. For example, married persons whose religion forbids divorce and remarriage will experience religious disapproval and condemnation as well as the same economic and social difficulties everyone else goes through. In the United States child custody almost invariably goes to the mother, and this presents an added emotional burden for the father. In Iran, in contrast, child custody goes to the father, which presents added emotional burdens for the mother. In India women experience greater difficulty than men in divorce because of their economic dependence on men, the cultural beliefs about women, and the patriarchal order of the family (Amato, 1994). And in Jordan it was only as recently as 2002 that a woman was granted a divorce for the first time. Before that, only men had been granted divorces (*New York Times,* May 15, 2002, p. A6).

In most of the United States, interpersonal friendships are drawn from a relatively large pool. Out of all the people you come into regular contact with, you choose relatively few of these as friends. With computer chat groups, the number of friends you can have has increased enormously, as has the range of geographic areas from which these friends can be chosen. In rural areas and in small villages throughout the world, however, you would have very few options. The two or three other children your age would become your friends; there would be no real choice, because these would be the only possible friends you could make.

Most cultures assume that relationships should be permanent or at least long-lasting. Consequently, it's assumed that people want to keep relationships together and will expend considerable energy to maintain relationships. Because of this bias, little research has studied how to move from one intimate relationship to another more effectively and efficiently. Culture even seems to influence the kind of love people want. For example, when compared to their Chinese counterparts, American men scored higher on ludic and agapic love and lower on erotic and pragma love. American men also are less likely to view emotional satisfaction as crucial to relationship maintenance (Sprecher & Toro-Morn, 2002).

Culture influences heterosexual relationships by assigning different roles to men and women. In the United States, men and women are supposed to be equal—at least that is the stated ideal. As a result, both men and women can initiate relationships and both can dissolve them. Both men and women are expected to derive satisfaction from their interpersonal relationships; and when that satisfaction isn't present, either person may seek to exit the relationship. In Iran, on the other hand, only the man has the right to dissolve a marriage without giving reasons.

Gay and lesbian relationships are accepted in some cultures and condemned in others. In some areas of the United States, "domestic partnerships" may be registered, and these grant gay men, lesbians, and (in some cases) unmarried heterosexuals rights that were formerly reserved only for married couples, such as health insurance benefits and the right to make decisions when one member is incapacitated. In Norway, Sweden, Belgium, the Netherlands, and Denmark, same-sex relationship partners have the same rights as married partners. As of this writing, only one U.S. state—Massachusetts—has issued marriage licenses to same-sex couples. And, as mentioned in the discussion of heterosexism in Chapter 6, in many countries same-sex couples would be considered criminals and could face severe punishment—in some cultures they could even face death.

Relationships and Technology

Perhaps even more obvious than culture is the influence of technology on interpersonal relationships. Clearly, online interpersonal relationships are on the increase. The number of Internet users is rapidly increasing, and commercial websites devoted to helping people meet other people are proliferating, making it especially easy to develop online relationships. Such websites as American Singles (www.americansingles.com), Friend Finder (www.friendfinder.com), Date (www.date.com), Match (www.match

E-Talk . ▪ . ▪ . ▪ . ▪

Online Romance

How would you describe the advantages and disadvantages (for *you*) of finding a romantic partner (potentially a life partner) through one of the Internet dating services?

.com), Yahoo! Personals (www.personals.yahoo), Lavalife (www.lavalife.com), and Where Singles Meet (www.wheresinglesmeet.com) number their members in the millions, making it especially likely that you'll find someone you'd enjoy dating.

And not surprisingly, there are websites (for example, www.comparedatingwebsites .com and www.homeandfamilyreview.com/dating.htm) that offer comparisons of the various dating websites, distinguishing between those that are best for serious daters who are looking for lifetime commitment from those that are for people who want to find someone for casual dating. Lavalife, for example, has a pull down menu where you can indicate whether you want a casual date, a relationship, or an intimate encounter. And of course there are dating websites for different affectional orientations and different religious preferences.

Some dating websites—eharmony.com and perfectmatch.com are perhaps the most notable—have members complete extensive scientific questionnaires about their preferences and personalities which helps further in successfully matching people.

Some of these websites, for example, Yahoo! Personals and Friend Finder, give free trials so you can test the system before registering or subscribing. And, to make these websites even more inviting, many of them offer chat rooms, dating and relationship advice, newsletters, and self-tests about love, relationships, and dating.

Clearly, many people are turning to the Internet to find a friend or romantic partner. And, as you probably know, college students are making the most of sites such as Facebook.com and MySpace.com to meet other students on their own campus. In one study of MOOs (online role-playing games), 93.6 percent of the users formed ongoing friendships and romantic relationships (Parks & Roberts, 1998). Some people use the Internet as their only means of interaction; others use it as a way of beginning a relationship and intend to supplement computer talk later with photographs, phone calls, and face-to-face meetings. Interestingly, a *New York Times* survey found that by 2003 online dating was losing its earlier stigma as a last resort for losers (June 29, 2003, p. A1).

Note that the importance of physical attractiveness enters the face-to-face relationship through nonverbal cues—you see the person's eyes, face, body—and you perceive such attractiveness immediately. In online relationships, just a few years ago, physical attractiveness could have only been signaled through words and descriptions (Levine, 2000). And in this situation the face-to-face encounter favored those who were physically attractive, whereas the online encounter favored those who were verbally adept at self-presentation. Today, with the numerous social networks such as MySpace, you can post your photo and reveal your attractiveness. Many of the online dating services (such as Friend Finder and Yahoo! Personals) now provide you with opportunities to not only post your photograph but also a voice introduction. Of course you still reveal more of yourself in face-to-face encounters, but the differences are clearly diminishing. Table 9.4 provides one example of the stages of Internet relationships.

Other research on Internet use finds that a large majority of users form new acquaintances, friendships, and romantic partnerships through the Internet. One study, published in 1996 (Parks & Floyd) found that almost two-thirds of newsgroup users had formed new relationships with someone they met online. Almost one-third said that they communicated with their partner at least three or four times a week; more than half communicated on a weekly basis. And, a study published in 2006 (Madden & Lenhart), found that 74 percent of Internet users who identify themselves as single and looking for romantic partners, used the Internet for this purpose.

Women, it seems, are more likely to form relationships on the Internet than men. An early study showed that about 72 percent of women and 55 percent of men had formed personal relationships online (Parks & Floyd, 1996). And women are more likely to use the Internet to deepen their interpersonal relationships (Fallows, 2005).

As relationships develop on the Internet, **network convergence** occurs; that is, as a relationship between two people develops, they begin to share their network of other communicators with each other (Parks, 1995; Parks & Floyd, 1996). This, of course, is similar to relationships formed through face-to-face contact. Online work

TABLE 9.4   Online Relationship Stages

This table represents one attempt to identify the stages that people go through in Internet relationships. As you read down the table, consider how accurately this represents what you know of online relationships. How would you describe the way Internet relationships develop?

STAGE	BEHAVIOR
1. Curiosity	You explore and search for individuals through chat rooms and other online sources.
2. Investigation	You find out information about the individual.
3. Testing	You introduce various topics, looking for common ground.
4. Increasing frequency of contact	You increase the breadth and depth of your relationship.
5. Anticipation	You anticipate face-to-face interaction and wonder what that will bring.
6. Fantasy integration	You create a fantasy of what the person looks like and how the person behaves.
7. Face-to-face meeting	You meet face-to-face, and reality and fantasy meet.
8. Reconfiguration	You adjust the fantasy to the reality and may decide to end the relationship or to pursue it more vigorously.
9. Already separated	If you decide to maintain the relationship, you explore ways you can accomplish this.
10. Long-term relationship	You negotiate the new relationship, whether it will be maintained in its online form or in a new face-to-face form.

Source: This table is adapted from Leonard J. Shedletsky and Joan E. Aitken, *Human Communication on the Internet.* Published by Allyn and Bacon, Boston, MA. Copyright © by Pearson Education. By permission of the publisher. Adapted by permission of the publisher.

groups also are on the increase and have been found to be more task oriented and more efficient than face-to-face groups (Lantz, 2001). Online groups also provide a sense of belonging that may once have been thought possible only through face-to-face interactions (Silverman, 2001).

ADVANTAGES OF ONLINE RELATIONSHIPS There are many advantages to establishing relationships online. For example, online relationships are safe in terms of avoiding the potential for physical violence or sexually transmitted diseases. Unlike relationships established in face-to-face encounters, in which physical appearance tends to outweigh personality, relationships formed through Internet communication focus on your inner qualities first. Rapport and mutual self-disclosure become more important than physical attractiveness in promoting intimacy (Cooper & Sportolari, 1997). And, contrary to some popular opinions, online relationships rely just as heavily on the ideals of trust, honesty, and commitment as do face-to-face relationships (Whitty & Gavin, 2001). Friendship and romantic interaction on the Internet are a natural boon to shut-ins and extremely shy people, for whom traditional ways of meeting someone are often difficult. Computer talk is empowering for those with "physical disabilities or disfigurements," for whom face-to-face interactions often are superficial and often end with withdrawal (Lea & Spears, 1995; Bull & Rumsey, 1988). By eliminating the physical cues, computer talk equalizes the interaction and doesn't put the disfigured person, for example, at an immediate disadvantage in a society in which physical attractiveness is so highly valued. On the Internet you're free to reveal as much or as little about your physical self as you wish, when you wish.

Another obvious advantage is that the number of people you can reach is so vast that it's relatively easy to find someone who matches what you're looking for. The situation is like finding a book that covers just what you need from a library of millions of volumes rather than from a collection holding only several thousand.

DISADVANTAGES OF ONLINE RELATIONSHIPS Of course, online relationships also have their disadvantages. For one thing, in many situations you can't see the other person. Unless you use a service that enables you to include photos or exchange photos or

E-Talk ■ ▪ ▪ ■ ▪ ■ ■ ▪

Staying Together

One study found that among people who met on the Internet, those who met in places of common interests, who communicated over a period of time before they met in person, who managed barriers to greater closeness, and who managed conflict well were more likely to stay together than couples who did not follow this general pattern (Baker, 2002). Based on your own experiences, how would you predict which couples would stay together and which would break apart?

" People are more frightened of being lonely than of being hungry, or being deprived of sleep, or having their sexual needs unfulfilled. **"**

—Fried Fromm Reichman

meet face-to-face, you won't know what the person looks like. Even if photos are posted or exchanged, how certain can you be that the photos are of the person or that they were taken recently? In addition, in most situations you can't hear the person's voice, and this too hinders you as you seek to develop a total picture of the other person. Of course, you can always add an occasional phone call to give you this added information.

Online, people can present a false self with little chance of detection. For example, minors may present themselves as adults, and adults may present themselves as children in order to conduct illicit and illegal sexual communications and, perhaps, arrange meetings. Similarly, people can present themselves as poor when they're rich, as mature when they're immature, as serious and committed when they're just enjoying the online experience. Although people can also misrepresent themselves in face-to-face relationships, the fact that it's easier to do online probably accounts for greater frequency of misrepresentation in computer relationships (Cornwell & Lundgren, 2001).

Another potential disadvantage—though some might argue it is actually an advantage—is that computer interactions may become all-consuming and may substitute for face-to-face interpersonal relationships in a person's life.

Perhaps the clearest finding that emerges from all the research on face-to-face and online relationships is that people will seek out and find the relationship that works best for them at a given stage in their lives. For some that relationship will be online, for others face-to-face, for still others a combination. And just as people change, their relationship needs and wants also change; what works now may not work two years from now, and what doesn't work now may be exactly right in a few years.

E-Talk ▪ ▪ ▪ ▪ ▪ ▪

Taking Safety Precautions

One study suggests that people who make friends on the Internet do take safety precautions such as protecting anonymity and talking on the phone before meeting face-to-face (McCown, Fischer, Page, & Homant, 2001). What safety precautions do you take in online friendships and romantic relationships?

The Telephone Breakup

Breaking up is never easy, and without interpersonal skills it's an extremely difficult interaction. As you read this dialogue, consider how you might have handled this if you were Chris and if you were Pat.

The Cast

Pat and Chris, in their late 20s, have been dating steadily for about eight months. Chris wants to break it off and so calls Pat.

The Context

Pat and Chris are in their respective homes, talking on the phone.

Chris: Hi, Pat, Chris.

Pat (coldly): Hi. Haven't heard from you all week.

Chris (hesitant and obviously nervous): Well, I've been meaning to call.

Pat (annoyed): Yeah, yeah. It's always the same story.

Chris: Look Pat I've been meaning to—

Pat (interrupting and still annoyed): How was Boston?

Chris: I need to say something.

Pat: Go ahead.

Chris: Things haven't been good with us, and I think we should maybe see other people.

Pat: What?

Chris: I mean still see each other but maybe not exclusively.

Pat (totally misreading Chris's intention): You mean you want to spend more time with your friends?

Chris: Well, yes. Well, I mean also maybe date others—you know, if something comes up.

Pat: Date others?

Chris: Yeah.

Pat: What did I do wrong? You've been seeing someone, haven't you? And behind my back. Well, tell me. Are you seeing someone?

Chris: No, not really.

Pat: Not really? What do you mean "really"?

Chris: I mean it's not serious.

Pat: So you are seeing someone.

Chris: Off and on, I guess; yeah, I kind of am.

Pat: So what did I do wrong?

Chris: It's nothing you did; it's me. I'm just not ready to get serious.

Pat: Serious. So we were serious. We date steady for eight months. And you break up by phone. I'm surprised you didn't text message me.

This chapter explored the nature of interpersonal relationships, including the stages relationships go through, the dark side of interpersonal relationships, relationship types and theories, and the role of culture and technology in relationships.

1. Interpersonal relationships may be viewed as occurring in stages. Recognize at least these: contact, involvement, intimacy, deterioration, repair, and dissolution.
2. In contact there is first perceptual contact and then interaction.
3. Involvement includes a testing phase (will this be a suitable relationship?) and an intensifying of the interaction; often a sense of mutuality, of connectedness, begins.
4. In intimacy there is an interpersonal commitment and perhaps a social bonding, in which the commitment is made public.
5. Some relationships deteriorate, proceeding through a period of intrapersonal dissatisfaction to interpersonal deterioration.
6. Along the process, repair may be initiated. Intrapersonal repair generally comes first (should I change my behavior?); it may be followed by interpersonal repair, in which you and your partner discuss your problems and seek remedies.
7. If repair fails, the relationship may dissolve, moving first to interpersonal separation and later, perhaps, to public or social separation.
8. Interpersonal relationships have both advantages and disadvantages. Among the advantages are that they stimulate you, help you learn about yourself, and generally enhance your self-esteem. Among the disadvantages are that they force you to expose your vulnerabilities, make great demands on your time, and often cause you to abandon other relationships.
9. Interpersonal relationships also have a dark side where violence becomes a part of the relationship. These behaviors and their effects need to be recognized and dealt with.
10. Among the major interpersonal relationships are friendship, love, family, and work relationships.
11. Friendship is an interpersonal relationship between two persons that is mutually productive and characterized by mutual positive regard.
12. Love—a romantic relationship existing between two people—comes in a variety of forms. Eros, ludus, storge, pragma, mania, and agape are some of the commonly distinguished types of love.
13. Family relationships are those existing between two or more people who have defined roles, recognize their responsibilities to each other, have a shared history and a prospect of a shared future, and interact according to a shared system of communication rules.
14. Among the workplace relationships that need to be considered are romantic relationships which have both positives and negatives.
15. Culture and technology both influence relationships in various and important ways. Relationships in one culture are very different from relationships in another culture and face-to face relationships are different from on-line relationships. Amid these differences, there are also similarities.

This chapter also considered a variety of skills. As you review these skills check those you wish to work on.

_____ 1. Relationship messages: Formulate messages that are appropriate to the stage of the relationship. Also, listen to messages from relationship partners that may reveal differences in perceptions about your relationship stage.

_____ 2. Relationship repair: Recognize the problem, engage in productive conflict resolution, pose possible solutions, affirm each other, integrate solutions into normal behavior, and take risks as appropriate.

_____ 3. Managing relationship dissolution: Break the loneliness–depression cycle, take time out, bolster self-esteem, seek support from others, and avoid repeating negative patterns.

_____ 4. Advantages and disadvantages of relationships: In evaluating, entering, or dissolving relationships, consider both the advantages and the disadvantages.

_____ 5. Violence in relationships: Become sensitive to the development of violence in a relationship and learn the ways to deal with this problem should it arise.

_____ 6. Friendships: Establish friendships to help serve such needs as utility, ego support, stimulation, and security. At the same time, seek to serve your friends' similar needs.

_____ 7. Romantic workplace relationships: Establish romantic relationships at work with a clear understanding of the potential problems.

_____ 8. Cultural and technology: Both culture and technology exert influence on all types of relationships, encouraging some and discouraging others, making some easy and some difficult.

Match the terms dealing with interpersonal relationships with their definitions. Record the number of the definition next to the appropriate term.

_____ friendship

_____ agape

_____ interpersonal repair

_____ equity theory

_____ social exchange theory

_____ family

_____ dissolution

_____ reciprocity

_____ emotional abuse

_____ relational dialectics theory

1. A type of friendship based on loyalty, self-sacrifice, and equality.

2. A selfless, compassionate love.
3. A relationship characterized by defined roles, recognition of mutual responsibilities, a shared history and a prospect of a shared future, shared living space, and rules for communicating.
4. An interpersonal relationship that is mutually productive and characterized by mutual positive regard.
5. Might include isolating, criticizing, or stalking.
6. A theory that all relationships can be defined by a series of competing opposite motivations or desires.
7. A stage in some relationships that involves recognizing problems and engaging in productive conflict resolution.
8. A theory of relationships postulating that people seek to get rewards commensurate with their costs.
9. A theory of relationships based on costs and rewards.
10. A stage in some relationships that involves interpersonal separation followed by social or public separation.

Four for Discussion

1. The "matching hypothesis" claims that people date and mate people who are comparable to themselves in physical attractiveness (Walster & Walster, 1978). When this does not happen—for example, when a very attractive person dates someone of average attractiveness—you may begin to look for "compensating factors," or attributes of the less attractive person that compensate or make up for his or her appearance. What evidence can you find to support or contradict this theory? Why do you think people date and mate people who are roughly equal in attractiveness?

2. Do you "comparison shop" (compare your own relationship against potential alternative relationships) regardless of the type of relationship you're in, or do you stop "shopping" when the relationship reaches a certain level of commitment?

3. It's been argued that you don't actually develop an attraction to people who are similar to you, but rather develop a repulsion toward those who are dissimilar (Rosenbaum, 1986). For example, you may exclude people who disagree with you from those with whom you might develop a relationship. You're therefore left with a pool of possible partners whose ideas are similar to yours. What do you think of this "repulsion hypothesis"?

4. Not surprisingly, a great deal of relationship maintenance takes place through e-mail (Stafford, Kline, & Dimmick, 1999; Howard, Rainie, & Jones, 2001). Because an increasing number of relationships develop online, and because online contact is so easy even when partners are widely separated geographically, this use of e-mail is likely to increase in frequency and importance. Incidentally, the use of e-mail to maintain relationships, is more common among women than men; women also find such e-mail contact more gratifying than do men (Boneva, Kraut, & Frohlich, 2001). What role does Internet communication play in your relationship life?

MyCommunicationLab Explorations

Explore www.mycommunicationlab.com to find exercises that will enable you to work actively with the concepts discussed in this chapter: (1) Analyzing Stage Talk, (2) Giving Repair Advice, (3) Til' This Do Us Part, (4) Applying Theories to Problems, (5) Male and Female, (6) Relational Repair from Advice Columnists, (7) How Can You Get Someone to Like You? (8) How Might You Repair Relationships? (9) Friendship Behaviors, (10) Mate Preferences: I Prefer Someone Who . . . , and (11) The Television Relationship. Relevant self-tests are

(12) What Do You Believe about Relationships? (13) How Committed Are You? (14) How Romantic Are You? and (15) What Type of Relationship Do You Prefer?

Visit also MyCommunicationLab for video clips on interpersonal relationships as well as additional exercises and study tools. These will give you additional perspectives on the different types of interpersonal relationships.

Explore our research resources at
www.researchnavigator.com.

Research
Navigator.com

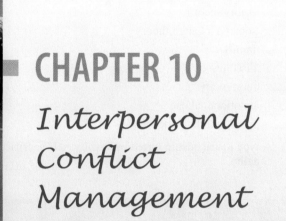

CHAPTER 10
Interpersonal Conflict Management

WHY READ THIS CHAPTER?

*B*ecause you'll **learn about:**
- the nature and types of interpersonal conflict.
- the stages of conflict management.
- the major strategies for conflict management.

*B*ecause you'll **learn to:**
- approach interpersonal conflict realistically and positively.
- manage conflict by moving effectively through its stages.
- engage in interpersonal conflict management using fair, productive, and proven strategies.

$\mathcal{P}$erhaps the most important of all your interpersonal interactions are those involving **conflict,** or dissension. Interpersonal conflict creates uncertainty, anxiety, and problems for the relationship but also, as you'll soon see, opportunities for improving and strengthening the relationship. And it is interpersonal conflict that most requires the skills of interpersonal communication. Appropriately, then, this final chapter focuses on this inevitable and often mishandled interpersonal interaction.

$\mathcal{W}$hat Is Interpersonal Conflict?

Interpersonal conflict is a special type of conflict, so we need here to define this type of conflict and to consider how it may focus on both content and relationship issues.

A Definition of Interpersonal Conflict

Interpersonal conflict is disagreement between or among connected individuals—coworkers, close friends, lovers, or family members. The word *connected* emphasizes the transactional nature of interpersonal conflict—the fact that each person's position affects the other person. The positions in interpersonal conflicts are to some degree both interrelated and incompatible.

Content and Relationship Conflict

Using concepts developed in Chapter 1, we can distinguish between content conflict and relationship conflict. *Content conflict* centers on objects, events, and persons in the world that are usually, though not always, external to the parties involved in the conflict. Content conflicts have to do with the millions of issues that we argue and

---

Listen to this

■ Listening to Conflict Messages

Perhaps the most difficult type of listening occurs in conflict situations, in which tempers run high and you may find yourself attacked. Yet it's in times of conflict that listening is especially crucial. Here are some suggestions for listening more effectively in these difficult circumstances.

- Act and think as a listener. Turn off the television, stereo, or computer; face the other person. Devote your total attention to the other person.
- Make sure you understand what the person is saying and feeling. Use perception checking (Chapter 4) and active listening techniques (Chapter 5).
- *Express* your support or empathy: "I can understand how you feel. I know I control the checkbook, and I realize that can create a feeling of inequality."
- If appropriate, indicate your agreement: "You're right to be disturbed."
- State your thoughts and feelings as objectively as you can; avoid criticism or blame.
- Get ready to listen to the other person's responses to your statement. After voicing your thoughts, be prepared to listen to the other person's response.

■ Applying Listening Skills

You're a new teacher at an elementary school. The parents of a student who has been doing very poorly and has created all sorts of discipline problems (in your opinion, she's a brat) complain that their daughter hates school and isn't learning anything. They want her transferred to another class with another teacher. What listening skills would you try to practice in your conversation with these parents?

What Do You Say

Escalating to Relationship Conflict

Your own interpersonal conflicts often start out as content conflicts but quickly degenerate into relationship conflicts and that's when things get ugly. You want to keep the argument and its eventual resolution focused on the content. **What Do You Say?**

fight about every day—the merit of a particular movie, what to watch on television, the fairness of the last examination or job promotion, the way to spend our savings.

Relationship conflicts are equally numerous and include clashes between, for example, a younger brother who refuses to obey his older brother, two partners who each want an equal say in making vacation plans, or a mother and daughter who each want to have the final word concerning the daughter's lifestyle. Here the conflicts are concerned not so much with some external object as with the relationships between the individuals—with issues like who is in charge, how equal are the members in a family relationship, or who has the right to set down rules of behavior.

Of course, content and relationship dimensions are always easier to separate in a textbook than they are in real life, in which many conflicts contain elements of both. For example, you can probably imagine both content and relationship dimensions in each of the "content" issues mentioned earlier. And yet certain issues seem more focused on content and others more focused on relationships. For example, intimacy and power issues (for example, who has the final say in financial matters or who takes the lead in sex encounters) are largely relational, whereas differences on political and social issues (for example, whom to vote for) are largely content focused.

Principles of Interpersonal Conflict

Interpersonal conflict is a complex and often difficult to understand process. The following principles will help clarify how interpersonal conflict works: (1) Conflict is inevitable—you can't avoid it; (2) interpersonal conflict can occur in computer-mediated communication as well as in face-to-face interaction; (3) conflict can have positive as well as negative effects; (4) conflict is heavily influenced by gender and culture; and (5) the style of conflict you use will have significant effects on your relationship.

Conflict Is Inevitable

Interpersonal conflict is a part of every interpersonal relationship, whether between parents and children, brothers and sisters, friends, lovers, or coworkers. If conflict doesn't exist, then the relationship is probably dull, irrelevant, or insignificant.

To appreciate the inevitability of interpersonal conflict, consider the broad range of topics on which relationship partners disagree to the point of conflict (Canary, 2003). For example, one study on the issues argued about by gay, lesbian, and heterosexual couples identified six major sources of conflict that were virtually identical for all couples (Kurdek, 1994). The issues are arranged here in order, with the first being the most often mentioned. Do you argue about these issues?

- *intimacy issues such as affection and sex*
- *power issues such as excessive demands or possessiveness, lack of equality in the relationship, friends, or leisure time*
- *personal flaws issues such as drinking or smoking, personal grooming, or driving style*
- *personal distance issues such as frequent absences or school or job commitments*
- *social issues such as politics, parents, or personal values*
- *distrust issues such as previous lovers or lying*

" It is seldom the fault of one when two argue. **"**
—Swedish proverb

Another study found that four conditions typically led up to couples' "first big fight": uncertainty over commitment, jealousy, violation of expectations, and personality differences (Siegert & Stamp, 1994). Among top managers in the business world, conflict most often revolved around issues of executive responsibility and coordination. Other conflicts focused on differences in organizational objectives, on allocation of resources, and on appropriate management style (Morrill, 1992). In a study of same-sex and opposite-sex friends, the four issues most often argued about involved problems with sharing living space or possessions, violations of friendship rules, difficulties in sharing activities, and incompatible ideas or opinions (Samter & Cupach, 1998).

Conflict Can Occur in Computer-Mediated Communication

Just as you experience interpersonal conflicts in face-to-face communication, you can experience the same kinds of conflicts online. A few conflict situations that are unique to online communication are noted here.

Sending commercial messages to those who didn't request them often creates conflict. Junk mail is junk mail; but on the Internet the receiver often has to pay for the time it takes to read and delete these unwanted messages. Even if there is no financial cost, there is still a loss of time.

Sending messages to an entire listserv when they're only relevant to one member may annoy members who expect to receive only messages relevant to the entire group and not personal exchanges between two people. This often occurs when someone sends a message seeking specific information; individual members may then reply not only to the person seeking the information but to the entire listserv. Sometimes the reply is simply "I can't help you with that question," a message relevant only to the person asking the question and not to the entire group.

Spamming often causes conflict. Spamming is sending someone unsolicited mail, repeatedly sending the same mail, or posting the same message in lots of newsgroups even when the message is irrelevant to the focus of some of the groups. Like commercial messages, these unwanted messages absorb recipients' valuable time and energy. Also, of course, spamming clogs the system, slowing it down for everyone.

Flaming, especially common in newsgroups, involves sending messages that personally attack another user. Frequently, flaming leads to flame wars in which everyone in the group gets into the act. Generally, flaming and flame wars prevent you from achieving your goals and are counterproductive.

Trolling, or putting out purposely incorrect information or outrageous viewpoints to watch other people correct you or get emotionally upset by your message, can obviously lead to conflict, though some see it as fun.

Another form of potential online conflict may be caused by ill-timed cell phone calls or text messaging. Often these messages interfere with more important matters, and they may easily be resented. And, of course, if you don't respond as the message sender thinks you should, conflict of a different sort can be generated.

Conflict Can Be Negative or Positive

Although interpersonal conflict is always stressful, it's important to recognize that it has both negative and positive aspects.

NEGATIVE ASPECTS OF INTERPERSONAL CONFLICT   Conflict often leads to increased negative regard for the opponent. One reason for this is that many conflicts involve unfair fighting methods and are focused largely on hurting the other person. When one person hurts the other, increased negative feelings are inevitable; even the strongest relationship has limits.

At times, too, conflict may lead you to close yourself off from the other person. When you hide your true self from an intimate, you prevent meaningful communica-

E-Talk . ▪ . ▪ . ▪ . ▪

Flaming

What specific kinds of messages do you consider flaming—"the practice of posting messages that are deliberately hostile and insulting to a discussion board (usually on the Internet). Such messages are called *flames*, and are often posted in response to *flamebait*" (TheFreeDictionary.com). What messages in face-to-face communication might you also consider flaming (cf. O'Sullivan & Flanagin, 2003)?

" Honest disagreement is often a good sign of progress. "
—Gandhi

tion from taking place. Because the need for intimacy is so strong, one or both parties may then seek intimacy elsewhere. This often leads to further conflict, mutual hurt, and resentment—qualities that add heavily to the costs carried by the relationship. Meanwhile, rewards may become difficult to exchange. In this situation, the costs increase and the rewards decrease, which often results in relationship deterioration and eventual dissolution.

POSITIVE ASPECTS OF INTERPERSONAL CONFLICT The major value of interpersonal conflict is that it forces you to examine a problem and work toward a potential solution. If the participants use productive conflict strategies, the relationship may well emerge from the encounter stronger, healthier, and more satisfying than before. And you may emerge stronger, more confident, and better able to stand up for yourself (Bedford, 1996).

Through conflict and its resolution we also can stop resentment from increasing and let our needs be known. For example, suppose I need lots of attention when I come home from work, but you need to review and get closure on the day's work. If we both can appreciate the legitimacy of these needs, then we can find solutions. Perhaps you can make your important phone call after my attention needs are met, or perhaps I can delay my need for attention until you get closure about work. Or perhaps I can learn to provide for your closure needs and in doing so get my attention needs met. We have a win–win solution; each of us gets our needs met.

Consider, too, that when you try to resolve conflict within an interpersonal relationship, you're saying in effect that the relationship is worth the effort; otherwise you would walk away from such a conflict. Usually, confronting a conflict indicates commitment and a desire to preserve the relationship.

Conflict Is Influenced by Culture and Gender

As in other areas of interpersonal communication, it helps to view conflict in light of culture and gender. Both exert powerful influences on how people view and resolve conflicts.

Ethical Fighting

Conflict strategies also have an ethical dimension, so you need to look at the ethical implications of the ways in which you engage in conflict. For example:

- What are the ethical implications of conflict avoidance? For example, is it unethical for one person to refuse to discuss issues of disagreement?
- Might it be ethical to force someone physically to accept your position in certain situations? Can you identify a situation in which it would be appropriate for someone to overpower another person to make the person accept his or her point of view?
- Are face-detracting strategies inherently unethical, or might it be appropriate to use them in certain situations? Can you identify such situations?
- When, if ever, might verbal aggressiveness be the logical and ethical choice?

What Would You Do?

At your stressful job you sometimes use coke with your colleagues. This happens several times a month, but you don't use drugs at any other times. Your partner—who you know hates drugs and people who use recreational drugs—asks you if you take drugs. Because your coke use is so limited, but mostly because you know that admitting it will cause a huge conflict in a relationship already having difficulties, you wonder what to say. Can you ethically lie?

CONFLICT AND CULTURE   Culture influences not only the issues that people fight about but also what people consider appropriate and inappropriate in terms of dealing with conflict. Researchers have found, for example, that cohabiting 18-year-olds are more likely to experience conflict with their parents about their living style if they live in the United States than if they live in Sweden, where cohabitation is much more accepted. Similarly, male infidelity is more likely to cause conflict between American spouses than in southern European couples. Students from the United States are more likely to engage in conflict with other U.S. students than with someone from another culture. Chinese students, on the other hand, are more likely to engage in conflict with non-Chinese students than with fellow Chinese (Leung, 1988).

The types of conflicts that arise depend on the cultural orientation of the individuals involved. For example, in collectivist cultures, such as those of Ecuador, Indonesia, and Korea, conflicts are more likely to center on violations of collective or group norms and values. Disagreeing in public or proving a colleague wrong in front of others and causing this person to lose face (and violate important cultural norms) is likely to create conflict.

Conversely, in individualist cultures, such as those of the United States, Canada, and western Europe, conflicts are more likely to occur when people violate individual norms; for example, if bonuses are not distributed according to merit (Ting-Toomey, 1985).

Americans and Japanese differ in their views of the aim or purpose of conflict. The Japanese (a collectivist culture) see conflicts and conflict resolution in terms of compromise; each side gains something and each side gives up something. Americans (an individualist culture), on the other hand, see conflict in terms of winning; it's an "I win, you lose" approach (Gelfand, Nishii, Holcombe, Dyer, Ohbuchi, & Fukuno, 2001). Also, different cultures seem to teach their members different views of conflict strategies (Tardiff, 2001). For example, in Japan it's especially important that you not embarrass the person with whom you are in conflict, especially if the disagreement occurs in public. This face-saving principle prohibits the use of such strategies as personal rejection or verbal aggressiveness. In another example, many Middle Eastern and Pacific Rim cultures discourage women from direct and forceful expression; rather, these societies expect more agreeable and submissive postures. Also, in general, members of collectivist cultures tend to avoid conflict more than members of individualist cultures (Dsilva & Whyte, 1998; Haar & Krahe, 1999; Cai & Fink, 2002).

Even within a given general culture, more specific subcultures differ from one another in their methods of conflict management. African American men and women and European American men and women, for example, engage in conflict in very different ways (Kochman, 1981). The issues that cause conflict and aggravate conflict, the conflict strategies that are expected and accepted, and the entire attitude toward conflict vary from one group to the other (Collier, 1991; Hecht, Jackson, & Ribeau, 2003).

The cultural norms of organizations also influence the types of conflicts that occur and the ways people may deal with them. Some work environments, for example, would not tolerate employees' expressing disagreement with high-level management; others might welcome it. In individualist cultures there is greater tolerance for conflict, even when it involves different levels of an organizational hierarchy. In collectivist cultures there's less tolerance. And, not surprisingly, the culture influences how the conflict will be resolved. For example, managers in the United States (an individualist culture) deal with workplace conflict by seeking to integrate the demands of the different sides; managers in China (a collectivist culture) are more likely to call on higher management to make decisions—or not to resolve the conflict at all (Tinsley & Brett, 2001).

CONFLICT AND GENDER   Do men and women engage in interpersonal conflict differently? One of the few stereotypes that is supported by research is that of the withdrawing and sometimes aggressive male. Men are more apt to withdraw from a conflict situation than are women. It has been argued that this may happen because men become more psychologically and physiologically aroused during conflict (and retain this heightened level of arousal much longer than do women) and so may try to distance themselves and withdraw from the conflict to prevent further arousal (Gottman & Carrere, 1994; Canary, Cupach, & Messman, 1995; Goleman, 1995a). Women, on the other hand, want to get closer to the conflict; they want to talk about it and resolve it. Even adolescents reveal these differences; in a study of boys and girls aged 11 to 17, boys withdrew more than girls but were more aggressive when they didn't withdraw (Lindeman, Harakka, & Keltikangas-Jarvinen, 1997). Similarly, a study of offensive language found that girls were more easily offended by language than boys but that boys were more apt to fight when they were offended by the words used (Heasley, Babbitt, & Burbach, 1995). Another study showed that young girls used more prosocial strategies than boys (Rose & Asher, 1999).

Other research has found that women tend to be more emotional and men more logical when they argue (Schaap, Buunk, & Kerkstra, 1988; Canary, Cupach, & Messman, 1995). Women have been defined as conflict "feelers" and men as conflict "thinkers" (Sorenson, Hawkins, & Sorenson, 1995). Another difference is that women are more apt to reveal their negative feelings than are men (Schaap, Buunk, & Kerkstra, 1988; Canary, Cupach, & Messman, 1995).

Among Mexican Americans, studies found that men preferred to achieve mutual understanding by discussing the reasons for the conflict, whereas women focused on being supportive of the relationship. Among Anglo Americans, men preferred direct and rational argument; women preferred flexibility (Collier, 1991). These, of course, are merely examples—but the underlying principle is that techniques for dealing with interpersonal conflict will be viewed differently by men and women.

Nevertheless, from a close examination of the research it would have to be concluded that the differences between men and women in interpersonal conflict are a lot less clear in reality than they are in popular stereotypes. Much research fails to find the differences that cartoons, situation comedies, novels, and films portray so readily. For example, several studies dealing with college students as well as with men and women in business found no significant differences in the way men and women engage in conflict (Wilkins & Andersen, 1991; Canary & Hause, 1993; Canary, Cupach, & Messman, 1995).

Conflict Styles Have Consequences

The way in which you engage in conflict has consequences for the resolution of the conflict and for the relationship between the conflicting parties. Figure 10.1 identifies five basic styles or ways of engaging in conflict and is especially relevant to understanding interpersonal conflicts (Blake & Mouton, 1985). Descriptions of the five styles, plotted among the dimensions of concern for self and concern for the other person, provide insight into the ways people engage in conflict and highlight some of the advantages and disadvantages of each style. As you read through these styles, try to identify your own conflict style as well as the styles of those with whom you have close relationships.

COMPETING: I WIN, YOU LOSE The competitive conflict style involves great concern for your own needs and desires, and little for those of others. As long as your needs are met, the conflict has been dealt with successfully (for you). In conflict motivated by competitiveness, you'd be likely to be verbally aggressive and to blame the other person.

This style represents an *I win, you lose* philosophy. As you can tell, this style might be appropriate in a courtroom or at a

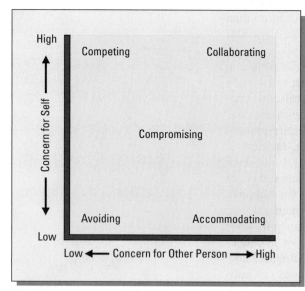

Figure 10.1
Five Conflict Styles
This figure is adapted from Blake and Mouton's (1985) approach to managerial leadership and conflict.

Source: R. R. Blake & J. S. Mouton, *The Managerial Grid III.* Gulf Publishing Company, 1985. Reprinted by permission of Grid International, Inc.

used-car lot, two settings where one person benefits from the other person's losses. But in interpersonal situations this philosophy can easily lead to resentment on the part of the person who loses, which can easily cause additional conflicts. Further, the fact that you win and the other person loses probably means that the conflict hasn't really been resolved but only concluded (for now).

AVOIDING: I LOSE, YOU LOSE   Conflict avoiders are relatively unconcerned with their own or with their opponents' needs or desires. They avoid any real communication about the problem, change topics when the problem is brought up, and generally withdraw from the scene both psychologically and physically.

As you can appreciate, the avoiding style does little to resolve any conflicts and may be viewed as an *I lose, you lose* philosophy. Interpersonal problems rarely go away of their own accord; rather, if they exist, they need to be faced and dealt with effectively. Avoidance merely allows the conflict to fester and probably grow, only to resurface in another guise.

" The aim of an argument or discussion should not be victory, but progress. "

—Joseph Joubert

ACCOMMODATING: I LOSE, YOU WIN   In accommodating you sacrifice your own needs for the needs of the other person(s). Your major purpose is to maintain harmony and peace in the relationship or group. This style may help maintain peace and may satisfy the opposition; but it does little to meet your own needs, which are unlikely to go away.

Accommodation represents an *I lose, you win* philosophy. And although this conflict style may make your partner happy (at least on this occasion), it's not likely to prove a lasting resolution to an interpersonal conflict. You'll eventually sense unfairness and inequality and may easily come to resent your partner and perhaps even yourself.

COLLABORATING: I WIN, YOU WIN   In collaborating you address both your own and the other person's needs. This conflict style, often considered the ideal, takes time and a willingness to communicate—and especially to listen to the perspectives and needs of the other person.

Ideally, collaboration enables each person's needs to be met, an *I win, you win* situation. This is obviously the style that, in an ideal world, most people would choose for interpersonal conflict.

COMPROMISING: I WIN AND LOSE, YOU WIN AND LOSE   The compromising style is in the middle: There's some concern for your own needs and some concern for the other's needs. Compromise is the kind of strategy you might refer to as "meeting each other halfway," "horse trading," or "give and take." This strategy is likely to result in maintaining peace, but there will be a residue of dissatisfaction over the inevitable losses that each side has to endure.

Compromise represents an *I win and lose, you win and lose* philosophy. There are lots of times when you can't both get exactly what you want. You can't both get a new car if the available funds allow for only one. And yet you might each get a better used car than the one you now have. So each of you might win something, though not everything.

Conflict Resolution Stages

The model in Figure 10.2 provides guidance for dealing with conflicts effectively. This five-stage model is based on the problem-solving technique first introduced by

John Dewey (1910) and still used by many contemporary theorists. The assumption made here is that interpersonal conflict is essentially a problem that needs to be solved. This model should not be taken as suggesting that there is only one path to conflict resolution, however. It is a general way of envisioning the process that should help you better understand how conflict works and how you can work toward resolving the conflict.

Before getting to the five stages of conflict, consider a few "before the conflict" suggestions.

- *Try to fight in private. You may not be willing to be totally honest when third parties are present; you may feel you have to save face and therefore must win the fight at all costs.*
- *Make sure you're both relatively free of other problems and ready to deal with the conflict at hand.*
- *Fight about problems that can be solved. Fighting about past behaviors or about family members or situations over which you have no control solves nothing; in fact, it's more likely to create additional difficulties.*

Define the Conflict

Your first and most essential step is to define the conflict. Here are several techniques to keep in mind.

- *Define both content and relationship issues.* Define the obvious content issues (who should do the dishes, who should take the kids to school) as well as the underlying relationship issues (who has been avoiding household responsibilities, whose time is more valuable).

Figure 10.2

The Stages of Conflict Resolution

This model derives from John Dewey's stages of reflective thinking and is a general pattern for understanding and resolving any type of problem.

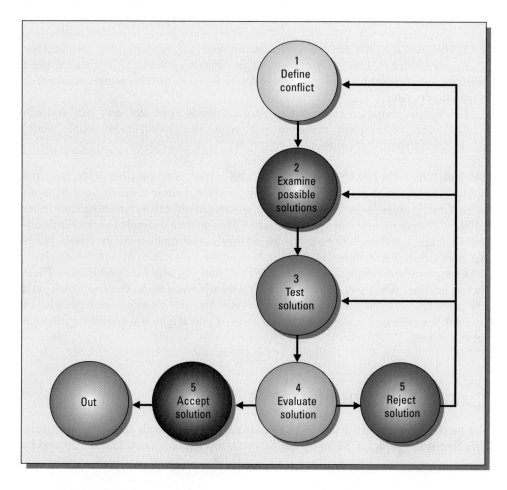

- *Define the problem in specific terms.* It's one thing for a husband to say that his wife is "cold and unfeeling" and quite another for him to say that she does not call him at the office, kiss him when he comes home, or hold his hand when they're at a party. Specific behaviors can be agreed on and dealt with, but the abstract "cold and unfeeling" remains elusive.
- *Empathize.* Try to understand the nature of the conflict from the other person's point of view. Once you have empathically understood the other person's feelings, validate those feelings when appropriate. If your partner is hurt or angry and you believe such feelings are justified, say so: "You have a right to be angry; I shouldn't have said that."
- *Avoid mind reading.* Don't try to read the other person's mind. Ask questions to make sure you understand the problem as the other person is experiencing it.

Let's take an example and work with it through the remaining conflict stages. This conflict revolves around Raul's not wanting to socialize with Julia's friends. Julia thinks her friends are wonderful and exciting; Raul thinks they're unpleasant and boring.

Examine Possible Solutions

The second step in conflict is to look for possible ways of resolving the issue. Because most conflicts can probably be resolved in a variety of ways, it's useful at this stage to identify as many solutions as possible.

As noted in the discussion of conflict styles earlier, win–win solutions are the ideal; so look for these whenever possible. Most solutions, of course, will involve costs to one or both parties (after all, someone has to take the dog out), so it's unlikely that solutions to real interpersonal problems are going to involve only rewards for both persons. But you can try to seek solutions in which the costs and the rewards will be evenly shared.

In our example, let's say Raul and Julia identify these possible solutions:

1. Julia should not interact with her friends anymore.
2. Raul should interact with Julia's friends.
3. Julia should see her friends without Raul.

Clearly solutions 1 and 2 are win–lose solutions. In 1, Raul wins and Julia loses; in 2, Julia wins and Raul loses. Solution 3, however, might be a possibility. Both might win and neither must necessarily lose. The next step would be to test this possible solution.

Test a Solution

Once you have examined all possible solutions, select one and test it out. First test the solution mentally. How does it feel? Are you comfortable with the solution? Will Raul be comfortable about Julia's socializing with her friends without him? Will Julia be comfortable socializing with her friends without Raul? Will she feel guilty? Will she enjoy herself without Raul?

Then test the solution in actual practice. Give the idea a fair chance. Perhaps Julia might go out once without Raul to try it out. Did her friends think there was something wrong with her relationship with Raul? Did she feel guilty? Did she enjoy herself? Did Raul feel jealous?

Evaluate the Solution

In the evaluation stage, ask whether the tested solution helped resolve the conflict. Is the situation better now than it was before the solution was put into operation? Share your feelings and evaluations of the solution.

■ What Do You Say
Confronting a Problem
Your next-door neighbor never puts out the garbage in time for pickup. As a result the garbage—often broken into by stray animals—remains until the next pickup. You're fed up with the rodents the garbage draws, the smell, and the horrible appearance. You're determined to stop this problem and yet not to make your neighbor hate you. **What Do You Say?** To whom? Through what channel?

Raul and Julia now need to share their perceptions of this possible solution. Would they be comfortable with this solution on a monthly basis? Is the solution worth the costs that each will pay? Are the costs and the rewards about evenly distributed? Might other solutions be more effective?

Critical thinking pioneer Edward deBono (1987) suggests that in evaluating problems or proposed solutions, you use six "thinking hats." With each hat you look at the problem or the solution from a different perspective. Here's how looking at Julia and Raul's problem with the six hats might work:

- *The fact hat* focuses attention on the facts and figures that bear on the problem. For example, How can Raul learn more about the rewards that Julia gets from her friends? How can Julia find out why Raul doesn't like her friends?
- *The feeling hat* focuses attention on the emotional responses to the problem. How does Raul feel when Julia goes out with her friends? How does Julia feel when Raul refuses to meet them?
- *The negative argument hat* asks you to become the devil's advocate. How might this relationship deteriorate if Julia continues seeing her friends without Raul or if Raul resists interacting with Julia's friends?
- *The positive benefits hat* asks you to look at the upside. What are the opportunities that Julia's seeing friends without Raul might yield? What benefits might Raul and Julia get from this new arrangement?
- *The creative new idea hat* focuses on new ways of looking at the problem. In what other ways can Raul and Julia look at this problem? What other possible solutions might they consider?
- *The control of thinking hat* helps you analyze what you're doing. It asks you to reflect on your own thinking. Have Raul and Julia adequately defined the problem? Are they focusing too much on insignificant issues? Have they given enough attention to possible negative effects?

Accept or Reject the Solution

If you accept a solution, you're ready to put this solution into more permanent operation. But if you decide, on the basis of your evaluation, that this is not the right solution for the conflict, then there are two major alternatives. First, you might test another solution. Perhaps you might now reexamine a runner-up idea or approach. Second, you might go back to the definition of the conflict. As the diagram in Figure 10.2 illustrates, you can reenter the conflict-resolution process at any of the first three stages.

Let us say that Raul is actually quite happy with the solution. He takes the opportunity of his evening alone to visit his brother. Next time Julia goes out with her friends, Raul intends to go to wrestling. And Julia feels pretty good about seeing her friends without Raul. She simply explains that occasionally she and Raul socialize separately and that both are comfortable with this.

After a conflict is resolved, it is not necessarily over. Consider a few "after the conflict" suggestions.

- Learn from the conflict and from the process you went through in trying to resolve it. For example, can you identify the fight strategies that aggravated the situation? Do you, or does your partner, need a cooling-off period? Can you tell when minor issues are going to escalate into major arguments?
- Attack your negative feelings. Often such feelings arise because unfair fight strategies were used (as we'll see in the next section)—for example, blame or verbal aggressiveness. Resolve to avoid such unfair tactics in the future, but at the same time let go of guilt and blame. Don't view yourself, your partner, or your relationship as a failure simply because you have conflicts.

Skill building *exercise*

Early Conflict Resolution

Here are a few conflict "starters," something someone might say to you that would signal the start of an interpersonal conflict. For each situation (a) write a productive response—that is, a response that will likely lessen the potential conflict—and (b) in one sentence explain what you hope this response will accomplish.

- You're late again. You're always late. Your lateness is so inconsiderate!
- I just can't bear another weekend of sitting home watching cartoon shows with the kids.
- Well, there goes another anniversary that you forgot.
- You think I'm fat, don't you?
- You never want to do what I want. We always have to do what you want.

Impending conflicts are often signaled at a stage when they can be confronted and resolved before they escalate and prove more difficult to resolve.

- Increase the exchange of rewards and cherishing behaviors. These will show your positive feelings and demonstrate that you're over the conflict and want the relationship to survive.

Conflict Management Strategies

In managing conflict you can choose from a variety of strategies, which we will consider here. Realize, however, that a variety of factors will influence the strategies you choose (Koerner & Fitzpatrick, 2002):

"Walking down here and asking if I can get you some more detergent from the store is just the beginning of my fence-mending agenda."

- the goals to be achieved
- your emotional state
- your cognitive assessment of the situation
- your personality and communication competence
- your family history

Understanding these factors may help you select more appropriate and more effective strategies to manage conflict with success. And, recent research finds, using productive conflict strategies can have lots of beneficial effects; conversely, using inappropriate strategies may be linked to poorer psychological health (Weitzman & Weitzman, 2000; Weitzman, 2001; Neff & Harter, 2002).

The *goals* (short-term and long-term) you wish to achieve will influence what strategies seem appropriate to you. If you merely want to enjoy the moment, you may want to simply "give in" and ignore the difficulty. On the other hand, if you want to build a long-term relationship, you may want to fully analyze the cause of the problem and to look for strategies that will enable both parties to win.

Your *emotional state,* too, will influence your strategies. You're unlikely to select the same strategies when you're sorry as when you're angry. When you are sorry, you're likely to use conciliatory strategies designed to make peace; when you're angry, you're more likely to use strategies that attack the other person.

Your *cognitive assessment* of the situation will exert powerful influence on your approach to managing conflict. For example, your attitudes and beliefs about what is fair and equitable will influence your readiness to acknowledge the fairness in the other person's position. Your own assessment of who (if anyone) is the cause of the problem also will influence your conflict style. You might also assess the likely effects of various potential strategies. For example, what do you risk if you fight with your boss by using blame or personal rejection? As a parent, do you risk alienating your teenager when you use force?

Your *personality and communication competence* will influence the way you engage in conflict. For example, if you're shy and unassertive, you may be more likely to want to avoid a conflict rather than fighting actively. If you're extroverted and have a strong desire to state your position, then you may be more likely to fight actively and to argue forcefully.

Your *family history* will influence the strategies you use, the topics you choose to fight about, and perhaps your tendencies either to obsess or to forget about interpersonal conflicts. Even in conflict people often imitate their parents; for example, if your parents argued about money or gave each other the silent treatment when conflict arose, you're likely to repeat these patterns yourself if you aren't mindful of your conflict strategies.

Win–Lose and Win–Win Strategies

As noted in the discussion of conflict styles, you can look at interpersonal conflict in terms of winning and losing. Obviously, solutions in which both parties win are the most desirable. Perhaps the most important reason is that win–win solutions lead to mutual satisfaction and prevent the kind of resentment that win–lose solutions often engender. Another reason is that looking for and developing win–win solutions makes the next conflict less unpleasant; conflict can more easily be viewed as "solving a problem" rather than as "fighting." Also, win–win solutions promote mutual face-saving; both parties can feel good about themselves. Finally, people are more likely to abide by the decisions reached in a win–win conflict than they are in win–lose or lose–lose situations. In sum, you can look for solutions in which you or your side wins and the other person or side loses (win–lose solutions). Or you

❝ Difficulties are meant to rouse, not discourage. The human spirit is to grow strong by conflict. ❞
—William Ellery Channing

Skill building *exercise*

Generating Win–Win Solutions

To get into the habit of looking for win–win solutions, consider the following conflict situations. For each situation (a) generate as many win–lose solutions as you can—solutions in which one person wins and the other loses; (b) generate as many possible win–win solutions as you feel the individuals involved in the conflict could reasonably accept; and (c) explain in one sentence the major difference between win–lose and win–win solutions.

1. For their vacation, Pat wants to go to the shore and relax by the water; Chris wants to go hiking and camping in the mountains.
2. Pat, who recently got a $3,000 bonus, wants to buy a new computer and printer; Chris wants to take a vacation.
3. Pat hangs around the house in underwear. Chris really hates this, and they argue about it almost daily.

Win–win solutions exist for most conflict situations (though not necessarily all); with a little effort win–win solutions can be identified for most interpersonal conflicts.

can look for solutions in which you and the other person both win (win–win solutions). Too often, we fail to even consider the possibility of win–win solutions and what they might be.

Take an interpersonal example: Let's say that I want to spend our money on a new car (my old one is unreliable) and you want to spend it on a vacation (you're exhausted and feel the need for a rest). Ideally, through our conflict and its resolution, we learn what each really wants. We may then be able to figure out a way for each of us to get what we want. I might accept a good used car, and you might accept a less expensive vacation. Or we might buy a used car and take an inexpensive road trip. Each of these win–win solutions will satisfy both of us; each of us wins, in the sense that each of us gets what we wanted.

Avoidance and Fighting Actively

Conflict **avoidance** may involve actual physical flight: You may leave the scene of the conflict (walk out of the apartment or go to another part of the office or shop), fall asleep, or blast the stereo to drown out all conversation. It also may take the form of emotional or intellectual avoidance, in which you may leave the conflict psychologically by not dealing with any of the arguments or problems raised.

Nonnegotiation is a special type of avoidance. Here you refuse to discuss the conflict or to listen to the other person's argument. At times nonnegotiation takes the form of hammering away at your own point of view until the other person gives in—a technique called "steamrolling."

Another form of avoidance is **gunnysacking.** The term *gunnysack* refers to the kind of burlap bag that years ago held potatoes. As a conflict strategy gunnysacking involves storing up grievances (as if in a gunnysack) and then unloading them on the other person—even when the grievances have nothing to do with the present conflict. As you can imagine, as a conflict strategy, gunnysacking is highly unproductive. The immediate occasion for unloading stored-up grievances may be relatively simple (or so it may seem at first); for example, you come home late one night without calling. Instead of arguing about this, the gunnysacker pours out a mass of unrelated past grievances. As you probably know from experience, however, gunnysacking often begets gunnysacking. Frequently the trigger problem never gets addressed. Instead, resentment and hostility escalate.

Instead of avoiding the issues, take an active role in your interpersonal conflicts. Involve yourself on both sides of the communication exchange. Be an active participant both as a speaker and as a listener; voice your own feelings and listen carefully to the voicing of your opponent's feelings. This is not to say that periodic moratoriums are not helpful; sometimes they are. But in general, be willing to communicate.

E-Talk ■ ■ ■ ■ ■ ■ ■ ■
E-Mail and Interpersonal Conflict

In what ways might e-mail enable you to avoid conflict more than a face-to-face situation might? Alternatively, in what ways might e-mail enable you to engage in conflict more actively than a face-to-face situation might? In what other ways is conflict through e-mail different from face-to-face conflict?

"She asked for a divorce, but I outsmarted her and ran into the next room."

Another part of active fighting involves owning your thoughts and feelings. For example, when you disagree with your partner or find fault with her or his behavior, take responsibility for these feelings. Say, for example, "I disagree with . . ." or "I don't like it when you. . . ." Avoid statements that deny your responsibility; for example, "Everybody thinks you're wrong about . . ." or "Chris thinks you shouldn't. . . ."

Focus on the present, on the here and now, rather than on issues that occurred two months ago. Similarly, focus your conflict on the person with whom you're fighting, not on the person's mother, child, or friends.

Defensiveness and Supportiveness

Although talk is preferred to force, not all talk is equally productive in conflict resolution. One of the best ways to look at destructive versus productive talk is to look at how the style of your communications can create unproductive **defensiveness** or a productive sense of **supportiveness**, an approach developed by Jack Gibb (1961) that is still used widely by communication and conflict theorists and interpersonal textbook writers. The type of talk that generally proves destructive and sets up defensive reactions in the listener is talk that is evaluative, controlling, strategic, indifferent or neutral, superior, and certain.

EVALUATION   When you evaluate or judge another person or what that person has done, that person is likely to become resentful and defensive and is likely to respond with attempts to defend himself or herself and perhaps at the same time to become equally evaluative and judgmental. In contrast, when you describe what happened or what you want, it creates no such defensiveness and is generally seen as supportive. The distinction between evaluation and description can be seen in the differences between you-messages and I-messages.

Evaluative You-Messages	Descriptive I-Messages
You never reveal your feelings.	*I sure would like hearing how you feel about this.*
You just don't plan ahead.	*I need to know what our schedule for the next few days will be.*
You never call me.	*I'd enjoy hearing from you more often.*

■ What Do You Say ?
Avoiding Conflict
Your work team members all seem to have the same conflict style: avoidance. When differing alternatives are discussed or there is some kind of disagreement, they refuse to argue for one side or the other or even to participate in the discussion. You need spirited discussion and honest debate if your team is going to come up with appropriate solutions. **What Do You Say?** To whom? Through what channel?

If you put yourself in the role of the listener hearing these statements, you probably can feel the resentment or defensiveness that the evaluative messages (you-messages) would create and the supportiveness from the descriptive messages (I-messages).

CONTROL   When you try to control the behavior of the other person, when you order the other person to do this or that, or when you make decisions without mutual discussion and agreement, defensiveness is a likely response. Control messages deny the legitimacy of the person's contributions and in fact deny his or her importance. They say, in effect, "You don't count; your contributions are meaningless." When, on the other hand, you focus on the problem at hand—not on controlling the situation or getting your own way—defensiveness is much less likely. This problem orientation invites mutual participation and recognizes the significance of each person's contributions.

STRATEGY   When you use **strategy** and try to get around other people or situations through **manipulation**—especially when you conceal your true purposes—others are likely to resent it and to respond defensively. But when you act openly and with **spontaneity,** you're more likely to create an atmosphere that is equal and honest.

NEUTRALITY   When you demonstrate **neutrality**—in the sense of indifference or a lack of caring for the other person—it's likely to create defensiveness. Neutrality seems to show a lack of empathy or interest in the thoughts and feelings of the other person; it is especially damaging when intimates are in conflict. This kind of talk says, in effect, "You're not important or deserving of attention and caring." When, on the other hand, you demonstrate empathy, defensiveness is unlikely to occur. Although it can be especially difficult in conflict situations, try to show that you can understand what the other person is going through and that you accept these feelings.

SUPERIORITY   When you present yourself as superior to the other person, you're in effect putting the other person in an inferior position, and this is likely to be resented.

"Honey, wake up! I just remembered something you did that annoyed the hell out of me!"

E-Talk · · · · · ·

Positiveness

One study found that, generally at least, people are more positive in dealing with conflict in face-to-face situations than in computer-mediated communication (Zornoza, Ripoll, & Peiró, 2002). Do you notice this to be true? If so, why do you think it's true?

Such **superiority** messages say in effect that the other person is inadequate or somehow second-class. It's a violation of the implicit **equality** contract that people in a close relationship have—namely, the assumption that each person is equal. The other person may then begin to attack your superiority; the conflict can easily degenerate into a conflict over who's the boss, with personal attack being the mode of interaction.

CERTAINTY   The person who appears to know it all is likely to be resented, so **certainty** often sets up a defensive climate. After all, there is little room for negotiation or mutual problem solving when one person already has the answer. An attitude of **provisionalism**—"Let's explore this issue together and try to find a solution"—is likely to be much more productive than **closed-mindedness.**

Face-Detracting and Face-Enhancing Strategies

Another dimension of conflict strategies is that of face orientation. Face-detracting or face-attacking strategies involve treating the other person as incompetent or untrustworthy, as unable or bad (Donohue & Kolt, 1992). Such attacks can vary from mildly embarrassing the other person to severely damaging his or her ego or reputation. When such attacks become extreme, they may be similar to verbal aggressiveness—a tactic explained below. So be especially careful to avoid "fighting words"—words that are sure to escalate the conflict rather than help to revolve it. Words like *stupid, liar,* and *bitch* as well as words like *always* and *never* (as in "you always . . ." or "you never . . .") invariably create additional problems.

One popular but destructive face-detracting strategy is **beltlining** (Bach & Wyden, 1968). Much like fighters in a ring, each of us has a "beltline" in interpersonal conflict. When you hit above the "belt," the person is able to absorb the emotional blow. When you hit below it, however, you can inflict serious injury. With most interpersonal relationships, especially those of long standing, you know where the beltline is. You know, for example, that to talk about Pat's infertility or Chris's failure to get a permanent job is to hit below the belt. This type of face-detracting strategy causes added problems for all persons involved in a conflict. Keep blows to areas your opponent can absorb and handle.

Another kind of face-detracting strategy is **blame**—attributing to the other person responsibility for whatever problem the relationship is facing. Consider, for example, a couple who are fighting over their child's getting into trouble with the police. Instead of dealing with the problem itself, the parents may blame each other for the child's troubles. Such blaming, of course, does nothing to resolve the problem or to help the child.

Skill building *exercise*

Responding to Confrontations

Sometimes you'll be confronted with an argument that you can't ignore and that you must respond to in some way. Here are a few examples of confrontations. For each one, write a response to the confrontation in which you (a) let the person know that you're open to her or his point of view and that you view this perspective as useful information, (b) show that you understand both the thoughts and the feelings that go with the confrontation, and (c) ask the person what he or she would like you to do about it.

1. You're calling these meetings much too often and much too early to suit us. We'd like fewer meetings scheduled for later in the day.
2. There's a good reason why I don't say anything. I don't say anything because you never listen to me anyway.
3. I'm tired of having to take care of everything to do with the kids—attending PTA, driving to soccer practice, checking homework, making lunch.

Confrontations can give you valuable feedback that will help you improve; if responded to appropriately, confrontations can actually improve your relationship.

Face-enhancing techniques involve helping the other person maintain a positive image—the image of a person who is competent and trustworthy, able and good. There is some evidence to show that even when you get what you want, say in a bargaining situation, it's wise to help the other person retain positive face. This makes it less likely that future conflicts will arise (Donohue & Kolt, 1992). Not surprisingly, people are more likely to make an effort to support someone's "face" if they like the person than if they don't (Meyer, 1994).

Generally, collectivist cultures like those of Korea and Japan place greater emphasis on face, especially on maintaining a positive image in public. Face is generally less crucial in individualistic cultures such as that of the United States. And yet there are, of course, many shadings to any such broad generalization. For example, in parts of China, whose highly collectivist culture puts great stress on face-saving, criminals are paraded publicly at rallies and humiliated before being put to death (Tyler, 1996). Perhaps the importance of face-saving in China gives this particular punishment a meaning that it could not have in more individualistic cultures. But be careful not to think of all individualist or collectivist cultures as similar. For example, one study indicated that Germans had more face concerns than Americans, although both are individualist cultures; and Chinese had more face concerns than Japanese, although both are collectivist cultures (Oetzel, Ting-Toomey, Masumoto, Yokochi, Pan, Takai, & Wilcox, 2001).

Confirming the other person's definition of self (Chapter 6), avoiding attack and blame, and using excuses and apologies as appropriate are some generally useful face-enhancing strategies.

" A slip of the foot may soon be recovered; but that of the tongue perhaps never. "
—Thomas Fuller

Verbal Aggressiveness and Argumentativeness

An especially interesting perspective on conflict has emerged from work on verbal aggressiveness and argumentativeness, concepts developed by communication researchers that have quickly spread to other disciplines—such as psychology, education, and management, among others (Infante, 1988; Rancer, 1998; Wigley, 1998; Rancer & Avtgis, 2006). Understanding these two concepts will help you understand some of the reasons why things go wrong and some of the ways in which you can use conflict to improve rather than damage your relationships.

VERBAL AGGRESSIVENESS   **Verbal aggressiveness** is an unproductive conflict strategy in which a person tries to win an argument by inflicting psychological pain, by attacking the other person's self-concept. The technique is a type of disconfirmation in that it seeks to discredit the individual's view of self. To explore this tendency further, take the following self-test of verbal aggressiveness.

Test *Yourself* ■ ■ ■ ■ ■ ■ ■ ■ ■ ■ ■ ■ ☑

How Verbally Aggressive Are You?

INSTRUCTIONS: This scale measures how people try to obtain compliance from others. For each statement, indicate the extent to which you feel it's true for you in your attempts to influence others. Use the following scale: 5 = strongly agree, 4 = agree, 3 = undecided, 2 = disagree, and 1 = strongly disagree.

_____ ❶ If individuals I am trying to influence really deserve it, I attack their character.

_____ ❷ When individuals are very stubborn, I use insults to soften their stubborness.

_____ ❸ When people behave in ways that are in very poor taste, I insult them in order to shock them into proper behavior.

_____ ④ When people simply will not budge on a matter of importance, I lose my temper and say rather strong things to them.

_____ ⑤ When individuals insult me, I get a lot of pleasure out of really telling them off.

_____ ⑥ I like poking fun at people who do things that are stupid in order to stimulate their intelligence.

_____ ⑦ When people do things that are mean or cruel, I attack their character in order to help correct their behavior.

_____ ⑧ When I am trying to influence others but nothing seems to work, I yell and scream in order to get some movement from them.

_____ ⑨ When I am unable to refute others' positions, I try to make them feel defensive in order to weaken their positions.

_____ ⑩ When people refuse to do a task I know is important without good reason, I tell them they are unreasonable.

HOW DID YOU DO? To compute your verbal aggressiveness score, simply add up your responses. A total score of 30 would indicate the neutral point: You are not especially aggressive but not especially confirming of the other either. If you scored about 35, you would be considered moderately aggressive; if you scored 40, or more, you'd be considered very aggressive. If you scored below the neutral point, you'd be considered less verbally aggressive and more confirming when interacting with others. In looking over your responses, make special note of the behaviors portrayed in the 10 statements, all of which indicate a tendency to act verbally aggressive. Note those unproductive behaviors that you're especially prone to commit.

WHAT WILL YOU DO? Because verbal aggressiveness is likely to seriously reduce communication effectiveness, you probably want to reduce your tendencies to respond aggressively. Review the times when you acted verbally aggressive. What effect did such actions have on your subsequent interaction? What effect did they have on your relationship with the other person? What alternative ways of getting your point across might you have used? Might these have proved more effective?

Source: From a 20-item scale developed by Infante and Wigley (1986) and factor analyzed by Beatty, Rudd, and Valencic (1999). See "Verbal Aggressiveness" by Dominic Infante and C. J. Wigley, *Communication Monographs* 53, 1986, and Michael J. Beatty, Jill E. Rudd, & Kristin Marie Valencic, "A Re-evaluation of the Verbal Aggressiveness Scale: One Factor or Two?," *Communication Research Reports*, 1999, Vol. 16, 10–17. Copyright © 1986 by the National Communication Association. Reprinted by permission of the publisher and authors.

ARGUMENTATIVENESS   Interestingly, perhaps the most general suggestion for reducing verbal aggressiveness is to increase your argumentativeness. Contrary to popular belief, argumentativeness is a quality to be cultivated rather than avoided. The term **argumentativeness** refers to your willingness to argue for a point of view, your tendency to speak your mind on significant issues. It's the mode of dealing with disagreements that is the preferred alternative to verbal aggressiveness (Infante & Rancer, 1995).

E-Talk · · · · · ·

Aggressiveness in Internet Communication

Are there certain types of Internet communication sites that are more likely to see verbal aggressiveness, and others that foster argumentativeness? How would you describe the state of verbal aggressiveness and argumentativeness on the Internet?

Test *Yourself*

How Argumentative Are You?

INSTRUCTIONS: This questionnaire contains statements about controversial issues. Indicate how often each statement is true for you personally according to the following scale: 1 = almost never true, 2 = rarely true, 3 = occasionally true, 4 = often true, and 5 = almost always true.

_____ ① While in an argument, I worry that the person I am arguing with will form a negative impression of me.

____ ② Arguing over controversial issues improves my intelligence.

____ ③ I enjoy avoiding arguments.

____ ④ I am energetic and enthusiastic when I argue.

____ ⑤ Once I finish an argument, I promise myself that I will not get into another.

____ ⑥ Arguing with a person creates more problems for me than it solves.

____ ⑦ I have a pleasant, good feeling when I win a point in an argument.

____ ⑧ When I finish arguing with someone, I feel nervous and upset.

____ ⑨ I enjoy a good argument over a controversial issue.

____ ⑩ I get an unpleasant feeling when I realize I am about to get into an argument.

____ ⑪ I enjoy defending my point of view on an issue.

____ ⑫ I am happy when I keep an argument from happening.

____ ⑬ I do not like to miss the opportunity to argue a controversial issue.

____ ⑭ I prefer being with people who rarely disagree with me.

____ ⑮ I consider an argument an exciting intellectual challenge.

____ ⑯ I find myself unable to think of effective points during an argument.

____ ⑰ I feel refreshed and satisfied after an argument on a controversial issue.

____ ⑱ I have the ability to do well in an argument.

____ ⑲ I try to avoid getting into arguments.

____ ⑳ I feel excitement when I expect that a conversation I am in is leading to an argument.

HOW DID YOU DO? To compute your score follow these steps:
1. Add your scores on items 2, 4, 7, 9, 11, 13, 15, 17, 18, and 20.
2. Add 60 to the sum obtained in step 1.
3. Add your scores on items 1, 3, 5, 6, 8, 10, 12, 14, 16, and 19.
4. Subtract the total obtained in step 3 from the total obtained in step 2.

Your score will range from a possible low of 20 to a high of 100. Scores between 73 and 100 indicate high argumentativeness; scores between 56 and 72 indicate moderate argumentativeness; and scores between 20 and 55 indicate low argumentativeness.

WHAT WILL YOU DO? The researchers who developed this test note that both high and low argumentatives may experience communication difficulties. The high argumentative, for example, may argue needlessly, too often, and too forcefully. The low argumentative, on the other hand, may avoid taking a stand even when it seems necessary. Persons scoring somewhere in the middle are probably the more interpersonally skilled and adaptable, arguing when it is necessary but avoiding arguments that are needless and repetitive. Does your experience support this observation? What specific actions might you take to improve your level of argumentativeness?

Source: From Dominic Infante and Andrew Rancer, "A Conceptualization and Measure of Argumentativeness" *Journal of Personality Assessment* 46 (1982): 72–80. Copyright 1982 Lawrence Erlbaum Associates, Inc. Reprinted by permission of Lawrence Erlbaum Associates, Inc., and the authors.

Some Differences between Argumentativeness and Verbal Aggressiveness

As you can appreciate, there are numerous differences between argumentativeness and verbal aggressiveness. Here are just a few (Infante & Rancer, 1996; Rancer & Atvgis, 2006).

■ What Do You Say
Talking Aggressively
Your partner is becoming more and more verbally aggressive, and you're having trouble with this new communication pattern. Regardless of what the conflict is about, your self-concept is attacked. You've had enough; you want to stop this kind of attack and yet to preserve the relationship. **What Do You Say?** Through what channel?

Argumentativeness	Verbal Aggressiveness
Is *constructive;* the outcomes are positive in a variety of communication situations (interpersonal, group, organizational, family, and intercultural).	Is *destructive;* the outcomes are negative in a variety of communication situations (interpersonal, group, organizational, family, and intercultural).
Leads to relationship *satisfaction.*	Leads to relationship *dissatisfaction,* not surprising for a strategy that aims to attack another's self-concept.
May *prevent relationship violence,* especially in domestic relationships.	May *lead to relationship violence.*
Enhances organizational life; for example, subordinates prefer supervisors who encouraged argumentativeness.	*Damages organizational life* and demoralizes workers on many levels.
Enhances parent–child communication and enables parents to secure greater cooperation.	*Prevents meaningful parent–child communication* and makes corporal punishment more likely.
Increases the user's credibility; argumentatives are seen as trustworthy, committed, and dynamic.	*Decreases the user's credibility,* in part because it's seen as a tactic to discredit the person rather than to address the argument.
Increases the user's power of persuasion in varied communication contexts and makes the user more likely to be seen as a leader	*Decreases the user's power of persuasion.*

Strategies for Cultivating Argumentativeness

Here are some suggestions for developing argumentativeness and for preventing it from degenerating into aggressiveness (Infante, 1988).

- Treat disagreements as objectively as possible; avoid assuming that because someone takes issue with your position or your interpretation, they're attacking you as a person.
- Center your arguments on issues rather than personalities. Avoid attacking a person (rather than a person's arguments), even if this would give you a tactical advantage—it will probably backfire at some later time and make your relationship or group participation more difficult.
- Reaffirm the other person's sense of competence; compliment the other person as appropriate.
- Allow the other person to state her or his position fully before you respond; avoid interrupting.
- Stress equality, and stress the similarities that you have with the other person or persons; stress your areas of agreement before attacking the disagreements.
- Express interest in the other person's position, attitude, and point of view.
- Avoid getting overemotional; using an overly loud voice or interjecting vulgar expressions will prove offensive and eventually ineffective.
- Allow people to save face; never humiliate another person.

The Unproductive Interpersonal Conflict

Here is a brief dialogue written to illustrate the unproductive conflict strategies discussed in the text as well as the failure to use their more productive counterparts. As you read this dialogue, identify the conflict strategies used by Chris and Pat so you can see how the strategies operate in an interactional context. How might the dialogue go if Chris and Pat used the principles of effective interpersonal communication and conflict management?

The Cast

Chris and Pat have been living together for the last four years and have been having problems throughout this time.

The Context

Pat is in the living room, reading. Chris enters.

Chris: It's me. Just came in to get my papers for the meeting tonight.

Pat: You're not going to another meeting, are you?

Chris: I told you last month that I had to give a lecture to the new managers on how to use some new research methods. What do you think I've been working on for the past two weeks? If you cared about what I do, you'd know that I was working on this lecture and that it was especially important that it go well.

Pat: What about shopping? We always do the shopping on Friday night.

Chris: The shopping will have to wait; this lecture is important.

Pat: Shopping is important, too, and so are the children and so is my job and so is the leak in the basement that's been driving me crazy for the past week and that I've asked you to look at every day since I found it.

Chris: Get off it. We can do the shopping anytime. Your job is fine and the children are fine and we'll get a plumber just as soon as I get the name from the Johnsons.

Pat: You always do that. You always think only you count, only you matter. Even when we were in school, your classes were the important ones; your papers, your tests were the important ones. Remember when I had that chemistry final and you had to have your history paper typed? We stayed up all night typing your paper. It's always been that way. You never give a damn about what's important in my life.

Chris: Look, just shut up. I just don't want to talk about it anymore. Forget it. I have to give the lecture and that's that.

Pat: The children were looking forward to going shopping. Johnny wanted to get a new record, and Jennifer needed to get a book for school. You promised them.

Chris: I didn't promise anyone anything. You promised them, and now you want me to take the blame. You know, you promise too much. You should only promise what you can deliver—like fidelity. Remember you promised to be faithful? Or did you forget that promise? Why don't you tell the kids that?

Pat: I thought we agreed not to talk about that. You know how bad I feel about what happened. And anyway, that was six months ago. What has that got to do with tonight?

Chris: You're the one who brought up promises, not me. You're always bringing up the past. You live in the past.

Pat: Well, at least the kids would have seen me enjoying myself—one enjoyable experience in eight years isn't too much, is it?

Chris: I'm leaving. Don't wait up.

This chapter examined interpersonal conflict, including key principles of interpersonal conflict, the distinction between content and relationship conflict, and conflict's positive and negative effects; the chapter explained a model of conflict resolution and described a variety of unproductive conflict strategies and their more productive counterparts.

1. Interpersonal conflict is disagreement between or among connected individuals. The positions in interpersonal conflicts are to some degree interrelated and incompatible.
2. Interpersonal conflict is inevitable and may focus on content and/or relationship issues.
3. Additional principles of interpersonal conflict are that conflict can be negative or positive; conflict is influenced by culture and gender; and conflict may be approached with different styles, each of which has different consequences.
4. Before the conflict, try to fight in private, be sure you're each ready to fight, know what you're fighting about, and avoid fighting about problems that cannot be solved.
5. A five-step model is often helpful in resolving conflict: Define the conflict, examine possible solutions, test a solution, evaluate the solution, and accept or reject the solution.
6. After the conflict, keep the conflict in perspective, challenge your negative feelings, and increase the exchange of rewards.
7. Unproductive and productive conflict strategies include win–lose and win–win approaches, avoidance and fighting actively, defensiveness and supportiveness, face-detracting and face-enhancing strategies, and verbal aggressiveness and argumentativeness.
8. To cultivate argumentativeness, treat disagreements objectively and avoid attacking the other person; reaffirm the other's sense of competence; avoid interrupting; stress equality and similarities; express interest in the other's position; avoid presenting your arguments too emotionally; and allow the other to save face.

This chapter also focused on the major skills for managing interpersonal conflict. Check those you wish to work on.

_____ 1. *Negatives and positives of conflict.* Approach conflict to minimize its negative aspects and to maximize the positive benefits of conflict and its resolution.

_____ 2. *Conflict, culture, and gender.* Approach conflict with the understanding of the cultural and gender differences in attitudes toward what constitutes conflict and toward how it should be pursued.

_____ 3. *Conflict styles.* Choose your conflict style carefully; each style has consequences. In relationship conflict, look for win–win solutions rather than solutions in which one person wins and the other loses.

_____ 4. *Content and relationship conflicts.* Analyze conflict messages in terms of content and relationship dimensions, and respond to each accordingly.

_____ 5. *Problem-solving conflicts.* Deal with interpersonal conflicts systematically as problems to be solved: Define the problem, examine possible solutions, test a solution, evaluate the solution, and accept or reject the solution.

_____ 6. *Active interpersonal conflict.* Engage in interpersonal conflict actively; be appropriately revealing, and listen to your partner.

_____ 7. *Talk, not force.* Talk about problems rather than using physical or emotional force.

_____ 8. *Supportive conflict.* Engage in conflict using a supportive approach, so as not to create defensiveness; avoid messages that evaluate or control, that are strategic or neutral, or that express superiority or certainty.

_____ 9. *Face-saving strategies.* Use strategies that allow your opponents to save face; avoid *beltlining,* or hitting opponents with attacks that they will have difficulty absorbing and will resent.

_____ 10. *Open expression in conflict.* Try to express your feelings openly rather than resorting to silence or avoidance.

_____ 11. *Present-focus conflict.* Focus your conflict resolution messages on the present; avoid gunnysacking, or dredging up old grievances and unloading these on the other person.

_____ 12. *Argumentativeness.* Avoid aggressiveness (attacking the other person's self-concept); instead, focus logically on the issues, emphasize finding solutions, and work to ensure that what is said will result in positive self-feelings for both individuals.

Match the terms dealing with interpersonal conflict with their definitions. Record the number of the definition next to the appropriate term.

_____ six hats technique

_____ accommodating

_____ argumentativeness

_____ gunnysacking

_____ beltline

_____ verbal aggressiveness

_____ compromising

_____ empathizing

_____ interpersonal conflict

_____ conflict resolution model

1. A disagreement between connected individuals.
2. An unproductive conflict strategy of storing up grievances and holding these in readiness to dump on the person with whom one is in conflict.
3. A person's level of tolerance for absorbing a personal attack.

4. A tendency or willingness to argue for a point of view.

5. A conflict strategy designed to maintain peace and harmony in the relationship.

6. Understanding the conflict from the other person's point of view.

7. A tendency to defend your position even at the expense of another person's feelings.

8. A set of procedures for dealing with conflict consisting of five steps: define the conflict, examine possible solutions, test a solution, evaluate the solution, and accept or reject the solution.

9. Varied ways of looking at a particular issue to give you different perspectives.

10. A style of conflict management concerned with both the self and the other.

Four for Discussion

1. One theory accounting for the male tendency to withdraw from conflict is that men experience flooding (a sense of being out of control, of extreme negative feelings of anger or rage) more easily and with less provocation than women (Gottman, 1993, 1994; Goleman, 1995a; Canary, Cupach, & Messman, 1995). Physiologically, flooding occurs at 10 heartbeats per minute more than normal and will remain high for some time, even after the conflict is "settled." The male tendency to withdraw from argument may, therefore, be due to a desire to reduce the effects of flooding. What do you think of this idea?

2. Are there certain types of issues that men are more likely to argue about than women? Are there certain types of issues that women are more likely to argue about? In one sentence, how would you describe the differences in the issues argued about by men and women?

3. How would you describe the conflicts in your family in terms of the productive and unproductive conflict strategies discussed in this chapter? How might your family's conflicts be resolved more effectively?

4. One of the most puzzling findings on relationship violence is that many victims interpret it as a sign of love. For some reason, they see being beaten or verbally abused as a sign that their partner is fully in love with them. Also, and equally puzzling, is that many victims blame themselves for the violence instead of blaming their partners (Gelles & Cornell, 1985). Why do you think this is so? What part does force or violence play in your own interpersonal relationship conflicts?

MyCommunicationLab Explorations

Explore www.mycommunicationlab.com to find two useful exercises on interpersonal conflict: (1) Analyzing a Conflict Episode and (2) How Do You Fight? Like a Man? Like a Woman?

Also visit MyCommunicationLab for other activities, study aids, and video clips on conflict and conflict resolution. Explore our research resources at www.researchnavigator.com.

Research Navigator.com

Glossaries

Glossary of Interpersonal Communication Concepts

abstract terms. Words that refer to concepts and ideas that have no physical dimensions (friendship, value, fear). *See also* **concrete terms.**

acculturation. The process by which your culture is modified or changed through contact with or exposure to another culture.

active listening. The process by which a listener expresses his or her understanding of the speaker's total message, including the verbal and nonverbal, the thoughts and feelings.

adaptors. Nonverbal behaviors that, when engaged in either in private or in public, serve some kind of need and occur in their entirety—for example, scratching one's head until the itch is relieved.

adjustment (principle of). The principle of verbal interaction that claims that effective communication depends on the extent to which communicators share the same system of signals.

affect displays. Movements of the facial area that convey emotional meaning such as anger, fear, and surprise.

affinity-seeking strategies. Behaviors designed to increase interpersonal attractiveness.

ageism. Discrimination based on age, usually against older people.

allness. The illogical assumption that all can be known or said about a given person, issue, object, or event.

alter-adaptors. Body movements you make in response to your current interactions; for example, crossing your arms over your chest when someone unpleasant approaches or moving closer to someone you like.

altercasting. Placing a person in a specific role for a specific purpose and asking that he or she assume the perspective of this specific role; for example, "As a professor of communication, please comment on. . . ."

ambiguity. The condition in which a message may be interpreted as having more than one meaning.

apprehension. See communication apprehension.

argumentativeness. A willingness to argue for a point of view, to speak one's mind. *Distinguished from* **verbal aggressiveness.**

artifactual messages. Messages that are conveyed by objects that are made by human hands. Art, color, clothing, jewelry, hairstyle, and smell would be examples of artifactual messages.

assertiveness. A willingness to stand up for your rights but with respect for the rights of others.

attention. The process of responding to a stimulus or stimuli; usually some consciousness of responding is implied.

attitude. A predisposition to respond for or against an object, person, or position.

attraction. The process by which one individual is emotionally drawn to another and finds that person satisfying to be with.

attraction theory. A theory holding that you develop relationships on the basis of three major factors: attractiveness (physical appearance and personality), proximity, and similarity.

attractiveness. A person's visual appeal and/or pleasantness in personality.

attribution. The processes by which we assign causation or motivation to a person's behavior.

avoidance. An unproductive conflict strategy in which you take mental or physical flight from the actual conflict.

backchanneling cues. Responses a listener makes to a speaker (while the speaker is speaking) but which do not ask for the speaking role; for example, interjections such as "I understand" or "You said what?"

barriers to intercultural communication. Physical or psychological factors that prevent or hinder effective communication.

behavioral synchrony. The similarity in the behavior, usually nonverbal (for example, postural stance or facial expressions) of two persons; generally taken as an indicator of liking.

belief. Confidence in the existence or truth of something; conviction.

beltlining. An unproductive conflict strategy in which one person hits the other at a vulnerable level—at the level at which the other person cannot withstand the blow.

blame. An unproductive conflict strategy in which we attribute the cause of the conflict to the other person or devote our energies to discovering who is the cause, avoiding talking about the issues at hand.

boundary marker. A **marker** that sets boundaries around or divides one person's territory from another's—for example, a fence.

breadth. The number of topics about which individuals in a relationship communicate.

censorship. Restrictions imposed on a person's right to produce, distribute, or receive various communications.

central marker. A **marker** or item that is placed in a territory to reserve it for a specific person—for example, the sweater thrown over a library chair to signal that the chair is taken.

certainty. An attitude of **closed-mindedness** that creates defensiveness among communicators. *Opposed to* **provisionalism.**

channel. The vehicle or medium through which signals are sent; for example, the vocal–auditory channel.

cherishing behaviors. Small behaviors you enjoy receiving from others, especially from your relational partner—for example, a kiss before you leave for work.

chronemics. The study of the communicative nature of time; of how a person's or a culture's treatment of time reveals something about the person or culture. Often divided into psychological and cultural time.

civil inattention. Polite ignoring of others (after a brief sign of awareness) so as not to invade their privacy.

closed-mindedness. An unwillingness to receive certain communication messages.

code. A set of symbols used to translate a message from one form to another.

coercive power. Power derived from an individual's ability to punish or to remove rewards from another person.

cognitive labeling theory. A theory of emotions that holds that emotional feelings begin with the occurrence of an event; you respond physiologically to the event, then you interpret the arousal (you in effect decide what it is you're feeling), and then you experience (give a name to) the emotion.

collectivist culture. A culture in which the group's goals are given greater importance than the individual's and in which, for example, benevolence, tradition, and conformity are given special emphasis. *Opposed to* **individualist culture.**

color communication. The use of color to communicate different meanings; each culture seems to define the meanings colors communicate somewhat differently.

communication. (1) The process or act of communicating; (2) the actual message or messages sent and received; (3) the study of the processes involved in the sending and receiving of messages.

communication apprehension. Fear or anxiety of communicating.

communicology. The study of communication, particularly the subsection concerned with human communication.

competence. "Language competence" is a speaker's ability to use the language; it is a knowledge of the elements and rules of the language. "Communication competence" generally refers both to the knowledge of communication and also to the ability to engage in communication effectively.

complementarity. A principle of **attraction** holding that you are attracted by qualities that you do not possess or wish to possess, and to people who are opposite or different from yourself. *Opposed to* **similarity.**

complementary relationship. A relationship in which the behavior of one person serves as the stimulus for the complementary behavior of the other; in complementary relationships, behavioral differences are maximized.

compliance-gaining strategies. Behaviors designed to gain the agreement of others, to persuade others to do as you wish.

compliance-resisting strategies. Behaviors directed at resisting the persuasive attempts of others.

computer-mediated communication. Communication between individuals that takes place through computer; usually refers to, for example, e-mail, chat groups, instant messaging, multiplayer video games.

concrete terms. Words that refer to objects, people, and happenings that you perceive with your senses of sight, smell, touch, hearing, or taste. *See also* **abstract terms.**

confidence. A quality of interpersonal effectiveness (and a factor in interpersonal **power**); a comfortable, at-ease feeling in interpersonal communication situations.

confirmation. A communication pattern that acknowledges another person's presence and indicates an acceptance of this person, this person's self-definition, and the relationship as defined or viewed by this other person. *Opposed to* **rejection** *and* **disconfirmation.**

conflict. A disagreement or difference of opinion; a form of competition in which one person tries to bring a rival to surrender; a situation in which one person's behaviors are directed at preventing something or at interfering with or harming another individual. *See also* **interpersonal conflict.**

congruence. A condition in which both verbal and nonverbal behaviors reinforce each other.

connotation. The feeling or emotional aspect of a word's meaning; generally viewed as consisting of evaluation (for example, good–bad), potency (strong–weak), and activity (fast–slow) dimensions. *Opposed to* **denotation.**

consistency. A tendency to maintain balance in your **perception** of messages or people; because of this process, you tend to see what you expect to see and to be uncomfortable when your perceptions run contrary to expectations.

contact. The first stage in **relationship development,** consisting of perceptual contact (you see or hear the person) and interactional contact (you talk with the person).

content and relationship dimensions. Two aspects to which messages may refer: the world external to both speaker and listener (content) and the connections existing between the individuals who are interacting (relationship).

context of communication. The physical, psychological, social, and temporal environment in which communication takes place.

conversation. Two-person communication, usually following five stages: opening, feedforward, business, feedback, and closing.

conversational management. The management of the way in which messages are exchanged in **conversation;** consists of procedures for opening, maintaining, repairing, and closing conversations.

conversational maxims. Principles that participants in **conversation** follow to ensure that the goal of the conversation is achieved.

conversational turns. The process of passing the speaker and listener roles back and forth during **conversation.**

cooperation. An interpersonal process by which individuals work together for a common end; the pooling of efforts to produce a mutually desired outcome.

cooperation (principle of). In **conversation,** an implicit agreement between speaker and listener to cooperate in trying to understand each other.

costs. Anything that you normally try to avoid—things you consider unpleasant or difficult. *Also see* **rewards.**

credibility. The degree to which people see a person as believable; competence, character, and charisma (dynamism) are major factors in credibility.

critical thinking. The process of logically evaluating reasons and evidence and reaching a judgment on the basis of this analysis.

culture. The lifestyle of a group of people; their values, beliefs, artifacts, ways of behaving, and ways of communicating. *Culture* includes everything that members of a social group have produced and developed—their language, ways of thinking, art, laws, and religion—and that is transmitted from one generation to another through communication rather than genes.

cultural assimilation. The process by which people leave behind their culture of origin and take on the values and beliefs of another culture; as when, for example, immigrants give up their native culture to become members of their new adopted culture.

cultural display. Signs that communicate a person's cultural identification, such as clothing or religious jewelry.

cultural display rules. Rules that identify what are and what are not appropriate forms of expression for members of the culture.

cultural rules. Rules that are specific to a given culture.

cultural sensitivity. An attitude and way of behaving in which you're aware of and acknowledge cultural differences.

culture shock. The reactions people experience at being in a culture very different from their own and from what they are used to.

cultural time. The meanings given to the ways time is treated in a particular culture.

date. An **extensional device** used to emphasize the notion of constant change and symbolized by a subscript: For example, John Smith$_{2000}$ is not John Smith$_{2007}$.

decoder. Something that takes a message in one form (for example, sound waves) and translates it into another form (for example, nerve impulses) from which meaning can be formulated. In human communication the decoder is the auditory mechanism; in electronic communication the decoder is, for example, the telephone earpiece. *Decoding* is the process of extracting a message from a code—for example, translating speech sounds into nerve impulses. *See also* **encoder.**

defensiveness. An attitude of an individual or an atmosphere in a group characterized by threats, fear, and domination; messages evidencing evaluation, control, strategy, neutrality, superiority, and certainty are thought to lead to defensiveness. *Opposed to* **supportiveness.**

delayed reaction. A reaction that a person consciously delays while analyzing the situation and evaluating possible choices for communication.

denial. One of the obstacles to the expression of emotion; the process by which you deny your emotions to yourself or to others.

denotation. The objective or descriptive aspect of a word's meaning; the meaning you'd find in a dictionary. *Opposed to* **connotation.**

depenetration. A reversal of penetration; a condition in which the **breadth** and **depth** of a relationship decrease.

depth. The degree to which the inner personality—the inner core of an individual—is penetrated in interpersonal interaction.

deterioration. In the stage model of relationships, the stage during which the connecting bonds between the partners weaken and the partners begin drifting apart.

dialogue. A form of **communication** in which each person is both speaker and listener; communication characterized by involvement, concern, and respect for the other person. *Opposed to* **monologue.**

direct speech. Speech in which the speaker's intentions are stated clearly and directly.

disclaimer. Statement that asks the listener to receive what you say without its reflecting negatively on you.

disconfirmation. The process by which someone ignores or denies the right of another individual even to define himself or herself. *Opposed to* **rejection** *and* **confirmation.**

dissolution. In the stage model of relationships, the termination or end of the relationship.

downward communication. Communication sent from the higher levels of a hierarchy to the lower levels—for example, messages sent by managers to workers or from deans to faculty members.

dyadic coalition. A two-person group formed from some larger group to achieve a particular goal.

dyadic communication. Two-person communication.

dyadic consciousness. An awareness on the part of the participants that an interpersonal relationship or pairing exists between them; distinguished from situations in which two individuals are together but do not see themselves as a unit or twosome.

dyadic effect. The tendency for the behaviors of one person to stimulate similar behaviors in the other interactant; often refers to the tendency of one person's self-disclosures to prompt the other also to self-disclose.

dyadic primacy. The significance or centrality of the two-person group, even when there are many more people interacting.

earmarker. A **marker** that identifies an item as belonging to a specific person—for example, a nameplate on a desk or initials on an attaché case.

effect. The outcome or consequence of an action or behavior; communication is assumed always to have some effect.

emblems. Nonverbal behaviors that directly translate words or phrases—for example, the signs for *OK* and *peace.*

emotion. The feelings we have—for example, our feelings of guilt, anger, or love.

emotional communication. The expression of feelings—for example, feelings of guilt, happiness, or sorrow.

empathy. A quality of interpersonal effectiveness that involves sharing others' feelings; an ability to feel or perceive things from others' points of view.

encoder. Something that takes a message in one form (for example, nerve impulses) and translates it into another form (for example, sound waves). In human communication the encoder is the speaking mechanism; in electronic communication the encoder is, for example, the telephone mouthpiece. *Encoding* is the process of putting a message into a code—for example, translating nerve impulses into speech sounds. *See also* **decoder.**

enculturation. The process by which culture is transmitted from one generation to another.

E-prime. A form of the language that omits the verb *to be* except when used as an auxiliary or in statements of existence.

equality. An attitude that recognizes that each individual in a communication interaction is equal, that no one is superior to any other; encourages **supportiveness.** *Opposed to* **superiority.**

equilibrium theory. A theory of **proxemics** holding that intimacy and physical closeness are positively related; as a relationship becomes more intimate, the individuals will maintain shorter distances between themselves.

equity theory. A theory claiming that people experience relational satisfaction when there is an equal distribution of rewards and costs between the two persons in the relationship.

et cetera (etc.). An **extensional device** used to emphasize the notion of infinite complexity; because you can never know all about anything, any statement about the world or an event must end with an explicit or implicit "etc."

ethics. The branch of philosophy that deals with the rightness or wrongness of actions; the study of moral values; in communication, the morality of message behavior.

ethnocentrism. The tendency to see others and their behaviors through your own cultural filters, often as distortions of your own behaviors; the tendency to evaluate the values and beliefs of your own culture more positively than those of another culture.

euphemism. A polite word or phrase used to substitute for some taboo or less polite term or phrase.

evaluation. A process whereby we place a value on some person, object, or event.

excuse. An explanation designed to lessen the negative consequences of something done or said.

expectancy violations theory. A theory of **proxemics** holding that people have a certain expectancy for space relationships. When that is violated (say, a person stands too close to you or a romantic partner maintains abnormally large distances from you), the relationship comes into clearer focus and you wonder why this "normal distance" is being violated.

expert power. Power that a person has because others believe the individual to have expertise or special knowledge.

expressiveness. A quality of **interpersonal effectiveness** that consists of genuine involvement in speaking and listening, conveyed verbally and nonverbally.

extensional devices. Linguistic devices proposed by Alfred Korzybski to make language a more accurate means for talking about the world. The extensional devices include **et cetera, date,** and **index.**

extensional orientation. A point of view in which primary consideration is given to the world of experience and only secondary consideration is given to labels. *Opposed to* **intensional orientation.**

face-saving messages. Communications that preserve or even enhance a person's self-image and self-respect.

facial feedback hypothesis. The hypothesis or theory that your facial expressions can produce physiological and emotional effects via a feedback mechanism.

facial management techniques. Techniques used to mask certain emotions and to emphasize others; for example, intensifying your expression of happiness to make a friend feel good about a promotion.

fact–inference confusion. A misevaluation in which a person makes an inference, regards it as a fact, and acts upon it as if it were a fact.

factual statement. A statement made by the observer after observation and limited to what is observed. *Opposed to* **inferential statement.**

family. A group of people with defined roles, recognition of mutual responsibilities, a shared history and future, shared living space, and rules for communicating.

fear appeal. The appeal to fear to persuade an individual or group of individuals to believe or to act in a certain way.

feedback. Information that is given back to the source. Feedback may come from the source's own messages (as when you hear what you're saying) or from the receiver(s)—in forms such as applause, yawning, puzzled looks, questions, letters to the editor of a newspaper, or increased or decreased subscriptions to a magazine. *See also* **negative feedback, positive feedback.**

feedforward. Information that is sent before a regular message, telling the listener something about what is to follow; messages that are prefatory to more central messages.

feminine culture. A culture that encourages both men and women to be modest, oriented to maintaining the quality of life, and tender. Feminine cultures emphasize the quality of life and so socialize their people to be modest and to emphasize close interpersonal relationships. *Opposed to* **masculine culture.**

flexibility. The ability to adjust communication strategies and skills on the basis of the unique situation.

focus group. An in-depth interview of a small group that aims to discover what people think about an issue or product.

force. An unproductive conflict strategy in which you try to win an argument by emotionally or physically overpowering the other person—either by threat or by actual behavior.

formal time. Temporal divisions that are measured objectively, such as seconds, minutes, hours, days, weeks, months, and years.

friendship. An interpersonal relationship between two persons that is mutually productive, established and maintained through perceived mutual free choice, and characterized by mutual positive regard.

fundamental attribution error. The tendency to overvalue and overweight the contribution of internal factors (i.e., a person's personality) to behavior, and to undervalue and underweight the contribution of external factors (i.e., the situation the person is in or the surrounding events).

gender display rules. The cultural rules that identify what are appropriate and what are not appropriate forms of expression for men and for women.

General Semantics. The study of the relationships among language, thought, and behavior.

gossip. Oral or written **communication** about someone not present, some third party, usually about matters that are private to this third party.

gunnysacking. An unproductive conflict strategy of storing up grievances—as if in a gunnysack—and holding them in readiness to dump on the other person in the conflict.

halo effect. The tendency to generalize a person's virtue or expertise from one area to other areas.

haptics. The study of touch or **tactile communication.**

heterosexism. Negative attitudes and beliefs about gay men and lesbians; the belief that all sexual behavior that is not heterosexual is unnatural and deserving of criticism and condemnation.

heterosexist language. Language that denigrates lesbians and gay men.

high-context culture. A culture in which much of the information in communication messages is left implied; it's "understood." Much information is considered to be in the context or in the person rather than explicitly coded in the verbal messages. **Collectivist cultures** are generally high context. *Opposed to* **low-context culture.**

high-power distance culture. Cultures in which power is concentrated in the hands of a few, and there's a great difference between the power held by these people and the power of the ordinary citizen. *See* **low-power distance culture.**

home field advantage. The increased power that comes from being in your own territory.

home territory. Territory in which an individual has a sense of intimacy and over which he or she exercises control—for example, a teacher's office.

hostile environment harassment. A type of **sexual harassment** in which verbal and nonverbal messages about sex make a worker uncomfortable.

illustrators. Nonverbal behaviors that accompany and literally illustrate verbal messages—for example, upward movements of the head and hand that accompany the verbal "It's up there."

I-messages. Messages in which the speaker accepts responsibility for personal thoughts and behaviors and states his or her point of view explicitly. *Opposed to* **you-messages.**

immediacy. A quality of **interpersonal effectiveness** that conveys a sense of contact and togetherness, a feeling of interest in and liking for the other person.

implicit personality theory. A theory of personality, complete with rules about what characteristics go with what other characteristics, that you maintain and through which you perceive others.

inclusion (principle of). The principle of verbal interaction holding that all members should be a part of (included in) the interaction.

index. An **extensional device** symbolized by a subscript and used to emphasize the assumption that no two things are the same; for example, even though two people may both be politicians, $politician_{1[Smith]}$ is not $politician_{2[Jones]}$.

indirect speech. Speech that hides the speaker's true intentions; speech in which requests and observations are made indirectly.

indiscrimination. A misevaluation that results when you categorize people, events, or objects into a particular class and respond to them only as members of the class; a failure to recognize that each individual is unique.

individualist culture. A culture in which the individual's rather than the group's goals and preferences are given greater importance. *Opposed to* **collectivist culture.**

inevitability. A principle of communication holding that communication cannot be avoided; all behavior in an interactional setting is communication.

inferential statement. A statement that can be made by anyone, is not limited to what is observed, and can be made at any time. *Opposed to* **factual statement.**

informal time. Temporal divisions that are approximate and that are referred to with such general terms as, for example, *forever, immediately, soon, right away, as soon as possible.*

information or **persuasion power.** Power that a person has because others see that individual as having significant information and the ability to communicate logically and persuasively.

information overload. A condition in which the amount or complexity of information is too great to be dealt with effectively by an individual, group, or organization.

in-group talk. Talk about a subject or in a vocabulary that some people present understand and others do not; has the effect of excluding those who don't understand.

insulation. A reaction to **territorial encroachment** in which you erect some sort of barrier between yourself and the invaders, such as a stone wall around your property, an unlisted phone number, or caller ID.

intensional orientation. A point of view in which primary consideration is given to the way things are labeled and only secondary consideration (if any) to the world of experience. *Opposed to* **extensional orientation.**

interaction management. A quality of **interpersonal effectiveness** in which the interaction is controlled and managed to the satisfaction of both parties; effectively managing conversational turns, fluency, and message consistency.

intercultural communication. Communication that takes place between persons of different cultures or between persons who have different cultural beliefs, values, or ways of behaving.

interpersonal communication. Communication between two persons or among a small group of persons and distinguished from public or mass communication; communication of a personal nature and distinguished from impersonal communication; communication between or among connected persons or those involved in a close relationship.

interpersonal competence. The knowledge of and the ability to communicate effectively in interpersonal interactions.

interpersonal conflict. Disagreement between two connected persons.

interpersonal effectiveness. The ability to accomplish interpersonal goals; interpersonal communication that is satisfying to both individuals.

interpersonal perception. The **perception** of people; the processes through which you interpret and evaluate people and their behavior.

intimacy. The closest interpersonal relationship; usually characterizes close **primary relationships.**

intimacy claims. Obligations incurred by virtue of being in a close and intimate relationship.

intimate distance. The closest distance in **proxemics,** ranging from touching to 18 inches.

intrapersonal communication. Communication with self.

involvement. The second stage in **relationship development,** in which you further advance the relationship, first testing each other and then intensifying your interaction.

irreversibility. A principle of communication holding that communication cannot be reversed; once something has been communicated, it cannot be uncommunicated.

jargon. The technical language of any specialized group, often a professional class, which is unintelligible to individuals not belonging to the group; shop talk. This glossary is an example of the jargon of part of the **communication** field.

Johari window. A diagram of the four selves (open, blind, hidden, and unknown).

kinesics. The study of the communicative dimensions of facial and bodily movements.

language. The rules of syntax, semantics, and phonology by which sentences are created and understood; *a language* refers to the sentences that can be created in any language, such as English, Bantu, or Italian.

leave-taking cues. Verbal and nonverbal signals that indicate a desire to terminate a conversation.

legitimate power. Power a person possesses because others believe he or she has a right—by virtue of his or her position—to influence or control their behavior.

linguistic relativity hypothesis. The theory that the language you speak influences your perceptions of the world and your behaviors and that therefore people speaking widely differing languages will perceive and behave differently.

listening. An active process of receiving aural stimuli consisting of five stages: receiving, understanding, remembering, evaluating, and responding.

love. A relationship with another person in which you feel closeness, caring, warmth, and excitement.

low-context culture. A culture in which most of the information in communication is explicitly stated in the verbal message rather than being left implied or assumed to be "understood." Low-context cultures are usually **individualist cultures.** *Opposed to* **high-context culture.**

low-power distance culture. Culture in which power is relatively evenly distributed throughout the citizenry. *See* **high-power distance culture.**

Machiavellianism. The belief that people can be manipulated easily; also, manipulative techniques or tactics one person uses to control another.

manipulation. An unproductive conflict strategy; a manipulative individual avoids engaging in open conflict but instead attempts to divert the conflict by being especially charming and getting the other person into a noncombative frame of mind.

manner principle. A principle of conversation that holds that speakers cooperate with listeners by being clear and by organizing their thoughts into meaningful and coherent patterns.

markers. Devices that signify that a certain territory belongs to a particular person. *See also* **boundary marker, central marker,** *and* **earmarker.**

masculine culture. A culture that views men as assertive, oriented to material success, and strong; such a culture views women, on the other hand, as modest, focused on the quality of life, and tender. Masculine cultures emphasize success and so socialize their people to be assertive, ambitious, and competitive. *Opposed to* **feminine culture.**

matching hypothesis. An assumption that you date and mate people who are comparable to yourself—who match you—in physical attractiveness.

meaningfulness. A principle of **perception** that assumes that the behavior of people is sensible, stems from some logical antecedent, and therefore is meaningful rather than meaningless.

mentoring relationship. A relationship in which an experienced individual helps train someone who is less experienced; for example, an accomplished teacher might mentor a younger teacher who is newly arrived or who has never taught before.

mere exposure hypothesis. The theory that repeated or prolonged exposure to a stimulus may result in a change in attitude toward the stimulus object, generally in the direction of increased positiveness.

message. Any signal or combination of signals that serves as a stimulus for a receiver. *See also* **stimulus.**

metacommunication. Communication about communication.

metalanguage. Language that refers to language.

metamessage. A message that makes reference to another message, such as "Did I make myself clear?" or "That's a lie."

micromomentary expressions. Extremely brief movements that are not consciously controlled or recognized and that are thought to be indicative of your true emotional state.

mindfulness. A state of awareness in which you are conscious of the logic and rationality of your behaviors and of the logical connections existing among elements.

mindlessness. A lack of conscious awareness of the logic or reasons behind your thoughts or behaviors.

mixed message. A message that communicates two different and often contradictory meanings; for example, a message that asks for two different (often incompatible) responses such as "leave me alone" and "show me more attention." Often, one meaning (usually the socially acceptable meaning) is communicated verbally and the other (usually the less socially acceptable meaning) nonverbally.

model. A representation of an object or process.

monochronic time orientation. A view of time in which things are done sequentially; one thing is scheduled at a time. *Opposed to* **polychronic time orientation.**

monologue. A form of **communication** in which one person speaks and the other listens; there's no real interaction among participants. *Opposed to* **dialogue.**

negative feedback. Feedback that serves a corrective function by informing the source that his or her message is not being received in the way intended. Looks of boredom, shouts of disagreement, letters critical of newspaper policy, and teachers' instructions on how better to approach a problem are examples of negative feedback and will (ideally) serve to redirect behavior. *See also* **positive feedback.**

network convergence. The blending or sharing of one individual's circle of friends with another person's circle of friends.

networking. Connecting with people who can help you accomplish a goal or help you find information related to your goal; for example, to your search for a job.

neutrality. A response pattern lacking in personal involvement; encourages defensiveness. *Opposed to* **empathy.**

noise. Anything that interferes with your receiving a message as the source intended the message to be received. Noise is present in communication to the extent that the message received is not the message sent.

nonallness. A point of view holding that you can never know all about anything and that what you know, say, or hear is only a part of what there is to know, say, or hear.

nonnegotiation. An unproductive conflict strategy in which an individual refuses to discuss the conflict or to listen to the other person.

nonverbal communication. Communication without words; communication by means of space, gestures, facial expressions, touching, vocal variation, or silence, for example.

nonverbal dominance. Nonverbal behavior through which one person achieves psychological dominance over another.

object-adaptors. Movements that involve manipulation of some object; for example, punching holes in a Styrofoam coffee cup, clicking a ball point pen, or chewing on a pencil.

object language. Language used to communicate about objects, events, and relations in the world (rather than about words as in **metalanguage**).

olfactory communication. Communication by smell.

openness. A quality of **interpersonal effectiveness** involving a person's willingness (1) to interact openly with others, self-disclosing as appropriate; (2) to react honestly to incoming stimuli; and (3) to own his or her own feelings and thoughts.

other talk. Talk about the listener or some third party. *Opposed to* **self talk.**

other-orientation. A quality of interpersonal effectiveness involving attentiveness, interest, and concern for the other person.

outing. The process whereby a person's affectional orientation is made public by another person without the gay man or lesbian's consent.

overattribution. The tendency to attribute to one or two characteristics most or even all of what a person does.

owning feelings. Taking responsibility for your own feelings instead of attributing them to others.

paralanguage. The vocal but nonverbal aspects of speech. Paralanguage consists of **voice qualities** (for example, pitch range, resonance, tempo); vocal characterizers (laughing or crying, yelling or whispering); vocal qualifiers (intensity, pitch height); and vocal segregates ("uh-uh" meaning "no," or "sh" meaning "silence").

pauses. Interruptions in the normally fluent stream of speech. Pauses are of two types: filled pauses (interruptions filled with such vocalizations as "er" or "um") and unfilled pauses (silences of unusually long duration).

peaceful relations principle. A principle of communication advising that you say only what preserves peaceful relationships with others.

perception. The process by which you become aware of objects and events through your senses.

perception checking. The process of verifying your understanding of some message, situation, or feeling.

perceptual accentuation. A process that leads you to see what you expect or want to see—for example, seeing people you like as better looking and smarter than people you don't like.

personal distance. The second closest distance in **proxemics,** ranging from 18 inches to 4 feet.

personal rejection. An unproductive conflict strategy in which you withhold love and affection and seek to win the argument by getting the other person to break down under this withdrawal.

persuasion. The process of influencing attitudes and behavior.

phatic communication. Communication that is primarily social; communication designed to open the channels of communication rather than to communicate something about the external world. "Hello" and "How are you?" in everyday interaction are examples.

physical noise. Interference that is external to both speaker and listener and that interferes with the physical transmission of a signal or message.

physiological noise. Interference within the sender or receiver of a message, such as visual impairments, hearing loss, articulation problems, and memory loss.

pitch. In relation to **voice qualities,** the highness or lowness of the vocal tone.

polarization. A form of fallacious reasoning in which only two extremes are considered; also referred to as black-and-white or either/or thinking or as a two-valued orientation.

politeness principle. A principle advising that you treat others respectfully.

polychronic time orientation. A view of time in which several things may be scheduled or engaged in at the same time. *Opposed to* **monochronic time orientation.**

positive feedback. Feedback that supports or reinforces the continuation of behavior along the same lines in which it is already proceeding—for example, applause during a speech, which encourages the speaker to continue speaking the same way. *See also* **negative feedback.**

positiveness. A characteristic of **interpersonal effectiveness** involving positive attitudes and the use of positive messages expressing these attitudes (as in complimenting others) along with acceptance and approval.

power. The ability to influence or control the behavior of another person; A has power over B when A can influence or control B's behavior; an inevitable part of interpersonal relationships.

power play. A consistent pattern of behavior in which one person tries to control the behavior of another.

pragmatic implication. An assumption that is logical (and therefore appears true) but is actually not necessarily true.

pragmatics. In interpersonal communication, an approach that focuses on communication behaviors and effects and on communication effectiveness.

primacy and recency. Giving more importance to that which occurs first (primacy) or to that which occurs last or more recently (recency).

primary affect displays. The communication of the six primary emotions: happiness, surprise, fear, anger, sadness, and disgust/ contempt.

primary territory. Areas that you consider your exclusive preserve—for example, your room or office.

process. Ongoing activity; communication is referred to as a process to emphasize that it's always changing, always in motion.

protection theory. A theory of **proxemics** holding that people establish a body-buffer zone to protect themselves from unwanted closeness, touching, or attack.

provisionalism. An attitude of open-mindedness that leads to the development of a supportive relationship and atmosphere. *Opposed to* **certainty.**

proxemics. The study of the communicative function of space; the study of how people unconsciously structure their space—the distance between people in their interactions, the organization of space in homes and offices, and even the design of cities.

proximity. As a principle of **perception,** the tendency to perceive people or events that are physically close as belonging together or representing some unit; physical closeness—one of the qualities influencing interpersonal **attraction.**

psychological noise. Mental interference in the speaker or listener, such as preconceived ideas, wandering thoughts, biases and prejudices, closed-mindedness, and extreme emotionalism.

psychological time. An emphasis on or orientation toward past, present, or future time; varies from person to person.

public distance. The farthest distance in **proxemics,** ranging from 12 feet to 25 feet or more.

public territory. Areas that are open to all people—for example, restaurants or parks.

punctuation of communication. The breaking up of continuous communication sequences into short sequences with identifiable beginnings and endings or stimuli and responses.

pupil dilation. The extent to which the pupil of the eye widens; generally, large pupils indicate positive reactions.

pupillometrics. The study of communication messages reflected by changes in the size of the pupils of the eyes.

Pygmalion effect. The condition in which you make a prediction of success, act as if it is true, and thereby make it come true (as when, for example, acting toward students as if they'll be successful influences them to become successful); a type of **self-fulfilling prophecy.**

quality principle. A principle of conversation that holds that speakers cooperate with listeners by saying what they think is true and by not saying what they think is false.

quantity principle. A principle of conversation that holds that speakers cooperate with listeners by being only as informative as necessary to communicate their intended meanings.

quid pro quo harassment. A type of **sexual harassment** in which employment opportunities (as in hiring and promotion) are made dependent on the granting of sexual favors.

racism. Negative attitudes and beliefs that individuals or a society as a whole hold about specific ethnic groups.

racist language. Language that denigrates, demeans, or is derogatory toward members of a particular ethnic group.

rate. In relation to **voice qualities,** the speed at which you speak, generally measured in words per minute.

receiver. Any person or thing that takes in messages. Receivers may be individuals listening to or reading a message, a group of persons hearing a speech, a scattered television audience, or machines that store information.

referent power. Power that a person possesses because others desire to identify with or be like that individual.

regulators. Nonverbal behaviors that regulate, monitor, or control the communications of another person.

rejection. A response to an individual that acknowledges the person but expresses disagreement. *Opposed to* **confirmation** *and* **disconfirmation.**

relational dialectics theory. A theory that describes relationships as defined by a series of competing opposite desires or motivations, such as the desires for autonomy and belonging, for novelty and predictability, and for closedness and openness.

relation principle. A principle of conversation that holds that speakers cooperate with listeners by talking about what is relevant and by not talking about what isn't.

relationship communication. Communication between or among intimates or those in close relationships; the term is used by some theorists as synonymous with **interpersonal communication.**

relationship development. The initial or beginning stage of a relationship; the stage at which two people begin to form an interpersonal relationship.

relationship maintenance. A condition of relationship stability in which the relationship does not progress or deteriorate significantly; a continuation as opposed to a dissolution (or an intensification) of a relationship.

relationship messages. Messages that comment on the relationship between the speakers rather than on matters external to them.

repair. In the stage model of relationships, a stage in which one or both parties seek to improve the relationship.

resemblance. As a principle of **perception,** the tendency to perceive people or events that are similar in appearance as belonging together.

response. Any bit of overt or covert behavior.

reward power. Power derived from an individual's ability to give another person what that person wants or to remove what that person wants removed.

rewards. Anything that you want, that you enjoy, and that you'd be willing to incur **costs** to obtain.

role. The part an individual plays in a group; an individual's function or expected behavior.

rules theory. A theory that describes relationships as interactions governed by a series of rules that a couple agrees to follow. When the rules are followed, the relationship is maintained; when they are broken, the relationship experiences difficulty.

schemata. Ways of organizing perceptions; mental templates or structures that help you organize the millions of items of information you come into contact with every day as well as those you already have in memory; general ideas about groups of people or individuals, about yourself, or about types of social roles. The word *schemata* is the plural of *schema.*

script. A type of schema; an organized body of information about some action, event, or procedure. A script provides a general idea of how some event should play out or unfold, the rules governing the events and their sequence.

secondary territory. An area that does not belong to you but that you've occupied and that is therefore associated with you—for example, the seat you normally take in class.

selective attention. The tendency to attend to those things that you want to see or that you expect to see.

selective exposure. The tendency to expose your senses to certain things and not others, to actively seek out information that supports your beliefs and to actively avoid information that contradicts these beliefs.

selective perception. The tendency to perceive certain things and not others; includes **selective attention** and **selective exposure.**

self-denigration principle. A principle of communication advising you to put the other person above yourself; to praise the other person rather than taking credit yourself.

self-talk. Talk about yourself. *Opposed to* **other talk.**

semantics. The area of language study concerned with meaning.

self-acceptance. Being satisfied with yourself, your virtues and vices, your abilities and limitations.

self-adaptors. Movements that usually satisfy a physical need, especially to make you more comfortable; for example, scratching your head to relieve an itch, moistening your lips because they feel dry, or pushing your hair out of your eyes.

self-attribution. A process through which you seek to account for and understand the reasons and motivations for your own behaviors.

self-awareness. The degree to which you know yourself.

self-concept. Your self-image, the view you have of who you are.

self-disclosure. The process of revealing something about yourself to another; usually refers to information that you'd normally keep hidden.

self-esteem. The value (usually, the positive value) you place on yourself; your self-evaluation.

self-fulfilling prophecy. The situation in which you make a prediction or prophecy and fulfill it yourself—for example, expecting a person to be hostile, you act in a hostile manner toward this person, and in doing so elicit hostile behavior in the person, thus confirming your prophecy that the person will be hostile.

self-monitoring. Manipulating the image you present to others in interpersonal interactions so as to create the most favorable impression of yourself.

self-serving bias. A bias that operates in the self-attribution process, leading you to take credit for the positive consequences of your behaviors and to deny responsibility for the negative consequences.

semantic noise. Interference created when a speaker and listener have different meaning systems; such noise can include language or dialectical differences, the use of jargon or overly complex terms, or ambiguous or overly abstract terms whose meanings can be easily misinterpreted.

sexism. Negative attitudes and beliefs about a particular gender; prejudicial attitudes and beliefs about men or women based on rigid beliefs about gender roles.

sexist language. Language derogatory to members of one gender, generally women.

sexual harassment. Unsolicited and unwanted verbal or nonverbal sexual messages.

sharpening. A process of message distortion in which the details of messages, when repeated, are crystalized and heightened.

shyness. A condition of discomfort and uneasiness in interpersonal situations.

signal and noise, relativity of. The principle of verbal interaction that holds that what is signal (meaningful) and what is noise (interference) is relative to the communication analyst, the participants, and the context.

signal reaction. A conditioned response to a signal; a response to some signal that is immediate rather than delayed. *Opposed to* **delayed reaction.**

signal-to-noise ratio. A measure of the relationship between meaningful information (signal) and interference (noise).

silence. The absence of vocal communication; often misunderstood to refer to the absence of communication.

silencers. Unproductive conflict strategies (such as crying) that literally silence your opponent.

similarity. A principle of **attraction** holding that you're attracted to qualities similar to your own and to people who are similar to you. *Opposed to* **complementarity.**

slang. Language used by special groups, often not considered standard in general society.

social comparison. The processes by which you compare yourself (for example, your abilities, opinions, and values) with others and then assess and evaluate yourself on the basis of the comparison; one of the sources of **self-concept.**

social distance. The next-to-farthest distance in **proxemics,** ranging from 4 feet to 12 feet; the distance at which business is usually conducted.

social exchange theory. A theory hypothesizing that you cultivate profitable relationships (those in which your rewards are greater than your costs) and that you avoid or terminate unprofitable relationships (those in which your costs exceed your rewards).

social penetration theory. A theory concerned with relationship development from the superficial to the intimate levels (**depth**) and from few to many areas of interpersonal interaction (**breadth**). *See also* **depenetration.**

source. Any person or thing that creates messages; for example, an individual speaking, writing, or gesturing, or a computer solving a problem.

speech. Messages conveyed via a vocal–auditory channel.

spontaneity. The communication pattern in which you say what you're thinking without attempting to develop strategies for control; encourages **supportiveness.** *Opposed to* **strategy.**

stability. Principle of **perception** that states that your perceptions of things and of people are relatively consistent with your previous conceptions.

static evaluation. An orientation that fails to recognize that the world is constantly changing; an attitude that sees people and events as fixed rather than as ever changing.

status. The level a person occupies in a hierarchy relative to the levels occupied by others. In the United States occupation, financial position, age, and educational level are significant determinants of social status.

stereotype. In communication, a fixed impression of a group of people through which we then perceive specific individuals. Stereotypes are most often negative but may also be positive.

stimulus. Any external or internal change that impinges on or arouses an organism.

stimulus–response models of communication. Models of communication that assume that the process of communication is linear, beginning with a stimulus that then leads to a response.

strategy. The use of some plan for control of other members of a communication interaction, often through **manipulation;** often encourages **defensiveness.** *Opposed to* **spontaneity.**

subjectivity. The principle of **perception** that refers to the fact that your perceptions are not objective but are influenced by your wants and needs, expectations and predictions.

superiority. A point of view or attitude that assumes that others are not equal to yourself; encourages **defensiveness.** *Opposed to* **equality.**

supportiveness. An attitude of an individual or an atmosphere in a group that is characterized by **openness,** absence of fear, and a genuine feeling of **equality.** *Opposed to* **defensiveness.**

symmetrical relationship. A relation between two or more persons in which one person's behavior serves as a stimulus for the same type of behavior in the other person(s); for example, a relationship in which anger in one person encourages anger in the other, or in which a critical comment by one person leads the other to respond in kind.

taboo. Forbidden; culturally censored; frowned upon by "polite society." Taboos may include entire topics as well as specific words—for example, death, sex, certain forms of illness, and various words denoting sexual activities and excretory functions.

tactile communication. Communication by touch; communication received by the skin.

temporal communication. The messages that your time orientation and treatment of time communicate.

territorial encroachment. The trespassing on, use of, or appropriation of one person's territory by another.

territoriality. A possessive or ownership reaction to an area of space or to particular objects.

theory. A general statement or principle applicable to related phenomena.

touch avoidance. The tendency to avoid touching and being touched by others.

transactional view. A view of communication as an ongoing process in which all elements are interdependent and influence one another.

uncertainty reduction theory. Theory that as interpersonal relationships develop, uncertainty is reduced; **relationship development** is seen as a process of reducing uncertainty about each other.

universal of interpersonal communication. A feature of communication common to all interpersonal communication acts.

unproductive conflict strategies. Ways of engaging in conflict that generally prove counterproductive; for example, avoidance, force, blame, silencers, gunnysacking, manipulation, personal rejection, and fighting below the belt.

upward communication. Communication sent from the lower levels of a hierarchy to the upper levels—for example, from line worker to manager or from faculty member to dean.

value. Relative worth of an object; a quality that makes something desirable or undesirable; ideal or custom about which we have emotional responses, whether positive or negative.

verbal aggressiveness. A method of arguing in which one person attacks the other person's **self-concept.**

visual dominance. The use of your eyes to maintain a superior or dominant position; for example, when making an especially important point, you might look intently at the other person.

voice qualities. Aspects of **paralanguage**—specifically, pitch range, lip control, glottis control, pitch control, articulation control, rhythm control, resonance, and tempo.

volume. In relation to **voice qualities,** the relative loudness of the voice.

you-messages. Messages in which you deny responsibility for your own thoughts and behaviors; messages that attribute your **perception** to another person; messages of blame. *Opposed to* **I-messages.**

Glossary of Interpersonal Communication Skills

abstractions. Use both abstract and concrete language when describing or explaining.

accommodation. Accommodate to the speaking style of your listeners in moderation. Too much mirroring of the other's style may appear manipulative.

active and inactive listening. Be an active listener: Paraphrase the speaker's meaning, express understanding of the speaker's feelings, and ask questions when necessary.

active interpersonal conflict. Engage in interpersonal conflict actively; be appropriately revealing, and listen to your partner.

advantages and disadvantages of relationships. In evaluating, entering, or dissolving relationships, consider both the advantages and the disadvantages.

allness. Avoid allness statements; they invariably misstate the reality and will often offend the other person.

analyzing your perceptions. Increase accuracy in interpersonal perception by identifying the influence of your physical and emotional states and making sure that you're not drawing conclusions from too little information.

anger management. Calm down as best you can; then consider your communication options and the relevant communication skills for expressing your feelings.

appreciating cultural differences. Look at cultural differences not as deviations or deficiencies but as the differences they are. Recognizing different ways of doing things, however, does not necessarily mean accepting them.

appropriateness of self-disclosure. When thinking of disclosing, consider the legitimacy of your motives, the appropriateness of the disclosure, the listener's responses (is the dyadic effect operating?), and the potential burdens such disclosures might impose.

argumentativeness. Avoid aggressiveness (attacking the other person's self-concept); instead, focus logically on the issues, emphasize finding solutions, and work to ensure that what is said will result in positive self-feelings for both individuals.

artifactual communication. Use artifacts (for example, color, clothing, body adornment, space decoration) to communicate desired messages.

body movements. Use body and hand gestures to reinforce your verbal messages.

channel. Assess your channel options (for example, face-to-face, e-mail, leaving a voicemail message) before communicating important messages.

checking perceptions. Increase accuracy in perception by: (1) describing what you see or hear and the meaning you assign to it and (2) asking the other person if your perceptions are accurate.

communicating assertively. Describe the problem, say how the problem affects you, propose solutions, confirm your understanding, and reflect on your own assertiveness.

communicating power. Avoid powerless message forms such as hesitations, excessive intensifiers, disqualifiers, tag questions, one-word answers, self-critical statements, overly polite statements, and vulgar and slang expressions.

communication apprehension management. To reduce anxiety acquire necessary communication skills and experiences, focus on prior successes, reduce unpredictability, and put apprehension in perspective.

communication options. In light of the inevitability, irreversibility, and unrepeatability of messages, assess your communication options before communicating.

confirmation. When you wish to be confirming, acknowledge (verbally and/or nonverbally) others in your group and their contributions.

conflict styles. Chose your conflict style carefully; each style has consequences. In relationship conflict, look for win–win solutions rather than solutions in which one person wins and the other loses.

conflict, culture, and gender. Approach conflict with an understanding of the cultural and gender differences in attitudes toward what constitutes conflict and toward how it should be pursued.

connotative meanings. Clarify your connotative meanings if you have any concern that your listeners might misunderstand you; as a listener, ask questions if you have doubts about the speaker's connotations.

content and relationship. Listen to both the content and the relationship aspects of messages, distinguish between them, and respond to both.

content and relationship conflicts. Analyze conflict messages in terms of content and relationship dimensions, and respond to each accordingly.

context adjustment. Adjust your messages to the physical, cultural, social–psychological, and temporal context.

conversational maxims. Follow (generally) the basic maxims of conversation, such as the maxims of quantity, quality, relations, manner, and politeness.

conversational rules. Observe the general rules for conversation (for example, keeping speaking turns relatively short and avoiding interrupting), but break them when there seems logical reason to do so.

conversational turns. Maintain relatively short conversational turns; after taking your turn, pass the speaker's turn to another person nonverbally or verbally.

cultural differences in listening. Be especially flexible when listening in a multicultural setting, realizing that people from other cultures give different listening cues and may operate with different rules for listening.

cultural identifiers. Use cultural identifiers that are sensitive to the desires of others; when appropriate, make clear the cultural identifiers you prefer.

cultural influences. Communicate with an understanding that culture influences communication in all its forms.

cultural influences on interpersonal relationships. Communicate with a clear recognition of the influence of culture on all types of relationships, encouraging some and discouraging others.

cultural sensitivity. Increase your cultural sensitivity by learning about different cultures, recognizing and facing your fears, recognizing relevant differences, and becoming conscious of the cultural rules of other cultures.

culture and perception. Increase accuracy in perception by learning as much as you can about the cultures of those with whom you interact.

dating statements. Date your statements to avoid thinking of the world as static and unchanging. Reflect the inevitability of change in your messages.

deciding to self-disclose. Consider the potential benefits (for example, self-knowledge, increased communication effectiveness, and physiological health) as well as the potential personal, relationship, and professional risks.

disclaimers. Use disclaimers if you feel you might be misunderstood. But avoid them when they're not necessary; too many disclaimers can make you appear unprepared or unwilling to state an opinion.

disconfirming language. Avoid sexist, heterosexist, racist, and ageist language, which is disconfirming and insulting and invariably creates communication barriers.

emotional communication. Communicate emotions effectively: (1) confront the obstacles to emotional expression; (2) describe your feelings, identifying; the reasons behind them; (3) anchor feelings to the present, and (4) own your feelings and messages.

emotional display. Express emotions and interpret the emotions of others in light of the cultural rules dictating what is and what isn't "appropriate."

emotionality in interpersonal communication. Recognize the inevitable emotionality in your thoughts and feelings, and include emotion as appropriate in your verbal and nonverbal messages.

emotional understanding. Identify and describe emotions (both positive and negative) clearly and specifically. Learn the vocabulary of emotional expression.

empathic and objective listening. Punctuate the interaction from the speaker's point of view, engage in dialogue, and seek to understand the speaker's thoughts and feelings.

empathic conflict. Engage in conflict with empathy rather than blame. Also, express this empathy ("I can understand how you must have felt").

empathy. Communicate empathy when appropriate: Resist evaluating the person, focus on the person, express active involvement through facial expressions and gestures, reflect back the feelings you think are being expressed, self-disclose, and address mixed messages.

ethnocentric thinking. Recognize your own ethnocentric thinking and be aware of how it influences your verbal and nonverbal messages.

evaluating. Try first to understand fully what the speaker means; then look to identify any biases or self-interests that might lead the speaker to give an unfair presentation.

expressiveness. Communicate active involvement by using active listening, addressing mixed messages, using I-messages, and using appropriate variations in paralanguage and gestures.

eye movements. Use eye movements to seek feedback, exchange conversational turns, signal the nature of your relationship, or compensate for increased physical distance.

face-saving strategies. Use strategies that allow your opponents to save face; avoid **beltlining,** or hitting opponents with attacks that they will have difficulty absorbing and will resent.

facial messages. Use facial expressions to communicate involvement. In listening, look to the facial expressions of others as cues to their emotions and meaning.

facts and inferences. Distinguish facts (verifiably true past events) from inferences (guesses or hypotheses), and act on inferences with tentativeness.

feedback. Listen to both verbal and nonverbal feedback—from yourself and from others—and use these cues to help you adjust your messages.

feedforward. Use feedforward when you feel your listener needs background or when you want to ease into a particular topic, such as bad news.

flexibility. Because no two communication situations are identical, because everything is in a state of flux, and because everyone is different, cultivate flexibility and adjust your communication to the unique situation.

friendships. Establish friendships to help serve such needs as utility, ego support, stimulation, and security. At the same time, seek to serve your friends' similar needs.

fundamental attribution error. Avoid the fundamental attribution error, whereby you attribute someone's behavior solely to internal factors while minimizing or ignoring situational forces.

gender differences in listening. Understand that in general, women give more cues that they're listening and appear more supportive in their listening than men.

giving space. Give others the space they need. Look to the other person for any signs of spatial discomfort.

high- and low-context cultures. Adjust your messages and your listening in light of the differences between high- and low-context cultures.

I-messages. Use I-messages when communicating your feelings; take responsibility for your own feelings rather than attributing them to others.

immediacy. Maintain immediacy through close physical distances and eye contact and by smiling, using the other person's name, and focusing on the other's remarks.

implicit personality theory. Bring your implicit personality theory to your mindful state to subject your perceptions and conclusions to logical analysis.

increasing assertiveness. Increase assertiveness by analyzing the assertive messages of others, rehearsing assertive messages, and communicating assertively.

indirect messages. Use indirect messages when a more direct style might prove insulting or offensive, but be aware that indirect messages also may create misunderstanding.

indiscrimination. Treat each situation and each person as unique (when possible) even when they're covered by the same label. Index key concepts.

individualist and collectivist cultures. Adjust your messages and your listening with an awareness of differences between individualist and collectivist cultures.

initial impressions. Guard against drawing impressions too quickly or from too little information and using initial impressions as filters; such filters can prevent you from forming more accurate perceptions on the basis of more information.

intensional orientation. Avoid intensional orientation. Look to people and things first and to labels second.

interaction management. Speak in relatively short conversational turns, avoid long and/or frequent pauses, and use verbal and nonverbal messages that are consistent.

intercultural communication. Become mindful of (1) differences between yourself and people who are culturally different, (2) differences within other cultural groups, and (3) cultural differences in meanings.

listening to the feelings of others. Empathize, focus on the other person, and encourage the person to explore his or her feelings.

making excuses. Repair conversational problems by offering excuses that demonstrate understanding, acknowledge your responsibility, acknowledge your regret, request forgiveness, and make clear that this will never happen again.

managing relationship dissolution. Break the loneliness–depression cycle, take time out, bolster self-esteem, seek support from nourishing others, and avoid repeating negative patterns.

masculine and feminine cultures. Adjust your messages and your listening to allow for differences in cultural masculinity and femininity.

meanings depend on context. Look at the context for cues as to how you should interpret the meanings of messages.

meanings in people. When you are deciphering meaning, the best source is the person; meanings are in people. When in doubt, find out—from the source.

message overload. Combat message overload by using and disposing of messages as they come to you, organizing, getting rid of extra copies, and distinguishing between messages to save and messages to throw away.

metacommunication. Metacommunicate when you want to clarify the way you're talking or what you're talking about by, for example, giving clear feedforward and paraphrasing your complex messages.

mindfulness. Increase your mindfulness by creating and recreating categories and being open to new information and points of view; also, beware of relying too heavily on first impressions.

negatives and positives of conflict. Approach conflict to minimize its negative aspects and to maximize the positive benefits of conflict and its resolution.

networking. Establish a network of relationships to provide insights into issues relevant to your personal and professional life, and be willing to lend your expertise to others.

noise management. Reduce physical, physiological, psychological, and semantic noise as best you can; use repetition and restatement and, when in doubt, ask if you're clear.

nonjudgmental and critical listening. Keep an open mind, avoid filtering out difficult messages, and recognize your own biases. When listening to make judgments, listen extra carefully, ask questions when in doubt, and check your perceptions before criticizing.

nonverbal communication and culture. Interpret the nonverbal cues of others with an awareness of the other person's cultural meanings (insofar as you can).

open expression in conflict. Try to express your feelings openly rather than resorting to silence or avoidance.

openness. Increase openness when appropriate by self-disclosing, responding spontaneously and honestly to those with whom you're interacting, and owning your own feelings and thoughts.

other orientation. Acknowledge the importance of the other person: use focused eye contact and appropriate facial expressions; smile, nod, and lean toward the other person.

overattribution. Avoid overattribution; rarely is any one factor an accurate explanation of complex human behavior.

packaging. Make your verbal and nonverbal messages consistent; inconsistencies often create uncertainty and misunderstanding.

paralanguage. Vary paralinguistic features to communicate nuances of meaning and to add interest and color to your messages.

perceptual shortcuts. Be mindful of your perceptual shortcuts so that they don't mislead you and result in inaccurate perceptions.

polarization. Avoid thinking and talking in extremes by using middle terms and qualifiers. But remember that too many qualifiers may make you appear unsure of yourself.

positiveness. Communicate positiveness by expressing your own satisfaction with the interaction and by complimenting others.

power distance. Adjust your messages and listening on the basis of the power-distance orientation of the culture in which you find yourself.

power plays. Respond to power plays with cooperative strategies: Express your feelings, describe the behavior to which you object, and state a cooperative response.

present-focus conflict. Focus your conflict resolution messages on the present; avoid gunnysacking, or dredging up and unloading old grievances.

problem-solving conflicts. Deal with interpersonal conflicts systematically as problems to be solved: Define the problem, examine possible solutions, test a solution, evaluate the solution, and accept or reject the solution.

receiving. Focus attention on both the verbal and the nonverbal messages; both communicate essential parts of the total meaning.

reducing uncertainty. Use passive, active, and interactive strategies to reduce uncertainty.

relationship messages. Formulate messages that are appropriate to the stage of the relationship. Also, listen to messages from relationship partners that may reveal differences in perceptions about your relationship stage.

relationship repair. Recognize the problem, engage in productive conflict resolution, pose possible solutions, affirm each other, integrate solutions into normal behavior, and take risks as appropriate.

relationship violence. Learn to recognize the patterns of behavior associated with relationship violence and become familiar with the strategies for dealing with it.

remembering. Identify the central ideas of a message, summarize the message in an easier-to-retain form, and repeat ideas (aloud or to yourself) to help you remember.

responding. Express support for the speaker by using I-messages instead of you-messages.

responding to others' disclosures. Listen actively, support the discloser, and keep the disclosures confidential.

romantic workplace relationships. Establish romantic relationships at work with a clear understanding of the potential problems.

self-awareness. Increase self-awareness by listening to others, increasing your open self, and seeking out information to reduce blind spots.

self-concept. See yourself, as objectively as you can, through the eyes of others; compare yourself to similar (and admired) others; examine the influences of culture; and observe and evaluate your own message behaviors.

self-esteem. Increase your self-esteem by attacking self-destructive beliefs, seeking out nourishing people, working on projects that will result in success, and securing affirmation.

self-fulfilling prophecy. Take a second look at your perceptions when they correspond very closely to your initial expectations; the self-fulfilling prophecy may be at work.

self-serving bias. Become mindful of giving too much weight to internal factors (when explaining your positives) and too little weight to external factors (when explaining your negatives).

sexual harassment management. Talk to the harasser; if this doesn't stop the behavior, then consider collecting evidence, using appropriate channels within the organization, and filing a complaint.

sexual harassment messages. Avoid behaviors that are sexual in nature, that might be considered unreasonable, that are severe or pervasive, and that are unwelcome and offensive.

silence. Examine silence for meanings just as you would eye movements or body gestures.

spatial and proxemic conversational distances. Maintain distances that are comfortable and that are appropriate to the situation and to your relationship with the other person.

stereotypes. Focus on the individual rather than on the individual's membership in one group or another.

supportive conflict. Engage in conflict using a supportive approach, so as not to create defensiveness; avoid messages that evaluate or control, that are strategic or inappropriately neutral, or that express superiority or certainty.

surface and depth listening. Focus on both verbal and nonverbal messages, on both content and relationship messages, and on statements that refer back to the speaker. At the same time, do not avoid the surface or literal meaning.

talk, not force. Talk about problems rather than using physical or emotional force.

time cues. Be alert for time cues on the part of the person with whom you're interacting. Be especially sensitive to the person's leave-taking cues—remarks such as "It's getting late" or glances at his or her watch.

touch and touch avoidance. Respect the touch-avoidance tendencies of others; pay special attention to cultural and gender differences in touch preferences.

turn-taking cues. Respond to both the verbal and the nonverbal conversational turn-taking cues given you by others, and make your own cues clear to others.

understanding. Relate new information to what you already know, ask questions, and paraphrase what you think the speaker said to make sure you understand.

Bibliography

Bibliography

Abel, G. G., & Harlow, N. (2001). *The stop child molestation book.* Xlibris. (www.stopchildmolestation.org/pdfs/study.pdf).

Acor, A. A. (2001). Employers' perceptions of persons with body art and an experimental test regarding eyebrow piercing (Doctoral dissertation, Marquette University, 2001). *Dissertation Abstracts International: Section B. The Sciences and Engineering, 61,* 3885.

Adrianson, L. (2001). Gender and computer-mediated communication: Group processes in problem solving. *Computers in Human Behavior, 17,* 71–94.

Albada, K. F. (2002). Interaction appearance theory: Changing perceptions of physical attractiveness through social interaction. *Communication Theory, 12* (February), 8–40.

Albas, D. C., McCluskey, K. W., & Albas, C. A. (1976, December). Perception of the emotional content of speech: A comparison of two Canadian groups. *Journal of Cross-Cultural Psychology, 7,* 481–490.

Albert, R., & Nelson, G. L. (1993, Winter). Hispanic/Anglo American differences in attributions to paralinguistic behavior. *International Journal of Intercultural Relations, 17,* 19–40.

Alberti, R. (Ed.). (1977). *Assertiveness: Innovations, applications, issues.* San Luis Obispo, CA: Impact.

Alessandra, T. (1986). *How to listen effectively. Speaking of Success* (videotape series). San Diego, CA: Levitz Sommer Productions.

Allen, J. L., Long, K. M., O'Mara, J., & Judd, B. B. (2003, September–December). Verbal and nonverbal orientations toward communication and the development of intracultural and intercultural relationships. *Journal of Intercultural Communication Research, 32,* 129–160.

Alsop, R. (2004, September 22). How to get hired: We asked recruiters what M.B.A. graduates are doing wrong. Ignore their advice at your peril. *Wall Street Journal,* p. R8.

Altman, I. (1975). *The environment and social behavior.* Monterey, CA: Brooks/Cole.

Altman, I., & Taylor, D. (1973). *Social penetration: The development of interpersonal relationships.* New York: Holt, Rinehart & Winston.

Amato, P. R. (1994). The impact of divorce on men and women in India and the United States. *Journal of Comparative Family Studies, 25,* 207–221.

Andersen, P. (1991). Explaining intercultural differences in nonverbal communication. In Larry A. Samovar & Richard E. Porter (Eds.), *Intercultural communication: A reader* (6th ed., pp. 286–296). Belmont, CA: Wadsworth.

Andersen, P. A., & Leibowitz, K. (1978). The development and nature of the construct touch avoidance. *Environmental Psychology and Nonverbal Behavior, 3,* 89–106.

Anderson, C. J., & Fisher, C. (1991, August). Male–female relationships in the workplace: Perceived motivations in office romance. *Sex Roles, 25,* 163–180.

Angier, N. (1995, May 9). Scientists mull role of empathy in man and beast. *The New York Times,* pp. C1, C6.

Argyle, M. (1988). *Bodily communication* (2nd ed.). New York: Methuen.

Argyle, M., & Henderson, M. (1984). The rules of friendship. *Journal of Social and Personal Relationships, 1,* 211–237.

Argyle, M., & Henderson, M. (1985). *The anatomy of relationships: And the rules and skills needed to manage them successfully.* London: Heinemann.

Argyle, M., & Ingham, R. (1972). Gaze, mutual gaze and distance. *Semiotica, 1,* 32–49.

Aronson, E., Wilson, T. D., & Akert, R. M. (1999). *Social psychology* (3rd ed.). Boston: Allyn & Bacon.

Aronson, J., Cohen, J., & Nail, P. (1998). Self-affirmation theory: An update and appraisal. In E. Harmon-Jones & J. S. Mills (Eds.), *Cognitive dissonance theory: Revival with revisions and controversies.* Washington, DC: American Psychological Association.

Asch, S. (1946). Forming impressions of personality. *Journal of Abnormal and Social Psychology, 41,* 258–290.

Ashcraft, M. H. (1998). *Fundamentals of cognition.* New York: Longman.

Aspinwall, L. G., & Taylor, S. E. (1993). Effects of social comparison direction, threat, and self-esteem on affect, evaluation, and expected success. *Journal of Personality and Social Psychology, 64,* 708–722.

Aune, K., Buller, D. B., & Aune, R. K. (1996, September). Display rule development in romantic relationships: Emotion management and perceived appropriateness of emotions across relationship stages. *Human Communication Research, 23,* 115–145.

Aune, R. K., & Kikuchi, T. (1993, September). Effects of language intensity similarity on perceptions of credibility, relational attributions, and persuasion. *Journal of Language and Social Psychology, 12,* 224–238.

Axtell, R. E. (1990). *Do's and taboos of hosting international visitors.* New York: Wiley.

Axtell, R. E. (1993). *Do's and taboos around the world* (3rd ed.). New York: Wiley.

Ayres, J., & Hopf, T. (1993). *Coping with speech anxiety*. Norwood, NJ: Ablex.

Ayres, J., & Hopf, T. (1995, Fall). An assessment of the role of communication apprehension in communicating with the terminally ill. *Communication Research Reports, 12,* 227–234.

Babcock, J. C., Waltz, J., Jacobson, N. S., & Gottman, J. M. (1993, February). Power and violence: The relation between communication patterns, power discrepancies, and domestic violence. *Journal of Marriage and the Family, 60,* 70–78.

Bach, G. R., & Wyden, P. (1968). *The intimacy enemy*. New York: Avon.

Balswick, J. O., & Peck, C. (1971). The inexpressive male: A tragedy of American society? *The Family Coordinator, 20,* 363–368.

Baker, A. (2002). What makes an online relationship successful? Clues from couples who met in cyberspace. *CyberPsychology and Behavior, 5,* 363–375.

Banerjee, N. (2005, January 23). Few but organized, Iraq veterans turn war critics. *The New York Times,* National Report, 16.

Barbato, C. A., & Perse, E. M. (1992, August). Interpersonal communication motives and the life position of elders. *Communication Research, 19,* 516–531.

Baringer, D. K., & McCroskey, J. C. (2000). Immediacy in the classroom: Student immediacy. *Communication Education, 49,* 178–186.

Barker, L. L., & Gaut, D. (2002). *Communication* (8th ed.). Boston: Allyn & Bacon.

Barker, L., Edwards, R., Gaines, C., Gladney, K., & Holley, F. (1980). An investigation of proportional time spent in various communication activities by college students. *Journal of Applied Communication Research, 8,* 101–109.

Barna, L. M. (1997). Stumbling blocks in intercultural communication. In L. A. Samovar & R. E. Porter (Eds.), *Intercultural communication: A reader* (7th ed., pp. 337–346). Belmont, CA: Wadsworth.

Barnlund, D. C. (1970). A transactional model of communication. In J. Akin, A. Goldberg, G. Myers, & J. Stewart (Eds.), *Language behavior: A book of readings in communication*. The Hague: Mouton.

Barrett, L., & Godfrey, T. (1988, November). Listening. *Person Centered Review, 3,* 410–425.

Barry, D. T. (2003, June). Cultural and demographic correlates of self-reported guardedness among East Asian immigrants in the U.S. *International Journal of Psychology, 38,* 150–159.

Barta, P. (1999, December 16). Sex differences in the inferior parietal lobe. Cerebral Cortex; www.wired.com/news/technology/0,1282,33033,00.html.

Bassellier, G., & Benbasat, I. (2004, December). Business competence of information technology professionals: Conceptual development and influence on IT–business partnerships. *MIS Quarterly, 28,* 673–694.

Basso, K. H. (1972). To give up on words: Silence in Apache culture. In Pier Paolo Giglioli (Ed.), *Language and social context*. New York: Penguin.

Baumeister, R. F., Bushman, B. J., & Campbell, W. K. (2000, February). Self-esteem, narcissism, and aggression: Does violence result from low self-esteem or from threatened egotism? *Current Directions in Psychological Science, 9,* 26–29.

Baxter, L. A. (1986). Gender differences in the heterosexual relationship rules embedded in break-up accounts. *Journal of Social and Personal Relationships, 3,* 289–306.

Baxter, L. A. (1988). A dialectical perspective on communication strategies in relationship development. In Steve W. Duck (Ed.), *Handbook of Personal Relationships*. New York: Wiley.

Baxter, L. A. (1990, February). Dialectical contradictions in relationship development. *Journal of Social and Personal Relationships, 7,* 69–88.

Baxter, L. A., & Simon, E. P. (1993, May). Relationship maintenance strategies and dialectical contradictions in personal relationships. *Journal of Social and Personal Relationships, 10,* 225–242.

Baxter, L. A., & Wilmot, W. W. (1984). "Secret tests": Social strategies for acquiring information about the state of the relationship. *Human Communication Research, 11,* 171–201.

Beach, W. A. (1990–1991). Avoiding ownership for alleged wrongdoings. *Research on Language and Social Interaction, 24,* 1–36.

Beatty, M. J. (1988). Situational and predispositional correlates of public speaking anxiety. *Communication Education, 37,* 28–39.

Beatty, M. J., Rudd, J. E., & Valencic, K. M. (1999). A re-evaluation of the verbal aggressiveness scale: One factor or two? *Communication Research Reports, 16,* 10–17.

Bedford, V. H. (1996). Relationships between adult siblings. In A. E. Auhagen & M. von Salisch (Eds.), *The diversity of human relationships* (pp. 120–140). New York: Cambridge University Press.

Beebe, S. A., & Masterson, J. T. (2000). *Communicating in small groups: Principles and practices* (6th ed.). New York: Longman.

Behzadi, K. G. (1994). Interpersonal conflict and emotions in an Iranian cultural practice: Qahr and Ashti. *Culture, Medicine, and Psychiatry, 18,* 321–359.

Beier, E. (1974). How we send emotional messages. *Psychology Today, 8,* 53–56.

Bell, R. A., & Buerkel-Rothfuss, N. L. (1990). S(he) loves me, s(he) loves me not: Predictors of relational information-seeking in courtship and beyond. *Communication Quarterly, 38,* 64–82.

Bell, R. A., & Daly, J. A. (1984). The affinity-seeking function of communication. *Communication Monographs, 51,* 91–115.

Ben-Ze'ev, A. (2003). Primacy, emotional closeness, and openness in cyberspace. *Computers in Human Behavior, 19,* 451–467.

Berg, J. H., & Archer, R. L. (1983). The disclosure–liking relationship. *Human Communication Research, 10,* 269–281.

Berger, C. R., & Bradac, J. J. (1982). *Language and social knowledge: Uncertainty in interpersonal relations.* London: Edward Arnold.

Berger, C. R., & Calabrese, R. J. (1975). Some explorations in initial interaction and beyond: Toward a theory of interpersonal communication. *Human Communication Research, 1,* 99–112.

Bernstein, W. M., Stephan, W. G., & Davis, M. H. (1979). Explaining attributions for achievement: A path analytic approach. *Journal of Personality and Social Psychology, 37,* 1810–1821.

Berry, J. W., Poortinga, Y. H., Segall, M. H., & Dasen, P. R. (1992). *Cross-cultural psychology: Research and applications.* Cambridge: Cambridge University Press.

Berscheid, E., & Reis, H. T. (1998). Attraction and close relationships. In D. Gilbert, S. Fiske, & G. Lindzey (Eds.), *The handbook of social psychology* (4th ed., Vol. 2, pp. 193–281). New York: W. H. Freeman.

Bishop, J. E. (1993, April 7). New research suggests that romance begins by falling nose over heels in love. *Wall Street Journal,* p. B1.

Blake, R. R., & Mouton, J. S. (1985). *The managerial grid III* (3rd ed.). Houston, TX: Gulf Publishing.

Blieszner, R., & Adams, R. G. (1992). *Adult friendship.* Thousand Oaks, CA: Sage.

Blumstein, P., & Schwartz, P. (1983). *American couples: Money, work, sex.* New York: Morrow.

Boase, J., Horrigan, J. B., Wellman, B., & Rainie, L. (2006). The strength of Internet ties. *Pew Internet & American Life Project* (www.pewinternet.org/).

Bochner, A. (1984). The functions of human communication in interpersonal bonding. In C. C. Arnold & J. W. Bowers (Eds.), *Handbook of rhetorical and communication theory* (pp. 544–621). Boston: Allyn & Bacon.

Bochner, A. P., & Yerby, J. (1977). Factors affecting instruction in interpersonal competence. *Communication Education, 26,* 91–103.

Bochner, A., & Kelly, C. (1974). Interpersonal competence: Rationale, philosophy, and implementation of a conceptual framework. *Communication Education, 23,* 279–301.

Bochner, S., & Hesketh, B. (1994, June). Power distance, individualism/collectivism, and job-related attitudes in a culturally diverse work group. *Journal of Cross-Cultural Psychology, 25,* 233–257.

Bok, S. (1978). *Lying: Moral choice in public and private life.* New York: Pantheon.

Bok, S. (1983). *Secrets.* New York: Vintage Books.

Boneva, B., Kraut, R., & Frohlich, D. (2001). Using e-mail for personal relationships: The difference gender makes. *American Behavioral Scientist, 45,* 530–549.

Borden, G. A. (1991). *Cultural orientation: An approach to understanding intercultural communication.* Englewood Cliffs, NJ: Prentice-Hall.

Bosmajian, H. (1974). *The language of oppression.* Washington, DC: Public Affairs Press.

Bourland, D. D., Jr. (1965–66). A linguistic note: Writing in e-prime. *General Semantics Bulletin, 32–33,* 111–114.

Bourland, D. D., Jr. (2004). To be or not to be: E-prime as a tool for critical thinking. *ETC: A Review of General Semantics, 61,* 546–557.

Bower, B. (2001). Self-illusions come back to bite students. *Science News, 159,* 148.

Bravo, E., & Cassedy, E. (1992). *The 9 to 5 guide to combating sexual harassment.* New York: Wiley.

Bresnahan, M. I., & Cai, D. H. (1996, March/ April). Gender and aggression in the recognition of interruption. *Discourse Processes, 21,* 171–189.

Bridges, C. R. (1996, July). The characteristics of career achievement perceived by African American college administrators. *Journal of Black Studies, 26,* 748–767.

Briton, N. J., & Hall, J. A. (1995). Beliefs about female and male nonverbal communication. *Sex Roles, 32,* 79–90.

Brody, J. E. (1991, April 28). How to foster self-esteem. *New York Times Magazine,* 26–27.

Brody, J. E. (1994, March 21). Notions of beauty transcend culture, new study suggests. *The New York Times,* p. A14.

Brody, L. R. (1985, June). Gender differences in emotional development: A review of theories and research. *Journal of Personality, 53,* 102–149.

Brown, P. (1980). How and why are women more polite: Some evidence from a Mayan community. In S. McConnell-Ginet, R. Borker, & M. Furman (Eds.), *Women and language in literature and society* (pp. 111–136). New York: Praeger.

Brown, P., & Levinson, S. C. (1987). *Politeness: Some universals of language usage.* Cambridge, UK: Cambridge University Press.

Brownell, J. (1987). Listening: The toughest management skill. *Cornell Hotel and Restaurant Administration Quarterly, 27,* 64–71.

Brownell, J. (2006). *Listening: Attitudes, principles, and skills* (3rd ed). Boston: Allyn & Bacon.

Bruneau, T. (1985). The time dimension in intercultural communication. In L. A. Samovar & R. E. Porter (Eds.), *Intercultural communication: A reader* (4th ed., pp. 280–289). Belmont, CA: Wadsworth.

Bruneau, T. (1990). Chronemics: The study of time in human interaction. In J. A. DeVito & M. L. Hecht (Eds.), *The nonverbal communication reader* (pp. 301–311). Prospect Heights, IL: Waveland Press.

Buber, M. (1958). *I and thou* (2nd ed.). New York: Scribners.

Bull, R., & Rumsey, N. (1988). *The social psychology of facial appearance.* New York: Springer-Verlag.

Buller, D. B., & Aune, R. K. (1992). The effects of speech rate similarity on compliance: Application of communication accommodation theory. *Western Journal of Communication, 56,* 37–53.

Buller, D. B., LePoire, B. A., Aune, K., & Eloy, S. (1992). Social perceptions as mediators of the effect of speech rate similarity on compliance. *Human Communication Research, 19,* 286–311.

Bunz, U., & Campbell, S. W. (2004). Politeness accommodation in electronic mail. *Communication Research Reports, 21,* 11–25.

Burgoon, J. K., & Bacue, A. E. (2003). Nonverbal communication skills. In J. O. Greene & B. R. Burleson (Eds.), *Handbook of communication and social interaction skills* (pp. 179–220). Mahwah, NJ: Erlbaum.

Burgoon, J. K., & Hoobler, G. D. (2002). Nonverbal signals. In M. L. Knapp & J. A. Daly (Eds.), *Handbook of interpersonal communication* (3rd ed., pp. 240–299). Thousand Oaks, CA: Sage.

Burgoon, J. K., Berger, C. R., & Waldron, V. R. (2000). Mindfulness and interpersonal communication. *Journal of Social Issues, 56,* 105–127.

Burgoon, J. K., Buller, D. B., & Woodall, W. G. (1996). *Nonverbal communication: The unspoken dialogue* (2nd ed.). New York: McGraw-Hill.

Burleson, B. R. (2003). Emotional support skills. In J. O. Greene & B. R. Burleson (Eds.), *Handbook of communication and social interaction skills* (pp. 551–594). Mahwah, NJ: Erlbaum.

Burleson, B. R., Holmstrom, A. J., & Gilstrap, C. M. (2005, December). 'Guys can't say *that* to guys': Four experiments assessing the normative motivation account for deficiencies in the emotional support provided by men. *Communication Monographs, 72,* 468–501.

Burnard, P. (2003). Ordinary chat and therapeutic conversation: Phatic communication and mental health nursing. *Journal of Psychiatric and Mental Health Nursing, 10,* 678–682.

Bushman, B. J., & Baumeister, R. F. (1998). Threatened egotism, narcissism, self-esteem, and direct and displaced aggression: Does self-love or self-hate lead to violence? *Journal of Personality and Social Psychology, 75,* 219–229.

Buss, D. M., & Schmitt, D. P. (1993). Sexual strategies theory: An evolutionary perspective on human mating. *Psychological Review, 100,* 204–232.

Butler, P. E. (1981). *Talking to yourself: Learning the language of self-support.* New York: Harper & Row.

Byers, E. S., & Demmons, S. (1999, May). Sexual satisfaction and sexual self-disclosure within dating relationships. *Journal of Sex Research, 36,* 180–189.

Cai, D. A., & Fink, E. L. (2002, March). Conflict style differences between individualists and collectivists. *Communication Monographs, 69,* 67–87.

Campbell, S. W., & Neer, M. R. (2001). The relationship of communication apprehension and interaction involvement to perceptions of computer-mediated communication. *Communication Research Reports, 18,* 391–398.

Canary, D. J. (2003). Managing interpersonal conflict: A model of events related to strategic choices. In J. O. Greene & B. R. Burleson (Eds.), *Handbook of communication and social interaction skills* (pp. 515–550). Mahwah, NJ: Erlbaum.

Canary, D. J., & Hause, K. (1993). Is there any reason to research sex differences in communication? *Communication Quarterly, 41,* 129–144.

Canary, D. J., Cupach, W. R., & Messman, S. J. (1995). *Relationship conflict.* Thousand Oaks, CA: Sage.

Cappella, J. N. (1993, March–June). The facial feedback hypothesis in human interaction: Review and speculation. *Journal of Language and Social Psychology, 12,* 13–29.

Carducci, B. J., with Zimbardo, P. G. (1996, November–December). Are you shy? *Psychology Today, 28,* 34–41, 64–70, 78–82.

Carli, L. L. (1999). Gender, interpersonal power, and social influence. *Journal of Social Issues, 55,* 81–99.

Carroll, D. W. (1994). *Psychology of language* (2nd ed.). Pacific Grove, CA: Brooks/Cole.

Castleberry, S. B., & Shepherd, C. D. (1993). Effective interpersonal listening and personal selling. *Journal of Personal Selling and Sales Management, 13,* 35–49.

Cate, R., Henton, J., Koval, J., Christopher, R., & Lloyd, S. (1982). Premarital abuse: A social psychological perspective. *Journal of Family Issues, 3,* 79–90.

Cawthon, S. W. (2001). Teaching strategies in inclusive classrooms with deaf students. *Journal of Deaf Studies and Deaf Education, 6,* 212–225.

Chadwick-Jones, J. K. (1976). *Social exchange theory: Its structure and influence in social psychology.* New York: Academic Press.

Chang, H., & Holt, G. R. (1996, Winter). The changing Chinese interpersonal world: Popular themes in interpersonal communication books in modern Taiwan. *Communication Quarterly, 44,* 85–106.

Chanowitz, B., & Langer, E. (1981). Premature cognitive commitment. *Journal of Personality and Social Psychology, 41,* 1051–1063.

Charlton, S. G. (2004) Perceptual and attentional effects on drivers' speed selection at curves. *Accident Analysis and Prevention, 36,* 877–884.

Chen, G. (1992). Differences in self-disclosure patterns among Americans versus Chinese: A comparative study. Paper presented at the annual meeting of the Eastern Communication Association, Portland, ME.

Chen, L. (1993). Chinese and North Americans: An epistemological exploration of intercultural communication. *Howard Journal of Communications, 4,* 342–357.

Cherulnik, P. D. (1979). Sex differences in the expression of emotion in a structured social encounter. *Sex Roles, 5,* 413–424.

Chesebro, J. L., & McCroskey, J. C. (1998). The relationship of teacher clarity and teacher immediacy with students' experiences of state receiver apprehension. *Communication Quarterly, 46,* 446–456.

Childress, H. (2004, May). Teenagers, territory and the appropriation of space. *Childhood: A Global Journal of Child Research, 11,* 195–205.

Christie, R. (1970). Scale construction. In R. Christie & F. L. Geis (Eds.), *Studies in Machiavellianism* (pp. 35–52). New York: Academic Press.

Chung, L. C., & Ting-Toomey, S. (1999). Ethnic identity and relational expectations among Asian Americans. *Communication Research Reports, 16,* 157–166.

Clement, D. A., & Frandsen, K. D. (1976). On conceptual and empirical treatments of feedback in human communication. *Communication Monographs, 43,* 11–28.

Cline, M. G. (1956). The influence of social context on the perception of faces. *Journal of Personality, 2,* 142–185.

Coates, J., & Cameron, D. (1989). *Women, men, and language: Studies in language and linguistics.* London: Longman.

Coats, E. J., & Feldman, R. S. (1996). Gender differences in nonverbal correlates of social status. *Personality and Social Psychology Bulletin, 22,* 1014–1022.

Cody, M. J. (1982). A typology of disengagement strategies and an examination of the role intimacy, reactions to inequity, and relational problems play in strategy selection. *Communication Monographs, 49,* 148–170.

Cohen, J. (2001, January 18). On the Internet, love really is blind. *The New York Times,* pp. G1, G9.

Cohen, J. (2002, May 9). An e-mail affliction: The long goodbye. *The New York Times,* p. G6.

Coleman, P. (2002). *How to say it for couples: Communicating with tenderness, openness, and honesty.* Paramus, NJ: Prentice-Hall.

Colley, A., Todd, Z., Bland, M., Holmes, M., Khanom, N., & Pike, H. (2004, September). Style and content in e-mails and letters to male and female friends. *Journal of Language and Social Psychology, 23,* 369–378.

Collier, M. J. (1991). Conflict competence within African, Mexican, and Anglo American friendships. In S. Ting-Toomey & F. Korzenny (Eds.), *Cross-cultural interpersonal communication* (pp. 132–154). Newbury Park, CA: Sage.

Collins, N. L., & Miller, L. C. (1994). Self-disclosure and liking: A meta-analytic review. *Psychological Bulletin, 116,* 457–475.

Cooley, C. H. (1922). *Human nature and the social order* (rev. ed.). New York: Scribners.

Coon, C. A., & Schwanenflugel, P. J. (1996). Evaluation of interruption behavior by naive encoders. *Discourse Processes, 22,* 1–24.

Cooper, A., & Sportolari, L. (1997). Romance in cyberspace: Understanding online attraction. *Journal of Sex Education and Therapy, 22,* 7–14.

Coover, G. E., & Murphy, S. T. (2000). The communicated self: Exploring the interaction between self and social context. *Human Communication Research, 26,* 125–147.

Coplin, B. (2004, June 10). For new graduates, "soft skills" are the secret weapon in job hunt. *USA Today,* p. 15A.

Cornwell, B., & Lundgren, D. C. (2001). Love on the Internet: Involvement and misrepresentation in romantic relationships in cyberspace vs. real space. *Computers in Human Behavior, 17,* 197–211.

D'Augelli, A. R. (1992, September). Lesbian and gay male undergraduates' experiences of harassment and fear on campus. *Journal of Interpersonal Violence, 7,* 383–395.

Darwin, C. (1872). *The expression of the emotions in man and animals.* Chicago: University of Chicago Press (reprinted 1965).

Davis, M. S. (1973). *Intimate relations.* New York: Free Press.

Davis, O. (1973). The English language is my enemy. In J. A. DeVito (Ed.), *Language: Concepts and processes* (pp. 164–170). Englewood Cliffs, NJ: Prentice-Hall.

Deal, J. E., & Wampler, K. S. (1986). Dating violence: The primacy of previous experience. *Journal of Social and Personal Relationships, 3,* 457–471.

Deaux, K., & LaFrance, M. (1998). Gender. In D. Gilbert, S. Fiske & G. Lindzey (Eds.), *The Handbook of Social Psychology* (4th ed., Vol. 1, pp. 788–828). New York: Freeman.

deBono, E. (1987). *The six thinking hats.* New York: Penguin.

DeCecco, J. (1988). Obligation versus aspiration. In J. DeCecco (Ed.), *Gay relationships.* New York: Harrington Park Press.

Dell, K. (2005, February 14). Just for dudes. *Time,* p. B22.

DePaulo, B. M. (1992). Nonverbal behavior and self-presentation. *Psychological Bulletin, 111,* 203–212.

Derlega, V. J., Winstead, B. A., Wong, P. T. P., & Greenspan, M. (1987). Self-disclosure and relationship development: An attributional analysis. In M. E. Roloff & G. R. Miller (Eds.), *Interpersonal processes: New directions in communication research* (pp. 172–187). Newbury Park, CA: Sage.

Derlega, V. J., Winstead, B. A., Wong, P. T. P., & Hunter, S. (1985). Gender effects in an initial encounter: A case where men exceed women in disclosure. *Journal of Social and Personal Relationships, 2,* 25–44.

DeTurck, M. A. (1987). When communication fails: Physical aggression as a compliance-gaining strategy. *Communication Monographs, 54,* 106–112.

DeVito, J. A. (1996). *Brainstorms: How to think more creatively about communication (or about anything else).* New York: Longman.

DeVito, J. A. (2003a, Fall). MEDUSA messages. *Etc: A Review of General Semantics, 60,* 241–245.

DeVito, J. A. (2003b, Spring). SCREAM before you scream. *Etc: A Review of General Semantics, 60,* 42–45.

DeVito, J. A., & Hecht, M. L. (1990). *The nonverbal communication reader.* Prospect Heights, IL: Waveland Press.

Dewey, J. (1910). *How we think.* Boston: Heath.

Dillard, J. P., & Marshall, L. J. (2003). Persuasion as a social skill. In J. O. Greene & B. R. Burleson (Eds.), *Handbook of communication and social interaction skills* (pp. 479–514). Mahwah, NJ: Erlbaum.

Dindia, K., & Fitzpatrick, M. A. (1985). Marital communication: Three approaches compared. In S. Duck & D. Perlman (Eds.), *Understanding personal relationships: An in-*

terdisciplinary approach (pp. 137–158). Thousand Oaks, CA: Sage.

Dindia, K., & Timmerman, L. (2003). Accomplishing romantic relationships. In J. O. Greene & B. R. Burleson (Eds.), *Handbook of communication and social interaction skills* (pp. 685–722). Mahwah, NJ: Erlbaum.

Dion, K. K., & Dion, K. L. (1993a, Fall). Individualistic and collectivist perspectives on gender and the cultural context of love and intimacy. *Journal of Social Issues, 49,* 53–69.

Dion, K. L., & Dion, K. K. (1993b, December). Gender and ethnocultural comparisons in styles of love. *Psychology of Women Quarterly, 17,* 464–473.

Dion, K., Berscheid, E., & Walster, E. (1972). What is beautiful is good. *Journal of Personality and Social Psychology, 24,* 285–290.

Dittman, D. A. (1997, December). Reexamining curriculum. *The Cornell Hotel and Restaurant Administration Quarterly, 38,* 3.

Dolgin, K. G., & Lindsay, K. R. (1999, September). Disclosure between college students and their siblings. *Journal of Family Psychology, 13,* 393–400.

Dolgin, K. G., Meyer, L., & Schwartz, J. (1991, September). Effects of gender, target's gender, topic, and self-esteem on disclosure to best and middling friends. *Sex Roles, 25,* 311–329.

Donohue, W. A., & Kolt, R. (1992). *Managing interpersonal conflict.* Thousand Oaks, CA: Sage.

Dorland, J. M., & Fisher, A. R. (2001). Gay, lesbian, and bisexual individuals' perception: An analogue study. *Counseling Psychologist, 29,* 532–547.

Douglas, W. (1994). The acquaintanceship process: An examination of uncertainty, information seeking, and social attraction during initial conversation. *Communication Research, 21,* 154–176.

Dovidio, J. F., Gaertner, S. E., Kawakami, K., & Hodson, G. (2002). Why can't we just get along? Interpersonal biases and interracial distrust. *Cultural Diversity and Ethnic Minority Psychology, 8,* 88–102.

Drass, K. A. (1986, December). The effect of gender identity on conversation. *Social Psychology Quarterly, 49,* 294–301.

Dresser, N. (1999). *Multicultural celebrations: Today's rules of etiquette for life's special occasions.* New York: Three Rivers Press.

Dresser, N. (2005). *Multicultural manners: Essential rules of etiquette for the 21st century* (rev ed.). New York: Wiley.

Drews, D. R., Allison, C. K., & Probst, J. R. (2000). Behavioral and self-concept differences in tattooed and nontattooed college students. *Psychological Reports, 86,* 475–481.

Dreyfuss, H. (1971). *Symbol sourcebook.* New York: McGraw-Hill.

Dsilva, M., & Whyte, L. O. (1998). Cultural differences in conflict styles: Vietnamese refugees and established residents. *The Howard Journal of Communication, 9,* 57–68.

Dunbar, R. I. M. (2004). Gossip in evolutionary perspective. *Review of General Psychology, 8,* 100–110.

Duncan, S. D., Jr. (1972). Some signals and rules for taking speaking turns in conversation. *Journal of Personality and Social Psychology, 23,* 283–292.

Dunn, D., & Cody, M. J. (2000). Account credibility and public image: Excuses, justifications, denials, and sexual harassment. *Communication Monographs, 67,* 372–391.

Duran, R. L., & Kelly, L. (1988). The influence of communicative competence on perceived task, social, and physical attraction. *Communication Quarterly, 36,* 41–49.

Eckstein, D., & Goldman, A. (2001). The couple's gender-based communication questionnaire (CGCQ). *Family Journal: Counseling and Therapy for Couples and Families, 9,* 62.

Eden, D. (1992, Winter). Leadership and expectations: Pygmalion effects and other self-fulfilling prophecies in organizations. *Leadership Quarterly, 3,* 271–305.

Eder, D., & Enke, J. L. (1991). The structure of gossip: Opportunities and constraints on collective expression among adolescents. *American Sociological Review, 56,* 494–508.

Edwards, K., & Smith, E. (1996). A disconfirmation bias in the evaluation of arguments. *Journal of Personality and Social Psychology, 71,* 5–24.

Ehrenhaus, P. (1988, March). Silence and symbolic expression. *Communication Monographs, 55,* 41–57.

Einstein, E. (1995). Success or sabotage: Which self-fulfilling prophecy will the stepfamily create? In D. K. Huntley (Ed.), *Understanding stepfamilies: Implications for assessment and treatment.* Alexandria, VA: American Counseling Association.

Ekman, P. (1985a). Communication through nonverbal behavior: A source of information about an interpersonal relationship. In S. S. Tomkins & C. E. Izard (Eds.), *Affect, cognition and personality.* New York: Springer.

Ekman, P. (1985b). *Telling lies: Clues to deceit in the marketplace, politics, and marriage.* New York: Norton.

Ekman, P., & Friesen, W. V. (1969). The repertoire of nonverbal behavior: Categories, origins, usage, and coding. *Semiotica, 1,* 49–98.

Ekman, P., Friesen, W. V., & Ellsworth, P. (1972). *Emotion in the human face: Guidelines for research and an integration of findings.* New York: Pergamon Press.

Elfenbein, H. A., & Ambady, N. (2002). Is there an in-group advantage in emotion recognition? *Psychological Bulletin, 128,* 243–249.

Ellis, A. (1988). *How to stubbornly refuse to make yourself miserable about anything, yes anything.* Secaucus, NJ: Lyle Stuart.

Ellis, A., & Harper, R. A. (1975). *A new guide to rational living.* Hollywood, CA: Wilshire Books.

Elmes, M. B., & Gemmill, G. (1990, February). The psychodynamics of mindlessness and dissent in small groups. *Small Group Research, 21,* 28–44.

Emmert, P. (1994). A definition of listening. *Listening Post, 51,* 6. Cited in Brownell (2006), p. 50.

Epstein, N., Pretzer, J. L., & Fleming, B. (1987). The role of cognitive appraisal in self-reports of marital communication. *Behavior Therapy, 18,* 51–69.

Epstein, R. M., & Hundert, E. M. (2002). Defining and assessing professional competence. *JAMA: Journal of the American Medical Association, 287,* 226–235.

Eriksen, J., & Lindsay, J. (1999). Unmarried cohabitation and family policy: Norway and Australia compared. *Comparative Social Research, 18,* 79–103.

Exline, R. V., Ellyson, S. L., & Long, B. (1975). Visual behavior as an aspect of power role relationships. In P. Pliner, L. Krames, & T. Alloway (Eds.), *Nonverbal communication of aggression.* New York: Plenum.

Fallows, D. (2005). How women and men use the Internet. Pew Internet & American Life Project (www.pewinternet .org/accessed, 1/6/2006).

Fehr, B. (2004). Intimacy expectations in same-sex friendships: A prototype interaction-pattern model. *Journal of Personality and Social Psychology, 86,* 265–284.

Fernald, C. D. (1995). When in London . . . : Differences in disability language preferences among English-speaking countries. *Mental Retardation, 33,* 99–103.

Fesko, S. L. (2001, November). Disclosure of HIV status in the workplace: Considerations and strategies. *Health and Social Work, 26,* 235–244.

Festinger, L. (1954). A theory of social comparison processes. *Human Relationships, 7,* 117–140.

Field, R. H. G. (1989, March). The self-fulfilling prophecy leader: Achieving the Metharme effect. *Journal of Management Studies, 26,* 151–175.

Finn, J. (2004). A survey of online harassment at a university campus. *English, 19,* 468–483.

Fischer, A. H. (1993). Sex differences in emotionality: Fact or stereotype? *Feminism and Psychology, 3,* 303–318.

Fisher, D. R. (1998). Rumoring theory and the Internet: A framework for analyzing the grass roots. *Social Science Computer Review, 16,* 158–168.

Fitzpatrick, M. A. (1983). Predicting couples' communication from couples' self-reports. In R. N. Bostrom (Ed.), *Communication yearbook 7* (pp. 49–82). Thousand Oaks, CA: Sage.

Fitzpatrick, M. A. (1988). *Between husbands and wives: Communication in marriage.* Thousand Oaks, CA: Sage.

Fitzpatrick, M. A. (1991). Sex differences in marital conflict: Social psychophysiological versus cognitive explanations. *Text, 11,* 341–364.

Fitzpatrick, M. A., Jandt, F. E., Myrick, F. L., & Edgar, T. (1994). Gay and lesbian couple relationships. In R. J. Ringer (Ed.), *Queer words, queer images: Communication and the construction of homosexuality.* (pp. 265–285). New York: New York University Press.

Floyd, J. J. (1985). *Listening: A practical approach.* Glenview, IL: Scott, Foresman.

Folger, J. P., Poole, M. S., & Stutman, R. K. (1997). *Working through conflict: A communication perspective* (3rd ed.). Boston: Allyn & Bacon.

Forbes, G. B. (2001). College students with tattoos and piercings: Motives, family experiences, personality factors, and perception by others. *Psychological Reports, 89,* 774–786.

Franklin, C. W., & Mizell, C. A. (1995). Some factors influencing success among African-American men: A preliminary study. *Journal of Men's Studies, 3,* 191–204.

Fraser, B. (1990). Perspectives on politeness. *Journal of Pragmatics, 14,* 219–236.

French, J. R. P., Jr., & Raven, B. (1968). The bases of social power. In D. Cartwright & A. Zander (Eds.), *Group dynamics: Research and theory* (3rd ed., pp. 259–269). New York: Harper & Row.

Friedman, J., Boumil, M. M., & Taylor, B. E. (1992). *Sexual harassment.* Deerfield Beach, FL: Health Communications.

Frone, M. R. (2000). Interpersonal conflict at work and psychological outcomes: Testing a model among young workers. *Journal of Occupational Health Psychology, 5,* 246–255.

Furlow, F. B. (1996, March/April). The smell of love. *Psychology Today, 29,* 38–45.

Furnham, A. (2004). Foreign students: Education and culture shock. *Psychologist, 17,* 16–19.

Furnham, A., & Bochner, S. (1986). *Culture shock: Psychological reactions to unfamiliar environments.* New York: Methuen.

Gable, M., Hollon, C., & Dangello, F. (1992). Managerial structuring of work as a moderator of the Machiavellianism and job performance relationship. *Journal of Psychology, 126,* 317–325.

Galvin, K., Bylund, C. L., & Brommel, B. J. (2004). *Family communication: Cohesion and change* (5th ed.). Boston: Allyn & Bacon.

Gamble, T. K., & Gamble, M. W. (2003). *The gender communication connection.* Boston: Houghton Mifflin.

Gelfand, M. J., Nishii, L. H., Holcombe, K. M., Dyer, N., Ohbuchi, K., & Fukuno, M. (2001). Cultural influences on cognitive representations of conflict: Interpretations of conflict episodes in the United States and Japan. *Journal of Applied Psychology, 86,* 1059–1074.

Gelles, R., & Cornell, C. (1985). *Intimate violence in families.* Newbury Park, CA: Sage.

Georges, J., et al. (2001). Functional relationships in the nuclear and extended family: A 16-culture study. *International Journal of Psychology, 36,* 289–300.

Gergen, K. J., Greenberg, M. S., & Willis, R. H. (1980). *Social exchange: Advances in theory and research.* New York: Plenum Press.

Gibb, J. (1961). Defensive communication. *Journal of Communication, 11,* 141–148.

Giles, H., Mulac, A., Bradac, J. J., & Johnson, P. (1987). Speech accommodation theory: The first decade and beyond. In M. L. McLaughlin (Ed.), *Communication yearbook 10* (pp. 13–48). Thousand Oaks, CA: Sage.

Gladstone, G. L., & Parker, G. B. (2002, June). When you're smiling, does the whole world smile with you? *Australasian Psychiatry, 10,* 144–146.

Goffman, E. (1967). *Interaction ritual: Essays on face-to-face behavior.* New York: Pantheon.

Goffman, E. (1971). *Relations in public: Microstudies of the public order.* New York: HarperCollins.

Goldin-Meadow, S., Nusbaum, H., Kelly, S. D., & Wagner, S. (2001). Gesture—psychological aspects. *Psychological Science, 12,* 516–522.

Goldsmith, D. J., & Fulfs, P. A. (1999). "You just don't have the evidence": An analysis of claims and evidence. In M. E. Roloff (Ed.), *Communication yearbook 22* (pp. 1–49). Thousand Oaks, CA: Sage.

Goleman, D. (1995a). *Emotional intelligence.* New York: Bantam.

Goleman, D. (1995b, February 14). For man and beast, language of love shares many traits. *The New York Times,* pp. C1, C9.

Gonzaga, G. C., Keltner, D., Lonhahl, E. A., & Smith, M. D. (2001). Love and the commitment problem in romantic relationships and friendships. *Journal of Personality and Social Psychology, 81,* 247–262.

Gonzalez, A., & Zimbardo, P. G. (1985). Time in perspective. *Psychology Today, 19,* 20–26. Reprinted in Guerrero, DeVito, & Hecht (1999), pp. 227–236.

Goode, E. (2000, August 8). How culture molds habits of thought. *The New York Times,* pp. F1, F8.

Goodwin, R., & Lee, I. (1994, September). Taboo topics among Chinese and English friends: A cross-cultural comparison. *Journal of Cross-Cultural Psychology, 25,* 325–338.

Gordon, T. (1975). *P.E.T.: Parent effectiveness training.* New York: New American Library.

Gosling, S. D., Ko, S. J., Mannarelli, T., & Morris, M. E. (2002, March). A room with a cue: Personality judgments based on offices and bedrooms. *Journal of Personality and Social Psychology, 82,* 379–398.

Gottman, J. M. (1993). *What predicts divorce: The relationships between marital processes and marital outcomes.* Hillsdale, NJ: Erlbaum.

Gottman, J. M. (1994). *Why marriages succeed or fail.* New York: Simon & Schuster.

Gottman, J. M. (2004). 12-year study of gay & lesbian couples. Retrieved March 25, 2006, from www.gottman.com/research/projects/gaylesbian.

Gottman, J. M., & Carrere, S. (1994). Why can't men and women get along? Developmental roots and marital inequities. In D. J. Canary & L. Stafford (Eds.), *Communication and relational maintenance* (pp. 203–229). San Diego, CA: Academic Press.

Gould, S. J. (1995, June 7). No more "wretched refuse." *The New York Times,* p. A27.

Graham, E. E. (1994). Interpersonal communication motives scale. In R. B. Rubin, P. Palmgreen, & H. E. Sypher (Eds.), *Communication research measures: A sourcebook* (pp. 211–216). New York: Guilford.

Graham, E. E., Barbato, C. A., & Perse, E. M. (1993). The interpersonal communication motives model. *Communication Quarterly, 41,* 172–186.

Graham, J. A., & Argyle, M. (1975). The effects of different patterns of gaze, combined with different facial expressions, on impression formation. *Journal of Movement Studies, 1,* 178–182.

Graham, J. A., Bitti, P. R., & Argyle, M. (1975). A cross-cultural study of the communication of emotion by facial, and gestural cues. *Journal of Human Movement Studies, 1,* 68–77.

Grandey, A. A. (2000). Emotion regulation in the workplace: A new way to conceptualize emotional labor. *Journal of Occupational Health and Psychology, 5,* 95–110.

Greif, E. B. (1980). Sex differences in parent–child conversations. *Women's Studies International Quarterly, 3,* 253–258.

Grice, H. P. (1975). Logic and conversation. In P. Cole & J. L. Morgan (Eds.), *Syntax and semantics: Vol. 3. Speech acts* (pp. 41–58). New York: Seminar Press.

Griffin, E., & Sparks, G. G. (1990). Friends forever: A longitudinal exploration of intimacy in same-sex friends and platonic pairs. *Journal of Social and Personal Relationships, 7,* 29–46.

Gross, R. (1991). *Peak learning.* Los Angeles: Jeremy P. Tarcher.

Gross, T., Turner, E., & Cederholm, L. (1987, June). Building teams for global operation. *Management Review,* 32–36.

Gu, Y. (1990). Polite phenomena in modern Chinese. *Journal of Pragmatics, 14,* 237–257.

Gudykunst, W. B. (1989). Culture and the development of interpersonal relationships. In J. A. Anderson (Ed.), *Communication yearbook 12* (pp. 315–354). Thousand Oaks, CA: Sage.

Gudykunst, W. B. (1993). Toward a theory of effective interpersonal and intergroup communication: An anxiety/uncertainty management (AUM) perspective. In R. L. Wiseman (Ed.), *Intercultural communication competence.* Thousand Oaks, CA: Sage.

Gudykunst, W. B. (1994). *Bridging differences: Effective intergroup communication* (2nd ed.). Thousand Oaks, CA: Sage.

Gudykunst, W. B. (Ed.). (1983). *Intercultural communication theory: Current perspectives.* Newbury Park, CA: Sage.

Gudykunst, W. B., & Kim, Y. W. (1992). *Communicating with strangers: An approach to intercultural communication* (2nd ed.). New York: Random House.

Gudykunst, W., & Nishida, T. (1984). Individual and cultural influence on uncertainty reduction. *Communication Monographs, 51,* 23–36.

Gudykunst, W. B., Nishida, T., & Chua, E. (1987). Perceptions of social penetration in Japanese–North American dyads. *International Journal of Intercultural Relations, 11,* 171–189.

Gudykunst, W., Yang, S., & Nishida, T. (1985). A cross-cultural test of uncertainty reduction theory: Comparisons of acquaintance, friend, and dating relationships in Japan, Korea, and the United States. *Human Communication Research, 11,* 407–454.

Gueguen, N. (2003, Summer). Help on the Web: The effect of the same first name between the sender and the receptor in a request made by e-mail. *Psychological Record, 53,* 459–466.

Guerrero, L. K., & Andersen, P. A. (1991). The waxing and waning of relational intimacy: Touch as a function of relational stage, gender and touch avoidance. *Journal of Social and Personal Relationships, 8,* 147–165.

Guerrero, L. K., DeVito, J. A., & Hecht, M. L. (Eds.). (1999). *The nonverbal communication reader: Classic and contemporary readings* (2nd ed.). Prospect Heights, IL: Waveland Press.

Gugerty, L, Rakauskas, M., & Brooks, J. (2004). Effects of remote and in-person verbal interactions on verbalization rates and attention to dynamic spatial scenes. *Accident Analysis and Prevention 36,* 1029–1043.

Haar, B. F., & Krahe, B. (1999). Strategies for resolving interpersonal conflicts in adolescence: A German–Indonesian comparison. *Journal of Cross-Cultural Psychology, 30,* 667–683.

Haga, Y. (1988). Traits de langage et caractère Japonais. *Cahiers de Sociologie Economique et Culturelle, 9,* 105–109.

Hajek, C., & Giles, H. (2003). New directions in intercultural communication competence: The process model. In J. O. Greene & B. R. Burleson (Eds.), *Handbook of communication and social interaction skills* (pp. 935–957). Mahwah, NJ: Erlbaum.

Hall, E. T. (1959). *The silent language.* Garden City, NY: Doubleday.

Hall, E. T. (1963). A system for the notation of proxemic behavior. *American Anthropologist, 65,* 1003–1026.

Hall, E. T. (1966). *The hidden dimension.* Garden City, NY: Doubleday.

Hall, E. T. (1976). *Beyond culture.* Garden City, NY: Doubleday.

Hall, E. T. (1983). *The dance of life: The other dimension of time.* New York: Doubleday.

Hall, E. T., & Hall, M. R. (1971, June). The sounds of silence. *Playboy,* pp. 139–140, 204, 206.

Hall, E. T., & Hall, M. R. (1987). *Hidden differences: Doing business with the Japanese.* New York: Doubleday.

Hall, J. A. (1984). *Nonverbal sex differences.* Baltimore: Johns Hopkins University Press.

Hall, J. A. (1996). Touch, status, and gender at professional meetings. *Journal of Nonverbal Behavior, 20,* 23–44.

Hall, J. A. (1998). How big are nonverbal sex differences? The case of smiling and sensitivity to nonverbal cues. In D. J. Canary & K. Dindia (Eds.), *Sex differences and similarities in communication: Critical essays and empirical investigations of sex and gender in interaction* (pp. 155–178). Mahwah, NJ: Erlbaum.

Hall, J. K. (1993). Tengo una bomba: The paralinguistic and linguistic conventions of the oral practice chismeando. *Research on Language and Social Interaction, 26,* 55–83.

Hancock, J. T. (2004). Verbal irony use in face-to-face and computer-mediated conversations. *Journal of Language and Social Psychology, 23,* 447–463.

Haney, W. (1973). *Communication and organizational behavior: Text and cases* (3rd ed). Homewood, IL: Irwin.

Harris, M. (1993). *Culture, people, nature: An introduction to general anthropology,* 6th ed. Boston: Allyn & Bacon.

Hart, F. (1990). The construction of masculinity in men's friendships: Misogyny, heterosexism and homophobia. *Resources for Feminist Research, 19,* 60–67.

Hart, R. P., Carlson, R. E., & Eadie, W. F. (1980). Attitudes toward communication and the assessment of rhetorical sensitivity. *Communication Monographs, 47,* 1–22.

Hastings, S. O. (2000). "Egocasting" in the avoidance of disclosure: An intercultural perspective. In S. Petronio (Ed.), *Balancing the secrets of private disclosures* (pp. 235–248). Mahwah, NJ: Erlbaum.

Hatfield, E., & Rapson, R. L. (1992). Similarity and attraction in close relationships. *Communication Monographs, 59,* 209–212.

Hatfield, E., & Rapson, R. L. (1996). *Love and sex: Cross-cultural perspectives.* Boston: Allyn & Bacon.

Havlena, W. J., Holbrook, M. B., & Lehmann, D. R. (1989, Summer). Assessing the validity of emotional typologies. *Psychology and Marketing, 6,* 97–112.

Hayakawa, S. I., & Hayakawa, A. R. (1989). *Language in thought and action* (5th ed.). New York: Harcourt Brace Jovanovich.

Hays, R. B. (1989). The day-to-day functioning of close versus casual friendships. *Journal of Social and Personal Relationships, 6,* 21–37.

Heasley, J. B., Babbitt, C. E., & Burbach, H. J. (1995). Gender differences in college students' perceptions of "fighting words." *Sociological Viewpoints, 11,* 30–40.

Heath, W. P., Stone, J., Darley, J. M., & Grannemann, B. D. (2003). Yes, I did it, but don't blame me: Perceptions of excuse defenses. *Journal of Psychiatry and Law 31,* 187–226.

Hecht, M. L. (1978a). The conceptualization and measurement of interpersonal communication satisfaction. *Human Communication Research, 4,* 253–264.

Hecht, M. L. (1978b). Toward a conceptualization of communication satisfaction. *Quarterly Journal of Speech, 64,* 47–62.

Hecht, M. L., Jackson, R. L., & Ribeau, S. (2003). *African American communication: Exploring identify and culture* (2nd ed.). Mahwah, NJ: Erlbaum.

Hendrick, C., & Hendrick, S. (1990). A relationship-specific version of the love attitudes scale. In J. W. Heulip (Ed.), *Handbook of replication research in the behavioral and social sciences* [special issue]. *Journal of Social Behavior and Personality, 5,* 239–254.

Hendrick, C., Hendrick, S., Foote, F. H., & Slapion-Foote, Michelle J. (1984). Do men and women love differently? *Journal of Social and Personal Relationships, 1,* 177–195.

Hesegawa, T., & Gudykunst, W. B. (1998). Silence in Japan and the United States. *Journal of Cross-Cultural Psychology, 29,* 668–684.

Hess, E. H. (1975). *The tell-tale eye.* New York: Van Nostrand Reinhold.

Hess, U., Kappas, A., McHugo, G. J., Lanzetta, J. T., et al. (1992, May). The facilitative effect of facial expression on the self-generation of emotion. *International Journal of Psychophysiology, 12,* 251–265.

Hewitt, J. P. (1998). *The myth of self-esteem: Finding happiness and solving problems in America.* New York: St. Martin's Press.

Hewitt, J., & Stokes, R. (1975). Disclaimers. *American Sociological Review, 40,* 1–11.

Hickson, M. L., & Stacks, D. W. (1993). *NVC: Nonverbal communication: Studies and applications* (3rd ed.). Dubuque, IA: William C. Brown.

Hofstede, G. (1997). *Cultures and organizations: Software of the mind.* New York: McGraw-Hill.

Hoft, N. L. (1995). *International technical communication: How to export information about high technology.* New York: Wiley.

Hofstede, G. (Ed.). (1998). *Masculinity and femininity: The taboo dimension of national cultures.* Thousand Oaks, CA: Sage.

Holmes, J. (1986). Compliments and compliment responses in New Zealand English. *Anthropological Linguistic, 28,* 485–508.

Holmes, J. (1995). *Women, men and politeness.* New York: Longman.

Honeycutt, J. (1986). A model of marital functioning based on an attraction paradigm and social penetration dimensions. *Journal of Marriage and the Family, 48,* 51–59.

Horenstein, V. D., & Downey, J. L. (2003). A cross-cultural investigation of self-disclosure. *North American Journal of Psychology, 5,* 373–386.

Howard, P. E. N., Rainie, L., & Jones, S. (2001). Days and nights on the Internet: The impact of a diffusing technology. *American Behavioral Scientist, 45,* 383–404.

Hupka, R. (1981). Cultural determinants of jealousy. *Alternative Lifestyles, 4,* 310–356.

Infante, D. A. (1988). *Arguing constructively.* Prospect Heights, IL: Waveland Press.

Infante, D. A., & Rancer, A. S. (1982). A conceptualization and measure of argumentativeness. *Journal of Personality Assessment, 46,* 72–80.

Infante, D. A., & Rancer, A. S. (1995). Argumentativeness and verbal aggressiveness: A review of recent theory and research. In B. R. Burleson (Ed.), *Communication yearbook 19.* Thousand Oaks, CA: Sage.

Infante, D. A., & Rancer, A. S. (1996). Argumentativeness and verbal aggressiveness: A review of recent theory and research. In B. R. Burleson (Ed.), *Communication yearbook, 19* (pp. 319–351). Thousand Oaks, CA: Sage.

Infante, D. A., Rancer, A. S., & Jordan, F. F. (1996, March). Affirming and nonaffirming style, dyad sex, and the perception of argumentation and verbal aggression in an interpersonal dispute. *Human Communication Research, 22,* 315–334.

Infante, D. A., Rancer, A. S., & Womack, D. F. (2002). *Building communication theory* (4th ed.). Prospect Heights, IL: Waveland Press.

Infante, D. A., & Wigley, C. J. (1986). Verbal aggressiveness: An interpersonal model and measure. *Communication Monographs, 53,* 61–69.

Ingram, M. P. B. (1998). A study of transformative aspects of career change experiences and implications for current models of career development (Doctoral dissertation, Texas A&M University, 1998). *Dissertation Abstracts International: Section A. Humanities and Social Sciences, 58,* 4156.

Insel, P. M., & Jacobson, L. F. (Eds.). (1975). *What do you expect? An inquiry into self-fulfilling prophecies.* Menlo Park, CA: Cummings.

Jackson, L. A., & Ervin, K. S. (1992, August). Height stereotypes of women and men: The liabilities of shortness for both sexes. *Journal of Social Psychology, 132,* 433–445.

Jacobson, D. (1999). Impression formation in cyberspace: Online expectations and offline experiences in text-based virtual communities. *Journal of Computer Mediated Communication, 5,* np.

Jaksa, J. A., & Pritchard, M. S. (1994). *Communication ethics: Methods of analysis* (2nd ed.). Belmont, CA: Wadsworth.

Jambor, E., & Elliott, M. (2005, Winter). Self-esteem and coping strategies among deaf students. *Journal of Deaf Studies and Deaf Education, 10,* 63–81.

Jandt, F. E. (2000). *Intercultural communication* (3rd ed.). Thousand Oaks, CA: Sage.

Jaworski, A. (1993). *The power of silence: Social and pragmatic perspectives.* Thousand Oaks, CA: Sage.

Johannesen, R. L. (1974, Winter). The functions of silence: A plea for communication research. *Western Speech, 38,* 25–35.

Johansson, W., & Percy, W. A. (1994). *Outing: Shattering the conspiracy of silence.* New York: Harrington Park Press.

Johnson, C. E. (1987). An introduction to powerful and powerless talk in the classroom. *Communication Education, 36,* 167–172.

Johnson, S. D., & Bechler, C. (1998). Examining the relationship between listening effectiveness and leadership emergence: Perceptions, behaviors, and recall. *Small Group Research, 29,* 452–471.

Johnson, S. M., & O'Connor, E. (2002). *The gay baby boom: The psychology of gay parenthood.* New York: New York University Press.

Joiner, T. E. (1994). Contagious depression: Existence, specificity to depressed symptoms, and the role of reassurance seeking. *Journal of Personality and Social Psychology, 67,* 287–296.

Joinson, A. N. (2001). Self-disclosure in computer-mediated communication: The role of self-awareness and visual anonymity. *European Journal of Social Psychology, 31,* 177–192.

Joinson, A. N. (2004, August). Self-esteem, interpersonal risk, and preference for e-mail to face-to-face communication. *CyberPsychology and Behavior, 7,* 472–478.

Jones, Q., Ravid, G., & Rafaeli, S. (2004, June). Information overload and the message dynamics of online interaction spaces: A theoretical model and empirical exploration. *Information Systems Research, 15,* 194–210.

Jones, S., & Yarbrough, A. E. (1985). A naturalistic study of the meanings of touch. *Communication Monographs, 52,* 19–56. (A version of this paper appears in DeVito & Hecht, 1990, pp. 235–244.)

Jourard, S. M. (1968). *Disclosing man to himself.* New York: Van Nostrand Reinhold.

Jourard, S. M. (1971). *Self-disclosure.* New York: Wiley.

Judge, T. A., & Cable, D. M. (2004). The effect of physical height on workplace success and income. *Journal of Applied Psychology, 89,* 428–441.

Kanner, B. (1989, April 3). Color schemes. *New York Magazine,* pp. 22–23.

Katz, S. (2003). In J. W. Henslin (Ed.), *Down to earth sociology: Introductory readings* (12th ed., pp. 313–320). New York: Free Press.

Kearney, P., Plax, T. G., Richmond, V. P., & McCroskey, J. C. (1984). Power in the classroom IV: Alternatives to discipline. In R. N. Bostrom (Ed.), *Communication yearbook 8* (pp. 724–746). Thousand Oaks, CA: Sage.

Kearney, P., Plax, T. G., Richmond, V. P., & McCroskey, J. C. (1985). Power in the classroom III: Teacher communication techniques and messages. *Communication Education, 34,* 19–28.

Keenan, E. O. (1976, April). The universality of conversational postulates. *Language in Society, 5,* 67–80.

Kennedy, C. W., & Camden, C. T. (1988). A new look at interruptions. *Western Journal of Speech Communication, 47,* 45–58.

Keyes, R. (1980). *The height of your life.* New York: Warner Books.

Kim, Y. Y. (1988). Communication and acculturation. In L. A. Samovar & R. E. Porter (Eds.), *Intercultural communication: A reader* (5th ed., pp. 344–354). Belmont, CA: Wadsworth.

Kim, Y. Y. (1991). Intercultural communication competence. In S. Ting-Toomey & F. Korzenny (Eds.), *Cross-cultural interpersonal communication* (pp. 259–275). Newbury Park, CA: Sage.

Kindred, J., & Roper, S. L. (2004). Making connections via instant messenger (IM): Student use of IM to maintain personal relationships. *Qualitative Research Reports in Communication, 5,* 48–54.

King, R., & DiMichael, E. (1992). *Voice and diction.* Prospect Heights, IL: Waveland Press.

Klein, J. (Ed.). (1992). The E-prime controversy: A symposium [Special issue]. *Etc.: A Review of General Semantics, 49.*

Kleinfield, N. R. (1992, October 25). The smell of money. *The New York Times,* pp. C1, C8.

Kleinke, C. L. (1986). *Meeting and understanding people.* New York: W. H. Freeman.

Kline, S. L., & Stafford, L. (2004, Winter). A comparison of interaction rules and interaction frequency in relationship to marital quality. *Communication Reports, 17,* 11–26.

Klineberg, O., & Hull, W. F. (1979). *At a foreign university: An international study of adaptation and coping.* New York: Praeger.

Kluger, J. (2005, January 9). The funny thing about laughter. *Time,* pp. A25–A29.

Knapp, M. L., & Hall, J. (1996). *Nonverbal behavior in human interaction* (3rd ed.). New York: Holt, Rinehart, & Winston.

Knapp, M. L., & Vangelisti, A. (2000). *Interpersonal communication and human relationships* (4th ed.). Boston: Allyn & Bacon.

Knapp, M., Hart, R. P., Friedrich, G. W., & Shulman, G. M. (1973). The rhetoric of goodbye: Verbal and nonverbal correlates of human leave-taking. *Speech Monographs, 40,* 182–198.

Knobloch, L. K., & Solomon, D. H. (1999, Winter). Measuring the sources and content of relational uncertainty. *Communication Studies, 50,* 261–278.

Kochman, T. (1981). *Black and white: Styles in conflict.* Chicago: University of Chicago Press.

Koerner, A. F., & Fitzpatrick, M. A. (2002, Fall). You never leave your family in a fight: The impact of family of origin of conflict behavior in romantic relationships. *Communication Studies, 53,* 234–252.

Kollock, P., & Smith, M. (1996). Managing the virtual commons: Cooperation and conflict in computer communities. In S. Herring (Ed.), *Computer-mediated communication: Linguistic, social, and cross-cultural perspectives* (pp. 109–128). Amsterdam: John Benjamins.

Komarovsky, M. (1964). *Blue collar marriage.* New York: Random House.

Koppelman, K. L., with Goodhart, R. L. (2005). *Understanding human differences: Multicultural education for a diverse America.* Boston: Allyn & Bacon.

Korda, M. (1975). *Power! How to get it, how to use it.* New York: Ballantine.

Korzybski, A. (1933). *Science and sanity.* Lakeville, CT: The International Non-Aristotelian Library.

Kposow, Augustine J. (2000, April). Marital status and suicide in the National Longitudinal Mortality Study. *Journal of Epidemiology and Community Health, 54,* 254–261.

Kramarae, C. (1974a). Folklinguistics. *Psychology Today, 8,* 82–85.

Kramarae, C. (1974b). Stereotypes of women's speech: The word from cartoons. *Journal of Popular Culture, 8,* 624–630.

Kramarae, C. (1977). Perceptions of female and male speech. *Language and Speech, 20,* 151–161.

Kramarae, C. (1981). *Women and men speaking.* Rowley, MA: Newbury House.

Kramer, R. (1997). Leading by listening: An empirical test of Carl Rogers's theory of human relationship using interpersonal assessments of leaders by followers. *Dissertation Abstracts International: Section A. Humanities and Social Sciences, 58,* 514.

Krivonos, P. D., & Knapp, M. L. (1975). Initiating communication: What do you say when you say hello? *Central States Speech Journal, 26,* 115–125.

Krohn, F. B. (2004). A generational approach to using emoticons as nonverbal communication. *Journal of Technical Writing and Communication, 34,* 321–328.

Kuhn, D., Weinstock, M., & Flaton, R. (1994). How well do jurors reason? Competence dimensions of individual variation in a juror reasoning task. *Psychological Science, 5,* 289–296.

Kurdek, L. A. (1994, November). Areas of conflict for gay, lesbian, and heterosexual couples: What couples argue about influences relationship satisfaction. *Journal of Marriage and the Family, 56,* 923–934.

Kurdek, L. A. (2003, August). Differences between gay and lesbian cohabiting couples. *Journal of Social and Personal Relationships, 20,* 411–436.

Kurdek, L. A. (2004, November). Are gay and lesbian cohabitating couples really different from heterosexual married couples? *Journal of Marriage and Family, 66,* 880–900.

Lachnit, C. (2001). Giving up gossip. *Workforce, 80,* 8.

Labott, S. M., Martin, R. B., Eason, P. S., & Berkey, E. Y. (1991, September/November). Social reactions to the expression of emotion. *Cognition and Emotion, 5,* 397–417.

Laing, M. (1993, Spring). Gossip: Does it play a role in the socialization of nurses? *Journal of Nursing Scholarship, 25,* 37–43.

Lakoff, R. (1975). *Language and women's place.* New York: Harper & Row.

Langer, E. J. (1989). *Mindfulness.* Reading, MA: Addison-Wesley.

Lantz, A. (2001). Meetings in a distributed group of experts: Comparing face-to-face, chat and collaborative virtual environments. *Behaviour and Information Technology, 20,* 111–117.

Lanzetta, J. T., Cartwright-Smith, J., & Kleck, R. E. (1976). Effects of nonverbal dissimulations on emotional experience and autonomic arousal. *Journal of Personality and Social Psychology, 33,* 354–370.

Larsen, R. J., Kasimatis, M., & Frey, K. (1992, September). Facilitating the furrowed brow: An unobtrusive test of the facial feedback hypothesis applied to unpleasant affect. *Cognition and Emotion, 6,* 321–338.

Lawson, W. (2005, November/December). Blips on the gaydar. *Psychology Today, 38,* 30.

Lea, M., & Spears, R. (1995). Love at first byte? Building personal relationships over computer networks. In J. T. Wood & S. Duck (Eds.), *Under-studied relationships: Off the beaten track* (pp. 197– 233). Thousand Oaks, CA: Sage.

Leaper, C., Carson, M., Baker, C., Holliday, H., et al. (1995). Self-disclosure and listener verbal support in same-gender and cross-gender friends' conversations. *Sex Roles, 33,* 387–404.

Leaper, C., & Holliday, H. (1995, September). Gossip in same-gender and cross-gender friends' conversations. *Personal Relationships, 2,* 237–246.

Leathers, D. G. (1997). *Successful nonverbal communication: Principles and applications* (2nd ed.). New York: Macmillan.

Lederer, W. J. (1984). *Creating a good relationship.* New York: Norton.

Lee, H. O., & Boster, F. J. (1992). Collectivism–individualism in perceptions of speech rate: A cross-cultural comparison. *Journal of Cross-Cultural Psychology, 23,* 377–388.

Lee, J. A. (1976). *The colors of love.* New York: Bantam.

Lee, K. (2000, November 1). Information overload threatens employee productivity. *Employee Benefit News, Securities Data Publishing,* p. 1.

Lemonick, M. D. (2005, January 17). A smile doesn't always mean happy. *Time,* p. A29.

Leung, K. (1988, March). Some determinants of conflict avoidance. *Journal of Cross-Cultural Psychology, 19,* 125–136.

Leung, S. A. (2001). Editor's introduction. *Asian Journal of Counseling, 8,* 107–109.

Lever, J. (1995, August 22). The 1995 advocate survey of sexuality and relationships: The women, lesbian sex survey. *The Advocate, 687/688,* 22–30.

Levine, D. (2000, August). Virtual attraction: What rocks your boat. *CyberPsychology and Behavior, 3,* 565–573.

Levine, M. (2004, June 1). Tell the doctor all your problems, but keep it to less than a minute. *The New York Times,* p. F6.

LeVine, R., & Bartlett, K. (1984). Pace of life, punctuality, and coronary heart disease in six countries. *Journal of Cross-Cultural Psychology, 15,* 233–255.

LeVine, R., Sato, S., Hashimoto, T., & Verma, J. (1994). Love and marriage in eleven cultures. Unpublished manuscript. California State University, Fresno. Cited in Hatfield & Rapson (1996).

Lewis, D. (1989). *The secret language of success.* New York: Carroll & Graf.

Lin, Y., & Rancer, A. S. (2003a, Spring). Ethnocentrism, intercultural communication apprehension, intercultural willingness-to-communicate, and intentions to participate in an intercultural dialogue program: Testing a proposed model. *Communication Research Reports, 20,* 189–190.

Lin, Y., & Rancer, A. S. (2003b, February). Sex differences in intercultural communication apprehension, ethnocentrism, and intercultural willingness to communicate. *Psychological Reports, 92,* 195–200.

Lindeman, M., Harakka, T., & Keltikangas-Jarvinen, L. (1997, June). Age and gender differences in adolescents' reactions to conflict situations: Aggression, prosociality, and withdrawal. *Journal of Youth and Adolescence, 26,* 339–351.

Lloyd, S. R. (2001). *Developing positive assertiveness* (3rd ed.). Menlo Park, CA: Crisp Publications.

Lukens, J. (1978). Ethnocentric speech. *Ethnic Groups, 2,* 35–53.

Lustig, M. W., & Koester, J. (2006). *Intercultural competence: Interpersonal communication across cultures* (6th ed.). New York: HarperCollins.

Lyons, A., & Kashima, Y. (2003). How are stereotypes maintained through communication? The influence of stereotype sharedness. *Journal of Personality and Social Psychology, 85,* 989–1005.

Ma, K. (1996). *The modern Madame Butterfly: Fantasy and reality in Japanese cross-cultural relationships.* Rutland, VT: Charles E. Tuttle.

Ma, R. (1992, Summer). The role of unofficial intermediaries in interpersonal conflicts in the Chinese culture. *Communication Quarterly, 40,* 269–278.

Mackey, R. A., Diemer, M. A., & O'Brien, B. A. (2000). Psychological intimacy in the lasting relationships of heterosexual and same-gender couples. *Sex Roles, 43,* 201–227.

Maas, D. F. (2002). Make your paraphrasing plagiarism proof with a coat of E-prime. *ETC: A Review of General Semantics, 59,* 196–205.

MacLachlan, J. (1979). What people really think of fast talkers. *Psychology Today, 13,* 113–117.

Madden, M., & Lenhart, A. (2006). Online dating. Pew Internet & American Life Project (www.pewinternet.org/, accessed 2/20/06).

Maggio, R. (1997). *Talking about people: A guide to fair and accurate language.* Phoenix, AZ: Oryx Press.

Mahaffey, A. L., Bryan, A., & Hutchison, K. E. (2005, March). Using startle eye blink to measure the affective component of antigay bias. *Basic and Applied Social Psychology, 27,* 37–45.

Malandro, L. A., Barker, L., & Barker, D. A. (1989). *Nonverbal communication* (2nd ed.). New York: Random House.

Mallen, M. J., Day, S. X., & Green, M. A. (2003). Online versus face-to-face conversation: An examination of relational and discourse variables. *Psychotherapy: Theory, Research, Practice, Training, 40,* 155–163.

Manes, J., & Wolfson, N. (1981). The compliment formula. In F. Coulmas (Ed.), *Conversational routine* (pp. 115–132). The Hague: Mouton.

Manniche, E. (1991). Marriage and non-marriage cohabitation in Denmark. *Family Reports, 20,* 9–35.

Mao, L. R. (1994, May). Beyond politeness theory: "Face" revisited and renewed. *Journal of Pragmatics, 21,* 451–486.

Marsh, P. (1988). *Eye to eye: How people interact.* Topside, MA: Salem House.

Marshall, E. (1983). *Eye language: Understanding the eloquent eye.* New York: New Trend.

Marshall, L. L., & Rose, P. (1987). Gender, stress and violence in the adult relationships of a sample of college students. *Journal of Social and Personal Relationships, 4,* 299–316.

Martin, G. N. (1998). Human electroencephalographic (EEG) response to olfactory stimulation: Two experiments using the aroma of food. *International Journal of Psychophysiology, 30,* 287–302.

Martin, M. M., & Anderson, C. M. (1995, Spring). Roommate similarity: Are roommates who are similar in their communication traits more satisfied? *Communication Research Reports, 12,* 46–52.

Martin, M. M., Anderson, C. M., & Mottet, T. P. (1999). Perceived understanding and self-disclosure in the stepparent-stepchild relationship. *Journal of Psychology: Interdisciplinary and Applied, 133,* 281–290.

Marwell, G., & Schmitt, D. R. (1967). Dimensions of compliance-gaining behavior: An empirical analysis. *Sociometry, 39,* 350–364.

Matsumoto, D. (1991, Winter). Cultural influences on facial expressions of emotion. *Southern Communication Journal, 56,* 128–137.

Matsumoto, D. (1994). *People: Psychology from a cultural perspective.* Pacific Grove, CA: Brooks/Cole.

Matsumoto, D. (1996). *Culture and psychology.* Pacific Grove, CA: Brooks/Cole.

Matsumoto, D., & Kudoh, T. (1993). American–Japanese cultural differences in attributions of personality based on smiles. *Journal of Nonverbal Behavior, 17,* 231–243.

McBroom, W. H., & Reed, F. W. (1992, June). Toward a reconceptualization of attitude–behavior consistency. *Theoretical Advances in Social Psychology* [Special issue]. *Social Psychology Quarterly, 55,* 205–216.

McCarthy, M. (2003). Talking back: "Small" interactional response tokens in everyday conversation. *Research on Language and Social Interaction, 36,* 33–63.

McConatha, J., Lightner, E., & Deaner, S. L. (1994). Culture, age, and gender as variables in the expression of emotions. *Journal of Social Behavior and Personality, 9,* 481–488.

McCown, J. A., Fischer, D., Page, R., & Homant, M. (2001). Internet relationships: People who meet people. *CyberPsychology & Behavior, 4,* 593–596.

McCroskey, J. C. (1970). Measures of communication-bound anxiety. *Communication Monographs, 37,* 269–273.

McCroskey, J. C. (1998). *Why we communicate the ways we do: A communibiological perspective.* Boston: Allyn & Bacon.

McCroskey, J. C. (2001). *An introduction to rhetorical communication* (8th ed.). Boston: Allyn & Bacon.

McCroskey, J. C., Booth-Butterfield, S., & Payne, S. K. (1989). The impact of communication apprehension on college student retention and success. *Communication Quarterly, 37,* 100–107.

McCroskey, J. C., & Wheeless, L. (1976). *Introduction to human communication.* Boston: Allyn & Bacon.

McDonald, E. J., McCabe, K., Yeh, M., Lau, A., Garland, A., & Hough, R. L. (2005, February). Cultural affiliation and self-esteem as predictors of internalizing symptoms among Mexican American adolescents. *Journal of Clinical Child and Adolescent Psychology, 34,* 163–171.

McGill, M. E. (1985). *The McGill report on male intimacy.* New York: Harper & Row.

McLaughlin, M. L. (1984). *Conversation: How talk is organized.* Newbury Park, CA: Sage.

McNamee, S., & Gergen, K. J. (Eds.). (1999). *Relational responsibility: Resources for sustainable dialogue.* Thousand Oaks, CA: Sage.

McNatt, D. B. (2001). Ancient Pygmalion joins contemporary management: A meta-analysis of the result. *Journal of Applied Psychology, 85,* 314–322.

Merton, R. K. (1957). *Social theory and social structure.* New York: Free Press.

Messick, R. M., & Cook, K. S. (Eds.). (1983). *Equity theory: Psychological and sociological perspectives.* New York: Praeger.

Messmer, M. (1999, August). Skills for a new millennium: Accounting and financial professionals. *Strategic Finance Magazine,* pp. 10ff.

Metts, S. (1989, May). An exploratory investigation of deception in close relationships. *Journal of Social and Personal Relationships, 6,* 159–179.

Metts, S., & Planalp, S. (2002). Emotional communication. In M. L. Knapp & J. A. Daly (Eds.), *Handbook of Interpersonal Communication* (3rd ed., pp. 339–373). Thousand Oaks, CA: Sage.

Meyer, J. R. (1994, Spring). Effect of situational features on the likelihood of addressing face needs in requests. *Southern Communication Journal, 59,* 240–254.

Midooka, K. (1990, October). Characteristics of Japanese style communication. *Media Culture and Society, 12,* 477–489.

Miller, G. R. (1978). The current state of theory and research in interpersonal communication. *Human Communication Research, 4,* 164–178.

Miller, G. R. (1990). Interpersonal communication. In G. L. Dahnke & G. W. Clatterbuck (Eds.), *Human communication: Theory and research* (pp. 91–122). Belmont, CA: Wadsworth.

Miller, G. R., & Parks, M. R. (1982). Communication in dissolving relationships. In S. Duck (Ed.), *Personal relationships: Vol. 4. Dissolving personal relationships* (pp. 127–154). New York: Academic Press.

Miller, S., & Weckert, J. (2000). Privacy, the workplace and the Internet. *Journal of Business Ethics, 35,* 255–265.

Miller, L. R. (1997, December). Better ways to think and communicate. *Association Management, 49,* 71–73.

Miner, H. (1956). Body ritual among the Nacirema. *American Anthropologist, 58,* 503–507.

Mir, M. (1993). Direct requests can also be polite. Paper presented at the annual meeting of the International Conference on Pragmatics and Language Learning, Champaign, IL.

Moghaddam, F. M., Taylor, D. M., & Wright, S. C. (1993). *Social psychology in cross-cultural perspective.* New York: W. H. Freeman.

Molloy, J. (1977). *The woman's dress for success book.* Chicago: Follett.

Molloy, J. (1981). *Molloy's live for success.* New York: Bantam.

Monahan, J. L. (1998). I don't know it but I like you. *Human Communication Research, 24,* 480–500.

Monk, A., Fellas, E., & Ley, E. (2004). Rapport-building activities in corner shop interactions. *Behaviour & Information Technology, 23,* 301–305.

Montagu, A. (1971). *Touching: The human significance of the skin.* New York: Harper & Row.

Moon, D. G. (1996, Winter). Concepts of "culture": Implications for intercultural communication research. *Communication Quarterly, 44,* 70–84.

Moon, Y. (2003). Don't blame the computer: When self-disclosure moderates the self-serving bias. *Journal of Consumer Psychology, 13,* 125–137.

Moore, A., Masterson, J. T., Christophel, D. M., & Shea, K. A. (1996). College teacher immediacy and student ratings of instruction. *Communication Education, 45,* 29–39.

Morreale, S. P., Osborn, M. M., & Pearson, J. C. (2000, January). Why communication is important: A rationale for the centrality of the study of communication. *Journal of the Association for Communication Administration, 29,* 1–25.

Morrill, C. (1992). Vengeance among executives. *Virginia Review of Sociology, 1,* 51–76.

Morris, D. (1977). *Manwatching: A field guide to human behavior.* New York: Abrams.

Morrow, G. D., Clark, E. M., & Brock, K. F. (1995). Individual and partner love styles: Implications for the quality of romantic involvements. *Journal of Social and Personal Relationships, 12,* 363–387.

Murstein, B. I., Merighi, J. R., & Vyse, S. A. (1991). Love styles in the United States and France: A cross-cultural comparison. *Journal of Social and Clinical Psychology, 10,* 37–46.

Naifeh, S., & Smith, G. W. (1984). *Why can't men open up? Overcoming men's fear of intimacy.* New York: Clarkson N. Potter.

Neff, K. D., & Harter, S. (2002, November). The authenticity of conflict resolutions among adult couples: Does women's other-oriented behavior reflect their true selves? *Sex Roles, 47,* 403–417.

Neimeyer, R. A., & Mitchell, K. A. (1988). Similarity and attraction: A longitudinal study. *Journal of Social and Personal Relationships, 5,* 131–148.

Nelson, J. E., & Beggan, J. K. (2004, May). Self-serving judgments about winning the lottery. *Journal of Psychology: Interdisciplinary and Applied, 138,* 253–264.

Neugarten, B. (1979). Time, age, and the life cycle. *American Journal of Psychiatry, 136,* 887–894.

Neuliep, J. W., Chaudoir, M., & McCroskey, J. C. (2001). A cross-cultural comparison of ethnocentrism among Japanese and United States college students. *Communication Research Reports, 18,* 137–146.

Ng, S. H., He, A., & Loong, C. (2004, September). Tri-generational family conversations: Communication accommodation and brokering. *British Journal of Social Psychology, 43,* 449–464.

Nicholas, C. L. (2004, Winter). Gaydar: Eye-gaze as identity recognition among gay men and lesbians. *Sexuality and Culture: An Interdisciplinary Quarterly, 8,* 60–86.

Nichols, M. P. (1995). *The lost art of listening: How learning to listen can improve relationships.* New York: Guilford Press.

Nichols, R. (1961). Do we know how to listen? Practical helps in a modern age. *Communication Education, 10,* 118–124.

Nichols, R., & Stevens, L. (1957). *Are you listening?* New York: McGraw-Hill.

Noble, B. P. (1994, August 14). The gender wars: Talking peace. *The New York Times,* p. 21.

Noller, P., & Fitzpatrick, M. A. (1993). *Communication in family relationships.* Englewood Cliffs, NJ: Prentice-Hall.

Nordhaus-Bike, A. M. (1999, August). Learning to lead. *Hospitals & Health Networks, 73,* 28ff.

Norton, R., & Warnick, B. (1976). Assertiveness as a communication construct. *Human Communication Research, 3,* 62–66.

Notarius, C. I., & Herrick, L. R. (1988). Listener response strategies to a distressed other. *Journal of Social and Personal Relationships, 5,* 97–108.

Nowak, K. L. (2003). Sex categorization in computer mediated communication (CMC): Exploring the Utopian promise. *Media Psychology, 5,* 83–103.

Oatley, K., & Duncan, E. (1994). The experience of emotions in everyday life. *Cognition and Emotion, 8,* 369–381.

Ober, C., Weitkamp, L. R., Cox, N., Dytch, H., Kostyu, D., & Elias, S. (1997). *American Journal of Human Genetics, 61,* 494–496.

Oberg, K. (1960). Cultural shock: Adjustment to new cultural environments. *Practical Anthropology, 7,* 177–182.

Oetzel, J., Ting-Toomey, S., Masumoto, T., Yokochi, Y., Pan, X., Takai, J., & Wilcox, R. (2001). Face and facework in conflict: A cross-cultural comparison of China, Germany, Japan, and the United States. *Communication Monographs, 68,* 235–258.

O'Hair, D., Cody, M. J., & McLaughlin, M. L. (1981). Prepared lies, spontaneous lies, Machiavellianism, and nonverbal communication. *Human Communication Research, 7,* 325–339.

Olaniran, B. A. (1994, February). Group performance in computer-mediated and face-to-face communication media. *Management Communication Quarterly, 7,* 256–281.

Olson, E. (2006, April 6). Better not miss the buss. *The New York Times,* G1–2.

Onishi, N. (2005, April 27). In Japan crash, time obsession may be culprit. *The New York Times,* pp. A1, A9.

Ono, H., & Zavodny, M. (2003). Gender and the Internet. *Social Science Quarterly, 84,* 111–121.

O'Sullivan, P. B., & Flanagin, A. J. (2003). Reconceptualizing 'flaming' and other problematic messages. *New Media and Society, 5,* 69–94.

O'Sullivan, P. B., Hunt, S. K., & Lippert, L. R. (2004). Mediated immediacy: A language of affiliation in a technological age. *Journal of Language and Social Psychology, 23,* 464–490.

Oswald, D. L., Clark, E. M., & Kelly, C. M. (2004, June). Friendship maintenance: An analysis of individual and dyad behaviors. *Journal of Social and Clinical Psychology, 23,* 413–441.

Otaki, M., Durrett, M. E., Richards, P., Nyquist, L., & Pennebaker, J. W. (1986). Maternal and infant behavior in Japan and America. *Journal of Cross-Cultural Psychology, 17,* 251–268.

Panyametheekul, S., & Herring, S. C. (2003). Gender and turn allocation in a Thai chat room. *Journal of Computer Mediated Communication, 9.*

Parker, J. G. (2004, September). Planning and communication crucial to preventing workplace violence. *Safety and Health, 170,* 58–61.

Parker, R. G., & Parrott, R. (1995). Patterns of self-disclosure across social support networks: Elderly, middle-aged, and young adults. *International Journal of Aging and Human Development, 41,* 281–297.

Parks, M. R. (1995). Webs of influence in interpersonal relationships. In C. R. Berger & M. E. Burgoon (Eds.), *Communication and social influence processes* (pp. 155–178). East Lansing: Michigan State University Press.

Parks, M. R., & Floyd, K. (1996). Making friends in cyberspace. *Journal of Communication, 46,* 80–97.

Parks, M. R., & Roberts, L. D. (1998). "Making MOOsic": The development of personal relationships online and a comparison to their off-line counterparts. *Journal of Social and Personal Relationships, 15,* 517–537.

Paul, A. M. (2001). Self-help: Shattering the myths. *Psychology Today, 34,* 60ff.

Payne, K. E. (2001). *Different but equal: Communication between the sexes.* Westport, CT: Praeger.

Pearson, J. C., & Spitzberg, B. H. (1990). *Interpersonal communication: Concepts, components, and contexts* (2nd ed.). Dubuque, IA: William C. Brown.

Pearson, J. C., West, R., & Turner, L. H. (1995). *Gender and communication* (3rd ed.). Dubuque, IA: William C. Brown.

Penfield, J. (Ed.). (1987). *Women and language in transition.* Albany: State University of New York Press.

Pennebacker, J. W. (1991). *Opening up: The healing power of confiding in others.* New York: Avon.

Penton-Voak, I. S., Jacobson, A., & Trivers, R. (2004, November). Populational differences in attractiveness judgments of male and female faces: Comparing British and Jamaican samples. *Evolution and Human Behavior, 25,* 355–370.

Peterson, C. C. (1996). The ticking of the social clock: Adults' beliefs about the timing of transition events. *International Journal of Aging and Human Development, 42,* 189–203.

Petrocelli, W., & Repa, B. K. (1992). *Sexual harassment on the job.* Berkeley, CA: Nolo Press.

Pilkington, C. J., & Richardson, D. R. (1988). Perceptions of risk in intimacy. *Journal of Social and Personal Relationships, 5,* 503–508.

Pilkington, C. J., & Woods, S. P. (1999). Risk in intimacy as a chronically accessible schema. *Journal of Social and Personal Relationships, 16,* 249–263.

Pilkington, N. W., & D'Augelli, A. R. (1995). Victimization of lesbian, gay, and bisexual youth in community settings. *Journal of Community Psychology, 23,* 34–56.

Piot, C. D. (1993). Secrecy, ambiguity, and the everyday in Kabre culture. *American Anthropologist, 95,* 353–370.

Pittenger, R. E., Hockett, C. F., & Danehy, J. J. (1960). *The first five minutes.* Ithaca, NY: Paul Martineau.

Placencia, M. E. (2004). Rapport-building activities in corner shop interactions. *Journal of Sociolinguistics, 8,* 215–245.

Plaks, J. E., Grant, H., & Dweck, C. S. (2005, February). Violations of implicit theories and the sense of prediction and control: Implications for motivated person perception. *Journal of Personality and Social Psychology, 88,* 245–262.

Plutchik, R. (1980). *Emotion: A psycho-evolutionary synthesis.* New York: Harper & Row.

Pornpitakpan, C. (2003). The effect of personality traits and perceived cultural similarity on attraction. *Journal of International Consumer Marketing, 15,* 5–30.

Porter, R. H., & Moore, J. D. (1981). Human kin recognition by olfactory cues. *Physiology and Behavior, 27,* 493–495.

Porter, S., Brit, A. R., Yuille, J. C., & Lehman, D. R. (2000, November). Negotiating false memories: Interviewer and rememberer characteristics relate to memory distortion. *Psychological Science, 11,* 507–510.

Powers, W. G., & Love, D. E. (2000). Communication apprehension in the dating partner context. *Communication Research Reports, 17,* 221–228.

Rainie, L., & Horrigan, J. (2005). A decade of adoption: How the internet has woven itself into American life. Retrieved February 20, 2006, from Pew Internet & American Life Project, www.pewinternet.org/PPF/R/148/report_display.asp.

Rainie, L., & Madden, M. (2006). Not looking for love: The state of romance in America. Retrieved February 20, 2006, from Pew Internet & American Life Project, www.pewinternet.org.

Rancer, A. S. (1998). Argumentativeness. In J. C. McCroskey, J. A. Daly, M. M. Martin, & M. J. Beatty (Eds.), *Communication and Personality: Trait Perspectives* (pp. 149–170). Cresskill, NJ: Hampton Press.

Rancer, A. S., & Avtgis, T. A. (2006). *Argumentative and aggressive communication: Theory, research, and application.* Thousand Oaks, CA: Sage.

Raney, R. F. (2000, May 11). Study finds Internet of social benefit to users. *The New York Times,* p. G7.

Rankin, P. (1929). Listening ability. Proceedings of the Ohio State Educational Conference's ninth annual session.

Rapsa, R., & Cusack, J. (1990). Psychiatric implications of tattoos. *American Family Physician, 41,* 1481–1486.

Raven, R., Centers, C., & Rodrigues, A. (1975). The bases of conjugal power. In R. E. Cromwell & D. H. Olson (Eds.), *Power in families* (pp. 217–234). New York: Halsted Press.

Rector, M., & Neiva, E. (1996). Communication and personal relationships in Brazil. In W. B. Gudykunst, S. Ting-Toomey, & T. Nishida (Eds.), *Communication in personal relationships across cultures* (pp. 156–173). Thousand Oaks, CA: Sage.

Reed, M. D. (1993, Fall). Sudden death and bereavement outcomes: The impact of resources on grief, symptomatology and detachment. *Suicide and Life-Threatening Behavior, 23,* 204–220.

Reisman, J. M. (1979). *Anatomy of friendship.* Lexington, MA: Lewis.

Reisman, J. M. (1981). Adult friendships. In Steve Duck & Robin Gilmour (Eds.), *Personal relationships: Vol. 2: Developing personal relationships* (pp. 205–230). New York: Academic Press.

Rhee, K. Y., & Kim, W-B (2004). The adoption and use of the Internet in South Korea, *Journal of Computer Mediated Communication, 9.*

Rich, A. L. (1974). *Interracial communication.* New York: Harper & Row.

Richmond, V. P., & McCroskey, J. C. (1998). *Communication: Apprehension, avoidance, and effectiveness* (5th ed.). Boston: Allyn & Bacon.

Richmond, V. P., Davis, L. M., Saylor, K., & McCroskey, J. C. (1984). Power strategies in organizations: Communication techniques and messages. *Human Communication Research, 11,* 85–108.

Richmond, V. P., & McCroskey, J. C. (1998). *Communication: Apprehension, avoidance, and effectiveness* (5th ed.). Boston: Allyn & Bacon.

Riggio, R. E. (1987). *The charisma quotient.* New York: Dodd, Mead.

Roberts, C. A., & Aruguete, M. S. (2000, February). Task and socioemotional behaviors of physicians: A test of reciprocity and social interaction theories in analogue physician–patient encounters. *Social Science and Medicine, 50,* 309–315.

Rockwell, S. C., & Singleton, L. (2002). The effects of computer anxiety and communication apprehension on the adoption and utilization of the Internet. *Electronic Journal of Communication, 12* (http://shadow/cios.org7979/journal\EJ\012\1\ 01212.html).

Roger, D., & Nesshoever, W. (1987, September). Individual differences in dyadic conversational strategies: A further study. *British Journal of Social Psychology, 26,* 247–255.

Rogers, C. (1970). *Carl Rogers on encounter groups.* New York: Harrow Books.

Rogers, C., & Farson, R. (1981). Active listening. In Joseph A. DeVito (Ed.), *Communication: Concepts and processes* (3rd ed., pp. 137–147). Englewood Cliffs, NJ: Prentice-Hall.

Rohlfing, M. E. (1995). "Doesn't anybody stay in one place anymore?" An exploration of the under-studied phenomenon of long-distance relationships. In J. T. Wood & S. Duck (Eds.), *Under-studied relationships: Off the beaten track* (pp. 173–196). Thousand Oaks, CA: Sage.

Rokach, A. (1998). The relation of cultural background to the causes of loneliness. *Journal of Social and Clinical Psychology, 17,* 75–88.

Rokach, A., & Brock, H. (1995). The effects of gender, marital status, and the chronicity and immediacy of loneliness. *Journal of Social Behavior and Personality, 19,* 833–848.

Rose, A. J., & Asher, S. R. (1999, January). Children's goals and strategies in response to conflicts within a friendship. *Developmental Psychology, 35,* 69–79.

Rosen, E. (1998, October). Think like a shrink. *Psychology Today,* pp. 54–59.

Rosenbaum, M. E. (1986). The repulsion hypothesis. On the nondevelopment of relationships. *Journal of Personality and Social Psychology, 51,* 1156–1166.

Rosenfeld, L. (1979). Self-disclosure avoidance: Why I am afraid to tell you who I am. *Communication Monographs, 46,* 63–74.

Rosengren, A., et al. (1993, October 19). Stressful life events, social support, and mortality in men born in 1933. *British Medical Journal.* Cited in Goleman (1995a).

Rosenthal, R., & Jacobson, L. (1968). *Pygmalion in the classroom.* New York: Holt, Rinehart and Winston.

Rosnow, R. L. (1977, Winter). Gossip and marketplace psychology. *Journal of Communication, 27,* 158–163.

Ross, H., Smith, J., Spielmacher, C. & Recchia, H. (2004, January). Shading the truth: Self-serving biases in children's reports of sibling conflicts. *Merrill-Palmer Quarterly, 50,* 61–85.

Ross, J. L. (1995). Conversational pitchbacks: Helping couples bat 1000 in the game of communications. *Journal of Family Psychotherapy, 6,* 83–86.

Rowatt, W. C., Cunningham, M. R., & Druen, P. B. (1999). Lying to get a date: The effect of facial physical attractiveness on the willingness to deceive prospective dating partners. *Journal of Social and Personal Relationships, 16,* 209–223.

Rowland-Morin, P. A., & Carroll, J. G. (1990). Verbal communication skills and patient satisfaction: A study of doctor–patient interviews. *Evaluation and the Health Professions, 13,* 168–185.

Ruben, B. D. (1985). Human communication and cross-cultural effectiveness. In L. A. Samovar & R. E. Porter (Eds.), *Intercultural communication: A reader* (4th ed., pp. 338–346). Belmont, CA: Wadsworth.

Rubenstein, C. (1993, June 10). Fighting sexual harassment in schools. *The New York Times,* p. C8.

Rubenstein, C., & Shaver, P. (1982). *In search of intimacy.* New York: Delacorte.

Rubin, R. B., Fernandez-Collado, C., & Hernandez-Sampieri, R. (1992). A cross-cultural examination of interpersonal communication motives in Mexico and the United States.

International Journal of Intercultural Relations, 16, 145–157.

Rubin, R. B., & Martin, M. M. (1994). Development of a measure of interpersonal communication competence. *Communication Research Reports, 11,* 33–44.

Rubin, R. B., Perse, E. M., & Barbato, C. A. (1988). Conceptualization and measurement of interpersonal communication motives. *Human Communication Research, 14,* 602–628.

Rubin, R. B., & Rubin, A. M. (1992). Antecedents of interpersonal communication motivation. *Communication Quarterly, 40,* 315–317.

Rundquist, S. (1992, November). Indirectness: A gender study of flaunting Grice's maxims. *Journal of Pragmatics, 18,* 431–449.

Saboonchi, F., Lundh, L. G., & Oest, L. G. (1999, September). Perfectionism and self-consciousness in social phobia and panic disorder with agoraphobia. *Behaviour Research and Therapy, 37,* 799–808.

Samovar, L. A., & Porter, R. E. (Eds.). (1991). *Communication between cultures.* Belmont, CA: Wadsworth.

Samter, W. (2003). Friendship interaction skills across the lifespan. In J. O. Greene & B. R. Burleson (Eds.), *Handbook of communication and social interaction skills* (pp. 637–684). Mahwah, NJ: Erlbaum.

Samter, W., & Cupach, W. R. (1998). Friendly fire: Topics variations in conflict among same- and cross-sex friends. *Communication Studies, 49,* 121–138.

Sanders, J. A., Wiseman, R. L., & Matz, S. I. (1991). Uncertainty reduction in acquaintance relationships in Ghana and the United States. In S. Ting-Toomey & F. Korzenny (Eds.), *Cross-cultural interpersonal communication* (pp. 79–98). Thousand Oaks, CA: Sage.

Sarwer, D. B., Kalichman, S. C., Johnson, J. R., Early, J., et al. (1993, June). Sexual aggression and love styles: An exploratory study. *Archives of Sexual Behavior, 22,* 265–275.

Satir, V. (1983). *Conjoint family therapy* (3d ed.). Palo Alto, CA: Science and Behavior Books.

Saunders, C. S., Robey, D., & Vaverek, K. A. (1994, June). The persistence of status differentials in computer conferencing. *Human Communication Research, 20,* 443–472.

Scandura, T. (1992). Mentorship and career mobility: An empirical investigation. *Journal of Organizational Behavior, 13,* 169–174.

Scealy, M., Phillips, J. G., & Stevenson, R. (2002). Shyness and anxiety as predictors of patterns of Internet usage. *CyberPsychology and Behavior, 5,* 507–515.

Schaap, C., Buunk, B., & Kerkstra, A. (1988). Marital conflict resolution. In Patricia Noller & Mary Anne Fitzpatrick (Eds.), *Perspectives on marital interaction* (pp. 203–244). Philadelphia: Multilingual Matters.

Schachter, S. (1964). The interaction of cognitive and physiological determinants of emotional state. In L. Berkowitz (Ed.), *Advances in experimental social psychology* (Vol. 1). New York: Academic Press.

Scheetz, L. P. (1995). Recruiting trends 1995–1996: A study of 527 businesses, industries, and governmental agencies employing new college graduates. East Lansing, MI: Collegiate Employment Research Institute, Michigan State University.

Scherer, K. R. (1986). Vocal affect expression. *Psychological Bulletin, 99,* 143–165.

Schmidt, T. O., & Cornelius, R. R. (1987). Self-disclosure in everyday life. *Journal of Social and Personal Relationships, 4,* 365–373.

Schoeneman, T. J., & Rubanowitz, E. E. (1985). Attributions in the advice columns: Actors and observers, causes and reasons. *Personality and Social Psychology Bulletin, 11,* 315–325.

Schott, G., & Selwyn, N. (2000). Examining the "male, antisocial" stereotype of high computer users. *Journal of Educational Computing Research, 23,* 291–303.

Schwartz, M., & the Task Force on Bias-Free Language of the Association of American University Presses. (1995). *Guidelines for bias-free writing.* Bloomington: Indiana University Press.

Scott, C. R., & Timmerman, C. E. (2005, December). Relating computer, communication, and computer-mediated communication apprehensions to new communication technology in the workplace. *Communication Research, 32,* 683–725.

Seiter, J. S., & Sandry, A. (2003, Fall). Pierced for success?: The effects of ear and nose piercing on perceptions of job candidates' credibility, attractiveness, and hirability. *Communication Research Reports, 20,* 287–298.

Sergios, P. A., & Cody, J. (1985). Physical attractiveness and social assertiveness skills in male homosexual dating behavior and partner selection. *Journal of Social Psychology, 125,* 505–514.

Shaffer, D. R., Pegalis, L. J., & Bazzini, D. G. (1996). When boy meets girl (revisited): Gender, gender role orientation, and prospect of future interaction as determinants of self-disclosure among same- and opposite-sex acquaintances. *Personality and Social Psychology Bulletin, 22,* 495–506.

Shaw, L. H., & Grant, L. M. (2002, December). Users divided? Exploring the gender gap in Internet use. *CyberPsychology & Behavior, 5,* (December), 517–527.

Shechtman, Z., Hiradin, A., & Zina, S. (2003, Spring). The impact of culture on group behavior: A comparison of three ethnic groups. *Journal of Counseling and Development, 81,* 208–216.

Sheese, B. E., Brown, E. L., & Graziano, W. G. (2004, September). Emotional expression in cyberspace: Searching for moderators of the Pennebaker disclosure effect via e-mail. *Health Psychology, 23,* 457–464.

Sherman, D. K., & Kim, H. S. (2005, January). Is there an "I" in "Team"? The role of the self in group-serving judgments. *Journal of Personality and Social Psychology, 88,* 108–120.

Shiu, E., & Lenhart, A. (2004). Pew Internet and American life project report: Instant Messaging. Retrieved July 29, 2005, from www.pewinternet.org/PPF/r/133/report_display.asp.

Shuter, R. (1990, Spring). The centrality of culture. *Southern Communication Journal, 55,* 237–249.

Siegert, J. R., & Stamp, G. H. (1994, December). "Our first big fight" as a milestone in the development of close relationships. *Communication Monographs, 61,* 345–360.

Signorile, M. (1993). *Queer in America: Sex, the media, and the closets of power.* New York: Random House.

Silverman, T. (2001). Expanding community: The Internet and relational theory. *Community, Work and Family, 4,* 231–237.

Singh, N., & Pereira, A. (2005). *The culturally customized web site.* Oxford, UK: Elsevier Butterworth-Heinemann.

Slade, M. (1995, February 19). We forgot to write a headline: But it's not our fault. *The New York Times,* p. 5.

Smith, C. S. (2002, April 30). Beware of green hats in China and other cross-cultural faux pas. *The New York Times,* p. C11.

Smith, M. H. (2003, February). Body adornment: Know the limits. *Nursing Management, 34,* 22–23.

Smith, R. (2004, April 10). The teaching of communication skills may be misguided. *British Medical Journal, 328,* 1–2.

Smith, A., & Williams, K. D. (2004). R U There? Ostracism by cell phone text messages. *Group Dynamics, 8,* 291–301.

Snyder, C. R. (1984). Excuses, excuses. *Psychology Today, 18,* 50–55.

Snyder, C. R., Higgins, Raymond L., & Stucky, Rita J. (1983). *Excuses: Masquerades in search of grace.* New York: Wiley.

Snyder, M. (1992, February). A gender-informed model of couple and family therapy: Relationship enhancement therapy. *Contemporary Family Therapy: An International Journal, 14,* 15–31.

Solomon, G. B., Striegel, D. A., Eliot, J. F., Heon, S. N., et al. (1996). The self-fulfilling prophecy in college basketball: Implications for effective coaching. *Journal of Applied Sport Psychology, 8,* 44–59.

Sommers, S. (1984). Reported emotions and conventions of emotionality among college students. *Journal of Personality and Social Psychology, 46,* 207–215.

Sondel, B. (1968). *To win with words.* New York: Hawthorn Books.

Song, I., LaRose, R., Eastin, M. S., & Lin, C. A. (2004). Internet gratifications Internet addiction: On the uses and abuses of new media. *CyberPsychology and Behavior, 7,* 384–394.

Sorenson, P. S., Hawkins, K., & Sorenson, R. L. (1995). Gender, psychological type and conflict style preferences. *Management Communication Quarterly, 9,* 115–126.

Spangler, D. L., & Burns, D. D. (2000). Is it true that men are from Mars and women are from Venus? A test of gender differences in dependency and perfectionism. *Journal of Cognitive Psychotherapy, 13,* 339–357.

Spitzberg, B. H. (1991). Intercultural communication competence. In L. A. Samovar & R. E. Porter (Eds.), *Intercultural communication: A reader* (pp. 353–365). Belmont, CA: Wadsworth.

Spitzberg, B. H., & Cupach, W. R. (1989). *Handbook of interpersonal competence research.* New York: Springer.

Spitzberg, B. H., & Hecht, M. L. (1984). A component model of relational competence. *Human Communication Research, 10,* 575–599.

Sprecher, S. (1987). The effects of self-disclosure given and received on affection for an intimate partner and stability of the relationship. *Journal of Social and Personal Relationships, 4,* 115–127.

Sprecher, S., & Toro-Morn, M. (2002, March). A study of men and women from different sides of earth to determine if men are from Mars and women are from Venus in their beliefs about love and romantic relationships. *Sex Roles, 46,* 131–147.

Stafford, L., Kline, S. L., & Dimmick, J. (1999). Homee-mail: Relational maintenance and gratification opportunities. *Journal of Broadcasting and Electronic Media, 43,* 659–669.

Steil, L. K., Barker, L. L., & Watson, K. W. (1983). *Effective listening: Key to your success.* Reading, MA: Addison-Wesley.

Steiner, C. (1981). *The other side of power.* New York: Grove.

Steinfatt, T. M. (1987). Personality and communication: Classic approaches. In J. C. McCroskey & J. A. Daly (Eds.), *Personality and interpersonal communication* (pp. 42–126). Thousand Oaks, CA: Sage.

Stephan, C. W., & Stephan, W. G. (1992, Winter). Reducing intercultural anxiety through intercultural contact. *International Journal of Intercultural Relations, 16,* 89–106.

Stephan, W. G., & Stephan, C. W. (1985). Intergroup anxiety. *Journal of Social Issues, 41,* 157–175.

Sternglanz, R. W., & DePaulo, B. (2004, Winter). Reading nonverbal cues to emotions: The advantages and liabilities of relationship closeness. *Journal of Nonverbal Behavior, 28,* 245–266.

Stewart, L. P., Cooper, P. J., & Stewart, A. D., with Friedley, S. A. (2003). *Communication and gender.* Boston: Allyn & Bacon.

Strassberg, D. S., & Holty, S. (2003). An experimental study of women's Internet personal ads. *Archives of Sexual Behavior, 32,* 253–260.

Strecker, I. (1993). Cultural variations in the concept of "face." *Multilingua, 12,* 119–141.

Strom, D. (2006, April 5). I.M. generation is changing the way business talks. *The New York Times,* D4.

Stritzke, W. G. K., Nguyen, A., & Durkin, K. (2004). Shness and computer-mediated communication: A self-presentational theory perspective. *Media Psychology, 6,* 1–22.

Stromer-Galley, J. (2003). Diversity of political conversation on the Internet: User's perspectives. *Journal of Computer Mediated Communication* 8 (http://jcmc.indiana.edu/vol8/issue3/stromergalley.html, accessed 6/21/2006).

Suler, J. (2004). The online disinhibition effect. *CyberPsychology and Behavior, 7,* 321–326.

Sutcliffe, K., Lewton, E., & Rosenthal, M. M. (2004, February). Communication failures: An insidious contributor to medical mishaps. *Academic Medicine, 79,* 186–194.

Szapocznik, J. (1995, January). Research on disclosure of HIV status: Cultural evolution finds an ally in science. *Health Psychology, 14,* 4–5.

Tannen, D. (1990). *You just don't understand: Women and men in conversation.* New York: Morrow.

Tannen, D. (1994a). *Gender and discourse.* New York: Oxford University Press.

Tannen, D. (1994b). *Talking from 9 to 5.* New York: Morrow.

Tannen, D. (2006). *You're wearing that? Understanding mothers and daughters in conversation.* New York: Random House.

Tardiff, T. (2001). Learning to say "no" in Chinese. *Early Education and Development, 12,* 303–323.

Tata, J. (2000). Toward a theoretical framework of intercultural account-giving and account evaluation. *International Journal of Organizational Analysis, 8,* 155–178.

Tavris, C. (1989). *Anger: The misunderstood emotion* (2nd ed.). New York: Simon & Schuster.

Thibaut, J. W., & Kelley, H. H. (1959). *The social psychology of groups.* New York: Wiley. Reissued (1986). New Brunswick, NJ: Transaction Books.

Timmerman, L. J. (2002). Comparing the production of power in language on the basis of sex. In M. Allen & R. W. Preiss (Eds.), *Interpersonal communication research: Advances through meta-analysis* (pp. 73–88). Mahwah, NJ: Erlbaum.

Ting-Toomey, S. (1981). Ethnic identity and close friendship in Chinese-American college students. *International Journal of Intercultural Relations, 5,* 383–406.

Ting-Toomey, S. (1985). Toward a theory of conflict and culture. *International and Intercultural Communication Annual, 9,* 71–86.

Ting-Toomey, S. (1986). Conflict communication styles in black and white subjective cultures. In Young Yun Kim (Ed.), *Interethnic communication: Current research* (pp. 75–88). Thousand Oaks, CA: Sage.

Tinsley, C. H., & Brett, J. M. (2001). Managing workplace conflict in the United States and Hong Kong. *Organizational Behavior and Human Decision Processes, 85,* 360–381.

Titlow, K. I., Rackoff, J. E., & Emanuel, E. J. (1999). What will it take to restore patient trust? *Business & Health, 17,* (6A), 61–64.

Trager, G. L. (1958). Paralanguage: A first approximation. *Studies in Linguistics, 13,* 1–12.

Trager, G. L. (1961). The typology of paralanguage. *Anthropological Linguistics, 3,* 17–21.

Traxler, A. J. (1980). *Let's get gerontologized: Developing a sensitivity to aging*. Springfield, IL: Illinois Department of Aging.

Tyler, Patrick E. (1996, July 11). Crime (and punishment) rages anew in China. *The New York Times*, pp. A1, A8.

Ueleke, W., et al. (1983). Inequity resolving behavior as a response to inequity in a hypothetical marital relationship. *Quarterly Journal of Human Behavior, 20*, 4–8.

Unger, F. L. (2001). Speech directed at able-bodied adults, disabled adults, and disabled adults with speech impairments. *Dissertation Abstracts International: Section B: The Sciences and Engineering (Hofstra University), 62*, 1146.

Urbaniak, G. C., & Kilmann, P. R. (2003, November). Physical attractiveness and the "nice guy paradox": Do nice guys really finish last? *Sex Roles, 49*, 413–426.

Uris, A. (1986). *101 of the greatest ideas in management*. New York: Wiley.

Vainiomaki, T. (2004). Silence as a cultural sign. *Semiotica, 150*, 347–361.

VanHyning, M. (1993). *Crossed signals: How to say no to sexual harassment*. Los Angeles: Infotrends Press.

Veenendall, T. L., & Feinstein, M. C. (1995). *Let's talk about relationships: Cases in study* (2nd ed.). Prospect Heights, IL: Waveland Press.

Velting, D. M. (1999). Personality and negative expectations: Trait structure of the Beck Hopelessness Scale. *Personality and Individual Differences, 26*, 913–921.

Victor, D. (1992). *International business communication*. New York: HarperCollins.

von Tetzchner, S., & Jensen, K. (1999). Interacting with people who have severe communication problems: Ethical considerations. *International Journal of Disability, Development and Education, 46*, 453–462.

Waddington, K. (2004). Psst—spread the word—gossiping is good for you. *Practice Nurse, 27*, 7–10.

Wade, C., & Tavris, C. (1990). *Learning to think critically: The case of close relationships*. New York: HarperCollins.

Wade, C., & Tavris, C. (1998). *Psychology* (5th ed.). New York: Longman.

Wade, N. (2002, January 22). Scent of a man is linked to a woman's selection. *The New York Times*, p. F2.

Walker, L. (1998). *Telephone techniques: The essential guide to thinking and working smarter*. New York: American Management Association.

Walster, E., & Walster, G. W. (1978). *A new look at love*. Reading, MA: Addison-Wesley.

Walster, E., Walster, G. W., & Berscheid, E. (1978). *Equity: Theory and research*. Boston: Allyn & Bacon.

Watzlawick, P. (1977). *How real is real? Confusion, disinformation, communication: An anecdotal introduction to communications theory*. New York: Vintage.

Watzlawick, P. (1978). *The language of change: Elements of therapeutic communication*. New York: Basic Books.

Watzlawick, P., Beavin, J. H., & Jackson, D. D. (1967). *Pragmatics of human communication: A study of interactional patterns, pathologies, and paradoxes*. New York: Norton.

Weathers, M. D., Frank, E. M., & Spell, L. A. (2002). Differences in the communication of affect: Members of the same race versus members of a different race. *Journal of Black Psychology, 28*, 66–77.

Weinberg, H. L. (1959). *Levels of knowing and existence*. New York: Harper & Row.

Weinstein, E. A., & Deutschberger, P. (1963). Some dimensions of altercasting. *Sociometry, 26*, 454–466.

Weitzman, P. F. (2001). Young adult women resolving interpersonal conflicts. *Journal of Adult Development, 8*, 61–67.

Weitzman, P. F., & Weitzman, E. A. (2000). Interpersonal negotiation strategies in a sample of older women. *Journal of Clinical Geropsychology, 6*, 41–51.

Werrbach, G. B., Grotevant, H. D., & Cooper, C. R. (1990, October). Gender differences in adolescents' identity development in the domain of sex role concepts. *Sex Roles, 23*, 349–362.

West, C., & Zimmerman, D. H. (1977, June). Women's place in everyday talk: Reflections on parent–child interaction. *Social Problems, 24*, 521–529.

Westwood, R. I., Tang, F. F., & Kirkbride, P. S. (1992). Chinese conflict behavior: Cultural antecedents and behavioral consequences. *Organizational Development Journal, 10*, 13–19.

Wetzel, P. J. (1988). Are "powerless" communication strategies the Japanese norm? *Language in Society, 17*, 555–564.

Wheeless, L. R., & Grotz, J. (1977). The measurement of trust and its relationship to self-disclosure. *Human Communication Research, 3*, 250–257.

Whitty, M. (2003). Cyber-flirting. *Theory and Psychology, 13*, 339–355.

Whitty, M., & Gavin, J. (2001). Age/sex/location: Uncovering the social cues in the development of online relationships. *CyberPsychology and Behavior, 4*, 623–630.

Wiederman, M. W., & Hurd, C. (1999, April). Extradyadic involvement during dating. *Journal of Social and Personal Relationships, 16*, 265–274.

Wigley, C. J., III. (1998). Verbal aggressiveness. In J. C. McCroskey, J. A. Daly, M. M. Martin, & M. J. Beatty (Eds.), *Communication and personality: Trait perspectives* (pp. 191–214). Cresskill, NJ: Hampton Press.

Wilkins, B. M., & Andersen, P. A. (1991). Gender differences and similarities in management communication: A meta-analysis. *Management Communication Quarterly, 5*, 6–35.

Wilmot, W. W. (1987). *Dyadic communication* (3rd ed.). New York: Random House.

Wilson, J. H., & Taylor, K. W. (2001). Professor immediacy as behaviors associated with liking students. *Teaching of Psychology, 28*, 136–138.

Wilson, R. A. (1989). Toward understanding e-prime. *ETC: A Review of General Semantics, 46*, 316–319.

Wilson, S. R., & Sabee, C. M. (2003). Explicating communicative competence as a theoretical term. In J. O. Greene

& B. R. Burleson (Eds.), *Handbook of communication and social interaction skills* (pp. 3–50). Mahwah, NJ: Erlbaum.

Winquist, L. A., Mohr, Cynthia D., & Kenny, David A. (1998, September). The female positivity effect in the perception of others. *Journal of Research in Personality, 32,* 370–388.

Witcher, S. K. (1999, August 9–15). Chief executives in Asia find listening difficult. *Asian Wall Street Journal Weekly, 21,* 11.

Witt, P. L., & Wheeless, L. R. (2001). An experimental study of teachers' verbal and nonverbal immediacy and students' affective and cognitive learning. *Communication Education, 50,* 327–342.

Wolak, J., Mitchell, K. J., & Finkelhor, D. (2003). Escaping or connecting? Characteristics of youth who form close online relationships. *Journal of Adolescence, 26,* 105–119.

Wolfson, N. (1988). The bulge: A theory of speech behaviour and social distance. In J. Fine (Ed.), *Second language discourse: A textbook of current research.* Norwood, NJ: Ablex.

Won-Doornink, M. (1985). Self-disclosure and reciprocity in conversation: A cross-national study. *Social Psychology Quarterly, 48,* 97–107.

Won-Doornink, M. (1991). Self-disclosure and reciprocity in South Korean and U.S. male dyads. In S. Ting-Toomey & F. Korzenny (Eds.), *Cross-cultural interpersonal communication* (pp. 116–131). Thousand Oaks, CA: Sage.

Wood, Julia T. (1994). *Gendered lives: Communication, gender, and culture.* Belmont, CA: Wadsworth.

Wright, J., & Chung, M. C. (2001, August). Mastery or mystery? Therapeutic writing: A review of the literature. *British Journal of Guidance and Counseling, 29,* 277–291.

Wright, P. H. (1978). Toward a theory of friendship based on a conception of self. *Human Communication Research, 4,* 196–207.

Wright, P. H. (1984). Self-referent motivation and the intrinsic quality of friendship. *Journal of Social and Personal Relationships, 1,* 115–130.

Wright, P. H. (1988). Interpreting research on gender differences in friendship: A case for moderation and a plea for caution. *Journal of Social and Personal Relationships, 5,* 367–373.

Yau-fair Ho, D., Chan, S. F., Peng, S., & Ng, A. K. (2001). The dialogical self: Converging East–West constructions. *Culture and Psychology, 7,* 393–408.

Yovetich, N. A., & Drigotas, S. M. (1999, September). Secret transmission: A relative intimacy hypothesis. *Personality and Social Psychology Bulletin, 25,* 1135–1146.

Yun, H. (1976). The Korean personality and treatment considerations. *Social Casework, 57,* 173–178.

Zimmerman, D. H., & West, C. (1975). Sex roles, interruptions and silences in conversations. In B. Thorne & N. Henley (Eds.), *Language and sex: Differences and dominance.* Rowley, MA: Newbury House.

Zornoza, A., Ripoll, P., & Peiró, J. M. (2002). Conflict management in groups that work in two different communication contexts: Face-to-face and computer-mediated communication. *Small Group Research, 33,* 481–508.

Zuckerman, M., Klorman, R., Larrance, D. T., & Spiegel, N. H. (1981). Facial, autonomic, and subjective components of emotion: The facial feedback hypothesis versus the externalizer–internalizer distinction. *Journal of Personality and Social Psychology, 41,* 929–944.

Zunin, L. M., & Zunin, N. B. (1972). *Contact: The first four minutes.* Los Angeles: Nash.

Credits

Index

Note: Italicized letters *f* and *t* following page numbers indicate figures and tables, respectively; italicized page numbers indicate glossary terms.

Intensional orientation, 144, *272, 280*
Interaction
    censoring, 99
    nonverbal, 154
Interaction management, *272, 280*
Interactional contact, 208
Interactional view, 4, *4f*
Interactive websites, 7
Intercultural communication, *272, 280. See also* Culture
    adjustments in, 51–52
    cultural differences in, 50–51
    culture shock and, 52–54
    defined, 43–45
    ethnocentrism in, 46–47, *48t*
    meaning differences in, 51
    mindfulness in, 49
    models of, *44f*
    relationships and, 54–55
    stereotyping and, 47–49
    uncertainty in, 50
Internet. *See* Computer-mediated communication
Interpersonal communication, *272. See also* Communication; specific form of communication (e.g. Nonverbal communication)
Interpersonal competence, *272. See also* Competence
Interpersonal conflict, *272. See also* Conflict
    active, *278*
Interpersonal effectiveness, *272. See also* Effectiveness
Interpersonal perception, 85, *272. See also* Perception
Interpersonal principles, 25
Interpersonal relationships. *See* Relationships
Interpersonal silence. *See* Silence
Interpretation
    of self, 61
    perception and, *85f,* 87–88
Interpretation-evaluation, 87–88
Intimacy, *208f,* 210–212, *272*
Intimacy claims, *272*
Intimate distance, 161, *161t, 272*
Intrapersonal communication, *272*
Intrapersonal repair phase, 213
Involvement in relationships, *208f,* 209–210, *272*
Irony, 125
Irreversibility of communication, 24, *272*

Jargon, *272*
Johari window, 61–64, *61f, 62f, 272*
Judgments
    listening and, 113
    paralanguage cues and, 166–167

Kinesics, *272*
Knapp's model of relationship stages, *215t*

Language, *272*
    cultural identifiers, 140–143
    heterosexist, 136, *271*
    racist, 135
    sexist, 138–139, *276*
    speech and language disorders, 181, *181t*
    symbolic nature of, 143–144
    verbal messages and, 124
Language competence, *272*
Last impressions, 94. *See also* Impressions
Leave-taking cues, *272*
Legitimate power, 22, *272*
Lesbians
    family structures of, 225
    heterosexism and, 135–136
    identifiers for, 141
    self-disclosure risks for, 71, 74
Linear view, 4, *4f*
Linguistic relatively hypothesis, *272*
Listening, 105–119, *272*
    active and inactive, 114–117
    active, skill exercise, 117
    avoiding, 113
    barriers to, reducing, 109
    competence and, *15f,* 16
    conversational cues for, *191f,* 192–193
    critical, *280*
    cultural differences in, *278*
    culture and, 117–118
    deaf and hearing people and, *107t*
    defined, 105
    depth, 113–114, *281*
    empathic, 111–112, *279*
    ethics in, 110
    gender and, 118–119, 127, *280*
    nonjudgmental, *280*
    nonjudgmental and critical, 113
    nonverbally, 158
    objective, 111–112, *279*
    obstacles to, skill exercises, 109
    problem-causing responses, *109t*
    purposes and payoffs of, 105
    reluctantly, 119–120
    self-disclosure and, 69, 73
    self-test of, 111
    stages of, 105–110, *106f*
    styles of, 110–117
    surface, 113–114, *281*
    to conflict messages, 241
    to disclaimers, 183
    to emotion, 198, *280*
    to empower, 66
    to new ideas, 5
    to others, 88, 198, *280*
    to self, 66
    to stage talk, 216

with power, 158
    without biases, 33
Listening cues, 119
Listserv, 6
Loneliness-depression cycle, 214
Love, *272. See also* Love relationships
Love relationships, 222–224
    cherishing behaviors in, 212
    cultural and gender differences in, 232–233
    excuses in, *187t*
    self-test of, 222–223
    types of, 223–224
    workplace romances, 228–229, *281*
Low-ambiguity-tolerance cultures, 42–43
Low-context cultures, 39–40, *272, 280*
Low-power-distance cultures, 41–42, *272*
Ludus love, 223
Lying, 154
    confronting, 126
    ethics and, 125

Machiavellianism, *272*
Mailing list group, 6
Making excuses, 188, *270, 280*
Male identifiers, 140–141
Managing relationship dissolution, *281*
Manic love, 224
Manipulation, conflict and, 255, *272*
Manner principle, 37, *272*
Markers, territoriality and, 162, *272*
Masculine cultures, 41, *272, 280*
Matching hypothesis, *272*
Maxims, conversational, *269, 279*
Meaning
    connotative, 124–125, *268, 278*
    context and, *280*
    cultural differences in, 51
    denotative, 124–125, *269*
    E-prime and, 143
    of colors, 173, *174t*
    of tactile communication, 165–166, 173–174
    people and, 124, *280*
Meaningfulness, *272*
Memory. *See also* Recall
    perception and, *85f,* 88–89
    smell and, 172
Mentoring relationships, *273*
Mere exposure hypothesis, *273*
Message overload, 11, *280*
Message surveillance, 22
Messages, *273. See also* Communication; specific form of communication (e.g. Nonverbal communication)
    censoring, 99
    types of, 10–12
Metacommunication, *273, 280*
Metalanguage, *273*
Metamessages, 11, *273*

Power distance, *281*
    computer-mediated communication and, 229
    cultural and, 41–42
Power plays, *274, 281*
Pragma love, 224
Pragmatic implication, *274*
Pragmatics, *274*
Present-focus conflict, *281*
Presenting yourself, 93
Preview of future messages, 183
Primacy effect, 93–94, *274*
Primary affect displays, *274*
Primary emotion, 195–196
Primary territories, 162, *274*
Principle of cooperation, *269*
Privacy
    civil inattention and, 160, *268*
    computer-mediated communication and, 211
Privileged language, 39
Problem-causing listening responses, *109t*
Problem-solving conflicts, *281*
Process, *274*
Projecting an image, 221
Protection theory, *274*
Provisionalism, *274*
Proxemic conversational distances, *281*
Proxemic distances, 160–162, *161t*
Proxemics, *274*
Proximity, *274*
Psychological noise, 13, *274*
Psychological time, 169, *274*
Public distance, 161–162, *161t, 274*
Public territories, 162, *274*
Punctuation of communication, *274*
Pupil dilation, *274*
Pupillometrics, *274*
Pygmalion effect, 93, *274*

Quality principle, 37, *274*
Quantity principle, 37, *274*
Questioning
    listening and, 116
    responding to, ethics in, 209
Quid pro quo harassment, 139, *271*

Race
    hate speech and, 109
    identifiers of, 141–143
    privileged language and, 39
    U.S. population by, 32–33
Racism, 135, *275*
Racist language, 135, *275*
Rate of vocal delivery, 166, 167, *281*
Reality, verbal messages and, 143–144
Recall, *85f,* 89. *See also* Memory
Receiver, 10, *10f, 44f, 275*
Receiving, *281*
    listening as, 106–107, *106f*

Recency effect, 93–94
Receptivity, 221
Reciprocity, 221
    in conversation, 191–193
Recovery stage of culture shock, 54
Reducing uncertainty, *281*
    intercultural communication and, 50
    perception and, 99–100
Referent power, 22, *275*
Regulators, 156, *157t, 275*
Rehearsal of assertive messages, 132
Rejection, *275*
    defined, 133
    direct, 128
    of conflict solution, *248f,* 250–251
    skill exercise, 134
Relation principle, 37, *275*
Relational dialectics theory, 214–215, *275*
Relationship communication, 216, *275*
Relationship conflict, 242
Relationship development, *275*
Relationship maintenance, *275*
Relationship messages, 19–20, *275, 281*
    skill exercise, 20
Relationship repair, *281*
Relationship violence, 217–220, *281*
    self-test of, 218
Relationships, 207–236. *See also* Love relationships; Workplace relationships
    advantages and disadvantages of, 216–217, *278*
    breadth of, *267*
    college students and, 224
    complementary, *268*
    computer-mediated communication and, 235
    conflict in. *See* Conflict
    content and, *268, 278*
    cultural influences on, 232–233
    deterioration of, *208f,* 212–213, *269*
    dissolution of, *208f,* 213–214, *281*
    ending of, 237
    excuses in, *187t*
    familial, 101, 224–228, *225t*
    friendships, 220–222
    in songs and greeting cards, skill exercise, 229
    intercultural, 54–55
    Interpersonally challenged family, 26–27
    nonverbal messages and, 154
    online, *235t*
    parental, 101
    power-distance in, 41–42
    proxemic distances and, 160–162, *161t*
    reluctant listening and, 119–120
    romantic, 222–224
    romantic workplace, *281*
    self-disclosure in, 71
    skill exercises, 212, 222
    spatial distance in, 222
    stage talk in, 216

    stages of, 207–216, *208f, 215f, 215t*
    technology and, 233–236
    theories of, 229–232
    uncertainty about, 99
    violence in, 217–220, 218
    where people meet, *209t*
Religion, 43
Religious identifiers, 142–143
Reluctant listening, 119–120
Remembering, *281*
    listening as, *106f,* 108
Repair, *275*
    of conversations, 186–188, *187t*
    of relationships, *208f,* 213, *281*
REPAIR process, 213
Resemblance, *275*
Resisting self-disclosure, 73–75
Responding, *281*
    listening as, *106f,* 108–110
    problem-causing listening responses, *109t*
    to emotion, 196, 200
    to good news of others, 197
    to self-disclosure, 72–73, *281*
Response, *275*
Reversing first impressions, 89
Reward, *275*
    of self-disclosure, 70–71
    social exchange theory and, 231
Reward power, 22, *275*
Risk
    in intimacy, 210–211
    in self-disclosure, 71
Roles, *275*
Romantic relationships. *See* Love relationships
Romantic workplace relationships, 228–229, *281. See also* Love relationships
Rules
    emotional communication and, 197
    of cultural display, 118, 173, 196, 197
    of family communication, 227
    of gender display, 196
    perceptual organization and, 86
Rules theory, 231–232, *275*
Rural computer-mediated communication, 33

Safety of computer-mediated communication, 236
Schemata, 86–87, *275*
SCREAM technique, 201–202
Scripts, 87, *275*
Secondary territories, 162, *275*
Secrets, 191
Selective attention, 85, *275*
Selective exposure, 85, *275*
Selective perception, 85, *275*
Self, 59–79. *See also* Others
    apprehension and, 75–79
    awareness of, 61–64, *61f, 62f*
    concept of, 59–61, *59f*